The Secret Chamber

Spiritual Wifery and the Doctrine of Christ

2nd Edition

Val Brinkerhoff

 Gratitude is expressed to Marti Grobecker, Kenneth Aaron Card, and Rock Waterman for their editing and other contributions.

Library of Congress Cataloging-in-Publication Data, Val Brinkerhoff, The Secret Chamber: Spiritual Wifery and the Doctrine of the Christ (second edition), 1st printing, March 12, 2019. 1. Polygamy, 2. Spritual Wifery, 3. Joseph Smith, 4. Brigham Young, 5. Mormonism, 6. Religion

2nd Edition, March 31, 2019, 284 pages
Printed in the United States of America
Publisher, Kindle Direct Publishing / ISBN-10: 1090268394 - ISBN-13: 978-1090268396
For copies, go to www.Amazon.com (in their search window, type in *The Secret Chamber: Spiritual Wifery*)
Type Style, Adobe Garamond

Front Cover

A golden ring, symbol of marriage has been placed over one of King David's Psalms in the Bible for this book cover. Light then casts a heart-shaped shadow on David's words of praise for God and His mercy. It is an appropriate symbol for both King David and the content of this book. The LORD compared David's heart to His own (1 Sam. 13:14). King David once had many wives and concubines, like some of the other kings in surrounding cultures. After David repented of his sins (1 Sam. 12:13), he turned his heart fully to "The Eternal" – the LORD Jesus Christ, God of the Old Testament (1 Kings 11:6). He did so with a broken heart and contrite spirit (Psalm 51:7 & 17). King David then put away his concubines and additional wives (see 2 Sam. 20:3), devoting himself solely to the living God and to one wife. His heart had been made new (chap. 7). This "mighty change" is a central feature of the Doctrine of Christ.

Forward, *Rock Waterman*

If this book had been available forty-odd years ago I might have changed my mind about becoming a Mormon Fundamentalist. To be clear, I never did join up with the Fundamentalists, but for a while I did think long and hard about it. This was in 1977, after I had I left my home in Anaheim, California to seek my fortune in Provo, Utah. (Yeah, you don't have to tell me. Nobody goes to Provo to seek their fortune. I know that now.) Anyway, I was 26 years old, a returned missionary, and still unmarried; one of those notorious "menaces to society, as I was constantly being reminded by the grownups in the Anaheim Stake. I figured maybe I could find a nice girl at BYU and settle down. Eventually circumstances led me to Utah, and Provo became my home. Being a bibliophile, I spent a lot of time at a used bookstore just south of the BYU campus called Grandpa's Books. It was owned by a young guy in his late twenties who favored long-sleeved flannel shirts, even in the summer. This was "Grandpa." He and I became pretty good friends, but it was quite some time before I learned his biggest secret.

One day I stopped in to browse and found the the owner's wife watching the store while he was taking care of business elsewhere. She and I ended up talking about this and that, and I learned that she and her husband were not actually native Utahns as I had assumed, but fairly recent converts from New Jersey, of all places. She told me they had moved to Utah to be closer to the church, and that after much study of church history, had concluded that plural marriage was the proper mode of living, and that it had been a mistake for the church to abandon the practice in 1890. In fact, the two of them had recently invited another young girl into their marriage, and were now "Independent Fundamentalists," which meant they weren't associated with any established fundamentalist sect.

My curiosity was piqued. I knew that generations of Utahns had grown up "living the principle," but what was it about polygamy that had attracted this otherwise normal couple from New Jersey to adopt it? I began reading books by fundamentalist authors who maintained that the church took a wrong turn when Wilford Woodruff effectively ended polygamy at the end of the 19th century. This made sense to me at the time, as I was astute enough to have noticed that the gifts of the spirit seemed to be largely absent in the modern LDS church. I was taught that we were a church that benefited from continuous revelation, yet I couldn't name an instance when a president of the church in my day ever claimed to have received one. If these guys were prophets, why didn't they ever prophesy? If they were seers, why didn't they offer to translate the missing fragments of the recently discovered Dead Sea Scrolls?

I had seen countless priesthood blessings given to the sick; I had given many myself. Yet I never saw anyone instantly healed after receiving one of these blessings. I wondered, why not? Mormon histories document healing blessings being instantly effective time after time during Kirtland/Missouri/Nauvoo era. Clearly the True Church today was not anything like it used to be. I was ready to agree with the conclusion of the fundamentalists; that God abandoned the Saints when the Saints abandoned plural marriage.

I know better now. It wasn't the *abandonment* of polygamy that brought the wrath of God down on the Saints, it was the *adoption* of that abominable practice in the first place. I had been looking for answers to that puzzle in the wrong time period, when it should have been obvious that the cursings began with the unauthorized takeover of the church by Brigham Young. As Val Brinkerhoff documents in the book you are now holding, the falling away of the Saints began with the insidious machinations of the Secret Chamber that had been operating without the Prophet's knowledge. This "secret priesthood" as they themselves called it, was led by Brigham Young, Willard Richards, and Heber C. Kimball. They were the *Secret Chamber* the Lord warned Joseph about in revelation. These usurpers were the architects of the conspiracy that led to the murders of the Prophet and his brother the Patriarch. The secret chamber members were in fact the authors of the cursed doctrine of plural marriage. They falsely claimed Joseph had revealed it to them, when in fact he warned the Saints repeatedly that it would prove the destruction of the Church.

In the spring of 1844, Joseph Smith instructed Nauvoo's stake president to initiate excommunication proceedings against these conspirators. But then the prophet made a fatal mistake. He had denounced plural marriage many times from the pulpit, but this time, in front of a congregation of three thousand Saints, he declared that he had learned that some men closest to him were guilty of this abominable practice and that he was preparing to rout them out. Three weeks later he was dead.

Rock Waterman is author of the popular blog puremormonism.blogspot.com *which documents the changes in the LDS church that began with the takeover by Brigham Young's illicit secret combination. Three years after arriving in Provo, Rock did find the girl of his dreams, the lovely Connie Bradfield, who to this day remains the* only *woman he has ever taken in marriage.*

The Secret Chamber

Spiritual Wifery and the Doctrine of Christ

Polygamy in Mormonism

Fruits in the Vineyard

This book is written to all Latter-day Saints or former Saints, either in or out of the church. It is focused on the complex subject of polygamy and how Satan used it to wreak havoc on the fullness of the gospel of Christ early on in church history, resulting in what the Book of Mormon calls our "awful situation" today.

The purpose of the fullness of the gospel of Christ at the beginning of Joseph's Restoration movement was to bring salvation to all those who would turn to Christ the LORD. He and the Father raised up the Prophet Joseph Smith for this purpose. Satan opposed the Restoration plan and used polygamy and Freemasonry early on to effectively stifle part of it, specifically the fullness portion of Christ's precious gospel. It has led to our awful situation today.

Joseph's primary mission was to bring forth more of God's priceless word in scripture, and specifically in two key works; (1) the Book of Mormon, and (2) Joseph Smith's inspired re-translation of the entire Bible. Together, God called them "**the fullness of my scriptures**" (see D&C 42:12, 15, 56-59). They were to go forth to world together, as one volume, along with the oracles or revelations contained in the Doctrine and Covenants. It was part of God's work through the Prophet Joseph to bring forth the fullness of the doctrine, gospel, and church of Christ - to the blessed remnant of Jacob and of Lehi on this land, and to repentant Jews and Gentiles everywhere. Unfortunately, the publication of both works did not happen in Joseph's lifetime. They didn't go out together in one volume.

Polygamy and other distractions introduced by Satan early on - via a secret combination, stopped this portion of Joseph's mission from being completed in his lifetime (see D&C 38:13 & 28). It eventually led to Joseph's murder, and that of his brothers Hyrum and Samuel Smith in 1844. It wouldn't be until 1867 that Joseph's entire re-translation of the Bible would finally be published, and by Joseph Smith's firstborn son, Joseph Smith III. He did so as the President of the RLDS church in Missouri. Unknown to most, Joseph Smith III, in collaboration with the U.S. Government in the late 19th century, helped eradicate the abomination of polygamy among the Saints in Utah Territory. He did so to clear his father's name from this practice, and to help remove the curses which polygamy had brought upon the Brighamite Saints. This is part of the untold story you are about to be exposed to.

Consulting God's word first and digging deeper into our history has resulted in my conclusion that the Prophet Joseph is innocent of polygamy. But even if he was not, the message of this book remains the same, one consistent with the Book of Mormon and other scripture. And that message is that polygamy is a whoredom that brings with it curses. Joseph's name has been used to promote a narrative that is **not** true, all for the sake of **gain** (1 Ne. 22:23). It continues today. If Satan and evil and designing men can get you and others to believe that Joseph was a polygamist, and that he deceived Emma and many others to live it, then it is easy to throw him out and embrace Brigham Young and his ways. For most, however, the false narrative of Joseph's polygamy *and* the clear practice of it by Brigham is a stumbling block that results in not only throwing Joseph out, the Book of Mormon he brought forth, and the church, but most importantly **Christ the LORD**. All can be flushed away and darkness wins. This book has been created that all the Saints, for or against polygamy, might come to **the truth**, and **He** is Jesus the Christ. **He is the way, the truth, and the life** (John 14:6). **He** as truth sets us all free, regardless of what Joseph and Brigham did or did not do.

The **key** to find **truth** about polygamy in this deceiving world is to turn to God for it in the **fullness** of His word. He has encouraged us to turn **first** to His written word in scripture (D&C 18:3), especially the Book of Mormon *along with* Joseph's re-translation of the Bible. We are then to turn to God's revealed word to us personally in **pure revelation**. We must pray fervently for clarity and truth from **the source** of all truth. Only with these two important witnesses together - can we overcome the lies, deception, and ignorance spread all around us - to find **light**. This is one of the first messages of the Book of Mormon. Lehi and Nephi his son found light at the Tree of Life, but only after they were first enveloped in darkness, led there by a **man** *dressed in white* (see 1 Nephi 8:5-11; 2 Ne. 7:10-11; Isa. 50:7-11). The light found was Jesus and His love. He then takes us to the Father (and later Mother). Lehi, Nephi, and others in the Book of Mormon tasted the sweet fruit of this Tree (God's love) and worked hard to bring others to it too.

Re-introducing readers to this pathway is a primary goal in this book. It is thus focused on three related themes; (1) **polygamy**, (2) **idolatry**, and (3) **the doctrine of Christ.** Addressing them together brings understanding of why things are they way they are, with so much lying, deception, and distraction, keeping us from partaking of **the Tree**. It was and is part of Satan's plan to destroy us by removing the fuller, saving portions of the doctrine and gospel of Christ. This work re-introduces readers to the important saving doctrines of Christ, revealing how they were modifed or removed when Brigham Young, and the Saints following him, embraced spiritual wifery.

Throughout history, Satan and his followers have opposed God's saving mission. When they organize into a **secret combination**, there is control, coercion, and often murder, all to get and keep "gain" (1 Ne. 22:23). Eighty-three scriptures in the Book of Mormon address secret combinations. They provide understanding of our current situation today. For most men, "gain" is sex, power, money, the honors of men, and the things of the world. When secret combinations rise up among us, all those under their control then become part of an **"awful situation."** We as Saints are currently in such a predicament, though far too many are not fully aware of it. All are invited to "awake and arise."

The phrase – "awful situation" - is addressed two times in the Book of Mormon (Mosiah 2:40 & Ether 8:24). King Benjamin, a wise, holy man in the book, revealed that it is to be in an **unsaved**, **unrepentant** state, unable to receive God's light. This is especially troubling in our day, as the great harvest of souls addressed in scripture is nearly upon us (see D&C 45:2, 56:16; Jer. 17:11). Towards the end of the Book of Mormon, Moroni tells us why so many are in this **awful**, **unsaved** condition. It is because of another "awful situation," the **secret combinations surrounding us** (Ether 8:24). They keep us in ignorance purposely for their gain. It isn't just governments that do this (national, state, and city). Secret agendas are fully entrenched in our educational institutions, in the media and entertainment industries, in schools (lower and higher education), *and* in churches. This is the clear message of the Book of Mormon. The book has solutions for us too. As the word of God, it can be trusted. Scripture is thus the lens we will first turn to in each of the ensuing chapters. They reveal the remaining curses we have inherited from our early polygamy.

The Prophet Mormon said that **all churches** in our day would be polluted (Morm. 8:36), and that those in them would be **ashamed of Christ**. The LORD Himself said that we would **deny** Him (2 Ne. 28:32), **reject** Him (2 Ne. 1:10), and **forsake** Him (Jer. 2:13; 17:5-14). The Book of Mormon addresses **us** as Latter-day Saints. Too many have believed that the prophets in this book are speaking of others. Instead, we are the ones who have been commanded by Christ to read the book, and especially the revealing words of Isaiah found in it (via 21 Isaiah chapters) along with the Bible. God's word in it collectively addresses our day, our **"awful situation."** Early **polygamy**, and the **idolatry** tied to it (in church and leader worship), has replaced the LORD Jesus Christ as our light in too many instances.

The Israelites of the Bible forsook God from time to time, so too believers in the Book of Mormon. The Latter-day Saints of early church history did so too, as too many do today. It began in subtle form when the man Joseph Smith was raised up to be a light to the people as their "Prophet, Seer, and Revelator," rather than seeking after our Savior (see 3 Ne. 18:24). Idolatry (placing faith and trust in "flesh" - mortal leaders) took on an even stronger role among the Nauvoo Saints when half of them followed Brigham Young and the Twelve west, out of Nauvoo and into polygamy. It cursed the Saints for some sixty years in Utah Territory, until a government crackdown stopped this whoredom for most. The early curse of this form of idolatry, however, remains with us. It is an institutional practice, reinforced with mantras like "follow the prophet," indoctrinated into our primary children at a very young age. Another mantra reinforcing this idolatry states, "we cannot and will not lead you astray." Neither statement is found in scripture. Both take our focus off of the LORD Jesus. To receive light, truth, and real salvtion, we must rely on Him as our ROCK.

Satan's introduction of the whoredom of polygamy early on in Mormonism has had a significant negative impact upon the Saints. Chief among many addressed hereafter, is our ignorance of the pathway to Salvation. It is an **"awful situation"** to remain in sin, darkness, and ignorance when salvation and significant progression thereafter is possible (see Mosiah 2:36-41). Because of pride, many Saints believe they already have salvation through their works and are thus not seeking the LORD and His salvation. I know, for I was in this **awful situation** for much of my life. I was deceived. For far too many, ordinances completed in the temple, and years of service in the church, are assummed indicators of at least some level of salvation. Wise virgins like Alma in the Book of Mormon eventually came to realize that their works were dead works, and that Christ the LORD was and is the only one providing us **redemption** on a personal, individual basis. Alma discovered this while listening to Abinadi. He shared his powerful witness of the living God. Alma then wisely left his sins and King Noah's court to seek and receive this salvation. He cried out to God for mercy (like Lehi in 1 Nephi 8:5-11) and then was made new in **Him**. This message repeats throughout the book that God has given us through Joseph the Prophet.

There are a number of key scriptures in the Book of Mormon that reveal its primary focus is two things: (1) **salvation** through Christ the LORD and how to receive it, and its polar opposite (2) the **secret combinations** that rise up among men to stop it. Those reading it are invited to "**awake** and **arise**." Before we can receive salvation and arise into our LORD's holy presence, we must first awaken to the "awful situation" we find oursevles in (our unsaved status). Much of this is a direct result of the curses upon us that arose from decades of polygamy in our early history.

As part of Joseph Smith's important mission, God had him bring forth the Book of Mormon first, because it clearly presents these two key messages to us. Both are desperately needed today. Both were corrupted to some degree in the Bible. Again, the first is, (1) the clear pattern of "**how** to be **saved or redeemed**" **of God**. And the second is, (2) the clear pattern of how Satan continually inhibits "the way of salvation" by **corrupting God's fullness of truth from within**, and often via **secret combinations** (organized evil). Polygamy was a significant part of Satan's plan to pollute the church in our early history, as we will see hereafter. It is thus a primary focus of this work. It also reveals the reasons for our present state. This work shines light into the darkness to fully expose it hereafter. Be open and prayerful, for many of these truths will be unfamiliar, even shocking. In the end, however, the truth sets us free.

In the four Book of Mormon events listed below, note that each of them features an individual or group escaping sin and corruption. Note that each situation is **marked by sexual immorality** (including polygamy), as part of a **secret combination** put in place by leaders for this and other forms of "gain." Each of them resulted in an awful situation, where the wise needed to (1) awaken to it first; (2) they are then encouraged to turn to **the LORD** in repentance; And in the end, (3) they departed from their predicament, their awful situation. For ancient Israel, they left Egypt and Babylon. Modern Israel today must do so *spiritually* first. Our salvation is at stake. We the modern Saints are the fifth group presented below, and are in the same awful situation addressed throughout scripture. We too are being tested and encouraged to grow via experience. We must be "wise" virgins and choose between two ways to awake and arise.

1. Lehi was committed to the LORD and had a vision of impending judgment on the city of Jerusalem. He took his family and departed wicked Jerusalem, as its leaders were oppressing the people with high taxes and practicing **whoredoms**, like those of David and Solomon of old (see Jacob 2:25). Lehi and Nephi turned their hearts fully to God and were preserved, taken to this new Promised Land, to raise up righteous seed or a branch of the house of Israel here, while the great city Jerusalem was destroyed.

2. Alma was a priest in King Noah's court of priests (the king replaced righteous priests with his own). They enjoyed the chief seats, living off the people with high taxes in order to support their lavish lifestyle, including **many wives** and concubines (Mosiah 11:1-8). Alma repented, leaving the King's court after hearing Abinadi's stirring testimony of Christ. He turned to God, then sought to awaken others to their **unsaved** condition. They came together in the wilderness, where they were free to pursue the LORD and His pure truths.

3. The *once* enlightened and believing Nephites allowed outside influences to corrupt them. They embraced both **secret combinations** and the **whoredom** of polygamy, whereas their enemy (the unbelieving Lamanites) loved the single wife each had, and their children. Jacob tells us that God allowed the Lamanites to destroy the entire Nephite civilization because of their *two great sins*. The LORD preserved a *remnant* of these people on this land **because** they did not embrace **either** of these sins. The book is written to *them*, and to Jews and Gentiles (see the Title Page).

4. God also brought the Brother of Jared and his people to this special land to escape the evil at the Tower of Babel. Like Jerusalem, **idolatry** and **whoredoms** were also rampant. In time, the same old plans of the evil one surfaced here, those tied to getting gain and using secret blood-oaths and murder to maintain it. This secret combination pattern is repeatedly used to topple kingdoms and start new ones, that sex, power, and money might be maintained by those in control. Eighty-three scriptures address this in the Book of Mormon.

5. Modern awakening Latter-day Saints are once again leaving *spiritual* Egypt and Babylon **to find the LORD** and escape darkness, corruption, and increasing sexual sin all around us. They are the "wise virgins" invited to be with Him in the Bridal Chamber. You and I must make difficult choices as we awake to this awful situation spoken of in the book, discovering **our** need for salvation, as secret combinations increase around us, keeping far too many from **truth**. And that truth is that we need to know God, receiving salvation and Him personally, and His other gifts.

Seeking Truth

Hereafter this book will present much that may be uncomfortable and unsettling. I have done my best to insure that it is truthful, but as in all things, you would be wise to consult God at every turn. He is the fountain of living waters. The LORD Jesus is also our primary source light as the father of our salvation (3 Nephi 18:24). His word tells us that truth is a dividing, powerful sword, forcing us one way or the other (Matt. 10:34). Do you want truth? Will you receive it? Many are happy to remain in ignorance, yet God has said that **we cannot be saved in ignorance** (D&C 131:6). In each chapter that follows, God's holy word in scripture is consulted first for **His** light and direction. The works of men in books, papers, and websites are then used for their added support. The *sources* chosen are very important. Too many of them have been corrupted by an agenda. Whether pro or anti-polygamy in their focus, each provides "evidence" that Joseph Smith had many wives or just one. Their opposing viewpoints quote many sources to support their claims, but rarely the fullnesss of God's word in scripture. The truth about polygamy can be a confusing mess, often full of lies and deception. The best place to start is always **God's written word**. I put my faith and trust in God, as did Nephi and Jeremiah (2 Ne. 4:34, 28:31; Jer. 17:5). The results are profound and revealing, and are backed up by the most trustworthy historical sources. The final word, however, is God's confirmation in **pure revelation** via prayer. It too is not consulted enough. Too few have learned to receive "pure" revelation – from God. Scripture tells us that in the mouth of these two or three witnesses, **all truth** is established (2 Cor. 13:1). Scripture and "pure" revelation are our two most important witnesses! Our courrupted history is a distant third.

For us to receive "pure" revelation, we must be clean, via heartfelt, sincere repentance and have an open, believing, and receptive heart. This **requires us to be free of our own biases**, called "**idols**" in scripture We as Latter-day Saints often hold many **idols in our hearts**, based on what our leaders and our Mormon culture have given us. These biases are called "**iniquities**" in scripture – passed down to us from "fathers, priests, and kings." They become part of our belief and tradition and have a profound affect upon our ability to **receive truth** ***in*** new, more accurate ideas.

WHO we believe determines What we believe.

Truth is obtained from the purest, uncorrupted sources. Because of the **iniquity** of **idolatry**, the Saints are conditioned to accept the narrative of "the arm of flesh" (mortal leaders) rather than God - in most all things, including polygamy. Sadly, this is one of the poorest sources of truth we have regarding this topic, primarily because of changes made to official church history, journals, and other sources, by those controlling this history immediately following Joseph Smith's murder. In ensuing chapters, we will see that **seven sources** of information for us (chap. 2) were modified to reflect a pro-polygamy stance, first under the direction of Brigham Young (chap. 2). Following the murder of the Smith brothers, a division arose among the Saints as to who should be their new leader. It was the succession crisis of 1844 (chap. 4). The most prominent dividing line for the Saints at Nauvoo at that time was **who to believe**. One's choice led them into two primary groups, those calling themselves "Brighamites" **or** "Josephites."

By 1846, the dividing line eventually led to their support of **or** rejection of **polygamy**. Early on the support and practice of it by leaders was *hidden* from the followers. It became more prominent among church leaders between 1844-and 46, after Joseph, Hyrum, and Samuel Smith were murdered. It was in the valleys of Utah Territory where Brigham Young finally let "**the cat out of the bag**" in 1852, informing the Saints that polygamy (and polyandry) had been practiced secretly in Nauvoo since the early 1840's (this is confirmed today by Church leadership). Half the Saints there rejected Brigham Young's leadership, his polygamy, and other new doctrines he began introducing to the people. These included not only polygamy, but Young's blood atonement doctrine, the Adam-God theory, the law of adoption, and other false doctrines, some in connection with a modified form of the temple endowment. The Josephites who remained behind wanted to stay true to Joseph Smith's early teachings and to the pure doctrines of Christ in the Book of Mormon. In time both groups latter lost focus on God and His will and became corrupted by the things of the world. It was and is a repeat of the apostasy – restoration cycle of scripture, occurring over and over again. What was needed then and today is a surer foundation, and that **Rock** is Christ the LORD. He is "**the way**." I choose to believe **Him** and trust **His word** first and foremost. With it there is clarity and hope rather than confusion.

Polygamy was practiced secretly in Nauvoo early on by a select few leaders until the three Smith brothers were murdered. Polygamy then exploded among the people at Nauvoo. Eight years later in Salt Lake (1852) the doctrine of "plurality of wives" was announced to the world as a **new tenet** or **doctrine** of the faith, part of Brigham's "**new order of things**." Thirteen different names would eventually be tied to this **whoredom**, many of them used to hide it from those around them *and* especially the Federal Government (p. 191). These deceptive names and the false **justification** tied to the practice - that Joseph Smith originated the practice - reflect the same old perversions of the Bible and the Book of Mormon. It is an unholy mix of religion with sex. The practice was later given the more acceptable title of "celestial" marriage. The Cochranites north of Boston called it "**spiritual wifery**." **Lies** leading to **deception** promoted the practice and maintained it. Satan is the father of all such lies (Moses 4:4).

Because of the division among the Nauvoo Saints early on, there are two sets of history to consult when researching polygamy. One reflects the modified, pro-polygamy stance of the Brighamite Saints that followed Brigham Young west to the Rocky Mountains. This is the one put forth by leadership of the LDS church today. The other history is that of the Josephites who refused to except Brigham Young as a leader, his polygamy, and other teachings. Once again, **who we believe determines what we believe**. Too many of the Brighamite Saints are unfamiliar with the other half of our history, the Josephite history, that of **the Smith family**. Their voices have been suppressed. Many have held the assumption that the Josephites left behind are not trustworthy, or that they are an "apostate" group that rejected Brigham Young and the church. This too is a lie, part of a labeling technique used to diminish, demean, discredit, downplay, or ignore *the opposing viewpoint*, as it most likely adds significant light to the story. The Josephite story **is** significant. It features **Joseph Smith's unmodified words**, and those of **the Smith family** generally. They have been underutilized and ignored by the Brighamite Saints. Hereafter, three primary sources are consulted for the polygamy information in this book which follows. It is a fascinating, enlightening journey.

1. **God** God's written word in *scripture* is consulted first. We must be careful to let it say what it says without bias or filtration. We must then consult His direct word via *pure revelation*, obtained by seeking **His will** and the **truth**, regardless of the resulting ramifications. This requires us to remove all **idols in our heart**, all assumptions, etc. The scriptures may include some sources that have been ignored (the full JST Bible), and some in the LDS canon of scripture that have been modified (Jacob 3:5), added to (D&C 132, or removed from it - the old D&C 101) by men, **without a vote** of priesthood quorums and church membership (see D&C 26:2; Mosiah 29:26; Alma 29:4; 1 Sam. 8:7). This is how our single pro-polygamy work (D&C 132) became part of our scripture.

2. **The Smith Family** The most truthful, unbiased sources relative to LDS polygamy originate in **the Smith family**, not in third party witnesses, produced decades *after* the fact, and by those with an *agenda*. We can use the unfiltered, unmodified words of their own mouths, not questionable witnesses who claim Joseph said one thing, while actually saying another. Hereafter we will consult the Prophet Joseph Smith Jr. and his brothers Hyrum, Samuel, and William Smith, and his sister Katharine Smith, along with Joseph's mother Lucy Mack Smith, his wife Emma Smith, and Joseph's firstborn son, Joseph Smith III. The words of **the Smith's** have been under-utilized by the Brighamite Saints out west, as they are **anti-polygamy** and are thus unpopular among the pro-polygamy groups today, led by the Utah LDS church and its leaders, of which I have been a member since age 8. I am a Brighamite by tradition, but a Josephite in belief. I have a leg in each camp and have come to under-stand both positions. Most importantly, I value God and the truth He gives. I let both sides have their say and then compare it to **God's word** in scripture. This helps in forming questions to take to the LORD for His confirmation, the pattern of all wise ones in scripture. Joseph read James 1:5-6 and prayed. I recommend it.

3. **Unmodified Sources of History** One must be very careful with the pro-polygamy history of the LDS church, as official LDS church sources have been modified to reflect the stance of Brigham Young early on (chap. 2). They are often questionable. This is the evaluation of some early, **official LDS Church historians** familiar with our early documents. Sadly, the less biased, unmodified sources on this subject are typically those obtained from non-LDS Church sources, those who separated from Brigham Young in Nauvoo. Like the Smith family, most of them claim Joseph Smith was innocent of polygamy, and that he was **framed** as its originator to **justify** its practice among the early Brighamite Saints, those fully committed to this whoredom early on.

The Important Message for Us in the Book of Mormon

In D&C 84, the Oath and Covenant of the Priesthood, the LORD informed the Saints that we remain under condemnation for not understanding *and* implementing the teachings of the Book of Mormon, and specifically its pathway to salvation – in the "fullness" of Christ's gospel. The condemnation is given us in verses 50 and 51, where God states boldly that those who do ***not*** **repent** and **come unto Him** are under "**the bongage of sin**." To overcome this, we have been given "the everlasting covenant" or the "**fullness**" of the gospel of Christ (D&C 66:2).

It is to obey God's will (see endnote 31). It is to embrace the pathway God lays out for us to receive a fullness of salvation **from Him**. Throughout scripture and in our early history, we see men modifying God's ways, adding things they desire (like polygamy). They then lift themselves up as **lights** before the people (priestcraft) for the sake of **gain**. The Book of Mormon was given that we might recognize this corrupt pattern. That book contains "the new covenant." In it we are reminded to "**repent** and **remember**" the original covenant in verse 57. There, God states:

> "And your minds in times past have been darkened because of *unbelief*, and because you have treated lightly the things you have received—Which vanity and unbelief have brought the whole church under condemnation. And this condemnation resteth upon the children of Zion, even all. And they shall remain under this condemnation until they **repent** and **remember the new covenant, even the Book of Mormon** and the former commandments which I have given them, not only to say, but to **do** according to that **which I have written**—That they may bring forth fruit meet for their Father's kingdom; otherwise there remaineth a scourge and judgment to be poured out upon the children of Zion" (D&C 84:54-57).

This scripture was given early on in **1832**. We have reaped portions of this scourge and judgment because of early choices. Fortunately there is always hope in Christ. Ten scriptures presented hereafter summarize the entire Book of Mormon message – and many in association with the polygamy of early Mormonism. In them and others we find that the Book of Mormon presents two primary messages; (1) **God's plan of salvation**, offered to us via His love - in an invitation, and (2) **Satan's secretive plan to stop it**, typically in association with secret combinations that oppress us and keep us ignorant of God's saving ways, all **for the sake of gain**. Clear knowledge of these two polar opposites represent "**the plain and precious things**" *edited out* of the Bible by evil and designing men. God thus raised up the Prophet Joseph Smith to *restore* these truths to us in the Book of Mormon *and* the Joseph Smith re-translation of the Bible. Both of these messages are tied to our **awful situation** today, that many remain unredeemed (Mosiah 2:36-41), because of the secret combinations that keep us ignorant of both things - for the sake of **their gain** (Ether 8:24).

The rise of polygamy among us, within a secret combination, is the subject of God's revelation in D&C 38:13 and 28. Few are aware of it. God called it "**the secret chamber**" there (chap. 3). It was put it place fully within the church at Nauvoo and led to the murder of three Smith brothers, that polygamy might be embraced. It is awful to **not** be fully aware of "**the way**" of salvation of our God, addressed most clearly in the Book of Mormon (chap. 7). In this inspired, merciful plan, we have opportunity to choose between **two ways**; one of God and one of men and Satan. The latter hides the truth in **secrecy**, seeking to control us for gain. The former is tied to God's love for us and features His simple, five-word invitation to receive salvation from **Him** directly, by rejecting corrupt ones that want control, the honors of men, and our money. **Jesus** is **the way**, **the truth**, and **the life** (John 14:6). He repeatedly invites us to receive Him and His best gifts. He repeatedly says, "**repent** and **come unto me**." It is a very efficient, five-word summary of His love, available to those who embrace His doctrine, His gospel, and His church (see D&C 10:67, 1828). Many simply call it - "**the doctrine of Christ**." Satan used polygamy and other things to corrupt it.

In the early chapters of the Book of Mormon, Lehi and Nephi were both shown a vision of the Tree of Life. It was a representation of the love of God and the pathway to the Tree where we can taste of its sweet, white fruit. Few get on this straight and narrow path. Most remain in the comfort of the great and spacious building (man's religion), primarily because it is **easier** to follow men rather than work to **know God**. Church leaders tell us, "we cannot and will not lead you astray." This results in idolatry and ignorance of **the salvation that is <u>only</u> obtained from God** - personally. We must cry out **to Him for salvation** as Alma did, not follow men. A type is given us in 1 Ne. 8:5-11, where a "**<u>man</u>**" dressed in a white robe invited Lehi to **follow <u>him</u>**. Lehi did so and was led into a dark and dreay wasteland (see 2 Ne. 7:10-11; Isa. 50:7-11). Lehi *cried out* **to God** in the darkness and was then **delivered by Him**!

> "And it came to pass that I saw a **man**, and he was dressed in a *white robe*; and he came and stood before me. And it came to pass that he spake unto me, and *bade me follow him*. And it came to pass that *as I followed him* I beheld myself that I was in a dark and dreary waste. And after I had traveled for the space of many hours *in darkness*, I began to pray unto the Lord that he would have mercy on me, according to the multitude of his tender mercies" (1 Ne. 8:5-8).

Later in his own vision, Lehi's son Nephi addressed our choice between the two ways - **men or God**, stating:

> "Behold **there are save two churches only**; the one is **the church of the Lamb of God**, and the other is the

> church of the devil; wherefore, whoso belongeth **not** to the church of the Lamb of God belongeth to that great church, which is the mother of abominations; and she is the whore of all the earth...and she had dominion over all the earth, among all nations, kindreds, tongues, and people...I beheld the church of the Lamb of God, and its numbers were **<u>few</u>**, because of the wickedness and abominations of the whore" (1 Ne. 14:10-13).

Too many remain in the great and spacious building. **Pride** is the number one reason, a sin among those in it. **Pride** leads to other sins, keeping many thinking they are already saved as God's special people. They thus do not seek for more, including real salvation from **God**, rather than men and their churches, **all** of which are **polluted** (Morm. 8:36).

> "ye do walk in the **pride** of your hearts...and all manner of iniquities; and **your churches, yea, even <u>every one</u>, have become polluted** because of the pride of your hearts. For behold, ye do love money, and your substance, and your fine apparel, and the adorning of your churches, more than ye love the poor and the needy, the sick and the afflicted. O ye pollutions, ye hypocrites, ye teachers, who sell yourselves for that which will canker, **why have ye polluted the holy church of God? Why are ye ashamed to take upon you the name of Christ**...?" (Morm. 8:36-38).

Once again, the primary purpose of secret combinations, leading to our "**awful situation**," is **gain**. It is hidden to keep us paying for it all. And as a result, we are given milk (little doctrine and distracting "dead works"), rather than saving meat. We are then left ignorant, **unredeemed** of God. Such are deceived, believing "all is well."

> "For the time speedily shall come that all churches which are built up to [1] get **gain**, and all those who are built up to [2] get power over the flesh, and those who are built up to [3] become popular in the eyes of the world, and those who seek [4] the lusts of the flesh and [5] the things of the world, and [6] to do all manner of iniquity; yea, in fine, all those who [7] belong to the kingdom of the devil are they who need fear, and tremble, and quake; they are those who must be brought low in the dust; they are those who must be consumed as stubble; and this is according to the words of **the prophet**" [who **is the Holy One of Israel**, v. 21] (1 Ne. 22:23).

Like the kings of the Bible, and the world in general, the kings in the book of Ether in the Book of Mormon sought for "**gain**" in power, money, and many wives and concubines. They turned to "the old plans," the **secret blood-oaths** of the evil one in Moses 5:29-31, along with murder, and placed burdens upon the people to get and keep this gain (see Ether 8:13-16, 21-26; 9:26; 10:33; Hel. 6:16-41). This Book of Mormon **pattern** was present with King Noah and King Riplakish, the latter "did afflict the people with his whoredoms and abominations" along with heavy taxes. So also his son King Morianton, and, "because of his many **whoredoms**...he was **cut off from the presence of the LORD**." Kings Akish, Riplakish, and Morianton in Ether 8-9, and King Noah of Mosaiah 11 are given us as **types** or **patterns** for why Joseph and Hyrum were murdered at Nauvoo. Wicked leaders seek power and many wives in their kingdoms. Such are **cut off** from God. They oppress others, murdering those in power to get and keep their "gain."

Seeing our day, the Father commanded the Son Jesus to address similar sins among the Saints of our day, those at Kirtland, Nauvoo, and Salt Lake. The ten sins He lists below are very revealing. Most of the Saints have **not** considered that they **<u>refer to us</u>** - past and present, as we will see in ensuing chapters. In God's wisdom, these sins are listed for us **five times** as a clear **witness** in (1) 3 Ne. 16:10, (2) 3 Ne. 21:19, (3) 3 Ne. 30:2, (4) Book of Commandments 4:5-6, and (5) D&C 123:12-13. In His mercy and love, God also shows us **how** to escape them in the last verse of 3 Nephi, in verse 2 of chapter 30. The message of all **five scriptures** is that following God leads us to light, whereas following men leads us to **lies**, **deception**, and their *curses* (2 Ne. 4:34, 28:31; Jer. 17:5).

> "And thus commandeth the Father that I [Jesus] should say unto **<u>you</u>**: At that day when the Gentiles [us] shall sin against *my gospel*, and shall **reject <u>the fulness</u> of my gospel**, and shall be lifted up in the **pride** of their hearts above all nations, and above all the people of the whole earth, and shall be filled with all manner of [1] **<u>lyings</u>**, and of [2] **<u>deceits</u>**, and of **mischiefs**, and all manner of **hypocrisy**, and **murders**, and **priestcrafts**, and **<u>whoredoms</u>**, **secret abominations**; and if they shall do all those things, and shall **reject the fulness of my gospel**, behold, saith the Father, I will bring **<u>the fulness</u> of my gospel** from among them. And then will I remember **my covenant** which I have made unto **my people**, O house of Israel, and I will bring **my gospel** unto them" (3 Ne. 16:10-11).

Who are "**my** people"? What is "**my** gospel" and its "**<u>fullness</u>**"?

"**Turn**, all ye Gentiles, from your wicked ways; and **repent** of your evil doings, of your [1] **lyings** and [2] **deceivings**, and of your *whoredoms*, and of your *secret abominations*, and your *idolatries*, and of your *murders*, and your *priestcrafts*, and your ***envyings***, and your *strifes*, and from all your *wickedness* and *abominations*, and **come unto me**, and be baptized in **my name,** that ye may receive a remission of your sins, and be filled with **the Holy Ghost**, that ye may be numbered with **my people** who are of the house of Israel" (3 Nephi 30:2).

Our sins as Saints are placed in a three-part listing *below*. Note especially that our LORD lists **lies** #1 and **deception** #2 at the start of all three lists (and two others, see pages 88-89). This is significant! Third Nephi 16:10 tells us that we will reject the "**the fullness**" of Christ's gospel, whereas 3 Nephi 30:2 tells us **what** this "**fullness**" **is**. And note too that the third sin listed in God's "top ten" listing in 30:2 is (3) "**whoredoms**." Polygamy and polyandry (as part of "**spiritual wifery**") were secretly practiced among select leaders in early church history until "the cat was let out of the bag" publically in Utah in 1852. Joseph, Hyrum, and Samuel Smith (the three murdered) were not among those practicing these things. They preached against them. To hide, protect, and maintain this part of their "gain," three sins were practiced repeatedly, those listed in 3 Nephi 30:2; (1) **lying,** (2) **deception**, and (3) **whoredoms**.

3 Nephi 16:10 (our Gentile **sins**)

we will reject the **fullness** of the gospel
and be lifted up in **pride**

and be filled with **lyings** (#**1**)
and **deceits** (#**2**)
and mischiefs
and all manner of hypocrisy
and murders
and priestcrafts
and **whoredoms**
and secret abominations

the **fullness** is taken from the Gentiles
and then given to the house of Israel

3 Nephi 21:14-21 (our Gentile sins)

wo unto the Gentiles except they **repent**
...And it shall come to pass that

all **lyings** (#**1**)
and **deceivings** (#**2**)
and envyings
and strifes
and priestcrafts
and **whoredoms** shall be done away

For it shall come to pass, saith the Father
...whosoever will **not repent** and **come unto my Beloved Son**, them will I cut off from among my people, O house of Israel

3 Nephi 30:2 (our Gentile **sins**)

Hearken of ye Gentiles, turn all ye Gentiles
from your wicked ways; and **repent** - of

all **lyings** (#**1**)
and **deceivings** (#**2**)
and **whoredoms**
and secret abominations
and idolatries
and murders
and priestcrafts
and envyings
and strifes
and all wickedness & abominations

and instead **come unto me**
and be baptized
and be filled with [fire &] the Holy Ghost
(this is the **fullness**, chap. 7)

Note also our LORD's mercy in 3 Nephi 30:2. He reminds us of the forgotten "*fuller*" pathway to His salvation in the same verse, telling us to "**turn**" or "**repent**" from these "evil doings" and "**come unto me**." We do this by being *physically* "**baptized unto repentance**" and in **His name**, that we might receive a second *spiritual* baptism by God Himself, one of fire, where we are literally purged of all our sins. This is where our sins are *fully* remitted. We are *sanctified* in this way, and then can receive the gift and power of the Holy Ghost - from God - to guide us back into His holy presence (see 2 Ne. 31 and 32). This is the "**fullness**" lost upon most of the Saints today! We can be numbered with those the LORD calls "**my people**" who "are of the house of Israel," the saved or **redeemed** ones. They are part of the church of the Lamb, *not* the churches of men (1 Ne. 14:10). Have you been made new in Christ?

I did not become aware of this pathway, nor experience it personally until the later years of my life. Most in the church today are unaware of how the second fiery baptism is received (see the instruction by Christ, John the Baptist, Joseph Smith, Nephi, and Alma on pages 242 - 245 in chap. 7). When one of the Twelve spoke at a recent Stake Conference in my area, he addressed 2 Nephi 31, but he did **not** address this second necessary *spiritual* baptism administered by God. Our Christian friends outside the LDS church call it being "**born again**," the central focus of 2 Nephi 31. Our collective ignorance of **the fullness** of **the way of salvation** of our God clearly illustrates how far we have drifted from "**the fullness**" Christ said **we would reject** in 3 Nephi 16:10. This "awful situation" can be remedied in the LORD's simple, five-word invitation – "**repent** and **come unto me**." We must do so in **His** way, with a *broken heart* and *contrite spirit* (3 Ne. 9:20). All our other works we perform are "**dead**" by comparison (2 Ne. 25).

This is the overlooked "**fullness**" of what He calls "**my** doctrine" and "**my** gospel" leading to entrance into "**my** church" (see 3 Nephi chapters 11 & 27). This "**fullness**" is summarized in five clear steps in chapter 7. The distraction of polygamy and new doctrines implemented by Young diminished the "fuller" things like the law of **real love** in "the law of consecration" *and* "the law of monogamy" (see D&C 42:2, 22-23, 30-37). **Lies** and **deception** are common threads found throughout this book and Satan's ways. They lead to *ignorance* of *our unredeemed state*, and of secret combinations that control us for gain. Satan was a *liar* and a *murderer* from the beginning (D&C 93:25; John 8:44). Seeing our day and the oppression caused by secret combinations surrounding us, Moroni stated:

> "O ye Gentiles, it is wisdom in God that these things should be shown unto **you**, that thereby **ye** may **repent** of your sins, and suffer not that these *murderous* **combinations** shall get above you, which are built up to get **power** and **gain**...when ye shall see these things come among you that ye shall **awake** to a sense of your **awful situation** because of this *secret* **combination** which shall be among you...for it is built up by the devil, who is the father of **lies**...even that same **liar** who hath caused man to commit murder from the beginning; who hath **hardened the hearts of men**..." (Ether 8:23-25).

Do not harden your heart to the truth of what follows. The wise, holy man known as King Benjamin was concerned for his people and their **unsaved** state. He loved his people. They are a type for the Saints today. He stated:

> "...if ye should transgress and go contrary to that which has been spoken, that ye do withdraw yourselves from the Spirit of the Lord, that it may have **no** place in you to guide you in wisdom's paths that ye may be blessed, prospered, and preserved...the man that doeth this, the same cometh out in open **rebellion** against God; therefore he listeth to obey the evil spirit, and becometh an enemy to all righteousness; therefore, the Lord has **no** place in him, for **he** dwelleth **not** in unholy temples. Therefore if that man **repenteth not**, and remaineth and dieth an enemy to God, the demands of divine justice do awaken his immortal soul to a lively sense of his own guilt, which doth cause him to shrink from the presence of the Lord, and doth fill his breast with guilt, and pain, and anguish, which is like an unquenchable fire, whose flame ascendeth up forever and ever. And now I say unto **you**, that mercy hath no claim on that man; therefore his final doom is to endure a never-ending torment...I pray that **ye should awake** to a remembrance of the **awful situation** of those that have fallen into *transgression*. And moreover, I would desire that **ye** should consider on the blessed and happy state of those that keep the commandments of God. For behold, **they** are blessed in all things, both temporal and spiritual; and if **they** hold out faithful to the end **they are received into heaven**, that thereby **they** may dwell with God in a state of never-ending happiness" (Mosiah 2:36-41).

Three chapters later in Mosiah 5, King Benjamin summed up his message. He had his people make a **covenant** with the LORD. Then they were "**spiritually begotten**" of God and became **His** sons and daughters. Their **hearts** had been changed through faith on **God's name**. They were **born again**. Then the King admonished them and us to be –

> "steadfast and immovable, always abounding in good works, that the LORD God Omnipotent may **seal you His**, that you may be **brought to heaven** [in this life], that ye may have **everlasting salvation and eternal life**" (Mos. 5:7 & 15).

Chapter 7 of this book is centered on "**the way** of salvation." In it there is hope, but **only** in Christ the LORD and **His** way. He states, "**repent** and **come unto me**" (see D&C 10:67-68, 93:1; 1 Ne. 10:18-19; 2 Ne. 9:23-24; 28:31-32; Jacob 1:7; Alma 5:33-34; Ether 4:7-19; Mor. 7:34; 3 Ne. 9:14, 22; 12:19-20, 23-24; 27:5-21; 30:2). It represents **the fullness** of **His** doctrine and **His** gospel, and includes those who then become part of **His** church. Chapters 1 through 6 hereafter address the rise and fall of polygamy among the Brighamite Saints, and what resulted.

An Introduction to Polygamy in Mormonism

Too often writings on the subject of polygamy utilize our corrupted, modified history. As we will see in chapter 2, Latter-day Saint history is very flawed, with manipulation, deletions and additions, all promoting the pro-polygamy agenda of those assuming power after the Smith brothers were murdered. To share **truth**, this work is grounded in scripture. God has directed us to **rely on His written word** *and* pure revelation from **Him** for all things (D&C 18:3). Satan and his followers hate God and want to destroy those who love and follow Him. Satan's favorite tools to destroy us are (1) pride, (2) idolatry, and (3) sexual sin. Secret combinations put them in place to spead their darkness.

1. The Sin of Pride

We need to know the truth about polygamy for many reasons. Because of pride, too many believe they already have truth and thus don't search for more. Pride pits our will against God's will. It is to seek one's own will, not "thine be done." The proud hearken to the precepts of men rather than the wisdom of God. They "love the praise of men more than the praise of God" (John 13:43). In choosing to **believe** *and* **trust God** - that **pride** is rampant among us as **He** said, we must choose to believe the Book of Mormon message that is written to **us. Pride** is the first sin mentioned by Jacob (son of Enos) in the book where he addresses "*the grosser crime*" of his people; their many wives and concubines, like the people of David and Solomon of the old world. According to Joseph Smith, the Book of Mormon is the **most correct book on earth**, and the **keystone** of our religion (HC 4:461). It clearly condemns polygamy and other sexual sin. Its words along with pure revelation from God, can bring us back to Him.

The Book of Mormon was written to *the remnant* of Jacob remaining on this land, along with *Jews*, and *Gentiles*. Most of us are in the third group, as Joseph Smith said (see D&C 109:60). Its words are to be likened unto us and our day (1 Ne. 19:23). In the Doctrine and Covenants the LORD tells us that the Book of Mormon is the "record of **a fallen people**" (D&C 20:9). The reason they fell (why *and* how) is one of the primary messages of the book. The Prophet Mormon stated, "Behold, the **pride** of this nation, or the people of the Nephites, hath proven their destruction" (Mor. 8:27). He added, "Beware of pride, lest **ye** become as the Nephites of old" (D&C 38:39). In the premortal council in heaven, it was **pride** that caused Lucifer, "a son of the morning," to fall (2 Ne. 24:12–15; D&C 76:25–27; Moses 4:3). At the end of this world, when God cleanses the earth by fire, the proud will be burned as stubble, whereas the meek shall inherit the earth (3 Ne. 12:5, 3 Ne. 25:1; D&C 29:9; JS—H 1:37; Mal. 4:1). All **pride** is sin. There is no such thing as righteous **pride**. Although it may have ties to self-centeredness, conceit, boastfulness, arrogance, or haughtiness, God uses the word **pride** to signal **enmity** toward Him and our fellowmen. Enmity means "hatred towards, hostility to, or in a state of opposition." Satan used **pride** to reign over us. In Jacob's denunciation of the whoredom of polygamy in Jacob chapters 2 and 3, he lists "**pride**" **first** - prior to other words associated with the sin of polygamy. It was, "a grosser crime." It was and is "wickedness," a "whoredom," and an "abomination."

At its core, **pride** is competitive in nature. With it we pit our will against God's superior understanding. It is "**my will** be done, and **not** thine." As Paul said, such "seek their own, not the things which are Jesus Christ's" (Philip. 2:21). It is to place **our will** in superior position to **God's will**. Doing so allows our heartfelt desires, appetites, and passions to go unbridled (Alma 38:12; 3 Ne. 12:30). **Pride** does not allow us to accept God's authority and His direction in our lives (Hel. 12:6), nor the truth of all things. We then pit our weaker perceptions of truth against God's much greater knowledge, love, and wisdom. Our enmity toward God is tied to rebellion, hard-heartedness, stiff-neckedness, being unrepentant, puffed up, and easily offended. When we are **prideful**, we wish God to agree with us. We aren't interested in **His will** - changing to agree with God. Enmity towards our fellowman causes us to elevate ourselves above others and diminish them. It is to be in competition with them, pitting our intellect, opinions, work, and talent against theirs (Hel. 6:17; D&C 58:41). In the pre-earth council, Lucifer placed his proposal in competition with the Father's plan, the one advocated by Christ (Moses 4:1–3). Lucifer desired honor above all others (2 Ne. 24:13). His **prideful** desire was and is to dethrone God (D&C 29:36; D&C 76:28).

Pride is also closely tied to selfishness, contention, and to secret combinations. They are built up to get gain, which is typically sex, power, money, and the honors of men (see 1 Ne. 22:23; Hel. 7:5; Ether 8:9, 16, 22–23; Moses 5:31). Secret combinations brought down the Jaredite nation, the Nephite civilization, and have been and will yet be the fall of many nations - us (Ether 8:18–25). As we will see in ensuing chapters, **pride** and secret combinations also led to many problems among the early Saints, including rejection of God's fullness, the murder of Joseph, Hyrum, and Samuel Smith, and the rise of polygamy thereafter for some sixty years, with all the resulting curses.

Pride continues to destroy individuals, groups, cities, and nations. "**Pride** goeth before destruction" (Prov. 16:18). It destroyed the Nephite nation completely and the cities of Sodom and Gomorrah (Moro. 8:27; Ezek. 16:49–50). The LORD Jesus spoke to the Prophet Joseph about **pride**, warning him to **not** fear or honor man more than God, stating, "For although a man may have many revelations, and have power to do many mighty works, yet if he boasts in his own strength, and sets at naught the counsels of God, and follows after the dictates of his **own will and carnal desires**, he must fall and incur the vengeance of a just God upon him" (D&C 3:4).

Too often the **prideful** stand more in fear of men's judgment than of God's judgment (D&C 3:6–7; D&C 30:1–2; D&C 60:2). They want "the praise of men more than the praise of God" (John 12:42–43). Jesus said He did, "always those things" that pleased God (John 8:29). Because of flawed reasoning, the **prideful** don't seek to take hold of the iron rod. It is God's pure revelation to us, along with His word in scripture (1 Ne. 8:19–28; 1 Ne. 11:25; 1 Ne.

15:23–24). Get rid of **pride**. Be humble. Receive the mighty change of heart by being born again in Christ Jesus, and obtain the Holy Ghost. Then go to God in prayer for answers on everything here. Know the truth. It will set you free.

2. Idoatry - Idols in our Hearts

Idolatry normally follows pride. In it we elevate men and things and diminish God. In it we come to fear man more than God. Satan is part of this. He is the great deceiver; a liar from the beginning. He and evil men desire that we remain in darkness, ignorance, and deception. The cover of this book features a heart-shaped illustration tied **to love of God**. To receive pure revelation from Him, directing us in this life, is one of the greatest blessings we can have. To receive it, we must love God with our whole heart, and remove all **idols** that may be there (our desire for other things). Our motives are a reflection of our heart and its condition. Jesus sought the Father's superior will and wisdom in all things (John 6:38). Pride causes us to place our desires ahead of those of God, and thus we receive lesser things, including deception. Scripture compares these desires to "**idols**" residing in the deep chambers of our heart. They drive our focus and actions. They can be things like fame, money, and position, or people, like actors, sports heros, or church leaders. If we do not value God above them, seeking a close relationship with Him, these things become an **idol** *replacing* **God**. When this happens, our ability to receive *pure* revelation from the source of all light and knowledge is severely impaired. We are then **cut off** from God (Psalm 66:18; Isa. 59:2). We then open ourselves up to *false revelation* from Satan, deceiving spirits, or our own mind. We may then get what we want, or what Satan and his servants want us to have, rather than what God, in His superior love and wisdom, wants us to receive. We may then live a **lie** having **strong delusion**, thinking we have received a revelation from Him, when we have **not**.

It is **very important** that we learn to discern between three voices that may be part of our "revelations." Having **idols** in our hearts often causes us to receive **according to our desires** (see Jacob 4:14; Alma 29:4; Isa. 66:2-4). Some are then given over to "**strong delusion**" (2 Thess. 2:10-12). To receive **pure revelation**, we must seek and receive it from God, by seeking **His will.** Nephi said, "I know that God will give liberally to him that asketh. Yea, my God will give me, **if I ask not amiss**" (2 Ne. 4:35). Asking "amiss" is not seeking God's will in our answers. This is the great overlooked key in understanding and receiving real **truth**. In addition to 2 Thess. 2:10-12, there are more scriptures that address removing all **the idols in our hearts** - that we might not be deceived – or given delusion or lies. They include Proverbs 23:7, Isaiah 66:2-4, Ezekiel 14:1-11, James 4:3, and Mormon 9:28. They are worthy of your study.

Removing false beliefs and traditions is also necessary to receive truth. Some are "iniquities" passed down to us from "fathers, priests, and kings" (family, church, and the state). Others came from life experience, work, reading and research, etc. Awakening to the truth of all things is necessary to receive salvation, as we cannot be saved in ignorance (D&C 131:6). The transition to truth can be traumatic, but in the end, truth frees us from the chains of ignorance.

It took time for the young Prophet Joseph and his companions to learn how to receive *pure*, undefiled revelation from God. Joseph Smith, Oliver Cowdery, and David Whitmer discovered early on, that when they received a "revelation," it could come from one of three sources - from (1) God, (2) from Satan and false or deceiving spirits, and (3) from their own minds. To receive *pure* revelation – or truth - from God alone, they had to be clean and open to **God's will** rather than seeking **their own**. Some of the earliest revelations in the Doctrine and Covenants were directed to Joseph, Oliver, and David as a group. David Whitmer (once second in command of the church) said:

> "How humble and contrite in heart a man must be to receive revelations from God: and how very weak man is, and how liable to be led into error, thinking at the time that he is doing God's will. At times when Brother Joseph would attempt to translate, he would look into the hat in which the stone was placed, he found he was spiritually blind and could not translate. He told us that his mind dwelt too much on earthly things, and various causes would make him incapable of proceeding with the translation. When in this condition he would go out and pray, and when he became sufficiently **humble before God**, he could then proceed with the translation. Now we see how very strict the Lord is; and how he requires **the heart of man to be just right** in His sight, **before he can receive revelation from him**."
>
> One specific false revelation is of particular interest. "Brother Hyrum said it had been suggested to him that some of the brethren might go to Toronto, Canada, and sell the copy-right of the Book of Mormon for considerable money [gain], and he persuaded Joseph to inquire of the Lord about it. Joseph concluded to do so. He had not yet given up the stone. Joseph looked into the hat in which he placed the stone, and received a revelation that some of

> the brethren should go to Toronto [or Kingston], Canada, and that they would sell the copy-right of the Book of Mormon. Hiram and Oliver Cowdery went to Toronto on this mission, but they failed entirely to sell the copy-right, returning without any money. Joseph was at my father's house when they returned. I was there also, and am an eye witness to these facts. Jacob Whitmer and John Whitmer were also present when Hiram Page and Oliver Cowdery returned from Canada."

> "Well, we were all in great trouble; and we asked Joseph how it was that he had received a revelation from the Lord for some brethren to go to Toronto and sell the copy-right, and the brethren had utterly failed in their undertaking. Joseph did not know how it was, so he enquired of the Lord about it, and behold the following revelation came through the stone: [1] 'Some revelations are of God: [2] some revelations are of men: and [3] some revelations are of the devil.' When a man enquires of the Lord concerning a matter, **if he is deceived by his own carnal desires, and is in error, he will receive an answer according to his erring heart, but it will not be a revelation from the Lord**. This was a lesson for our benefit and we should have profited by it in future more than we did" (David Whitmer, An Address to All Believers in Christ, pps. 30 - 31).

The **idols** in our heart may include churches and their leaders. We raise them up and put too much trust in them, rather than taking what they say to a higher source – God. Consult His word in scripture. Consult Him personally, but first remove all false beliefs you may hold as an idol in your heart ("we cannot and will not lead you astray"). To avoid lies and deception, turn to God or be **cursed** (2 Ne. 4:34; 28:31; Jer. 17:5). Satan influenced secret combinations to rise up all around us. To overcome them, two things are in order; (1) believe God's word in scripture that the wheat and the tares **are growing together** in and out of the church, and turn fully to God for light (3 Ne. 18:24).

Sexual Sin

Idolatry is often tied to sexual sin, which replaces selfless, holy love with selfish unholy indulgences. Those in power often use it gratify their own lusts. It was first called "**spiritual wifery**" in early LDS Church history. It later came to be known as "plural marriage" and then "*celestial marriage*." Outsiders call it polygamy. God calls it an "abomination" and a "whoredom" in Jacob 2. The term "**spiritual wifery**" effectively describes the use of a religious environment to justify sex. In it, religion is used for self gratification, **not** charity and charitable service. Regardless of its name, sexual sin has been used by Satan for thousands of years to destroy God's work and his people. It effectively **cuts off** those practicing it from God and His Spirit. They are then left in darkness and ignorance. The first six presidents of the Utah LDS Church following Joseph Smith were polygamists. We have little or no revealed truths from these men, including new scripture, prophecy, or revelation. Joseph Smith, on the other hand, was very fruitful. The scriptures he brought forth are a testament to his fruitful relationship with God.

Fruits on the Trees of the Vineyard

In referring to His servants and the people they lead, God said, "**by their fruits ye shall know them**" (Mat. 7:16-20). Today, the State of Utah – capital of Mormonism - is known for many things, including beautiful mountains, red desert landscapes, a number of National Parks, the Great Salt Lake, the Mormon Tabernacle Choir, the Osmonds, and **polygamy**. For many, polygamy is the first thing that comes to mind when "Utah" is brought up in a conversation. Sadly, our state is also known as the scam capital of the country. We are a trusting people. Too often, however, our trust is placed in men, not God. God's healing hand is desperately needed here and throughout the world. Much of our present "awful situation" is the result of following men who embraced the abomination of polygamy, rather than seeking the LORD and His ways. Today, the State of Utah has abnormally high rates of child physical and sexual abuse, including satanic ritual abuse (or SRA). Our pornography addiction is at epidemic levels. Utah ranks #1 in on-line porn subscriptions, according to Harvard Economics professor Benjamin Edelman. And abortions in Utah are on the rise (3,200 per year and growing [2017]). Prescription drug abuse (including anti-depressants) is very high in Utah, as are our teen suicide rates. We are among the leading states in a number of these categories. There is also an increasing exodus of from the Church as detailed in a 2013 report (see endnote 4).

Polygamy did bring curses upon the church early on. The lies and deception of the current church narrative is foremost among them. It asserts that Joseph Smith was a polygamist. It is a stumbling block that has caused many to leave the church, and in greater numbers than ever. Many do not feel the Spirit in their meetings, as focus is often upon leaders and the church itself, rather than Christ. At present, we have the lowest growth rate for the church in our recorded history (see endnote 4). There are other signs of trouble among us too, such as various types of sexual dysfunction, potentially reflecting generational curses passed down to us from the early polygamy years. They include men wielding unrighteous dominion over the women in their lives, along with incest, unnatural affection, and plenty of broken marriages, not to mention many polygamous groups around us. We are nearing the end of **the fourth generation** from the time polygamy was first implemented in early church history. Thus, it is time for truth to be revealed and the oppressive chains upon many to be broken. Those who accept the blood of Christ in their lives will be freed and find healing, as our LORD's arms are extended to all those who will come to Him.

These things, combined with widespread unbelief among the Saints, and an **unsaved** condition for far too many of us - are the "fruits" we as trees are bearing in the LORD's vineyard. These bitter fruits are in direct opposition to what could be occurring in Utah - the headquarters of the Brighamite branch of the Church of Jesus Christ of Latter-day Saints. Some are also the natural result of immersing ourselves in modern-day Babylon. God charged the early Saints to become a light to the world instead. The LORD said that He, "will not spare any that **remain** in Babylon" (D&C 64:24). We can only be lights if we remove ourselves from the false traditions and lies that are pervasive among us. This is what Lehi and his family did, along with Alma, a priest in King Noah's employ. They left spiritual Babylon and turned their hearts wholly to the living God. With it, there was healing and salvation. It requires us to "awake" before we can "arise," however, requiring hard truths to be addressed, the reason for this book. Its focus is not just polygamy and its origins in the Church, but original, pure doctrines, and the later substitutes for them. Many of these new doctrines emerged after Brigham Young's takeover. Scripture reveals a link between pride, idolatry, polygamy, and false doctrine. They in turn led to the murder of three Smith brothers, and the cursed condition of many today.

God has said that we as trees in His vineyard are to "bear fruit meet for **the Father's kingdom**" (D&C 84:58). Many trees are bearing bitter fruit, perhaps tied to curses originating in the polygamy of our ancestors. They have continued to the third and fourth generations (see Mosiah 13:11-14; Ex. 20:5). In the Book of Mormon, Abinadi called King Noah and his priests to repentance. They were living off the high taxes they placed upon the people to support their lavish lifestyle. It included many wives and concubines. Abinadi stated:

> "And now I read unto you the remainder of the commandments of God, for I perceive that they are not written in your **hearts**; I perceive that ye have studied and taught **iniquity** the most part of your lives…for I the Lord thy God am a jealous God, visiting the **iniquities** of the fathers upon the children, unto the third and fourth generations of them that hate me; And showing **mercy** unto thousands of them that **love me** and keep my commandments" (Mosiah 13:11-14).

A search of the word "**iniquity**" reveals that it is found 1,129 times in scripture; 330 times in the Old Testament, 231 times in the Book of Mormon, and 20 times in the D&C. It is tied to three things:

> Is is "**premeditated moral sin** worthy of punishment," those directly opposing "virtue, morality, and goodness."
>
> It is also associated with "**generational curses**" passed down to us from our fathers, priests, and kings, those whom many look to in their idolatry. From them we have received false teachings and traditions.
>
> The word iniquity is also tied to "**inequality**," where some place themselves above others in pride, causing an increase in oppression.

Pride is at the root of iniquity and most sin, the first thing Jacob spoke of in his address on the evils of polygamy. Polygamy in early Mormonism involves *all three types* of "**iniquity**." It has resulted in too many of the Saints remaining unredeemed (Mos. 2:40-41). Three times we are warned that, "**the harvest is come and our souls are not saved**" (D&C 45:2, 56:16; Jer. 17:11). God and His word invite us to "awake and arise" and come out of Babylon and be **redeemed – of Him.** To do so, we must remove all kinds of deception – including the belief that we are saved in ignorance or our "dead works" - including church callings, church service, and temple work. It is through Christ's blood, His grace and mercy that we are redeemed, **not** anything we do, other than *turning* to Him in **repentance**. Nephi invited us to become "*alive* in Christ" (see 2 Ne. 25:25-30), developing a relationship with Him, that we might *abide* in Him as the True Vine, bearing fruit abundantly. Note the last-days fulfillment of the parable of the wise and unwise virgins in D&C 45:56-58.

> "And at that day, when I shall come in my glory, shall the parable be fulfilled which I spake concerning the ten virgins. For they that are **wise** *and* [1] have received **the truth**, and [2] have taken **the Holy Spirit** *for their guide*, and [3] have **not been deceived**—verily I say unto you, **they** shall **not** be hewn down and cast into the fire [with other unfruitful trees] but shall abide the day. And the earth shall be given unto **them** for an inheritance..."

In the 1999 movie the Matrix, the main character *Neo* (a type for Christ – the "*one*" – the same letters as "*Neo*") is a disillusioned, unhappy computer hacker. He knows something is wrong in his life. It is because he is **asleep** - to the reality of his **awful situation**. He is given the choice to know **the truth** or remain *asleep* by one who has **awakened** – Morpheus (a type for a true prophet). *Neo* and all the human beings (us) that are **not** awake are being *used* by the machines to generate electricity **for them**, just as secret combinations today use the masses for "**gain**" of every kind. Morpheus offers Neo a *blue pill* (remaining in the happy **deception** of "wonderland"), or the *red pill* (**the truth** and its difficult ramifications). Morpheus tells *Neo*, "After this, there is **no** turning back. You take the blue pill, the story ends (everything remains as it is). You wake up in your bed and **believe whatever you want to believe** [the state of most today]. You take the red pill – I show you how deep the rabbit hole goes. Remember, all I'm offering is **the truth**." In reading this book, I believe you are taking the red pill and entering into a many faceted rabbit hole, with ramifications.

In addressing our deceptive history, the main characters in it, and the events tied to the rise, fall, and remaining curses associated with polygamy, the remedy to our "**awful situation** is also presented. It is contained in "the fullness" of the **doctrine**, **gospel**, and **church** of Christ (chap. 7). The fuller portions of it have been diminished, pushed aside, and modified. They will be re-introduced here side by side with the darkness that removed it. These doctrines include:

The "new and everlasting covenant," what it is (endnote 31) and what it became following Joseph's murder
What the "fullness of the gospel" of Christ is, and how we rejected it in connection with "the doctrine of Christ"
How to be made new in Christ, by obtaining the "mighty change of heart," or being "born again" in Him
What the "endowment of power from on high" really is, and what it has become because of polygamy
What the Holy Ghost is and how to obtain it, according to God's words and instruction
What "the sealing power" really is, in connection with "the promises made to the fathers"

The journey to explore these saving doctrines *and* the truth about polygamy in our history, are introduced side by side in eight chapters, each about thirty pages in length, plus the endnotes at the end of the book.

In Chapter 1, **God's Word and Will**: *Is Polygamy of the LORD?* we begin our journey for truth regarding polygamy in Mormonism. It must begin with God's word and will, not man's flawed thinking. God's word is the standard to be consulted, in all of scripture, not just a few select verses used out of context. With it we **can** determine if God encouraged, condoned, or condemned those who had more than one wife in the Bible, the Book of Mormon, and early church history, and discover **why**. Specific scriptures used by pro-polygamists are also carefully examined in context to determine if polygamy is ordained of God, past, present, or future.

Chapter 2 follows, entitled, **Historical Truth**: *The Origin of Polygamy*. This chapter addresses our messy history, one modified to support the agenda of pro-polygamists that took control of the Utah church following the murder of the three Smith brothers (Joseph, Hyrum, and Samuel Smith). In it we see how our "doctored" records were used to frame Joseph Smith as a polygamist by those using his name and standing to **justify** their own early secret practice of it. Secret combinations control information. Seven information sources were *or* are used to **deceive**. They include:

1. Modifying scripture – *what God has to say*, by modifying, adding to, and removing relevant statements in scripture
2. Modifying Joseph Smith's personal journals and history in the same way – *what Joseph had to say*
3. Modifying official church history in the similar ways – *what our official record has to say*
4. Modifying - *what Joseph Smith's mother had to say* in her biography (gathered up, modified, and republished by Young)
5. Creating false affidavits and stories to prop up polygamy (mostly between 1860-90) – *what others supposedly said*
6. Creating a false narrative in Nauvoo's two newspapers (one civil, one religious) – *the fake news presented to the Saints*
7. *Continuing the false narrative today* - via sermons, press releases, magazines, books (including a *new* four-volume church "history"), supportive websites, and church owned media outlets (KSL, Deseret News, etc.).

A more accurate history reveals how the Prophet Joseph fought against all forms of spiritual wifery (and other false doctrines) early on at Kirtland, and how this effort continued right up until his murder at Nauvoo, along with the words of Hyrum and others. Joseph's voice (in accurate statements) and that of the entire Smith family has been supressed and ignored for far too long. We will hear from the Smiths and others in this and later chapters.

Chapter 3 is entitled, **The Secret Chamber**: *New Doctrine.* This chapter addresses a secret combination that rose up at Nauvoo within the church, one prophesied by our LORD in D&C 38. Its focus was supporting the secret practice of "spiritual wifery" (using religion to justify sexual sin), and getting other gain. The words "secret chamber" represent more than just an organized group with evil intent. It is also tied to desires held in the secret chambers **of our hearts**. Because spiritual wifery was opposed by Joseph, he and those who could have taken over following his death (Hyrum and Samuel Smith) were also murdered that the practice might continue, and so that others outside the Smith bloodline might lead the Church. Spiritual wifery began at Kirtland. It was secretly practiced by some leaders at Nauvoo, finally becoming an institutional practice as part of marriage in Utah, one *required* for exaltation under Young. What began as "spiritual wifery," became marriage to multiple wives in "celestial marriage."

Chapter 4 is entitled, **Succession Crisis:** *Legitimate Heir or Usurper?* This chapter focuses on who was to lead the Saints following the murders of the Smith brothers, in God's forgotten choice in the Smith bloodline. Another took power after the murders in crafy ways, cleverly going against God's word in scripture. In a unique twist, Joseph Smith's firstborn son, the one anointed and blessed to succeed him, finally published his fathers' re-translation of the Bible. He also eradicated polygamy in Utah with help from the U.S. Government. Two over-looked court cases support his legal right to succession in leadership, also revealing how his father's name and mission were free from polygamy.

Chapter 5 features a discussion of **The Nauvoo Masonic Temple**: *New Temple Theology.* In it we will see the transition that occurred from Joseph Smith's inspired vision for a "house of the LORD" at Nauvoo, to a new temple theology that emerged after Joseph's murder, one featuring a mix of Joseph's teachings, with modified Elijah doctrine from two pro-polygamy publications, along with Freemasonry influences, all in support of plural marriage "sealings."

In Chapter 6, **Our Awful Situation**: *Modern Doctrine*, we look at the awful situation the Utah Saints have inherited as a result of embracing polygamy as a people for some sixty years, in Brigham's "new order of things." Ten assumptions held by many Saints are addressed one by one, revealing the truths tied to these assumptions and how many things, including church doctrine have changed since the early restoration movement of Joseph Smith.

Chapter 7, **The Doctrine of Christ** & *Rejecting God's Fulness*, provides hope in addressing the most important message of the Book of Mormon. It is salvation **in Christ** and how to receive it. We do so by embracing the fullness of His doctrine and His gospel. We then become part of His church. It is laid out in the early teachings of Joseph Smith and in what the LORD called "**the fullness** of **my** *scripture*." Joseph's primary mission was to bring forth this knowledge. Key portions of this "fullness" were suppressed when many became focused upon polygamy and other worldly things.

Chapter 8 concludes the book, providing hope in Christ, but only as pride, idolatry, unbelief, and sin are removed through our repentance and turning fully to God. It is entitled, **A Coming Reformation**: *Inviting Zion.* It concentrates on what must occur to bring about Zion among the pure in heart. The endnotes provide additional clarifying insights.

The Prophet Joseph taught, "For there are many yet on the earth among **all** sects, parties, and denominations, who are **blinded by the subtle craftiness of men**, whereby they **lie** in wait to **deceive**, and who are only kept from **the truth** because they **know not where to find it**—Therefore, that we should waste and wear out our lives in **bringing to light all the hidden things of darkness**, wherein we know them; and they are truly manifest from heaven" (D&C 123:12-13). Nephi said, "O Lord, **I have trusted in thee**, and I will trust in thee forever. I will **not** put my trust in the arm of flesh; for I know that **cursed is he that putteth his trust in the arm of flesh**. Yea, **cursed is he that putteth his trust in man** or maketh flesh his arm. Yea, I know that God will give liberally **to him that asketh**. Yea, my God will give me, if I **ask not amiss**; therefore I will lift up my voice unto thee; yea, I will cry unto thee, my God, **the rock** of my righteousness. Behold, my voice shall forever ascend up unto thee, **my rock** and mine everlasting God. Amen" (2 Nephi 4:34-35).

The LORD Jesus holds His arms out to you and I, continually inviting us to, "**repent** and **come unto me**" (D&C 10:67-68, 93:1; 1 Ne. 10:18-19; 2 Ne. 9:23-24; 28:31-32; Jacob 1:7; Alma 5:33-34; Ether 4:7-19; Mor. 7:34; 3 Ne. 9:14, 22, 51; 11:14; 12:19-20, 23-24; 27:5-21; 30:2).

He really is the answer as our source of **light** (3 Ne. 18:24).

Chapter One

God's Word and Will

Is Polygamy of the LORD?

God said that in the mouth of two or three witnesses all **truth** is established (2 Cor. 13:1; Deut. 17:6; D&C 6:28). The written word in scripture and pure revelation are our two best sources of truth we have regarding polygamy. In their purity, they do not contradict one another (TPJS p. 215), especially if we seek and obtain God's will rather than our own. This chapter is divided into these two witnesses and relies on God's holy word in scripture to first establish truth in the multiple wives doctrine. It was called "spiritual wifery" early on in Church history, a term used by the Cochranites of Saco Maine. Using scripture (Part I), in conjunction with pure revelation from God (Part II), we can best determine if the LORD sanctioned polygamy in the Old Testament, in the Book of Mormon, at Nauvoo, and later in Utah. As we turn to God first and seek His truth, rather than the teachings of men, surprisingly clear answers emerge. The key is to let scripture say what it says, without interpretation based upon a personal agenda or desire. All idols within our heart, including the desire for *or* against polygamy - must be removed. Following our search of scripture to seek God's perspective, we should then seek confirmation of our interpretation of the written word via sincere prayer. These two consistent and mutually supportive witnesses will combine when we seek God's word and will, **not** our own. This is the great key to obtain truth!

A third witness addressed hereafter is history. It is also useful, though frequently subject to biases, agendas, and thus modification. Most of the Saints consult the pro-polygamy "Brighamite" history put forth by the LDS Church, those that went west with Brigham Young. It is significant that one half of the Saints at Nauvoo did not follow Brigham Young west nor embrace his "new order of things" in polygamy. Relatively few consult the anti-polygamy "Josephite" history, kept by those who stayed behind, including most of the Smith family. These two histories are diametrically opposed and reveal much in the struggle between these groups. Polygamy was a central dividing factor.

Part I: God's Written Word in Scripture

The condition of our heart, and the desires within it, determine whether we obtain truth from God or something else. The desires held in the secret chambers of our heart determine whether two people in the Church view the same scripture in unity or in opposing ways. Scripture calls these desires "idols in our heart." They determine where "revelation" comes from; (1) God, (2) Satan and false spirits, or (3) or our own mind. All light and truth originates in God, not flawed men, including this author. Scripture informs us that the LORD Jesus is our **rock** and the fountain of "**living waters**" (a type for "pure revelation" from Him and our Father and Mother in scripture). Christ the LORD is also the light and life of the world. As we turn to Him for truth - by seeking His word and will, we can obtain the sweet, white fruit of the Tree of Life, rather than the corrupted fruit of men and the tree of knowledge. Written scripture represents God's word to all. Pure revelation is His word to you, personally.

The problem is, too many men don't want God's truth, nor do they seek it. They want their own beliefs to be validated and their own will to be done. This is **pride**, the first trait addressed in connection with the polygamists of Jacob 2. The humble seek Christ's will, as He sought and seeks the Father's will (Alma 42:7; Rom. 10:1-4; Mat. 6:33). Another problem is accepting **truth** once it is given, and doing so from God's perspective rather than ours. Too often the arm of flesh has biases based on an agenda. They originate in the idols we hold in "the secret chambers" of our own hearts. Our individual agendas are **rooted** in our own unique experiences, traditions, and beliefs, some of which are false. These are part of the **iniquities** passed down to us from "fathers, priests, and kings." The prideful know more than God. The humble seek His will to remove tainted perspectives, known in scripture as "the idols of our heart" (Prov. 23:7, Isa. 66:2-4, Ezek. 14:1-11, 2 Thess. 2:10-12, James 4:3, Jacob 4:14, Alma 29:4 & Morm. 9:28).

Throughout many verses in the Bible, the Book of Mormon, and other scripture, polygamy is sin. It originates in the carnal desires of mainly men. In the foundational source of our faith, the Book of Mormon the Prophet Jacob used five negative words or phrases to address it in an important order. He tells us that polygamy came among men because of (1) "**pride**." This led to the people committing (2) "a **grosser crime**" tied to (3) "**wickedness**." God then referred to it as a (4) "**whoredom**" and (5) an "**abomination**" before His face (see Jacob chapters 2 & 3). Jacob later made it clear that God preserved their Lamanite brethren (though unbelievers) because there was love between husbands and wives and their children, in non-polygamous relationships (Jacob 3:7). The corrupted Nephites were eventually wiped off this land, because of the **secret combinations** they embraced, and the **whoredom** of **polygamy** tied to it. Note that whoredoms and secret combinations are ranked with **priestcraft** and **murder** as some of the most wicked things in 3 Nephi 16:10, 21:19, and 30:2.

In contrast to the many scriptures condemning the practice, there are only a handful used by pro-polygamists to support it. The most notable may be the incorrect interpretations of Jacob 2:30, the Levirate law of Deuteronomy 25, Isaiah 4:1, and Section 132 of the Doctrine and Covenants. Each of them is refuted hereafter, using God's word to determine His will and understanding. These scriptures, in combination with others, are often used by pro-polygamists to negate all the others that clearly speak out against the practice. Collectively, they reveal that polygamy, concubines, adultery, homosexuality, and other sexual sins are unacceptable to the LORD. To understand what is being expressed in His word as a whole, we must seek His will rather than our own. Otherwise we will go off in many directions, following the idols of our own hearts, and the false revelations that can originate in them.

The Book of Mormon, together with the inspired Joseph Smith re-translation of the Bible is what the LORD called "*the fullness* of **my scriptures**" in D&C 42:12, 15, 56 and 59. Two notable things are given us in both books; (1) Greater clarity in what "the way of salvation" is – or how to be saved or redeemed of the LORD; And (2) The significant role of the evil one in stopping us from receiving God's salvation, and often because of secret combinations and their lies and deception. These opposing things have been suppressed or removed from the Bible (see Moses 1:23; Luke 11:52; 1 Ne. 13:26-29, 32-40, 14:23). Evil and designing men removed many "**plain** and **precious** things" from the Bible. Salvation requires knowledge of both light and darkness. God said we cannot be saved in ignorance (D&C 131:6). He added that all things are to be established by two or three witnesses (2 Cor. 13:1). For our purposes here, they are the JST Bible, the Book of Mormon, and God's pure revelation to us. Relying on the arm of flesh for truth results in **curses**, according to 2 Nephi 4:34. They result in idolatry, ignorance, and deception.

Besides removing the simple and sacred truths of how to be saved in pure form, clear references to organized evil and darkness among us in **secret combinations**, have also been removed. The clearer JST version of Genesis in the Book of Moses, for example, reveals the deceptive tactics of Satan, especially in Moses chapter 5. There we learn that secret combinations placed among men significantly thwart God's work in redeeming His children. The Book of Mormon negates this ignorance by providing a clear pathway to redemption in the teachings of Nephi, Abinadi, Alma, Mormon, and Moroni. Together, the JST version of the Bible and the Book of Mormon reveal how polygamy and other sins, including murder, were put in place by secret combinations to destroy God's great work in bringing about "the immortality and eternal life of man" (Moses 1:39). Hereafter we will see that God did not require, command, nor condone the whoredom known as "spiritual wifery," "polygamy," or "plural marriage" among us, or among any other people in scripture. Instead, sexual sin has been a tool of the adversary to corrupt God's saving work from the very beginning. It began in our history at Kirtland among new converts brought there. It then took root secretly at Nauvoo among leaders, and finally became an institutionalized practice in in Utah, one required for exaltation.

The primary purpose of the Prophet Joseph Smith's mission was to bring forth more of God's precious word, to inform God's people of these two opposing forces, one of light and one of darkness. They represent God's work to save us and Satan's plan to destroy us. God said that relying on His written word in scripture keeps "**the gates of hell**" from "prevailing against us." The following scriptures address the importance of **God's word** as a guide for us.

> "And whoso treasureth up **my word, shall not be deceived**" (JST Mat. 1:37).
>
> "If ye continue in **my word**, then are ye **my disciples** indeed; And **ye shall know the truth**, and the truth shall make you free" (John 8:32).
>
> "Behold I give unto you **a commandment**, that you <u>**rely upon the things which are written**</u>; for in them are all things written, concerning **my church**, **my gospel**, and **my rock**. Wherefore if you shall build up **my church** and **my gospel**, and **my rock** [rather than the teachings of men], the gates of hell shall **not** prevail against you" (early unchanged 1833 Book of Commandments, now D&C 18:3-6; see also JST Mat. 16:16-19 & 2 Ne. 4:32-35).
>
> "For you shall live by **every word** that proceedeth forth from the mouth of **God** [not man]. For **the word of the Lord is truth**, and whatsoever is truth is **light**, and whatsoever is light is **Spirit**, even the Spirit of **Jesus Christ**. And the Spirit giveth light to every man that cometh into the world; and the Spirit enlighteneth every man through

the world, that hearkeneth to **the voice of the Spirit**. And every one that hearkeneth to the voice of the Spirit cometh unto **God**, even **the Father**" (D&C 84:44-47; see also Mat. 4:4; 2 Ne. 32:1-6).

Raising Up Righteous Seed

God desires that his people become righteous and holy, through repentance and the atonement of Christ, that such might be blessed with His greatest gifts, including eternal life. He desires that men and women raise up their children, their righteous seed or posterity, on promised, covenant lands, where there is opportunity for peace, prosperity, and protection, and where His doctrine and His truth may be taught. The LORD's definition of "righteous seed" can also be numerous "seed" as promised to Abraham and Sarah. Polygamy, however, was not necessary for Abram and Sarai to have posterity "as numerous as the stars of heaven." Scripture reveals that when this couple turned their hearts fully to God, as marked by the **new names** He gave them in "Abraham" and "Sarah," they were then able to have this promise fulfilled. The LORD Jesus came to earth through their blessed bloodline, that all those on earth might be blessed in Christ's redeeming work - His atonement (see Abr. 2:11; 3 Ne. 20:25; 1 Ne. 15:18, 22:9; D&C 110:12). The LORD came through the birthright son Isaac, and his son Jacob, who was renamed Israel. He was not born in the blood lineage of Sarai's handmaid Hagar, the concubine of Abram, nor their son Ishmael. Sadly, the whole world has reaped cursings, hatred, and war from the jealousy born of these two opposing bloodlines, one through Hagar and one through Sarah. This great curse followed the corruption of God's law of marriage - of one man and one woman (see D&C 42:22-23). In time they escaped the iniquities of idolatry and polygamy in their surrounding culture!

The Book of Mormon condemns the practice of multiple wives using the law of witnesses (2 Cor. 13:1). There is (1) the bad example of the Nephites (Jacob ch. 2-3) as seen in King Noah and his priests (Mosiah 11:2-14; see also Hel. 2:12-13). Much earlier, on this same Promised Land, there was (2) the Jaredites (Ether 10:5). Both cultures were destroyed because they allowed secret combinations to rise up among then. Both allowed polygamy and other sexual sin to flourish too. A third later group, (3) is the wicked Gentiles of our day (including the Gentile Latter-day Saints). In 1832, the Saints were collectively placed under condemnation for not relying on *the New Covenant* as contained in the truths of the Book of Mormon. We remain under this same condemnation today (see D&C 84:49-59). Multiple prophecies address another cleansing of this Promised Land (see Ether 2:7-12, 8:15-26; JST Mat. 21:51-56).

Note that polygamy was not used to raise up a large quantity of "righteous seed" in the following verses, where the people multiplied quickly (2 Ne. 5:13, Jarom 1:8, Mos. 2:2, 9:9, 23:20, Alma 50:18, 62:48, Hel. 3:8, 11:20, 4 Ne. 1:10, 23). Instead, in the Book of Mormon, God said he brought Lehi and his family to this choice, Promised Land to raise up a "**righteous branch**" of Israel, the **spiritual** *seed* of God. We can become His seed when we are spiritually "born again" in Christ, becoming his sons and daughters (Mosiah 5), as He is the Father of our salvation through the atonement (Ether 3:14, 4:12-15; Mos. 15:1-2, 15). Brigham Young's polygamy was centered on physical seed, not the more important **spiritual** component addressed in much of scripture.

In our Bible dictionary, the word "**holiness**" refers to "**moral character**" (Lev. 11:44; 19:2; 21:8; Isa. 6:3–8). The children of Jacob or Israel were to be holy in character because the God of Israel was and is holy (Jer. 7:4–7; Matt. 5:48). The Law of Holiness (Lev. 17–26) shows how the Israelites often attempted to obtain it by means of ceremonial observances (outward ordinances) to secure holiness of character. The attempt failed because they began observing the letter of the law and neglected the spirit. They attached more importance to the ceremonial ordinances than to the moral and the spiritual. The result was a lapse into formalism. We have inherited the same curse.

In Lehi's case, he and his blessed seed escaped to a new Promised Land, one free of the sins of David and Solomon and other wickedness in the old world (verses 25, 32; Jacob 3:4, 6; 3 Ne. 15:19-20). They were to separate themselves from evil of all kinds, including polygamy. Here they were to embrace "**the everlasting covenant**" or "the fullness of the gospel" of Christ and its truths (see endnote 31). This "**fullness**" is about coming to Christ and being redeemed or saved through Him. Jacob, spoke on behalf of the LORD using the phrase, "thus saith the LORD" two times:

> "Wherefore, thus saith the LORD, I have led this people forth out of the land of Jerusalem, by the power of mine arm, that I might raise up unto me **a righteous branch** from the fruit of the loins of Joseph [of Egypt]. Wherefore, I the LORD God will **not** suffer that this people shall do **like unto them of old**. Wherefore, my brethren, hear me, and hearken to the word of the LORD: For there shall **not** any man among you **have save it be one wife**; and concubines he shall have **none**; For I, the LORD God, delight in the chastity of women. And

whoredoms are an **abomination** before me; thus saith the LORD of Hosts. Wherefore, this people shall keep my commandments, saith the LORD of Hosts, or cursed be the land for their sakes" (Jacob 2:25-29 [5 verses]; see also 3 Ne. 15:19-20).

God separated Lehi and his family from this particular wickedness and others in Jerusalem (3 Ne. 15:19-20). He also addressed "the chastity of women," saying "**whoredoms** are an **abomination** before me." He added, "this people shall keep my commandments, or **cursed** be the land for their sakes." Then in verse 30 we read:

"For if I will, saith the LORD of Hosts raise up seed [a righteous people] unto me I will command **my people** [God is our King and Law Giver and He commands that we have **one wife** only, 2:27, 3:5-6]; otherwise they [the people] shall hearken unto these **things** [the many wives abomination, like David and Solomon]" (Jacob 2:30).

The added words in the brackets [ ] above provide great clarity to Jacob 2:30. The word "**thing**" or "**things**" is used four times in the later part of Jacob 2, each time in connection with **sin** or **negative things**. It is found in verses 14, 23, 30 and 34. All these "**things**" are **sinful** (see below). This scripture is twisted by pro-polygamists to provide an "escape clause" or "justification" to practice polygamy, thus God's will and understanding must be sought, not that of man. The "**things**" in this context are:

1. **Pride** In verses 22-30, Jacob did not want his people to "persist in these [prideful] **things**" (v. 14).
2. **Grosser Crime** Jacob had to speak to his people "about a grosser crime" they were embracing (v. 22).
3. **Iniquity** Jacob's people "began to wax in iniquity" (v. 23).
4. **Whoredoms** Jacob said "they seek to excuse themselves in committing whoredoms" (v. 23).
5. **Abomination** And because of "the **things** which were written concerning David and Solomon his son [many wives & concubines], which **thing** was abominable before me" (vs. 23-4).
6. **Hearkening to these things** Jacob's people were hearkening "unto these [negative] **things**" (v. 30).
7. **Sinful things** Jacob tells them, "ye have done **things** which ye ought not to have done" (v. 34).

Word links *connect* Jacob 2:30 to two unique prophecies of the LORD in D&C 38:13 and 28 (1831), and 3 Nephi 16:10! Verse 13 of D&C 38 states, "And now I show you a **mystery**, a **thing** which is had in **secret chambers**, to bring to pass even your destruction in process of time, and ye knew it not." Verse 28 adds, "And again, I say unto you that the enemy in the **secret chamber** seeketh your lives." This was fulfilled ten years later at Nauvoo when a *secret combination* rose up there to practice spiritual wifery (spiritual Babylon, D&C 133:14). The LORD stated that it was the "**mystery**" or "**thing**" had in the darkness of **secret chambers** to bring about the destruction of Joseph Smith *and* the fullness of the gospel of Christ he had brought forth. The LORD also prophesied that the Gentiles (Saints and others) would reject the fullness of His gospel in embracing these "**things**." After listing eight sins, He stated,

"and if they [the Gentile Saints and others] shall do all those **things**" and shall **reject the fullness of my gospel**, behold, saith the Father, I will bring **the fullness** of **my gospel** from among them" (3 Ne. 16:10).

This is exactly what happened. It is the sandy foundation which many of the the Saints are on. These "**things**" are part of a "**mystery**" (secret), tied to great "*iniquity*" (2 Thess. 2:7), in connection with "**mystery Babylon**" (or a **secret combination**, Rev. 17:5), involving "**the wresting of scripture**" to *justify* polygamy (D&C 10:63-64; Jacob 2:23). There are 91 scriptures utilizing the word "**mystery**." A total of 88 of them are positive (like "mysteries of godliness"), whereas only 3 are negative, those related to the "**secret things**" of Jacob 2:30 (see D&C 10:63-64; 2 Thess. 2:7; Rev. 17:5). Emma Smith said, "it was **secret things** which had cost Joseph and Hyrum their lives" (William Clayton journal, 15 Aug., 1844). The LORD's prophecy in 3 Nephi 16:10 addressed our rejection of the fullness of His gospel and Joseph's "destruction" or murder. Note again Jacob's words:

"they **understand not the scriptures**, for they seek to **excuse themselves** in committing **whoredoms**, because of the **things** which were written concerning David, and Solomon his son. Behold, David and Solomon truly had **many wives** and **concubines**, which **thing** was **abominable** before me, saith the Lord" (*Jacob 2:23-24).*

David and Solomon did "**things**" which were sinful. Today, many supporting polygamy "**wrest scripture**" or "**understand not the scriptures**" (Jacob 2:23; D&C 10:63-64). Many *want* to believe the wording of just one verse in Jacob 2, which for them, leaves the door open to practice polygamy (verse 30 being an "escape clause" for them), whereas the context of the five scriptures immediately before and after it are clearly anti-polygamy, tied to this abomination existing in Jerusalem, and the sorrow and mourning of God's daughters there *and* among Jacob's people in the New World. Too often verse 30 is twisted or "**wrested**" to *excuse* or **justify** polygamy. When we seek God's will rather than our own, we see that this verse is about following God's **command**, *not* a justification for polygamy. It references Lehi coming to this Promised Land to raise up his family in **righteousness**. They did so by separation from the wicked **things** at Jerusalem (see 3 Ne. 3:15, 19-20). The Israelites there practiced what God had forbidden: unlawful polygamy, divorce, and remarriage (see Mat. 19:3-9). This is further supported in Jacob chapter 3.

Most of Jacob 2 is about **separation** from evil, and specifically the multiple wives and concubines of men like King Noah, who came later (Mosiah 11, compare the first 8 verses to Brigham Young and those following him). Verse 30 of Jacob 2 is not an escape clause from God's law of marriage (D&C 42:22-23). The key for its correct interpretation or for any scripture, is, (1) context (surrounding verses), and (2) God's intended will and instruction, not our "**wresting**" and *justifying* interpretation of it. To receive **truth**, we must first **want it**. God has it. Those supporting polygamy, are looking for *justification* for their own viewpoint, and because of this "*idol in their heart*," they see Jacob 2:30 through their own filter (see Mosiah 2:11 & 13:11). All **idolatry** must be removed to find or understand **His** intended meaning. This is one reason there are so many Christian churches today. They come from differing interpretation of the same scriptures, all of them based on "idols" that various individuals support. Too many use Jacob 2:30 as an opening for multiple wives, along with Section 132 of the D&C. For Latter-day Saints today, one primary idol is – our leaders. They say Joseph was a polygamist, and that he taught Brigham and the Twelve all about it. We have believed them, and believed their version of scripture. King David was a polygamist, but in time he eventually learned the hard lesson that it was not of God (addressed hereafter). He then said:

> "It is better to **trust in the Lord** than to put confidence in man" (Psalm 118:8).

Nephi said trusting men brings "curses" (2 Ne. 4:34). David's wise words may be the exact center scripture of the Bible. Again, note the five descriptive words (in order) that Jacob used to define the whoredom of polygamy in Jacob chapter 2. These five "**things**" include, (1) "**pride**," (2) "**grosser crimes**," (3) "**iniquity**," (4) "**whoredoms**," and (4) "**abominable**." They are associated with the Nephites in Jacob 2, along with two of Israel's kings, David and Solomon, and their additional wives and concubines (the reason God did not condemn Abraham or Jacob for their additional wives in Jacob 2 is revealed hereafter). Jacob's five condemning descriptions of the sexual sin among his people are contrasted with the words "**righteous branch**" (of the house of Israel or Jacob) in verse 25. Context and **God's will** are the two key features that must be taken into consideration in this and all scripture.

Finally, in the last five verses of Jacob chapter 2, immediately following verse 30 (31-35), there are more strong words used by Jacob to condemn all sexual practices that go against God's will. They include the following negative words and phrases; "sorrow, mourning of the daughters, wickedness, abominations of their husbands, cries of the fair daughters…against the men, lead away captive the daughters of my people, sore curse, destruction, commit whoredoms like them of old, great condemnation, greater iniquities than the Lamanites, our brethren, Ye have broken the hearts of your tender wives, and lost the confidence of your children, because of your bad examples before them, and the sobbings of their hearts ascend up to God against you," and "many hearts died, pierced with deep wounds."

Women and children suffer the most under the whoredom and abomination of polygamy. Christ came to this earth to relieve the pain, suffering, and oppression that wicked men put upon others. Turning to Him and His ways provides hope, peace, and love. Note the four points below that keep us in ignorance and darkness. They lead to being **deceived** by crafty men who "**lie in wait to deceive**" – for the sake of "**gain**." They are:

(1) **Pride**, believing we are safe in our present situation

(2) Practicing **idolatry** (looking to man first and foremost for light and direction, rather than God) and other sin, separating us from God

(3) Not seeking and receiving the gift and power of **the Holy Ghost** in our lives, as a result of not seeking for and receiving the cleansing power of the baptism of fire and the Holy Ghost (being born again in Christ – "the mystery . . . which is Christ in you," Col. 1:27).

(4) Not knowing how to receive *pure* **revelation** *from* **God**, that we might discern truth from error among the diverse and often false teachings and doctrines of men, they whose hearts may be far from God

Receiving pure, undefiled revelation from God - the source of light - begins with removing ourselves from Babylon and its **idolatry** – trusting in men and things. As we leave behind our pride, which often keeps us believing we are correct in our false teachings and traditions, and then **repent** and **come unto Christ** – seeking truth from Him rather than our own or that of other men, we can then be gifted or endowed with the power of **the Holy Ghost** as our "comforter" or guide. It comes after being born again in Christ (chap. 7). This is the promise given to all wise virgins, those who have obtained **oil** in their lamps. It aids us in correctly interpreting scripture. God said:

> "For they that are wise and have received the **truth**, and have taken **the Holy Spirit for their guide**, and have **not** been **deceived**—verily I say unto you, they shall not be hewn down and cast into the fire, but shall abide the day" (D&C 45:57).

Sadly, too many of the Saints "are **deceived** *by the craftiness of men*," and thus inherit lesser kingdoms in the hereafter (see D&C 76:75). We can only receive the important gift or "endowment" of the Holy Ghost if we remove the obstacles of pride and idolatry, and instead turn to God and cultivate a "broken heart and a contrite spirit." With "the mighty change of heart" that comes from being redeemed of God in His fiery baptism of us, we then have no more desire to sin or do evil, but to seek the LORD's will in all things.

Too few understand this pathway, known in scripture simply as "**the way**" or "**the way of salvation**" of our God. Too few obtain - and hold on to - the iron rod (God written and revealed word), and thus they don't arrive at the great Tree in this life. They then wander in strange paths, amidst mists of darkness, following **men** instead of God (1 Ne. 8:5-8). Many are persuaded to remain there by fear – fear of men pointing their fingers at them from the great and spacious building. **Such fear men more than God**. Such rely on "the arm of flesh" and are thus frequently **deceived**.

Polygamy Among the Early Patriarchs & Kings of the Bible

When God's will is sought, truth emerges. If we seek our own will (the idols in the heart), we seek justification to obtain them. God said we are judged by our works, along with the desires of our heart (D&C 137:9). Many pro-polygamist men among the Saints today, seek to be part of this practice. They use the following justifications for it.

(1) The first justification for Latter-day Saint polygamy is normally **the Old Testament Patriarchs**, including the kings over Israel in Saul, David, Solomon, and others. Jacob 2 judges many of them harshly for it.

(2) The second is typically our modified Latter-day Saint **history**, changed by Brigham Young and those sympathetic to the practice to promote a pro-polygamy stance. They claim it was Joseph Smith who first lived and taught the practice. This provides them justification to practice it too, now or in the future.

(3) The words of **church leaders** that were polygamists (especially **the six Presidents** following Joseph Smith) provides a third justification. The most prominent are Presidents Brigham Young and John Taylor, and Apostle Orson Pratt. Their words are addressed in later chapters. The Prophet Joseph Smith's words counteract them!

(4) Private interpretation of select scripture, rather than the whole body of scripture, is also used to justify the practice, especially **Section 132** of the Doctrine and Covenants. Evidence provided hereafter suggests that much of Section 132 was modified and written by Brigham Young. Incorrect interpretation Jacob 2:30 is also used to justify polygamy, while ignoring both context and the vast majority of other scripture that speaks out against it. Deception often comes because we hold an idol within our heart. This is the important, ignored message of each of the following important scriptures; Isaiah 66:2-4, Ezekiel 14:1-11, 2 Thessalonians 2:10-12, James 4:3, Jacob 4:14, Alma 29:4, and Mormon 9:28. They can help us receive *pure* revelation, if we want **truth**.

Did God command polygamy in specific situations? Was it practiced according to His will anywhere in scripture? Were any inspired "revelations" tied to its practice, and were they from God or a false source (one's own mind or a false, deceiving spirit)? The first question to ask is: **do we really want the truth**? **Will you receive it** if it is given?

A young Joseph Smith went to the woods to seek God's wisdom as the result of reading James 1:5. Both James and the Prophet Joseph said that going to God is the best way to obtain truth. Seeking God's will rather than our own will leads us to **truth** from Him. It really is that simple. God's word and will is found throughout scripture. Too many don't want it, however. As we will see hereafter, His consistent command is to have one wife. The stories of polygamy and concubines in the Bible, along with more recent LDS history, feature significant negative consequences tied to having more than one wife, especially for women and children.

In the Bible we see how imperfect mortal men like Abram, Jacob, and David, influenced by the surrounding culture, eventually turned from the practice. They did so when their hearts were finally turned wholly to God in complete submission. When this happened, when they were "born again" in Him, **they gave up the practice.** Pro-polygamists ignore this. The LORD then gave them new names to accompany their **rebirth** in Him. It was an important marker for their "**mighty change of heart.**" They then "put away" polygamy and their concubines. This is a significant truth overlooked by those who use the ancient patriarchs to justify their practices. While there was polygamy among some of them, it was also eliminated in most cases later on. As we will see hereafter, God condemned this practice when men initiated it to **multiply wives** to themselves – for selfish reasons (David and Solomon in the Old Testament, and Noah and Riplakish in the Book of Mormon). In cases like that of Abram and Jacob, however, God did *not* condemn the practice among **them**, but *nor* did he approve it. It was the result of **the wives** of both men **initiating the practice**, because of their infertility, or for competitive reasons. A heavy price was paid to live it thereafter. Brigham Young and the Twelve at Nauvoo and Salt Lake initiated the practice for their own gratification. The women did not initiate it, nor did God. It was thus a whoredom and an abomination before Him. Let us begin with Adam and Eve.

Adam & Eve

In the second chapter of the Bible, we read of God's law of marriage. "Therefore shall a man leave his father and his mother, and shall cleave unto his wife: and they shall be one flesh" (Gen. 2:24, see also Gen. 1:27 and Moses 3:24). God began the human family with the marriage of the one man Adam with one woman, **not** a harem of women. Things began to change with their son Cain, however. This is especially clear in the Joseph Smith re-translation of Genesis. We call it the Book of Moses. There, the influence of Satan is made very clear, a record **removed** from the Bible along with other "**plain and precious things**" (by evil and designing men), like the clear plan of salvation found in Moses 6:52, 57-68. Because of wickedness, Moses' record of these things, "is not had among the children of men" (Moses 1:23). We read there of one of high station who was cast down to earth because of **pride**. God said, "And he became Satan, even the devil, the father of all **lies**, to **deceive** and to blind men, and to lead them captive at his will, even as many as would not hearken unto *my voice* [nor *my will*]" (Moses. 4:4).

The first record of **polygamy** in the Bible is tied to Lamech, a third generation son from Cain, the first addressed in the book to **willfully rebel** against God, in a covenant or **oath** with Satan. He was also part of the first **secret combination**. Cain, his ancestor was the first to **murder**. Cain's brother Abel was murdered for gain. Lamech married two wives. There may have also been homosexuality, with murder again (see Genesis 4:23-24; Moses 5:51). He too "entered into a covenant with Satan, wherein he became Master Mahan" (meaning "**destroyer**," v. 49). He was "master of that great **secret** which was administered unto Cain by Satan." In Genesis (the first book of the Bible), God defines the true model of marriage. Satan twisted it, giving us a plurality of wives to appease man's **carnal** nature. Because of this, God has had to define marriage as one man and one woman again and again all throughout scripture. While D&C 42:22-23 and 49:16 conform with God's instruction, D&C 132 does not. It came later from Brigham Young in 1876. He put it into the D&C without a vote of the church, also removing older anti-polygamy Section 101.

Many believe homosexuality (an increasing evil in our day) is a part of a great secret combination spreading throughout our land today, perhaps part of initiation into some secret combinations, along with murder. We read in Moses 5 that "every man" in this dark, secret combination in Lamech's day, "**knew** his brother" (Moses 5:51). The same word "**knew**" is used four times in Moses 5 and 6 to coincide with *sexual intercourse* (see verses 2, 16, and 42 of Moses 5, along with Moses 6:2). Polygamy, homosexuality, and murder are all tied to serving Satan in the book of Moses, along with fear-based **secret blood-oaths** or covenants made with him, where one "swears by the throat" or neck. God works by love and invitation, not by force and fear. Sinful things are often done in **secret** (see Moses 5, verses 44-47). The opposite is to love God, our fellow man, and thus to receive light. It is to obtain and practice charity, the pure love of Christ, after one turns to God fully, receiving "the mighty change of heart" (see Mosiah 4:2-3, 9-12; 5:2, 7-15; Alma 5:7, 12-14, 16-26, 49; 7:14-15; 36-3-27).

The JST translation of the Genesis account of Adam and Eve reveals many insights, primarily tied to the rise and spread of secret combinations among their later children, after they were redeemed of God. Prior to this, Moses chapter 1 begins with Satan trying to overpower Moses in verses 16-21. We learn that Satan has no glory and that he came to "**deceive**" Moses. This is important, as Moses is the source of the Genesis account of the creation, and the Adam and Eve story. In verse 23 of Moses chapter 1 we read:

> "And now of this thing [Moses interaction with Satan] Moses bore record; but **because of wickedness** it [evil and designing men who **changed** scripture] is not had among the children of men" (Moses 1:23).

In Moses 4 we learn that Satan is the father of all **lies**. He deceives men, leading those who will not hearken to God's voice. He **lied** to Eve, telling her there was no penalty for partaking of the forbidden fruit (Moses 4:4, 10). Satan's **lies** are tied to **secrecy**, **blood oaths** (made to Satan and other men), as part of a **secret combination** put in place to get **gain** and **murder**. It is especially clear in Moses chapter 5. The footnote of Moses 1:23 takes us to JST Luke 11:52.

> "Woe unto you, lawyers! For ye have taken away the key of knowledge, **the fullness of the scriptures**; ye **enter not** in yourselves **into the kingdom**; and **those who were entering in**, ye hindered" (JST Luke 11:52-53).

They then point fingers at those who are "entering in" – those holding onto **the rod** of revelation from God and His word. They are making their way to God, as symbolized in the sweet, white fruit of the Tree of Life. It is the joy they experience in God's love there. Corruption of God's written word in the Bible – in the removal of many "plain and precious things" - is addressed in these two verses (Moses 1:23 & JST Luke 11:52-53, and in 1 Ne. 13:). It is where (1) Satan's secret methods of darkness are revealed (Moses chapters 4 & 5), and (2) it is also where God's light-filled plan of salvation for his children is also revealed in its **fullness** (Moses chapters 5-8; see also Moses 1:39). They represent **the doctrine of the two ways** (as taught by Moses in Deut. 30:16-19); the choice between a fullness of light, or its absence in darkness. Our choice leads to blessing or cursing. In Moses 5:44, we learn of the first polygamist in the Bible (he was also a murderer). His name was Lamech - the sixth generation from Adam. He "took unto himself two wives" (Moses. 5:44). Lamech slew Irad to keep a secret a secret blood oath in place.

> "For Lamech having entered into a covenant with Satan, after the manner of Cain, wherein he became Master Mahan, master of that great **secret** which was administered unto Cain by Satan; and Irad, the son of Enoch, Having known their **secret**, began to reveal it unto the sons of Adam. Wherefore Lamech, being angry, slew him, not like unto Cain his brother Abel, for the sake of getting **gain**, but he slew him for **the oath's sake**. For, from the days of Cain, there was a s**ecret combination**, and their works were in the dark, and they *knew* every man *his brother*" (Moses 5:49-51).

The LORD then cursed Lamech and his house for their **abominations**. Lamech's wives also rebelled against him.

> "And thus the works of darkness began to prevail among all the sons of men. And God **cursed** the earth with a sore **curse**, and was angry with the wicked, with all the sons of men whom he had made; For they would not hearken unto **his voice**, nor believe on **his** Only Begotten **Son**, even him whom he declared should come in the meridian of time, who was prepared from before the foundation of the world. And thus the Gospel began to be preached…"(Moses 5:55-58).

Abraham & Sarah (Abram & Sarai prior to conversion)

The destructive, on-going strife between Jews and Arabs today, including the hatred leading to terrorism and the Jewish Holocaust, can largely be traced to the jealousy that began with Sarai and her concubine Hagar. Sarai brought her handmaid to Abram, because she was aged *and* barren. It was her idea, not God's nor Abram's. She desperately wanted children. Idolatry and polygamy (with concubines) were pervasive in their culture and the cultures of those around them. Sarai's proposal thus represented a great temptation to Abram. Though Abram had escaped the idolatry of his father, he consented to the desires of his wife. Hagar then became a concubine to Abram, a surrogate mother. No scripture says that it was God's plan, nor that of Abram, though Abram did *submit* to Sarai's *will,* and perhaps without checking in with God first. Although the LORD promised Abram and Sarai children, as numerous as the stars of heaven or the sands of the seas, this would come naturally, within God's timing *and* change to their hearts, signaled by God giving them "**new names**" as part of a new conenant relationship with God. Hagar and her child Ishmael preceded this covenant relationshp.

Sarai and Abram become impatient, taking their childless condition into their own hands, rather than waiting *in faith* patiently upon the LORD and His miraculous power. Doubt may have entered into their minds as much time passed without the heir God promised them, an heir they desperately wanted. God did **not** punish the couple in this thing, as sorrow and trouble **naturally came** to them (and to the later posterity of Jacob) when stife developed between the women (Sarai and Hagar) and their posterity.

After Ishmael was born, trouble between Sarai and Hagar grew. Sarai wanted Hagar banished from her presence. Ismael and Hagar were eventually forced to leave, according to Sarai's wishes, supported by God (Gen. 21:8-21). In time, their decisions and the resulting troubles led Sarai and *Abram* to **turn** their hearts fully to God and His ways in a **covenant** relationship with Him (Gen. 17:19, 21), signaled by their **new names**. It was **then** that *Abraham* **sent away** *Sarah's* bondwoman Hagar **at God**'s direction (see Galatians 4:22-31, Gen. 21:8-21). The couple put away **idolatry** *and* **polygamy**, as part of the surrounding culture, turning to God wholly in their conversion. Note that God put an "**h**" in their names. This *5th* letter of the Hebrew alphabet is tied to *covenant* making and to *life* (physical), and the promise of *eternal life* (spiritual). It was **then** that Sarah *miraculously* conceived Isaac in her old age. God had given the name for the child to the couple via the angel He sent; **Isaac** (Hebrew meaning "*to laugh*"). He would become the **birthright** child of Abraham, a child of "**the promise**," the firstborn son of Sarah. The firstborn son Ishmael through Hagar the concubine, was not a "child of promise." She was not a legal wife. Paul the Apostle later referred to the **change of heart** of Abraham and Sarah and their later **covenant** with God (see Galatians 4:22-31). It resulted in "**the children of promise**" (the Israelites) through Jacob, their grandchild (another heir of "the promises"). Jacob also had a **change of heart**, part of his later conversion to God (addressed hereafter).

While Sarah was alive, it does not appear that Abraham married another woman. We read of Sarah's death in Genesis 23:1-2. Two chapters later we read that Abraham married Keturah, who is mentioned four times in the Bible, two times each in Genesis 25 and 1 Chronicles 21. Keturah may have first been a "*concubine*" (Gen. 25:6; 1 Chron. 1:32) and then *after* Sarah's death a "*wife*" (Gen. 16:3, 25:1). The relationship was not on a par with that of Sarah, mother of the promised son Isaac (Gen. 17:15-22), as the sons of the concubine Keturah were latter sent away (v. 6), as was Ishmael, both with gifts, whereas Isaac was given "all Abraham had" (Gen. 25:5). This is similar to Bilhah, Jacob's concubine-wife (Gen. 30:4, 35:22, 37:22), who did not rival Rachel or Leah. Thus, Bible writers referred to both Keturah and Bilhah as both *wives* and *concubines*. Some researchers believe they held an "in-between" position, unlike the separation existing between the two with David and Solomon. Other scholars and Rabbis believe Hagar *was* Keturah, and that Keturah was a new name given her, tied to change in her in association with the *pleasantness* of "incense." Many believe the *plural* "concubines" in verse 6 is a mistranslation, as no other concubine but Keturah is addressed elsewhere. Abraham was thus not a polygamist, but he may have transgressed in the extenuating circumstances involving the concubine Hagar, as he and Sarah's actions may not have reflected God's will.

In addition, some claim Abraham bore false witness on two occasions, claiming Sarah as a sister. It was a command from God in Abraham 2:24-25, designed to protect him, as husbands were sometimes killed by powerful rulers in surrounding cultures to obtain their beautiful wives (part of ancient kings "**multiplying wives**"). Sarah was very beautiful. She was born of Haran, the brother of Abraham's father. When Haran died, Abraham's father Terah took Sarah as his own daughter. Thus Sarah was technically both Abraham's niece and his **step-sister**. Two powerful men wanted Abraham's beautiful "sister." One was Pharaoh in Egypt. He took Sarah as a wife while she was barren (he did not kill Abraham). We do not know if there was intimacy between Sarah and the Pharaoh. Some suggest God made Sarah barren to protect her from children through this foreign leader. Another king also took Sarah as wife for a time. In both cases Sarah was returned, and both times these kings enriched Abraham with additional animals to make up for their acts, once it was found out that Abraham was her husband, not her brother. Though Abraham was imperfect, He loved God and attempted to follow Him, once He knew what was right. In his **covenant-relationship** with God, Abraham had one wife; Sarah then Keturah.

Some suggest there may have been another concubine besides Hagar. In Genesis 25:6 we read that the sons of Abraham's concubines (plural) were also sent away. The Bible only tells us of Ishmael, however. An ancient book known as "the Austrian Chronicle" reveals that an additional concubine may have been named Susanna. Was this an inserted book to justify polygamy? In it Hagar and the sons of *both concubines* were sent away. Again in this book, the damage had already been done. Hagar and her posterity never forgot. Ever since then, the whole world has been affected by the jealousy, hatred, and war between the posterity of Hagar and Sarah, a leftover from polygamy.

Why did God **not** condemn Abraham in Jacob 2? **Abraham did not initiate the practice**, though he did *submit* to his wife in it. Abraham did not desire more wives as did David and Solomon. He had one love, Sarah. It was Sarah's idea to have surrogate children through Hagar. Though they may have lacked faith or been impatient, their desires were essentially good, especially after they turned to their hearts wholly to God. As Abraham hearkened to his wife in this thing (like Adam in the Garden of Eden), both men had to **live with the consequences** of hearkening to their wives rather than to God. Neither seemed to have consulted God. It was Sarai who initiated this relationship, because she was aged *and* barren. The desires of the heart of both the wife and the husband were basically good. She then brought her concubine to her husband, a **cultural tradition** (**not** a law or command of God). Eve partook of the fruit in her own temptation and choice, and brought this fruit to her husband. He partook, hearkening to Eve, and thus both coupless paid a price. **God did not condemn them**, as difficult natural consequences followed their choices.

Isaac & Rebekah

Isaac is an important type for Christ. His father Abraham was tested to see if he would offer his precious son Isaac as a sacrifice to God. It was a supreme test, as Abraham saw the sacrifices of his father in connection with his idolatry. As a youth, Abram was nearly offered up to false gods. Fortunately Abraham passed this test. Isaac was a righteous man. He was **not** a polygamist, nor does he appear to have had one or more concubines. Isaac had one love and one wife - Rebekah. Isaac also lived in one land, and had only **one name** - given him of God before he was born. An angel gave this name to his parents. Speaking to Abraham, the angel said, "your wife Sarah shall bear you a son, whom you shall call Isaac" (Gen. 17:19). This name means, "to laugh." It reflects Sarah's reaction to the angel's announcement that they would have a child in their advanced age (Gen. 17:17). Isaac observed the trouble that his parents endured because of multiple "wives" in the strife between Sarah and Hagar. And though Rebekah was barren for a time (like Isaac's mother), Isaac **trusted** God to intervene. Rebekah and he did **not** take things into his own hands to have children through a handmaid (as did Sarah and Abraham). Instead, Isaac "**pleaded** with the Eternal on behalf of his wife" for a child (Gen. 25:21). God listened to Isaac and he and Rebekah soon become parents of the twins Esau and Jacob. The **birthright** blessing that Isaac obtained was eventually passed on to Jacob and then to Joseph, one of his twelve sons. Note that in each case the **birthright** blessing was not given to the *firstborn* son (Ishmael, Esau, or Reuben respectively), but to a later, younger son. Both types of sons ("*firstborn*" versus "*birthright*") receive different types of blessings.

Isaac's loyalty and commitment to Rebekah were admirable, especially within a culture that encouraged men to take multiple wives or concubines to increase family size, and at nearly any cost. His *righteous* character also remained consistent throughout his life. This may be one important reason why he served as **a type for Christ**, the one perfect man that was sacrificed that we all might live, typified in Abraham's near sacrifice of Isaac. Both men demonstrated their full **submission** to God (Gen. 22:7-8). Many believe Isaac demonstrated a willingness to be such a sacrifice too, a symbol of the future Lamb of God, who descended to this earth for the same purpose. Isaac's wife Rebekah serves as a type for the church, the bride of Christ. Scripture tells us that she loved Isaac *before* she ever saw him, while far away in another land (Gen. 24). We too must love the LORD with our whole heart if we are to see Him.

Jacob & Rachel

Jacob's name means "**supplanter.**" Though it was God's will that Jacob receive the **birthright** blessing instead of his older brother Esau, there was some *deception* involving both Isaac and his mother to see that it occurred. This *deception* was then returned to Jacob, as Leah was forced upon him by the *deception* of Laban his father in law. He **supplanted** Jacob's promised, beloved wife, Rachel, with his elder daughter Leah. According to God's marriage laws, Jacob could have rejected Leah and put her away as soon he discovered the *deception*, but he didn't do so. He was merciful. God was also merciful to Jacob. He did not condemn him for his extra wife, and thus he is not mentioned in Jacob 2, as Jacob did **not** seek to "**multiply wives**" to himself as did David and Solomon. Like Abraham, two of Jacob's wives were offered to him by his existing wives, Leah (given him through *deception*), and then Rachel. Both were brought to him for *infertility* reasons as part of child-bearing competition among them, as handmaids of Leah and Rachel.

Jacob did not send away Leah, nor the children from her and the handmaids. Though the Bible record is limited, we do know that Jacob lived with both wives, and had children by their handmaids (concubines to him). This occurred because the wives had *infertility* issues, like Abraham and Sarah. The cultural tradition was that because of the woman's desire for children, she could have surrogate children through the concubine. David and Solomon as powerful men (kings) abused this *cultural tradition*, "**multiplying wives**" to themselves. They made it about **their desires**, **not the desires of <u>barren women to have children</u>.**

At the start, there was *competition* between the women to provide children for Jacob. The concubines became part of this. Later there may have been a peaceful covenant relationship maintained between the sisters and the concubines. Anciently, this covenant required the surrogate mother (the concubine) to give her child to the wife because of her barrenness. Once again we read of no punishment by God upon Jacob and his wives and concubines, as Jacob had been **deceived** by Laban, and **it was the women** who *consented* and *initiated* the extra wives relationship, **not the man**. Like Abraham, Jacob did **not** *initiate* the additional wives relationship. Note also, that there was no command from God to become part of it either, **nor** condemnation of it. The deception of his father in-law, *and* Jacob's long years of service, were apparently punishment enough.

Like his grandfather Abraham, Jacob eventually **turned** his heart fully to God. His **conversion** occurred at "Peniel" (Hebrew for "face" or "vision of God") in Genesis 32:24-30. There we read of the vision of "Jacob's ladder" extending to heaven. It was at this time that Jacob put **idolatry** out of his house, fully *submitting* to the one true God (Gen. 35:2-4). We know God appeared to him there and changed his **name** to "Israel," which means "*one who overcomes*" or one who "*prevails with God*." It reflects two things; (1) Jacob's new, "**mighty change of heart**," and (2) a new **covenant** relationship with God. Because of his great faith, Jacob had parted the veil separating him from the God of heaven. He prevailed in his "*wrestle*" with God. His later birthright son Joseph also "*prevailed*" with God (see JST Gen. 48:10). Following his "**renewal**," some suggest God may have assisted Israel in living His higher **covenant** law by taking his second wife Rachel home (Gen. 35:19). This left Jacob with Leah, his first wife. Though there was no command from God to take the wives and concubines, once Jacob was fully converted to Him, Jacob did not cast away those whom he cared for, nor the children of the wives and concubines he had grown to love, as he took them **prior to his covenant relationship with God**. Some suggest that when Jacob went to Egypt, his additional wives and concubines were not with him.

Joseph and Asenath

In the Prophet Joseph Smith's patriarchal blessing, he is told that he is a literal descendant of four covenant "fathers"; Abraham, Isaac, Jacob, *and* **Joseph** (of Egypt). Joseph, son of Jacob and Rachel, was a valiant, visionary son (second youngest), and the *birthright* son of Jacob. He was given a coat or robe of many marks (symbols) to signify this birthright. His brothers (through *other* wives) were jealous of his gifts and his father's love for him, and thus sold him into Egyptian slavery. In Genesis we learn that while working as a slave in Potiphar's house, He resisted the sexual advances of Potiphar's wife and was thrown into prison because of her false accusation of Joseph. Later after rising to second in command under Pharaoh, Joseph met the adopted daughter of an Egyptian priest at Heliopolis, also called Potiphar. Like Joseph, she too was not Egyptian, but of the blood of Israel (or Jacob), through Jacob's only daughter Dinah (her mother was Leah). Joseph and Isaac wisely saw the trouble that additional wives brought and did not take additional wives themselves. It was **not** part of God's *divine sanction* for any of the Patriarchs from Adam to Moses, nor of the Prophets from Moses to Malachi. Neither do we find the practice among the Twelve Apostles chosen by the LORD in the New Testament! This is significant.

Dinah became involved with Shechem, a non-Israelite prince and they had a child through this union named Asenath. Because the child was illegitimate, she was sold into Egypt too, ending up in the home of the Egyptian priest at Heliopolis. He and his wife were apparently childless. Note that both Asenath *and* Joseph were both sold and taken to Egypt. This is how the LORD preserved the bloodline - He brought Asenath to Joseph. She was a unique beauty in all of Egypt, called "the Jewel of the Nile." After meeting and falling in love with Joseph, she gladly accepted his God, the God of her ancestry and was greatly blessed. Before her wedding to Joseph, she was covered with bees and then honey. According to one author, "the bees were a symbol of His anointing her as the mother of many nations and an elect woman of God. She was in the image of Sarah, the wife of Abraham." When Asenath gave birth to the twins, Manasseh and Ephraim, the first had dark black-brown hair and the second, red-brown hair. Through her loins the earth would be blessed in the spreading of the Gospel, "like the bees spread out to gather pollen and bring it back to the hive" (see Anonymous, https://purerevelations.files.wordpress.com/2017/05/temporal-dispensations-051017-1.pdf - pps. 99-108; http://www.johnpratt.com/items/docs/lds/meridian/2000/puzzle_ans.html and Hugh Nibley, Abraham in Egypt, Deseret Book, pps. 625-38).

Many of the Saints are descendants of Joseph of Egypt and his only wife Asenath through their twins Manasseh and Ephraim. Lehi and his posterity on this land are thought to descend through the lineage of Manasseh, the older *firstborn* son. Lehi pronounced the **covenant** blessings of Joseph of Egypt on his youngest, sixth son, also named

Joseph in 2 Nephi chapter 3. These promises will soon be fulfilled and perhaps with another Joseph, soon to rise up (see 2 Ne. 3:24). These promises are tied to our day and us (see Gen. 37; JST Gen. 48-50; Deut. 33, and 2 Ne. 3).

David & Bathsheba

Early on, the popular warrior-king David had several wives, like King Saul before him. There is no record of fertility issues with the first wives. It was a cultural tradition for a powerful, prideful king to satisfy his desires, as this is what kings in the surrounding, *idolatrous* cultures did. They "**multiplied wives**" to themselves. David followed this pattern and paid a price for it. After his great sin in taking Bathsheba, by having her husband killed in putting him on the frontlines of battle, David repented (1 Sam. 12:13). He too eventually **turned** his heart fully to "The Eternal" (1 Kings 11:6), doing so with a **broken heart** and a **contrite spirit** (see Psalm 51:7 & 17). **He then put away his multiple wives** and concubines (2 Sam. 20:3). Nevertheless, the consequences of his actions remained. And unlike Abraham and Jacob (whose wives *initiated* the practice), **there was condemnation** ***and*** **punishment** from God for David's actions (lustful desires, adultery, and murder), and natural consequences resulting from them (see Jacob 2:23-25). We read in 2 Samuel 12:9-12:

> "Now therefore, the sword shall never depart from thine house; because **thou hast despised me**, and hast **taken the wife of Uriah** the Hittite **to be thy wife**."

David also went against God's law relative to Israel's leaders in Deuteronomy 17:17, "Neither shall he **multiply wives** to himself!" There was a heavy price to pay for what David did in both of these instances, and a legacy left. According to Emma Smith, her husband Joseph stated:

> "David was not raised from the dead when the righteous came forth at the time of Christ's resurrection, because he **put Uriah to death**, and the crimes of *polygamy* and *murder* always go together" (Saints Herald, 48:184).

Emma believed polygamy was the root cause of her husband's murder. It wasn't because Joseph was practicing polygamy and hiding it from Emma and others, as we shall see in latter chapters. He was murdered because he had threatened to expose all those within the church practicing it at Nauvoo, including members of the Twelve. His plan was to completely root it out from the Church.

King David "despised" God by taking Bathsheba (already married) as an additional wife, and by having her innocent husband killed in battle. Therefore the sword was never to depart from his house or family thereafter. It was a **curse**. At that time David's house consisted of additional wives and the children from them. They were taken as part of David's **conquests, not** in God officiating in the new divinely sanctioned relationships.

God told David, "Thus saith the Eternal, Behold, I will raise up evil against thee out of thine own house." God added, "and I will take thy wives before thine eyes, and give them unto thy neighbor, and he shall lie with thy wives in the sight of this sun. For thou didst it **secretly**: but I will do this thing before all Israel, and before the sun [openly]." David's own son Absalom actually did this, lying with his father's former wives (2 Sam. 16:21-22). It was a great sin. God allowed David to take Saul's wives as He allowed Absalom, David's son to take his (David's) wives. He gave them power to take them. **Both Absalom and David transgressed God's law!** Polygamists take these actions and twist them to their favor. Remember that Saul had died, his wives widowed, whereas David took Uriah's wife while he was alive. God may have allowed wives to be taken in **conquest**, but not part of His *divine sanction.*

Later David repented. "And David said unto Nathan, I have sinned against the Eternal" (I Samuel 12:13). We read his private prayer of **repentance** to God in Psalm 51, the prayer of *a broken heart* and *a contrite spirit.* Significantly, David then **turned** from both *polygamy* and from his *concubines*! We read in 2 Samuel 12:9-12, "And Nathan said unto David, The Eternal also hath put away thy sin; thou shalt not die." There was a three-fold price to pay for David's sin. It included; (1) Continual war (or the sword) in David's house; (2) The taking of the son born of his adultery (2 Sam. 12:13); Joseph Smith then informs us of the third curse; (3) "Although David was a King he never did obtain the spirit & power of Elijah & the Fullness of the Priesthood, & the priesthood that he received & the throne & kingdom of David is to be taken from him & given to another by the name of David in the last days, raised up out of his lineage" (Joseph Smith, TPJS, p. 339). The scriptural record is clear. In the end, David **put away** his ten concubines.

> "And David came to his house at Jerusalem; and the king took **the ten women his concubines**, whom he had

left to keep the house, and put them in ward, and fed them, **but went not in unto them**. So they were **shut up** unto the day of their death, living in widowhood" (*no sexual relations*, 2 Sam. 20:3).

David then went "**fully after the Eternal**" (1 Kings 11:6). He became "a man after God's own **heart**" (the cover of this book is tied to David's new heart). David was left with Bathsheba as his only legitimate wife. Many scholars believe Michal (an earlier wife who didn't like "his dancing before the LORD") may have died by this time (2 Sam. 6:23). Like Jacob, God may have cleared the way for Bathsheba to become David's single, **legal wife**. In these things we see that God was merciful *and* just. He had laws and commandments that were to be kept.
David's son, Solomon did the opposite of his father. He started out righteously, relying on God and His will. Then, "when Solomon was old," he acquired a record number of women in his harem (**multiplying wives** unto himself). Solomon's many wives and concubines turned away his **heart** from God, and sadly, to their idols. "Solomon did evil in the sight of the Eternal" (1 Kings 11:6). There was *polygamy* and *concubines* in the leadership of ancient Israel once again. The resulting *idolatry* was especially offensive to God. It led to the nation of Israel being broken up, divided, and scattered. As we will see later on, *idolatry, polygamy,* and *murder* in Latter-day Saint history at Nauvoo led to a scattering of the Saints too, and in seven different directions.

God's Law of Marriage in Scripture (a short summary)

Unlike the Book of Mormon, the D&C, and Joseph's re-translation of Genesis, the Old Testament is less clear in addressing polygamy. Though God may not have punished Abram, Jacob, and David early on for their additional wives or concubines in the Old Testament, there are no sanctioning statements from Him for it there either. The limited statements condemning it, suggests that it may have been tolerated there in rare cases, or that scripture was changed. We do know that David, Solomon, and other kings in Israel were condemned for multiplying wives unto themselves (see Deut. 17:14, 17; Jacob 2:22-35). This is very clear in the Book of Mormon, a book that has had much less editing (see Jacob 2 and 3). Equally clear is *God's definition of marriage* and **His law** for it in all of scripture. It features **one wife** (see Gen. 2:24; Ex. 20:17; Moses 3:24; Mat. 19:5; Eph. 5:31; D&C 42:22-23, 49:15-17). Negative examples of multiple wives or concubines have an asterisk* hereafter. Examples of divorce feature two asterisks.**

God has never commanded a "plurality of wives" to anyone. He is the same yesterday, today and forever, when it comes to moral integrity. Proverbs 14:5 reads, "A faithful witness will not lie; but a false witness will utter lies." God said He would give us a "pattern" in all things, including His law for marriage (D&C 52:14; 63:13-16). Note the following three key scriptures, supported by four key witnesses.

A. "**Thou shalt love thy wife with all thy heart**, and **shalt cleave unto her** and **none else**. And he that looketh upon a woman to lust after her shall deny the faith, and shall not have the Spirit; and if he repents not he shall be cast out" (D&C 42:22 -23, Feb. 9, 1831. It was called "embracing the law of the Church."

B. "Wherefore, it is lawful that he should have **one wife**, and they twain shall be one flesh, and all this that the earth might answer the end of its creation; And that it might be filled with the measure of man, **according to his creation before the world was made"** (D&C 49:16-17, March 1831).

C. "Inasmuch as this church of Christ has been reproached with **the crime of fornication**, **and polygamy**: we declare that we believe, that one man should have **one wife**; and *one woman*, but *one husband*, except in case of death, when either is at liberty to marry again" (D&C 101:4, 1835 canonized edition, removed by Brigham Young in 1876).

Witness #1: Adam & Eve (Gen. 2:18 & 24) "And the LORD God said, It is not good that the man should be alone; I will make him an help meet [singular] for him . . . Therefore shall a man leave his father and his mother, and **shall cleave unto his wife**: [singular] and they shall be one flesh" (Gen. 2:18 & 24).

Witness # 2: Noah and His Sons (Gen. 7:5-7, 13) "And Noah went in, and his sons, and his wife, [singular] and his sons' wives [singular] with him, into the ark, because of the waters of the flood . . . In the selfsame day entered Noah, and Shem, and Ham, and Japheth, the sons of Noah, and Noah's wife, and the three wives of his sons with them, into the ark" (Gen. 7:7, 13).

Witness # 3: Lehi and His Sons (1 Ne. 7:1, 16:7-8) "AND now I would that ye might know, that after my father, Lehi, had made an end of prophesying concerning his seed, it came to pass that the Lord spake unto him again, saying that it was not meet for him, Lehi, that he should take his family into the wilderness alone; but that his sons should take daughters to wife, [singular] that they might raise up seed unto the Lord in the land of promise" . . . And it came to pass that I, Nephi, took one of the daughters of Ishmael to wife; and also, my brethren took of the daughters of Ishmael to wife; and also Zoram took the eldest daughter of Ishmael to wife. And thus my father had fulfilled all the commandments of the Lord which had been given unto him. And also, I, Nephi, had been blessed of the Lord exceedingly" (1 Ne. 7:1; 16:7-8).

"And now it came to pass that the people of Nephi, under the reign of the second king, began to grow **hard in their hearts**, and **indulge themselves somewhat in wicked practices, such as like unto David of old desiring many wives and concubines**, and also Solomon, his son" (Jacob 1:15).

"Wherefore, thus saith the Lord, **I have led this people forth out of the land of Jerusalem**, by the power of mine arm, that **I might raise up unto me a righteous branch** (seed) from the fruit of the loins of Joseph. Wherefore, **I** the Lord God **will not suffer** that this people (which includes latter-day Israel) **shall do like unto them of old**. Wherefore, my brethren, hear me, and hearken to the word of the Lord: **For there shall not any man among you have save it be one wife**; and concubines he shall have none; For I, the Lord God, delight in the chastity of women. And **whoredoms** are an **abomination** before me; thus saith the Lord of Hosts" (Jacob 2:25-28).

"Wherefore, **this people shall keep my commandments**, saith the Lord of Hosts, or **cursed** be the land for their sakes. For if I will, saith the Lord of Hosts, raise up seed unto me, I will command my people; otherwise (meaning therefore) they shall hearken unto these things" (Jacob 2:29-30).

"And now it came to pass that Zeniff conferred the kingdom upon Noah, one of his sons; therefore Noah began to reign in his stead; and **he did not walk in the ways of his father**. For behold, **he did not keep the commandments of God**, but he did walk after **the desires of his own heart**. And he had **many wives and concubines**. And he did cause his people to commit sin, and do that which was **abominable** in the sight of the Lord. Yea, and they did commit **whoredoms** and all manner of wickedness" (Mosiah 11:1-2)

Witness # 4: Joseph Smith, His Sons & His People (D&C 49:15-17) "...marriage is ordained of God unto man. Wherefore, it is lawful that he should have one wife, and they twain shall be one flesh, and all this that the earth might answer the end of its creation; And that it might be filled with the measure of man, according to his creation before the world was made (D&C 49:15-17, March 1831).

"Nevertheless, I give commandments, and many have turned away from my commandments and have not kept them. There were among you adulterers and adulteresses; some of whom have turned away from you, and others remain with you that hereafter shall be revealed. Let such beware and repent speedily, lest judgment shall come upon them as a snare, and their folly shall be made manifest, and their works shall follow them in the eyes of the people. And verily I say unto you, as I have said before, he that looketh on a woman to lust after her, or if any shall commit adultery in their hearts, *they shall not have the Spirit*, but shall deny the faith and shall fear" (D&C 63:13-16, Aug. 1831).

A month and a day before Joseph's murder (June 27, 1844), he spoke to a large group in Nauvoo. He started out by reading 2 Corinthians 11, a warning to some of the apostles and others present who were secretly practicing polygamy and accusing him of teaching and living it. Joseph said, "For such are false apostles, deceitful workers, transforming themselves into the apostles of Christ. And no marvel; for Satan himself is transformed into an angel of light. Therefore it is no great thing if his ministers also be transformed as the ministers of righteousness; whose end shall be according to their works" (2 Cor. 11:13-15). He added, "What a thing for a man to be accused of committing adultery, and having seven wives, when I can only find one. I am the same man, and as innocent as I was fourteen years ago" (HC 6:408-412, Sunday, May 26, 1844).

General Overview Scriptures (more detail)

Genesis 2:24 "And the LORD God said, It is not good that the man should be alone; I will make him an help meet [singular] for him . . . Therefore shall a man leave his father and his mother, and **shall cleave unto his wife**: [singular] and they shall be one flesh" (Gen. 2:18 & 24).

Exodus 20:17 The 10th Commandment states, "You shall not covet your neighbour's **wife** [singular].

Deuteronomy 17:17 God forbade the leaders of Israel to have many wives. He said, "When thou art come unto the land which the Eternal thy God giveth thee, and shalt possess it, and shalt dwell therein, and shalt say, I will set a king over me, like as all the nations that are about me. . . . **Neither shall he multiply wives** to himself, that his heart turn not away" (Deut. 17:14, 17). It is spoken of as "this law" in verses 18 and 19.

2 Samuel 13 Sibling rivalries resulted from the sons of David's different wives (see also 1 Kings 2).

Malachi 2:14 "… the LORD hath been witness between thee and the **wife** of thy youth, against whom thou hast dealt treacherously; yet is she thy companion, and the **wife** of thy covenant" (see also the discussion on Tithing, chap. 6 in connection with the priests of Israel being *unfaithful* to God and their wives in polygamy).

1 Kings 11:1–3 Solomon's excessive number of *wives* led him into *idolatry.*

Matthew 19:5 "For this cause shall a man leave father and mother, and shall cleave to his **wife**: and they twain shall be one flesh."

Mark 10:7 "For this cause shall a man leave his father and mother, and cleave to his **wife**."

Ephesians 5:31 "For this cause shall a man leave his father and mother, and shall be joined unto his **wife**, and they two shall be one flesh."

1 Timothy 3:2 In this verse, polygamy is forbidden among church elders (leaders). Paul wrote: "each man should have his own **wife**, and each woman her own **husband**" (1 Cor. 7:2). "A bishop [elder, overseer, preacher, minister] must be blameless, the husband of **one wife**" (I Tim. 3:2)…Let the deacons be the husbands of **one wife**…" (v. 12).

2 Nephi 9:44-45, Jacob 1:19, 2:2 These verses address Jacob "**shaking his garments**" **free of the blood and sins of the Nephites**, those whom he had taught the law of monogamy to. He spoke out against the "grosser crime" or **whoredom** of many wives and concubines among his people, and the **abomination** it became by seeking to excuse it doctrinally via the examples of David and Solomon. Joseph Smith **shook his garments free of the blood and sins of his people too**, because of spiritual wifery and other iniquities in his "**last charge**" to the Council of Fifty (see p. 113 & endnote 16). So did Paul the Apostle in Acts 18:6, and Moroni in his warning to us in Ether 12:37-40.

Jacob 1:7, 15; 2:2-5, 22-35* These verses use strong language to condemn polygamy. Jacob first shares things that are "most precious," that we are to "come unto Christ, and partake of the goodness of God," that we "might enter into his rest" (Jacob 1:7). He then addresses the wicked practices of David and Solomon and their many wives and concubines (Jacob. 1:15). He preached repentance among the Nephites to remove the stain of blood and sin from his garments (2 Ne. 9:44-45, Jacob 1:19; 2:2-5), something Joseph Smith also did in the Spring of 1844 during his 'last charge**" to leaders (see endnote 16), as did Paul the Apostle (18:6). The Nephites of Jacob's day were developing (1) "**heard hearts**" and "**pride**" (Jacob 2:20, 22), were committing (2) a "**grosser crime**" (than that of the Lamanites, v. 22), were (3) becoming "**wicked**" (v. 1:15) in (4) their practice of "**whoredoms**" (v. 2:23). It was (5) a great "**abomination**" before God (v. 2:24). Verses 25 and 30 provide reasons why Lehi and his family depart Jerusalem, that a "**righteous branch**" of the house of Israel (through Joseph) might be set up on this land. It was accomplished via their physical separation from the evil there. God's command in Jacob chapters 2:21, 27, 29 and 34, and 3:5-6 is:

> "…hearken to the word of the LORD: For there shall not any man among you have **save it be one wife**; and **concubines he shall have none**" (Jacob 2:27, Witness #3, page 28).

Jacob 3:5-6* The LORD through Jacob stated that the Lamanites were more righteous than the Nephites for they didn't forget the commandment of the LORD to have but **one wife. "Behold, the Lamanites . . . are more righteous than you; for they have not forgotten the commandment of the Lord, which was given unto our **fathers**" (plural, 1830 version). In the 1981 printing of the Book of Mormon, the word "**fathers**" (plural) was changed to *"father"* (Lehi only). Thus, in reality, all the "**fathers**" were given this same commandment, that "they should have save it were **one wife**, and concubines they should have *none*, and there should not be **whoredoms** committed among them. And now, this commandment they observe to keep; wherefore, because of this observance, in keeping this commandment, the Lord God **will not destroy them**, but will be merciful unto them; and one day they shall become a blessed people."

Helaman 15:7-8 "...as many of them as are brought to the knowledge of the truth, and to know of the wicked and **abominable** *traditions* of their fathers, and are led to believe the holy scriptures, yea, the prophecies of the holy prophets, which are written, which leadeth them to faith on the Lord, and unto repentance, which faith and repentance bringeth a change of heart unto them . . ."

3 Nephi 30:2 In this scripture God appears to clearly address the Saints and polygamy, listing this sin as a "**whoredom**" after first listing lies and deception to protect it. God said, "Turn, all ye Gentiles, from your wicked ways; and **repent** of your evil doings, of your [1] **lyings** and [2] **deceivings**, and of your [3] **whoredoms**, and of your *secret abominations*, and your *idolatries*, and of your *murders*, and your *priestcrafts*, and your *envyings*, and your *strifes*, and from all your wickedness and abominations, and **come unto me**, and be baptized **in my name**, that ye may receive a remission of your sins, and be filled with the Holy Ghost, that ye may be numbered with **my people** who are of the house of Israel." This scripture also summarizes the fulness of Christ's doctrine, gospel, and church (chap. 7).

D&C 42:22-24 "Thou shalt love thy **wife** with all thy heart, and shalt *cleave unto her* and **none else**. And he that looketh upon a woman to lust after her shall *deny the faith*, and shall **not have the Spirit**; and if he repents not he shall be cast out. Thou shalt not commit adultery; and he that committeth adultery, and repenteth not, shall be cast out" (1831). Significantly, Section 42 is called "**the law**" in this and other sections of the D&C. Section 42 is where we find *the higher law* of real **love** in both "the law of consecration" *and* the law of "monogamy."

D&C 49:15-17 "And again, verily I say unto you, that whoso forbiddeth to marry is not ordained of God, for marriage is ordained of God unto man. Wherefore, it is lawful that he should have **one wife**, and they twain shall be one flesh, and all this that the earth might answer the end of its creation" (1831). Creation is not possible in homosexual relationships. This was the law of God, implemented before the world was made.

D&C 63:12–16 "I, the Lord, am not pleased ... I gave commandments and many have turned away from **my commandments** and have not kept them. There were among you *adulterers* and *adulteresses*; some of whom have turned away from you, and others remain with you.... And verily I say unto you, as I have said before, He that looketh on a woman to lust after her, or if any shall commit adultery in their hearts, they shall **not have the Spirit**, but shall *deny the faith*" (1831).

D&C 101 (1835 canonized edition, removed by Brigham Young in 1876) "...as this church of Christ has been reproached with **the crime of fornication, and polygamy**: we declare that we believe, that one man should have **one wife**; and *one woman*, but *one husband*, except in case of death, when either is at liberty to marry again" (1835).

***Kingly Corruption**

Though there were good kings in the Book of Mormon, including King Benjamin, Mosiah, and Lamoni, the Bible features many kings who oppressed the people they were to serve. In addition to heavy taxes, their sins and iniquities were often passed down to the people. King David and Solomon of the Bible and King Noah, Akish, and Riplakish of the Book of Mormon reveal how kings influenced their people negatively. Murder was sometimes used to protect what they valued, including the king's many wives. All was supported by high taxes upon the people.

Jacob 1:15* "...the people of Nephi...began to grow hard in their hearts, and indulge themselves somewhat in **wicked practices, such as like unto David of old desiring **many wives** and **concubines**, and also Solomon, his son" (Jacob 1:15, see also Deut. 17:14, 17).

Jacob 2:23-24* "...they [the Nephites, those later at Nauvoo, and some today] **understand not the scriptures, for they seek to **excuse themselves** in committing **whoredoms**, because of the **<u>things</u>** which were written concerning David, and Solomon his son Behold, David and Solomon truly had **many wives** and **concubines**, which **<u>thing</u>** was **abominable** before me, saith the Lord."

Mosiah 11:2* In the book of Mosiah, Abinadi addressed the **wickedness of king Noah and how it was affecting his people. He stated, "For behold, he [king Noah] did **not** keep the commandments of God, but he did walk after the desires of his own **heart**. And he had **many wives** and **concubines**. *And he did cause his people to commit sin*, and do that which was **abominable** in the sight of the LORD. Yea, and they did commit **whoredoms** and all manner of

wickedness." Wicked kings cause their people to sin (Mos. 29:17) and they are very difficult to dethrone (Mos. 29:21). We must not look to men, kings and other leaders for truth, but only God (see 2 Ne. 4:34; Psalm 118:8; Jer. 2:13), otherwise we practice idolatry, which often leads to sexual perversion. Such was the plight of ancient Israel repeatedly. Baal worship is a good example (endnote 1). The Prophet Abinadi was murdered (burned alive at the stake) for preaching against the sins (including sexual sins) of King Noah and his priests.

Mosiah 13:11* Speaking to Noah and his wicked priests, Abinadi said, "And now I read unto you the remainder of the commandments of God, for I perceive that they are not written in your **hearts; I perceive that ye have studied and taught **iniquity** the most part of your lives." The word *iniquity* in scripture is very often tied to moral or sexual sins, those that are premediated and worthy of punishment. They are passed down to ancestors.

Ether 10:5, 7 & 11* Like the kings of the Bible and the world in general, four kings in the Book of Mormon sought for "gain," which was power, money, and many wives and concubines. They turned to "the old plans," the secret blood-oaths of the evil one in Moses 5:29-31, along with murder, and burdens upon the people (see Ether 8:13-16, 21-26; 9:26; 10:33; Hel. 6:16-41). King Riplakish "did afflict the people with his **whoredoms and **abominations**" along with heavy taxes. So also his son King Morianton, and, "because of his many **whoredoms**...he was **cut off from the presence of the LORD**." Kings *Akish, Riplakish,* and *Morianton* in Ether 8-9, and King *Noah* of Mosaiah 11 are given us as types for why Joseph and Hyrum were murdered. Each sought power and many wives in their own kingdoms and were thus cut off from God. The first eight verses of Mosiah 11 are types for Brigham Young.

D&C 1:3 "And the rebellious shall be pierced with much sorrow; for their **iniquities** shall be spoken upon the housetops and their secret acts shall be revealed" (D&C 1:3). Those in a "carnal state...are in the bonds of *iniquity*" (Alma 41:11). This prophecy is being fulfilled in our day, as the sexual sins of those in government, in Hollywood, and in churches are being revealed via satellite technology to viewers throughout the world.

***Matthew 19:3* "Divorcing" and "putting her away" are often confused in the Bible. The lone reason for a lawful divorce is adultery. Some are simply put away or separated. We read in Matthew, "The Pharisees also came unto him, tempting him, and saying unto him, Is it lawful for a man to put away [the Greek word apoluo is used here, meaning G630 - divorce] his wife for every cause? And he answered and said unto them, Have ye not read, that he which made them at the beginning made them male and female [singular], And said, For this cause shall a man leave father and mother, and shall cleave to his wife: and they twain shall be one flesh? Wherefore they are no more twain, but one flesh. What therefore God hath joined together, let not man put asunder."

The Israelites in the city of Jerusalem practiced what God had forbidden: unlawful polygamy, divorce, and remarriage. On this, Jesus said, "Moses [not God] because of the hardness of your hearts suffered you to put away your wives: but from the beginning it was not so. And I say unto you, Whosoever shall put away [divorce] his wife, except it be for fornication, and shall marry another, committeth adultery: and whoso marrieth her which is put away doth commit adultery" (Mat. 19:8-9). There are many clarifying examples of lawful separation versus divorce in scripture. See http://www.christianpoly.org/divorce.php On this useful webpage we read, "Divorce" and "Put or send away" are not the same thing. A man who wanted to divorce his wife had to do two things. He had to write her a bill of divorcement and then send her away or put her away (Deut. 24:1-4, Mark 10:4). A man who found that his wife had been unfaithful to him did not write her a bill of divorcement as she and the other man were stoned. Malachi and Matthew chapter five were all about men who were **putting or sending away their wives without just cause**. Men were sending away their wives without writing a bill of divorcement even though their wives were not guilty of adultery. God hates the putting away (without divorce) because it always involves sin. In one case the sin of the wife for being unfaithful and in the other the sin of the husband for putting his wife away without just cause or a bill of divorcement. The act of putting away a wife without a bill of divorcement is equivalent to separation only.

Mixing Religion with Idolatry & Sexual Sin: *Reproach upon Christ's Teachings*

God said that we would **deny** Him (2 Ne. 28:32), **reject** Him (2 Ne. 1:10), and **forsake** Him (Jer. 2:13), along *with the power of the Holy Ghost* (2 Ne. 28:26, 31). Mormon said we would be ashamed of him (Morm. 8:36). Twisting or "wresting" God's words is a form of rejection (see D&C 10:63). One of the most common ways we as Saints diminish Christ is idolatry. In the Old Testament we see the frequent worship of Baal among the Israelites (endnote 1). It is a good example of the relationship of five things, one following after another; (1) pride, (2) idolatry, (3) sexual sin, (4) a secret combination rising up to protect it, and then (5) murder of those working against it. This five-fold path of darkness has occurred repeatedly throughout history. It led to the murder of Joseph, Hyrum, and Samuel Smith. Not only did ancient Baal worship include worshipping a false god or lord of this world, but it also involved sexual perversion, complete with child sacrifice (the innocent blood of a firstborn child was offered up to Baal).[1]

Sexual perversion remains a huge evil infesting our world today too, as pedophilia, child sex slavery, and acceptance of LGBT lifestyle are rampant. The great Prophet Elijah stood alone as the LORD's servant in putting this great sin away in ancient Israel, destroying Baal worship and the 450 priests who kept it in place (1 Kings 16-19). It came among the people because of its leaders (King Ahab and Queen Jezebel). This couple replaced the living God with Baal to satisfy their worldly ways. The people followed the King. He was heavily influenced by his wicked wife.

In America today, nearly 60 million abortions have been performed "legally" since the Supreme Court passed Roe versus Wade in 1973. It is a form of child sacrifice, strengthening dark forces in our day via the innocent blood of children, and often in connection with sexual sin. In Utah, there is an average of 3,200 abortions a year, a number that is growing. Note the following two scriptures, one ancient, one modern. Both address idolatry and the use of religion – and God's name - to justify sexual sin. Polygamy under Brigham Young did the same thing. He later made polygamy a requirement for exaltation. The phrase "spiritual wifery" – used by the Cochranites of Saco Maine, describe this abominable mix of religion with sexual sin, an iniquity passed down to us from our fallen fathers, priests, and kings.

In the early portion of Revelation, the LORD addresses seven New Testament churches that were departing from Him because of **idolatry** and **sexual sin**. It was resulting in what Paul called "*another gospel*" (see Gal. 1:6-9). The LORD first addressed the Ephesian Saints who were leaving their "first LOVE" - Jesus Christ (vs. 4). In verses 1 -7 of Revelation 2, the LORD invited the Ephesus Saints to repent and "**do the first works**" or the foundational acts of faith, repentance, baptism, and receiving the Holy Ghost, a fullness of His gospel (see 3 Ne. 30:2). The LORD made one exception for those at Ephesus. He was not happy with their "deeds," but he congratulated them for **not** doing as the Nicolaitans did at Pergamos. They were using **spiritual things** (religion) to *justify* changes to God's "**doctrine**." The Saints at Pergamos practiced sexual sins, mixing them with idolatrous religious practice. It became **doctrine** and was thus a great "**abomination**." Note the LORD's words below to the Saints at Ephesus, a city known for its great **temple** and its **idolatry** in connection with getting "**gain**" (see also Acts 16:16, 19, 19:26-27; 1 Ne. 22:23).

> "I know thy works…how thou canst not bear them which are **evil**: and thou hast tried them which *say they are apostles, and are not,* and hast found them *liars*…Nevertheless I have somewhat against thee, because thou hast left thy first love [the love of Jesus Christ as God]. Remember therefore from whence thou art fallen, and **repent**, and do the first works; or else I will come unto thee quickly, and will remove thy candlestick out of his place, except thou **repent**. But this thou hast, that thou hatest *the deeds* of **the Nicolaitans**, which I also hate…But I have a few things against thee, because thou hast there them that hold *the doctrine* of Balaam [Baal worship and its sexual sins], who taught Balac to cast a stumbling block before the children of Israel, to *eat things sacrificed unto idols*, and to commit **fornication**. So hast thou also them that hold **the doctrine of the Nicolaitans**, which thing I hate" (Rev. 2:4-6, 14-15).

Some research suggests that the Nicolaitans were early Christians who claimed Nicolas had received a *revelation* that led him to participate in idolatrous sexual practices (see Irenaeus, Epiphanius, Hippolytus). Brigham Young also claimed a revelation for his polygamy (see pps. 45, 51). Joseph never claimed a revelation on polygamy! Nicolas was said to be one of seven deacons in the early New Testament Church (Acts 6:5). The Nicolaitans were said to follow him into "*unrestrained indulgences*" or "**love feasts**" in two cities known for *idolatry*, Ephesus and Pergamos. **Their religious rites involved sex** and were also called "*Balaam's error*" (see Jude 4-16; 2 Peter 2:2-21). The "**Nicolaitan rites**" featured *feasting on unclean things sacrificed to idols*, followed by **fornication in religious rites.** The later Cochranites of Saco Maine utilized a similar mix of **religion** (with foot washing), *followed by sexual sin.* Early converts among the Cochranites were brought back to Kirtland Ohio as early as 1832. It then spread among the Saints, exploding in Nauvoo after Joseph, Hyrum, and Samuel Smith were murdered. Jude and Enoch addressed 200 fallen angels whose sexual sins with mortal women resulted in a race of gaints that the great flood was meant to remove. The Earth herself cried to her Creator to have these pollutions removed from her by way of the atonement of The Righteous One (see Moses 7:48).

Other research suggests that the word "Nicolaitan" comes from two Greek words "**Nike**" and "**Laos**." Nike is the Greek winged Goddess of Victory, while Laos is Greek for "laity," meaning "devotees," or "followers." In Greek mythology, Nike's function was to evangelize for Zeus and ascribe to him the honor and glory of *all other gods*, displacing them that he might be worshipped instead. Zeus is often pictured on a throne with Nike behind him putting a crown of laurel on his head, a symbol of his victory over all other deities. Zeus is comparable to Bel of Babylon or Baal of the Phoenicians. Idolatrous Baal worship was a constant problem for Israel. Elijah defeated the 450 prophets of Baal in 1 Kings 18. Some say the Nicolaitans had ties to Greek and Roman temple cults, those involving temple prostitutes, along with the Dionysian mysteries. The Nicolaitans brought **reproach** to the title "Christian" after Christ's death. The Brighamite practice of polygamy also brought great **reproach** upon the Church of Jesus Christ of Latter-day Saints. In Acts 27:22 we read, "For as concerning this sect [the Christians], we know that everywhere it is *spoken against*." It is no different for the Mormons who succombed to simililar practices, using God's name vainly, and later Joseph Smith's name for the practice, freeing Brigham and the Twelve from the real culpability. The Apostle Paul spoke of **reproach** on the early church in Hebrews 11:26 and 13:13, so too the LORD. Peter prophesied that **damnable heresies** would be brought into the Christian church, saying, "and many shall follow their *pernicious* ways, by reason of whom the way of truth shall be evil spoken of" (2 Pet. 2:1-2).

The LORD used the word "**reproach**" in the original D&C Section 101 (removed by Brigham Young), in connection with the words "**adultery**" and "**fornication**." They begun to enter into the church in 1832 with the infusion of Cochranite converts to Kirtland from Saco Maine. The stain of **polygamy** brought **reproach** upon the early Saints because of the same mix of **religion** with **sexual sin**! Joseph Smith's name was then used to falsely *justify* the practice, adding credibility to the deviant behavior of men like Dr. John Bennett in Nauvoo. Bennett was a physician, former Mayor of Nauvoo, and assistant to Joseph Smith in the First Presidency. Bennett tried to seduce a number of women, offering them abortions if needed (a modern tie to ancient child sacrifice). Bennett falsely claimed that Joseph Smith taught him and others **spiritual wifery**. Like other later leaders, Bennett did so to *justify* his seductions. Confronted later in Nauvoo in a public trial by Joseph about this, Bennett denied that Joseph taught such things and sought his forgiveness! Note the LORD's warning to future Bishop Newel K. Whitney in D&C 117, below. In 1838, Whitney is chastised for his connection to the **secret abominations** of the Nicolaitan band.

> "Let my servant Newel K. Whitney be ashamed of *the Nicolaitane band* and of all their **secret abominations**, and of all his littleness of soul before me, saith the Lord, and come up to the land of Adam-ondi-Ahman, and be a bishop unto my people, saith the Lord, *not in name* but in **deed**, saith the Lord" (D&C 117:11).

This revelation for Whitney was given to Joseph Smith at Far West on July 8 of 1838, the year that *secret enforcers* and their **secret oaths** among "the Danites" were used to support revenge, theft, and even murder on the enemies of the Saints. Their coercion methods stirred up a lot of trouble for the Saints. **Secret oaths** were later used at Nauvoo to keep **spiritual wifery** in place. They later became part of the temple "endowment" put in place by Brigham Young. Whitney would later become part of this **secret combination** (chap. 5, D&C 38:11, 28). Whitney had been a member of the Meridian Orb Masonic Lodge #10 in Plainesville, Lake County, Ohio. Brigham Young and Heber C. Kimball were also Masons before joining the Church. The Masons make extensive use of **secret oaths**. A total of 1,492 men joined this brotherhood in five Masonic lodges in the Nauvoo area. They made **blood-oaths** to one another to protect their **secret rites** and later their *spiritual wifery* (secret oaths were part of the Danite band of the Mormons, the Freemasonry they adopted, and the new Brighamite temple endowment he and Heber put in place). "**Secret combination**" *blood oaths* first surface in Moses 5. They were also made by the 200 "Watchers," those who descende to earth in the Book of Enoch as "fallen angels," after they lusted after mortal women. They made covenants to support each other **in their sin** (which included taking many wives). The oaths were made atop Mt. Hermon in northern Israel (see pps. 164-65, chap. 5). One of the main reasons the Book of Enoch was removed from the Bible was the removal of these **plain** *and* **precious** truths - of *how* evil is put in place among men, via *secret combinations* and their *blood oaths*. It is why the LORD brought forth the Book of Mormon with its 83 references to *secret combinations*, and why he had Joseph re-translate the Bible (the largest part of it being Genesis, see Moses 5).

Note the ancient to modern timeline below, a result of pride, idolatry, whoredoms, and murder, often in connection with secret combinations and their oaths. These sins cut the people off from God (3 - 4 generations). Child sacrifice remains today in abortions. Scripture says promised covenant lands (east & west) are swept clean of such things.

1. *Lamech loved Satan more than God* — multiple wives, every man knew his brother, murder, cut off
2. *Watchers descend to take many wives* — in Enoch's day 200 "Watchers" make evil covenant on Mt. Hermon
3. *Baal worship (false "Lord") with Asherah* — cult of fertility - ritual sex, firstborn child sacrificed to Baal, cut off

4. *Temple Prostitutes (Venus, Aphrodite)* sexual sin in connection with religious worship, cut off
5. *The Nicolaitan Chrstians* feast of unclean food with ritual sex thereafter, cut off
6. *Mormon Polygamy under Young* sexual sin mixed with religion - polygamy eventually tied to exaltation
7. *Abortion & same-sex relationships today* worship of sex with child sacrifice in abortion

Six Scriptures Used to Support Polygamy

Many scriptures speak plainly against polygamy and other sexual sin. Some among us claim the following six sets of scripture make allowance for it; (1) 1 Kings 15:5, (2) 4th Nephi 1:11, (3) Isaiah 4:1, (4) Jacob 2:30, (5) Genesis 38, and (6) D&C 132. Only one of them features taking a single second wife *lawfully* (#5, but not *many* wives). It is called the **Levirate Law,** part of "the lesser law" of Moses (D&C 42 features "the higher law" of consecration and monogamy).

1. 1 Kings 15:5 – *One Major Sin?* This verse states, "Because David did that which was right in the eyes of the LORD, and turned not aside from any thing that he commanded him all the days of his life, save only in the matter of Uriah the Hittite." A number of other scriptures counteract this statement. David was an imperfect man. He sinned with his many wives and concubines, according to Deuteronomy 17:14, 17, and especially Jacob 2:23-24. We know that David later repented, putting away his ten concubines once he turned his heart fully to God (see 2 Sam. 20:3). Because we do **not** have a record of David receiving a command of the LORD to take extra wives, we must rely on Jacob 2 and 3 for greatest understanding of his story.

2. Isaiah 4:1 - *Removing Spiritual Reproach* Isaiah 4 follows a chapter tied to war and thus the depletion of men. It states, "And in that day seven women shall take hold of one man, saying, We will eat our own bread, and wear our own apparel: only let us be called by thy name, to take away our reproach." Because the ratio of men to women was very uneven in this particular situation, some believe God will allow one righteous man to have more than one wife, because they desire it, and because God allows it, knowing the man's heart. It should be noted again that the man did not initiate the practice Abraham or Jacob, the women did.

This Isaiah verse may represent a lower, first level *physical* meaning addressing the needs of women and children after war has depleted the male population. The extreme, extenuating circumstances appear to have caused the women there to request or accept polygamy as a necessary alternative, if they were to have children, overcoming the *reproach* of being childless, and to have male companionship (though perhaps severely limited). There is no evidence that God approves it, nor does He condemn it. There is no indication of the righteousness of those involved. In Mosiah 21:17 we read about "a great number of women, more than there was of men; therefore King Limhi commanded that every man should impart to the support of the widows and their children, that they might not perish with hunger; and this they did because of the greatness of their number that had been slain." King Limhi did not command the men to take the women as additional wives, but only to impart to them in **charity**.

There may be another higher (*spiritual*) meaning for Isaiah 4:1, based on marriage symbolism throughout the Bible. The ultimate **reproach** for women (the bride – symbolic of the Christian church, women and men) to be taken away, is not infertility, but **the reproach of sin**. Christ, the Bridegroom - the one man in Isaiah 4:1 - can do that for each of us if we come to Him in love, and with broken heart and contrite spirit. The seven women of Isaiah 4:1 are thought to represent **the seven churches** addressed in Revelation chapters 2 and 3. Each of them wanted to be called by the name of Christ, to be His **bride**, and could do so if their *shame* or "**reproach**" (because of sin) was removed. Like all the prideful (the first negative quality mentioned in Jacob's denouncement of polygamy in the Book of Mormon), *they arrogantly wanted to do things their own way*, keeping some sin, *because of the idols they maintained in their hearts.* They wanted to feed themselves their own bread, instead of being fed on the bread of Christ. They want to clothe themselves in their own apparel, instead of being clothed in the righteousness of Christ.

Isaiah 4:1 may thus be tied to **seven arrogant or prideful churches** (the number 7 is tied to a "fullness" or being "complete") **in the last-days all wishing to be the bride of Christ** (like the 7 split-off churches that arose after Joseph's murder[2]). They want to practice their own version of religion for selfish motives, but also want to have the LORD's salvation too. They want to be called "Christian" or be called by His Name, yet they want to do things their own way, to stay in the sins they enjoy, and be saved too. Such want to have it *both ways.* Those who will be the Bride of Christ cannot be lukewarm, nor cold. They must be on fire for him and His will and ways (see Rev. 3:15-17), as exemplified by the baptism of fire and the Holy Ghost. It occurs as we turn our hearts wholly to God.

3. Jacob 2:30 – *Separation from Babylon* The Prophet Joseph said, "I told the brethren that the Book of Mormon was the most correct of any book on earth, and the keystone of our religion, and a man would get nearer to God by abiding by its precepts, than by any other book" (*History of the Church,* 4:461). Why then do we ignore it and the covenant it represents? Such rebellion lead to our **condemnation** in D&C 84:57. A careful review of word usage in Jacob chapters 2 and 3 is revealing. Jacob is an important prophet in the Book of Mormon. Speaking of himself and his older brother Nephi, he said that they "had many revelations, and the spirit of much prophecy; wherefore, we knew of Christ and his kingdom . . ." Both men had been to heaven, becoming sure witnesses of Jesus Christ and His reality. Both "labored diligently" thereafter among their people that they "might persuade them to come unto Christ, and partake of the goodness of God, that they might enter into his rest" (Jacob 1:6-7), which is the glory of His personal presence (D&C 84:24). This is the whole reason for the Book of Mormon, that we might partake of His **redemption**, His love and gifts, and come to know Him as they did.

Jacob made it clear that the Lamanites, though they were *unbelievers*, were preserved of God on this land, and would be until our day, for one simple reason; **they kept the commandment to have but one wife** and they loved them and their families, whereas the Nephites, supposed believers in God, had turned their hearts from God in favor of *additional* **wives** and *allowed* **secret combinations** to come upon them. They were thus *destroyed* (see Jacob 3:4-9). Lehi and his family were brought to this land that a *righteous branch* of the house of Israel might be preserved here, without the stain of *polygamy* as practiced in Jerusalem and elsewhere (Jacob 2:24-26; 1 Ne. 7:1). Following these verses we have the most misinterpreted scripture in the Book of Mormon (v. 30). It provides *justification* or an "*excuse*" for some to take additional wives, that they might "raise up seed unto me" (along with Genesis 38:8). Interpreting verse 30 wrongly negates the rest of Jacob's words by those seeking "to **excuse** themselves in committing **whoredoms**."

> "For if I will, saith the LORD of Hosts raise up seed unto me [a righteous people] I will command my people [God is our King and Law Giver and He commands that we have one wife only, 2:27, 3:5-6]; otherwise they [the people] shall hearken unto these **<u>things</u>** [the many wives abomination, like David and Solomon]" (Jacob 2:30). Jacob's and the LORD's use of the word "**<u>things</u>**" is detailed on pages 22-23.

If we love the LORD, we will honor His command and will in all things. Again, the primary problem is often *idolatry. We have idols in our hearts* and we *trust in ourselves and other men* **more than God**. Joseph received a revelation from God explaining how he could also receive false revelation - from deceiving spirits or his own mind. God said to Him, Oliver Cowdery, and David Whitmer; "Some revelations are of God: some revelations are of men: and some revelations are of the devil." According to Whitmer, "When a man enquires of the Lord concerning a matter, if he is deceived by his own carnal desires, and is in error, he will receive an answer according to his erring heart, but it will not be a revelation from the Lord" (Joseph Smith in David Whitmer, An Address to All Believers in Christ, p. 31).

We are to become the seed of the Righteous, a special name-title for Jesus Christ – the Father of our salvation (see Moses 7:45 & 47). This is the message of King Benjamin to his people in Mosiah chapters 1-5. When we are spiritually born again in Christ, we become His sons and daughters. We then take upon us His name. We are redeemed by Him as He alone performed the Atonement on our behalf. The LORD talks about us being His seed in this regard in Isaiah 53:10, Mosiah 14:10-14, and 15:10-12. In Mosiah 14:10 (Isaiah's words in 53:10), the Prophet Abinadi stated, "When thou shalt make his soul an offering for sin **he shall see his seed**." The children of the LORD Jesus Christ are those who believe in Him and live His gospel. They are given power to become his sons and his daughters, and are thus adopted into His family through Abraham, the father of the faithful. Abinadi stated:

> "Behold I say unto you that whosoever has heard the words of the prophets, yea, all the holy prophets who have prophesied concerning the coming of the LORD—I say unto you, that all those who have hearkened unto their words, and believed that the LORD would redeem his people, and have looked forward to that day for a remission of their sins, I say unto you, that **these are his seed**, or they are the heirs of the kingdom of God. For these are they whose sins he has borne; these are they for whom he has died, to **redeem** them from their transgressions. And now, are they not **his seed**? Yea, and are not the prophets, every one that has opened his mouth to prophesy, that has not fallen into transgression, I mean all the holy prophets ever since the world began? I say unto you that they are **his seed**. And these are they who have published peace, who have brought good tidings of good, who have published salvation; and said unto Zion: The God reigneth!" (Mos. 15:10-14).

Overall, the context of Jacob 2:30 is not about having many children via polygamy, but about Lehi and His family *separating themselves from the sins of Babylon* (like polygamy), that they might become **a righteous branch** of the house of Israel on this special Promised Land. They, like all of us are to be born again in Christ Jesus, becoming **His seed** – His sons and daughters. This scripture ignores other statements by Jacob in chapters 2 and 3, and other anti-polygamy scriptures elsewhere. Joseph Smith spoke out against the whoredom. He has no known children by polygamous wives. His lack of more children via polygamy goes against one of Young's primary justifications for it - "*to raise up seed*" or have many children in it. Young favored polygamy and had 57 children via 16 of his 55 wives.

Other Notable Spiritual "Seed" Scriptures

"In thy seed [Abraham, through Christ] shall all the kindreds of the earth be blessed" (Abr. 2:11; 3 Ne. 20:25 & 1 Ne. 15:18; 22:9; D&C 110:12
"Thy seed also had been as the sand" (1 Ne. 20:19; Isa. 48:19).
Like Abraham, Joseph Smith's seed was to be a blessing to many (D&C 124:58)
This land is consecrated to the seed of Lehi (2 Ne. 10:19)
The remnant seed of Jacob shall be gathered in – in the last-days (3 Ne. 5:23-24)
Those renewed in Christ become the seed of Abraham, father of the faithful (D&C 84:34)
The children and seed of Abraham must be led out of the bondage of sin by power (D&C 103:17)
Those who keep God's law have a continuation of the seeds forever (D&C 132:19)

God's love for us and our love of Him keeps us in "**the way**." The first four of the Ten Commandments are tied to idolatry. Commandment #1 states, "Thou shalt have no other gods before me. Thou shalt not make unto thee any graven image, or any likeness of any thing that is in heaven above, or that is in the earth beneath, or that is in the water under the earth. Thou shalt not bow down thyself to them, nor serve them: for I the LORD thy God am a jealous God, visiting the iniquity of the fathers upon the children unto the third and fourth generation of them that hate me; And shewing mercy unto thousands of them that love me, and keep my commandments" (Ex. 20:3-6).

We read of the promise of a **curse** to come upon this land, polluting it, and upon the Saints, to "the third and fourth generation" in D&C 124:46-50 (see also Jacob 3:3-4), if we did not honor God in this and other commandments. One of these "other commandments" was to complete the Nauvoo House and the Nauvoo Temple in the timeframe God had given them. If they did not do this, the LORD said, "ye shall be rejected as a church with your dead" (D&C 124:31-32). Note Psalm 78 in this regard. It is the LORD's desire that we might set our, "hope in God and not forget the works of God, but keep his commandments: And might not be as their fathers, a stubborn and rebellious generation; a generation that set not their heart aright, and whose spirit was not steadfast with God" (Psalm 78:7-8).

To hearken to "the word of the LORD" or God's command, is to receive and understand scripture and His commandments to individuals personally in pure revelation. In Jacob 2:21, 29 and 34, and 3:5-6, the Nephites sought, "to **excuse** themselves in committing **whoredoms**, because of the things which were written concerning David, and Solomon his son." God's commandment throughout scripture is to have one wife only (see v. 27). Jacob **shook his garments free of the blood, sins, and iniquities of the people he had taught** – the primary **grosser crime** being **many wives and concubines** (see 2 Ne. 9:44-45, Jacob 1:19, 2:2). Both Paul the Apostle (Acts 18:6) and Joseph Smith (in his "**last charge**") did the same thing as a sign and warning for their people (p. 113 & endnote 16).

4. 4th Nephi 1:10-11 – *The Levirate Law in the Book of Mormon?* Some believe verses 10 and 100 of 4th Nephi hint of plural wives in the Book of Mormon. "And now, behold, it came to pass that the people of Nephi did wax strong, and did multiply exceedingly fast, and became an exceedingly fair and delightsome people. And they *were married*, and *given in marriage*, and were blessed according to the multitude of the promises which the LORD had made unto them" (4 Ne. 1:10-11). Those favoring polygamy claim the phrases "*given in marriage*" and "*multiply exceedingly fast*" both point to lawful polygamy. In 4 Nephi 3 we read that the people were living the higher Law of Consecration, thus some pro-polygamists associate the higher law of love in "consecration" with what they believe is a higher law of marriage. This is false reasoning. D&C 42, called "**the law**" (see the Preface) featured two "**higher laws**," the "**law of consecration**" and the "**law of monogamy**." Only the Levirate Law portion of the "lesser" Mosiac Law allowed for a second wife, in a rare exception. They were not to *multiply wives* to themselves (Deut. 17:17).

Once again, the correct interpretation of any verse of scripture requires (1) context (surrounding scriptures), and (2) seeking and obtaining God's will and meaning, not our own based upon the idols held in our own heart. Ambiguity should encourage us to seek clarification from God via *pure revelation.* This goes for two other Book of Mormon scriptures that some force into being associated with polygamy. They are 1 Nephi 5:1 and the use of "my mother" there, in connection with 1 Nephi 18:17-18, in connection with Lehi's two youngest sons, Jacob and Joseph. Pro-polygamists claim they were born of a different mother. They believe Nephi's use of the word "my mother" in Nephi 5:1, and "their children" and "their mother" in verses 17 and 19 hint at plural marriage for father Lehi. Nephi's use of the phrase "my father" in verse 17 for Lehi appears to negate this interpretation. Why would Jacob, as one of these sons, speak out against another wife for his father Lehi in Jacob 2 and 3, if he had taken Ishmael's wife in a Levirate arrangement? She already had children, and thus no need to "raise up seed" to her dead husband (see Gen. 38 below).

5. Genesis 38 – *The Levirate Law* Genesis 38 gives us the Levirate law. Some suggest it is the only legal and lawful way in scripture – within God's **lesser** Mosiac law – for a man to have an additional wife (one). It encouraged a widowed woman to marry the brother of her dead husband that they might raise up seed **to his dead brother**. It was centered on preserving the widow's dead husband's "**name** in Israel," via a firstborn son given him by his brother In Deuteronomy 6:25, we read, "And it shall be, that the firstborn which she beareth shall succeed in the name of his brother which is dead, that **his name be not put out of Israel**." A man could refuse to take his brother's widow as a second wife, but he was penalized for it (see verses 7-10). Those believing this law was inspired of God suggest it wasn't about the man, but about the woman and her desire for children, all in connection with "**raising up seed**" **unto the one who had died.** Though the Levirate Law was not the whoredom of multiple wives and concubines practiced by many kings in the ancient world, it may have been *another way of justifying polygamy*, an open door to it by ungodly men with poor motives. Others believe it was part of the fallen culture surrounding the people. We should pray to know if the Levirate law was of God or a part of changed scripture. The Prophet Jacob said:

> "For Behold, thus saith the Lord; This people [the Nephites] begin to wax in *iniquity*: **they understand not the scriptures**, for **they seek to excuse themselves** in committing **whoredoms** concerning David and Solomon" (Jacob 2:23).

Because men, anciently and today "**understand not the scriptures**," they find ways to *twist* them to *justify* their own lustful desires (D&C 10:63:64; 2 Thess. 2:7; Rev. 17:5). Jacob 2:30 is one such verse for many LDS pro-polygamists. Some *do not* or *will not* "**see**" what the words say. The Levirate law may be another example. Unholy intent (idols in the heart) cover the truth like a veil, so that some *believe a lie. Did or does marrying a dead brother's wife and raising up children for him come from God?* The term Levirate is derivative of the Latin word levir, meaning "husband's brother." Some **excuse** this practice believing that it was a way to care for the widow, allowing her to have children through the dead husband's brother. **Why does a dead husband need children**? It is true that women had few rights in the ancient world, and without a husband, a woman's plight as a widow was of great concern, especially if she had children to care for (see Mosiah 21:17). In verses 8 through 10 of Genesis 38, we read of Onan, one of Judah's sons. He was to;

> "Go in unto thy brother's wife [the brother was now dead], and marry her, and **raise up seed to thy brother**. And Onan knew that the seed [children] should not be his; and it came to pass, when he went in unto his brother's wife, that he spilled it on the ground, lest that he should give seed to his brother. And the thing which he did displeased the LORD; wherefore he slew him also" (see v. 7).

This is one of three known scriptures where the phrase "**raising up seed**" is tied to having physical children, rather than becoming a **spiritual** *son* or *daughter* of Christ. Note also that the LORD "slew him" for doing this. This is a very harsh punishment. Additional scriptures tied to the Levirate Law are found in Deut. 21:15-17, 25:5-10; Lev. 18:17; Ruth 4:7; Mat. 22:23-30; Mark 12:19-25; And Luke 16:17. Some say Jacob 2:30 has potential Levirate connections as the Nephites were living the Mosaic Law on this land. Prayer in pure revelation is needed to discern truth from error.

Part II: D&C 132 - Pure versus False Revelation

Brigham Young and LDS Church leaders today claim that Section 132 of the D&C is a revelation (supporting polygamy) given to Joseph Smith on July 12 of 1843. Brigham Young first made this claim publically in **1852**, eight years after Joseph's murder. The so-called 132 "revelation" was published in the Deseret News in August of 1852.

Later in 1865 and 1874, Young changed this story. Before addressing this sixth document (now part of our canon of "scripture"), we should first review God's words relative to receiving *pure* revelation – from **Him**.

God said He wants us to rely on **His word** to keep the gates of hell from prevailing against us (see D&C 18:3-6). His word in writing (scripture) and in *pure* revelation are invaluable. Because, "all have not *faith*" (the faith necessary to receive God's revelation), many "seek…words of wisdom…out of the **best books**…" (D&C 88:118). Too many turn from both types of God's "word" and instead turn to "the arm of flesh" - *scholars* and *church leaders.* Both are falible. God's word says that trusting in "*the arm of flesh*" leads to curses (see 2 Ne. 4:34 & 28:30-31). In Christ's day they were the Rabbis. Faith and trust in God is needed to receive pure revelation from Him. The Prophet Joseph taught, "The best way to obtain truth and wisdom is not to ask it from books, but to go to God in prayer, and obtain divine teaching" (TPJS p. 191). "It is the privilege of the children of God to come to God and get revelation" (Words of Joseph Smith, p. 13). Joseph added, "Salvation cannot come without revelation. It is in vain for anyone to minister without it" (WJS, p. 10). "If we have any claim on our Heavenly Father for anything, it is for knowledge . . . Reading the experience of others, or the revelation given to them, can never give us a comprehensive view of our condition and true relation to God . . . Could you gaze into heaven five minutes [visions], you would know more than you would by reading all that ever was written on the subject" (TPJS p. 324). God said, "If any of you *lack wisdom*, let him ask of God, that giveth to all men liberally, and upbraideth not; and it shall be given him."

Deception – *tied to Desires in the Heart*

Like Joseph's false revelation with Oliver and David, all of us can receive revelation from one of three sources, based on the desires of our hearts; (1) the Lord, (2) Satan and false spirits, or (3) our own voice or mind. All of us can be deceived, especially if we don't seek God's will and wisdom. We read in Proverbs 23:7, "For as he thinketh in his heart, so is he." James stated, "Ye ask, and receive not, because **ye ask amiss**, that ye may **consume it upon your lusts**" (James 4:3; Morm. 9:28). The phrase "lusts of the flesh" is not tied to just sexual perversion here, but our own **heartfelt desires** *or* **lusts** in our mortal tabernacle. Some can be good, but not necessarily in line with God's will for us. If we want pure revelation from God, we must be willing to receive His will and fully submit to it.

Like Joseph, all of us have to learn line upon line. Whitmer added, "When a prophet, or any other man, prays to God and asks wisdom concerning a matter, his conscience will reveal an answer to him just according to the desires of his heart. If his desires are in any way carnal, he being deceived, an answer will be revealed to him accordingly; and he will think it is the revealed will of God." This is the "**strong delusion**" addressed in seven scriptures (2 Thess. 2:10-12, Isa. 66:2-4, Ezek. 14:1-11, James 4:3, Jacob 4:14, Alma 29:4 & Morm. 9:28). He added, "It is Satan who deceives the man, but God permits it because of the wicked desires of the man, and it is right and just in God's wisdom to permit the persistent transgressor to be led off and deceived by a delusive false doctrine" (see David Whitmer, *An Address to All Believers in Christ*, http://www.utlm.org/onlinebooks/address1.htm (pps. 42-43).

Paul, in 2 Thess. 2:11, stated: "And for this cause God shall send them **strong delusion**, that they should **believe a lie.**" Why would God allow this? Verses 10 and 12 give the reason why; "because they received not the love of the truth."... because they "but had pleasure in *unrighteousness*" – in their *carnal desires.* In Isaiah 66:2-4, the Lord said that the people, "have chosen their own ways, *and their soul delighteth in their* abominations, I will also choose their delusions." Note the following verses from JST Ezekiel 14. Joseph changed one word, adding the "not" at the end.

> "Thus saith the Lord GOD; Every man of the house of Israel that setteth up his idols in his heart, and putteth *the stumbling block* of his *iniquity* before his face, and cometh to the prophet; I the LORD will answer him that cometh according to the multitude of his idols; That I may take the house of Israel in their own heart, because they are all estranged from me through their idols. Therefore say unto the house of Israel, Thus saith the Lord God; Repent, and turn yourselves from your idols; and turn away your faces from all your abominations. For every one of the house of Israel, or of the stranger that sojourneth in Israel, which separateth himself from me, *and setteth up his* idols in his heart, and putteth *the stumblingblock* of his *iniquity* before his face, and cometh to a prophet to enquire of him concerning me; I the LORD will answer him by myself: And I will set my face against that man, and will make him a sign and a proverb, and I will cut him off from the midst of my people; and ye shall know that I am the LORD. And if the prophet be deceived when he hath spoken a thing, I the LORD have **not** deceived that prophet, and I will stretch out my hand upon him, and will destroy him from the midst of my people Israel" (JST Ezek. 14:3-9, the non-JST version does is missing the word "**not**").

Finally, note Alma 29. "God…granteth unto men according to their desire, whether it be unto death or unto life; yea, I know that he allotteth unto men, yea, decreeth unto them decrees which are unalterable, according to their wills, whether they be unto salvation or unto destruction" (Alma 29:4, see also Jacob 4:14).

Let us now look at D&C 132 closely, a very damaging document which Young called a "revelation." He put it into the Doctrine and Covenants *thirty-two years* **after** Joseph Smith was murdered (1876). He said it was given to the Prophet Joseph on July 12th of 1843, and yet in 1865, Young told Ulysses S. Grant's Vice Presidential candidate Shuyler Colfax that it was he (Young) who received the D&C 132 revelation on polygamy, **not** Joseph (see p. 42). The Prophet Joseph never presented any revelation on polygamy to the Saints. It was Young who made D&C 132 part of the Doctrine and Covenants, even though the priesthood quorums and the Saints in Young's day were **not** allowed to vote it in *or* out of their canon of scriptures in 1876 as "law." This was Young's decision alone, an action going against God's direction in this and other books of scripture. The LORD said, "All things shall be done by common consent in the church, by much prayer and faith..." (D&C 26:2, see also Mosiah 29:26; Alma 29:4; 1 Sam. 8:7).

6. D&C 132 - *Modified Revelation* What we now call Section 132 appears to be a composite construction of both Brigham Young and Joseph Smith. It represents Brigham Young's "coming out" document, produced to justify his version of spiritual wifery among the Saints in the early 1840's in Nauvoo, one he and some in the Twelve had been practicing secretly since the early 1840's. It was used to cement polygamy in place as an official church doctrine, one required for exaltation. Young used the word "**justify**" in the very first verse of D&C 132 to "**excuse**" his acts.

> "Verily, thus saith the Lord unto you my servant Joseph, that inasmuch as you have inquired of my hand to know and understand wherein I, the Lord, **justified** my servants Abraham, Isaac, and Jacob, as also Moses, David and Solomon, my servants, as touching the principle and doctrine of their having many wives . . . " (D&C 132:1).

Nowhere do we find a document stating that Joseph "inquired" of the LORD on the subject of polygamy! And nowhere does the LORD **justify** *anyone in scripture practicing polygamy*, and especially in the way Brigham, David, or Solomon did! It was Brigham Young that justified his version of spiritual wifery in these very words in D&C 132:1, using *his own words* to counteract what the LORD said in Jacob chapter 2, verse 23. It reads:

> "This people [the Nephites and then the early Saints] begin to wax in iniquity; **they understand not the scriptures**, for **they seek to excuse themselves** in committing whoredoms, because of the things which were written concerning David, and Solomon his son."

Twenty-four years after publishing Joseph's supposed "revelation" in the Deseret News (1852), Young put it into the 1876 version of the Doctrine and Covenants, calling it Section D&C 132 (he died a year later). In this same year he removed older Section 101 (which was anti-polygamy). Both actions were done without a vote of any priesthood quorum or the vote of the church. God's government is not to be a dictatorship. It is to feature involvement by the Saints. Brigham Young, Orson Pratt, and Joseph F. Smith all claimed that Oliver Cowdery, author of Section 101, was secretly a polygamist. Like Joseph, He could not defend himself against this false charge, as both men were dead.

In the Temple Lot Case of 1894 (chap. 4), Joseph and Emma Smith's firstborn son, Joseph Smith III testified that when any purported revelation was received by "the primitive church" established by his father (not the later changed one by Brigham Young), *it had to pass each of three priesthood quorums first, and by a unanimous vote, before going before the Saints for a fourth.* This represented **four total votes**; (1) the First Presidency, (2) the Quorum of the Twelve Apostles, and (3) the Quorum of the Seventies. If each of the previous branches of church government (equal in power to another, D&C 107) **unanimously approved** the revelation as being "of God," then the revelation was passed on to (4) church members for their vote. If a majority of the membership approved the revelation, it was then canonized as **a law** of the church and published in the Doctrine and Covenants [see chap. 4 & Abstract 50, 1894 Temple Lot Case].

Section 101 was not a revelation given Oliver, but a statement he penned. It was approved and **voted on by the whole church**. This statement was put into our canon of scripture to fight the perception that the Saints approved of secretly practicing polygamy (some were at the time, 1835). The Manifesto was also a "statement" put into the D&C to later stop the practice of polygamy among the Saints by church President Wilford Woodruff (1890). Pres. Joseph F. Smith produced a second Manifesto fourteen years later in 1904 (as many polygamous marriages were still being performed in the church). Both Manifestos were statements, **not revelations** from God (see chap. 6). Old Section

101 was originally called "**the Article on Marriage**" and was part of Joseph's early effort to fight polygamy in the early days of the church (1833). It had four primary parts, featuring God's *higher* law of marriage (see D&C 42:22-23). It remains with God's *higher* law of real love in the "law of consecration," both found in Section 42 of the D&C. The Preface of Section 42 refers to it as – "The Law." Note the content of its four verses:

1. The first verse addressed "civilized nations" having laws pertaining to **the marriage ceremony**, one solemnized in **a public meeting** (not a secretive, private act, which most polygamous marriages were).
2. It was to be celebrated with prayer and thanksgiving and be conducted by the Holy Spirit via a High Priest or Elder. The woman was to stand left of the man, both facing the one performing the marriage. They were directed to keep themselves "**wholly for each other**."
3. A church clerk was to **keep a record** of the marriage.
4. The fourth verse was the most revealing, stating, "…as this church of Christ has been **reproached** with **the crime of fornication**, and **polygamy**: we declare that we believe, that **one man should have one wife**; and *one woman*, but *one husband*, except in case of death, when either is at liberty to marry again."

Brigham Young saw to it that Section 101 was removed, when he put Section 132 into the D&C, both actions without any vote. When questioned about this unlawful action in The Temple Lot Case, later President Wilford Woodruff, a witness for the Utah church, stated, "I do not know why it was done. It was done by the authority of whoever presided over the Church, I suppose. Brigham Young was the President then." Lorenzo Snow, President of the Quorum of the Twelve testified in this trial, "the entire authority of the church rested upon the Twelve. Brigham Young [President of this quorum at the time of Joseph's martyrdom] was made President of the Church afterwards" [Abstract 323]. William Blair stated the LDS church had materially changed the functioning of the First Presidency by making it **subservient** to the Quorum of the Twelve Apostles [Abstract 111]. In D&C 107, the LORD laid out four equal quorums to govern the church. The Quorum of the Twelve was one of them, charged to be **traveling missionaries** *out in the mission field*, preaching Christ and His gospel, **not** administrators (see Assumption #2 chap. 6).

A Composite Re-Construction

Section 132 of the Doctrine and Covenants appears to be a composite re-construction, given us by two men; an unpublished collection of potential "revelations" given to Joseph Smith (mostly likely at different times), mixed with Brigham Young's "revelation" on polygamy and his additions decades later, all to support polygamy. Portions of it are consistent with God's word elsewhere (like verses 22-25), while other portions of it contradict other scripture. Young's additions are not doctrinal (addressed hereafter) and violate God's own law of two or more witnesses for all things (2 Cor. 13:1). In a scholarly language analysis of Section 132 presented hereafter, some of the wording of Section 132 reflects **two different voices**, including that of Brigham Young. His words reflect the state of his heart at that time. He wanted polygamy to be fully entrenched among the Saints. Joseph's potential portion of this "revelation" may have originated during his re-translation of the Bible between 1830 and 1834. Hyrum Smith apparently told, "the Nauvoo City Council that the 1843 revelation pertains to ancient polygamy, not to modern times" (Quinn, Mormorn Heirarchy, p. 645). We do not know today what this early reference revealed, but it surely was consistent with other scripture, or confusion would result.

Joseph knew the doctrine of the Book of Mormon did not support polygamy. Jacob 2 reveals that David and Solomon were **not** justified in *their* practice of polygamy (see Jacob 2:22-26), as Jacob's people were "**excusing** themselves" because of "the things that were written." This may be the primary reason we have these statements in the Book of Mormon – to help us discern the truth of this practice and *other things* among us today. If Joseph enquired of the LORD inappropriately about polygamy (desiring it – an idol in his heart), while re-translating portions of the Old Testament dealing with the additional wives of Abraham, David, Solomon, and others, the carnal desires of his heart could have led him into receiving a false revelation (from his own mind or from Satan or false spirits). God warned Joseph about carnal idols in his heart (D&C 3:4). It could have led to a desire that a revelation be received supporting or justifying it. He would then be asking "amiss" or not according to God's will. We know that Joseph, Oliver, and David Whitmer all experienced receiving a false revelation together in early Church history. This important experience teaches us that all mortals, including leaders, are susceptible to deception. As addressed later in this chapter (regarding the angel and the sword story), discernment of truth and darkness is a key tool we must all learn to exercise. Some believe that such a deception explains why Joseph's portion of the "revelation" was never published or brought before the Saints to be canonized. Others in the Brighamite camp suggest the Saints weren't ready for what they justify as being higher law.

As noted earlier, Nicholas of the early Christian Nicolaitans (Rev. 2:4-6; D&C 117:11) justified his practice of sexual sin by stating that he had received a "*revelation*" from God to support it. Later we will see that Brigham Young, Lorenzo Snow, and John Taylor (all polygamists) claimed that they too – like Nicholas - all received *revelations supporting polygamy* (see Jer. 23:16; Ezek. 13:2 & Lam. 2:14). I believe they were (false) revelations used to justify their sexual sin with religious rites. Practicing this abomination cut them off from heaven and pure sources of truth. God tells us that we are cut off from Him when there is (1) lust after another (D&C 42:22-23; 63:13-16), when there is (2) desire for power over others (D&C 121:34-35), and one (3) seeks money from people for spiritual things (Mosiah 18:24-26, see also p. 191). Both the Nicolaitans and the early Mormons caused "*reproach*" to come upon their version of the Christian church, but at different points in time. Satan provided *false revelations* to corrupt the things of God in New Testament times, *and* in early Church history. The LORD warned Joseph Smith and the Saints about following the dictates of ones "own will and carnal desires" in D&C 3 (1828), verses 1-9. This section references the loss of the 116 pages of the early Book of Mormon manuscript tied to Lehi. God said that Joseph, like all mortals, could fall:

> "And behold, how oft you have transgressed the commandments and the laws of God, and have gone on in the persuasions of men. For, behold, you should not have **feared man more than God**. Although men set at naught the counsels of God, and despise his words—Yet you should have been faithful; and he would have extended his arm and supported you against all the fiery darts of the adversary; and he would have been with you in every time of trouble. Behold, thou art Joseph, and thou wast chosen to do the work of the Lord, but because of transgression, if thou art not aware thou wilt fall."

This warning does not imply that Joseph had a false revelation on polygamy, but it is a remote possibility. Following the murder of the Smith brothers, Young modified whatever was given to Joseph Smith in his early "revelation" (in the 8 years between 1844 and the time the revelation was first published in the Deseret News in 1852). Young's vocabulary, writing style, and doctrinal focus, were all a part of his reconstructed portion of 132. This is clearly evident in the research of Master's candidate Enid DeBarthe, addressed hereafter.

A Fabricated Document

Section 132 stands alone as the only LDS scripture clearly rejecting the doctrine and gospel of Christ in other scripture, especially Jacob in the Book of Mormon! The following seven items refute the divinity of D&C 132.

1. *No Original Manuscript Exists for D&C 132* We have only a "copy" of the D&C 132 "revelation," and it was made by an avowed polygamist, Joseph Kingsbury. Corroborating testimony for the existence of an original is supplied only by other polygamists like William Clayton and Brigham Young. Various references to the original, if there was one, imply that it was much shorter in length than D&C 132.

2. *Young Claimed He Received 132, not Joseph* In a meeting with U.S. Vice Presidential candidate Shuyler Colfax (June 17, 1865; Ulysses S. Grant was the Presidential candidate), Young said **he received** the polygamy revelation, **not** Joseph Smith. In his private journal, Colfax recorded that Young brought up the subject of polygamy, stating, "the revelations of the Doctrine and Covenants **declared for monogamy**, but that polygamy was a later revelation *commanded* by God **to him** and a few others, and *permitted* and *advised* to the rest of the church" (Shuyler Colfax journal entry, quoted in The Western Galaxy, Vol. I, p. 247).

3. *Brigham Young Wrote Much of D&C 132* There is strong evidence suggesting Brigham Young authored much of Section 132, as his writing style is clearly evident in it (see below). Note especially the **threats against Emma Smith** in D&C 132 (v. 54). She is also referred to as a "handmaid" (or female servant) in this same verse. Young considered Emma an enemy. He trashed her in various public venues, including a very public general conference address, whereas God referred to Emma as "**my daughter**" (D&C 25:1).

4. *It Was Not Voted on to be Included into our Canon of Scripture* Young put Section 132 *into* our scripture in 1876 without a Church vote of priesthood quorums or Church members. In the same year he removed anti-polygamy Section 101, that was voted on by three priesthood quorums and the whole church. Leaders had previously put Section 101 into the D&C to counteract the rise of sexual sins into the church. It coincided with the influx of

Cochranite converts to Kirtland in the early 1830's. It and other new Sections necessitated that the "Article on Marriage" be placed in the new 1835 edition of the Doctrine and Covenants. It helped convince members and non-members that Mormons were Christian people and were not to engage in abominations like adultery and polygamy. Leaders in 1835 presented this new Section to a general assembly of the church on August 17 of that year. It was canonized as scripture and remained there for 41 years until 1876, when original Section 101 was taken out by Brigham Young. Verse 4 of it acknowledges that the church had been "reproached with the crime of fornication, and polygamy." We should remember that the word "reproach" was tied to the early Christians in the New Testament church who followed Nicholas and his *false revelation* into sinful sexual practices. He justified the sex using religious rites among his followers. Section 101 was a declaration of the doctrine held by the whole Church. It was not a revelation. It was written by Oliver Cowdery and approved in a vote by the church on August 17, 1835.

According to Apostle Orson Hyde, Joseph taught, "There is a way by which all revelations purporting to be from God through any man can be tested. Brother Joseph gave us the plan. Says he, 'When all the quorums are assembled and organized in order, let the revelation be presented to the quorums. If it pass[es] one let it go to another. And if it pass[es] that [one], to another, and so on until it has passed all the quorums. And if it pass[es] the whole without running against a snag, you may know it is of God...Brother Joseph said, 'Let no revelation go to the people until it has been tested here'" (Times and Seasons, vol. 5, no. 17, 15 Sept. 1844, pps. 649–50).

5. *There Are No Corroborating Witnesses for its False Doctrine* God gave us the law of witnesses to prove and support His doctrines, those which make up His gospel and church. It states that, "in the mouth of two or three witnesses shall every word be established" (2 Cor. 13:1). There are no other scriptural witnesses of Brigham Young's plural marriage doctrine in the Bible, Book of Mormon, or other scripture. D&C 132 stands alone as the sole foundation of it in current LDS theology. The foundational book of our faith (the Book of Mormon) condemns the practice of polygamy (see Jacob 2 & 3; Mos. 11:2), as does God's higher law as given us in D&C 42:22-23 and 49:16. God's word in scripture tells us that a house divided against itself cannot stand (Mat. 12:22-28).

Four False Doctrines There are at least four false doctrines taught in D&C 132 in connection with, (a) the promotion of polygamy as a new doctrine, one replacing God's law of monogamy in D&C 42:22-23; (b) Brigham's "new and everlasting covenant of [plural] marriage" (verses 6 & 19) which replaces God's "everlasting covenant" - which is the fullness of His gospel (endnote 31 & D&C 1:15, 22:1, 45:9, 49:9, 66:2, 76:101, 133:57). This "fullness" begins with the two baptisms and the gifting of the Holy Ghost (D&C 6:15; 33:11-15; 39:6); (c) D&C 132 promotes the new doctrine of "exaltation" in connection with polygamy. There is no second witness for this anywhere in scripture. The word "exaltation" can only be found in one other place in the D&C, for example, in connection with lifting up of Zion (see D&C 124:9), and it does not address entering the highest level of the celestial kingdom. Brigham Young made polygamy essential for his version of exaltation. And last (d) D&C 132 claims that only one man on earth at the time has *the sealing power* (v. 7), while the LORD stated that both Joseph and Hyrum Smith held this same power (D&C 124:124). Section 132 also suggests that the Holy Spirit of Promise (in connection with *the sealing power*) is dispensed by a man holding proper priesthood authority. This contradicts other scriptures that teach that the Holy Spirit of Promise is sent forth from the Father (D&C 76:53) to bind on earth and in heaven, that which men do symbolically on earth. Thus it only points to this greater spiritual power wielded by God (see chap. 7).

Other Errors D&C 132 has many errors in it revealing that it was constructed by a weak man with an agenda. Verse 3, for example addresses Isaac as being justified in his polygamy even though he was married to **one wife only**, Rebekah. In verse 3 we read, "for all those who have this [polygamous] law revealed unto them must obey the same." Those who don't are damned. There are plenty of those who did not abide this law, including Isaac, Joseph of Egypt, Joseph Smith Senior, and many others. Are they then "damned"?

Verses 34-35 address scripture inaccurately, saying, "God commanded Abraham, and Sarah gave Hagar to Abraham to wife." God did **not** command Sarah to take Hagar to wife. It was Sarah who wanted Abraham to take Hagar, and it was Abraham that followed her suggestion, by not trusting in LORD's miraculous power and His timing. Both were in error. There is *no record of Abraham praying about this decision*, or he being commanded by God to do so. Note also that Joseph Smith did not make any substantive changes regarding these verses in the inspired re-translation of this Genesis story.

Note also the confusing doctrine of verse 61 of D&C 132, that if a woman is "vowed to no other man, then is he justified" in taking her as another wife. Of Brigham's first three wives, two remained married to other men. Today the Church claims Joseph was sealed or married to other married women. Both men thus violated this law.

6. *Not Published in Joseph's Lifetime* Joseph Smith did not publish this material as canonized scripture in his lifetime. This would normally mean it was of questionable value. In April of 1844, two months prior to his murder, Hyrum

said that we must not accept *any doctrine that is contrary to scripture.* "If any man writes to you, or preaches to you, doctrines contrary to the Bible, the Book of Mormon, or the Book of Doctrine and Covenants, set him down as an *imposter*" (Times and Seasons, Vol. 5, p. 490). One of Sidney Rigdon's primary responsibilities as given to him by the LORD in Section 35:23 was to "call on the holy prophets [scripture] to *prove his* [Joseph's] *words, as they shall be given him.*" Sidney Rigdon fought "spiritual wifery" in Nauvoo and was excommunicated for it by Young.

In addition, God said that only Joseph could receive revelation **for the Church** as a whole (D&C 43:3-7). Apostle Brigham Young's revelation promoting polygamy was said to be given him during his English mission in 1839-40 (it s provided hereafter). Joseph was not murdered until four years later in 1844. God said, "But, behold, verily, verily, I say unto thee, **no one shall be appointed to receive commandments and revelations in this church excepting my servant Joseph Smith**, Jun., for he receiveth them even as Moses" (D&C 28:2; 43:3). Brigham did not reveal that he had a "revelation" on polygamy (in 1839-40) until **1874**, however. Once again, it provided "justification" for him.

7. *James Whitehead Testimony in the Temple Lot Case* James Whitehead took over many of William Clayton's duties at the beginning of 1843, after Clayton was accused of using church funds inappropriately in buying and selling church properties. Clayton remained in Joseph's service, looking after church real estate, according to the testimony of James Whitehead in the Temple Lot Case of 1893-94. Whitehead's testimony reveals that "the [132] revelation" shown to Whitehead in the spring of 1848 by Bishop Newell K. Whitney at Winter Quarters - purporting to be Joseph's Smith revelation on polygamy today, was in reality "a revelation" or Joseph's "thoughts" (written down by another) on "the doctrine of sealing." It had nothing to do with polygamy, according to Whitehead. He stated:

"I saw what they claimed was it, or what purported to be it, published in the Book of Doctrine and Covenants [D&C 132], by Brigham Young in Salt Lake [1876]. But the one published in the Book of Doctrine and Covenants by the Utah Church was not the one that Bishop Whitney showed me at Winter Quarters. It was not the same at all. It was entirely changed. It was so changed that it sanctioned polygamy, and that change was made by the Brighamites. For there was no such thing in it when I read it . . . it sanctions and imposes polygamy on the church, but there was no such thing in the revelation that Whitney showed me...It did not have the same language at all. I knew, that, when I read it I considered that they had got that revelation from Bishop Whitney, and had changed it and added to it, it had nothing to do with polygamy when I read it at Winter Quarters. . ." Whitehead also addressed the much shorter length of the "sealing" revelation he was shown by Whitney in 1848, "The document was about as much as would fill both sides of a sheet of foolscap, about three sides of a sheet of paper like that." Section 132 of the D&C today is long at 3,522 words (8 or more typed pages).

In addressing his knowledge of Joseph's marriage to Emma, Whitehead stated, "When I lived at Nauvoo, I resided, maybe, three hundred yards from where Joseph Smith's house was, I saw him there frequently, perhaps not every day, but almost every day, that he was in Nauvoo. I was there in his office, as his private secretary, at the time he was killed. I was in his office on that day, and was keeping the books at that time. **Joseph Smith had one wife** and her name was Emma; I do not know any other woman who claimed to be the wife of the prophet, there at Nauvoo, nor at any other place . . . There was never any woman who came to me, or Joseph Smith in my presence, during the time of my employment as his private secretary, for money, claiming that she was the wife of Joseph Smith, except his wife Emma. There was no entry of that kind ever made on the books [that he kept], of money paid by me or by him to any woman claiming to be his wife, except Emma (James Whitehead testimony, Temple Lot Case, pps. 474-77).

DeBarthe's Important Language Analysis

Though the document we call D&C 132 has some truths in it, perhaps provided by the Prophet Joseph Smith, it also has many additions, most likely from Brigham Young, as the later portions of D&C 132 use language, phraseology, and words that are inconsistent with Joseph Smith, words and intent that are clearly those of Brigham Young.

Enid S. DeBarthe carefully scrutinized Section 132 in her Master's Thesis completed at Northern Illinois University in 1969. It is very revealing. DeBarthe's research concentrated on specific word usage, like "anointed," "espouse," "exaltation," "eternal lives," "damned," and "destroy" in Section 132, versus curious absence of more common words in scripture like "repent." They are the added words of Brigham Young, not Joseph Smith or the LORD. The rare word "exaltation," for example, was associated with polygamy by Young. Under his leadership, polygamy became a requirement for what he called "exaltation," or to be part of the Celestial Kingdom of God. This doctrine is embraced by many Fundamentalist Mormons today. Young stated:

"Now **if any of you will deny the plurality of wives**, and continue to do so, I promise that **you will be damned**" (Journal of Discourses, vol. 3, p. 266). He added, "The only men who become Gods, even the Sons of

God, are those who enter into polygamy" (Journal of Discourses, vol. 11, p. 269).

DeBarthe also addressed other unique phrases found in Section 132, like, "must," "stay herself," or "accounted unto him for righteousness," phrases that are believed to have originated in Brigham Young. She also studied sentence structure characteristics, including nouns, verbs, dependent clauses, etc. DeBarthe also researched how the language of Section 132 made use of prepositional phrases, "neologisms, pleonasms, and tautologies." She examined total words per sentence and finally style, particularly the writing style of Joseph Smith versus that of Brigham Young.

The result is very telling. Barthe's research clearly points to Section 132 being consistent with the unique language of Brigham Young, via a comparison of his writings and that of others, especially the Prophet Joseph Smith (including revelations given to Joseph). She reveals that Joseph's writing style was and is "affirming," calling men "to repentance and inviting them to seek righteousness and truth." Young, on the other hand, has a style involving force, insistence, and coercion, and that laws must be obeyed (this is consistent with his use of former Danites as enforcers in Nauvoo and Salt Lake City, men like Hosea Stout and hitman Bill Hickman, and the coercive techniques used by his "deacons" upon suspected "dissenters," including intimidation by "the whitling and whistling brigade," and "anointings" using human excrement from "aunt peggy's privy closet"). Young made extensive use of "*idoms*," "*redundancies*," and "*valedictory*" phrases that clearly brand the concepts of Section 132 to him. Some would call it "*strongman*" tactics. Young's language reflects his own strong, coercive will, not that of God or Joseph.

In addition to contradictory doctrine, Section 132 also features threats of destruction against Emma (vs. 54, 63-65), threats that she must conform to the practice. These are inconsistent with God's love and His desire that we have agency or choice. God invites. Satan uses fear and force. The threats are consistent with one as "Mahan," a "master of the great secret," a "mastermind destroyer." Young hated Emma and spoke evil of her in his various remarks. This led to years of animosity among many of the Saints towards this noble woman.[3] In his October 1866 General Conference address, Young offered up a rebuke of the widow Emma and a lie, stating that she attempted to murder Joseph, and that he (Joseph) said she was "the most wicked woman on this earth." Young castigated the *harmless widow* of the Prophet Joseph Smith, stating:

> "To my certain knowledge, Emma Smith is one of **the damnedest liars** I know of on this earth; yet there is no good thing I would refuse to do for her, if she would only be a righteous woman; but she will continue in her **wickedness**. Not six months before the death of Joseph, he called his wife Emma into a **secret** council, and there there he told her the truth, and called upon her to deny it if she could. He told her that the judgments of God would come upon her forthwith if she did not **repent**. He told her of the time she undertook to **poison** him, and he told her that she was **a child of hell**, and literally **the most wicked woman** on this earth, that there was **not one more wicked than she**" (6-8 Oct., 1866, 36th Semi-Annual Conference, Bowery, G. S. L. City. [Deseret News Weekly 15:364, 10/10/66, p 4-5 and 15:372, 10/17/66, p 4-5; MS 28:764, 774).

The murdered Prophet Joseph was not present to refute Section 132 - or any other modifications that have now become part of our history. Though the early portions of D&C 132 have ties to some scripture, the later portions of Section 132 are often dark and confusing. Some verses clearly go against other scripture, especially the founding document of our faith – the Book of Mormon - and the words of the LORD and Jacob there. This sets up confusion. Section 132 provides a reason for splinter groups "to do their own thing." As noted earlier, Section 132 begins with a false question in verse 1, which contradicts what the LORD had already revealed in the Book of Mormon. It states:

> "Verily, thus saith the LORD unto you my servant Joseph, that inasmuch as you have inquired of my hand to know and understand wherein I, the LORD, **justified** my servants Abraham, Isaac, and Jacob, as also Moses, David and Solomon, my servants, as touching the principle and doctrine of their having many wives and concubines" (D&C 132:1).

The LORD already revealed that David and Solomon were **not justified** in their polygamy in Jacob 2:22-26. He said Jacob's people were "**excusing themselves**" because of "the things that were written." Brigham's verse 1 question in D&C 132 is a *blatant rejection* of God's teachings in the Book of Mormon. Young was excusing himself and others in the Twelve who were secretly practicing "spiritual wifery," beginning in 1841. God does not contradict Himself. He said, "And if a house be divided against itself, that house cannot stand" (Mark 3:25). Note also Jacob 1:15.

"And now it came to pass that the people of Nephi, under the reign of the second king, began to grow hard in their hearts, and **indulge** themselves somewhat in wicked practices, such as like unto David of old desiring many wives and concubines, and also Solomon, his son" (Jacob 1:15).

"And now I make an end of speaking unto you concerning this pride. And were it not that I must speak unto you concerning a **grosser crime**, my heart would rejoice exceedingly because of you. But the word of God burdens me because of your **grosser crimes**. For behold, thus saith the LORD: This people begin to wax in **iniquity**; they understand not the scriptures, for they **seek to excuse themselves** in committing **whoredoms**, *because of the things things which were written concerning David, and Solomon his son.* Behold, David and Solomon truly had many wives and concubines, which thing was **abominable** before me, saith the LORD. Wherefore, thus saith the LORD, I have led this people forth out of the land of Jerusalem, by the power of mine arm, that I might raise up unto me a *righteous branch* from the fruit of the loins of Joseph. Wherefore, I the LORD God will **not suffer** that this people shall do like unto them of old" (Jacob 2:22-26).

Section 132 was Removed from the D&C for a Time

In 1930, James E. Talmage, a senior member of the Twelve at the time, authored a book for the church entitled, "Latter-day Revelation." It contained, "Sections and parts of Sections from the Doctrine and Covenants, the sections comprising scriptures of *general* enduring value…" According to Talmage, its purpose was, "to make the strictly doctrinal parts of the Doctrine and Covenants of easy access and reduce its bulk." Portions of many D&C Sections were removed, those tied to individuals at various times without ties to doctrine. Its introduction read, "This little book contains . . . selections comprising Scriptures of general and enduring value, given as the Word of the LORD through the First Elder and Prophet in the present dispensation . . ." The most noteworthy of these non-doctrinal omissions, was all of **Section 132** and 136, both believed to originate in Brigham Young. Those remaining, at least in part, include, Sections 1, 2, 4, 7, 13, 18, 19, 20, 22, 27, 29, 38, 42, 43, 45, 46, 50, 56, 58, 59, 63, 64, 65, 68, 76, 84, 87, 88, 89, 93, 98, 101, 107, 110, 119, 121, 124, 130, 131, 133 and 134. Fundamentalist Mormons were outraged with the removal of **132** at this time, "accusing the [LDS] church of changing the scriptures" (at least the one they used to *justify* their polygamy). Pres. Grant (an early polygamist) then ordered the work immediately "withdrawn" from sale and the remaining copies "shredded to avoid further conflict with the fundamentalists." (see Newell G. Bringhurst, "Section 132: Contents and Legacy" in The Persistence of Polygamy, John Whitmer Books, 2010, pps. 83-84).

Brigham Young went to great lengths to "**justify**" the practice of polygamy (see verses 1 & 59-60). Section 132 is just one of many efforts by Young to do so. The official LDS church narrative today is that Section 132 was a revelation given to Joseph Smith on July 12, 1843. Young's own statements refute this. In 1874, for example, he stated that he had a pro-polygamy vision or revelation while on his mission to England, and that Joseph had said nothing to him about the practice prior to this point in time. This was in 1839-41 (see p. 48, #2B). Other than this statement, there are no other details on Young's revelation available. His own statements reveal that his revelation **preceded** the supposed one he said Joseph Smith was given, and by three to four years. Emma Smith consistently refuted the stories of Young and Richards surrounding D&C 132. She had nothing to hide and knew Joseph better than any man on the earth. Note also that **God said only Joseph was to receive revelation for the Church** (D&C 28:2).

Five Additional False Justifications for Polygamy

1. Patriarchal Order - *A Higher Law* Some believe early polygamy in the LDS Church was part of a secret "higher order" of priesthood among the Apostles first, and then later lay members in Utah. This goes hand in hand with pride and special excuses or justification. Titles tied to those possessing "the secret priesthood" include those in "the holy order," "the Quorum of the Anointed," and those part of "the ancient order of things." They originally taught that Joseph Smith was part of this ancient order, as practiced by the Old Testament Patriarchs. Later on they justified departing from Joseph's teachings, as lies were introduced saying that he was a fallen prophet. Pride placed them in higher standing, as select chosen ones that were privileged to live a higher way.

In addition, many polygamists claim that early church leaders were restoring the ancient ways of the Biblical patriarchs, and that this included polygamy. They say it was part of "the restoration of all things." What they do not mention is that Brigham Young, Heber C. Kimball, and Parley P. Pratt also practiced *polyandry.* Where is there evidence of this perversion in the Bible among the ancient patriarchs? Was it to be restored too?

2. Justifications, Exceptions, Excuses & Contradictions Many justify breaking a commandment, like God's law to have one wife only (see 2 Ne. 28:8-9), using the example that God killed many in the Bible, but He commanded us to not kill. It is a favorite reason why atheists do not believe in God. Nephi's killing of Laban in the Book of Mormon is often cited by pro-polygamists as a good example of why the Saints can be monogamists most of the time, while polygamists in other special circumstances (because of a **higher law** or **special circumstance**). It is a "justification" or "escape clause" to do more important, "higher" things. Justification for lies and deception were used to cover the practice of "higher things" (polygamy) at Nauvoo. Later in Utah this became an institutional practice to hide polygamy from the Federal Government. Thirteen different deceptive "code words" were used to hide polygamy. An article detailing these code words was published in an 1886 issue of the Deseret News (see p. 191).

Pride leads many to believe their actions are an exception to God's law. Pro-polygamists, citing Nephi's experience with Laban, say God is the great law-giver, and that He can change the rules anytime He wants. If, in His wisdom, a previous law needs to be broken in order to fulfill a "higher law," then He can authorize it for the greater good. This is exactly what the polygamists did later on at Nauvoo.

Two Supportive Publications on Polygamy Besides citing their "secret" or "greater priesthood" (the Patriarchal priesthood of the ancient Patriarchs in the Old Testament), two publications were used in early church history to **justify** taking as many wives as one wanted; (1) The first was entitled *The Peacemaker*, printed on the press of the *Times and Seasons* in Nauvoo in 1842, without Joseph Smith's knowledge or permission. His name was also printed on its front cover; (2) The second was printed by a British Latter-day Saint and sold in the Millennial Star office of the church in Liverpool England in 1843. It was entitiled *The Testament of the Twelve Patriarchs, the Sons of Jacob.* Both publications are addressed in chapter 5.

3. A Test Some claim that polygamy was used by the LORD as a test for Joseph Smith and others, as Joseph taught against the practice, just as Abraham abhorred and spoke out against human sacrifice, having nearly experienced sacrifice himself at the hands of his father and others. A test of worthiness requiring Joseph to break one of God's commandments can be confusing (see endnote 30). Following God's direction is a must, however.

4. Create Spirit Bodies Another *justification* for polygamy attributed to Brigham Young is his claim that additional wives for the Father are needed to create many *spirit bodies* that are later tabernacled on the earth into mortal bodies. In the King Follett Discourse Joseph Smith refuted this, teaching that intelligence or Spirit is self-existant and co-equal with God. They are not created by God, but have co-existed **with** Him since the very beginning (Abr. 3:18). Certain of the intelligences were drawn to God and His companion and their great love. They chose to participate in God's great plan of happiness (progression), becoming His sons and daughters *through their* **choices** (not a creation act). Multiple wives for Father is not necessary for the Spirits or Intelligences to *gather* to them. A plan and choice is. Choosing to be part of Father's great plan of happiness is comparable to how we become the sons and daughter of the LORD Jesus here, by **choosing** to repent and accept His atonement on our behalf (Mosiah 5). Joseph said, "God Himself found Himself in the midst of spirits and glory. Because He was greater He saw proper to institute laws whereby the rest, who were less in intelligence, could have a privilege to **advance** like Himself. So He took in hand to save the world of Spirits" (the King Follett Discourse). He added, "The Father *called* all spirits before him at the creation of man, and **organized** them" (Ehat and Cook, *Words of Joseph Smith,* p. 9, Aug. 1839). "At the first organization in heaven we were all present and saw the Savior chosen and appointed, and the plan of salvation made and we sanctioned it" (*Words of Joseph Smith*, p. 60, Jan. 1841). "The spirits of men are eternal . . . They are organized according to that Priesthood which is everlasting" (HC 4:575, April 1842). "He who rules in the heavens when he has a certain work to do calls the Spirits before him to organize them" (*Words of Joseph Smith*, May 1843). "**Giving it** [the intelligence] **a tabernacle was to arm it against the power of Darkness**" (Words of Joseph Smith, p 62).

5. Subtle Polygamy Scriptures It is clear throughout this chapter that God prefers one wife for one man in most all marriages. There may be rare situations where God allows for more. The stories of Abraham, Jacob, and David before he got carried away, may be examples. So too Isaiah 4:1 and two other scriptures; 2 Sam. 12:1-18, and Moses 8:12 and 27. In the 2 Samuel story, David is chastised for taking Uriah's wife. He is told by God through the Prophet Nathan, "I gave your master's house to you, and your master's wives into your arms." David then took more, *multiplying wives* to himself, including Uriah's wife.

Some say Moses 8:12 may imply a different mother or wife for Shem than for other sons of Noah in verse 12. It reads, "he [Noah] begat Shem of her who was the mother of Japheth." The danger of these possible exceptions is that men like Brigham Young find *justification* in them, even though they do not follow the pattern in scripture, where God's will must be sought in addition to the welfare of others in real love.

The Pro-Polygamy "Revelations"

There are five total *so-called* "**revelations**" used to support polygamy in the LDS church. They are addressed hereafter. What unites all of them is that they are put forth by *pro-polygamists*, and each of them coming forth *years* **after** Joseph's murder. Joseph was thus unable to defend himself or fight against these claims. Besides being *non-contemporary* sources, they are also *non-credible* sources, especially because their content goes against God's word *and* patterns in scripture!

1. 1852 – *Joseph's Supposed Pro-Polygamy Revelation* As addressed earlier, it was in 1852 that Brigham Young announced that Joseph Smith had a pro-polygamy "revelation" on July 12th of **1843**. This so-called "revelation" was printed by Young in the Deseret News that same year. His statements reflect a changing narrative over time.

2. 1874 - *Young Makes Three Announcements to the Saints* Young "let the cat out of the bag" to the Utah Saints (to use his own words) with three polygamy related announcements in 1874.

A. Young never did announce to the Saints what he privately told U.S. Vice Presidential candidate Shuyler Colfax in **1865**, that D&C 132 was a revelation to Him, **not** to Joseph Smith!

B. Instead, he originally claimed that he had a pro-polygamy revelation while on his **1839-41** English mission. No specific date is tied to it, and the actual words of the "revelation" have never been published. Young stated, "While we [Brigham & ten of the Twelve Apostles] were in England, (in 1839 and 40) I think, the LORD manifested to me by vision and his Spirit, things [concerning "spiritual wifery'] that I did not then understand. I never opened my mouth to any one concerning them, until I returned to Nauvoo; **Joseph had never mentioned this; there had never been a thought of it in the Church that I ever knew anything about at that time**, but I had this for myself, and I kept it to myself. And when I returned home, and Joseph revealed those things to me [a lie] then I understood the reflections that were upon my mind while in England. But this (communication with Joseph on the subject) was not until after I had told him what I understood— this was in 1841" (Brigham Young, Deseret News, July 1, **1874**).

C. He added that many of the Twelve were practicing polygamy secretly at Nauvoo in the early **1840s**. Today the church confirms that there were secret ("confidential") "plural marriages" going on in Nauvoo in the early **1840's**.

D. He also suggested a new earlier date for Joseph Smith's pro-polygamy "revelation," stating that it was in the early **1830's**, not the July 12, **1843** date he originally gave in his **1852** Deseret News announcement. Young also claimed that the prior 1843 date was the year William Clayton "**recorded**" the revelation.

Some suggest Young changed the narrative to protect Heber C. Kimball, his friend and counselor in the First Presidency. Information was apparently coming forth about the Apostles practicing polygamy earlier than **1843**, including news that Heber's second wife (his first polygamous wife) was brought back from England by him following his mission in 1841 (Kimball had a wife in Nauvoo). The earlier date for Joseph's "revelation" provided **justification** for the Apostles polygamy prior to 1843 (and Joseph's revelation) and Heber's new additional English wife (she was pregnant by him when arriving in Nauvoo).

3. 1886 - *John Taylor's Pro-Polygamy Revelation* In 1887 the son of Pres. John Taylor discovered a document in his father's personal papers (after his death) that some believe is an **1886** pro-polygamy Taylor "revelation." Though later repudiated by the LDS church, Mormon fundamentalists (polygamists) have used Pres. Taylor's private "revelation" to **justify** their pro-polygamy beliefs. This is partly because it is consistent with Young's modification of "the New and Everlasting Covenant," where he made it a covenant tied to plural marriage, replacing what God taught in scripture, that it is "the fullness of the gospel" of Christ (see endnote 31 and D&C 6:15; 22:1; 33:11-15; 39:6; 66:2 & chapter 6). Taylor's purported "revelation" was given him in 1886, while Taylor was church President. The document was never publically revealed during his life. Its language is similar to that of D&C 132. The works of Abraham are those tied to "**righteousness**," not polygamy. The document reads, "My son John, you have asked me concerning **the New and Everlasting Covenant** how far it is binding upon my people. Thus saith the Lord: All commandments that I give must be obeyed by those calling themselves by my name unless they are revoked by me or by my authority, and how can I revoke an **everlasting covenant**, for I the Lord am everlasting and my **everlasting covenants** cannot be abrogated nor done away with, but they stand forever. Have I not given my word in great plainness on this subject? Yet have not great numbers of my people been negligent in the observance of my law and the keeping of my commandments, and yet have I borne with them these many years; and this because of their weakness—because of the perilous times, and furthermore, it is more pleasing to me that men should use their free agency in regard to these matters. Nevertheless, I the Lord do not change and my word and my covenants and my law do not, and as I have heretofore said by my servant Joseph: All those who would enter into my glory must and shall obey my law. And have I not commanded men that if they were Abraham's seed and would enter into my glory, they must do the works of

Abraham. I have not revoked this law, nor will I, for it is everlasting, and those who will enter into my glory must obey the conditions thereof; even so, Amen" (Sept. 27, 1886).

4. 1887 / *The Angel with the Sword Story* In May of 1887, four decades after Joseph's murder, pro-polygamists came forward with *false* claims that the Prophet Joseph said an angel came to him three times, **commanding** him to take additional wives. This story was part of sixteen pages of affidavits and testimonies published by the church (43 years after Joseph's murder) – that have now become Joseph Smith's *false* history. Some of the affidavits promote the *false* belief that polygamy was introduced into the church by the angel's three visits to Joseph in the early 1830s (much like how the Book of Mormon came to be). This *false* story claims that Joseph refused to obey the angel until the LORD sent him with a sword, threatening to "**destroy**" Joseph if he did not take additional wives.

The assertion that the LORD sent an angel to **force** Joseph to obey His pro-polygamy message, directly opposes God's higher way of *invitation*, *persuasion*, and *choice*, in connection with **love** (see D&C 121:37). It is Satan and his servants that use **fear**, **force**, and **coercion**. This story is more typical of Brigham Young. It also opposes Joseph's own constant, public fight against polygamy. On the one hand we have Joseph's *first-hand, contemporary published* testimonies, given *while he was yet alive*, all of them revealing that he was clearly against the practice. Opposing them we have **the four decades old** 1887 affidavits and other doctored accounts put forth later by LDS Church leaders, all produced by *pro-polygamists* decades **after** Joseph's murder. He could no longer defend himself. The angel story doesn't align with God's pattern of **choice**. In addition, Joseph never spoke of this angel and sword story! It is another lie manufactured with his name tied to it, all to **justify** the whoredom of polygamy.

According to apostle Lorenzo Snow's *false* affidavit, Joseph Said, "unless he [Joseph] moved forward and established plural marriage, his Priesthood would be taken from him and he should be destroyed!" Lorenzo's sister Eiza R. Snow said, "This testimony he not only bore to my brother, but also to *others*—a testimony that cannot be gainsayed" (Lorenzo Snow statement to Eliza, see Biography and Family Record of Lorenzo Snow [1884], pps. 69–70). Lorenzo Snow's affidavit was produced in **1887**, forty-three years after Joseph Smith's murder (so too the affidavits of Joseph Bates Noble *and* Benjamin F. Johnson). As we will see in ensuing chapters, the 1880's were a critical time for propping up polygamy. The Federal Government was threatening to remove polygamy from the Saints at that time. Young and other leaders needed to prove that **polygamy was an <u>original tenet</u> of the faith founded by the Prophet Joseph**, so that they could convince the Federal authorities that the Saints had a right to practice polygamy as part of religious freedom. Numerous false affidavits were manufactured for this purpose between 1870 and 1890, especially in the 1880's. President Woodruff later issued the Manifesto (1890).

Mary Elizabeth Lightner also put forth the false "Angel with the Sword" story. She said Brigham Young sealed her to Joseph in February of 1842 (she was married at the time). This is over a year **before** Brigham said Joseph had his revelation on polyygamy (July 12, 1843). This false revelation says there is "never but one man on the earth" who has the sealing power on earth (v. 7). According to his scenario, Brigham was conveniently given this power before God gave the revelation to Joseph. This is one of many "holes" found in the desperate stories put forth in the numerous false affidavits of the 1880's, all to prove polygamy was an original "tenet" of the faith (chapters 2 & 4).

5. 1899 / *Lorenzo Snow's Pro-Polygamy Revelation* Like Brigham, Lorenzo Snow claimed or implied that he too had a pro-polygamy "revelation" while serving as a missionary in England (though later in the mid-1840's). "There is no man that lives that had a more perfect knowledge of the principle of plural marriage, its holiness and divinity, than what I had. It was **revealed** to me before the Prophet Joseph Smith **explained** it to me. I had been on a mission to England between two and three years, and before I left England I was perfectly *satisfied* in regard to something connected with plural marriage" (Lorenzo Snow, Deseret Semi-Weekly News, June 6, 1899). Like Young, Snow never provided the specific words or the date of his "revelation." Neither men were church Presidents at the time of their "revelation." Both men made their "revelation" announcements decades after Joseph was murdered. These men were in England, living away from both Joseph and their wives. When an individual holds an idol in their heart (like polygamy), they can receive false spirits in false revelation. Paul said, "…because they received not the love of the **truth**, that they might be saved. And for this cause God shall send them **strong delusion**, that they should believe a lie: That they all might be damned who believed not the truth, but had pleasure in *unrighteousness*" (2 Thess. 2:10-12). Young, Taylor, and Snow received "**strong delusion**" (2 Thess. 2:10-12) because of their support for polygamy – **an idol in their hearts**. It led them to lead the Saints into "damnable heresies" (see 2 Peter 2:1). All three men were Masons and part of the secret chamber at Nauvoo (chap. 3). All three became Presidents of the church and were polygamists. Young had 55 wives, Taylor had 16, and Snow 9.

Joseph's Printed Warnings about *False* Revelations & Spirits

The Prophet Joseph warned the Saints repeatedly about *false revelations* that contradict existing *true revelations* and *scripture.* False spirits mix truth with lies *and* flattery, making us feel good, supporting our pride. As an early editor of the Times and Seasons, Joseph published an article entitled, "Try the Spirits." In it he warned the Saints against *mistaking false angels of Satan for true angels* from God. He feared that the Saints were being *deceived* into believing false revelations through them, as he, too had been deceived on occasion. Joseph's article on "Try the Spirits" was so important that it filled over five and one-half pages of this issue of the Times and Seasons (see also D&C 129). According to Joseph, should any statement delivered by an angel **contradict a former true revelation from God**, that message is from a false spirit or from Satan. God's house is a house of order, not confusion. Joseph wrote, "There have also been ministering angels in the church which were of satan appearing as an angel of light:— A sister in the State of New York had a vision who said it was told her that if she would go to a certain place in the woods an angel would appear to her - she went at the appointed time and saw a glorious personage descending arrayed in white . . . Many true things were spoken by this personage and many things that were false.—How it may be asked was this known to be a bad angel?...by his **contradicting a former revelation** (*Times & Seasons* 3 [Apr. 1, 1842], p. 747).

Paul and Peter both warned us of false teachings and false spirits. Truth is **consistent with scripture** already given (D&C 132 is not). Paul said, "But though we, or an angel from heaven, preach **any other gospel** unto you than that which we have preached unto you, let him be accursed" (Gal. 1:8–9). He added, "But there were false prophets also among the people, even as there shall be false teachers among you, who privily shall bring in **damnable heresies**, even denying the Lord that bought them…Having eyes full of **adultery**, and that cannot cease from sin; beguiling unstable souls: an heart they have exercised with covetous practices; cursed children; Which have forsaken the right way, and are gone astray, following *the way of Balaam*…who loved the wages of unrighteousness" (2 Peter 2:2, 14-15).

"The way of Balaam" or "*Balaam's error*" in other scriptures is associated with **false revelation** tied to sexual sin, as with the Nicolaitans. Brigham took his modified *spiritual wives* doctrine in D&C 132 and made it part of the "new and everlasting covenant" of plural marriage, one that now takes precedence over God's "everlasting covenant" as found in the Book of Mormon, the Bible, and the Doctrine and Covenants (see D&C 6:15; 22:16; 33:11-15, 39:6; 66:2). The real "everlasting covenant" has nothing to do with polygamy, but everything to do with Salvation in Christ by following God's **will** and wisdom (see JST Gen. 9:21; Mosiah 5:5, 8, 18:10; 2 Ne. 32:3, 6; D&C 22 & 84:35-48). This "fullness" is rejected in Brigham's "new order of things" (see D&C 132, verses 4, 6, 19, 26, 27, 41 & 42). It is one reason we are under condemnation for rejecting, "the new covenant, even [that "fullness of the gospel of Christ" found in] the Book of Mormon" (D&C 84:55 & 57). Joseph said we cannot be saved in ignorance (D&C 131:6).

The false affidavits tied to "the angel and sword" story are in direct conflict with Joseph's warning concerning discernment of spirits. *Nothing published during Joseph's lifetime supports this lie.* It should be noted that Lorenzo Snow's family was related to the Youngs, the Nobles, and the Beamans by way of polygamy! Lorenzo's sister, Eliza R. Snow, became one of Brigham Young's plural wives later on. Young also married Louisa Beaman (Joseph Bates Noble's sister-in-law). Lorenzo's brother, Erastus Snow, was married to Artemesia Beaman, who was Louisa Seaman's sister. Joseph Bates Noble married Mary Adeline Beaman, who was also a sister to Louisa and Artemesia (see Boyack, A Nobleman in Israel, 21). All were deeply involved in polygamy. The angel story justified all of their polygamy. "**Justify**" is the word Brigham inserted into the very first verse of D&C 132, along with verses 59 and 60. The LORD said David and Solomon were **not** justified in their multiple wives. They sought "**to excuse themselves** in committing whoredoms." God said this practice was "**abominable** before me" (Jacob 2:23-24).

Note the justification used by the LDS Church today on one official website, claiming it was "*divine instruction*" given Joseph. "In 1831, Church founder Joseph Smith made a *prayerful inquiry* about the ancient Old Testament practice of plural marriage. This resulted in the *divine instruction* to reinstitute the practice as a religious principle" (https://www.mormonnewsroom.org/topic/polygamy). Both statements are a **lie**. There is **no** statement by Joseph anywhere that he approached the LORD in prayer on the subject of plural marriage! He fought against it.

The LORD listed "**lies**" and "**deception**" first and second in five scriptures tied to **the sins of our day**; (1) 3 Nephi 16:10, (2) 3 Nephi 21:19, (3) 3 Nephi 30:2, (4) Book of Commandments 4:5-6, and D&C 123:12-13 (see also D&C 45:57). Joseph's name was used to "get gain" (1 Ne. 22:23), including the honors of men, power, money, and sex.

Chapter Two

Historical Truth

The Origin of Polygamy

Throughout scripture there is opposition in all things, with good pitted against evil. An angel told Nephi that there are save **two churches only**; the church of the lamb of God, with few in it, and the all inclusive church of the devil (1 Ne. 14:10). It is full of people kept in darkness, ignorance, and sin. Many of them are deceived into thinking "all is well," and that they are saved when they are not. Moses instructed his people about the opposition that exists in all things. In scripture it is called "the doctrine of the two ways." Moses told Joshua that as soon as he and the Israelites crossed over the Jordan River into the Promised Land, that he was to place all the tribes of Israel on two opposing mountains in what is now the area of Shechem, in northern Israel. Moses instructed Joshua to place six tribes on Mt. Ebal to the east, and the other six tribes on the opposing mountain, Mt. Gerizim to the west (Deut. 27). Joshua was then to recite **the law** God had given Moses and all Israel to all the people - as he stood in the valley in between the two mountains. From this point on, the law was to be read again to them every 7th Sabbatical Year. The six tribes on Ebal, the higher mountain in the east, recited all the **cursings** that would come upon them if the people turned away from God. The six tribes on Mt. Gerizim to the west, recited all the **blessings** they would enjoy if they remained true to the living God (Deut. 28).

The choices of Israel then, and ours today, lead to either blessing or cursing, life or death (see Deut. 30:19). Making good choices requires good information - **the truth**. Satan always tries to dilute it, pollute it, or take it away. As soon as God provided light in the early Restoration efforts of the Prophet Joseph, Satan immediately came to *take it away* (D&C 93:39). It is a primary message in this book. **Polygamy** was an important tool Satan used to pollute the early church and its real history. This chapter begins the process of explaining how. It is divided into four parts. *Part I* takes us back to Lamech, the first polygamist in scripture and his secret combination with Satan. The evil one used a secret combination to corrupt the people of God, doing so then and throughout human history. Murder, polygamy, and homosexuality were part of it. *Part II* addresses how early church history was changed by those who were practicing polygamy secretly at Nauvoo. The changes were put in place to point us falsely to Joseph Smith as the origin of the practice. His name provided **justification** for it. *Part III* presents evidence that Joseph Smith was a monogamist instead. *Part IV* features his words and those of other Smith family members, showing how they consistently fought polygamy. *Part V* examines how Satan used spiritual wifery with things like Freemasonry to pollute early Mormonism in the first part of the 19th century. This discussion serves as a bridge into the rising up of the secret chamber at Nauvoo, addressed by the LORD in D&C 38 in the following chapter.

Part I: The Origin of Polygamy

The first record of polygamy we have is given us by the Prophet Joseph Smith in his inspired re-translation of the Bible, and specifically Genesis. Most refer to it as the JST. Joseph began re-translating the Bible six months after he completed the Book of Mormon in 1830. The Book of Moses resulted from this important work. It provides much of the early content of the temple endowment. In Moses chapter 5 we are given the first record of **polygamy** in verse 44, where Lamech, the seventh generation son from Adam took two wives, Adah and Zillah. Like Cain, Lamech is an evil man. He too made a **covenant with Satan** and then **murdered** two men, one of them was his great grandfather Irad. Unlike Cain who murdered for the sake of "**gain**," Lamech's second murder was because of the **blood-oath** he made with Satan. Like Cain, Lamech was part of a **secret combination** too. The **secret blood-oaths** with Satan and with others in the **secret combinations** are used for **secrecy** and to cover serious **sin**.

> "And Lamech took unto himself **two wives**; the name of one being Adah, and the name of the other, Zillah . . . For Lamech having entered into **a covenant with Satan**, *after the manner of Cain*, wherein he became **Master Mahan, master of that great secret** *which was administered unto Cain by Satan*; and *Irad*, the son of Enoch, having known their **secret**, began to reveal it unto the sons of Adam. Wherefore Lamech, being angry, *slew him*, **not** like unto Cain, his brother Abel, for the sake of **getting gain**, but he slew him for **the oath's sake**. For, from the days of Cain, there was a **secret combination**, and their works were in the **dark**, and they **knew** *every man his brother*" (Moses 5:44, 49-51).

These and other verses of Moses 5 are packed with important insights. There is **darkness**, **secrecy**, **a blood-oath**, **polygamy**, **murder**, **a secret combination**, and the phrase – "*they* **knew** *every man his brother*." The three previous uses of the word "**knew**" in Moses 5 (vs. 2, 16 & 42) address sexual relations between Adam and Eve. The fourth one, however, is tied to the brotherhood of those in the **secret combination**. Many believe it represents a form of *initiation* into this **secret** brotherhood, one involving *homosexuality.*

Sexual sin has been a primary component of idolatrous worship throughout scripture. In the Old Testament there was Baal worship with its sexual sin and child sacrifice (abortion today). Satan used sexuality and idolatry to continually corrupt the Israelites. The great Prophet Elijah eliminated this practice in 1 Kings 18, bringing down fire from heaven to destroy the 450 priests of Baal. Believers were continually influenced by surrounding cultures, including the temple rites of the Greeks and the Romans with their temple prostitutes. Satan used similar influence with the early Christian church at Ephesus in the New Testament. There the Christian leader Nicolas led many of the Saints in religious rites that involved idolatry, fornication, and adultery. It brought reproach to the early church. John the Revelator and the LORD addressed it as "the Nicolaitan rites" or "Balaam's error" (see p. 34).

The Power of the Word

The Prophet Joseph's primary mission in the Restoration was to bring forth or "**restore**" more of God's **word**, and in its purity and "**fullness**" (D&C 5:4). It is very useful in fighting darkness and evil. Alma said:

> "And now, as the preaching of **the word** had a great tendency to lead the people to do that which was just—yea, it had had **more powerful effect** upon the minds of the people than the sword, or anything else, which had happened unto them—therefore Alma thought it was expedient that they should try the virtue of the word of God" (Alma 31:5).

Joseph brought forth the Book of Mormon first. In 1 Nephi 13:25-29 we read that many "plain" (simple, important truths) and "precious" (sacred) things were removed from the Bible by evil and designing men. It, in combination with the JST version of the Bible (June 1830 to July 1833), **restores** much of **the fullness** of the gospel of Christ back to us. Too few know what this "**fullness**" is. Chapter 7 is dedicated to it.

In D&C 42 (1831, called "the law"), God began revealing **the fullness** or the greater portion of His gospel to the early Saints at Kirtland through Joseph. It included both the higher law of unconditional love known as "the law of consecration" (vs. 31-39) and the higher law of marriage in monogamy (vs. 22-23). Both were eventually rejected by the Saints at Nauvoo, along with other parts of this **fullness** (chapters 5-7). It was a fulfillment of God's prophecy in 3 Nephi 16:10, where He said that we the Gentile Saints and others would reject this "**fullness**." Polygamy was a significant part of the reason why it was rejected. This is partly explained in another prophecy God gave us 2,000 years later in D&C 38. Speaking of the powers of darkness prevailing on the earth, causing **silence** and ignorance to reign, God told Joseph Smith in 1831:

> "behold, the *enemy is combined.* And now I show unto you a *mystery*, a **<u>thing</u>** which is had in **secret chambers**, to bring to pass **even your destruction** in process of time, and ye knew it not…I say unto you that the enemy in **the secret chambers seeketh your lives**…ye know not the *hearts* of men in *your own land*" (D&C 38:12-13, 28-29).

That "**<u>thing</u>**" was **polygamy**. Joseph was destroyed because of it just as God said. Jacob in the Book of Mormon used the word "**<u>thing</u>**" four times in Jacob chapter 2 to negatively connect it with other words like "*pride, grosser crime, iniquity, whoredomes, abomination,* and *cursed*," all to get his people to removed this serious sin from them.

The LORD used the word "**<u>things</u>**" in 3 Nephi 16:10, stating that, "if they [the Gentile Saints and others] shall do all those **<u>things</u>**" **and shall reject the fullness of my gospel**, behold, *saith the Father*, I will bring **the fullness** of **my gospel from among them**." This is exactly what happened. Both the Book of Mormon (Jacob 3:5, "Fathers" to "Father"), and the Doctrine and Covenants (older 101 removed, 132 put in, both without a vote) have been modified to promote polygamy. The most dramatice changes and the greatest number of them, have been to our church history. The great darkness of secret combinations - that place sin among us in subtle and deceptive fashion - is one of two primary things present in **the fullnesss** of the gospel of Christ, **the fullness** that Satan attempts to take away from followers of Christ. Addressing both the JST and the Book of Mormon, Joseph said, "many important points touching the **salvation** of man, had been taken from the Bible, or lost before it was compiled" (HC 1:245.). Joseph restored many "plain" (simple) and "precious" (sacred) truths, tied to (1) how to receive **salvation** from God, and (2) how Satan tries to stop it. He does so by keeping man in darkness, ignorance, and sin – a pattern very apparent in the secret combination of Moses 5, and in the 83 references to secret combinations in the Book of Mormon. Evil men don't want us to believe that Satan is real. They don't want information about their secret oaths and other sinister methods to come out into the light. They want us ignorant and easily controlled. God said, "It is impossible for a man to be saved in ignorance" (D&C 131:6). We must know God's path to salvation **and** Satan's ways to stop it.

Today the Utah Saints have a limited selection of the Joseph Smith Translation available in our LDS scriptures, as the Community of Christ holds the copyright to the whole volume. Too few Saints are aware of the limited verses we do have, let alone Joseph's entire selection of re-translated Bible verses, 3,410 of them. The keys to unlock the fuller truths of Christ's gospel are available to "the elect" who search out God's holy word in what He calls "**the fullness of my scriptures**" (see D&C 42:15, 56 and 59 & D&C 93:53; 94:10; 104:58 & 124:89). History shows that the LORD wanted the JST version of the Bible and the Book of Mormon to "**go to the world together, in a volume by itself**." They were to be "**printed together**" (HC 1:341) in **one volume**. It would fulfill Ezekiel 37:15-17, the two sticks coming together to provide the fullness given to Judah (the JST Bible) *and* Joseph (the Book of Mormon).

God told Joseph Smith, "And I give unto you a commandment, that then ye shall teach them unto all men; for they shall be taught unto all nations, kindreds, tongues, and people" (D&C 42:56-58). Note, that they were and are to be "**my law** to *govern* **my church**" (D&C 42:59). According to Joseph, "**the salvation of the elect**" was dependent upon the **fullness** in them being delivered to believers (see D&C 35:20). Some say Joseph's prophecy in the Far West Record has been fulfilled. In it he stated, "God had often sealed up the heavens because of covetousness in the Church . . . and except the Church **receive the fulness of the Scriptures that they would yet fail**" (Far West Report, p. 16, TPJS, Deseret Book, p. 9).

What the LORD called "**the fullness of my scriptures**" (D&C 42:15, 56 and 59 & D&C 93:53; 94:10; 104:58 & 124:89) still hasn't went out to the world as one volume with regard to the Brighamite Saints. By 1867, however (23 years after Joseph's murder), the Josephite Saints published the full JST version of the Bible to go with the Book of Mormon, the D&C, and the Pearl of Great Price. Emma had kept the 500-page manuscript for the JST in safe keeping until she and her son brought it forth, fulfilling a significant portion of the Prophet Joseph's mission. Finally 120 years later in 1979, Robert J. Matthews (a wise educator) obtained permission to use a portion of the JST for the Brighamites. It amounts to 16 total pages (a miniscule portion of the 3,410 total verses available), as the Community of Christ (formerly the RLDS church) retains the copyright to the full version. Satan used spiritual wifery to effectively thwart this work early on, keeping many Saints from the fullness of God's word (see 3 Ne. 16:10).

Many believe Joseph's restoration movement was all about bringing forth a church – the one we know today. The LORD informs us instead, that Joseph's primary mission was to bring forth more of God's precious **word** - in the Book of Mormon, the Joseph Smith re-translation of the Bible, and the oracles now contained in the Doctrine and Covenants (see endnote 27), and the Lectures on Faith (now removed from the D&C without a vote of the church). The fullness of God's precious word contains the fullness of His law, His priesthood, and His gospel. Those embracing them become part of a very simple definition of God's church, those as He said, who "**repent** and **come unto me**" (see D&C 10:67). This is the pattern in 3 Nephi, where Christ provided a fullness of His word, detailing His doctrine and His gospel. Those embracing them are His church. He brings us into it.

Part II: Brighamite versus Josephite History

Following Joseph's murder in 1844, the Nauvoo Saints had to choose between the strength of Brigham Young and his "new order of things," or the original teachings of Joseph Smith. It was a fairly clear choice by 1846, go with Brigham and the Quorum of the Twelve west, or stay behind without a clear leader. The dividing line wasn't just about leadership though, but also about **doctrine** and what one believed. From 1844-46, it became clear to some that choosing Brigham also meant choosing polygamy and other new doctrines he was putting forth. About half the Saints rejected Young and the new ways, and as a result, we as "Brighamite" Saints are only familiar with one half of the story, a half that has been controlled and modified to reflect a particular narrative – that Joseph was a polygamist.

There are many viewpoints, stories, and "histories" available addressing polygamy, as presented on the Internet, in books, and via the official narrative of the LDS church. **WHO we believe in determines WHAT we believe**. Secret combinations control all the information sources in order to **lie** and **deceive** for gain. They include seven things:

1. Modifying what God has to say in scripture
2. Modifying Joseph Smith's personal journals & history
3. Modifying official church history
4. Modifying Lucy Mack Smith's biography
5. Creating false affidavits & stories to prop up polygamy
6. Creating a fake news in Nauvoo's two newspapers
7. Continuing the false narrative today in modern media

It is only logical that Latter-day Saints would turn to the church's leaders and official history for it. Relying on "the arm of flesh" more than God and His word is dangerous, however, leading to curses as God tells us (see 2 Ne. 4:34, 28:31; Jer. 17:5). This is how and why the **deception** has occurred, a **cursing** for our idolatry. Our history is **not** trustworthy. History has always been written and modified by those in charge, as the truth is too messy and powerful, having at least two sides. Those in charge want **one narrative** presented, theirs. Brigham Young saw to it that his pro-polygamy narrative was put forth, the one saying that Joseph Smith was responsible for it among the Saints. It is a lie!

In 2017 the church announced a new "*transparent*" history rewrite. The last one published was in 1930 by B.H. Roberts. The new history features a four-volume set, with one volume published each year for four years, from 2018 (now available) to 2021. Elder Steven E. Snow, church Historian and Recorder, said these four volumes will be, "**transparent**, **honest**, and **faithful**," with controversial aspects of church history covered in the context of the entire story. The promise to be "transparent," "honest" and "faithful" implies that our prior history hasn't been. It represents a third rewrite since the days of Joseph Smith. The first begun prior to Joseph's murder. The second continued in 1844, when Brigham Young had Willard Richards, William Clayton, Mark Forscutt, and others made modifications to the first history, changes that coincided with Young's pro-polygamy agenda. Forscutt chose to follow Young west, but later left Utah after Young put significant pressure on him to take plural wives. Forscutt later revealed how the history was modified. Harvard educated and respected LDS historian Richard bushman stated, "I think for the church to remain strong, it has to reconstruct its narrative. **The dominant narrative is not true.** It can't be sustained. So, the Church has to absorb all this new information or it will be on **very shaky ground**, and that's what its trying to do. And it will be a strain for a lot of people, older people especially. It has to change. Elder Packer had a sense of protecting the little people, the scholars were the enemy of this faith…The price of protecting the grandmothers, was the loss of the grandsons" (see https://www.youtube.com/watch?v=uKuBw9mpV9w

Sadly, most active Latter-day Saints today believe Joseph Smith was a polygamist because Brigham and those who followed him said it was so. The Prophet Joseph and the entire Smith family provide an entirely opposite perspective, one closely tied to the teachings given us in scripture. This is best presented in a three-volume set of books, entitled *Joseph Smith Fought Polygamy* (https://restorationbookstore.org). The Utah Saints have trusted what Brigham Young and leaders after him in the Utah church have said about Joseph, rather than Joseph's own words, or those of others in the Smith family. The Smiths proclaim Joseph's innocence. They include his mother, Lucy Mack Smith, his brothers Hyrum, Samuel, and William Smith, his sister Katharine Smith, and Joseph and Emma's firstborn son Joseph Smith III. Their important testimonies are consulted hereafter. They have generally been swept under the rug in the Brighamite agenda, as they promote an opposing viewpoint. There are two sides to this story, that of the Brighamites and the Josephites. The dividing line was polygamy, doctrine in general, and Brigham Young's leadership.

Latter-day Saint "history" is often very fragmented, confusing, and with many contradictions. Some stories have changed over time. It is messy and faulty because it has been based on one primary lie – that Joseph Smith was a polygamist. Additional lies have multiplied to protect this first one, all attempting to prove that Joseph originated the practice. It has been done because Joseph's name gives credibility or "justification" to this early whoredom in Nauvoo. The Book of Mormon describes it as a whoredom and an "abomination." The false Brighamite narrative is a primary reason why so many have and are leaving the LDS church. Many feel betrayed. Church growth was at an all time low in 2017 – a 1.4% growth rate.[4] It is one of many causes of concern for the wise.

The Brighamite Saints have been indoctrinated with the narrative of those taking control of the church, after the three Smith brothers were murdered in Nauvoo. Many today are rejecting this narrative, as the curses tied to it have endured to the fourth generation from Joseph Smith (see 2 Ne. 4:34, 28:31). The remaining chapters of this book are about how this curse has been manifested among us (see endnote 4). The rejection doesn't have to be of "the church," of "Joseph Smith," or of "God." For some it is all three. What must be rejected is the lies. As we saw in the Introduction, the LORD - in addressing our day and us, provided three listings of sins that must be removed among us for light to return. They are 3 Nephi 16:10, 21:19, and 30:2. The first sin atop each list is "**lyings**." The second is "**deceits**" or "**deceivings**." Lies keep people in ignorance, typically for the sake of "gain" (1 Ne. 22:23). Nephi said:

> "For the time speedily shall come that all churches which are built up to get gain, and all those who are built up to get power over the flesh, and those who are built up to become popular in the eyes of the world, and those who seek the lusts of the flesh and the things of the world, and to do all manner of iniquity; yea, in fine, all those who belong to the kingdom of the devil are they who need fear, and tremble, and quake; they are those who must be brought low in the dust; they are those who must be consumed as stubble; and this is according to the words of the prophet" (1 Ne. 22:23, "the Prophet" is Jesus Christ – our rock and source of light, see verses 20-21).

Wise virgins, with pure intent, a desire for truth, and oil in their lamps, can avoid deception in their pathway back to God by turning to Him first and foremost, not men (including this author). I have chosen to believe God and the Prophet Joseph and others in the Smith family. Doing this immediately places one in opposition to the Brighamite narrative. This shouldn't be the case.

Brighamites Versus Josephites

As information unfolds in this and other chapters of the book, the most trustworthy historical evidence reveals that the Prophet Joseph Smith did not practice polygamy, but that other leaders did, specifically some in the Twelve, beginning at Nauvoo and even earlier in Young's case. They justified their secret practice of it by claiming that Joseph Smith began the practice secretly among them. More credible evidence – first-hand contemporary evidence - reveals that Brigham Young and others implemented the practice secretly in Nauvoo first, prior to Joseph's murder. Joseph and Hyrum were fighting against it. The secrecy contributed to the murder of both men and their brother Samuel. To truly understand our history, we must **separate** Joseph Smith and the Smith family (the Josephites), from leadership over the Twelve at Nauvoo led by Brigham Young and those that followed him (the Brighamites). The dividing line was and is – polygamy, first known among the Saints as "**spiritual wifery**." Our history was modified to protect it.

According to a number of LDS historians, the official history of the church is a huge mess, reflecting both the sins of weak or evil men, along with the triumphs of incredible people. Following the murder of Joseph, Hyrum, and Samuel Smith in 1844, church history was **revised by Brigham Young** to reflect a pro-polygamy agenda. The Prophet Joseph Smith was made out to be a polygamist to justify the secret practice of it by many of the early Twelve. Pres. Young employed Willard Richards, William Clayton, Mark Forscutt, and others to modify as many historical documents as possible to support polygamy as an official church doctrine. Joseph's name was then used to **justify** the early practice of polygamy, along with those following Young into it at Nauvoo and later Utah. This agenda has required more lies to cover the first. Not only is our history greatly tarnished in this way, but so too a number of early important Christ-centered doctrines. They thave been diminished over time. What the early doctrines were, versus what they have become, is an important part of this work in later chapters (chap. 7).

Since President Young took power, the Brighamite church has embraced a number of false narratives. To our own detriment, the Utah Saints have not consulted with the Josephites and their version of history because of pride and mistrust. Both were implanted within us to divide us and to **discredit them**; a favorite ploy to keep us from the truth. Those who stayed behind in the various branches of the original restoration movements embraced the Book of Mormon and the early doctrines of Joseph Smith. They are not "apostates" or unenlightened; on the contrary, they often hold many precious insights into our history. Too often we are the ones unaware of basic historical facts. Many of those staying behind were more seasoned in the gospel of Christ and recognized problems with polygamy and other teachings promoted by Brigham Young in his "new order of things."

As we will see in chapter 4, two very public court cases in 1880 and 1894 reveal that the Reorganized Church of Jesus Christ of Latter-day Saints (led at the time by Joseph Smith's firstborn son Joseph Smith III) was determined to be the legal successor to the truths of what the original founder, Joseph Smith Junior had taught and brought forth. In their final verdicts both judges determined that the Brighamite church of Utah had failed to continue with the teachings of its founder, primarily because of its later focus upon polygamy. This occurred after the Smiths were murdered. Few are aware of these things as it is not part of the current church narrative.

The devisive and superior attitude held by some Utah Brighamites over the Josephites of Missouri should end. This pride is addressed throughout the Book of Mormon. Those who stayed behind have preserved an entirely different history, one where Joseph Smith is innocent of polygamy. Many among them have believed his words, whereas the Utah Saints have believed Brigham Young's words instead. The current Brighamite narrative put forth by our leaders suggests that Joseph Smith was a polygamist and a polyandrist, and that he said one thing in public while doing another in private. The Prophet of the Restoration has been thrown under the bus on official church websites and in various publications. Joseph Smith is not a liar, a cheat, nor a fraud. In 1838 the LORD saw that a secret combination would arise among the Saints (see D&C 38:13 and 28). He provided a plan to counteract it with a future "endowment of power from on high" – the gift of the Holy Ghost (verses 31-42). The secret chamber rose up at Nauvoo and was responsible for the murder of Joseph and his two brothers. It is addressed in the next chapter. Joseph was innocent of polygamy! The fruits in Joseph's life reveal his connection with God, not the abominable practices Jacob spoke of in Jacob chapters 2 and 3. As *the* Prophet of the Restoration, Joseph Smith brought forth the Book of Mormon, the JST version of the Bible, the Pearl of Great Price, and nearly all the revelations in the Doctrine and Covenants. He also said he never practiced polygamy! His mother, his wife, his brothers and sisters, and his son Joseph say the same. They are **first-hand contemporary witnesses** of him, his life, and his marriage. We can go to God in prayer to confirm or reject the testimonies of the Smiths.

Joseph Smith never stated that he had a revelation on or encouraging polygamy, though Young and others put that false narrative forth years after his murder. Instead, Joseph spoke out against spiritual wifery repeatedly. He fought it openly much of his life, excommunicating some from the church for it right up until his murder. We have many statements by him and others to reflect this – but typically they are easier to find in the Josephite history, the one most Saints don't consult. Joseph was framed as a polygamist by those who first implemented spiritual wifery secretly among the Nauvoo Saints, and all to justify their own secret practice of it. They included Brigham Young and some of the Twelve before his murder. Eventually all the Twelve embraced polygamy.

Many stories were manufactured thereafter to cover up the secret practice of polygamy in Nauvoo. They repeat the false narrative that the Saints were run out of Nauvoo by persecutors, but **never was it** because of the **spiritual wifery** being practiced by some leaders, nor the secrecy, deception, division, sin, and murder among the Saints. Sadly these things are a part of the more truthful, untold story. As we will see hereafter, although there was persecution from outsiders, some of it was warranted by the actions of our own people - especially among the leaders (see 3 Ne. 16:10; 30:2). Many of the Josephite Saints remained behind unmolested. Those that did go west were often new European converts of Brigham Young and the Twelve in the British Isles, along with those who chose to embrace his strong leadership. Many new converts did not know polygamy was part of the church until years later. Those leaving Nauvoo also left the United States as Joseph prophesied (p. 69), that Brigham might establish his own kingdom free of government involvement, where polygamy could be installed unrestrained. Unlike the more seasoned Saints, the new converts had zeal, loyalty, and trust in their leaders, those who taught them, and to the church itself, more so than God and His word and will. The **idolatry** of unseasoned Saints led them to follow Brigham into the sin of polygamy.

Records Taken West

Like the records in the Vatican, many historical documents tied to our history are off limits to the average Saint, as well as serious researchers and historians today. It doesn't encourage trust. Only select portions of Joseph Smith's history have been released to the public. What is most telling is that the remaining members of the Smith family did not go west with Brigham Young, nor did some of the more experienced Saints at Nauvoo. Many rejected Brigham Young and his "new order of things." They include four of the twelve apostles (in bold hereafter) at Nauvoo; Brigham Young, Heber C. Kimball, Orson Hyde, George A. Smith, **William B. Smith**, Wilford Woodruff, Parley Pratt, Orson Pratt, **Lyman Wight**, **John E. Page**, John Taylor, and **Amasa Lyman**. Others separating from Young include Nauvoo Stake President William Marks, Joseph Smith's private secretary James Whitehead, and Nauvoo Temple architect William Weeks. Many of them joined the RLDS church, including **1,557** church members by 1849 (see the research of Susan Easton Black, https://dcms.lds.org/delivery/DeliveryManagerServlet?dps_pid=IE5412785).

Joseph's plans to prove his innocence through diligent record-keeping was thwarted by Brigham Young's editors. They gathered up all the official church records and as many of Joseph Smith's personal papers as possible, so that all of it would end up in Brighamite control in Utah. They could then be hidden away or modified. Most remain in church vaults today. Joseph Smith III (firstborn son of Joseph and Emma), explained what happened to his father's personal history:

> "At the death of my father, Joseph W. Coolidge was appointed administrator of the estate.... The private and personal correspondence of my father, many books and some other matters of personal character were in his office in care of Willard Richards and others, clerks and officials. These were either retained by the administrator upon his own responsibility; or were **refused to my mother's demand** at the direction of the Twelve; the latter we were at the time led to believe.... In answer to **repeated demands** for my father's private papers, journal and correspondence, made by my mother, there was an invariable denial (Edward W. Tullidge, Life of Joseph the Prophet, 744–745).

Fortunately, the manuscript for the inspired Joseph Smith re-translation of the Bible remained with Emma, hidden away in the lower, secret portion of a two-tiered chest in her bedroom. This important manuscript was not modified by Young's editors. For a time, those holding the copyright to this work called themselves, "The Reorganized Church of Jesus Christ of the Latter-day Saints. Today they call themselves the Community of Christ. The LDS Church headquartered in Utah has been given permission to use some 16 pages of various verses out of the entire re-translated Bible. Much more is available. Young's control of his version of history is reflected in a statement about our official History of the Church, designed originally to instill confidence in it. Historian B.H. Roberts stated:

> "...since the death of the Prophet Joseph, the history has been carefully **revised under the strict inspection of President Brigham Young**, and **approved by him**. We therefore, hereby bear our testimony to all the world... that the History of Joseph Smith is true, and is *one of the most authentic histories ever written*" (B. H. Roberts, History of the Church, 1:5-6).

Lies to Support Spiritual Wifery & More

One of the most troubling things discovered in writing this book, has been the tremendous amount of **lying** and **deception** that has occured to protect polygamy and power. With the practice now mostly gone, the deception has continued to protect this falsified history, and the church and its leaders. Lying and deception for a "higher cause" was used early on to conceal polygamy from the Federal Government via thirteen different names for it. Deception then became an *institutional practice* (see p. 190). Many left and are leaving the church because of it, some 2,000 plus in August of 2018 alone. According to a number of historians employed by the LDS Church, our history is far from "authentic." Assistant Church Historian Charles Wesley Wandell has much to say about our corrupt "official" history.

> "The official History of the Church of Jesus Christ of Latter-day Saints [the Documentary History of the Church, or DHC] was published in book form under the direction of the First Presidency in 1902. The introductory assurance that, "**no historical or doctrinal statement has been changed**" is demonstrably wrong. Over-shadowed by **editorial censorship, hundreds of deletions, additions, and alterations**, these seven volumes are not always reliable...The nineteenth-century **propaganda mill** was so adroit that few outside Brigham Young's inner circle were aware of the **behind-the-scenes alterations so seamlessly stitched into Church history**."

Wandell had first-hand knowledge of how and why our history was modified. He worked directly with Dr. Willard Richards in Nauvoo! Following Richards return from his English mission, he became the Church Historian and Recorder. Wandell expressed shock at the **many changes made to Joseph's personal diary**, by Richards, Clayton, and others. Commenting on the vast number of changes made in this historical work, as it was being serialized in the Deseret News, Wandell noted:

> "I notice the interpolations because having been employed in the Historian's office at Nauvoo by Doctor Richards, and employed, too, in 1845, in compiling this very autobiography, I know that after **Joseph's death his memoir was 'doctored' to suit the new order of things** [polygamy], **and this, too, by the direct order of Brigham Young to Doctor Richards and systematically by Richards. The Quorum of the Twelve, under Brigham Young's leadership, began altering the historical record shortly after Smith's death. Contrary to the introduction's claim, Smith did not author the History of the Church.** At the time of his 1844 death [murder], the narrative had been written up to 5 August 1838" (Richard S. Van Wagoner, Sidney Rigdon: A Portrait of Religious Excess, Signature Books [Salt Lake City, 1994], p. 322).

There are five favorite deception methods employed to deceive people and keep them ignorant of the truth. All five of them have been employed to make Joseph Smith out to be a polygamist (see the 15 lies, Assumption #7, chap. 7).

1. Ignore or bury the **truth** (lock it away in vaults, bury it in complexity, or rarely address it)
2. Discredit, demean & diminish other credible souces of **truth** (those in the Smith family)
3. Distract and divert others from the **truth** (keep people busy or distracted with other things)

*4. Modify existing **truths** (change official history, private journals, etc.)

5. Create new false records and narratives to negate **truth** (via false affidavits, stories, and statements)

One of Many Doctoring Examples – "Joseph forbids it [polygamy] and the practice thereof"

One of the most important journal entries by the Prophet Joseph Smith, in connection with polygamy, is his October 5, 1843 entry, recorded by William Clayton. It has been modified to promote polygamy. He and Joseph were walking the public streets of Nauvoo together on this date. Clayton recorded an **anti**-polygamy statement by Joseph. Ten years later it was changed by historians under Brigham Young's direction to reflect a **pro**-polygamy stance, then put in the official History of the church. Both versions are presented hereafter.

In their effort to falsely prove that Joseph was a polygamist, church historians deleted **ten** key words from Joseph Smith's original statement (below), then add **forty-nine** other words. Based on the Joseph Smith's Papers timeline for this compilation, the illustrated example (see below) would have probably been edited sometime between 1853-1855, after George A. Smith took over duties for the deceased Willard Richards. Both Willard Richards and George A. Smith were Freemasons, Apostles, and members of the secret chamber at Nauvoo. Both men became counselors in the First Presidency to Brigham Young. The entry does not describe a public moment, but instead Joseph's **private journal** entry, made by his personal scribe William Clayton, after the two walked the public streets of Nauvoo. It occurred **three months after July 12, 1843**, *the supposed date* that Brigham Young said Joseph had the pro-polygamy revelation, now known as D&C 132. Modern LDS scholars with access to church archives found both statements. Joseph's original, undoctored quotation is in "an untitled journal of 278 manuscript pages," as identified in the handwriting of Willard Richards (secret chamber member), another scribe of Joseph. Richards recorded:

> "Walked up and down St[reet] with Scribe and gave instructions to try those who were preaching, teaching, or ~~practicing~~ the doctrine of plurality of wives on this Law. **Joseph forbids it and the practice thereof**. No man shall have but **one wife**" [rest of page blank, page 116], Scott H. Faulring, ed., An American Prophet's Record: The Diaries and Journals of Joseph Smith, 417). See also, Van Wagoner, *Sidney Rigdon*, 292.

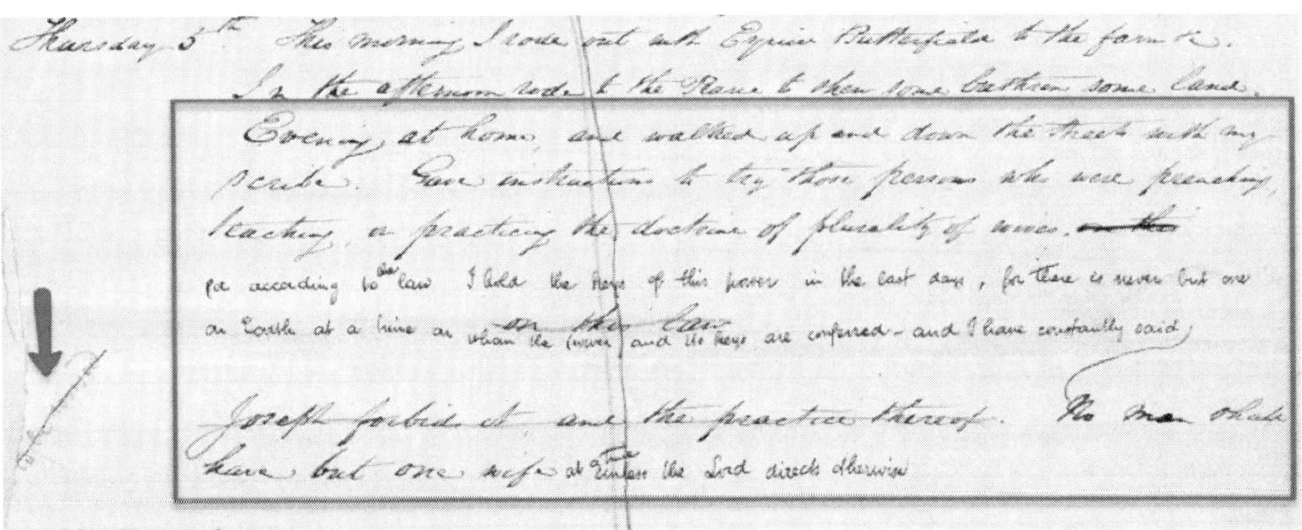

Thursday 5th This morning I rode out with Esquire Butterfield to the farm &c.
In the afternoon rode to the Prairie to shew some brethren some land.
Evening at home and walked up and down the streets with my scribe. Gave instructions to try those persons who were preaching, teaching, or practicing the doctrine of plurality of wives. ~~on this~~
for according to the law I hold the keys of this power in the last days, for there is never but one on Earth at a time on whom the power and its keys are conferred – and I have constantly said ~~on this law~~
Joseph forbids it and the practice thereof. No man shall have but one wife at a time unless the Lord directs otherwise

Fauling (trained in history at BYU and elsewhere) pointed out that the rest of the page was blank, allowing for future "doctoring." The edited version above (supporting polygamy) is the one that ended up in the official History of the Church, volume 3, p. 46 (changes made 1853-55). It states:

"Gave instructions to try those persons who were preaching, teaching, or practicing the doctrine of plurality of wives; for, according to the law, I hold the keys of this power in the last days; for there is never but one on earth at a time on whom the power and its keys are conferred; and I have constantly said no man shall have but one wife at a time, unless the Lord directs otherwise" (History of the Church 6:46).

The changed historical document (among many) illustrated on the preceeding page was discovered in the Joseph Smith Papers project, though difficult to now find there. A transcription of the relevant, changed text appears in it. Note the "to be revised" statement near the arrow at the illustration's lower left. They appear in a different scribe's handwriting, which appears to match that of the revisions made. The revisions change the whole meaning of Joseph's words. The definitive words "Joseph forbids it" and "the practice thereof" are crossed out and replaced with verbiage similar to what is found in D&C 132. The edited version was changed to say what is found in the outline area of the illustration on the next page. The 1850's editor left **extra space** around the part where Joseph unequivocally forbids the practice of plural marriage. This was a favorite tactic of Freemasonry devotee Heber C. Kimball. He [Kimball] and Young had editors like William Clayton carried out this form of editing repeatedly. It is a pattern found in many "official" historical documents from the Nauvoo era. Clayton modified a number of entries in the Masonic Lodge book #2 as well. Some of these modifications include post-dating and ante-dating entries, as well as omitting other entries. One of these modified entries involved ten names, two of them being Joseph Smith and Sidney Rigdon. They were men not admitted to the Freemasonry Lodge at the time. Kimball and Young were both members of "the craft" before joining Mormonism. The Lord uses the word "**craft**" in *mostly negative ways* in scripture (Psalm 83:1-4; Dan. 8:25; Mark 14:1; Alma 35:3; Hel. 2:4; D&C 76:75, 106:6, 123;12; JSH 1:75). It comes from the Hebrew "*Aram,*" meaning "**serpent**, *subtle, crafty,*" or "*shrewd.*" Satan inspires "**secret**" or "*hidden*" things (from the Hebrew "*sod*"), like his blood-oaths with Cain. For more on the Oct. 5, 1843 journal entry, and this particular edit, see:

1. http://www.josephsmithpapers.org/paper-summary/journal-december-1842-june-1844-book-3-15-july-1843-29-february-1844/123
   Joseph Smith's anti-polygamy personal journal statement, entered July 15, 1843.
2. http://www.josephsmithpapers.org/paper-summary/history-draft-1-march-31-december-1843/143
   An editor's plans for modifying this journal entry to make it pro-polygamy.
3. http://www.josephsmithpapers.org/paper-summary/history-1838-1856-volume-e-1-1-july-1843-30-april-1844/118
   The final modified journal entry establishing a pro-polygamy stance in LDS church history.

By October of 1843, known irregularities in the record keeping of Nauvoo Masonic Lodge and other concerns led to the denial of a charter for the Mormon Lodge and a revocation of its dispensation. Minute Book 2, once housed in the Nauvoo Masonic Lodge cornerstone, was obtained by Pres. David O. McKay in 1954 and now resides in church vaults in Salt Lake City. It may have much to say. Changing stories typically revolves around lies to protect the guilty. The changing stories tied to how and when polygamy originated in the church are evident in the statements hereafter. Though Joseph Smith never claimed to have had a revelation on polygamy, Brigham Young claimed that he did have one on polygamy, and many years after Joseph was murdered. Additional so-called "evidence" used by the church to support the narrative that Joseph was a polygamist is presented in the following statements by William Clayton, Orson Pratt, and Brigham Young.

"Now, I say to you, as I am ready to testify to all the world, and on which testimony I am most willing to meet all the Latter-day Saints and all apostates, in time and through all eternity, I did write the revelation on celestial marriage given through the Prophet Joseph Smith on the 12th of July, 1843 (William Clayton Journal, said to be written in 1842-46, July 12, 1843 entry).

Though dated as 1843, Clayton's wording suggests a much later date, perhaps as late as 1874, when Young made new claims tied to it. According to Clayton, he, Hyrum, and Joseph were the only ones present when he wrote down this revelation in the Whitney Store. Two of these "witnesses" are conveniently dead. Neither supported polygamy. Official Church sources today claim that the open practice of polygamy - as part of doctrine - occurred in 1852 in Utah, or 22 years after the Book of Mormon was published. This foundational document speaks out against it clearly (see Jacob 2 & 3). Under the direction of Brigham Young, Apostle Orson Pratt published The Seer in the same year (1852), a pro-polygamy document distributed by the Church. In 1859, Apostle Pratt stated:

"Thirteen years after the publication of the Book of Mormon [1830], the same Prophet…received a revelation upon marriage, which commanded certain individuals in this Church to take unto themselves a plurality of wives for time and all eternity; declaring that it is a righteous principle, and was practiced by inspired men in time of old"

(JD 6:362, July 24, 1859).

In 1879, Apostle Pratt added, "...the revelation on polygamy was not given until some thirteen years after the rise of this Church [1830], and that was after we had been driven and smitten and scattered to and fro, here and there, by the hands of our enemies, hence, it was not for that we were persecuted" (JD, 17:111-12, June 14, 1879).

This and Pratt's prior statement reveals that for 20 years (1859 to 1879), Elder Pratt understood that Joseph Smith's revelation on polygamy was neither received by - nor given to - Joseph Smith, until 1843! Both of Pratt's statements align with the story of William Clayton. Young's 1874 public statement about his revelation on polygamy while in England opposes Orson's statements. He claimed he [Brigham] received a revelation while serving in England (1839-40) that justified the practice of polygamy (see p . 48, 2B). And he said Joseph had never mentioned anything about polygamy to him or others **prior to it**, and that there **had never been a thought of polygamy in the church at that time**. From 1874 forward, the story changed – that the revelation was **only recorded** on July 12th of 1843 by Clayton. In other words, Joseph had received this revelation much earlier, in the early 1830s.

Cats & Kittens in and out of the Bag

Pres. Brigham Young's new, changed 1874 story opened a can of worms. The cat was now out of the bag leading to a lot more kittens. First, according to Pres. Young, God was now giving revelations to Young, not the Prophet Joseph, and for a new church-wide doctrine, even while Joseph was yet alive (God said only Joseph was to receive revelations for the church, see D&C 28:2; 43:3). Secondly, Brigham's supposed revelation on polygamy came **before** 1843, before Joseph's supposed revelation (now D&C 132). Third, Brigham took full responsibility for having the first revelation on polygamy for the whole church, while he was on a mission in England in 1839-40, as he said Joseph "never mentioned it," and "there had never been a thought of it in the Church." Fourth, later in 1899, Pres. Lorenzo Snow later backed up Brigham's story, claiming that he too had a revelation on polygamy while in England supporting the practice (Deseret Semi-Weekly News, June 6, 1899).

According to Kerran, "The omissions, deletions, and unidentified additions tell us much more of what transpired than do those items that remained in their original form. Moreover, there is much more truth to be had in the journals of Heber C. Kimball and William Clayton than in all of the church's written history combined. Also, Brigham's "compiled history" (referred to as Brigham's Manuscript History or Journal) was helpful in exposing the extent to which he and his religious progeny rewrote history to fit their narrative. Toward the end of 1839 to the beginning of 1843, the period that both temple worship and spiritual wifery were infused into Joseph's church in Nauvoo, the personal journals of Joseph, Heber, and Brigham go silent: a veritable black-out period for recordkeeping—peculiar activity for a peculiar record keeping people...Luckily, I came upon a document that exposes not only irregularities in the recordkeeping of the Nauvoo Lodge (Masonic), but also in the Masonic Temple documents. These records were created, manipulated, partially destroyed, and then pilfered by Heber Kimball and William Clayton, and taken to Salt Lake. This not only explains why their journals go silent (they were extremely busy doing something else), but it also puts the LDS history regarding the temple and temple endowment into a more reasonable, clear, and common-sense perspective."[5] Karren added, "In the post-Brigham spin-room, they had one mission: find something on Joseph that creates a preponderance of impropriety that we can spin into plural marriage."[6] And that one thing used by the church in the late 1800's was the fragmentary Fanny Alger story. She was a 15-year old young woman working for the Smith Family. She apparently had a crush on Joseph. Emma and Joseph were aware of it. She had to be dismissed because of it. Some took note and the rumors spread.

One of these Fanny Alger rumors was later used by the Church to frame Joseph as a polygamist in the early 1830's. It was a letter written from from one former anti-Mormon preacher to another, with a plan to accuse Joseph of something, so that they could diminish his influence over members of their churches, former members that were converting to Mormonism. It took money out of their pockets as preachers. They also wanted to bring about Joseph's fall. The accusations and plans of these two anti-Mormon preachers, is hardly strong evidence. Nevertheless, the Fanny Alger story began to take root. It was later utilized by Brighamite leaders to incriminate Joseph, that they might justify themselves in the practice, having been part of it since the 1840's.

The year 1835 is given by pro-polygamists for a possible secret marriage date for Joseph and Fanny, performed by Oliver Cowdery. In 1838, Cowdery was excommunicated from the Church, and at real odds with Joseph. He does not say anything about Joseph and Fanny in his church court, but supposedly does so in a letter to his apostate brother Warren. In that supposed letter, Oliver accuses Joseph of a "dirty, nasty affair." There is no marriage. The story that a marriage or "sealing" occurred was later put in place to overcome the possible embarrassment of adultery, rather than "plural marriage." Note the words of researcher Brian Hales about the Fanny Alger evidence. He is one of the premiere pro-polygamy LDS scholars, and yet his own words reveal real problems with the Fanny Alger "evidence."

> "To date, nineteen different references to the Joseph Smith-Fanny Alger relationship have been identified in the historical record. Hopefully more will come to light in the future. An analysis of the various narratives shows that the first reference was written on January 21, 1838, probably two to three years after the event; no contemporaneous records have been located. Also, fifteen of the accounts were composed at least thirty-seven years after the incident; thirteen of the narratives are secondhand. The first published reference to Fanny Alger by her full name occurred in 1881, although her first name was used in an 1875 anti-Mormon book, Wife No. 19, written by Ann Eliza Webb Young in 1875. Regardless, most Church members would not have known anything about her until Andrew Jenson mentioned her as "one of the first plural wives sealed to the Prophet" in his 1887 article in the Historical Record" (Hales, Joseph Smith Polygamy Vol. 2, 2008, p. 369).

The Fanny Alger "evidence" is nothing more than a proposed plan to stop Joseph from taking converts away from two anti-Mormon pastors, in a letter from one to the another. It contained their false accusations against Joseph. This shoddy "evidence" would never stand up in a reputable court of law.

Since the Nauvoo days, the Prophet Joseph Smith has become a scapegoat and a stone of stumbling for many, all to protect the current narrative. It is no longer necessary. Truth about our real history would stop much of the bleeding (so many leaving the Church). Truly, as Moroni said, Joseph's name has been had for both good and evil. Speaking of the night of the angel's first visit to Joseph on Rosh Hashanah of 1823, the Prophet Joseph stated, "He [the angel] called me by name, and said unto me that he was a messenger sent from the presence of God to me, and that his name was Moroni [or Nephi, depending on the source];[7] that God had a work for me to do; and that my name should be had for good and evil among all nations, kindreds, and tongues, or that it should be both good and evil spoken of among all people" (Joseph Smith History 1:33).

False Affidavits, Statements & Stories – *Justifying "Celestial Marriage"*

In the later part of the 19th century, many "manufactured" affidavits, statements, and stories began popping up, all tied to the supposed polygamy of the Prophet Joseph Smith, including his many so-called wives. Apostle Joseph F. Smith served in the church historians office for a time. He later collected many affidavits from Assistant church Historian Andrew Jensen, and others. Falsified Affidavits were part of this shady effort. It was done to counter mounting pressure to stop the practice of "plurality of wives" from the U.S. Government, in association with the Prophet's Joseph's firstborn son, Joseph Smith III, President of the RLDS church. The lying was seen as a way to preserving a higher calling, leading to *institutional lying* (see p. 190 and the 15 lies of Assumption #7, chap. 7). He encouraged the U.S. Government to put great pressure upon the Utah Saints to abandon polygamy. This political pressure followed prior efforts by him and his two brothers, Alexander Hale Smith and David Hyrum Smith, to return the Utah Saints to their father's original teachings via missionary work. Each of the three Smith sons of Joseph and Emma would make three trips to Utah for this purpose. The pressure of new laws enacted by Congress to stop polygamy finally resulted in Wilford Woodruff's Manifesto in 1890, and then fourteen years later Pres. Joseph F. Smith's second Manifesto of 1904 (see chap. 4) Both were statements issued by the President of the church to appease the U.S. Government. They were not "thus saith the LORD revelations" from God. The Manifestos eventually helped end the practice of polygamy in the LDS church.

It was in the late 19th century that the church produced the largest quantity of questionable documents, including false affidavits to prove to the Federal Government that polygamy was an original **tenet** or doctrine of the church that Joseph Smith put in place. It didn't work. It was in the 1880's, for example, or some forty years after Joseph's murder, that the bulk of these false documents were produced. Church leaders believed that the affidavits, in combination with modified stories and doctored church history would show that Joseph Smith had been practicing polygamy for years. They hoped it would thus ensure their religious freedom to continue practicing polygamy. The lying in these falsified reports was justified to protect a believed "higher cause" in "Celestial" plural marriage." One Deseret News article featured thirteen code names that were subsequently employed by the Saints to protect or lie about polygamy in the late 19th century (see p. 190). They were part of the **lies**, **deceptions**, and **whoredoms** the LORD spoke of in 3 Nephi 16:10, 21:19 and 30:2.

Created some forty years after the events in them suposedly occurred, the fake affidavits feature amazing recall of very specific events and stories, most tied to the Prophet Joseph Smith's plural "wives." Not only are they from non-contemporary sources, but most were produced by biased polygamists, many of them apparently under pressure from higher-ups. Some appear to be pre-made documents, needing only signatures. Andrew Jensen, LDS assistant church historian is tied to many, if not most of these bogus documents (others are connected to Joseph F. Smith, who worked in the historian's office for a time). With scrutiny, most of the affidavits are easily discredited, tied to fearful polygamists and sloppy, fake history. It is a sad testament to those desperate to protect polygamy.

Responding to similar pressure at this time, a number of faith-promoting falsified stories appeared in association with Brigham Young, Wilford Woodruff, and Lorenzo Snow, all Presidents of the church. One was the sworn affidavit of Lorenzo Snow (with supportive statements by his sister Eliza Snow), where he said an "angel with the sword" appeared to Joseph Smith, leading him to finally embrace the practice of polygamy. Another story was that of Brigham Young's and his supposed transfiguration before the Saints in Nauvoo during the 1844 succession crisis. False witnesses in this story state that Brigham looked and sounded like the Prophet Joseph Smith, while he stood before the Nauvoo Saints, addressing his qualifications to lead them after the Smith's were murdered. This story was desgined to lift up Young as a credible leader over the Saints, and again **used** the power of Joseph Smith name (here his voice and appearance) to **justify** Brigham Young's rise to power. There was also the story of the Founding Fathers visiting Wilford Woodruff in the St. George Temple (see http://puremormonism.blogspot.com/2013/04/wilford-woodruffs-pants-are-on-fire.html). All three stories were produced many years after the fact. All three stories have proven to be complete frauds by a number of researchers (see https://www.dialoguejournal.com/wp-content/uploads/sbi/articles/Dialogue_V34N0102_171.pdf). All three men were polygamists, Freemasons, and part of the secret chamber at Nauvoo (next chapter).

Polygamy did not Begin nor End with a Revelation from God

The sons of Joseph and Hyrum Smith, both named Joseph Smith (after the founding Prophet), were later part of the end of the practice of polygamy (with the aid of the U.S. Government). They were cousins. They opposed each other in their support or rebuke of polygamy. Both became Presidents of their respective churches (Joseph F. Smith of the Utah church and Joseph Smith III of the RLDS church in Missouri). Because polygamy was often the focal point of authenticity and succession arguments for decades between those of the Brighamite church west, and those of the Josephite church east, and because polygamy was of interest to the non-Mormon public, the pro and con polygamy battle between these two cousins spilled over into the public domain in the early part of the 20th century. It occurred in a publication appropriately entitled "*Arena*" in 1902 and 1903.

Two years later in 1904 the U.S. Senate began investigating whether Apostle Reed Smoot could or should take his Senate seat for the state of Utah, as many in Utah Territory were still practicing this outlawed form of marriage. In trying to win support for Senator Smoot so that he might help secure Statehood for Utah, LDS President Joseph F. Smith issued a "Second Manifesto" in August of 1904. It informed the Brighamite Saints that the practice of plural marriage had to end. He showed his supposed resolve in this by dismissing two of the twelve Apostles who had married additional wives after Woodruff's "Manifesto" of 1890 (one was John W. Taylor, son of former church President John Taylor). Both men believed they would eventually return to the Twelve when the controversary settled down (they were apparaently told they would be readmitted some time after the hearings). Addressing both the Manifestos of 1890 and 1904 provides insights to the lying and deceptions associated with polygamy in Mormonism.

Woodruff's 1890 Manifesto

Some lies are told blatantly, while other things, "assumed" to be true, persist among us because those in power don't want them corrected. They can be **useful assumptions** (see chapter 6). Uncorrected assumptions are a form of deception. The perception by many Saints that the 1890 Manifesto was a revelation from God is one of many of these. It was not a "revelation" but a statement penned by later church leader Charles W. Penrose **for** Pres. Woodruff. Thomas J. Rosser, a missionary in Wales in 1908, asked mission president Charles Penrose if the 1890 Manifesto was a "revelation" from God. Penrose replied, "Brethren, I will answer that question, if you will keep it under your hats. I...wrote the manifesto with the assistance of Frank J. Cannon and John White... Wilford Woodruff signed it to beat the devil [the U.S. Government] at his own game." The document was submitted to a committee of three non-LDS Judges for refinement; Charles S. Zane, C.S. Varian, and O.W. Powers. They changed the wording slightly, after which it was recopied by a clerk named Green (Samuel Taylor, *The Rocky Mountain Empire*, New York, NY, MacMillan, 1978, p. 35. See also D. Michael Quinn, *LDS Church Authority and New Plural Marriages*, 1890-1904, *Dialogue: A Journal of Mormon Thought*, Spring 1985).

Lies and **deception** are often used to protect a believed "higher cause." It may be to protect "tender testimonies," the warts in church history, to preserve the image of the church and its leaders for effective missionary work or other purposes, and to protect **power** (endnote 16). The practice is thought to have begun with polygamy and the necessity to evade laws enacted by the Government. Some 250 polygamous marriages are believed to have been performed after the 1890 Manifesto, many with full knowledge of church leadership. Because of mistrust of church leaders, the 1904 Smoot investigation of polygamy by Congress lasted more than three years (1904-1907), resulting in over 3,000 pages of sworn testimony. It included LDS church history, theology, and much more. The reputation of the Utah church decreased substantially across the nation after the hearings. The decline began with the very first testimony of Pres. Joseph F. Smith. He and others twisted their words on many occasions. Four examples of polygamy related dishonesty follow. There are many more such stories, all **justified** because many had come to *falsely believe* they were protecting a doctrine that had been revealed to Joseph Smith by God, then put in place by Brigham Young.

(1) Pres. Smith employed deception by performing a secret polygamous marriage for Abraham H. Cannon and Lilian Hamlin while at sea on the way to Catalina Island. Because it was performed on water, some believe it permitted him to say that he had not performed a marriage "in" the U.S. or "on U.S. soil."

(2) Church historian B.H. Roberts was elected to the U.S. House of Representatives after Utah became a state. The House voted to exclude him, as an investigation revealed that Roberts was engaged in a polygamous marriage that occurred after the 1890 Manifesto. He was thus declared unfit for office after U.S. citizens signed a petition that was presented to Congress demanding Roberts be denied his seat. In D&C 134:1, we read, "We believe that governments were instituted of God for the benefit of man; and that he holds men accountable for their acts in relation to them."

(3) Apostle John W. Taylor (son of former Pres. John Taylor) married Janet Maria Wooley as his third wife only four days after the Manifesto was presented and accepted in LDS general conference. The couple married in a carriage in Liberty Park at night in Salt Lake City. The family intentionally backdated the marriage to October 10, 1889. He also married Rhoda and Roxie Welling on August 29th 1901 (11 years after the Manifesto). The ceremony was performed at the Taylor home in Farmington, Utah. Joseph F. Smith, who was acting as a counselor in the First Presidency at the time, gave permission.

(4) The son of Wilford Woodruff, Abraham Owen Woodruff, married 18 year-old Eliza Avery Clark as a plural wife in 1901 (11 years **after** his father presented the Manifesto).

Smith's 1904 Manifesto

LDS church President Joseph F. Smith (son of Hyrum Smith, whose wife [Mary Fielding Smith] later married Heber C. Kimball, a polygamist) was a proponent of polygamy. Nevertheless, in the end he helped officially end polygamy in Utah with what is known as "the second Manifesto" in 1902. He thus followed his anti-polygamy cousin, the Josephite RLDS church president Joseph Smith III from Missouri (son of Joseph and Emma Smith), in adding the final blow to polygamy in Utah. The two Josephs had been battling it out for decades. Now their last battle was in a very public forum in 1902 and 1903 in the publication entitled *Arena.*

Pres. Joseph Smith III (RLDS) published a number of arguments in *Arena* against polygamy, including the accusation that polygamy originated with his father. He did so by wisely quoting from God's word in the Book of Mormon and the Articles of Faith. Both works were brought forth by his father. He also added the testimony of his mother Emma, and others, as they had intimate knowledge of the Prophet prior to his murder. Pres. Joseph F. Smith (LDS) countered, stating that the Utah church was enjoying continuing **revelation**, and that **polygamy had begun with a revelation from God**. He added that because plural marriage was introduced in a **revelation** first recorded on July 12 of 1843, his cousin's quotations of pre-1840 texts like the Book of Mormon were irrelevant. He followed up this faulty reasoning, stating that **continuing revelation was also responsible for the end of polygamy in Wilford Woodruff's "Manifesto" of 1890.** Both statements are proven false by his own words and those of others. Pres.

Smith's (LDS) testimony in the Reed Smoot Congresssional hearings negated his continuing revelation statement. Under oath he testified that the current apostles of the Utah LDS church he led were selected by other men, **not** by God in **revelation** (see Assumption #3, chap. 6). In addition, his 1904 Manifesto was like Woodruff's, in that it was a "statement" by him, not a **revelation** from God.

Five things combined to counteract the faked affidavits, stories, and statements of the 1880's, and the modified records brought from Nauvoo, all of them designed to justify Brigham's version of polygamy in Utah territory in the later 19th century. They included; (1) General moral outrage of polygamy by Federal officials and the American public; (2) Fear that Brigham Young's growing anti-government theocracy was a threat to the nation; (3) The work of President Joseph Smith III of the RLDS church (the firstborn son of the Prophet Joseph Smith), who spoke out against polygamy consistently for some 30 years, encouraging many Government officials to enforce laws already on the books, as well as create new ones to end the practice; And last, two laws were put in place by Congress. The first was the (4) 1882 Edmunds Act, and (5) the 1887 Edmunds and Tucker Act. Both enforced anti-polygamy laws in Utah Territory. The latter resulted in seized church property and many polygamists put in prison who were found guilty of "illegal cohabitation." They resulted in the official demise of polygamy in 1890 in Wilford Woodruff's Manifesto. President Joseph Smith III's efforts to eliminate polygamy (with aid by the U.S. Government) was further cemented by two very important public court cases in 1880 and 1894. These are addressed in chapter 5.

Current LDS church leadership is not to blame for many early changes to documents, or the false affidavits and stories created in the 19th century. They have inherited them, and sometimes added to them, like the 1981 change of Jacob 3:5 – from "fathers" (plural) to "father," the commandment for them all to have "**one wife**" in the Book of Mormon. Our leaders today have opportunity and responsibility to address the many lies originating with Brigham Young and others, if they will. Chief among them is the lie that Joseph Smith was a polygamist, and that he gave the keys of power to this practice to them in "the last charge" (endnote 16). It is those *outside* the church in the Josephite tradition who have provided the best evidence to support his innocence. God provides confirmation in Joseph's gifts.

Part III: Joseph Smith was a Monogamist

Either Joseph was the monogamist Prophet of the Restoration, or he was a liar, a fraud, and a cheat. Today, official LDS church websites put forth the false narrative that the Prophet Joseph Smith had many wives, and took them behind Emma's back (deception). They say some of his wives were married at the time to other men (polyandry). In addition, these sites claim that one of Joseph's earliest wives was Fanny Alger, taken at age 15, in either adultery or polygamy (pedophilia). Contrasting these lies, Joseph and the Smith family continually claimed his **innocence**. Joseph brought others to church courts for their polygamy right up until his murder. And as a sign from God to us, he exhibited many gifts and fruits of the Spirit. They were real. He did not fake them. Joseph was **not** a liar, a cheat, an adulterer, a polygamist, a polyandrist, nor a pedophile. To embrace this false narrative requires that the Prophet of the Restoration be thrown under the bus – and by those who have the most to gain from it.

In speaking of His chosen servants, God said, "by their **fruits** ye shall know them" (Mat. 7:16-20). The Prophet Joseph demonstrated that he was a gifted seer, revelator, and translator, bringing forth both ancient and modern scripture. He also demonstrated many gifts of the Spirit and received many significant revelations. He brought forth the Book of Mormon, the JST version of the Bible, the Pearl of Great Price, and the oracles in the Doctrine and Covenants (including the Lectures on Faith). He did amazing things in bringing forth the restoration of the fullness of the gospel of Christ. Joseph was also an imperfect mortal man. Nevertheless, in 1829, after sincere repentance, turning fully to Christ, he and Oliver Cowdery received the lesser priesthood, and then baptized each other. Immediately thereafter, they experienced what Alma did in the Book of Mormon – "**the mighty change of heart**" in the baptism of fire and the Holy Ghost. Joseph Smith had love for God and the Saints with his new heart. It is the single biggest difference between him as the first Prophet of the Restoration and Brigham Young, its second, pro-polygamy leader.

The "born again" status of Joseph and Oliver was before there was an official church organization (1830), one done according to the laws of men in New York State (see Assumption #9, chap. 6 & JS History 1:72-74). The LORD's church, as decribed by Him in D&C 10:67 was present and working effectively in 1828 and 1829. The gifts and fruits of the Spirit were clearly evident. This is because both Joseph and Oliver came in "**at the gate**" the LORD required, **not some other way**, like the robber and thief (John 10:1; 1 Ne. 31 & 32; D&C 22:2, 43:7). It is the same gate all of us must come through. It is "**the way** of salavation of our God" (chap. 7). It is **the way** the LORD requires, via a broken, repentant heart and a contrite, humble spirit. Because of humility and heartfelt repentance, Joseph received the necessary gifts of the Spirit to lead the Restoration movement - to bring again the LORD's way of doing things.

No leader since Joseph can rival his contributions. His most important attribute was **love.** It is one of the fruits of the Spirit. God empowered Joseph Smith to help bring forth the fullness of the gospel of Christ in the latter-days for the salvation of many. What "**the fullness**" is and how it was lost is addressed in succeeding chapters. We will see that as soon as God dispensed greater light to the Saints in the early 1830's, Satan then came to take it away (D&C 93:39). Wicked men helped the evil one do it. Especially useful, as a corrupting influence, was spiritual wifery. Sexual sin is a great weakness for many men. Satan used it to cut many of the Saints off from God early on.

Joseph Smith brought forth the Book of Mormon, which is a decidedly **anti-polygamy** book. It is the foundational document of our faith, along with the Joseph Smith re-translation of the Bible. Joseph had just one wife, Emma Smith. This is the consistent testimony of both of them, and other Smith family members. I choose to believe them rather than those practicing polygamy, those continually justifying their abominations via Joseph's *supposed* practice of it. The excellent work of Richard and Pamela Price provides a substantial body of evidence to back up the statements of Joseph, Emma, and many others. Their website and their three-volume book set, entitled, *Joseph Smith Fought Polygamy* provides the clearest evidence for this (see https://restorationbookstore.org). Their words are also consistent with God's word in scripture. It is ironic that the strongest evidence presented to us in defending the Prophet Joseph Smith and his message as a monogamist, comes from those outside the LDS church.

Contrast this with official LDS church websites and publications, and information presented at the three church universities named after Brigham Young. There, official descriptions of Joseph Smith state that he was a polygamist and a polyandrist. They suggest that he secretly practiced what the Book of Mormon calls a **whoredom** and an **iniquity**, while publically preaching against it. Justifying it with changed doctrine is a great **abomination**. The gifts and fruits of the Spirit were clearly present in Joseph's life. He was not a liar, a cheat, or a fraud.

Eight Reasons Why Joseph is Innocent

To believe that the Prophet Joseph was a polygamist, requires us to accept significant inconsistencies in the church narrative, ever since Brigham took power. There are at least eight of these inconsistencies. The Twelve led the Saints into polygamy. That is the great secret. It is a great abomination according to the Book of Mormon. The LORD said they "polluted mine holy grounds" (D&C 124:46), and thus brought upon themselves "cursings, wrath, indignation, and judgments, upon your own heads, by your follies, and by all your abominations, which you practice before me, saith the LORD" (verse 48). Eight points below reveal Joseph's innocence. **WHO** we believe determines **WHAT** we believe. Do you believe Joseph Smith or Brigham Young?

(1) *The Smith's Own Words* First, there are numerous, first hand, contemporary sources showing that Joseph Smith consistently denied that he was a polygamist, including Joseph's own words and those of Emma and Hyrum Smith. We have their public speeches and written words that preach against this abomination (see endnote 3). God said we may know his servants by their fruits. The gifts and fruits of the Spirit were evident in Joseph's life, a clear sign of his connection with God, his love for the Saints, and his desire to create Zion.

(2) *No Children from Joseph Except Through Emma* DNA testing thus far reveals that there are no known children from Joseph Smith by any woman other than Emma Smith. She bore Joseph 9 children. A primary purpose of polygamy (according to some who advocate it) is to raise up righteous seed. Where are the children from Joseph's supposed polygamous unions? Brigham Young had 56 children from 16 of his 55 wives. Heber C. Kimball had 66 children by 17 of his 43 wives. Willard Richards had 11 children via 8 of his 11 wives. All total, the 3 men of the First Presidency in Utah had 109 wives, and 133 children.

(3) *No First-hand Contemporary Evidence of Joseph being a Polygamist* It is significant that the Church has no first-hand, contemporary sources of evidence showing that Joseph Smith was involved in spiritual wifery. Instead, non-contemporary sources surfacing many years after the fact are used, and from poor second and third-hand sources. They are often polygamists, employed to prop up the practice, and by "ascusers" with conflicting testimonies. Some of these sources are by anti-Mormons, again with an agenda. As a whole, these sources are suspect at best, many of them sloppy, fabricated documents, produced decades after the fact by second and third-hand false witnesses.

(4) *Poor Evidence via Joseph's Enemies* Joseph's enemies often provide us excellent, first-hand, contemporary evidence of their own guilt as secretive polygamists. It is presented in their private journals, which may counteract public statements made by them. Joseph's enemies were part of a secret combination at Nauvoo called by some in it, "the secret chamber" (leadership in the Twelve and those assisting them [enforcers and hitmen] (1841-46). The journals of those in it were kept by Brigham Young, Heber C. Kimball, and Willard Richards (the First Presidency later in Utah), William Clayton, and other secretaries to both Joseph Smith and Brigham Young. The enforcers and hitmen employed by church leaders also kept private journals. They included men like Hosea Stout, Chief of Police at Nauvoo, and hitman Bill Hickman later in Salt Lake. Their journals and that of others reveal use of fear, coercion, violence, and murder to protect spiritual wifery among leadership. These private writings often reveal the truth behind their own secret actions. In Wilford Woodruff's Journal, for example, we read about Brigham Young's indictment for murder in Salt Lake City by a U.S. Marshall in 1859. No trial was ever held in connection with it (see Wilford Woodruff's Journal, vol. 7, pages 45 & 52).

(5) *Modified "Official" History* Much of Latter-day Saint church history has been modified to support the claim that Joseph was a polygamist, and by those taking power following his murder. There are a number of significant examples (see pps. 60-61). This modified history is in direct opposition to that of the Smiths. Willard Richards became the official Church Historian and Recorder when he returned to Nauvoo from his English mission, a position he held until his death. Later in Utah he was the first Editor for the Deseret News. He and William Clayton and others became spin masters for Brigham.

(6) *Public Disciplinary Action* Joseph Smith identified and disciplined a number of people publically in adulterous relationships at Nauvoo and elswhere. This was part of his effort from 1842 to 1844 to root out polygamy and other sexual sin from Nauvoo and other cities, with the help of Hyrum, William Marks (Stake President), and the Nauvoo Stake High Council. These efforts continued right up until his murder. Four months prior to their murder in February of 1844, co-Presidents of the church Joseph and Hyrum Smith excommunicated Hyrum Brown of Michigan for practicing polygamy. Joseph's plans to stop polygamy among the Saints with President Marks, and specifically their effort right at the end to bring suspected polygamous Apostles before church courts is thought to be the primary motive for his murder and that of Hyrum and Samuel Smith.

(7) *William Smith - the Wild Card* Apostle William Smith admitted practicing spiritual wifery in his last speech as an Apostle, just before Brigham Young excommunicated him. Secretaries for Brigham Young documented his speech and other actions. The church does not use these primary, contemporary sources as they are very revealing. As we will see in chapters 3 and 4, William was part of "the secret chamber" at Nauvoo for a time. He knew that Brigham Young was directing it all. And even though there were times when he and Joseph did not see eye to eye (they got into physical altercations), William did not identify Joseph as a polygamist before or after his murder. William did use Joseph's name to justify his practices, as did most others. After his three brothers were murdered, William turned on the secret chamber, exposing their secret acts. His firsthand knowledge of the secret chamber speaks volumes about the guilt of Brigham Young and the Twelve (the secret chamber) and their lies about Joseph.

(8) *God as a Witness* God is the best witness of whether Joseph Smith was truthful, or a liar, cheat, and fraud, saying one thing in public and doing another thing in private. God said we may know his servants by their fruits. The gifts and fruits of the Spirit were evident in Joseph's life; a clear sign of his connection with God, his love for the Saints, and his desire to create Zion. Besides God's prophecies (like D&C 38), which came true and are yet unfolding, we have another important witness from Him. He does not open the heavens to those practicing abominations, those lying about them, those in secret combinations that use fear, coercion, secret blood-oaths, Danite-like enforcement, and murder to cover their actions. The heavens are sealed up to such individuals (2 Ne. 27:5). Even if Joseph Smith was guilty of some form of introduction of the practice of polygamy among the Saints, his guilt or innocence does not change the focus of this work – and that is that polygamy or infidelity is nearly always conceived in **the secret chambers** of one's **heart. It did not originate with a command from God.**

Part IV: Joseph Consistently Battled Polygamy

Like Abinadi, Joseph Smith preached repentance and faith in Christ the LORD. Being mortal, he made mistakes too. There are always at least two sides to any story. If we listened to only Hillary Clinton, we would believe her lies, and believe that she is innocent of all wrongdoing tied to her and her husband over the last 25 years. The same is true of Brigham Young versus Joseph, Emma, and Hyrum Smith. Our own idolatry today, in lifting up the arm of flesh over

God, causes many to rely upon one viewpoint with regard to church history; the history given us by Brigham Young and others under his control. Most have not searched out the words of others opposing him, those with more truth. The Smith family story needs to be told.

The "doctoring" of church history was widespread under Young's direction. Joseph's story was changed and so to that of his mother. She wanted her voice heard. Even her biography was modified by Brigham Young. For truth to emerge, we must pay more attention to the words of those outside the secret chamber, including the Smith family, and our other brothers and sisters in Christ, those who rejected the polygamy of Brigham Young. These people stayed behind or went elsewhere. **The Smith family** is the best source of truth on what really happened in Nauvoo. See -

Joseph Smith Fought Polygamy	https://restorationbookstore.org/jsfp-index.htm
William & Katherine Smith writings	http://olivercowdery.com/smithhome/WmSmith1.htm
Joseph Smith writings	http://www.olivercowdery.com/smithhome/smithhis.htm

Israel A. Smith, grandson of the Prophet Joseph Smith, said, "Joseph Smith was the greatest victim of fraud and conspiracy of the last 500 years. Nothing like it in recorded history. He was simply lied about when something had to be done to justify. . . polygamy" (Letter to Pamela Price, Sept. 17, 1956). Hereafter some of Joseph's teachings are presented (for those of Hyrum, Emma, Samuel, and Katharine Smith, see endnote 3).

On May 26 of 1844, a month and a day prior to his murder, the Prophet Joseph spoke up to defend himself against an accusation of polygamy and other crimes by William Law, former member of the First Presidency. Joseph began his sermon by reading from 2 Corinthians 11:13-15. It was a warning to some of **the apostles** and others who were secretly practicing spiritual wifery. It reads, "For such are **false apostles**, **deceitful workers**, **transforming themselves into the apostles of Christ**. And no marvel; for Satan himself is transformed into an angel of light. Therefore it is no great thing if **his ministers** also be transformed as the ministers of righteousness; whose end shall be according to their works." They became Joseph's enemies, Satan giving them his power (p. 113 & endnote 16).

> "When facts are proved, truth and innocence will prevail at last. My enemies are no philosophers: they think that when they have my spoke under, they will keep me down; but for the fools, I will hold on and fly over them. God is in the still small voice. In all these affidavits, indictments, it is all of the devil-all corruption. Come on! ye prosecutors! ye false swearers! All hell, boil over! Ye burning mountains, roll down your lava! for I will come out on the top at last...The God and Father of our LORD Jesus Christ, which is blessed for evermore, knoweth **that I lie not** [1 Cor. 11:31]...Another indictment has been got up against me [a polygamy indictment]. It appears a holy prophet [William Law] has arisen up, and he has testified against me [causing the polygamy indictment to be brought forth]...God knows, then, that the charges against me are false. **I had not been married scarcely five minutes,** and made one proclamation of the Gospel, before it was reported that I had seven wives. I mean to live and proclaim the truth as long as I can. This new holy prophet [William Law] has gone to Carthage and swore that I had told him that I was guilty of adultery. This spiritual wifeism! Why, a man dares not speak or wink, for fear of being accused of this...William Law...swears that I have committed adultery. I wish the grand jury would tell me who they [the alleged wives] are—whether it will be a curse or blessing to me...A man asked me whether the commandment [revelation] was given that a man may have seven wives; and now the new prophet has charged me with adultery...Wilson Law [William's brother] also swears that I told him I was guilty of adultery...I have rattled chains before in a dungeon for truth's sake. I am innocent of all these charges, and you can bear witness of my innocence, for you know me yourselves.... **What a thing it is for a man to be accused of committing adultery, and having seven wives, when I can only find one. I am the same man, and as innocent as I was fourteen years ago** [when charged with polygamy shortly after his marriage to Emma Hale]; and I can prove them all perjurers" (HC 6:408, 410–411, **May 26, 1844**)

In February of 1844, or four months prior to the murder of Joseph and Hyrum, co-Presidents of the Church Joseph and Hyrum Smith excommunicated Hyrum Brown of Michigan. Their statement in the Times and Seasons read:

> "As we have lately been credibly informed that a member of the Church of Jesus Christ of Latter-day Saints, a man by the name of Hyrum Brown, has been teaching polygamy and other false and corrupt doctrines in the County of Lapeer, State of Michigan; this is to notify him and the church in general that he has been cut off from the church for his iniquity," Signed, Joseph Smith, Hyrum Smith, Presidents of the Church, Feb. 1844, Autobiography of

Elder R.C. Evans, p. 331).

"I preached in the grove and pronounced **a curse** upon all **adulterers** and **fornicators**, and unvirtuous persons and those who have made **use of my name** to carry on their **iniquitous** designs" (Grove Sermon, Apr. 10, **1842**). Joseph **cursed** those betraying him in "**the Last Charge**" given to the Council of Fifty (p. 113, endnote 16).

"Bennett went to some of the females in the city, who knew nothing of him but as an honorable man and began to teach them that promiscuous intercourse between the sexes was a doctrine believed in by the Latter Day Saints, and that there was no harm in it; but this failing, he had recourse to a more influential and desperately wicked course; and that was to persuade them that myself and others of the authorities of the Church not only sanctioned but practiced the same wicked acts…He was well aware of the consequences of such willful and base falsehoods, if they should come to my knowledge, and consequently endeavored to persuade his dupes to keep it a matter of secrecy, persuading them there would be no harm if they should not make it known" (Times and Seasons, 3:840 July 1, **1842**).

"[John Bennett] reached out his hand to Br. Joseph and said, will you forgive me, weeping at the time; he said Br. Joseph, I am guilty, I acknowledge it, and I beg of you not to expose me, for it will ruin me; Joseph replied, Doctor! **why are you using my name to carry on your hellish wickedness? Have I ever taught you that Fornication and adultery was right, or polygamy or any such practices? He said you never did**" (Hyrum Smith, Affidavit May 1842, Times and Seasons 3 [August 1, **1842**]).

"To the church of Jesus Christ of Latter Day Saints in Caldwell county, Know assuredly Dear brethren, that it is for the testimony of Jesus, that we are in *bonds* and in *prison*...Was it for committing adultery? **We are aware that false and slanderous reports**…respecting this thing…and spread by the dissenters, who are extremely active in spreading **foul and libilous reports** concerning us; thinking thereby to gain the fellowship of the world...Satan taking advantage of this has transfigured it into **lasciviousness, a community of wives**, which things are an **abomination** in the sight of God….contrary to the law of God, which says, "Thou shalt not commit **adultery**, Thou shalt **not covet thy neighbors wife**." "He that looketh upon a woman to **lust** after her has committed adultery already in his heart"…Now if any person has represented any thing otherwise than what we now write they have willfully misrepresented us" (*Times and Seasons* 1 [April **1840**]: 82–85, a letter Joseph wrote to the Saints on Dec. 16, 1839, in response to an accusation that he was a polygamist).

"Do the Mormons believe in having more wives than one? **No, not at the same time**. But they believe, that if their companion dies, they have a right to marry again" (The Elders' Journal 1, Nov. **1837**, 28).

Three of Joseph Smith's Prophecies tied to Polygamy

Joseph prophesied that because of polygamy, the Saints would have to leave the United States (another curse). It was just prior to his murder, that Joseph went to William Marks, Nauvoo Stake President, saying that he would bring the polygamists to trial before the High Council, and that Pres. Marks must expel those practicing this whoredom from the Church. Elder Marks later testified:

"He [Joseph] said 'it eventually would prove the overthrow of the church, and we should soon be obliged to **leave the United States**, unless it could be speedily put down'" (RLDS History of the Church 2:733).

Joseph also prophesied two times about his own murder, and a third time about living to see Jesus Christ. The first was indirect, stating that murder and polygamy go hand in hand. The second was very direct, addressing who would kill him and why. The third was published in the D&C. According to Emma Smith, Joseph stated:

"David was not raised from the dead when the righteous came forth at the time of Christ's resurrection, because he put Uriah to death, and the crimes of polygamy and murder always to together" (Saints Herald, 48:184).

"There are those among you who will **betray me soon**; in fact, you have plotted to deliver me up to the enemy **to be slain**" (Joseph Smith, June 23, 1844, from an interview of Katharine Smith Salisbury [Joseph's sister], by I.G. Davidson, Fountain Green, Ill., May 1894, http://olivercowdery.com/smithhome/BroBill/KStestimony.htm).

Harrison Sagers & the Warning to the Twelve

In 1843, Joseph Smith became aware of the adultery of Harrison Sagers, and tried him publicly in two courts—the church's High Council and the Nauvoo Municipal Court. Harrison Sagers was charged with seduction of the sister of his wife Lucinda. The Prophet Joseph presided at the first church hearing. The charge stated that he had told a young woman that the doctrine of spiritual wifery was right, according to Joseph Smith. This is the same justification that Dr. John Bennett, Chauncey Higbee, Brigham Young and others used in their spiritual wifery.

Sager's legal wife, Lucinda, announced that her husband Harrison had deserted her, doing it in the very public forum of the first and only issue of the Expositor. There we read an unusual advertisement by Lucinda Sagers against her unfaithful husband Harrison. The advertisement read, "One Cent Reward. WHEREAS my husband, the Rt. Rev. W. H. Harrison Sagers, Esq., has left my bed and board without cause or provocation, this is to notify the public not to harbor or trust him on my account, as I will pay no debts of his contracting" (Lucinda Sagers, Nauvoo Expositor, June 7, 1844, 3). Tried in 1843, Harrison Sagers continued his infidelity through 1844 and beyond.

In Joseph Smith's journal for November 25,1843, we read of the Nauvoo High Council meeting, where **he warned all those present, including some of the Twelve, to be virtuous**. Joseph wrote, "In the evening the High Council sat on the case of Harrison Sagers, charged with seduction, and having stated that I had taught it was right. Charge [by Sagers against Joseph was] not sustained. I was present with several of the Twelve, and gave an address tending to do away with every evil, and **exhorting them** [the Twelve] **to practice virtue and holiness before the Lord**; told them that the Church had not received any permission from me to commit fornication, adultery, or any corrupt action; but **my every word and action has been to the contrary**. If a man commit adultery, he cannot receive the celestial kingdom of God. Even if he is saved by any kingdom, it cannot be the celestial kingdom. I did think that the many examples that have been made manifest, such as John C. Bennett's and others, were sufficient to show **the fallacy of such a course of conduct**. I condemned such actions in toto, and warned the people present against committing such evils; for it will surely bring a **curse** upon any person who commits such deeds" (HC 6:81).

In Joseph's journal entry, of the Sagers' public High Council hearing, we learn that several of the Twelve present were practicing polygamy secretly in 1843. **Joseph did not give Sagers, or any other individual, authority to practice polygamy**. By November of 1843, it is believed that Apostles Brigham Young, Parley P. Pratt, Heber C. Kimball, and Orson Hyde had already married plural wives. Joseph Smith's warning words were directed to them and others.

Following Joseph's murder, Sagers followed Brigham Young to Utah. Church records show that in addition to Lucinda Sagers, Harrison had also married **nine** other women; Olive Amanda Wheaton, Ruth Adelia Wheaton, Lucy Marilla Wheaton, Sarah Lovena Bailey, Harriet Emmaline Barney, Frances Cornelia Adams, Mary___, Elizabeth____, and Marion Browning Smith. **None of them were Sagers' wives during Joseph Smith's lifetime** (see LDS Family Group Record, Genealogical Data, for William Henry Harrison Sagers). Harriet Emmaline Barney bore him four children. She separated from Sagers and married Brigham Young. Her children with Sagers were sealed to Brigham (see James H. Crockwell, Brigham Young and His Wives [Salt Lake City, Utah: The F. W. Gardiner Co., 1896], 38; The Utah Genealogical and Historical Magazine 11 [April 1920]: 133). Thus, Brigham Young married a woman that had been a plural wife of Sagers, who had been involved with polygamy since the days of Dr. John Bennett.

During the last seven months of his life, Joseph Smith spent time trying to convict Sagers and others of polygamy. Like Bennett, Higbee, and Young, Sagers placed the blame for their plural marriages on the teachings of Joseph. The words of Emma, Hyrum, and Samuel Smith refute them (see chap. 2 & endnote 3).

Emma & the Hot Iron

As Relief Society President over the whole Church, Emma spoke out repeatedly against spiritual wifery in Nauvoo. And like Hyrum Smith's public speech at China Grove, Emma Smith tried to stop the practice among the Saints by giving her "Virtue Will Triumph" public speech to all the women of the city and the church. Like her husband and Hyrum, She knew that Brigham Young was the prime promoter of spiritual wifery in Nauvoo. Young participated in it secretly by at least 1842. Nearly all of those who did so, justified their practices by using Joseph's name.

Years later, Velma Bradshaw, a close friend to the firstborn granddaughter of Joseph and Emma, stated that one day Joseph Smith, "came into the Mansion House for his noontime meal, while Emma [his wife] was ironing. Joseph told her that Brigham Young and others were talking favorably about plural marriage. Emma knew he was being pressured by those men. She picked up the hot iron and held it close to Joseph's face and said, 'Do you see this iron? If you don't want your face scarred with this iron, don't scar your heart.'" Some believe Emma's words may have alluded to the following scripture:

> "Now the Spirit speaketh expressly, that in the latter times **some shall depart from the faith**, giving heed to **seducing spirits, and doctrines of devils**; speaking **lies** in hypocrisy; having their conscience seared as with **a hot iron**" (1 Tim. 4:1–2).

According to Velma Bradshaw it was, "Aunt Emma [Emmeline – the first grandchild of Emma and Joseph Smith] who spoke of this event. She said it took place in the Mansion House in late 1843 or early 1844. Velma was a close friend of Emma Josepha Smith McCallum, who was the firstborn daughter of Joseph Smith III and his first wife Emmeline (the first wife died). Emmeline was the first grandchild of Joseph and Emma Smith.[8]

At the time of Joseph Smith's murder, Young, Kimball, and several of the Apostles and other leaders were secretly involved in spiritual wifery. From 1842 to 1844, Joseph was continuously involved in trying to rid the Nauvoo Saints of the practice. By spring of 1844 Joseph decided to directly expose all the polygamists he knew of openly, including those in the Twelve. To do so, Joseph sought out Nauvoo Stake President and High Priest William Marks for needed help. Within weeks both Joseph and Hyrum were murdered (see RLDS History of the Church 2:733–734). One month later, Samuel Smith was also murdered. By the date of the martyrdom (June 27, 1844), Brigham Young had four wives. The first two polygamous wives were still married to other men when he took them (polyandry). Young's first legal wives were, (1) Mary Ann Angell Young; (2) Mrs. William Seely (Lucy Ann Decker Seely Young); (3) Mrs. Henry Cobb (Augusta Adams Cobb Young, baptized into the church in 1832 by Samuel Smith); And (4) Harriet Elizabeth Cook Campbell Young.[9] The latter three were taken secretly, before Joseph's murder.

Young's actions and those following him is one main reason why official Church websites and publications accuse the Prophet Joseph Smith of the very things Young was guilty of, though in subtle form. He is accused of polyandry, along with polygamy and perhaps adultery and pedophilia (Fanny Alger). Being "justied" is the word Brigham Young used (out of context) in the first verse of his recontructed work known as D&C 132.

David and Solomon were **not justified** in this practice by God anywhere in scripture! In Jacob 2:23 we read, "This people [the Nephites and the Saints in early Church history] begin to wax in iniquity; they understand not the scriptures, for they seek to **excuse** themselves in committing whoredoms, because of the things which were written concerning David, and Solomon his son."

Emma & Lucy Mack Smith Statements on Joseph & Polygamy

The women of early Mormondom (and the children) were affected most negatively by polygamy. Their voices need to be heard. Two knowledgeable and trustworthy women regarding the events at Nauvoo include Emma Smith, wife of the Prophet Joseph, and his mother Lucy Mack Smith. Both paid a dear price for their devotion to the Prophet Joseph and their unwavering knowledge that he was innocent of the stain of polygamy. Brigham referred to the widow Emma as the world's biggest liar in a General Conference address in Utah. He said Joseph would have to go get her in hell (see p. 45). Mary Fielding Smith, on the other hand, former wife of Hyrum Smith and mother of Joseph F. Smith, polygamist and sixth president of the church, is praised for following Brigham west. Only ten weeks after Hyrum's murder she turned on the anti-polygamy efforts of her husband, becoming the fourth polygamous wife of Heber C. Kimball. She died seven years later.[10] Hyrum fought polygamy right up until his murder, speaking out against the practice in his last General Conference at Nauvoo.

Emma Smith: An Elect Lady and President of the Female Relief Socity

Emma was a valiant, intelligent leader, dedicated and true to her husband. She was interviewed by a number of people who came to Nauvoo following the murder of her husband. A small collection of statements by her in these interviews is included hereafter (see also endnote 3). In answer to the question of when did Emma first see the so-called "revelation" on polygamy, the one falsely attributed to her husband, she said, "Right here in Nauvoo in the year 1853, published in…a paper called The Seer, by Orson Pratt of the Utah Church" (J.S. Chrestensen interview).

In another interview, Emma added, "There was no revelation on either polygamy, or spiritual wives." The spiritual wives system, according to her husband, "was contrary to the will of heaven...He had no other wife but me." When Joseph asked Emma if she had heard rumors about him and polygamy, Emma said that Joseph told her that, "they were without foundation; that there was no such doctrine, and never should be with his knowledge, or consent. I know that he had no other wife or wives than myself, in any sense, either spiritual or otherwise" (Joseph Smith III interview of his mother).

In answer to a question about whether Brigham would lead the church after Joseph's death, Emma responded, "I would pity the people that should follow Brigham as a leader." Then, in answer to another question as to why Young's followers should be pitied, Emma said that Joseph answered, saying, "Because he would lead them to hell." Twelve others in Nauvoo said Joseph repeated this opinion of Brigham on other occasions. In her last physical meeting with Brigham Young, Emma told him, "You know too that Joseph in my presence told you [Brigham] that you had been teaching such things [spiritual wifery] while he was alive, and that he commanded you in the name of the LORD, to teach them no more, or judgments would overtake you" (Mark Forscutt interview. Forscutt was a secretary to Brigham Young in Utah, until Brigham insisted that he take a plural wife. Forscutt refused and was forced to escape from Utah to save his life).

Three months before her husband was murdered, President Emma Smith of the female Relief Society of the church at Nauvoo spoke out. Emma stated that the spiritual wives system introduced at Nauvoo by Bennett and others was dealing, "**a death blow at the hal'owed marriage covenant**...Resolved unanimously, That while we render credence to the doctrines of Paul that neither the man is without the woman neither is the woman without the man in the LORD, yet we raise our voices and hands against John C. Bennett's "spiritual wife system" as a scheme of profligates to seduce women...wherefore, while the marriage bed, undefiled is honorable, let polygamy, bigamy, fornication, adultery, and prostitution, be frowned out of the hearts of honest men to drop in the gulf of fallen nature" (public speech by Emma, The Voice of Innocence, Mar. 20, 1844).

Lucy Mack Smith: Matriarch of the Smith Family

In 1845, Lucy Mack Smith dreamed that her son William was in trouble. He had been speaking out on the secret ativities of Brigham Young, Heber C. Kimball and others of the Twelve and their polygamy. Lucy said she heard a voice telling her to "awake, awake, for thy only son that thou hast living, they for his life have laid a snare...**I saw William in a room full of armed men and he having no weapons**. They have crushed him down, if it had not been for the power of God; and many of the family would have been cut off, the LORD have softened their hearts. **Two** amongst them **had blacker hearts** than the rest...Brigham Young and Kimball know it is so, and dare not deny it...Thy son William he shall have power over the churches, he is father in Israel over the Patriarchs..." (Dean C. Jessee, ed., The John Taylor Nauvoo Journal, Jan. to Sept. 1845, BYU Studies, no. 3, pps. 63-64).

In that same year, Apostle William Smith was in fact brought before an intimidating group of church leaders (Brigham and many of the Twelve) and others, all brought together on the third floor of the Masonic Lodge to confront him. He stated that to his surprize, "some fifty or sixty policemen all armed with their Bowie knives, pistols, and hickory clubs" had gathered there. It was a warning to him of the path he was then pursuing (see statement #2, William Smith's Proclamation to the Saints, pages 130-33).

A year later, Lucy wrote a letter to Brigham Young and his representatives in 1846, stating that she was enduring much because her children were a higher priority than Brigham Young and the Twelve. Both Lucy and Emma Smith were removed from their homes, and their former support from the church was withheld from them, all because of this priority. Lucy stated, "the last thing that Brigham said to me was, I should have a home and be provided for, in all my wants...but you restrict my conscience, put limits to my affections [for her son William], **threaten me with poverty**, if I do not drive my children from my door because [of] the recent insult and abuse, that has been heaped upon them without measure, but I grieve for them, I am old...Yet I must not complain...although my children have been the Fathers and Founders of the Church, and spent their all in its service...I am called upon to banish from my home the few of my family who are left as my only solace, as you so proudly and wickedly ask me to do, **or my support shall be withheld from me**...You would have me forsake my children in order that you may give me a living...a mother has to forfeit all nature's ties, to cut asunder the cords of affection that bind her to her children, **or she shall not have a subsistence**...Give me a deed to a house and lot and advance the Quarterly sum [originally agreed upon]...I have no means, no food but coarse corn meal and I am old and feeble in health...Let this be a sufficient rebuke from your Mother in Israel" (Ronald Romig, Lucy's Nauvoo, John Whitmer Books, pps. 71-2).

Two months later in May of 1846, Lucy sent a letter to James Strang, stating, "I...have been disfranchised from the church by the Twelve, and much abused by their infatuated followers. Time would fail me to mention all of the

The Cochranite movement *justified* fornication and adultery *within religious rites*. Some of the first Cochranite converts were baptized by missionaries Orson Hyde and Samuel H. Smith (Joseph's brother) in **1832**. Coming to Kirtland Ohio, they brought some Cochranite traditions with them into Mormonism. Satan used this age-old mix of religion with the lusts of the flesh to corrupt the church.

Brigham Young served at least two missions to the Boston - Saco area. He was given permission by the Nauvoo Stake High Council to travel there alone. Two church conferences were held in Saco Maine, home of the Cochranites, between 1834-36. In these conferences, nine of the Apostles were exposed to the practice. The LORD warned Joseph and the Saints that Satan wanted to destroy them in an early message in **1831** in D&C 38. It addressed "a *mystery*, a **thing** which is had in **secret chambers**." That "**thing**" was "*spiritual wivery*." Six scriptures were given the Saints between **1830** and **1833** tied to God's higher law of monogamy. They were D&C 19:25; 38:13-14 & 28; 42:22-23; 49:15-16; 63:12-16 *and* verse 4 of the original D&C 101. This Section was known as "**the Article on Marriage**."

> "Inasmuch as this Church of Christ has been **reproached** with the crime of **fornication**, and **polygamy**: we declare that we believe that one man should have **one wife**" (D&C 101:4).

Two years later in 1837, in another effort to stop the Cochranite influence from gaining further ground into the church, the Seventies Quorums at Kirtland published their own statement against *spiritual wifery* among the Saints. Their resolution asserted, "That we have no fellowship whatever with any elder belonging to the quorums of the Seventies who is **guilty of polygamy**" (Messenger and Advocate 3: 511, May, 1837). Forty years later in 1876, President Brigham Young removed Section 101 from the D&C (without a church vote), the same year he replaced it with pro-polygamy Section 132, a supposed revelation given to Joseph Smith on July 12th of 1843. For more on the Cochranite influences, see *Joseph Smith Fought Polygamy*, https://restorationbookstore.org/jsfp-index.htm

English Incubation Period

Polygamy in Mormonism appears to have had additional roots in the English missions of Brigham Young, Heber C. Kimball, Willard Richards, William Clayton, and others between 1839-41. These men would become senior members of the secret chamber later in their return to Nauvoo. Young and some of the other members of the Twelve had already been exposed to spiritual wifery in the Boston and Saco areas. They were now away from their wives and Joseph and Hyrum for an extended period. They were also held in high esteem by most of those whom they were teaching. The conditions were ripe for experimentation with spiritual wifery by at least Young, Kimball, and Clayton. They were married men. Young's cousin, Willard Richards found his first wife while serving his mission there.

Europe was fertile ground for both polygamy and Freemasonry in the early 1800's. Polygamy was an especially popular subject of discussion in religious and university circles in Germany, England, and the U.S. at this time. Polygamy became an acceptable practice among some small groups in these countries. A number of books published in England reveal that it was a popular subject of discussion for some time prior to the arrival of the Apostles, first in 1837, and then in force between **1839-45**. Note the books below. The last one was sold in church offices in Liverpool.

1. Johannes Lyser, *Polygamia Triumphtrix* (Europe: 1682)
2. T. T. Payen, *The Cases of Polygamy, Concubinage, Adultery, Divorce, etc., Seriously and Learnedly Discussed* (London: 1732)
3. Delany Patrick, *Reflections on Polygamy* (London: 1739)
4. John Towers, Polygamy Unscriptural (London: 1780)
5. James Cookson, *Thoughts on Polygamy Including Remarks on Theolyphtora and Its Scheme* (Winchester, England: J. Wilkes for the author, 1782)
6. William Hepworth Dixon, *Spiritual Wives*, 2 vols. (London, 1868)
7. English, LDS elder & author, Samuel Downes' reprint of an ancient Greek Manuscript, entitled, *The Testament of the Twelve Patriarchs, the Sons of Jacob* (1843).

Latter-day Saint Samuel Downes apparently showed the pro-polygamy book, *The Testament of the Twelve Patriarchs, the Sons of Jacob*, to a number of church leaders in England. It presented Jacob's plural marriage and concubines as godly, stressing *the unique* **patriarchal priesthood** of the ancient Patriarchs of the Old Testament. Some 100 copies of it were sold in the church's Millennial Star office in Liverpool England. A short review of it was published in The Millennial Star 4 (October 1843, 96). Reprinted by Downes (an "elder" in a local LDS Ward), the book was dedicated to a Patriarch in Manchester. Downes stated, "Having shewn it to many of **my brethren**, and it having met with their approbation, they are wishful to possess themselves of it also. I now at their solicitation for the church, and for mankind in general, **send it forth unto the world**" (his new "Preface" to The Testament of the Twelve Patriarchs).

In a meeting later in Uath where Brigham first introduced new Section 132 to the Saints in 1852 (and where Joseph's name was falsely attached to it), Apostle Orson Pratt gave a stirring sermon citing the ancient practices of the Patriarchs of the Old Testament as a primary reason for reinstituting the same practice in modern times among the Saints (Orson Pratt JD 1 [1854]: 53–66). Pratt would eventually take ten wives. Four of them were from the British Isles (Utah Genealogical Magazine 27 [1936]: 113–114). Pratt authored *The Seer* (by request of Brigham Young), believing that polygamy was the most efficient way for the Lord to raise up a righteous and numerous people (see Breck England, *The Life and Thought of Orson Pratt*, 175). Later in Utah, another influential book on polygamy would be promoted among the brethren of the Twelve. This one was printed on the Times and Seasons press.

Justified Experimentation

The experimentation with spiritual wifery by the some of the Twelve in England did not involve plural marriage, at least yet. It began in adultery and fornication. One Seventy serving in England with the Twelve observed curious behavior by Young with one woman there. He accused Young of adultery (endnote 12). In addition, numerous journal entries by William Clayton reveal his love for a mistress he had during his mission there. His wife and children are absent from this same journal. The entries involve references to foot washing in connection with intimacy which followed, a clear tie to Cochranite spiritual wifery.

In 1841 Heber C. Kimball brought his first polygamous wife back to Nauvoo with him from his English mission. This was two years before Joseph's supposed "revelation" on polygamy (1843). Like two of Brigham's early polygamous wives, she too was married to another man at the time. Her name was Sarah Peak Noon, apparently baptized just before boarding the boat to America. She had Heber's child in Nauvoo. Their child died at an early age, so too the those of Young and Clayton. They were taken like the child of David and Bathsheba in the Old Testament, the one conceived in adultery. The secrecy of Sarah Peaks pregnancy and marriage to Heber wasn't kept for long, however.

Thirty-five years later in Utah (1874) Young knew that these and other historical events might come forth to reveal the truth about Heber C. Kimball's additional wife in 1841. Young moved into action to protect the First Presidency and his long-time friend Heber. Young and Kimball were friends and Freemasons prior to their baptisms into the church. Heber was especially committed to the Masonic brotherhood, also called "the craft." At this point in time in Utah, Young was President, Heber was First Councilor, and Willard Richards was Second Councilor (with 109 wives between them). To protect Heber and the 1852 lying announcement that Section 132 was a revelation given Joseph on July 12 of 1843, Young appears to have put forth a new narrative in 1874. He spoke of a vision or revelation he had on polygamy while serving in England, and *for the first time* (35 years after it supposedly occurred). Some suspect this "revelation" (occurring sometime between 1839 and 1840) was cover for Heber's pregnant wife, brought to Nauvoo in 1841, and perhaps cover for William Clayton's journal entries which addressed his mistress, Sarah Crooks. *No specific date* was tied to Young's "revelation" and its actual content *was never revealed*. His 1874 statement read:

> "While we [Brigham & ten of the Twelve Apostles] were in England (in 1839 and 40) *I think*, the LORD manifested to me by vision and his Spirit, things that I did not then understand. I never opened my mouth to any one concerning them, until I returned to Nauvoo; **Joseph had never mentioned this; there had never been a thought of it in the Church that I ever knew anything about at that time**, but I had this for myself, and I kept it to myself. And when I returned home, and Joseph revealed those things to me [a lie] then I understood the reflections that were upon my mind while in England. But this (communication with Joseph on the subject) was not until after I had told him what I understood— this was in 1841" (Brigham Young, Deseret News, July 1, **1874**).

Young's new narrative opened up a large can of worms. Receiving a revelation for the whole church in place of Joseph went against God's word in D&C 28:2 and 43:3. In addition, the "revelation" went against Young's former 1852 justification for polygamy - that Joseph began plural marriage among the Saints via a July 12, 1843 "revelation." Young then put Section 132 into the Doctrine and Covenants in 1876, without a vote from the church.

Lies were thus used to support polygamy from the very beginning. Reports today suggest Young took his first plural wife in 1842 at Nauvoo, when he was 41 years old. She was 20 and remained married to her first husband (polyandry).

This precedes Joseph's "*supposed revelation*" by a year. At age 42 (1843) Young married 3 more women, including a 19-year-old and 15-year-old. He thus had four wives prior to Joseph's murder (2 remained married to previous husbands). In the latter part of 1844, **after** *the murders*, he added 10 more wives, 3 of whom were teenagers. One was 15-year old Clarissa Caroline. Two years **after** *the murders* in 1845, he added 21 more wives, 2 of them teenagers. And he added 20 more wives during a single month in 1846, 5 of them in a single day (Feb. 3), their ages being 55, 42, 41, 36, and 18. At age 45, Young married 1 additional wife. She was 16. Finally, in his 60's, Young married 5 more wives, 3 of whom were in their early 20's. All told, Brigham Young had taken 55 wives, 9 of whom were teenagers on their wedding day (5 were 15-17 years of age), and 20 of whom were in their 20's. He later divorced 10 of them.

In the *six months* following the murder of the three Smith brothers (from June to December of 1844), Brigham Young went from 4 wives to 14. Heber C Kimball went from 2 wives to 10. It was an explosion of spiritual wifery, Brigham's way. There were 56 new plural marriages in 1845 alone by church members. By 1846, the "spiritual wives" movement expanded 5-fold - to 255 plural wives (*Nauvoo Roots of Mormon Polygamy, 1841-46: A Preliminary Demographic Report*, p 32). The three men leading the secret chamber at Nauvoo ended up with **109** total wives as **the First Presidency** of the church in Utah. Young had 55 wives, Kimball had 43, and Richards had 11.

How could Young and others in the Twelve in England go against the clear teaching of Joseph Smith and Jacob 2 in the Book of Mormon and other scripture? The answer may involve two things; (1) Brigham Young taught that the apostles had a special priesthood, that of the **Patriarchal Order** of the ancient Patriarchs in the Old Testament, allowing them to have as many wives and concubines as they wanted. This priesthood involved a special **sealing doctrine** provided by Elijah (this false doctrine was borrowed from the book *The Peacemaker* printed at Nauvoo, see chap. 5). This new doctrine became part of the modified temple endowment Young put in place to promote polygamy after Joseph's murder. Young used this **special priesthood** as justification for polygamy later in 1852 when he wrote verse 1 of Section 132. The very first verse of this Section uses the word "*justified*" in connection with Joseph's *supposed* inquiry to the LORD about doing the works of Abraham, Isaac, Jacob, Moses, David, and Solomon, an inquiry, "touching the principle and doctrine of their having many wives and concubines" (D&C 132:1).

And (2) Young and others may have begun teaching that Joseph was a **fallen prophet**, partly because he didn't support Young's view on priesthood, and because Joseph **later** admitted that the Spirit was not with him *the last few days of his life* because he returned to Nauvoo after originally heading west to avoid trouble in Carthage. Young stated:

> "If Joseph . . . had followed the Spirit of revelation in him he never would have gone to Carthage . . . and never for one moment did he say that he had had **one particle of light in him** *after* he started back from Montrose to give himself up in Nauvoo. This he did through the persuasion of others . . . if Joseph had followed the revelations in him he would have followed the shepherd instead of the shepherd's following the sheep."

In his own manuscript diary of the Nauvoo Legion, Joseph said, "*contrary to the council of the Spirit* . . . I am now no more than another man." This was repeated in a School of the Prophets meeting later in Utah by Colonel Stephen Markham. Abraham O. Smoot, one of Nauvoo's police officers, stated years later that Joseph, "went as a lamb to the slaughter, in opposition to his better judgment, and the Spirit of God in his heart, at the time" (for all three statements, see Quinn, *Mormon Hierarchy*, Signature Books, p. 145). This loss of the Spirit was just *days* before his murder, not the years of secret polygamy that had taken place in Nauvoo after the Twelve return from England (1841 to 1844). Joseph's loss of the Spirit the last few days of his life was expanded to the last few years of his life, as a convenient **justification** for Young and others, those who took charge of the practice of this whoredom. It was Young who approved all sealings of multiple women to any one man at Nauvoo. Apostle William Smith was later chastised for not seeking Young's approval in his early plural marriages.

Moving Forward with Decisions

In the Encyclopedia of Mormonism we read one modern report about the mission of the Twelve in England. It stated that being separated from Joseph and Hyrum Smith, the Twelve had to make decisions on their own. One of them was making Willard Richards an apostle, a relatively new English convert. Another was beginning the practice of spiritual wifery, there. Willard was a cousin of Brigham Young. He, Brigham, and Heber were all related by blood or marriage. They would later become the First Presidency in Utah. The Encyclopedia of Mormonism states: "On April 14, 1840, in Preston, they ordained Willard Richards an apostle and sustained Brigham Young as "standing president" of their quorum." Joseph & Hyrum Smith weren't consulted for this ordination. In the June 1987 issue of the Ensign magazine, we read of a letter (most likely manufactured years later) said to be written by Brigham Young to Willard Richards (also in England at the time) in September of 1840. According to Ronald K. Esplin, "Although he [Brigham] *had several times written* [to Joseph Smith in the States] for direction, by early September [1840], some five months into his mission, President Young still had no answers. With a detailed report to the First Presidency in September, he [Brigham] asked again for counsel on a series of **pressing questions**. He also knew that he could not await a reply." There is no record of attempted contact with Joseph. Brigham said:

> "Our motto is **go ahead**. Go ahead - & ahead we are determined to go – till we have conquered every foe. So come life or come death we'll go ahead, but tell us **if we are going wrong** & we will right it" (*The Historian's Corner: The Willard Richards and Brigham Young 5 September 1840 Letter from England to Nauvoo*," BYU Studies, Spring 1978, p. 475).

Brigham later claimed that another pressing concern while in England was moving forward with spiritual wifery, and acting on the revelation he had been given. He may have viewed his special priesthood as an apostle as supportive of this move, as he held the priesthood of the ancient patriarchs of the Old Testament. Young stated that **because he had received no word from Joseph, he moved forward**, believing Joseph *and* God were **bound** to sustain him.

> "If I do not know the will of my Father, and what He requires of me in a certain transaction, if I ask Him to give me wisdom concerning any requirement in life, or in regard to my own course, or that of my friends, my family, my children, or those that I preside over, **and get no answer** from Him and then do the very best that my judgment will teach me, **He is bound to own and honor that transaction**, and He will do so to all intents and purposes" (JD 3:205, this reasoning is similar to that used with the "revelation" on blacks in the church receiving the priesthood in 1978, see Assumption 3, chap. 6).

God is **not** bound by the weak understanding and corrupt will of men. We are bound by His decrees. Young's claim of a "revelation" was used to deceive many into following him into the same practice. "Covered heads" (2 Ne. 27:5; Isa. 29:10) has prevailed since then. The humble and repentant who look to God in all things, can receive God's guidance – according to His will, but the LORD is never bound by our limited understanding, or our will. Our decisions too often manifest "the idols in our heart." Jeremiah's lament in chapter 23 applies to this "awful situation."

> "For both prophet and priest are **profane**; yea, in my house have I found their wickedness, saith the LORD...Mine heart within me is broken because of the prophets...**they commit adultery**, and walk in **lies**: they strengthen also the hands of evildoers...they are all of them unto me as Sodom, and the inhabitants thereof as Gomorrah...they speak **a vision of their own heart**, and **not** out of the mouth of the LORD... I have **not** sent these prophets...I have not spoken to them, yet they prophesied...I have heard what the prophets said, that prophesy **lies** in my name, saying, I have dreamed...they are prophets of the deceit *of their own heart*; Which think to cause my people to forget my name by their dreams...as their fathers have forgotten my name for **Baal**...Therefore, behold, I am against the prophets, saith the LORD...Behold, I am against them that prophesy **false dreams**, saith the LORD, and do tell them, **and cause my people to err by their lies**...yet I sent them not, nor commanded them...And I will bring an everlasting **reproach** upon you, and a perpetual shame...(Jer. 23, select verses 1-40).

The justification of special *patriarchal* priesthood and the rumor that Joseph was a fallen prophet were later used at Nauvoo to spread the practice among select church leaders. This occurred on their return from their English missions (1841). By 1844, the Law group, with their strong grievances against Joseph, were used by those in the secret chamber - to effectively spread rumors about Joseph's fallen status and his supposed secret practice of spiritual wifery. To the surprise of the apostles, however, the Law group was also spreading the news that **some of the Twelve were also practicing polygamy** and **polyandry** with Joseph. This truth was told in the first and only issue of *The Expositor.* The Law group and the apostles were both pushing their own agendas. Both used Joseph's name for justification, leading to his murder and the establishment of polygamy as official LDS church doctrine. The Lord told Joseph, "They draw near to me with their lips; but their hearts are far from me, they teach for doctrines the commandments of men, having a form of godliness, but they deny the power thereof." Joseph continued, "He again forbade me to join with any of them" (JS-History 1:19-20).

Chapter Three

The Secret Chamber

New Doctrine

This chapter addresses "the secret chamber" addressed by the LORD in a prophecy in D&C 38, the one that rose up at Nauvoo ten years later to destroy Joseph and the fullness of the gospel of Christ. This chapter is divided into three parts; *Part I* addresses why and how the false Brighamite narrative has come to dominate the world of the Latter-day Saints. *Part II* addresses the role of secrecy in Satan's destructive influences at Nauvoo. *Part III* addresses the secret chamber there and the murder of the Prophet Joseph and his brothers Hyrum and Samuel Smith.

Part I: Why the False Brighamite Narrative?

The false narrative of church leadership that Joseph was a polygamist has been promoted ever since Nauvoo. Why? The first reason may be to **keep "gain"** in place (power, money, the honors of men, D&C 121), in connection with avoiding concern over **the succession of power and authority** from Joseph Smith to Brigham Young, and then the Twelve today (chap. 4). The second reason may be **avoiding embarrassing truths** - of what really happened at Nauvoo. It was Brigham Young and the Twelve who were responsible for raising themselves up as leaders over the whole church (he was President over the Twelve at Nauvoo). They became like King Noah and his priests in the Book of Mormon, living in luxury off the people with their many wives (see Mosiah 11:1-8). They became "lights" for the people, replacing Christ the LORD. It is priestcraft.

> "He commandeth that there shall be no priestcrafts; for, behold, priestcrafts are that **men preach and set themselves up for a light unto the world,** that they may **get gain and praise of the world**; but they seek not the welfare of Zion" (2 Ne. 26:29).
>
> "Behold **I am the light which ye shall hold up—that which ye have seen me do**" (3 Ne. 18:24).

This **idolatry** continues today and is a significant **sin** in the church ("follow the Prophet," "we cannot and will not lead you astray"). Their **sitting in the chief seats** today goes against God's clear instruction in D&C 107. They were to be **traveling missionaries**, like Paul the Apostle, not administrators. God set up four **equal** priesthood quorums (the Quorum of the Twelve being one of them), so that power would not be abused by one body (the Twelve) or by one man (the corporation President - the church was incorporated in 1923). This takeover occurred after Joseph's murder (see chap. 6). No vote was offered church membership to approve this new leadership model.

The idolatry in trusting in men (uninspired leaders), rather than turning to God and His word (scripture and personal revelation) is the root cause of continuing ignorance by so many, and other resulting curses which the Brighamite Saints have inherited. Nephi and others have stated that **curses follow those who put their "trust in the arm of flesh"** (2 Ne. 4:34; 28:31; Jer. 17:5). God's word tells us that the truth will eventually be shouted from the rooftops (see Luke 12:3; D&C 1:3). That time is now. Generational curses have been upon us for four generations, and upon many good people - because of the **iniquities** of those leading us (scripture calls them "fathers, priests, and kings"), *and* because the Saints followed Brigham and eight of the Twelve blindly into this abomination, without consulting God (his word in scripture and his personal word to each of us in pure revelation). This idolatry remains. The curses can end (see Mosiah 13:13; Ex. 34:6-7; Deut. 5:8-10) as we are at the end of this fourth generation since the murder of Joseph, Hyrum, and Samuel Smith. The hope expressed in the 2018 LDS General Conference provides an open door for substantive change to occur, but only if we reexamine our messy history and embrace truth. God has it. He is truth. He said, **I am the way, the truth, and the life**: no man cometh unto the Father, but by me" (John 14:6).

Academics, researchers, and regular Saints wishing to uphold leadership are expected to conform to the faulty historical narrative of Brigham Young and the version of history he and later church leaders have given us. Support for this false narrative is presented us in papers, books, speeches, and websites. Embracing truth, however, requires us to consult other sources. It is like listening to CNN versus FOX news. Both claim to be sincere and truthful, yet the results are polar opposites of one another. Embrcing truth can be messy. One must have courage. It requires a willingness to embrace uncomfortable things and **fear** (honor, love, and respect) God more than men. Doing so can lead to a needed healing among us, and greater unity of all those in Joseph's "Restoration" movement (the Brighamites, the Josephites, the Hedrickites, and others), if there is humility, repentance, and a focus upon God for light, not men. The result will be a dramatic change in our relationship with the living God and with each other, as we seek to experience the "mighty change of heart" that only God can give us. With new hearts, peace can then truly exist among us, and we will be set free by God's truth, embracing His doctrine, His gospel, and thus become part of His church. It is the one seen in vision by Joseph the Prophet and by John the Revelator, as symbolized on the exterior of the Nauvoo Temple. It is the Millennial church of the Bride or Lamb – the church of the Firstborn.

Many good people, because of love for the LDS church and respect for its leaders have not questioned Brigham Young and what happened at Nauvoo. Elder Nelson's recent charge to love God first, and then each other, has opened the door to seek God's **truth** first. It is an essential first step in removing our idolatry (trusting men more than God). It was the idolatry of early converts that looked to Young and the Twelve for guidance rather than God. This idolatry led them to follow Young and eight of the Twelve west and into their polygamy. Those who rejected Brigham Young and his new order of things stayed behind or went elsewhere. They represented one half of all the Saints. They too have a history. It is very different than the Brighamite narrative, but involves the same historic events.

Today, official LDS church websites put forth the false narrative (**lies**) that the Prophet Joseph Smith had many wives, and took them behind Emma's back (**deception**). They say some of his wives were married at the time to other men (polyandry). In addition, these sites claim that one of Joseph's earliest wives was Fanny Alger, taken at age 15, in either adultery or polygamy with a youth (pedophilia). Contrasting these statements, Joseph and the Smith family proclaim Joseph's innocence. Joseph brought others to church courts for their polygamy right up until his murder. And as a sign from God to us, the Prophet Joseph exhibited many gifts and fruits of the Spirit (speaking of His servants, God said, "by their fruits ye shall know them," D&C 5:2, 93:36, 88:11; Mat. 7:16). Joseph Smith was not a liar, a cheat, an adulterer, a polygamist, a polyandrist, nor a pedophile. To embrace this horrible false narrative requires the beloved Prophet of the Restoration to be thrown under the bus by those who have the most to gain from it.

The Prophet Joseph brought forth the Book of Mormon, which he said was "the most correct book," the "keystone of our religion" (Joseph Smith, HC 4:461). It is decidely **anti**-polygamy. It also states that the primary purpose behind men gathering together in secret combinations is to get "gain" (1 Ne. 22:23). Cain murdered his brother Abel to get gain (see Moses 5:29-31). Lamech murdered his great grandfather for the sake of a blood oath in a secret combination (Moses 5: 51). The unmodified history kept by those following Joseph reveals that Brigham Young and select leaders among the Twelve at Nauvoo put "spiritual wifery" in place secretly in the early 1840's. He and those following him were much like King Noah and his priests (see Mosiah 11:1-8). The gain for these men included more than sexual pleasures. Brigham took all power over the church in crafty ways (chap. 4). Two weeks after Joseph's murder the Twelve increased tithing upon the Saints exempting themselves from paying it. He and the Twelve lived well in Utah. Brigham had two mansions with 55 wives. Besides many wives, money, and power, they received the honors of men.

Perks today include corporate salaries, book deals, and being treated like a celebrity. Some are good people. Others are wolves in sheep's clothing. The Savior and John the Baptist were killed by those leading the ancient church. Joseph and his two brothers were too. Paul the Apostle is a much better model. He was a vailant minister of and for Christ. He gloried in his trials for the LORD. He was a traveling missionary, the primary role of one of Twelve, as laid out by the LORD in D&C 107. Paul did not sit in the chief seats like Noah and his priests. Paul willingly endured "stripes above measure, in prisons more frequent, in deaths oft" for the LORD Jesus Christ (see 2 Cor. 11:23-31). He preached repentance and faith on the LORD Jesus! Like King Benjamin, Paul's desire – because of love for God and his fellow man - was not to obtain the things of the world, but to brings souls to the living God.

Mantras "like follow the Prophet" and "we cannot and will not lead us astray" help prop up the current idolatry. They are part of the inherited, idolatrous, false traditions, tied to a false history that leaders don't sin and can't lead people astray. **All men sin and need repentance**. So says God in scripture. The prophets of scripture preach repentance and faith on the LORD. God corrected the Prophet Joseph Smith on multiple occasions (see D&C 3:6-11; 5:21-22; 35:17-18; 64:5; 93:47). **No mortal is infallible**. The atonement of Christ is for all, and so is pure revelation, if we will turn to God and seek it. We should be praying about everything that is taught us – to avoid **deception**.

Some of leaders know full well that Brigham Young is the weak link in a chain of **deception** that has driven knowledgeable Saints from the church. Many of his early teachings have been repudiated by later church leaders. This includes not only polygamy, but the Adam-god theory, Young's blood atonement doctrine, his denial of priesthood to blacks, and his tirades against the noble widow of the Prophet Joseph, Emma Smith. Young's polygamy, his controversial life, his statements and teachings represent another reason why a new and more "transparent" third LDS history rewrite was announced officially by the church in 2017. Leaders say it will be *more* transparent and honest, implying that thus far, the history hasn't been either. Truth is needed to counteract the exodus from the church and its record low growth rate (endnote 4). Utah also has very high rates for teen suicide, drug abuse, pornography addiction, and SRA (Satanic Ritual Abuse) among church members. Much of this is tied to the curses brought on by making polygamy an institutional practice under Brigham Young, and by enforcing lies to protect it ever since.

The primary solution for most of our problems is turning to Jesus Christ, our Redeemer. He continually invites us to "**repent** and **come unto me**." He is THE source of light. We need to trust Him, His word in scripture, and His *pure* revelation. After years of research, I have chosen to believe the words of His servant Joseph Smith and the words of Emma, Hyrum, Samuel, and William Smith among others, rather than what has been fed us by Brigham Young and those following him into polygamy. The Smith's fought polygamy. The fruits of Joseph's life and his actual behavior (not the lies) speak volumes. It all comes down to **who we trust and believe, who we put our faith in. This determines what we believe.** God's word repeatedly tells us **not to put our trust in "the arm of flesh"** - **men** (2 Ne. 4:34, 28:31; Psalm 118:8; Jer. 2:13). We can listen to them, but we should always test their words and actions against the scriptures and *pure* revelation, which we are entitled to receive, especially after receiving the Holy Ghost. Too few Saints have been made new, receiving the Holy Ghost. This is why God gave us D&C 38, the warning about **the secret chamber** (verses 13 and 28). He also gave the early Saints the opportunity to "**escape the power of the enemy**" by being *born again* (sanctified) in Him and then receiving His "endowment of power from on high" – and from Him, in the gift and power of the Holy Ghost. This gives us power to discern truth from error, along with true shepherds *from* false ones. Receiving this gift was tied to the future building of the house of the LORD at Kirtland and its dedication (see verses 31-42, chap. 5). When we ignore God's wisdom and His invitation to repent and come to Him, and reject Him by raising up weak men as our light instead, trouble and **curses** result. Humble true prophets in scripture always point us to God, not to themselves. And they always tells us what we need to do - **repent**.

Three Secret Combination Sources: *Restoring Plain & Precious Things*

God said that in the mouth of two or three witnesses, all truths are established (2 Cor. 13:1; D&C 6:28). There are three important books addressing *secret combinations* today; (1) **The Book of Mormon**, having **83** references to them, more than any other book of scripture; (2) **The Book of Moses** (chapters 1 & 5), coming from Joseph's re-translation of Genesis; And (3) **The Book of Enoch** is mentioned over 100 times in the Bible, removed from it in the 4th century (seven copies of it were found among the Dead Sea Scrolls, and have been found elsewhere as well). Some say this important book was removed by Rabbis because of its *hidden* knowledge (mysteries), as the unwashed masses were unworthy or unable to comprehend it. Yet they left another book of "mysteries" *in* the Bible, the book of Revelation. "Plain and precious things" in the Book of Enoch were removed to protect evil and designing men in power, as it revealed **the secret blood oaths** they made with Satan and each other (Moses 1:23, 41; 4:4; 1 Ne. 13:32; 2 Ne. 3:9, 9:21, 27-29; JST Luke 11:53; D&C 18:3). These **oaths**, combined with murder, greatly aided crafty men in "getting gain" (power, sex, money & the honors of men), all at the expense of the people. Equally important, they helped Satan and evil men establish **dominion** over the lives of others. This great evil then spread among the nations.

> "And the angels [the Watchers] . . . saw and lusted after them [beautiful women on the Earth], and said to one another: 'Come, let us choose us wives from among the children of men and beget us children.' And Semjâzâ, who was their leader, said unto them: 'I fear ye will not indeed agree to do this deed, and I alone shall have to pay the **penalty** of a great sin.' And they all answered him and said: 'Let us all **swear an oath**, and all **bind** ourselves by mutual imprecations not to abandon **this plan** but to do this thing.' Then **sware** they all together and **bound** themselves by mutual imprecations upon it. And they were in all *two hundred*; who descended [in the days] of Jared on the summit of Mount Hermon, and they called it Mount Hermon, because they had **sworn** and **bound** themselves by mutual imprecations upon it" (see Enoch 4:1-8).

The first Bible record we have of **secret combinations**, **blood oaths**, *polygamy*, and perhaps *homosexuality*, is seen early on with Cain and his posterity in Moses 5. They are inspired by Satan. We have this knowledge today, because God had Joseph *re-translate* the whole Bible *after* Joseph finished bringing forth the Book of Mormon. Both books **restore many "plain and precious things" removed from the Bible**. Both, along with the book of Enoch address how evil and designing men protect one another and their primary source of power – the **secret blood oaths** given them of

Satan. All three books were created for our day, when this evil would rise up in strength. Note the words of the first chapter of Enoch:

> "The words of the blessing of Enoch, wherewith he blessed the elect [and] righteous, who will be living **in <u>the day of tribulation</u>**, when **<u>all the wicked</u>** [and godless] **<u>are to be removed</u>**. And he took up his parable and said - Enoch a righteous man, **whose eyes were opened by God**, saw the vision of the Holy One in the heavens, [which] the angels showed me, and from them I heard everything, and from them I understood as I saw, **but not for this generation, but for <u>a remote one</u>** [our day] **<u>which is for to come</u>**" (1 Enoch 1:1-2).

The Evil One was a *liar* and *deceiver* from the beginning. He wants us ignorant (through *lies* and *deception*), and thus easily controlled. Knowledge for the illuminated elite and ignorance for the masses provides them power. In Genesis (and with more clarity in Moses 5), Satan put Cain under an **oath** with him that he might obtain *all* that his brother Abel had. The pattern of making an **oath** - and with **God's name**, and to **do evil** (or good) is a principle of **power and dominion**, understood by good men *and* evil men in antiquity. Their **oaths were sealed by God's name**, as He is the great Lawgiver. He must keep and honor His own law – without change - or He would cease to be God (Morm. 9:19). By placing someone under an **oath** and **sealing** it in or by **God's name**, a covenant relationship of **power** and **dominion** is *legally* created, one that is bound by **God's law** and maintained in His **courtroom** on high. There Satan is the accuser and Christ is our advocate with the Father, the Great Judge (D&C 29:5, 45:3-4; Mor. 7:28; Rom. 8:34).

Knowledge of these things was had among evil ones like Lucifer (a fallen angel), "the Watchers" (200 fallen angels), and "the Gadianton robbers" and others in the Book of Mormon. They were given this knowledge **by Satan directly**. Evil men today have an advantage, in that they have an understanding of this portion of God's **law**, His **heavenly court system**, and the **power** behind **God's name as a covenant seal**. Again, this knowledge was given to wicked leaders by Satan. It is knowledge lost among most of the religions of men today, those corrupted by Satan and men who use these oaths today. Most are kept ignorant of them. God in His great wisdom and mercy saw our "awful situation" today and decreed from His courtroom on high that all secret combinations will be destroyed (Ether 8:22).

Power & Control via Fear

Satan placed Cain under a **secret blood oath** with him – and by the **name of God**. Fear of **the penalty** tied to this **oath** was a motivating force, making use of **fear, control**, and **coercion** – to shape behavior and enforce his will.

> "And it came to pass that Cain took one of his brothers' daughters to wife, and they loved Satan more than God. And Satan said unto Cain: **Swear unto me by thy throat**, and *if thou tell it thou shalt die*; and **swear** thy brethren **by their heads**, and by the living God, that they tell it not; for if they tell it, **they shall surely die**...And I will deliver thy brother Abel into thine hands. And Satan **sware** unto Cain that he would do according to his commands. And all these things were done in **secret**. And Cain said: Truly I am **Mahan**, the master of this **great secret**, that I may **may murder and get gain**. Wherefore Cain was called **Master Mahan**, and he gloried in his wickedness...And Cain was **shut out** from the presence of the Lord...For, from the days of Cain, there was a **secret combination**, and their works were in the **dark**, and they **knew** *every man his brother*...For [they] entered into a covenant with Satan, after the manner of Cain, wherein he [Lamech and others] became **Master Mahan**, master of that great **secret** which was administered unto Cain by Satan... And thus the works of **darkness** began to prevail among all the sons of men (Moses 5:29-31, 41, 51, 55; Ether 8:15-16; Hel. 6:16-41).

The "**penalties**" within Freemasonry *and* Mormonism (in the LDS temple endowment until 1990, see chap. 5) consisted of three types of **death by mutilation**. The **penalties** were promised results upon those **who didn't keep the oath** *or* **if one revealed the secrets** tied to them **to others**. In this way Satan was able to **control** others by **fear** and **coercion**, and thus obtain **<u>legal</u> dominion over them** under God's own law, as he [Cain and all who enter into such **oaths**] do so freely and within a **<u>legally binding</u> relationship with Satan**.

In this covenant relationship there is also an **<u>exchange of life</u>** (Lev. 17:11, see pps. 178-79, 182-83). God creates all **life** and then provides **eternal life** to those who keep "the everlasting covenant" made with Him *in love*. It is a covenant **to do <u>His will</u>** (see Mosiah 5:5, 8; JST Gen. 9:12). *Secret blood*-**oaths** with Satan and other men are just the opposite. They result in *spiritual* **death** (*separation* from God) and even *physical* **murder**, by way of fear and coercion, not love. God wants our hearts, whereas Satan and evil men want "gain," demanding also obedience and our *lives* if we do not adhere to their ways. The Aztecs took the beating heart from live victims upon their temples. Some who take life, consume the blood of their victims. Today there is pedophilia, SRA, and many *abortions* – a form of modern child sacrifice, like that for Baal anciently. It combined the murder of innocent children with sexual sin and idolatry; three great evils increasing today. Evil ones use murder and sacrifice of the innocent to provide them power and longevity. It is growing stronger, as witnessed in the January 2010 celebration in New York City (with lit up buildings) tied to the passage of new State laws allowing for late-term abortions, right up to birth. In the Book of Enoch we read about "the Watchers" some 200 rebellious angels who caused great trouble on the earth. One was "the chief" of the **secret blood-oath**. In it he taught "the smitings of the **embryo in the womb**, **that it may pass away**" (Enoch 69:12-13).

Through our LORD"s blood atonement (Lev. 17:11 & with our repentance), we can be made clean, wearing white rather than filthy garments in God's courtroom. We can claim victory over Satan, placing our right foot on his neck, and then raise the sword of truth high into the air. Satan and evil men want **dominion** – the **power** to do as they please and at our expense. Fear, control, and murder are all part of their kingdom of evil. Such have the "*mark, sign, token, omen*" or "**oath**" of Cain upon them (see Strong's Concordance #226, from the Hebrew word "avah" – "*oth*"). The "*Cain principle*" or "mark of Cain" is the mixing of our own **will** with the things of God, creating the false, corrupt religions of men dominating today. Able sought the LORD's will, doing his sacrifice God's way. It was thus accepted.

In the Reed Smoot hearings before Congress, one Latter-day Saint revealed what the fear-based penalties of Mormonism were, those made via **secret blood oaths** in temples. They are nearly exactly the same as those found in Freemasonry, and are administered for the same reasons, (1) not keeping one's **oath**, or (2) revealing the **secret oath and its penalties** to others. The administration of the penalty was part of Brigham Young's "Blood Atonement" doctrine. In 1904, the Chicago Daily Herald (see "Church Bloody Oath," Dec. 23, 1904) reported that under **penalty of mutilation**, Mormons made *secret bloody* **oaths** in their endowment houses or temples. Testifying under *oath* there, J.H. Wallis said the resulting penalty was **physical mutilation** in three ways; [1] "That the throat be cut from ear to ear and the tongue be torn off; [2] That the breast be cut asunder and the heart and entrails be torn from the body; And [3] That the body be cut asunder at the middle and the bowels be cut out." He added, "That if demanded [and by covenant] we will *give all we possess* to the support of **the church**." For specific Masonic oaths, signs, grips, and their mutilation penalties, for fear, control, vengeance, and murder, see http://www.ephesians5-11.org/handshakes.htm

Satan has always worked by fear and control that he might have **dominion** over us. God works by love and invitation. It is by these and other "fruits" that we can know if something or someone (including true or false prophets) are of God, as God's love casts out all fear (1 John 4:18). Two excellent sources to gain understanding of the Watchers in the Book of Enoch, the blood oaths of Satan, and the power in God's name in oath-making, is Rob Kay's three-part blog post series at, http://mormonyeshiva.blogspot.com See Part I - Dec. 30, 2018, Part II - Jan. 6, and Part III - Jan. 9, 2019. For God's courtroom and how we can participate in it, see Ian Clayton, *Realms of the Kingdom*, chap. 9.

Joseph's stance against the practice of spiritual wifery at Nauvoo by members of the Twelve cost him his life along with his two brothers Hyrum and Samuel. They were murdered by those who made similar **oaths** for their gain. In D&C 123, Joseph said *we should* – "waste and wear out our lives in bringing to light **all the hidden things in darkness**, where we know them." He said our fathers "have inherited **lies**," and that there is great *corruption* and *iniquity* among us. It is an "iron yoke" and a "strong band." He added that these things are had among "**all** sects, parties, and denominations" (see 2 Ne. 28:11; Morm. 8:36). Even the elect "are *blinded* by the *subtle craftiness* [Masonry is called "the Craft) of men, whereby they **lie** in wait to **deceive**, and who are only kept from the truth, because they know not where find it" (D&C 123:7-17; 76:75; Psalm 83:1-4, see p. 62).

The Utah Saints today have only 16 pages of Joseph's inspired *re-translation* of **the entire Bible** in their scriptures. The few we have *were selected for us* by leaders, and all by *permission* from the RLDS Church. The Prophet Joseph Smith purposely placed *the final 1844 manuscript* of this **re-translation** in the hands of his wife Emma - **<u>for safe-keeping</u>, not** to Brigham Young, another church leader, or an historian. Young tried to obtain the re-translation from Emma on a number of occasions. She refused, also refusing to follow him west. She and the Smith children (and many other Saints in Nauvoo) later joined the RLDS Church, believing it was closer to Joseph's teachings than Brigham's "new order of things." In 1878, Orson Pratt, as official Church Historian, one of the Twelve, and a polygamist, put together a new LDS Book of Moses from a *copyrighted* and *printed* RLDS JST Bible as his **primary source**. Pratt knew that the older LDS 1851 version of this book was incomplete, created from two early periodicals only, *The Evening and the*

Morning Star and *The Times and Seasons.* Robert Matthews (Dean of BYU's Dept. of Religion), stated, "With few exceptions, the [later LDS] 1878 *printing* of the Pearl of Great Price was **remarkably close** to the 1867 [RLDS] printed Inspired Version [of the Bible], and both of them generally, but not exactly, resemble the text of the **later** [copyrighted] **manuscript** of the **new translation** . . . " Matthews added, "Elder Pratt used the [*copyrighted* and] **printed 1867 Inspired Version as his basic source** for the Moses material when he prepared the [later LDS] 1878 edition of the Pearl of Great Price." Neither Pratt then, nor the LDS Church today, acknowledges the *copyrighted* RLDS material Pratt borrowed from, as his *primary source*! Pratt made *changes* too. One of these is verse 39 of Moses chapter 5 below, *the* chapter tied to *secret combinations* and their *secret blood oaths.* It shows he changed the word "**oath**" to "**iniquities**." Was this ordered by Brigham Young? All changes to God's words as given us by Joseph, are in **bold**.

Original 1867 RLDS JST Text "Behold, **you have** driven me out this day from the face of **men**, and from **your** face shall I be hid **also**; ... And it shall come to pass, **everyone** that **finds** me will slay me because of **my oath**," for these things are not hid from the LORD."

Modified 1878 LDS Book of Moses Text - Orson Pratt "Behold **thou hast** driven me out this day from the face of **the Lord**, and from **thy** face shall I be hid; ... and it shall come to pass, **that he** that **findeth** me will slay me, because of mine **iniquities**, for these things are not hid from the LORD" (the "iniquity" *was* "the oath" with Satan).

One researcher believes Joseph offered up his life freely to God at Nauvoo for the *iniquities* of the Saints, hoping the LORD would have mercy on them. The secret combination God prophesied of in D&C 38 took real root ten years later in Nauvoo in the early 1840's. It was put in place so that polygamy might expand among the men of the secret chamber (eight of the twelve apostles), that they might have power and money in addition to many wives. Brigham Young made polygamy the official doctrine of the church later in Utah, and one required for exaltation. He directed many men to take additional wives, including my great grandfather on my father's side. Many had no desire for it and wouldn't do it, men like Young's secretary and historian Mark Forscutt, and Navuoo Temple architect William Weeks. Both men and their families escaped Utah Territory and Young's control. They feared for their lives. Out of honor for the position of church president (and idolatry), too many acquiesed to Young, including men like Bill Hickman, one of Young's enforcers or hit men. Many feared Pres. Young in Utah Territory as he had great power over his growing kingdom in the west. Fear of leaders, of loosing standing, or membership in the church, rather than **fearing God** (love, honor, and respect) remains a problem today. It is an effective tool keeping us under control. In scripture it is a part of idolatry, allowing others to reign over us rather then the great King who truly loves us. Again, God invites with love. Satan and those following him use fear, control, coercion, and revenge (see D&C 121:34-46).

By the end of the 19th century, the U.S. government finally removed the whoredom of polygamy from the Saints. Joseph and Emma's firstborn son Joseph Smith III saw the problem up close. He helped remove this curse from the Brighamite Saints via pressure from the Federal Government (see chap. 4). This helped to restore God's original marriage covenant among our ancestors. The marriage covenant between a husband and his wife has been greatly damaged by the passed down iniquities tied to polygamy. It has resulted in generational curses and dysfunction among us. Many men in the LDS church have an unspoken fantasy of extra wives obtained in the Milllennium and in heaven. This inherited lie is also held by many Muslim men, in the promise of a future harem of virgins in heaven. Satan has planted such lies in men's hearts. They continue to thwart the development of healthy marriage relationships today.

Joseph's brother, Apostle William Smith, was not murdered by the secret chamber. He was once part of it (and one of six at Nauvoo to call this secret combination "the secret chamber"). He was the only member of the original Smith family to embrace Brigham's notion of secret priesthood that allowed the Twelve and those they selected to have multiple wives. Those part of the secret chamber used their secret priesthood to take as many wives as they wanted (the so-called patriarchal priesthood of the Old Testament patriarchs). The early secret sexual practices of Cochranite spiritual wifery were made more palatable later on via Mormon marriage, but *with* mutliple wives. From 1841 on, this "new order of things" was put in place secretly, by Brigham and the Twelve, and then protected with the secret blood oaths and penalities borrowed from Freemasonry (see Moses 5:29-31). They became part of Young's modified version of Joseph's temple endowment (chap. 5), and were also used by Young's Danite-like enforcers, the Nauvoo Police, and other enforcers later in Utah.

Information Control

William Smith was aware of all the dirt and revealed it in his writings. Few consult them today. After the murder of his three brothers, William turned on the secret chamber, exposing much of the darkness he witnessed within it. He later wrote a number of letters to the Nauvoo Saints in 1845 (pages 131-37). Some were published in the Warsaw Signal, a newspaper that often ran anti-Mormon articles. He used other newspapers too. Excommunicated by Young because he was revealing too much, William had no other way to reach the Saints and inform them of what was actually going on at Nauvoo. William knew that Young had men in his inner circle that collectively controlled **all information** among the Saints, including; (1) the official history of the church, (2) Joseph Smith's private history (journals and biography), (3) the civil records, and (4) offiical church publications like the Times and Seasons. Joseph's personal and church records were gathered and taken to Utah, then modified to protect the pro-polygamy narrative.

The editors were Willard Richards, William Clayton, and John Taylor. Others were added later on. By modifying these early records, and controlling other information given the Saints (in local newspapers), Young had power to make it appear as though the Prophet Joseph instituted polygamy secretly among the Saints. Those in the secret chamber believed that if the Prophet Joseph could be seen as the one who implemented polygamy among the Saints, then the Twelve would be **justified** in their secret practice of it later on. Young and Kimball officially let this "cat of the bag" in Utah from 1852 to 1874. Apostle Willard Richards (#3 in the secret chamber) was both **the church historian** and **the clerk for the Nauvoo Municipal Court** following his return to Nauvoo. He and John Taylor convinced Joseph *to destroy the Expositor press, putting Joseph and Hyrum in jail.* Richards *was there when both men were murdered.* Richards also did **the autopsy** on the bodies afterwards, and he did **the report** of his findings too. In addition, Richards also wrote up **the official church report on the murders** of Joseph and Hyrum. John Taylor (#4 in the secret chamber) **edited and printed both of the Nauvoo newspapers**; the *Nauvoo Neighbor* (a more political paper, which he owned), and the *Times and Seasons* (the official religious newspaper of the church). Thus those in the Nauvoo secret chamber controlled nearly all the information fed to the Nauvoo Saints, and all under Brigham Young's direction.

William Clayton was a **private secretary to Joseph Smith**, recording nearly all of his daily activities. He was also a **recorder for the Nauvoo Masonic Lodge** in 1843, after John Bennett was removed from this lodge duties. Clayton was a **useful spy** for the secret chamber. Brigham Young was the mastermind in control of it all. He was "master of the great secret." In the Book of Moses this is called "Mahan" meaning "destroyer" (see Moses 5:29-31). Collectively these and other men created a whole new history that covered their actions, a hisotry supporting polygamy. Charles Wesley Wandell (an assistant to Willard Richards) later revealed this editing. Similar secretive control and editing continued in the historians office in Utah with others like historian Mark Forscutt. He eventually rejected Young's "*new order of things*," joining the RLDS church. Historian Scott Faulring later helped to reveal much of this editing too. It is important to remember the LORD's warning to us today in 3 Nephi 30:2, where (1) "**lies**" and (2) "**deception**" are the first things listed in His description of our day, followed by (3) "**whoredoms**." See also the similar description in 3 Nephi 21:19, and in 16:10 where these and other descriptive terms - like "priestcraft," "secret abominations," and "murder" are tied to our rejection of "**the fulness**" of the gospel of Christ, in trade for **gain** - the things of the world.

Lies and Deceptions for the Saints

Secret combinations are put in place by Satan and evil men in high places - to **murder** and "**get gain**" (Moses 5:32; 1 Ne. 22:23; Ether 8:23; Mark 8:36; Acts 16:16,19; 1 Tim. 6:5-6; Prov. 1:19, 3:13-14, 15:27, 28:8; Isa. 33:15, 56:11; Dan. 11:39; Ezek. 22:12-13). They put forth an innocent public face, especially at the lower levels of their organizations, but at the higher levels the truth of their real intent emerges. This is addressed in detail in chapter 5.

Lying and **deceptio**n are favorite tools of *secret societies.* Our LORD has repeatedly tried to wake us up to various things, encouraging us to "**awake** and **arise** and go forth." Many scriptures have been sprinkled here and there, that when put together form a very troubling, completed puzzle. It reveals our "**awful situation**" - that, (1) *we are surrounded by* **secret combinations** (Ether 8:24) that #1 **lie** and #2 **deceive**, keeping us in *ignorance* for the sake of *their* **gain** (1 Ne. 22:23). And as a result, (2) we are in a second "**awful situation**," an *unsaved condition* (Mos. 2:40). We are bound down by "*awful chains*" and must "*awake, awake* from a *deep sleep*" (2 Ne. 1:13). And we must do so quickly, as the great last-days **harvest of souls** is right around the corner! Three times the warning states, "*the harvest is come* and **our souls are <u>not saved</u>**" (D&C 45:2, 56:16 & Jer. 17:11). God loves and encourages the "**wise** virgins" to be informed *and* **saved**, spiritually and physically. He is the Great Deliverer for those who turn to Him.

In the first *five* of the *seven* scriptures hereafter, the LORD addresses the sins among us as **LATTER-DAY SAINTS**, along with those of the world. Note that He lists "**lies**" *first*, followed by "**deception**" *second* - in all *five* lists! Other sins among us then follow, things like "**whoredoms**" (early polygamy). The order in God's listings is significant, given to help **wise** virgins "**awaken**" to our "*awful situation*" and the great cleansing that is coming soon. The LORD stated:

1. "And thus commandeth the Father that **I** should say unto **you**: At that day *when* the Gentiles shall sin against **my gospel**, and shall **reject** *the fullness of* **my gospel**, and shall be *lifted up* in the **pride** of their *hearts* above all nations, and above all the people of the whole earth, and shall be filled with all manner of **lyings**, and of **deceits**, and of *mischiefs,* and all manner of *hypocrisy,* and *murders,* and *priestcrafts,* and *whoredoms,* and of *secret abominations*; and if they shall do all those things, and shall **reject** *the fullness of* **my gospel**, behold, saith the Father, **I** will bring *the fullness of* **my gospel** *from among them*" (3 Nephi 16:10).

2. "And **I** will pluck up thy groves out of the midst of **thee**; so will **I** destroy *thy cities.* And it shall come to pass that all **lyings**, and **deceivings**, and *envyings,* and *strifes,* and *priestcrafts,* and *whoredoms*, shall be done away. For it shall come to pass, saith the Father, that at that day *whosoever will* **not repent** and **come unto my Beloved Son**, *them* will **I** cut off from among **my people**, O house of Israel" (3 Nephi 21:18-20).

3. "Hearken, O **ye Gentiles**, and *hear the words of* **Jesus Christ**, the Son of the living God, which he hath commanded **me** that **I** should speak concerning **you**, for, behold he commandeth me that **I** should write, saying: **Turn**, *all ye Gentiles, from your wicked ways*; and **repent** of *your evil doings*, of *your* **lyings** and **deceivings**, and of *your whoredoms,* and of *your secret abominations,* and *your idolatries,* and of *your murders,* and your *priestcrafts,* and *your envyings,* and *your strifes,* and from all *your wickedness* and *abominations* [changing my doctrine], and **come unto me**, and be baptized in **my name**, that **ye** may receive *a remission of your sins* [by being born again in me] and be filled with **the Holy Ghost** [the endowment of power from on high], that ye may be numbered with **my people** who are of *the house of Israel*" (3 Nephi 30:1-2).

4. "And thus, if the people of *this generation* harden **not** their hearts, **I** will work a *reformation* among *them*, and **I** will put down all **lyings**, and **deceivings**, and *priestcrafts,* and *envyings,* and *strifes,* and *idolatries,* and *sorceries,* and all manner of *iniquities*, and **I** will establish **my church**, like unto the church which was taught by **my disciples** in the days of old. And now if this generation *do* harden their hearts against **my word**, behold **I** will deliver them up unto Satan, for he reigneth and hath power at this time, for he hath got great hold upon the hearts of the people of *this generation*: and **not** *far from the iniquities of Sodom and Gomorrah*, do they come at this time: and behold the sword of justice hangeth over **their** heads, and if **they** persist in the hardness of their hearts, the time cometh that it must fall upon **them**" (1833 Book of Commandments, 4:5-6, *removed* and *replaced* with D&C 5:19).

5. While in Liberty Jail, the Prophet Joseph wrote the following to the Saints: "It is an *imperative duty* that **we** owe to God, to angels, with whom **we** shall be brought to stand, and also to ourselves, to our wives and children, who have been made to bow down with grief, sorrow, and care, under the most damning hand of *murder, tyranny,* and *oppression,* supported and urged on and upheld by the influence of that spirit which hath so strongly riveted **the creeds of the fathers**, who have **inherited lies,** upon the hearts of the children, and filled the world with *confusion*, and has been growing stronger and stronger, and is now *the very mainspring of all corruption*, and the whole earth groans under the weight of its *iniquity* [passed down *false teachings* and *traditions* from our "fathers, priests, and kings"]. It is an *iron yoke*, it is *a strong band*; they are the very *handcuffs*, and *chains*, and *shackles*, and *fetters* of hell. Therefore it is an *imperative duty* that **we** owe, not only to our own wives and children, but to the widows and fatherless, whose husbands and fathers have been *murdered* under its *iron* hand; Which dark and blackening deeds are enough to make hell itself shudder, and to stand aghast and pale, and the hands of the very devil to tremble and palsy. And also *it is an imperative duty* that we owe to all the rising generation, and to all the pure in heart—For there are many yet on the earth **among all sects, parties**, and **denominations**, **who are blinded by the subtle craftiness of men**, whereby they **lie** in wait to **deceive**, and who *are only* kept from **the truth** *because they know not where to find it*—Therefore, that **we** *should waste and wear out our lives in bringing to light all* **the hidden things of darkness**, *wherein we know them*; and they are truly manifest from heaven—These should then be attended to with great earnestness. *Let no man count them as small things*; for there is much which lieth in futurity, pertaining to the saints, *which depends upon these things.* You know, brethren, that a very large ship is benefited very much by a very small helm in the time of a storm, by being kept workways with the

wind and the waves. Therefore . . . let us cheerfully do all things that lie in our power; and then may we stand still, with the utmost assurance, to see the salvation of God, and for **his arm** *to be revealed*" (D&C 123:7-17).

6. "**He** [the LORD] that descended is the same also that ascended up far above all heavens, that **he** might fill all things. And **he** gave some, apostles; and some, prophets; and some, evangelists; and some, pastors and teachers [in scripture and a few sprinkled among us]; For the *perfecting* of the saints [the **wise** virgins], for the *work* of the ministry, for the *edifying* of the body of Christ: Till *we all* come in the *unity of the faith*, and *of the knowledge of* **the Son of God**, unto a *perfect man*, unto the measure of the stature of *the fullness* **of Christ**: That we henceforth be *no more* **children**, *tossed to and fro*, and *carried about with* **every wind of** [false] **doctrine**, by **the sleight of men**, and [their] cunning **craftiness**, whereby they **lie** in wait to **deceive**" (Ephesians 4:10-14).

In the final *seventh* scripture hereafter, our LORD has provided a **5**-*part* scripture instructing **us** on *how* to return to His holy presence (there are many of these scattered throughout God's holy word). The number 5 is a *covenant* number tied to *life*, *eternal life*, and **His** "**grace**" – symbolized in the **5** nails driven into His body for us. Each of these **5**-part scriptures address **5** *steps* to return to **Him**. D&C 93:1 may be the best known of these among the Latter-day Saints. Here is one more tied to **not** *being* **deceived** by *crafty men* among us, that we might be prepared for God's return.

7. "For **they** [1] *that are* **wise** [virgins – who "*repent* and *come unto me*"] and [2] have received **the truth** [Jesus Christ as their light *and* His words], and [3] have taken **the Holy Spirit** *for their guide* [been "born again" in Christ, receiving the gift and power of the Holy Ghost – "*the endowment of power from on high*" to guide them], and [4] have **not been deceived** [by the lies and deceptions of crafty secret combinations surrounding us] - verily I say unto you, [5] **they** shall **not** be *hewn down* and *cast into the fire*, but shall *abide* the day" (D&C 45:57) of God's return. See also *Moses 4:4*.

God said there are **tares** among the wheat, **wolves** in sheep's clothing. They are the **men in white** *deceiving* many, leading them into *darkness* (see 1 Ne. 8:5-8). Leaders of many Christian organizations today are part of Freemasonry and their *secret blood-oaths*. God saw the insidious control rising up in Joseph Smith's day, and Mormon and Moroni saw that it has come to dominate our day even more. Fortunately we have God's word in *the Book of Mormon*, *the JST Bible* (specifically *the Book of Moses*), and *the Book of Enoch*, all available to the **wise** virgins. I choose to believe God, the prophets in these special books, *and* the words of Joseph, Emma, Hyrum, and William Smith, rather than Brigham Young and those that followed him into polygamy. The most truthful early sources are from the Josephites, those choosing to stay behind at Nauvoo, as the "official" Brighamite history has been modified to **deceive** us, just like God said, while other *plain* and *precious* parts are hidden away or swept under the rug, all to promote the early pro-polygamy message, and to now promote an equally wicked and *idolatrous* message – that modern *false* prophets part of "the Great and abominanble church" are our *light* - in *priestcraft* – rather than God's precious **word** in scripture!

Fortunately, our powerful and just Judge, King, and Savior will *destroy* all secret works of darkness in the near future. Note His statements and promises below.

> "**I, the Lord, the king of heaven**, will be their **king**, and **I** will be a **light** unto them forever, *that hear my words*" (2 Ne. 10:14, see also 3 Ne. 18:24).
>
> "For the time soon cometh that the fulness of the wrath of **God** shall be poured out upon all the children of men; for he will **not** suffer that the wicked shall destroy the righteous . . . for thus saith **the prophet**, they shall be saved, even if it so be as by fire . . . all they who fight against Zion shall be *cut off* . . . all those who will **not hear that prophet** shall be *cut off* from among the people . . . And now I, Nephi, declare unto you, that **this prophet** of whom Moses spake was **the Holy One of Israel** . . . For the time speedily shall come that **all churches** which are [1] built up **to get gain**, and all those who [2] are built up to get power over the flesh, and those who [3] are built up to become popular in the eyes of the world, and those who [4] seek the lusts of the flesh and [5] the things of the world, and [6] to do all manner of iniquity; yea, in fine, [7] all those who belong to the kingdom of the devil are they who need fear, and tremble, and quake; they . . . must be brought low in the dust; they are those who must be **consumed as stubble**; and *this is according to the words of* **the prophet**" (2 Ne. 22, portions of 16-17, 19-21 & 23; see also 1 Ne. 22:13 & 2 Ne. 10:15).
>
> "*. . . they who are not for me* **are against me**, saith our God" (2 Ne. 10:16).

Russel M. Nelson is now the President of the Church. Note his words in the October 2014 General Conference. "Our sustaining of prophets is a personal commitment that we will do our utmost to uphold **their prophetic priorities**. *Our sustaining* is an **oath**-like indication that we recognize their calling as a prophet *to be legitimate* and **binding upon us**" (Russell M. Nelson, Sustaining the Prophets, Oct. 2014, General Conference Address).

When we sing the song, "*Follow the Prophet*," **the LORD Jesus** is the one we must *hear* and *obey* as "**The Prophet**." In 1 Nephi 22, **He** is listed there *seven times* with *this title*. Our covenant in "**the New and Everlasting Covenant**" (JST Gen. 9:21, Mosiah 5:5, 8, 18:10; 1 Ne. 22:20; 2 Ne. 1:13, 9:21, 10:24, 32:3, 6 & endnote 31) is with **Him – to do His will** as our **head** (Mosiah 5:8; Eph. 1:22, 4:15, 5:23), **not** any weak, vain man that is lifted up as a false light in priestcraft and idolatry before us (3 Ne. 26:29; 3 Ne. 18:24). We are not to be **bound** to such a man, but instead we are to be sealed to Christ the LORD as our **head** (Mosiah 5:15). He alone performed the atonement for us. He alone saves us. Crafty men **lie** and **deceive** for **gain**. As "The Prophet," Jesus said churches "**built up to get gain**" (see 1 Ne. 22:23, 28:3; 2 Ne. 26:20-23; Morm. 8:33; Book of Commandments, 4:5-6 1833; D&C 10:46-70) "**shall be as stubble**." His judgment is near, as Nephi stated that there "are save to **two churches** only," the one of the Lamb of God and the one of Satan (1 Ne. 14:10). The great and abominable church will be destroyed. Addressing our day, Nephi said those leading corrupt churches "**hide their counsels** from the Lord; and *their works shall be* **in the dark**" . . . "they have **all gone out of the way . . . their churches** have become **corrupted**" (2 Ne. 28:3-22). Mormon added, "**your churches, yea, even every one, have become polluted** . . . ye do love money . . . more than ye love the poor and the needy, the sick and the afflicted . . . ye hypocrites . . . why have **ye polluted** the holy church of God? Why are **ye ashamed** to take upon you **the name of Christ**?" (Morm. 8:36-38).

Part II: Secrecy – *The Start of Secret Chamber*

Secrecy can be dangerous. Nothing done in secret bears good fruit. Sin, infidelity, and spiritual wifery breed in it. Satan uses secrecy along with fear and force to oppose God's better way of love, openness, invitation, and free will. As stated earlier, 83 scriptures in the Book of Mormon are tied to "secret combinations." There are only four in the Doctrine and Covenants (D&C 38:13, 28, 42:64, 117:11 & 123:7-13), and two of them use the phrase "**secret chamber**." They reference the secret brotherhood that brought polygamy into the church, ending with the murder of Joseph, Hyrum, and Samuel Smith. Apostle William Smith was part of the secret chamber for a time. He is one of the first to describe those following Brigham Young at Nauvoo as "Brighamites." William was an imperfect man – like all men, but he has blesssed us with many important **truths**. The Brighamite church claims he is an unreliable source, one with mental problems. This is a typical discrediting tactic, used by those with something to hide. They diminish, attack, and discredit the opposition. Much of what William has to say in chapter 4 is invaluable.

Brigham Young led half of the Nauvoo Saints outside the borders of the United States, where Church leadership could begin revealing to the Saints their secret sexual practices, those beginning at Nauvoo. The practice later came to be called "plural marriage" and eventually "celestial marriage." It began as spiritual wifery - sex *justified* by new false, religious doctrine. From 1846 to 1852, Young slowly introduced the Saints to what he and others had been secretly practicing. The Brighamite version of polygamy was a modification of Jacob Cochran's spiritual wifery, but on a much grander and safer scale – through officially sanctioned, lawful marriage – then made "**sacred**" in temple marriage "sealings" where mutliple wives were "**sealed**' to one man.

Over time, nearly all the men of Nauvoo embraced the secret blood-oaths in the brotherhood of Freemasonry. Some 1,492 men, including nearly all Church leadership eventually supported them in five Masonic lodges in the area. A Masonic Hall was completed and dedicated in Nauvoo, whereas the "temple" and the Nauvoo House were never finished. Curses followed the Saints for not focusing on the LORD's directives and for falling into grevious sins (D&C 124). The secret blood-oaths of the Danites, the Cochranites, the Masons, and now the Mormons, reflected the desires held in the secret chambers of some men's hearts. Those in the secret chamber at Nauvoo were seeking the lusts of the flesh and the things of the world rather than what God was offering them. Others believed polygamy was a higher principle practiced by those with greater priesthood. Secret blood-oaths were used at Nauvoo to implement Brigham's version of Cochranite spiritual wifery, first among the Twelve and then among the Saints. Similar blood-oaths have been used since the days of Cain to enforce the will of evil ones and cover their actions. These oaths with penalties eventually showed up in Brigham's Young's version of the temple endowment (the penalties tied to these oaths were removed in 1990, see pps. 178-81). The LORD spoke out against secrecy in strong terms, saying:

"I spake **openly** to the world; I ever taught in the synagogue, and in the temple, whither the Jews always restort; and in **secret** have I said nothing" (John 18:20).

"But I say unto you, **Swear not at all**; neither *by heaven* [in God's name], for it is God's throne: Nor by the earth; for it is his footstool: neither by Jerusalem; for it is the city of the great King. Neither shalt thou **swear** *by thy head* because thou canst not make one hair white or black. But let your communication be Yea, yea; Nay, nay; for whatsoever is *more than this cometh of* **evil**" (Mat. 5:34-36; JST Mat. 5:37-39; 3 Ne. 12:34-37; Moses 5:29-31).

James, the half-brother of the LORD, said, "**above all things**, my brethren, **swear not**, neither by heaven, **neither by** the earth, **neither by any other oath**" (James 5:12).

"For nothing is **secret**, that shall not be made manifest; neither any thing **hid**, that shall not be known and come abroad" (Luke 8:17).

"Take no part in the unfruitful works of **darkness**, but instead **expose** them" (Eph. 5:11; D&C 123:7-17).

Emma said, "it was **secret** things which had cost Joseph and Hyrum their lives" (William Clayton journal, 15 Aug., 1844).

Secret combination scriptures show forth **evil** intent in the heart, to get **gain** – in power, money, and the lusts of flesh (see 2 Ne. 9:9, 10:15; 3 Ne. 6:27-30; Alma 37:22-33; Hel. 6:15-26, 36-37; Morm. 8:26-40; Ether 8:15, 20-25; D&C 38; 42:63-64, 45:64, 117:11, 123:13; Moses 5:29-31, 49, 51, 6:15). A quick scan of the 83 scriptures tied to secret combinations in the Book of Mormon point us to the following concepts, all surfacing in Nauvoo between 1841 - 46.

1. **The Secret Chamber of the Heart** – the seat of our desires
   a. The choice to **love** God or Satan, results in blessing or cursing, life or death – "the two ways" (Deut. 28-30)
   b. Early example - Abel versus Cain – follow **the will** of God or Satan (covenant with God, blood-oath –Satan)
   c. Later example Joseph Smith versus Brigham Young

2. **A Secret Combination** – a brotherhood or society
   a. The Gadianton Robbers in the Book of Mormon
   b. The Illuminati, the Freemasons, the Elite Bankers of Europe and America
   c. Brigham Young and some of the Twelve

3. **Secret Plans and Works** – to get gain
   a. Getting Gain: Power, Money, Sex, the Honors of Men, etc. (1 Ne. 22:23)
   b. Control: Fear, coercion, intimidation, blood-oaths, murder / Control of media, history, eductation, doctrine
   c. Murder

5. **Public Results** – cursings
   a. Cut off from God (Ether 10:11) / See also page 193
   b. Curses rather than blessings
   c. Destroyed

Ancient Israel was frequently removed from their promised, covenant lands in the east (Deut. 19:8-9), because they rejected God and His covenant with Abraham and his righteous posterity. The Book of Mormon addresses three peoples who have been and will be **removed** from this promised, covenant land, the land given to Joseph of Eygpt and his posterity – by covenant. They are, (1) the Jaredites (Ether 2:7-12, 8:16-26), (2) the Nephites (Hel. 2:12-13), and the future destruction of **the Gentiles** on this land (America, JST Mat. 21:35-56; Ether 2:7-12, 8:15-26). God **decreed** that He will be King over a righteous people on this land, a promise repeated by Moroni (Ether 2:9-12), by Alma (Alma 37:31, 4515-16), by Nephi (2 Ne. 1:7), and by Mormon (Morm. 1:17). Destruction results in the descending pattern of pride, idolatry, sexual sin, secret combinations, and then murder (see the ten cursings in 2 Ne. 9:27-28).

The Battle Lines are Drawn

God's word tells us that there is opposition in all things (2 Ne. 2:11). A war is raging between light and darkness everywhere, between our LORD and Satan, and those that follow them. It is very real. Wickedness, as part of secret combinations in high places, is being exposed in the highest levels of our national government, in Hollywood, in the news media, as well as other settings. It will also be exposed in our schools and our church too, as the darkness is widespread. In speaking of evil surrounding us, God said:

> "So do not be afraid of them, for there is nothing **concealed** that will not be disclosed, or **hidden** that will not be made known. What I tell you in the **dark**, speak in the daylight; what is **whispered** in your ear, proclaim from the roofs" (Mat. 10:26, see also Luke 12:3 & D&C 1:3; D&C 123:7-17).

Mormon and Moroni in the Book of Mormon saw our day and spoke of the secret combinations that would surround us. Eight of these scriptures address **murder**. Moroni described it as an "**awful situation**" (Ether 8:24).

> "And whatsoever nation shall uphold such secret combinations, to get power and **gain**, until they shall spread over the nation, behold, **they shall be destroyed**; for the Lord will not suffer that the blood of his saints, which shall be shed by them, shall always cry unto him from the ground for vengeance upon them and yet he avenge them not. Wherefore, O ye Gentiles, it is wisdom in God that these things should be shown unto you, that thereby ye may **repent** of your sins, and suffer not that these murderous combinations shall get above you, which are built up to **get power and gain**—and the work, yea, even the work of destruction come upon you, yea, even the sword of the justice of the Eternal God shall fall upon you, to your overthrow and destruction if ye shall suffer these things to be. Wherefore, the Lord commandeth you, when ye shall see these things come among you that ye shall awake to a sense of your **awful situation**, because of this secret combination which shall be among you . . . [and] come unto the fountain of all righteousness and be **saved**" (Ether 8:22-26).

Earlier in this same chapter of Ether, we read that Jared rebelled against his father King Omer, because his heart was set upon the kingdom of his father, and upon the riches, power, and "the glory of the world" (vs. 1-7). With "flattering words" first, and then with force, Jared took control of his father's kingdom and then held him captive. Jared's brothers made war on him for the sake of their father, freeing him. Jared pleaded with them for his life. His brothers allowed him to live. Jared's daughter, seeing her father's sorrow, asked him - have you not read – "the record which our fathers brought across the great deep? Behold, is there not an account concerning them of old, that they by their **secret plans** did obtain kingdoms and great glory?" (Ether 8:9).

Jared's daughter, knowing that her beauty could beguile wicked men, suggested to her father that she could dance before Akish, and that if he [Akish] would deliver the head of king Omer to Jared, Akish could have Jared's daughter as a wife. Thus, by **murder**, **intrigue**, and **sexual favors**, her father Jared could retake the kingdom, have power, riches, and the honors of men. We then read about those making **secret oaths** with one another to get power.

> "And Akish did administer unto them the **oaths** which were given by them of old who also sought power, which had been handed down even from Cain, who was a **murderer** from the beginning. And they were kept up by the *power of the devil to administer these oaths* unto the people, to **keep them in darkness**, to help such as **sought power** *to* **gain power**, *and* **to murder**, *and* **to plunder**, *and* **to lie**, *and to commit all manner of wickedness* and **whoredoms**...And it came to pass that they formed a **secret combination**" (Ether 8:15-18).

Joseph, Hyrum, and Samuel Smith were murdered so that Young and the Twelve might take power, controlling the kingdom, have riches, the honors of men, and most importantly, multiple wives. Their "new order of things" made use of Danite-like coercion and control techniques, and the secrecy of Satan's **blood-oaths** to protect it all, the teachings of the Cochranite movement, Freemasonry, and eventually Brigham's modified temple endowment.

Four Secret Combinations Rise Up – *all using Joseph Smith's Name and God's Name*

Secret combinations organize to get gain; power sex, money, and the honors of men. There are four of them tied to Joseph Smith and the early church. They used Joseph's name to justify it all. The first **secret combination** was formed in Missouri in 1838 to protect the Saints. Three of the final four were at Nauvoo between 1841 to 1846. The last four have ties to spiritual wifery, where accusations were made that Joseph originated polygamy among the Saints. All of them protected their "gain" via **secretive, blood-oaths** among one another, combined with fear, intimidation, coercion, violence, and even murder. Secret blood-oaths and their blood penalties are part of Freemasonry. Many of the early Saints were part of this all male-fraternity. Later in the Nauvoo area, five Masonic lodges were established.

1. *The Danites - Power* In 1838 the Danites entered into **secret blood-oaths** with one another to avenge the Latter-day Saints against their "Gentile" enemies in Missouri. The Danites were Mormon men who wanted to protect the Saints. This later expanded to protect the church, its leaders, and *their* teachings, including polygamy. In time their controlling methods were directed towards those Saints that did not **conform** to Brigham's "new order of things." Some of the early Danites were also Freemasons, a brotherhood that also made use of *secret blood-oaths* to protect one another. These blood-oaths would later become part of Brigham's version of the early temple endowment (chap. 5).

At first, Joseph Smith supported the initial efforts of the Danites for justice. Later in Liberty Jail, he spoke out against their practices, calling them a "secret combination," as they were going too far. The Danites began taking revenge on Latter-day Saints too, those who disagreed with them or certain church leaders (like Young and the Twelve later at Nauvoo). Conformity was maintained by coercion. These tactics were employed upon David Whitmer, God's choice to be one of the three witnesses to the Book of Mormon (and second in command to Joseph Smith in Missouri for a time). David Whitmer stated that, "a certain oath was to be administered to all the brethren to bind them to support the heads of the church in everything they should teach [right or wrong]. All who refused to take this oath were considered dissenters" (David Whitmer, An Address To All Believers In Christ, 1887, pp. 27-28). Today we call some who stand up for truth "apostates."

The Danites also went after David's brother John Whitmer, Oliver Cowdery, W.W. Phelps, and Lyman E. Johnson. **They were not allowed to think differently or disagree**. All of these men were run out of select areas of Missouri in 1838 as part of an official Danite Manifesto. It demanded that "**the dissenters**" depart portions of Missouri. Other names for these early church enforcers included "the Daughters of Zion" and "Destroying Angels." Thomas Marsh, former President of the Twelve, and David Whitmer, former head of the church in Missouri, both left the church, citing discomfort with Danite coercion and their blood-oaths as reasons for leaving the faith. Like Whitmer, Marsh noted that some men swore oaths, "to support the heads of the church in all things that they say or do, whether right or wrong."Whitmer was later *labeled* a "**dissenter**" or "**apostate**." This same label today remains an effective weapon to silence those who speak up, whether in politics or church affairs.

In 1838 Joseph spoke out against secret works of darkness, stating, "Thus we find that there has been frauds and secret abominations and evil works of darkness going on leading the minds of the weak and unwary into confusion . . . and palming it all the time upon the presidency, while mean time the presidency were ignorant as well as innocent of these things, which were practicing in the church in our name" (Joseph Smith, Dec. 1838, Times and Seasons, Vol. 1 No. 6, April 1840). Later, when Joseph and others were in Liberty Jail, he issued a reminder of the danger of the secrecy of blood oaths. He said:

> "We farther caution our brethren against the impropriety of the organization of bands or companies, by **covenants, oaths, penalties, or secrecies**...And let our covenants be that of the everlasting covenant, as it is contained in the Holy Writ, and the things which God has revealed unto us. Pure friendship always becomes weakened the very moment you undertake to make it stronger by **<u>penal oaths</u>** and **<u>secrecy</u>**. Your humble servants intend FROM HENCEFORTH to disapprobate everything that is **not** in accordance with the fullness of the gospel of Jesus Christ, and which is not of a bold, frank and upright nature" (Times and Seasons, July, 1840). He added, "No quorum in the Church was entirely exempt from the influence of those **false spirits** who are striving against me for the mastery; even **some of the Twelve** *were so far lost to their high and responsible calling* as to begin to take sides **secretly with the enemy**" (Joseph Smith, HC 2:488).

2. *The Bennett Group – Spiritual Wifery* (1841-42) This group wanted to practice adultery using Joseph Smith's name and his supposed teachings on polygamy to justify it. They were led by Dr. John Bennett, Nauvoo Mayor and Assistant to Pres. Joseph Smith for a time. The group also included Chauncey and Francis M. Higbee (sons of the church historian Elias Higbee). Joseph Smith's name was used as a scapegoat by those in this group to justify their immorality. Bennett, for example, convinced several women to have sex with him using the justification "that Joseph had such revelations and commandments [supporting the practice], and that they were of God" (The Wasp, July 27, 1842). Dr. Bennett even offered abortions to the women if they would succomb to his desires. When the seductions of Bennett and the Higbees came to light, Joseph tried to work with the guilty men at first. He later excommunicated Dr. Bennett from the church and disciplined others within the group. Joseph eventually sued Chauncy Higbee (a lawyer) in a public, non-Mormon court to expose what he knew was really happening in Nauvoo. Had Joseph been secretly practicing polygamy, this public trial would have exposed him **as well**. The actions of the Bennett group were reported in local Nauvoo newspapers, but revealing facts and testimony by the Prophet Joseph Smith **were withheld by John Taylor, owner, editor, and printer of the two Nauvoo Newspapers** (one religious, one civil). Taylor was

a secret chamber member. This occurred twice with court cases involving Joseph Smith. Following the murder of the Smith brothers, Taylor also ran three negative stories on Joseph's brother William Smith to discredit him (William was an Apostle and Patriarch to the Church), when he challenged Brigham Young for church leadership.[13]

3. *The Law Group – Spiritual Wifery, Power & Reform (1843-44)* The Law group was led by Dr. William Law, a former member of the First Presidency, and Wilson Law his brother. The Higbee brothers were part of it too, as were the Foster brothers, and others. They collectively desired to remove Joseph Smith from church leadership for a number of reasons, including his private excommunication of four members of the Law group, his supposed secret practice of spiritual wifery with some of the Twelve, and his teaching of false doctrine (15 allegations are listed in it).[14] At first, some in this group wanted to hide their **spiritual wifery**, attributing it to Joseph Smith. Later they wanted to expose Joseph's crimes and that of the Twelve. **Like most of the Saints, they believed Joseph directed the Twelve to practice spiritual wifery secretly at Nauvoo**. At first they desired to reform the church and return to Joseph's earlier teachings. Later they tried to start their own church. They believed Joseph Smith was a fallen prophet and was leading the church into errors in both the secret practice of spiritual wifery and other false teachings. The Law group was being fed lies by secret chamber members (the Twelve), all to encourage their actions against Joseph's supposed crimes, and to protect their own spiritual wifery.

The Law group eventually purchased and set up their own newspaper, **The Expositor**, to expose what they believed were Joseph's crimes *and* those in the Twelve. This was necesssary, as secret chamber member and Apostle John Taylor owned, edited, and printed both of Nauvoo's newspapers. One officially represented the church – the *Times and Seasons*, the other – *The Nauvoo Neighbor* represented a more civil or political viewpoint. In the latter years at Nauvoo, Brigham Young was calling the shots behind the scenes, not Joseph, all to protect spiritual wifery among a growing number of men at Nauvoo. Nearly all of the men in Nauvoo were Masons. Secret oaths and Danite-like coercion kept everything in place.

Though Dr. Bennett was expelled from the church in 1842 for practicing spiritual wifery, leaving Nauvoo, the young Higbee brothers remained. Others soon joined them because of their grievenances against Joseph Smith, whether perceived or real. These were reinforced by the lies fed them by the secret chamber. The complaints of the Law group were economic, political, or personal. Joseph, for example, had disciplined some in the group in church courts for adultery, stealing, and other sins. Joseph became frustrated by the mounting lies about him and his growing list of troubles from traitors within and outside the church. He then did two things that led to his incarceration and eventual murder. First he **privately** excommunicated four members of the Law group, going against church policy. This was followed by his later order as Nauvoo Mayor to **destroy the press** that had printed the first edition of The Expositor in June of 1844. It **listed all 15 grievances** against Joseph and the Twelve (lies and truths, see endnote 18).

The Law group knew that some among the Twelve were secretly practicing spiritual wifery at Nauvoo. They believed Joseph had to be leading them (**lies fed them by the secret chamber reinforced this**). They planned to expose them all in the Expositor. Two members of the secret chamber, Apostles Willard Richards and John Taylor were "plants" to see that this did not happen. They coerced Joseph Smith into signing the order to destroy the press. We know this because Apostle William Smith (once part of this secret combination too) witnessed this event in the home of Joseph and Emma Smith (chap. 4). Joseph's destruction of the press resulted in his permanent removal from power. Other things were lost then too.

Francis Higbee lost his reputation in the church as a result of his adultery and Joseph's excommunication of him. He lost his relationship with Sidney Rigdon's daughter as a result. Francis had contracted a veneral disease after visiting a prostitute. Prior to the press being destroyed, Joseph went to see Francis while he lay incapacitated in bed, that he might smooth things over. The strife, hate, and revenge had grown too far, however. In time, the Law group formed a conspiracy to kill Joseph.

In one court case, A.B. Williams of the Law group sued Joseph Smith. His affidavit stated, "Joseph H. Jackson said that Doctor (Robert) Foster, Chauncy Higbee and the Laws were red-hot for a conspiracy, and he should not be surprised if in two weeks there should be not one of the Smith family left in Nauvoo" (Times and Seasons 5:541, May 15, 1844). Eventually, former church leader William Law declared himself the head of the "Reformed Mormon Church." He called Francis Higbee and others to be his Apostles, and called for elders to have their licenses renewed under him. They may have also helped in raising the mob at Carthage, the mob blamed for killing Joseph and Hyrum Smith. As we will see hereafter, their efforts dovetailed perfectly into the hands of the secret chamber, that the Smiths might be removed from power.

4. *The Nauvoo Apostles, led by Brigham Young – Spiritual Wifery* The apostles in Nauvoo were led by Brigham Young as President of the Twelve. His close friend was Heber C. Kimball. Both men were friends and Masons before joining

the church. Eight of the apostles chose to follow Young and Heber into polygamy. In time four rejected Young and polygamy and left the Twelve or were excommunicatedd from the church by Young. He, Kimball, Richards, and Taylor made up the leadership of "**the secret chamber**." Kimball was especially devoted to "the craft" (a word used negatively by the LORD in many scriptures, see p. 59). Kimball set up the five Nauvoo Masonic Lodges, an effective way in which Satan corrupts Christianity. Note the breakdown of **the secret chamber** below (D&C 38).

Leaders Brigham Young, Heber C. Kimball, Willard Richards, and John Taylor
Followers Parley P. Pratt, Orson Hyde, George A. Smith, Wilford Woodruff, and Orson Pratt
Those Rejecting the Secret Chamber Lyman Wight, John E. Page, Amasa Lyman, and *William B. Smith

The reason there are thirteen men is that Orson Pratt was excommunicated and then reinstated later on. William Smith was part of the secret chamber (and spiritual wifery) for a time then rejected it later. The serect chamber began rising up there in 1841, after the Apostles returned from their English missions. Some were fully aware of what was going on (the leadership), while others were not.

The apostles spent considerable time together in England, without Joseph and Hyrum leading them, and without their wives, all between 1839-41. Some appear to have experimented in spiritual wifery there, specifically Brigham, Heber, and William Clayton (he was not an apostle). There may have also been planning for what might occur later at Nauvoo. In 1874 Brigham Young claimed that he had a revelation in England, confirming the divine status of polygamy. He used craftiness and an iron hand to take control in Nauvoo, intimidating dissenters with fear, coercion, and violence. The secret blood-oaths of the Danites, the Cochranites, and Freemasonry helped Young keep the secrets in place for a time. Former Danite enforcers were put to work as Nauvoo policemen in the 1840's for Young and other secret chamber members. They included men like Orrin Porter Rockewell, and Hosea and Allen Stout in Nauvoo, and Bill Hickman later in Utah.

Four increasingly severe control measures were used by the secret chamber to warn, intimidate, and abuse suspected dissenters among the Saints or the general popluation. Murder was their last resort. Speaking of the first level "whittlers," Young observed that "at the corner of every block a deacon is found atttending to his duty" and "every part of the city is watched with the strictest care" (Quinn, Mormon Hierarchy, p. 182). The "deacons" were not 12-year old boys, but men ranging in age from 17 to 60. They were intimidators, used to get others to conform or leave.

Brigham's Control Agents

1. The "**whittling and whistling brigade**" was a group of men that stood very near suspected "dissenters," whistling while they used their large bowie knives (some with 14" blades) to whittle wood or sticks. This tactic was used to intimidate suspected enemies, warning them or driving them from Nauvoo. Brigham Young made Hosea Stout head of "the Whistling and Whittling Brigade." Stout reported directly to Brigham Young, as President of the Twelve. Many believe Stout poisoned Samuel Smith one month after the murders of Joseph and Hyrum. Samuel was in line to replace Joseph as head of the church, if he and Hyrum were taken out (chap. 4).

2. Other suspected "dissenters" were marked or "**anointed**" with human excrement from "**Aunt Peggy's privy cabinet**" (an outhouse). The phrase "Aunt Peggy" was code, tied to acts of revenge, intimidation, and coercion.

3. More serious "**dissenters**" or "**apostates**" were beaten by select members of **the Nauvoo police** force or by Brigham Young's bodyguards. They included former Danites. Hosea Stout was Chief of Police and a primary enforcer for Young at Nauvoo and later in Salt Lake.

4. Some were murdered. Bill Hickman was one of Young's primary enforcers or "hitmen" in Salt Lake City. Hosea Stout and Bill Hickman both kept personal journals detailing their secret acts (including murder) for Brigham Young (Orrin Porter Rockwell did not keep a journal). On March 13, 1847, speaking of a "dissenter" from Young's instructions, Hosea stout wrote that the appropriate outcome would be to, "**cut him off** - behind the ears - according to **the law of God** in such cases" (Quinn, Mormon Hierarchy, p. 658). Cutting the throat was part of temple covenants and *penalties* made until 1990 (see chap. 5). It was a sign of why and how the hit would take place.

Brigham's "**blood atonement**" doctrine (which became prominent in Utah Territory in the 1856-57 "Reformation" movement and thereafter), was marked by *cutting the throat* of victims, in connection with a Masonic inspired **blood-**

oath that was later put into Young's version of the temple endowment (chap. 5). The various names for Young's "**hit men**" (used as code words later in Utah Territory), included "Brigham's boys" (Hickman), "Be hoys" (Stout), "Minutemen," "Destroying Angels," "Life Guards," "Strikers," and "Wolfhunters." Many labeled as "dissenters" or "apostates" included thousands leaving Utah during the 1856-57 "Reformation" period. Blood atonement was sometimes preached as the only hope for murderers, adulterers, *and* the apostates, including those making the blood-oath in the temple endowment (the related *penalties* tied to it were removed in 1990, see chap. 5). Those wanting to leave Utah (many of whom were unable to pay back their PEF loans) were labeled as "*apostates*" for speaking out about abuses they saw and experienced under Brigham's "new order of things." Young required written approval to leave during these early days. His enforcers were sent to get many to return, or at least pay back their debt.

The earliest enforcers in the church were "the Danites" of Missouri in **1838**. They made use of **blood-oaths** in their revenge of persecutors of the Saints. This revenge sometimes involved murder and taking the property of their enemy. The secret oaths typical of the Cochranites, the Freemasons, and the early Danites, later became part of Young's version of the temple endowment in 1846. They were also useful in enforcing the secrecy of polygamy in the Nauvoo years. Young and the Apostles following him, modified Cochranite spiritual wifery into a more acceptable form among the Saints, doing so within legal and lawful marriage (but with multiple wives). "Spiritual wifery" among the Cochranites involved various types sexual sin (adultery, polyandry, and swapping marriage partners). Among the Saints, this age old practice later came to be known as "plural marriage" and finally "celestial marriage" among the Utah Mormons. It involves the same old sins of the Bible; use of false religion to justify sexual sin. This **whoredom** is also called an **abomination** in Jacob 2 and 3, because it inovolved changed doctrine, a perversion of the original "doctrine of Christ" (chap. 7).

In 1843, Young preached in the Boston area among the Cochranites again. He returned to Nauvoo bringing with him Augusta Adams Cobb, a married woman, who had been baptized earlier amid the Cochranites by missionaries Samuel Smith (another brother of Joseph and Hyrum) and Orson Hyde (Journal of Orson Hyde, pp. 16–17; *American Heritage,* Feb. 1965, pp. 50–55). Young married Augusta as his second plural wife. (third overall). Augusta never divorced her first husband (polyandry). It is believed that Young secretly married three polygamous wives, including Augusta, before Joseph's murder. Records reveal that seven of the Apostles also had plural wives prior to Joseph's murder. Although the Nauvoo Apostles denounced John Bennett's sexual escapades, they claimed Joseph was the author of their new system of spiritual wifery, which required *special* priesthood. Joseph's supposed teachings and actions *justified* theirs. In Utah in 1852, President Young "*let the cat out of the bag*," telling the Saints that the Twelve had been secretly practicing what they then called plural marriage since the early 1840's. Today **the church confirms this**. It was all a great **secret**. Later in 1874, Young would claim that he had a revelation while performing missionary labors in England (1839-40) to begin the practice, even while the Prophet Joseph was alive and preaching against it.

The secret combination dominating our government today utilizes numerous intelligence agencies along with the power of the U.S. military to **enforce** its will around the globe. The LORD will eventually use the wicked to destroy the wicked here in our day (Morm. 4:5; Psalm 34:21). It may be Russia, China, and Islamic militants who do so.

Getting and Keeping Gain: *The Smiths versus Organized Opposition*

Sex, power, money, and the honors of men are typically the *gain* (1 Ne. 22:23) sought for in secret combinations. Pride, lies and deception often lead to murder to get and keep gain. After the murder of the three Smith brothers, the Mormon version of spiritual wifery spread quickly in Nauvoo, and thereafter in Utah, until Brigham Young made polygamy an official church practice in 1852, one required for exaltation. For some thirty years thereafter, "plural marriage" spread throughout the isolated communities of the mountain-west, most of them outside the borders and control of the United States of America. The U.S. government eventually stopped the practice. Only then did Utah territory become a state. Many of the curses from the Nauvoo days remain with us.

Some believe the real issue politicians had with 19th Century Mormons wasn't polygamy and its moral issues, but Brigham Young's and the church's theocratic control over economics, politics, and the natural resources of the region (for their own "**gain**"). They believed the Saints were too independent, with ability to prosper on their own. Key parties most concerned about their independence were *the banking establishment*, *railroad tycoons*, and *federal bureaucrats* and *politicians*, all of which were tied together in what the Book of Mormon calls, "**the great and abominable church**." Polygamy among the Mormons was thus a secondary issue to money. It was used, however, to exploit negative public opinion against the Saints, while also initiating legal pressure on them that would eventually **stop their independent development**. Their plan was to subdue and **control** the Saints. In time the legal status of the church was revoked (because of polygamy), and all church assets fell into the hands of the federal government. The legal-entity church that Joseph Smith established in 1830 was dissolved, never to be re-established in the way the LORD had desired.

The "church" that Joseph tried to establish no longer exists today, though parts remain. Not only did Brigham change much of it by embracing spiritual wifery, with all it resulting ramifications, but by 1923, President Heber J. Grant (also a polygamist) changed the status of the church to a 501c3 **corporation** in 1923. The President of "The Corporation Sole" today owns, personally and completely, all property and assets of "the church." He makes decisions for us as President without need for revelation or a "common consent" vote from membership (D&C 26:2, see chap 6).

Joseph Smith fought spiritual wifery where he could between 1841 and 1844. He was nearly powerless, however, as the Twelve held increasingly more power, and as greater numbers of men were becoming part of the secret chamber to practice what men like Young, Kimball, and Bennett had started. The coersive tactics and blood-oaths used by the Cochranites, the Danites, and the new brotherhood of Freemasonry helped maintain the secret implementation of spiritual wifery among the Nauvoo Apostles first, and then the Saints later on in Utah. The same blood-oaths with penalites later became part of Young's modified temple endowment and "celestial marriage." The LORD saw it all coming in 1831 in a revelation to Joseph Smith (D&C 38). Six different individuals spoke of "**the secret chamber**." They included The LORD, Apostle William Smith, Sidney Rigdon, Emma Smith, and two secretaries for Brigham Young. It addresses Satan's plan to destroy Joseph Smith, the Saints, and the Church. The LORD said:

> "Thus saith the Lord your God...all flesh is corrupted before me; and the powers of darkness prevail upon the earth, among the children of men...Which causeth silence to reign, and all eternity is pained, and the angels are waiting the great command to reap down the earth, to gather the tares that they may be burned; and, behold, **the enemy is combined**. And now I show unto you a *mystery*, a **thing** which is had in **secret chambers**, to bring **to pass even your destruction** in process of time, and ye knew it not...I hold forth and deign to give unto you...a land of promise...ye shall possess it again in eternity...in time ye shall have no king nor ruler, for I will be your king and watch over you. Wherefore, hear my voice and follow me, and you shall be a free people, and ye shall have no laws but my laws when I come...be one; and if ye are not one ye are not mine. And again, I say unto you that **the enemy in the secret chambers seeketh your lives**. Ye hear of wars in far countries, and you say that there will soon be great wars in far countries, but *ye know not the hearts of men in your own land*...And that **ye might escape the power of the enemy**, and be gathered unto me a righteous people, without spot and blameless – Wherefore, for this case I gave unto you the commandment that ye should go to the Ohio; and there I will give unto you **my law**; and there you shall be **endowed with power from on high**...but beware of pride, lest ye become as the Nephites of old...And go ye out from among the wicked. Save yourselves. Be ye clean that bear the vessels of the LORD. Amen" (D&C 38 select verses).

The "**thing**" protected by the Nauvoo secret chamber is given us in Jacob 2 of the Book of Mormon. It is an important word link. It is the "**abomination**," "**whoredom**," and "**iniquity**" of polygamy, as seen in the four uses of the word "**thing**" or "**things**" in Jacob 2, verses 23, 24, 30 and 34 (see pages 22-23 and Ezra 10:2). This "**grosser crime**" came because of "pride" and "wickedness" and led to the "awful situation" addressed by Moroni in Ether 8:24 – a secret combination that murdered Joseph and his two brothers, all to keep polygamy in place. Both Jacob and Joseph Smith *shook their garments free* of the sins of their people for practicing this whoredom (see p. 113, endnote 16).

For the Saints today, the generational curses originating in this "**iniquity**" have been passed down to us from "fathers, priests, and kings" (Josh. 24:2; D&C 93:39; Mosiah 11:7). They led to an additional, but more serious "awful situation" – **ignorance** amidst this darkness. It is ignorance of our own unsaved or unredeemed state, and when God's harvest of souls is very near us. Too many of the Saints today simply don't know what it means to be saved. They thus don't seek it.. Instead, too many have been deceived by **the craftiness of men** – including leaders - into worshipping other things (D&C 76:75; 123:12; Psalm 83:1-4, see p. 59). They are lifted up as our light in place of Christ (idolatry). As a result, too many remain ignorant and unredeemed, full of pride, thinking they are already saved when they are not. It is the result of pride and idolatry, and an "all is well" attitude. True prophets teach us to **repent** and **come unto Christ**. Salvation in the fullness of the doctrine of Christ is addressed in chapter 7

Gain versus Waxing Strong in the Spirit

Inspired leaders like King Benjamin, King Mosiah, and Alma the elder and the younger – all taught against receiving payment for preaching. They supported themselves financially with their own hands, and taught that **the Spirit** would attend them as they sacrificed for the Lord and those they serve without "filthy lucre" (Titus 1:11). Later in Mosiah we read that those who sacrifice to teach the sheep have God's **grace** with them. They then "**wax strong in the Spirit**, having the knowledge of God, that they might teach with power and authority from God" (see Mosiah 18:26; Alma 30:32-35). Leaders who serve from the heart, rather than for gain, are gifted with the Lord's Spirit! Others are cut off.

There are many scriptures stating that payment should not accompany preaching (see 2 Nephi 26:20, 25, 27, 29-31; Jacob 2:13-19; Mosiah 2:14, 18:24-26, 27:5; Alma 1:3, 4:8-12, 30:32-35, 60:36; Hel. 13:28-29; Mormon 8:32-33, 36-41; D&C 38:25-27; 42:29-31; 52:40; 70:14; 83:6; 84:78-86, 103; 105:1-5; Acts 20:34; 1 Cor. 9:18; Jer. 7:6, all of chapter 23; Ezek. 22:25-29; all of chapter 34; Amos 6:1-6; and Micah 3:1-12). Especially useful is Mosiah 18:26. In it we read that those practicing priestcraft are **cut off** from God and His pure revelation, especially if they (1) **lust** after others (D&C 42:22-23; 63:13-16), (2) desire **power** over others (D&C 121:34-35), and (3) seek **money** from the people (Mosiah 18:24-26, see also p. 191). "Gain" became a primary motivation for Young and the Twelve at Nauvoo.

Moroni, seeing our day, said that "they [secret combinations] are had among all people" (Ether 8:20), and that they are led by Satan. He inspires corrupt men to pervert nearly all things, including governments, schools, and churches. Men in high places make covenants with each other and with Satan. They shield each other from our view by putting forth an innocent public "face" to **deceive** us for **gain** (1 Ne. 22:23). Gain is defined in scripture as "the things of the world" and "the honors of men" (D&C 121:34-35), including sex, power, and money. When men value these things above God and his truths, they are cut off from Him. The lesser public "face" appears innocent, but above the underlings (who are often very good people), there is something more sinister at the top.

The Innocent Public Face	*Higher Power Behind It*
The Catholic church & the White Pope	The Jesuits & the Black Pope
Lower level Freemasony	Upper level Freemasonry
World governments	Corrupt leaders, Secret Service & the military
Unpaid local leaders (Bishops, Stk Pres.)	Paid corporate executives

Nephi's vision of the Tree of Life (chapters 11-14) reveals that in time, God's wrath will be poured out on the great whore Babylon - the great and abominable church of the devil (see 1 Ne. 14:6-17). There are billions of Muslims, Buddhists, and Hindus in this world, and many millions of Christians, including Latter-day Saints. There are only a few in the church of the Lamb, however (1 Ne. 14:12). It is "because of the wickedness and abominations of the whore who sat on many waters." She keeps the people deceived, ignorant, and unsaved. Satan and his minions celebrate it and laugh. The sheep pay for the gain of the shepherds. God destroyed evil upon the earth in the time of Noah with water. In our day He will do it again with fire. The cleansing of the earth in this manner mirrors our own path of redemption. There is first a lesser watery baptism, followed by fiery rebirth in Christ thereafter. Cleansed, we are then gifted with the Holy Ghost. We then hold on to the iron rod (revelation from God) to make it to the Tree and its sweet fruit. It is the glory and majesty of the love of God! This simple, pure doctrine is suppressed today.

The Gates of Hell Open Wide

It is good to remember that God said that in the mouth of two or three witnesses all truth would be established (see 2 Cor. 13:1; D&C 6:28). Two of the most trustworthy witnesses are; (1) God's written word in scripture, and (2) God's revealed word in pure revelation. They do not counteract one another. In the Book of Commandments, the LORD spoke to the early Saints about His word and the gates of hell. They opened wide at Nauvoo.

> "Behold I give unto you a **commandment**, that **you rely upon the things which are written**; for in them [the plates] are all things written, concerning **my church**, **my gospel**, and **my rock**. Wherefore if you shall build up **my church** and **my gospel**, and **my rock** [rather than the teachings of men], the gates of hell shall **not** prevail against you" (early unchanged 1833 Book of Commandments, now D&C 18:3-6).

In Jerusalem, our LORD asked His servants:

> "...whom say ye that I am? And Simon Peter answered and said, Thou are the Christ, the Son of the living God.

And Jesus answered and said unto him, Blessed art thou, Simon Barjona; for flesh and blood [man] hath not revealed this unto thee, but my Father who is in heaven. And I say also unto thee, That thou are Peter; and upon **this rock** [Jesus Christ, and pure revelation from the Father and me] I will build **my church**, and the gates of hell shall not prevail against it" (JST Mat. 16:16-19).

In praise and worship, Nephi prayed:

"May the gates of hell be shut continually before me, because that my heart is broken and my spirit is contrite! Oh LORD, wilt thou not shut the gates of thy righteousness before me…O LORD, will thou encircle me around in the robe of thy righteousness…Oh LORD, **I have trusted in thee**…I will not put my trust in the arm of flesh…for I know that **cursed** is he that putteth his trust **in man** or maketh flesh his arm…Yea, I know that God will give liberally to him that asketh. Ye my God will give me, **if I ask not amiss**; therefore will I will lift up my voice unto thee, **my God**, **the rock** of my righteousness. Behold, my voice shall forever ascend up unto thee **my rock** and mine everlasting God. Amen" (2 Ne. 4:32-35).

In these three verses we learn that (1) inspired scripture and (2) pure revelation comes to us from **the rock** that must be our foundation – Jesus Christ and the Father. The wise virgins with pure hearts – and oil in their lamps - build on this rock, rather than the words of imperfect men, which can open the gates of hell. The Saints were cursed in Nauvoo and forced from the land God had given them, because they rejected Christ the LORD, in favor of Brigham Young and the Apostles - and their polygamy. The idolatry of raising up men in replacement of Christ for the sake of gain is **priestcraft** (2 Ne. 26:29; 3 Ne. 18:24). This **iniquity**, along with 60 years of polygamy, has led to our **awful situation** today. It explains why "the gates of hell" continue to prevail among many.

Brigham Young's Legacy

Brigham Young has a public face upon official Church websites and publications. One web page reads, "In his lifetime, Brigham Young supervised the trek of between 60,000 to 70,000 pioneers to the Salt Lake Valley; founded 400 settlements; established a system of land distribution later ratified by Congress; served as the first territorial governor of Utah for two terms, as first superintendent of Indian Affairs of Utah Territory, and as Church President for 30 years" (see https://history.lds.org/article/pioneer-story-brigham-young-an-american-moses?lang=eng Although there is truth in these statements, there is much more to Brigham's story.[15] We know he was a strong leader. He, in fact, had an iron hand. Some call him a modern-day Moses because he led many of the Saints westward in the exodus from Nauvoo, settling much of the western U.S. It is true that he established a new kingdom outside the boundaries of the U.S. in Utah territory. It allowed him and the Twelve to practice polygamy freely. By the time of his death, Young's final tally of wives was 55. Only Heber C. Kimball, his friend and counselor in the First Presidency, rivaled him with 43 wives. Intimidation, coercion, and blood atonement were employed to protect it all.

Though Young was mostly uneducated, there are now three church universities named after him; one in Utah, Idaho, and Hawaii. They were **not** named for the proven Prophet, Seer, and Revelator Joseph Smith, but for Young. He was a prolific builder, like King Noah in the Book of Mormon, and all at the expense of the people. He built the St. George Temple and oversaw construction of other temples, including the Salt Lake Temple, though he died before it was completed. He also built many Tabernacles and Ward Houses. Young's primary legacy involves three things; (1) the polygamy he put in place among the Saints, and marked by his 55 wives; (2) the unchallenged power he wielded in Utah; And (3) the wealth he acquired via the expanding business interests of the church. The last two allowed him to build many spacious buildings. At the time of his death, Young's assets were in excess of one million dollars, much of it borrowed (taken) from the Church he oversaw. He is very comparable to King Noah of the Book of Mormon, as a number of parallels exist between both men. Both had many wives, all power, and much wealth. Both taxed the people heavily to build "many elegant buildings" (see first 8 verses, Mosiah 11). Young ended up with two mansions, one in Salt Lake, one in St. George. His widows went to the church for help after he died, but with little success.

The deaths of both men are comparable too. Abinadi prophesied that King Noah and his priests would die in the same manner in which they *murdered* him (Mosiah 13:10). Many believe Young's sudden death in 1877 was brought on by *poison*, administered by one of his wives. Samuel Smith, brother of Joseph and Hyrum, is believed to have been murdered by *poison* too, one month after the murder of his two brothers. The poison was most likely administered by Brigham Young's hit man, Hosea Stout; Nauvoo's Chief of Police and Young's body guard (Samuel's murder is addressed at the end of this chapter). He acted by the order of Young. The murders would continue in Utah territory, part of his "blood atonement" doctrine. The Mountain Meadows Masssacre was one such legacy.

Entering in at the Gate

Unlike Joseph Smith, Brigham Young does not appear to have "**entered in at the gate**" the LORD chose (2 Ne. 31:13-18). Christ is that gate. It must be evident in (1) how we approach the LORD **spiritually**, and (2) in what we do **physically** in this life. God said:

> "Verily, verily, I say unto you, He that entereth **not** by the door into the sheepfold, but climbeth up **some other way**, the same is a **thief** and a **robber**" (John 10:1).

God said, "he that is **ordained of me shall come in at the gate**" (D&C 43:7). Young took power, control, and many wives through deception, intrigue, and murder in the secret chamber. Christ the LORD is the gate to all the blessings of heaven. He employs no servant there (2 Ne. 9:41). All of us must come humbly to Him and pass His judgment here to receive the gifts of the Spirit from Him. Only then can we abide in the True Vine and bear sweet fruit in Him. We read in 1 Nephi 13:40, "**All men must come unto Him, or they cannot be saved.**" There is no record of Young receiving the baptism of fire and Holy Ghost as did Joseph Smith (JSH1:72-74). The sign of this "mighty change of heart" is one important characteristic of Christ the LORD - **love**. Young never claimed he saw Christ. God wants each of us to bear, "fruit meet for the Father's [Celestial] kingdom" in the gifts and fruits of the Spirit (D&C 84:58). Otherwise, we inherit lesser glory, being "deceived by the craftiness of men." This is the message of D&C 76:75 and 123:12 (see p 62). Brigham Young was one of these deceivers.

In 2 Nephi 31:17-18, we read that baptism of water, followed by the baptism of fire and the Holy Ghost - is **the gate** we must pass through to be on the path to receive sanctification, the Holy Ghost, and finally eternal life. It is not understood well today nor taught openly, except in God's word. We must seek the LORD and His will, not our own, in full submission to Him - to be sanctified and receive the precious gifts of the Holy Ghost. Brigham was a strong, prideful, self-willed man. Scripture informs us that seeking the things of the flesh, or power over others, or money in church service, each **cut us off** from God's Spirit (see the listing p. 191). Scripture addresses this relationship of our heartfelt desires and obtaining the Spirit of God (see D&C 42:22-23; 63:13-16, 121:34-35 & Mosiah 18:26).

Choices cause us to be cut off from God. We then do not enter in at the gate. The gates of hell prevailed against Young and those following him (gates are places of judgment in scripture). Condemnation and curses upon the Saints resulted. Many in the Twelve became wolves in sheep's clothing, seeking their own welfare rather than that of the sheep in Zion (2 Ne. 26:29). Speaking to similar religious leaders of His day, the LORD said:

> "But woe unto you, scribes and Pharisees, hypocrites! for ye shut up the kingdom of heaven against men: for **ye neither go in yourselves, neither suffer ye them that are entering to go in**" (Mat. 23:13).
>
> "Woe unto you, lawyers! For ye have taken away the key of knowledge, the fullness of the scriptures; **ye enter not in yourselves into the kingdom; and those who were entering in, ye hindered**" (JST Luke 11:53).

We have no revelation from God designating Brigham Young as the next leader over the Saints. Unlike Joseph and Hyrum (Prophet and Patriarch over the church), both of whom held the sealing power (see D&C 124:57-59, 91-95, 123-25), the LORD does not appear to have given Brigham Young nor the Twelve this gift, or other spiritual gifts of note. To be **chosen** by God to actually receive various gifts from Him, the giver of the gifts must become their focus, not the things of the world and the honors of men (see D&C 121:34-35). God said:

> "And this ye shall know assuredly—that there is **none other appointed** unto you to receive commandments and revelations until he [Joseph] be taken, **if he abide in me**. But verily, verily, I say unto you, that none else shall be appointed unto this gift except it be through him; for if it be taken from him he shall not have power except to appoint another in his stead. And this shall be a law unto you, that **ye receive not the teachings of any** that shall come before you as revelations or commandments; And this I give unto you that **you may not be deceived**, that you may know **they are not of me**. For verily I say unto you, that **he that is ordained of me shall come in at the gate** and be ordained as I have told you before, to teach those revelations which you have received and shall

receive through **him whom I have appointed**" (D&C 43:3-7).

There is no record of Brigham Young entering in **at this gate** either – that of who would lead the Church. As we will see in chapter 4, Young took all power by another way, via **craftiness** (D&C 76:75, 123:12) He was not ordained to this position, nor approved by the LORD, nor Joseph Smith. And neither his revelation on polygamy in England, nor Joseph's supposed revelation (D&C 132) were ever voted on by church membership for inclusion in scripture. Such a vote requires four groups; three priesthood quorums (the 1st Pres., the Twelve, the Seventy) and the Saints as a body.

Part III: The Secret Chamber at Nauvoo (1841-46)

As addressed earlier, it was in 1831 that the LORD used the phrase "secret chamber" two times in D&C 38 to describe what was coming. It is associated with secret gathering places where evil plans are hatched, and to the secret chambers of the heart, where these plans originate. Though false revelations can be (1) placed in our minds, or (2) come from Satan or false spirits, they often originate in the deepest, secret chambers of our hearts – in the idols we hold there (see Jer. 23:16; Ezek. 13:2 & Lam. 2:14). To receive pure revelation from God, we must "ask not amiss." Instead, we should come to God in real humility and complete submission to **His will**. This requires faith, trust, and love for God, rather than being focused upon our own will. The list of "idols of the heart" scriptures is provided once again. They are essential to understand as we learn to receive pure revelation from God, not other sources. They include, Prov. 23:7, Isa. 66:2-4, Ezek. 14:1-11, 2 Thess. 2:10-12, James 4:3, Jacob 4:14, Alma 29:4, and Morm. 9:28. Speaking of the powers of darkness prevailing on the earth, causing **silence** to reign, God told Joseph in 1831:

> "behold, the enemy is combined. And now I show unto you a *mystery*, a **thing** which is had in **secret chambers**, to bring to pass **even your destruction** in process of time, and ye knew it not…I say unto you that the enemy in the secret chambers **seeketh your lives**…ye know not the *hearts* of men in your own land" (D&C 38:12-13, 28-29).

God told Joseph about Satan's plans for his destruction earlier in D&C 5:33 and 10:6. Besides these references, there is only one other reference to the "secret chamber" in scripture. It is Matthew 24:24-26. It describes **false prophets** deceiving "the very elect" in a place where Christ the LORD *is not.* Note too, that there are 91 scriptures utilizing the word "**mystery**," 88 of them are positive (like "mysteries of godliness"), whereas only 3 are negative, those related to the focus of Jacob 2:30 – the whoredom of polygamy (see D&C 10:63-64; 2 Thess. 2:7; Rev. 17:5). All three of these scriptures are related to the "**mystery**" or "**thing**" kept secret in England and Nauvoo – spiritual wifery (pages 22-23). It is a great "**iniquity**" (2 Thess. 2:7), an **abomination**, in connection with "**mystery Babylon**," a secret combination (Rev. 17:5). Those promoting it "**wrest scriptures**" to **justify** their actions (D&C 10:63-64; Jacob 2:23).

The Secret Priesthood & Temple Endowment Sealings

Having returned from England, a number of early statements by Young and Kimball reveal that they believed they were part of a new "**secret** patriarchal priesthood" that allowed them and others in the Twelve to practice *spiritual wifery* in Nauvoo in 1841. The book on the ancient patriarchs sold at the Millennial Star office in Liverpool supported this. Another book printed in Nauvoo – *The Peacemaker* – would be even more influential among the Twelve. It addressed the sealing power of the great Prophet Elijah; power to seal wives to husbands for "time and eternity." These doctrines, combined with the rites of Freemasonry at Nauvoo became a dominant force moving polygamy forward among the Twelve (see chap. 4).

By 1844, and just before the murder of Joseph and Hyrum, those involved with the new **secret** priesthood and the Joseph's new temple rites grew to include many church leaders. Most were part of Freemasonry. A growing percentage were Apostles. Many of them were together in England. The **secrecy** surrounding it all was fulfillment of the LORD's prophecy ten years earlier in 1831 (D&C 38). Besides Young, early participants in spiritual wifery at Nauvoo included Heber Kimball, John Taylor, Willard Richards, Parley Pratt, Orson Pratt, G. A. Smith, William Smith, and Orson Hyde. Three leaders, Amasa Lyman, Lyman Wight, and John E. Page were not part of the **secret chamber** there. Secrecy has made clear separation difficult at specific points in time.

Others participating in *the spiritual wives* movement at Nauvoo included William Clayton (scribe for Joseph), Hosea Stout (Chief of Police), Bishops George Miller and Newel K. Whitney, and others. The Masonic brotherhood or "craft," with its **secret** blood-oaths, helped maintain the **secrecy** of the early *spiritual wives* movement. So too the **secret** priesthood and its new temple rites (chap. 5). Another prophetic warning of a coming secret combination is found in D&C 117:11 (1838, Far West). There, God told Newel K. Whitney that he was to remove himself from the **secret** abominations of the Nicolaitans (Rev. 2:6). He apparently ignored this warning. Only those in the **secret chamber** had the **secret** Patriarchal priesthood necessary to participate in the practice, and all under the direction of Brigham Young. He was Master Mahan (see Moses 5:29-31). These things were opposed by Joseph and Hyrum Smith. On May 23 of 1843, William Clayton (Joseph Smith's scribe and a spy for Heber) recorded that he had;

> "conversed with H.C.K. [Heber C. Kimball] concerning a plot that is being laid to entrap **the brethren of the secret priesthood** by bro. H[yrum]. and others" (William Clayton Journal, May 23, 1843, 1842-46 journal).

Six days later on May 29th of 1843, Clayton wrote about William Smith specifically, and the fact that he was beginning to take matters into his own hands. Apostles William Smith and George Adams (both members of "**the secret priesthood**" at this time) were marrying additional wives to some men secretly – and without the oversight and permission of Brigham Young (after Joseph's murder he would later claim to have the sole authority of Elijah's sealing power to join multiple women to one man). Clayton wrote of a special prayer circle, in which, "The subjects prayed for were many, especially that the LORD would over-rule the movements of Wm. Smith who is endeavoring to ride the Twelve down" (William Clayton Journal, 29 May, 1845). Eventually apostles William Smith and John Page departed Nauvoo for their own safety. Both men were eventually excommunicated from the church by Young.

Following their English missions, many of the Twelve began participating in Brigham's "*new order of things*." They were also involved in fundraising for construction of both the Nauvoo house and what we call today, "the Nauvoo Temple." The Masonic Lodge building was also going up. The Prophet Joseph saw the construction of all three buildings as useful for the poverty-stricken Saints. Following Joseph's death there would also be work on the mansions for Brigham, Heber, and others in the Twelve. In time, five Masonic lodges were eventually installed in and around Nauvoo, serving some 1,492, mostly Mormon men. Joseph had frequently complained that work on "the Nauvoo house" was not advancing fast enough, because of other priorities by the Twelve. That priority was their own mansions (see Hagai 1), two Masonic buildings, and spiritual wifery.

Theft, Embezelment & Counterfeiting Among the Twelve

In the multiple wives doctrine of Young, Kimball, and the Twelve, sexual sin was justified with new religious beliefs (addressed in chap. 5). Satan has always used the lusts of the flesh to corrupt God's work. This lust for the things of the world also included wealth and power. It causes division and strife. The poor are forsaken. By 1843, Joseph Smith confronted Brigham Young and others in the Twelve, accusing them of embezelment of some $200.00 a day that had come up missing. The Twelve (nearly all Masons) had been charged by Joseph Smith to collect funding from the Saints for construction of the Nauvoo House (a hotel-like structure) and the new Temple. Many were pocketing portions of the donations they were collecting from the Saints. Joseph was most concerned for the quick completion of "the Nauvoo House" and the temple he had seen in vision; the exterior patterned after John's revelation in JST Revelation 12. Neither building would be completed by the time the Saints left Nauvoo.

Joseph was noting in 1843 that collected funds were disappearing, and thus payments to laborers on the two higher priority buildings were not able to be made. Joseph cared for the Saints and knew that many of them were desperate for money to support themselves. Joseph believed the funds were being embezelled by the Twelve. Both Hyrum Smith and those in the Law group were aware that the embezelment was also tied to the secrecy of blood oaths. Resolution 10 and 11 in the first and only issue of the Expositor (printed by the Law group, endnote 15) addressed embezzlement and how the blood-oath penalties were tied to the secrecy in how the funds were taken and used.

In May of 1843, Joseph Smith stated, "Of the twelve apostles chosen in Kirtland and ordained under the hands of Oliver Cowdrey, David Whitmer and myself, there have been but two but what have lifted their heel against me—namely Brigham Young and Heber C. Kimball" (May 28, 1843, HC 5:412). That same year, Joseph accused Brigham Young and others of the Twelve of embezzlement of funds collected by the Twelve. William Clayton wrote about it.

> "The next business [of the Nauvoo High Council] was appointing the Twelve on their mission &c. He [Joseph] showed the injustice of Elders collecting funds for the Temple in as much as they rarely brought them there. The conference must contrive some measures to put the Twelve under bonds, for a **true return of monies** received by them (William Clayton Journal, 1842 – 1846).

In an April 6, 1843 meeting, Joseph Smith said:

> "It is not right that all the burden of the Nauvoo House should rest on a few individuals and we will now consider the propriety of sending the Twelve [Apostles] to collect names for the Nauvoo House. There has been too great latitude in individuals for the building of the [Masonic] Temple to the exclusion of the Nauvoo House. It has been reported that **the Twelve have wages $200 per day for their services**. I never heard this till recently and I do not believe I have ever known their having any thing. I go in for **binding up the Twelve**. Let this conference institute an order to this end and let **no more pay money** or stock into the hands of the Twelve except the payer transmit the account immediately **to the Trustee in trust and no man else** /but the Twelve [Apostles]/ have authority to act as agents for the Temple and Nauvoo House…I propose that you send moneys for the Temple by the Twelve [Apostles] some or all; or some agent of your chosing and if you send by others and the money is lost, tis lost to yourselves. I cannot be responsible for it…"(Scott Faulring, 1989, An American Prophet's Record: Diaries and Journals of Joseph Smith, 1842-43, pps. 328-29, in protest, Young refused to sit on the stand).

Because some $200 a day was disappearing, Hyrum Smith accused those embezeling the money of using secret blood-oaths to keep their theft secret.

> "A man who formerly belonged to the Church revealed to me there are a band of men and some strong in the faith of the Doctrine of the Latter-day Saints, and some who do not belong to the Church / were bound by **secret oaths** & c. / that **it is right to steal from anyone who does not belong to the Churc**h if they gave ¼ part to the [Masonic] Temple. If they did not remain stedfast **they ripped open their bowels** and gave them to the cat fish and they are the very Gadianton robbers of the last days" (HC [RLDS] 2:644-45).

In addition to embezzlement, Apostle William Smith believed Young and others used the plight of some women with children as an excuse to take them as polygamous wives via their secret priesthood, using the embezzled funds to then support them. Young and others in the Twelve were apparently building mansions for themselves at this time with the funding. William Smith stated:

> "Young's first plural wife, Lucy Seely, was a young woman separated from her ill husband, with two little children to support. **That the church funds have been misapplied, I have no hesitation in asserting**, for of necessity I have been made acquainted with the fact, that several houses have been tilled up with women who have been secretly married to Brigham Young, H. C. Kimble [Heber C. Kimball], and Willard Richards—women with little children in their arms, who had no means of support except from the tithing funds...(William Smith, A Proclamation, Warsaw Signal, Oct. 22, 1845).

One of the first signs of trouble in any society is how the poor are cared for. God rained down fire and brimstone upon Sodom and Gomorrah, not just for their sexual perversions, but because the poor and needy were ignored (see Ezek. 16:49). Many converts from Europe came to Nauvoo with very little money. Young and others of the Twelve built themselves mansions after the three Smith brothers were murdered. Embezzlement may have helped with this. The leaders had corrupted themselves, like King Noah and his priests. They put heavy taxes on the people to support their lavish lifestyle, complete with multiple wives and concubines.

The Law Group & the Secret Chamber: *Two Conspiracies at Once Leading to the Smith Murders*

Trouble really started to ramp up for Joseph and potentially the Twelve three months prior to his murder. On March 27, 1844, M. G. Eaton and A. B. Williams submitted sworn court affidavits that prominent men in the LDS Church and in the city of Nauvoo had formed a conspiracy against Joseph, Hyrum, the entire Smith family, *and* the Apostles. Eaton and Williams revealed that the conspirators were "the Law group." They were accusing Joseph and Hyrum of polygamy and threatened to kill Joseph and every member of the Smith family. Some in the group wanted revenge on Joseph Smith for their *private* excommunication from the Church by him. Eaton and Williams testified that the conspirators were William Law (Joseph's former counselor in the First Presidency), his brother Wilson Law, Attorney Chauncy L. Higbee, and his brother Francis M. Higbee, Dr. Robert and Charles Foster, Joseph H. Jackson, and others. Eaton and Williams were unaware that a second group, **the secret chamber members** (most of the Twelve Apostles) were also conspiring against Joseph and Hyrum Smith, and *how they might silence them*, as the Smith's knew that Brigham and some of the Twelve were the masterminds behind the spiritual wives movement since 1841.

According to the affidavits, the Law group conspirators claimed that it wasn't just Joseph and Hyrum who were involved with polygamy, but select members of the Twelve too. They believed church leaders were secretly engaged in both polygamy and polyandry. This was one of fifteen "resolutions" that they wanted addressed, resolutions printed in the first and only issue of the Expositor in June 7th of 1844. Other resolutions in The Expositor focused on Joseph's fallen status for teaching false doctrine, the use of blood-oaths to secure funding for the new temple, and other complaints. The Apostles had much to fear if this newspaper continued printing damaging claims. They could be discovered. Joseph Smith knew that the Twelve and the Law group were both using his name for their own agendas. The Twelve did so to justify their spiritual wifery and to bring in new converts to the practice. The Law group (like the secret chamber) wanted to destroy Joseph. Both wanted power. It was a serious conspiracy.

No matter how often and how hard Joseph denied that he had additional wives, most of the Saints would not believe him, as the Apostles were denying their involvement in it and condemning publicly, while secretly practicing it. Many of the Nauvoo Saints were brought into the church by the apostles in the British Isles. They believed the apostles were simply following Joseph's example and directions, if they were in fact involved with polygamy, and that the secrecy was necessary at this time. **They could not separate Joseph from the Twelve**. This is the case with most of the Saints today too. The apostles then *and* today use this perception to their advantage. Equally important at Nauvoo, some apostles in the secret chamber were feeding the Law group lies to create added hostility towards the Smiths.

Those in the secret chamber feared that the Law group could **expose** them as well. They knew that the Law group had plans to purchase a press to begin printing a new publication that would expose what they believed was happening in Nauvoo. The Law group believed that Joseph Smith and the Twelve were behind it all, and that the new secret things Joseph had been teaching (tied to the new endowment, the Council of Fifty, etc.) revealed that he was a fallen prophet (see D&C 3:9). Much of what was published in the first and only issue of *The Expositor* had good intentions. This is evident in the paper's fifteen "resolutions," where a desire to preserve the original truths of the Gospel of Christ was expressed. The Law group was not privy to Joseph's framing by the secret chamber.

The secret chamber had to act quickly to stop more publicity by the Law group, publicity that could result in their prosecution by civil authorities and potential jail time on charges of bigamy. Joseph Smith's growing knowledge of the secret polygamy and polyandry among the Twelve was less of a threat to them, until they learned that he was about to have Nauvoo Stake President William Marks begin church courts against them. They also knew that Joseph was preparing to appear before a grand jury to clear his name of all charges tied to the crime of polygamy. It would be very public and there Joseph could expose those in the Twelve practicing spiritual wifery. They could be imprisoned.

Publicly the apostles aligned themselves with Joseph Smith to stand against the practice. Privately, those part of the secret chamber were developing plans to silence him permanently. Apostle John Taylor and Willard Richards were both important cogs in these plans. Taylor was editor and printer of Nauvoo's two newspapers. One was the church's official paper – the Times and Seasons (Joseph Smith was the original editor of it), and the other was the Nauvoo Neighbor - a more politically minded civil publication. As an apostle, he had a double responsibility to both speak and publish the truth. What he did not reveal in his two newspapers was just as important as what he printed, however (see endnote 14). Instead of reporting the complete truth, Taylor did two things; (1) In a May 15,1844, *Times and Seasons* article, where Joseph's May 8 court case was reported, Taylor falsely portrayed Nauvoo as a peaceful and flourishing city. In addition, he deleted a critical portion of the affidavit by M. G. Eaton, when it was published in both papers, stating, "some expressions are too indecorous for insertion." His deletion removed an important link in the chain of events that showed that it was the apostles who were introducing polygamy officially into the LDS church in the early 1840's, not the Prophet Joseph Smith and his brother Hyrum.

A reading of the Eaton affidavit reveals that Chauncy Higbee had been sharing with Eaton and the Law group allegations against Joseph **and the Twelve about their spiritual wives system**, including how church elders had married a number of wives, while some were still married to prior husbands (polyandry). At this point in the affidavit, Eaton asked Higbee a question. Eaton's question to Higbee was **deleted by Taylor in both newspaper accounts**. In addition, attorney Chauncy Higbee's entire reply to Eaton was also left out. It is believed specific names were given along with specific actions that would do tremendous damage to the Twelve. This testimony is no longer available. Taylor's editing was one of many reasons why the Law Group decided to purchase their own press, the one that would eventually print the lone issue of *The Expositor.*

The case of Francis M. Higbee versus Joseph Smith

By mid-May of 1844, Joseph Smith was arrested on the charges made by Francis M. Higbee of the Law group. This 20-year old had gotten involved with John Bennett and his spiritual wifery. In his $5,000 court case against Joseph, Francis made a number of false claims. They continue to be used by the LDS church today to prove Joseph was a polygamist. The story and its claims have a number of twists. By this time Francis had contacted a venereal disease from a French prostitute from Warsaw. He was now very sick in bed. Dr. Bennett had been treating him. Prior to his sickness he had been seeing Nancy Rigdon, the daughter of President and Sister Sidney Rigdon. Nancy later stopped seeing Francis. In his suit against Joseph, Francis claimed that the Mormon Prophet had assailed the virtue of Nancy and that he had asked her to be one of his spiritual wives. Bennett wrote a whole espose' on it. This is where Apostle Willard Richards of the secret chamber became part of the whole story.

Richards was the official Church Historian and Recorder. He took this job after returning to Nauvoo from his English mission. It insured that all of Joseph's actions could be watched and that Church history could be modified the way Brigham Young desired. Richards personally delivered a letter to Nancy Rigdon and in Richards own handwriting, **claiming that Joseph Smith had dictated it to him**. It was a letter asking Nancy to be Joseph's wife (it can be viewd at https://restorationbookstore.org/articles/nopoligamy/jsfp-visionarticles/JSFP-Vision71.htm). Apostle Willard Richards never denied that he wrote and delivered the letter to Nancy Rigdon. In contrast, Joseph stated clearly that he was not its author. Church historians after Joseph's murder ignored Joseph's denial of authorship, and after they copied the letter directly from Bennett's book in *The History of the Saints,* they falsely attributed it to Joseph the Prophet. To further attribute the letter to Joseph, they called it an essay and gave it the title of "Happiness." They also printed a false statement about the letter (see *History of the Church* 5:134–136). In referencing this letter, which they knowingly copied from Bennett's slanderous book on Mormon polygamy, they wrote to trusting Latter-day Saints:

> "It is not positively known what occasioned the writing of this essay; but when it is borne in mind that at this time the new law of marriage for the Church-marriage for eternity, including plurity of wives under some circumstances - was being introduced by the Prophet, it is very likely that the article was written with a view of applying the principles here expounded to the conditions created by introducing said marriage system" (HC, 5:134).

To defend himself against Francis Higbee's false claims, Joseph submitted the Eaton and William's affidavits as evidence for his own defense. He claimed that the Higbees, the Laws, and others were in a conspiracy against him (see Times and Seasons 5 [May 15, 1844]: 541–542). More importantly, the affidavits also revealed that **polygamy among the Twelve was one of the subjects that the Law group was determined to expose before the public**. The polygamy charges Francis Higbee made against Joseph could easily bring the polygamy of some of the apostles into question in a public court case. Something had to be done to silence Joseph and the new newspaper known as *The Expositor.*

By this time the Law group had purchased their printing press, knowing that Taylor and his newspapers were tied to Brigham and the Twelve (the secret chamber). With their own press, the Law group could expose what they believed was going on with both Joseph *and* the Twelve. The Law group was unaware that Joseph was innocent and that the secret chamber members were feeding them lies to speed Joseph's arrest and downfall. He had become the scapegoat for both groups. **Both were using Joseph's name to push their own agendas.** With the new press in place, the leaders of the secret chamber had to act quickly. They needed to get Joseph and Hyrum into jail quickly. They also needed to stop the new newspaper from revealing too much about them. With Joseph and Hyrum in jail, they could be put away by a faceless, nameless mob, incited for them by the Law group and their new newspaper. To keep too much information from coming forth in the new paper, the plan of the secret chamber required apostle John Taylor, a Nauvoo City Council member (and publisher), along with apostle Willard Richards, to pressure Joseph into signing an order to destroy the Law group's new printing press (this occurred June 10, 1844).

This plan was implemented just after the first issue of the Expositor was published (June 7, 1844). It excited much public interest against Joseph. More issues of the newspaper, however, would do great damage to the Twelve. A meeting of Taylor and Richards with Joseph occurred in the Smith family home. There Joseph and Emma were having breakfast. Apostle William Smith just happened to be there too. Taylor and Richards came to seek immediate action by Joseph (as Nauvoo's Mayor) in destroying the troublesome new press. They weren't interested in preserving Joseph's reputation, as much as their own, and that of the Twelve. They coerced Joseph into signing this order. In the meeting, Relief Society President Emma Smith brought up her belief that Young, Kimball, Taylor and others were encouraging women in Nauvoo to join them in their spiritual wives movement. It was then that Joseph vowed to get Nauvoo Stake President William Marks involved in bringing those guilty in the Twelve before a church court. Days latter Joseph met with Marks to begin proceedings against them. Joseph and Hyrum were murdered two weeks later.

Joseph's Order to Destroy the Expositor Press

Those in the secret chamber knew that the destruction of the Expositor press violated the sacred laws of freedom of the press. They were convinced it would lead to the imprisonment and potential murder of Joseph and Hyrum Smith. In 1879, former Apostle William Smith, then an old man, sent a letter to his nephew, Joseph Smith III (then President of the RLDS Church), in which he (William) revealed three important things tied to Joseph and Hyrum's murder by the secret chamber. He stated:

(1) That many of the Apostles were teaching polygamy among the Nauvoo Saints secretly prior to Joseph's murder. Emma Smith (President of Relief Society over the whole Church) had concerns that spiritual wives doctrines were being shared with women under her care in Nauvoo in 1844. William quoted Emma, stating that, "some complaint had been made to her [Emma Smith] by females whom she had visited, that John Taylor, Willard Richards, and Brigham Young had been teaching some doctrines among the Saints privately that was going to ruin the Church, unless there was a stop put to it, as it was contrary to the law and rules governing the Church. Your father remarked that he would attend to the matter as soon as he got through with his troubles with the Laws and Fosters. But mark you their conversation took place only a few days previous to your father's death."

(2) That two church Apostles - John Taylor and Willard Richards - had put pressure on the Prophet Joseph (as Mayor of Nauvoo) to get him to sign the order (by the City of Nauvoo) to destroy the press (Taylor also served on Nauvoo City Council). William knew this because he was present when both things occurred at the home of Joseph and Emma Smith. He was there to have breakfast with Joseph and Emma. William stated:

> "What fixes the stain of guilt upon these parties named in this letter making them more criminally murderous, is the part that the City Council at Nauvoo took in getting up the ordinance which resulted in the destruction of the Expositor press. And I wish here to name the fact that the principal instigators in getting up that ordinance were **men who feared the revelations that this organ** (Expositor) was about to make of their secret and ungodly doings to the world. The persons who were most conspicuous in the work, and were the means of bringing on the scenes that finally resulted in the bloody tragedy which took place at Carthage Jail were no other than John Taylor and Willard Richards, **who by constant importunities** prevailed upon your father to sign his own death warrant by placing his name to that accursed ordinance which resulted in his death and the death of your Uncle Hyrum. To these importunities of Richards and Taylor **I was a witness, and was present** when Richards brought in the book containing the ordinance and asked for your father's signature to make it a law in the City of Nauvoo. I remonstrated with Richards at the time, against my brother Joseph putting his name down in such a place, as it would most certainly result in his death. Richards, failing to secure your father's name at this time, both he and Taylor **called on your father the next morning**, with feigned tears of desperation, expatiating upon the great necessity of having that Expositor removed, as a means to the further growth and prosperity not only of the City of Nauvoo, but of the cause of the Church abroad. Thus these men, with the sophistry of their lying tongues, like wolves in sheep's clothing, ensnared the prophet from off his watch tower, and led him as a lamb to the slaughter, they promising, also, **to be his assistants in case he should fall into trouble, as a result of his name being placed to that ordinance. This accounts for the whys and the wherefores, that Taylor and Richards were both in jail at the time your father and your uncle Hyrum were murdered**" (William. B. Smith. Kingston, Caldwell Co., Mo., March 25th, 1879, published in The Saints' Herald 26 [April 15, 1879], p. 117).

(3) Richards and Taylor were in Jail with Joseph to see that he and Hyrum were killed. William stated, "Thus these men…led him as a lamb to the slaughter, they promising, also, to be **his assistants in case he should fall into trouble**, as a result of his name being placed to that ordinance…" The conspiracy against the Smith's had been strengthening over the years. William said, "Thus you see, by the secret workings and secret doings of these men for years gone by, the Church was robbed of her prophet and patriarch, by a most hellish plot that had been in vogue for not only months, but years previous to the time of their deaths" (see https://restorationbookstore.org/articles/nopoligamy/jsfp-vol2/2chp14.htm).

Ridding the Church of Iniquity

In his last days at Nauvoo, the Prophet Joseph was determined to rid the church of the iniquity of spiritual wifery, intertwined with other secret things creeping into the church. Standing with him was Emma, Hyrum and Samuel Smith, along with William Marks, Nauvoo Stake President, and a few others. One week before his murder (June 20th), the prophet Joseph removed his garment just before his murder, directing all the Twelve to do the same.[16] The vast majority of the Saints tie this to not wanting the sacredness of the garment to be exposed to those who might take his life. If this was the case, why did he want all the Twelve to remove their garments too?

Today, most Latter-day Saints are unaware of the war going on behind the scenes between the Smiths and Brighamites in the secret chamber. The opposing parties were standing their ground in more determined fashion. Just weeks before the martyrdom, Joseph decided to bring the battle out into the open. By the spring of 1844, Joseph was fully informed of certain Apostles that were secretly teaching and practicing spiritual wifery. His brother William, once a part of it, was a significant aid. According to Nauvoo Stake President William Marks, Joseph had approached him (early June, 1844) to start the prosecution of some leaders in church courts. Joseph told Marks he planned to bring the guilty to trial before the Nauvoo Stake High Council, including some of the leading Apostles. Marks later testified:

> "I met with Brother Joseph. He said that he wanted to converse with me on the affairs of the church, and we retired by ourselves. I will give his words verbatim, for they are indelibly stamped upon my mind. He said he had desired for a long time to have a talk with me on the subject of polygamy. He said it eventually **would prove the overthrow of the church, and we should soon be obliged to leave the United States**, unless it could be speedily put down [the Brighamite Saints went to Utah Territory, which was outside the U.S. boundaries then existing]. He was satisfied that it was a cursed doctrine, and that there must be every exertion made to put it down. He said that he would go before the congregation and proclaim against it, and I must go into the High Council, and he would prefer charges against those in transgression, and I must sever them from the church, unless they made ample satisfaction. There was much more said, but this was the substance. The mob commenced to gather about Carthage in a few days after, therefore there was nothing done concerning it. After the Prophet's death, I made mention of this conversation to several, hoping and believing that it would have a good effect; but to my great disappointment, it was soon rumored about that Brother Marks was about to apostatize, and that all that he said about the conversation with the Prophet was a tissue of lies" (RLDS History of the Church 2:733).

Joseph expressed to Pres. Marks some things he regreted. One was that he had not pursued action against the guilty parties sooner. Another was the growing secrecy in Nauvoo within Freemasonry and the early temple rites. There may have also been concern with the growing dependency the Saints had upon him, rather than development of a personal life-line to God for revelation. Many of Joseph's words were being twisted and used against him. He was not a micro manager, but instead sought out those who could assist him. He then allowed them to do their work. In hind sight he wished he had been more involved in some ways. Joseph focused upon his own work and simply didn't spend much time with the guilty parties at Nauvoo. It was his brother William who informed him of what was going on behind his back. Joseph planned to reveal it all and was waiting for the opportune time to do so, with the help of the council of fifty. Towards the end, and seeing all the trouble polluting what he had tried to implement among the Saints, Joseph then relied more on the Council of Fifty for assistance. He turned over the burden of making things right upon them, rather than the Twelve. Unfortunately many of the Council of Fifty were not available to help him. Joseph's desire to expose the Twelve and others with Pres. Marks was made known to the secret chamber. Shortly thereafter he and Hyrum were taken out. His brother Samuel was removed a month later.

By 1852 (eight years later), Young publicly proclaimed that Joseph Smith had left a revelation commanding the church to practice Young's version of spiritual wifery (he told VP candidate Shuyler Colfax that he received the revelation, see p. 42). He would later make the practice a requirement for exalation in the Kingdom of God. The apostles in the secret chamber became the vehicle through which this abomination entered into the church. This is the **great secret**. It was part of a "**mystery**, a **<u>thing</u>** which is had in **secret chambers**" that God said was designed to destroy Joseph in the "process of time" (see D&C 38:13). Few today "know the hearts of men" in our own land (D&C 38:28).

The Testimony of Joseph's Sister Katherine

Three days before his murder (Saturday June 23, 1844), Joseph gave a sermon to thousands of Saints gathered at the Stand in Nauvoo to hear him speak. Joseph's younger sister Katharine was there. Joseph knew that those among the leadership seated behind him were seeking to take his life, that they might control the church. This is evident in Joseph's words given in his last public speech at Nauvoo. Katherine Smith Salisbury was there. She stated that some 3,000 people had gathered to hear Joseph. "I was in Nauvoo a few days before my brothers were brought to Carthage, where they met their death. I shall never forget that Saturday, June 23, 1844, when I last saw my brothers alive. I heard Brother Joseph's last sermon, delivered to a great audience in Nauvoo -- the largest crowd I have ever seen -- in the open air, for no house would hold the people. I might say that it was more in the nature of a **prophecy** than a sermon, or rather its conclusion was, for as he finished he turned [and] stood facing some of the high priests and Elders sitting there -- church dignitaries who were seated on the platform behind him and told them that there was seated on the speaker's stand beside him those who were conspiring to deliver him up to the enemy . . . to take his life, and who would be responsible for his death." Joseph said:

> 'There are those among you **who will betray me soon**; in fact, you have **plotted to deliver me up to the enemy to be slain**.'

Katherine added, "The truth of this prophecy is of history. He was betrayed, and by his own alleged best friends. These same fellows attempted to assume the reigns of the church at his death. They not only attempted this, but they attempted to introduce obnoxious teachings into the church" (Katharine Smith Salisbury statement, I.G. Davidson interview, Fountain Green, Ill., May 1894, http://olivercowdery.com/smithhome/BroBill/KStestimony.htm).

The Murder of Joseph, Hyrum & Samuel Smith

Three Smith brothers - Joseph, Hyrum, and Samuel Smith - spoke out against polygamy, while a fourth brother, Apostle William Smith, embraced it for a time. Joseph and Hyrum held primary leadership positions because of promised blessings of the LORD tied to lineal blood descent. They were co-leaders over the church at the time of their murders (see D&C 124:91-96, 123-25). Hyrum was Patriarch (the highest office in the church) and Joseph was Prophet. Both held the sealing power. In our scriptures, the Lord referred to these two men as "prophets, seers, and revelators" (not the Twelve - they were to become chosen to receive other gifts, if they remained faithful). Both men held the sealing power in case one or the other died. Young and those in the secret chamber knew this, and thus both were murdered simultaneously, that any claim to lead the church via the Smith bloodline (or their sealing power) might be forfeited. The LORD's clear promises to the Smith bloodline are addressed in the next chapter.

Insiders within the secret chamber murdered Joseph and Hyrum at Carthage, not the Carthage Greys and the mob. The latter simply provided a convenient diversion from the truth. Masons with their blood-oath commitments to secrecy were among those with Joseph and Hyrum in jail, and those part of the mob.

The Carthage Conspiracy

Some suggest that the Prophet Joseph Smith offered up his life as a sacrifice to answer for the sins of the Nauvoo Saints. Moses did a similar thing (see Ex. 32). They suggest he may have allowed himself to go to Carthage, knowing he was going there like a lamb to the slaughter. He may have done so because he genuinely loved God and the Saints, and desired them to be spared from additional judgments. **Love** is what separated Joseph from Brigham. Joseph's wife Emma Smith stated that it was **secret** things that killed her husband and his brothers – those in the secret chamber. Joseph's murder fulfilled the LORD's prophecy in D&C 38:13 and 28. Eight of the scriptures tied to secret combinations in our canon of scripture listed hereafter in italics involve **murder** (*2 Ne. 9:9, 10:15*; 3 Ne. 6:27-30; *Alma 37:22-33; Hel.* 2:8, *6:15-26,* 36-37; *Morm. 8:26-40*; Ether 8:15, 20-25; *D&C 38:11, 28*; 42:63-64, 45:64, 117:11, 123:13; ***Moses*** 5:29-31, 49, 51, *6:15*).

The questions surrounding the murders that follow, help in finding answers, including who murdered Joseph and Hyrum and how? The guilty parties may have been Willard Richards and John Taylor. Both were part of the secret chamber at Nauvoo. Both were Masons. Both were polygamists. Both were in jail with the Smith brothers. Richards later conducted the autopsy on both bodies. He also provided the final report on all that was connected to the murders, reporting on the event as an eye-witness, and as the official church recorder and historian. He had complete control over what was given to the Saints about it. These are all very convenient, allowing him to cover the truth if necessary. According to William Smith, days earlier, both Richards and Taylor coerced Joseph into signing the Nauvoo City order to destroy the press that printed the Expositor. This led to Joseph's arrest and incarceration. Hyrum accompanied Joseph there. In 1879, William explained how Joseph was arrested in a letter to Joseph Smith III.

"The Church was robbed of her prophet and patriarch, by a most hellish plot that had been in vogue for not only months, but years previous to the time of their deaths...I wish to here name the fact that the principal instigators in getting up that ordinance [the order signed by Mayor Joseph Smith to destroy the press] were men who **feared the revelations** that this organ (the Expositor) was about to make of their secret and ungodly doings to the world. The persons who were most conspicuous in this work. . .were no other than John Taylor and Willard Richards, who by **constant importunities prevailed upon your father to sign his own death warrant** . . . Thus these men. . . ensnared the prophet from off his watch tower, and led him like a lamb to the slaughter" (William Smith in *Saints Herald*, April 15, 1879, p. 117).

In this same letter, William stated that the Apostles were secretly teaching spiritual wifery among the Saints. He knew this - as he had been one of them, **once a part of the secret chamber** in Nauvoo under Brigham Young. Emma's statement at this breakfast meeting with Richards and Taylor that "some complaint had been made to her (as President of the female Relief Society) by females whom she had visited, that John Taylor, Willard Richards, and Brigham Young, had been teaching some doctrines among the Saints privately that was going to ruin the Church." Joseph's answer was that, "he would attend to the matter as soon as he got through with his trouble with the Laws and Fosters." This breakfast meeting immediately followed the publication of the first and only issue of *The Expositor*. Some two weeks before his murder, Joseph went to Nauvoo Stake President William Marks and asked him to start church court procedings against all those who were practicing spiritual wifery. They were mainly those called as apostles. **Joseph and Hyrum were murdered soon thereafter**! The threat of bringing leading Apostles before church courts is a **strong motive** for the murders at Carthage, where a nameless, faceless mob could be blamed for it.

A reconstruction of what may have occurred inside the jail is included hereafter. It has been put together via a variety of sources. Though only conjecture, it is based on some of the facts, my own research, that of a top historian on the Smith Family, the visions of two trusted friends, and the following informative video; https://www.youtube.com/watch?v=pTuu6Y6C0o4&t=4320s It should be noted that Pres. Dallin Oaks (of the Church's First Presidency today) and Marvin Hill wrote a book about the Carthage murders, entitled *The Carthage Conspiracy*. The video uses this same title. Pray to know the truth of what follows.

1. *Motive* The motive behind the Carthage Jail murders appears to have been gain, wherein a secret alliance of like-minded men saw to it that spiritual wifery would continue. Power, money, and the honors of men may have also been motives of those who eventually took charge of the church. Joseph Smith, with William Marks assisting him as Stake President, was about to expose the polygamous apostles. They had been protecting each other via secret blood-oaths, like those of the Cochranites, the Danites, and the Freemasons. It was patterned after a much earlier blood-oath, implemented by Cain and Satan (see Moses 5:29-31; Ether 8:15-16; Hel. 6:16-41). Brigham Young, Willard, and others among the Twelve had the most to gain from the murders. Young, Kimball, and Richards eventually came to lead the church in Utah, where polygamy became a central doctrine tied to exaltation for some 60 years. Young's "new order of things" in the New and Everlasting Convenant (of plural marriage) replaced the doctrine of Christ, which is the Everlasting Covenant (following God's will, endnote 31).

Young may have put forth the master plan for the murders as Master Mahan, with Richards and Taylor carrying it out. These two men may have also organized a mob from the Masonic Lodge to be part of the conspiracy, if their plan failed. The murders apparently stopped them from being ousted from leadership in front of the Council of Fifty, which would have convened soon had Joseph lived.

2. *Easy Removal for a Mob Shooting* Why were Joseph and Hyrum not locked up in the secure area of the Jail that had bars? This may have been part of the plan to murder the Smiths all along. It allowed the Carthage Greys (about 60 men from the Warsaw militia) to reach the Smiths easily and then take them down below, where a nameless, faceless mob could line them up against the wall and shoot them, if Richards and Taylor were unsuccessful, or vice-versa. With blackened faces and many guns, it would be difficult to identify specific shooters, excepting the ballistics between the guns of the mob and those of Richards, Taylor and the Smith brothers.

3. *Guns Smuggled into the Jail* Guns were smuggled into the jail and into the hands of Taylor, Richards, and the Smiths. Some believe Richards got one pistol and Joseph two. One of Joseph's pistols may have been a .44 caliber boot pistol brought to him by John Fulmer (he visited the night before the murders). The other appears to have been a .28 caliber smaller pistol given him by Cyrus Wheelock. He visited Joseph and Hyrum the next morning – the day of the murders. Wheelock's pistol may have been John Taylor's gun. Taylor (a gun nut) had loaned it to Wheelock

earlier. It is thought to have been a .28 caliber 6-shooter pocket pistol, an Allen's Patent Revolver or "Pepperbox." Joseph may have given Fulmer's single shot .44 caliber "boot pistol" to Hyrum. Around 1:30 pm on the day of the murders (occurring about 5 pm), Willard Richards went out of the jail to get a bottle of Whiskey (saying he had an upset stomach). This is believed to be when Richards was given a .36 caliber Allen's Patent Revolver (a "Dragoon" model), the preferred gun of officers in militias (half the caliber of the rifles used by the Carthage Greys - the mob).

4. *Backup Plan* Why were John Taylor and Willard Richards with the Smiths in jail? Both men were Apostles, pro-polygamists, Freemasons, and part of the secret chamber. More importantly, they were part of Brigham's innermost circle. Getting Joseph to sign the order to destroy the Expositor press appears to have been part of the plan to murder the Smiths while in jail. Taylor and Richards were key to the plan. If there was trouble, the Carthage Greys (and the Freemason brothers among them) could finish the job. Joseph's firing on those coming up the narrow stairs one at time effectively stopped the initial Carthage Greys attack, forcing plan B to go into effect.

5. *Smoking Guns* Ballistics (body wounds) tied to the weapons used may reveal much in the Smith murders.

A. Joseph Smith had a .28 caliber Allen's Patten Revolver or "Pepperbox," pistol with six rounds, brought to him by Cyrus Wheelock the day of the murders. He fired three shots into two men coming up the stairway.

B. Hyrum Smith may have used the .44 caliber single shot boot pistol given to him by Joseph. Joseph got it from John Fuller the night before.

C. John Taylor is believed to have used a .36 caliber Allen's Patent Revolver (the Dragoon model favored by officers in the militia). It was originally smuggled to Joseph Smith. It is not known how John Taylor got it.

D. The .69 caliber of the single shot musket rifles normally used by militias at this time were over 6 feet long with the bayonet attached. They would have been difficult to use in the small stairway of the jail. And they would have done tremendous damage to the bodies of Joseph and Hyrum, as a nearly ¾" lead ball deforms in flight, tearing flesh dramatically on entry. The holes in the bodies suggests use of both small and large caliber weapons.

The two smaller pistols may have been used to severely injure Joseph and Hyrum, or kill them. They were the .36 caliber gun Richards got from an outsider just before the murders, and John Taylor's gun smuggled to Joseph - the small .28 caliber Pepperbox 6-shooter.

6. *The Inside Job* Richards (as the Doctor doing the autopsy), said Hyrum was shot in the back from one of the Carthage Greys outside. They were below and to the southeast, the only entry point for bullets being the window or the door to the room. The jail walls are too thick for bullets to enter through them. The Greys had to shoot from below and to the right of where Hyrum's body was found, as this is where the nearest window was. The bullet in Hyrum's back traveled a straight line to his right vest pocket, striking his pocket watch. This direct line through his body dismisses a bullet from the outside, which would have required the ball to turn in three directions; (1) going up into the room from the window in the south part of the room, (2) turning left to enter Hyrum, and (3) leveling off to go straight through Hyrum's back and through his chest to strike the watch. The windows in this room were south of Hyrum's body. After Hyrum was shot in the back, he may have then turned around and struggled with Taylor, when a second ball from Taylor's gun (the .36 caliber obtained by Richards earlier) may have grazed his chest while going up into Hyrum's throat.

In Dr. Willard Richard's later autopsy report, he said Hyrum was first shot in the face by a musket ball while standing near the door. The militia muskets of the Carthage Greys were .69 caliber and would have blown a huge hole in Hyrum's face and head – as this caliber is nearly ¾" of an inch in diameter. A soft lead ball really tears up flesh. Richards said that while Hyrum was lying on the floor, one of the Carthage Greys used their 6-foot long single-shot musket to shoot Hyrum again. This person would have to be at floor level for his ball to graze Hyrum's chest and then go up into his throat.

We know one ball hit Taylor's pocket watch. It was of small caliber, not a huge .69 caliber musket ball from one of the Carthage Greys, but Joseph's small .28 caliber Pepperbox pistol – from Taylor's own gun that was smuggled to him by Cyrus Wheelock that morning! Historic pictures of this watch show a small bullet hole just above center. Later pictures in church publications show the pocket watch without hands, but with the very small caliber hole still evident. After striking Taylor in the pocketwatch, did Joseph send two balls into Taylor's body; one in the lower leg just below his knee and another in his thigh? We know a fourth ball hit Taylor's hip, perhaps by one of the Carthage Greys, as this was a larger wound.

It is not known how Joseph was killed, through Richards and Taylor are prime suspects. We know two balls hit Joseph from the front. The Greys re-entering the room may have also fired upon him. Richards is thought to have thrown Joseph's body out of the second-floor window as described hereafter. In summary, I believe John Taylor shot Joseph. Hyrum may have then turned on Taylor and while doing so, he was shot by Willard Richards.

7. *Body Location* The walls of the jail are too thick for balls to pass through them (2-3 feet of stone). Thus the window and the door to the room are the only ways for bullets to enter. The window to the room is south from where Hyrum's body was found (just behind the wood door leading to the stairway).

Joseph's body was found below, propped against the exterior east wall of the Carthage Jail. How did he get there? According to eyewitnesses who saw him exit the second-floor window area, Joseph's head came out first, then his right arm, then his right leg, his body falling to the ground. Some suggest Willard Richards pushed Joseph's dead body out the window. Richards own statement after the fact states, "As his feet went out the window, my head went in …balls whistling all around." How was Willard Richards not hit by these balls? I believe it is because it didn't happen as he reported. Richards needed to prove that Joseph was killed by the mob down below, not him.

8. *Autopsy Coverup* Dr. Willard Richards conveniently conducted the autopsies of the bodies of Joseph and Hyrum Smith. He may have done so to cover up some of the most damaging evidence of his false story; the ballastics tied to the wounds in not only the Smith brother's bodies, but those of John Taylor. They are from different caliber weapons, including the small caliber pistols smuggled into the jail.

9. *False Reports* Dr. Willard Richards also wrote up the historical report on the murders, as he was there and was the official church historian and recorder following his mission in England. He survived the attack at the jail, not a single bullet hole in his endowment robe.

As a "believeable" Apostle, Richards created a story that seemed plausable. Some pieces of the puzzle don't fit. We have not looked into them more carefully because we have trusted him and those in the secret chamber who carried it out. Some reports of this event suggest that just before he was shot, Joseph went to the window and raised his arms to the square, reciting the Masonic call of distress as his last words to his Masonic brothers. Others say both he and Hyrum knelt, reciting the Masonic distress call.

This may be another manufactured story by Brigham Young, Heber C. Kimball, and Willard Richards, the three Masons that would become the First Presidency of the church later in Utah. Joseph was a reluctant Mason, not fully committed to the brotherhood as was Heber C. Kimball and others. Joseph's only known comment about Masonry was, "the secret of Masonry is to keep a secret."

We know that one week before the murders, Joseph Smith removed his garment, asking the Twelve in an emergency letter to remove theirs and destroy them too (June 20). Was Joseph's order a repudiation of many new **secret** things in Nauvoo, like the blood-oaths of Masonry, the secret meetings of the Council of 50 and the Quorum of the Anointed, and some of the mysteries part of the new temple endowment? We know Willard Richards refused to remove his garment. In retelling the story of the murders, some have made a connection between the garment Richards wore and his complete protection from any bullets, thus initiating the belief that the garment provides protective power (D&C 135:2, see Quinn, The Mormon Hierarchy, pps. 145-47).

The Murder of Samuel Smith

Bishop Samuel Smith appears to have been murdered one month after his two brothers to keep him from assuming leadership over the church. He may have been poisoned by former Danite Hosea Stout, Brigham Young's personal bodyguard. In an address Young gave in 1857, he stated, "William Smith has asserted that I was the cause of the death of his brother Samuel, when brother Woodruff, who is here to day, knows that we were waiting at the depôt in Boston to take passage east at the very time when Joseph and Hyrum were killed. Brother Taylor was nearly killed at the time, and Doctor Richards had his whiskers nearly singed off by the blaze from the guns. In a few weeks after, Samuel Smith died, and I am blamed as the cause of his death" (JD 6:77). There are clues pointing to Samuel Smith's murder in the following statements. "Samuel Harrison Smith, born in Tunbridge, Vt., March 13, 1808. Died July 30, 1844, broken hearted, and worn out with persecution. Aged 36. The righteous are removed from the evils to come" (Times and Seasons, Vol. 5, No. 24, p. 760). From the family history of Joseph Smith, we read, "Hyrum & Joseph was Murdered Carthage Jail in Hancock Co[,] Illinois. Samuel Smith died in Nauvoo, supposed to have been the Subject of Conspiracy by Brigham Young" (William Smith Notes, 1875, Vogel, Early Mormon Documents, p. 488).

Brigham Young and Heber C. Kimball claim they were not in Nauvoo at the time of the murders of Joseph and Hyrum. Some records suggest they were conveniently campaigning away from Nauvoo for Joseph Smith as President of the United States. Others say the run for the Presidency was a sham, and that Young was spotted one evening at Nauvoo. The journal entires for Young and Kimball tell us that they started back as soon as they heard the news. There is no sadness or love expressed in these statements. Very little is said at all, and what is *not* said speaks volumes. Meanwhile, several potential leaders were positioning themselves to take the reins of leadership in Nauvoo. The most popular replacement was Samuel Smith, brother of Joseph and Hyrum. William Clayton recorded Joseph declaring his brother Samuel his **successor** should he and Hyrum be killed (succession in the Smith bloodline is addressed in the next chapter). On October 6 of 1844, just months after the murders, Brigham Young asked, "Did Joseph ordain any man to take his place? He did. Who was it? It was Hyrum, but Hyrum fell a martyr before Joseph did. If Hyrum had lived he would have acted for Joseph" (HC 7:288). In a July 11, 1844 meeting, Samuel Smith claimed he was to lead the Church. This was recorded by William Clayton on July 12 of 1844 (see An Intimate Chronicle, p. 138). He wrote:"Joseph has said that if he and Hyrum were taken away **Samuel H. Smith would be his successor**." Two weeks later, Samuel was dead, another suspected murder by the secret chamber. It was Richards who insisted that nothing should be decided until Brigham Young returned to Nauvoo. Many members of the church did not want to wait, however, and **support was gathering for Samuel Smith's potential leadership.** For Young, Kimball, and Richards, this was a real problem, as Bishop Samuel Smith was much against polygamy. It was looking like Samuel might become the next leader. He denounced the sinful practice of "spiritual wifery."

Historian Michael Quinn explains what happened next. "Then Samuel Smith suddenly became violently ill and died on 30 July 1844 [about one month after the murders of Joseph and Hyrum]. This added suspicion of murder to the escalating drama. Council of Fifty member and physician John M. Bernhisel told [Apostle] William Smith that anti-Mormons had somehow poisoned his brother. William learned from Samuel's widow that **Hosea Stout**, a Missouri Danite and senior officer of Nauvoo's police, **had acted as his brother's nurse**. Stout had given him 'white powder' medicine daily until his death. Samuel became ill within days of the discussion of his succession right, and by 24 July was 'very sick.' There had been enough talk about Samuel's succession claims that the newspaper in Springfield, Illinois, reported: 'A son of Joe Smith [Sr.] it is said, had received the revelation that **he was to be the successor of the prophet**.' William Smith eventually concluded that Apostle Willard Richards asked Stout to murder (his brother) Samuel H. Smith. **The motive was to prevent Samuel from becoming church president before Brigham Young and the full Quorum of Twelve arrived** (in Nauvoo). William's suspicions about Stout are believable since Brigham Young allowed William Clayton to go with the pioneer company to Utah three years later only because Stout threatened to murder Clayton as soon as the apostles left. Clayton thus regarded Hosea Stout as capable of homicide and recorded no attempt by Young to dispute that assessment concerning the former Danite." Stout was also one of Young's enforcers, not only in Nauvoo but later in Salt Lake City (with Bill Hickman and others).

Quinn continued, "Samuel's daughter also believed her father was murdered. 'My father was undoubtedly poisoned,' she wrote. '**Uncle Arthur Millikin was poisoned at the same time-the same doctors were treating my father** and Uncle Arthur at the same time. **Uncle Arthur discontinued the medicine-without letting them know that he was doing so**. (Aunt Lucy [Smith Millikin] threw it in the fire). Father continued taking it until the last dose-he spit out and said he was poisoned. But it was too late-he died.' Nauvoo's sexton recorded that Samuel Smith died of 'bilious fever,' the cause of death listed for two children but no other adults that summer. This troubling allegation should not be ignored but cannot be verified. Nevertheless Clayton's diary confirms the efforts of Richards to avoid the appointment of a successor before his first cousin Brigham Young arrived. Stout's diary also describes several occasions when **Brigham Young and the apostles seriously discussed having Hosea 'rid ourselves' of various church members considered dangerous to the church and the apostles**. Stout referred to this as 'cut him off-behind the ears-according to the law of God in such cases.' When the Salt Lake 'municipal high council' tried Hosea Stout for attempted murder, he protested that '**it has been my duty to hunt out the rotten spots in the Kingdom**.' He added that he had 'tried not to *handle* a man's case *until it was right*.' Evidence does not exist to prove if the prophet's brother was such a 'case' Stout handled" (D. Michael Quinn, The Mormon Hierarchy: Origins of Power, pps. 152-153). With the Smith brothers gone, Brigham Young said he came to power to *temporarily* fulfull a need. He later kept that power. How did it all happen, as God said:

> "For this anointing have I put upon **his head**, that **his blessing** shall also be put upon the head of **his posterity after him**. *And as I said unto Abraham concerning the kindreds of the earth, even so I say unto my servant Joseph:* In thee **and in thy seed** shall the kindred of the earth be blessed. Therefore, let my servant Joseph and **his seed after him have place in that house**, from generation to generation, forever and ever, saith the Lord" (D&C 124:57-59).

Chapter Four

Succession Crisis: Legitimate Heir or Usurper?

Who Should Lead & Why

We know God chose Joseph Smith Jr. to lead the Restoration movement early on. But who was **the LORD's choice** to lead the church after its Patriarch, Prophet, and their brother (a Bishop) were murdered? The answer has direct ties to the rise of polygamy among the Saints, and its eventual demise at the end of the 19th century. Both are linked to the succession crisis of 1844 at Nauvoo. To find the truth of what happened, we must again turn first to God and His word. Trusting in Him appears to be the chiastic center scripture of the Bible. It reads:

> "It is better to **trust in the LORD** than put confidence in man" (Psalm 118:8).

The LORD has much to say about who should lead His people, and how the transition of one leader of His church to the next is to proceed. Ancient traditions, along with many scriptures, including seven in the D&C address it. Because too many trust in men and their **lies** and **deception**, *secret combinations* often rise up to put others in power. Those who take power resort to whoredoms and other sin, forcing the people to pay for it. In time others become involved in the sins themselves. Many in the culture then descend into darkness until God finally has to intervene to save the innocent. This is why we had the great flood, and why the Book of Mormon addresses the apostasy and restoration cycle over and over again. We are currrently in the descent phase of this same cycle. Our cleansing will be by fire. Men often want power *so they can sin*. Nephi in the Book of Mormon called it "gain." It is defined by seven characteristics in 1 Nephi 22:23, including "the lusts of the flesh" and "the things of the world." Polygamy was this focus for corrupt leaders in early church history. King Noah and his priests are a type for Brigham and the Twelve at Nauvoo, and the Saints in Utah. It is the dirty little secret swept under the rug today. The sexual sins today are as bad as ever. Children are now involved in them. It is called pedophilia (child sexual abuse and slavery), and is widespread among the elite of the world. It is a focus of secret combinations today. A huge underground ring of evil is present among world leaders in governments, the entertainment industry, and even churches. God is about to bring a great cleansing once again.

The same basic pattern began with Cain. He loved darkness more than light and turned to Satan in the world's first secret combination for this gain. He murdered his brother Abel for it. Throughout world history and scripture, kingly power is sought to get and keep gain. Sons are put in prison or sent away by the fathers to keep them from rising up to kill the king and replace him. A rare exception was the smooth transition of power from King Benjamin to his son Mosiah. The difference in the Mosiah chapters was **love** of God and one another. King Benjamin and his people turned to God, becoming His sons and daughters. They were a peaceful, righteous people.

Today, the Utah Saints have a President to lead them, a man chosen by his seniority in the Quorum of the Twelve. This tradition began with Brigham Young and has continued ever since. A more inspired pattern is presented us in scripture. We need only to consult God and His word to recognize it.

> "I will give unto you a **pattern** in all things, that **ye may not be deceived**; for Satan is abroad in the land, and he goeth forth **deceiving** the nations" (D&C 52:14, see also 24:19.).

God's pattern for succession in church leadership is given in at least eight sets of modern scripture addressed hereafter (see D&C 28:2; 43:2-7; 86:7-10; 107:16-17, 40-41; 110:12; 113:8; 124:57-59 & 2 Nephi 3). They are focused on **His choice** of a leader, and then **lineal** or **patriarchal bloodline** succession thereafter – **not** "seniority in the Twelve." The Prophet Joseph Smith put lineal succession in place via the anointing and blessing of his firstborn son Joseph Smith III to succeed him. Prior to it, and before he understood this pattern fully, Joseph prepared David Whitmer and then Oliver Cowdery to potentially succeed him. Later he prepared his brothers Hyrum and Samuel Smith to succeed him, and then finally his firstborn son Joseph Smith III. Because the older Smith's were murdered, and because the sons of Joseph and Emma were too young to lead during the succession crisis of 1844-46, others stepped forward, including Sidney Rigdon, James Strang, and Brigham Young to temporarily lead (Joseph Smith III was only eleven when Joseph was murdered). They were fully aware of the anointing and blessing of Joseph Smith III, and expected him or his brother David to be their next leader – at some future point. It necessitated another to lead in the interim. It did not happen in Utah, but it did in Missouri in 1860. This is when Joseph Smith III finally accepted an invitation to lead what later would be called The Reorganized Church of the Jesus Christ of Latter-day Saints (now the Community of Christ).

Lineal succession is an important, forgotten portion of our doctrine, one supported by not only God's word, but by two unique court cases at the end of the 19th century. Hereafter, this history is addressed chronologically in the three divisions of this chapter. In *Part I: The Usurper,* we observe how Brigham Young as President of the Quorum of the Twelve took power, so that polygamy could be fully entrenched among the Saints. We will see Young's crafty methods to follow portions of the letter of the law in D&C 107, but not its Spirit. And we will see how Young handled the challenge of Joseph Smith III to lead the Saints, once he got older.

In Part II: Legitimate Heir, the specifics of God's lineal succession pattern is discussed as found in the Bible, the Book of Mormon, and the Doctrine and Covenants. This pattern was utilized in the anointing and blessing of Joseph Smith III to succeed him. It was performed by those occupying the three presiding offices of the Patriarchal, Melchizedek, and Aaronic orders of priesthood at Nauvoo; Hyrum as Patriarch, Joseph as Prophet, and Newel K. Whitney as Presiding Bishop. We will also see how this ordinance fulfilled three prophecies tied to this young man's future role in completing portions of his father's unfinished mission. Then in *Part III: An Explosion of Polygamy & Other Change,* we will witness the curses that came among the Brighamite Saints for not comforming to God's word and will, and instead accepting Brigham Young as their leader. It meant embracing his new version of the church, which focused on polygamy. We begin with the succession crisis of 1844.

Part I: The Usurper – *The Succession Crisis Power Grab*

There were six viable candidates to lead the church after the murder of the three Smith brothers. Joseph Smith had ordained two of them earlier to succeed him; David Whitmer and Oliver Cowdery. Both were then out of the church. Only one of the six fell in line with both God's word in scripture, and with the Prophet Joseph's actions - Joseph Smith III (#1 below). Brigham Young (#6, and the **only** polygamist) stepped in quickly to take charge of the church.

(1) **Joseph Smith III,** Joseph and Emma's firstborn son / God's choice to lead the church is given us in eight scriptures provided on pages 115-16, all part of the lineal (patriarchal) succession pattern. The Prophet Joseph Smith followed this pattern in preparing his son Joseph Smith III to succeed him.

(2) **William Marks**, Nauvoo Stake President / Pres. Marks was Emma's choice as *the* church leader. This is because she knew he had local jurisdiction of the Nauvoo stake according to D&C 107. Emma trusted Pres. Marks and knew that her son, Joseph Smith III was too young to lead the Church (see also endnote 17).

(3) **Lyman Wight**, close, trusted friend of the Prophet Joseph / Wight was chosen by God at the Morley Farm Conference to see Him and the Son. He was invited to receive the Melchizedek Priesthood and ordained a high priest there too. He was committed to the Law of Consecration. Though #2 in seniority in the Council of Fifty, he left Nauvoo for Texas, taking some of the Saints with him. They rejected Young's leadership.

(4) **Sidney Rigdon**, former First Counselor in the First Presidency / He was an important advisor to Joseph Smith early on in church history, one very familiar with scripture. He and Strang were Young's primary rivals.

(5) **James Strang**, charismatic preacher and lawyer / He led a group of Saints to Michigan, as one of many who chose not to follow Brigham Young west. Many of the Smiths considered following him including some of the Smiths for a time. Strang later ended up practicing polygamy and was murdered, also by insiders.

(6) **Brigham Young**, President of the Quorum of the Twleve Apostles / The succession claim of Brigham Young to lead the church, as President of the Quorum of the Twelve. It did **not** rest on his calling as an "apostle" for they were to be "traveling missionaries" away from the Stakes of Zion - preaching the gospel of Christ. They were **not to be** administrators over the whole church (see D&C 107). Today the church claims that before he died, Joseph Smith commissioned the Twelve to govern and preserve not only the church, but also the **secret** rites of the temple, the theocratic Council of Fifty, various priesthood keys, and unique teachings that he supposedly introduced at Nauvoo about God, mankind, and especially polygamy, as part of Brigham Young's modified endowment. In reality, "**the last charge**" at the private **meeting** of the Council of Fifty in the spring of 1844 (perhaps March 23, after the anointing and blessing of Joseph Smith III) was **to** the Council of Fifty, that they were to lead out in cleansing the church, **not** the Twelve, as a growing portion of the Twelve, and their involvement in spiritual wifery was the problem (see p. 113, endnote 16 & Assumption #7, chap. 6).

A Supposed Temporary Takeover

Some say that to avoid division, Brigham and the Twelve took charge *temporarily*. Taking power is like raising taxes, they never go back down. I believe it was the plan of the secret chamber members all along to get the power and keep it, for the purpose of making polygamy an institutional practice. Quinn makes it all out to be very innocent, stating, "The Latter-day Saints voted on 8 August 1844 to preserve the LDS Church from fragmentation by **sidestepping** the succession question: there were too many seemingly unresolvable succession claims for various men to be the sole successor to Joseph Smith, and the church membership simply voted to **defer** that question by turning to the Quorum of Twelve to '**act in its place**' as the priesthood quorum that had the full powers and authority of Joseph Smith. In an epistle of 15 August 1844, the Quorum of Twelve also indicated to the members that the question of appointing a successor to Joseph could be **deferred indefinitely**, rather than risk disrupting the church by trying to choose among various succession contenders: 'Let no man presume for a moment that his [Joseph Smith's] place will be filled by another; for, *remember he stands in his own place,* and always will' (*Times and Seasons,* 15 Aug. 1844, p. 618)" (D. Michael Quinn, *Joseph Smith III's 1844 Blessing and the Mormons of Utah*, p. 79).

It is clear in the events addressed hereafter that President Young of the Quorum of the Twelve pushed all competition aside, taking power in "**crafty**" ways to support and maintain polygamy (he was secretly practicing it at the time with others in the secret chamber). The LORD uses the word "craft" or "craftiness" in scripture in association with **secrecy**, **intrigue**, and **deception**, and typically in connection with **secret blood-oaths**, like those used by Freemasons, the Danites, and those in Cochranite spiritual wifery (see D&C 76:75, 106:6, and 123:12). Young succeeded in downplaying the strengths of the other candidates and attacking them, especially Sidney Rigdon. Later the distance between Rigdon, Young and the Twelve increased, primarily because of the **iniquities** Rigdon addressed among church leaders. William Clayton recorded Rigdon's comments, stating:

> "Last evening the Twelve and some others met together with Elder Ridgon to investigate his course. He came out full against the Twelve and said he would **not** be controlled by them. They asked him for his license, and he said he would give that if he must **expose** *all the works of* **the secret chambers** and all the **iniquities** of the church" (Clayton Journal, Wed., 4 Sept. 1844).

We now focus on the two most relevant candidates to lead the church - in connection with God's word; Joseph Smith III and Brigham Young. For more on the other candidates, see D. Michael Quinn, The Mormon Heirarchy: Origins of Power, chapters 5 and 6.

God's Direction in D&C 107: *Equality in Four Priesthood Quorums*

The LORD set up **four equal** priesthood quorums to lead the church administratively in D&C 107 (1835). Two of these priesthood quorums were to lead the Saints in the stakes of Zion *at home*, and two more were to lead the Saints *in the mission field.* The LORD put checks and balances in place both at home and away (like the U.S. Constitution which He also inspired, D&C 101:80. **One quorum** or **one man** was **not** to hold all **power**. Unfortunately, this is exactly what happened and what now remains as the leadership model in the Brighamite church in Utah.

The two equal quorums to lead the local Stakes were; (1) the First Presidency, and (2) the Stake High Councils of the church headed up by a Stake President. The remaining two equal priesthood quorums to lead in the missionary field were; (3) the Twelve, and (4) the Seventy. Brigham Young understood all of this. He took control quickly and in three crafty ways to negate it. In doing so, he eventually became the sole leader of the church, with the Twelve to support him; a type for **King Noah** and his priests, and their many wives. Young and the Twelve were part of their own kingdom beyond the borders of the United States. Two of the leading members of the secret chamber at Nauvoo became his counselors in the First Presidency there; Heber C. Kimball and Willard Richards. They had 109 wives between the three of them. Brigham's rise to power was accomplished by raising up the Twelve as the sole administrators over the whole church, lessening the role of the other three **equal** priesthood quorums, as stipulated by the LORD in D&C 107. They helped him because they got power too. Then, as President over the Twelve, he took sole command over the church, doing so in the following four crafty ways.

1. *The Claim to Temporarily Lead* Though not directly involved in the murders of the three Smith Brothers, Young had the most to gain from them. Because of them, the Smith family bloodline did not immediately lead the church. The anointed and blessed firstborn son of Joseph and Emma - Joseph Smith III, was only eleven years old at this time

(June 1844). Alexander Hale Smith was 6 years old then, and Emma was five months pregnant with David Hyrum Smith. Young was fully aware of the blessing of Joseph Smith III. He claimed to step in to "temporarily" lead until Joseph Smith III (or David) took over at an older age. History shows that Young never gave up this power.

2. *Removing Remaining Threats* Brigham Young quickly eliminated all remaining non-Smith threats to his rise in power. These included the following actions.

A. He released the senior leader of the Quorum of the Anointed or Holy Order (the secret priesthood)

B. He released the senior leader of the Council of Fifty

C. He overcame all other potential rival "strong men" to lead the church. They were William Marks – Stake President, the leader over the local governance priesthood quorum – the Stake High Council. The other quorum, the First Presidency was dissolved with the murders of Joseph and Hyrum. Young also overcame Sidney Rigdon by discrediting him. Rigdon was a former member of the First Presidency (now dissolved).

3. *Modification of Priesthood Quorums* Young was fully aware of the church governance parameters set up by God in D&C 107 (for maintaining equal authority among four quorums). He went around them by cleverly modifying the membership of various priesthood quorums in Nauvoo (via mass ordinations), so that the Quorum of the Twelve Apostles (for which he was President), could oversee them all. These sweeping changes met the letter of the law of D&C 107, but clearly not the Spirit of it. Young's actions helped him to successfully raise up the Twelve, who were to be traveling missionaries away from the stakes of Zion, to become the leading administrative body over the church at home, instead of the two local priesthood quorums (the First Presidency and the Stake High Councils). Because he was the current President of the Twelve, he could become the sole leader over the church. As stated earlier, Brigham Young's crafty changes *remain in force today.*

4. *The False Claim that "the Last Charge" was a Transfer of Power to the Twelve* Young also utilized the later lie (via modified historical documents) that the Prophet Joseph's "**last charge**" was a transfer of all keys of priesthood power to the Twelve, done in a private meeting with them prior to Joseph's murder. In reality it was a private meeting with **the Council of Fifty**, where the Prophet Joseph removed all *responsibility* of their sins from him, by placing the *responsibity* for them squarely on the shoulders of those present, those part of spiritual wifery at Nauvoo, including some in the Twelve. Joseph removed these sins in an ancient symbolic rite involving the "shaking" of his garments - free from the blood and sins of his generation. It is similar to the "shaking off of dust" from one's feet against those who reject the gospel of Christ. These two acts throughout scripture absolves the one doing it (under inspiration) from the responsibility of the sins of those taught correct doctrine (like the law of monogamy, D&C 42:22-23).

The truest account of what happened during Joseph's "**last charge**" is apparent in an unmodified letter from Benjamin F. Johnson (Joseph's close friend *and* confidant) to George Gibbs. In the non-doctored version of this account, Johnson supplies two important details *edited out* of the "official" church history account. The first (1) is that this was a private meeting of **the Council of Fifty**, not the Twelve alone, and that many of the Twelve were present (including some in the secret chamber); And (2) that Joseph performed a dramatic sign, symbolizing the removal of guilt from him for the sins of many at Nauvoo - those practicing spiritual wifery. He did so by vigorously shaking his clothing, while saying, "**I now shake my garments clear and free from the blood of this generation and of all men**" (see endnote 16). Joseph taught the Saints correct doctrine about marriage and was removing the stain of polygamy from him, laying it instead upon those who were guilty of it at this time (Spring 1844).

Paul the Apostle in teaching the Jews to repent and come unto Christ, and Jacob of the Book of Mormon who taught his people to abandon the whoredom of many wives and concubines – also "shook" their garments free of the sins of those they taught. They are excellent examples of this important act and its real meaning. The Jews were threatening to kill Paul for preaching Christ to them (see Acts 18:6), whereas Jacob was aware of "the abominable thoughts" and hard hearts of his people. He knew of their pride and their desire to *justify* or *excuse* the sins of David and Solomon that were rising up among his people, the Nephites. Jacob shook off these sins and "iniquities" in the following important scriptures (see **2 Ne. 9:44-45** and **Jacob 1:19, 2:2**). Jacob, Moroni (Ether 12:37-40), Paul (Acts 18:6), and Joseph Smith shook their garments free of the blood and sins of those they taught, including us.

In one of the later doctored accounts of Joseph's **last charge**, it is claimed that all keys of power were transferred from Joseph to Brigham and the Twelve. Young later claimed to have sole charge of "**the sealing power**" because of this act. Joseph knew God's revelation in D&C 107 and its equal powers doctrine. Note also that there was no **vote** by other priesthood quorums or general church membership giving the Twelve all power in this secret meeting (see D&C 26:2; Mosiah 29:26; Alma 29:4; 1 Sam. 8:7).

Brigham Young eventually tried to excommunicate Stake President William Marks, knowing that Joseph had come to him in the last few weeks of his life with a plan to bring Brigham and other guilty members of the Twelve up before **the Council of Fifty** and the Nauvoo High Council, on charges of practicing spiritual wifery secretly. Others were aware of this, including Sidney Rigdon. The Council of Fifty was given responsibility by Joseph to watch over the church and clean things up, not the Twelve, as they had many guilty among them. See also endnote 17.

> "It is a fact, so well known, that **the Twelve** and their adherents have endeavored to carry on this **spiritual wife business in secret**... and have gone to the most shameful and desperate lengths, to keep it from the public...How often have these men and their accomplices stood up before the congregation, and called God and all the holy Angels to witness, that there was no such doctrine taught in the church; and it has **now** come to light, by testimony which cannot be again said, that at the time they thus dared heaven and insulted the world, they were living in the practice of these enormities; and there were multitudes of their followers in the congretation at the time who knew it" (Sidney Rigdon, *Messenger and Advocate*, 1 October 15, 1844).

Ignoring God's Will in D&C 107 *& Statements by the Propeht Joseph*

Seeking power, Brigham Young ignored God's "equal authority" parameters among the four priesthood quorums of D&C 107. He acted boldly, moving 2,500 priesthood brethren quickly into quorums which the Twelve had jurisdiction over. Thus he as President of the Twelve could oversee them all. This included the Seventy, those who were to assist the Twelve out in the mission field, away from the stakes of Zion. In D&C 107, the Seventies Quorum was equal to the Quorum of the Twelve, **not** beneath them. Young usurped all power via both mass-priesthood ordinations *and* movement of the men in them. In just one of these moves, **400** males under 35 years old (including all deacons, teachers, and priests) were made a Seventy in **a single day** on October 8, 1844!

Young's crafty plan first negated the equal power of the local Nauvoo Stake High Council via three additional bold moves. The Stake High Council was under its leader Pres. William Marks (he was anti-polygamy and anti-Young). Young took away the priesthood brethren in the High Council from under the direction of Pres. Marks, placing them all in new Seventies Quorums that Young set up, quorums that were under the **new**, more powerful leadership of the Twelve, a quorum Young oversaw. Young started by ordaining 63 subordinate members of the First Quorum of Seventy as presidents of nine local quorums of Seventy on Sept. 29 of 1844. This vacated the Seventy's first quorum, which the LORD in D&C 107:26 said, was "**equal** in authority" with the Quorum of the Twelve. Days later at the October 7 conference, Young then released William Marks as Stake President of the Nauvoo Stake. Young even tried to excommunicate Marks, accusing him of Apostasy, but the Stake High Council would not do it (Nov. 30, 1844).

The next day, Young ordained **400** men to the office of Seventy on this day alone! This mass ordination included all former deacons, teachers, priests, and every elder under the age of thirty-five. This new large Seventies quorum now accounted for 80% of all males in Nauvoo – or some 35 quorums of Seventy. Young had succeeded in removing them from the jurisdiction of the Stake High Council (which had authority over "elders"). These new Seventies supposedly all fell under the jurisdiction of the Twelve, which resulted in a net transfer of **2,500** males **away** from the local Nauvoo High Council **to** the Quorum of the Twelve, led by President of the Twelve Brigham Young.

Young next removed 85 High Priests from the jurisdiction of the Nauvoo High Council by sending them abroad to preside over various branches of the church. There is no revelation in the D&C giving the Twelve jurisdiction over High Priests. Appointed now as Branch Presidents in the mission-field, these High Priests then fell under the leadership of the Quorum of the Twelve, no matter where they were physically. Three months later, Young then called another 50 High Priests as missionaries, also outside the jurisdiction of the Nauvoo High Council.

In addition to God's words, Young also ignored the Prophet Joseph's words. "The Twelve shall have **no right** to go into Zion or any of its stakes and there undertake to **regulate the affairs** thereof **where there is a standing high council**. But it is their duty to *go abroad* and regulate all matters relative to the different branches of the church." Conversely, the prophet cautioned the high council that they were to stay off the apostles turf, "No standing high council has authority to go into the *churches abroad* and *regulate the matters thereof*, for this belongs to the Twelve" (Joseph Smith, Kirtland Council Minute Book, p. 112). It should be noted that Joseph Smith chose his brother Hyrum to lead with him as President, as Hyrum was taken from **the Stake High Council**, not from among the Twelve. Joseph reorganized the First Presidency **several times**, but never **once** did he ever call one from the Twelve to replace one of his counselors. Instead Joseph chose this new administrator from the Stake High Council, as the Apostles were never to be administrators, but traveling missionaries, like Paul the Apostle. Joseph ordained his brother Hyrum to become co-president of the church with him, as Hyrum was a member of the standing High Council! Joseph stated, "If I should now be taken away, I had accomplished the great work the Lord had laid before me, and that which I had desired of the Lord; and that I had done my duty in organizing the High Council, through which council the will of the Lord might be known on all important occasions, in the building up of Zion, and establishing truth in the earth" (HC 2:124). See also endnote 17.

Neutralizing Other Remaining Threats

With the local Nauvoo High Council now disarmed (one of the four equal quorums), Young then released the senior leaders of two important groups that might challenge him. They were the Quorum of the Anointed (or Holy Order), and the Council of Fifty. Men leading both groups did so via *seniority* (age). Though Brigham Young was 24th in Seniority in the Council of Fifty, he was then President of the Twelve. Lyman Wight (#2 in Seniority in the Council of Fifty, a loyal friend to Joseph Smith and an outspoken critic of Brigham) did not challenge Young for church leadership. Instead he left for Texas with some of the Saints. Young moved quickly, **secretly** admitting **21** new people to what was called the Holy Order (or Quorum of the Anointed). **Twelve** of these new members were **female polygamous wives** (now 57% of the Order). Many of those in this order were part of "the secret priesthood," heavily involved in spiritual wifery. According to Quinn, "This was the beginning of Young's effort to make polygamy an institution," something that would later occur in Utah (see Quinn, *Mormon Hierarchy*, Signature Books, p. 176). Two months later Young **removed** from the Council of Fifty those he knew opposed him. They included William Marks, Sidney Rigdon, Lyman Wight, James Emmett, Samuel James, George J. Adams, and Lorenzo E. Wasson (Emma Smith's nephew). He also dropped every non-Mormon from the Council of 50.

Young's power grab did not go unnoticed. Many thus parted with the church that Joseph had worked so hard to establish. James Whitehead, Joseph Smith's private secretary during the last two years of Joseph's life, was one of many who would not follow Young. They included four of the Twelve Apostles and Stake President William Marks. Many of those who rejected Brigham Young were the more seasoned Saints, whereas the new converts from Europe, converted to the faith by Young and the Twelve, generally stayed with them. In all, there were some seven different factions of the church created at this time (see endnote 2). About half went with Brigham Young westward.

The administrative power Young and the Twelve took at Nauvoo, is retained by the Twelve today, as they no longer primarily serve as traveling missionaries, sent out into the world, to bear witness of Christ and his literal reality. All one has to do to see that this is contrary to God's will, is to observe in scripture what the original Apostles in the New Testament did, along with the twelve "disciples" in the Book of Mormon. They were traveling missionaries like Paul the Apostle. Brigham did not follow the pattern the LORD put in place. Instead, the Brighamite apostles now sit in the chief seats, overseeing the whole church as administrators rather than preaching Christ in the mission field. For sixty years in early Utah Territory, they had many wives, like King Noah and his priests (Mosiah 11). The Saints are to judge the fruits of their leaders that they might not be deceived (see 3 Ne. 14:16; Mat. 7:16-20; D&C 84:58).

Young succeeded in taking control of the church in large measure because he had help in ascending to power by those in the secret chamber, most of whom were also his brothers in Freemasonry. They also wanted "the honors of men" and "the things of the world" (see D&C 121:35). Their chief priority was not "**the welfare of Zion**" but **priestcraft** for the sake of "**gain**." They took blood-oaths to support one another in this and other practices, as Cain did in Moses 5:29-31. The blood-oaths were part of the Danite-like coercion methods put in place in Nauvoo, the secret priesthood (to promote polygamy), and the Masonic brotherhood. They were also part of early Cochranite spiritual wifery. Young later incorporated them into his version of the temple endowment. In 1990, they were removed from the temple ritual. The reasons are addressed in chapter 5.

Young's rise to power was complete when he finally became church President later in Utah. He first suggested forming a First Presidency separate from the Quorum of the Twelve in October of 1847. At that time apostle Wilford Woodruff believed a new revelation would have to be given, written, and canonized for this to happen. In time, however, Young, Kimball, and Richards, all related by blood or polygamous marriage, eventually became the First Presidency. Quinn states, "From 1844 to 1847 the quorum had alsmost exclusively an **administrate** role, far from its 1835 definitions [of traveling missionary work, as given by God in D&C 107]. Brigham Young wanted to 'liberate' the quorum to be away from church headquarters as evangelical apostles while he and two others led the church as **presidential apostles**" (Quinn, *Mormon Hierarchy*, p. 248). See also endnote 17.

After much opposition in a five-hour meeting held on the 5th of December, **1847**, those apostles *present* finally succumbed and voted to form a new First Presidency. There was no revelation given as Woodruff and others desired, but instead a general feeling that this was right. Young's power grab that began with Joseph's murder was now complete. Quinn stated, "**Years later** Hyde and Young said the vote occurred because of *a divine manifestation.* In April **1860** [13 years later] Young told the apostles; 'At O. Hyde's *the power* came upon us, *a shock* that alarmed the neighborhood.' He added that the previously hesitant [Orson] Pratt 'believed when the Revelation was given to us.' Hyde expanded on that at the October conference by affirming that the apostles organized the First Presidency because *the voice of God declared*: '*Let my servant Brigham step forth and receive the full power of the presiding Priesthood in my Church and kingdom.*' By contrast, Woodruff later said he did '**not remember** any particular manifestations at the time of the organization of the Presidency.' His diary mentions nothing unusual about the 5 December meeting, and the minutes mention nothing extraordinary" (Quinn, Mormon Hierarchy, p. 249).

To maintain this new power, Young used strongmen to enforce his will. This occurred at Nauvoo and continued later in Utah. He used his blood atonement doctrine to justify it. It sometimes involved murder. His enforcers at Nauvoo included former Danites Hosea Stout (Chief of Police at Nauvoo), and Orrin Porter Rockwell (former bodyguard to Joseph Smith). Bill Hickman would later become the most notable and notorious hit man for Young in Utah territory. His biography is worth reading (*Brigham's Destroying Angel*).

Towards the end, Joseph had strong words against Brigham. Apostle William Smith said, "I heard my brother Joseph declare before his death, that Brigham Young was a man, whose passions, if unrestrained, were calculated to make him *the most licentious man in the world*, and should the time ever come, said he, that this man should lead the church, he would certainly lead it to destruction" (William Smith, Proclamation, Warsaw Signal, Oct. 22, 1845). This statement is backed up by eleven other individuals, all of whom claimed that Joseph said Brigham would lead the church into destruction if given the chance.[17] The LORD said it was Joseph Smith who was to appoint another in his stead – if this need arose - in D&C 43, and only if he [Joseph] did not abide in God. It was his task alone as God's servant. According to William Clayton, Joseph's scribe for a time, Joseph's brother Samuel Smith, was one potential candidate to lead should Joseph or Hyrum be taken. Young knew this. Samuel was thus taken out a month after the murders of Joseph and Hyrum.

Part II: The Legitimate Heir – *Joseph Smith III*

It is a significant, overlooked fact that the LORD chose Joseph Smith *and* **the Smith bloodline to lead the church** in the early Restoration movement, part of the **lineal** or **bloodline succession** found throughout scripture. Few are aware of it because of the false Brighamite narrative we have inherited, one giving the Twelve all power in the LDS church today. There are many Bible scriptures tied to the God's law with **Firstborn son inheritance** (which can be lost due to sin), including of course, the Savior Jesus Christ as God's **Firstborn Son**. These scriptures include: Ex.4:22; Num. 27:8-11; 2 Sam. 7:12-16, 24, 29; Psalm 2:7-9, 89:27; Prov. 19:14; Heb. 1:5; Rev. 1:5. God's will is given us in 8 *modern* bloodline succession scriptures, all ignored by Brigham. Three marked by an * point to a "Joseph" who is to rise up in our day as part of the "restoration of all things" in connection with the future establishment of Zion.

1. **D&C 28:2 & 5** "…**no one shall be appointed** to receive commandments and revelations in this church **excepting my servant Joseph Smith Jun.**, for he receiveth them even as Moses."

2. **D&C 43:2-7** "ye have received a commandment for **a law** unto **my church**, through him **whom I have appointed** unto to you to receive commandments and revelations **from my hand** – that **there is none other appointed unto you to receive commandments and revelations until he be taken, if he abide in me . . . none else shall be appointed unto this gift except** it be **through him**; for if it be taken from him he shall not have power **except to appoint another in his stead**. And this shall be **a law** unto you, that ye **receive not the teachings of any** that shall come before you as revelations or commandments; And this I give unto you that you may **not be deceived**, that you may know **they are not of me**. For verily I say unto you, that **he** that is **ordained of me shall come in at the gate** and be ordained as I have told you before, **to teach those revelations which you have received** and **shall receive through him whom I have appointed**."

***3. D&C 86:7-10** The wheat and the tares have been growing together (Brighamites and Josephites and others). The "**priesthood continued through the lineage** of your fathers." Some are "**lawful heirs according to the Flesh** and have been hid from the world with Christ in God – Therefore **your life and the priesthood have remained**, and **must needs remain through you and your lineage** until the restoration of all things spoken by the mouths of all the holy prophets since the world began."

4. **D&C 107:16-17, 40-41** "The order of this priesthood was confirmed to be **handed down from father to son, and rightly belongs to the literal descendants of the chosen seed**, to whom the promises were made. This order was instituted in the days of Adam, and **came down by lineage**..."

5. **D&C 110:12** "Elias appeared [in the Kirtland house of the LORD], and committed the dispensation of the gospel of Abraham, saying that in **us and our seed** all generations after us should be blessed." Joseph and Oliver received this vision and kept it to themselves as the LORD required.

***6. D&C 113:8** In answer to a question about the meaning of Isaiah 52 and the phrase "Put on thy **strength**, O Zion," the LORD told the Prophet Joseph that it "had reference to those whom God should *call* in the last days, who should hold **the power of priesthood to bring again Zion**, and **the redemption of Israel**; and to put on her **strength** is to put on **the authority of the priesthood**, which she, Zion, has **a right to by lineage**; also to **return to that power which she had lost**" (D&C 113:8).

7. **D&C 124:57-59** The "anointing have I put on his **[Joseph's] head**, that **his blessing shall also be put upon the head of his posterity after him**...In thee **[Joseph]** and **in thy seed** shall the kindred of the earth be blessed. Therefore, let **my servant Joseph and his seed** after him have place in that house [the Nauvoo House] from generation to generation, forever and ever saith the LORD."

***8. 2 Nephi 3** This chapter addresses important **promises** made to **Joseph** of Egypt, a patriarchal father with Abraham, Isaac, and Jacob, and those through Lehi and his preserved posterity in the Book of Mormon, who also inherit them through Lehi's youngest son **Joseph**. The Prophet **Joseph's** patriarchal blessing mentions all four of these ancient fathers. In them we are reminded of specific important promises made to **Joseph** of Egypt, a special one beloved of the LORD (Gen. 37:6-9, JST Gen. 48:6; Gen. 49:1, 22-26; Gen. 50; Deut. 33:17; 1 Ne. 15:12-14), along with other latter-day **servants**, all having "**believing blood**" ("tame" versus "wild" branches in the tree). This chapter is Lehi's patriarchal blessing on (1) his youngest son **Joseph** (v. 1 & 3). In addition, it appears to point to, (2) **Joseph of Egypt** (v. 4); (3) **The Prophet Joseph Smith**, a choice seer bringing many to God's covenants (v. 7), doing none other work (v. 8), and who is great like Moses (v. 9); and potentially (4) **Joseph Smith III** (the Prophet's firstborn son), who brought forth more of God's word (the JST Bible), unto the convincing of the word which has already gone forth in the Bible and the Book of Mormon (v. 11). He lives a long life, as those wishing to destroy him are confounded (v. 14). He has the same name as his father (v. 15); (5) The followers of **Joseph F. Smith** today (great-grandson of the Prophet **Joseph** Smith through his son Alexander Hale Smith) suggest he may also be addressed in this verse, said to be the English-speaking spokesman (v. 18-19) for another raised up like Moses in our day (v. 17, thecauseofzion.org); And (6) There may also be a "future Indian Prophet" named "**Joseph**," (v. 24). He was addressed in the original footnote to verse 24 until 1909 as a "future Indian Prophet." It was created by Apostle Orson Pratt in 1876. He and brother Parley P. Pratt, along with Oliver Cowdery, David Whitmer, and Spencer W. Kimball all believed verse 24 addressed a future leader of the loins of Lehi through his youngest son "**Joseph**" (v. 23-24). This footnote was changed to "**Joseph** Smith" in 1909. One tribe of white Indians in Central America has had forty consecutive "**Josephs**" as their leader in a row (an honored name-title there). Many believe 2 Nephi 3:24 addresses this "future Indian Prophet" and from this tribe. Moroni quoted verse 24 to the Prophet **Joseph** Smith on his first visit to the young Prophet on Rosh Hashanah (Sept. 22) of 1823, as part of some 40 total quoted verses to him (only five of these are given us in JSH 1, at the back of our LDS scriptures).

The name "**Joseph**" has ties to one who is a *restorer, protector, guardian,* or *preserver.* Besides the three "**Joseph Smiths**" addressed in this book, the Bible features **Joseph** of Eygpt, a *protector* and *preserver* of the whole family of Jacob. The historian **Joseph**us *preserved* Israelite history. The stepfather and *guardian* of Jesus was named **Joseph** (husband of Mary). **Joseph** of Arimathea *preserved* and *protected* the body of Christ after the crucifixion.

Suppressed Knowledge

Brigham Young and others in the secret chamber were fully aware of God's Bible inheritance laws *and* Joseph Smith III's anointing and blessing, but it did not stop him from usurping **power** – the first type of "**gain**" most men seek, as it leads to all others. Note also that two of the apostles **in** the secret chamber were present when young Joseph III was anointed to succeed his father. They were John Taylor and Willard Richards. Many in Utah in the 19th century (including some leaders) longed for the day when Joseph Smith III or David Hyrum Smith would come to Utah and take the reins of the church. Brigham Young made eight known statements tied to Joseph Smith III and three more in connection with David Hyrum Smith. The first of the two below occurred in 1866. Young said:

> "It would be his right to preside over this Church if he would only walk in *the true path* of duty" (which for Young involved **polygamy**; see transcript, unpublished Brigham Young sermon, Oct. 7, 1866).
>
> "If one of Joseph's children takes the lead of the Church he will come and place himself at the head of this Church, and I will receive him as willing as anyone here" (Quote of Brigham Young in Edmunds C. Briggs diary, Oct. 1863 RLDS archives, for all eight statements, see Quinn, The Mormon Hierarchy, pps. 226-243).

Brigham Young was **not** appointed by the LORD through the Prophet Joseph to lead, nor did he "**come in at the gate**" as the LORD requests. He came up "**some other way**." And according to the LORD own words, he was thus a "**thief** and a **robber**" (John 10:1). He did not meet any of the four requirements for leadership outlined in scripture, including the most important - personal righteousness (humility, love, keeping the commandments, etc.). Young's statements and his invitation to both of Joseph's sons (Joseph III & David) to come take their place at the head of the church in Utah was not sincere. It required them to accept his version of the church – including polygamy, and he knew they would not do it. **All three sons** of Joseph and Emma traveled to Utah on missions (three occasions each) to re-claim the Utah Saints. David Hyrum stated that they were "poor deceived souls." The Utah Brighamite Saints accused the Josephites of being apostate, because they did not follow Young west. This too was a lie.

Many of the Saints in North America have ties to the bloodline blessings promised the two sons of Joseph of Egypt (see JST Gen. 48). Those of European descent here inherit blessings tied to Joseph's *birthright* son Ephraim, where many Native people on this land typically receive promised blessings through Joseph's *firstborn* son Manasseh. Both sons were born in Egypt – as twins. The blessings have been passed down through Lehi and his sons in the Book of Mormon (Lehi is thought to be of the bloodline of Manasseh), whereas the women they married may have been of Ephraim's bloodline through Isahmael (1 Ne. 7). Joseph's posterity possesses "**believing blood**" as heirs of "**the promises**" made to the fathers (Abraham, Issac, Jacob, and Joseph). We are to turn our hearts to these "**promises**."

The Royal Legitimate Heir

In 1831, the LORD revealed to Joseph that his successor, a legitimate heir, was to be appointed by him (the Prophet Joseph). This is clear in D&C 43:2-7 and other scriptures presented previously. From that point on, Joseph's choices for who to potentially follow him were based on lineal bloodline succession within the Smith family. As things worsened for Joseph at Nauvoo, he prepared his brothers to succeed him, and then finally his firstborn son. Brigham Young was fully aware of lineal succession through Joseph Smith III. Young skirted all of it.

On October 6 of 1844, just months after the murders of the three Smith brothers, Brigham Young asked, "Did Joseph ordain any man to take his place? He did. Who was it? It was Hyrum, but Hyrum fell a martyr before Joseph did. If Hyrum had lived he would have acted for Joseph" (see HC 7:288). Following the murder of his two brothers, Samuel Smith claimed he too was to lead the church in a meeting on July 11. This was recorded by William Clayton on July 12 of 1844 (see *An Intimate Chronicle*, p. 138). He wrote, "Joseph has said that if he and Hyrum were taken away Samuel H. Smith would be his successor." **Two weeks** later, Samuel was murdered, most likely by poisoning. Young understood the threat of the Smith bloodline to his leadership and to his implementation of spiritual wifery among the Saints. Later in Utah in 1847, Young claimed that he too had a right to lead because of bloodline, saying, "I am entitled to the Keys of the priesthood according to lin[e]age and blood." Young was a sixth cousin to the Prophet Joseph Smith, while Heber C. Kimball was a fifth cousin, and Willard Richards a fourth cousin.

Lineal, bloodline succession is a clear pattern in scripture, after one is first chosen by God Himself to lead the people at the beginning. The Father chose His Son Jesus to come to earth to save us. He had the necessary traits to do so, the most important being pure **love**, along with intelligence and other traits, most of it passed down through God Himself to His Son. The Prophet Joseph taught that when Gentiles are born again in Christ, their blood is **literally changed**. He stated, "the effect of the Holy Ghost upon a Gentile, is to purge out the old blood, and make him actually of the seed of Abraham. That man that has none of the blood of Abraham (naturally) must have a **new creation by the Holy Ghost**" (TPJS pps. 149-50). Such become of **the blood of Israel**, a **new creature** in Christ. Alma described the process using two primary phrases; being "born again" and receiving "the mighty change of heart" (see chap 7). Such are sanctified, then filled with God's **love**. They can then serve like the wise, holy man known as King Benjamin. He supported himself while serving the people with real love. Opposing his leadership style were men like King Noah and King Riplakish. Both were polygamists. They desired power and taxed the people heavily to live off them in luxury with their many wives. Brigham did the same.

THE King - Legitimate Right to Rule & Reign in Israel

Before proceeding further, it is important to first acknowledge **God as King**. The LORD Jesus Christ, as Firstborn Son of God the Father - on the Earth, is King over His whole creation. He came into this world via a virgin birth as the Firstborn son of Mary, too. He will eventually be the King of **His** Millennial **kingdom** on this earth. It will occur as wise virgins – His bride - remove their idolatry and turn to Him as the living God. He is the Head of **His** church. Imperfect men on the earth, some of them evil, lead men's churches on earth.

The Three Overturns - Changes in Leadership on Earth There are many scriptures tied to lineal, bloodline succession of those leading **God's kingdom** on earth. They can be divided into three categories of who leads us; (**1**) **The LORD is to lead His people.** In the Bible, they are the house of Jacob or Israel. They eventually rejected **Him**, desiring kings like the nations surrounding them (see 2 Sam. 8:7); (**2**) **The Gentile**s then inherited God's kingdom on the earth for a time. Eventually they (**us**) reject Him and the fullness of His gospel (see 3 Ne. 16:10); (**3**) A last-days Davidic servant prepares the way for the return of **the LORD Jesus - as King over the earth.** At His Second Coming, heavenly Kingship then returns back to **the God of Jacob or Israel**. What is happening among us, the Brighamite Latter-day Saints - must be viewed in the larger fulfillment of the "**promises made to the fathers**" (chap. 5). The Gentile saints reject God and His fullness, for men and their ways (3 Ne. 16:10). It is thus taken back to the house of Israel (the bloodline of Jacob scattered throughout the earth). The **Gentiles who repent and come unto Christ** can be adopted into this purer bloodline and be saved (see chap. 7). The **three transitions of power** in lineal bloodline succession are called "**overturns**" by the Prophet Ezekiel (chap. 21). The peaceful and just heavenly kingdom of God will occur when we turn our hearts fully to God and **His** ways.

> "And thou, profane wicked prince of Israel, whose day is come, when iniquity shall have an end, Thus saith the Lord God; Remove **the diadem**, and take off *the crown*: this shall not be the same: exalt him that is low, and abase him that is high. I will **overturn, overturn, overturn**, it: and it shall be no more, until **he** [Christ] **come whose right it is**; and I give it him" (Ezek. 21:25-27, a "diadem" is a cloth, turban like headpiece with studded jewels in it. It is a sign of a legitmate heir. Earthly crowns are used by usurpers).

1. *The First Overturn* **God** (Christ) is the **heavenly King** over the Israelite people until they reject Him. He then allows them to have an earthly king like the nations surrounding Israel (2 Sam. 8:7). It is a form of idolatry. The kingship bloodline of David is promised to Judah in an everlasting covenant (2 Sam. 6; Gen. 49 [lion]). Further corruption of the Israelites causes **Judah to lose the crown to Gentiles** (of the **Joseph** line), as Zedekiah and the Israelites are taken into captivity. King Benjamin of the Book of Mormon is a type for the heavenly King God, whereas King Noah is a type for mortal kings and their idolatry and other sins (wives and concubines).

2. *The Second Overturn* The **Gentiles** (of **Joseph**) have the crown for a time through both of his sons; *Manasseh* (*firstborn son* in the New World west) and *Ephraim* (*birthright son* in the British Isles east). **Judah** and **Joseph** are reconciled, the breach healed (Ezek. 37). Two sticks (two peoples & their records) come together to bear testimony of Christ the LORD and the fullness of His saving gospel in the JST Bible (east) and the Book of Mormon (west). God calls it "*the fullness of* **my scriptures**" (D&C 42:12, 15, 56-59).

A. *Zedekiah's son Mulek* establishes Kings (through Judah) in the New World (west) when his seed is mixed with those of Lehi of **Manasseh** (*the firstborn* son of Joseph of Egypt, west). See Omni 1:14-19, Helaman 6:10, 8:21-22, Mosiah 25:2 and 2 Nephi 3.

B. *Zedekiah's daughter Teia Tephi* establishes Kings and Queens (through Judah) in the British Isles when her seed is mixed with that of **Ephraim** (*the birthright* son of Joseph of Egypt, east).

3. *The Third Overturn* **Christ** (through the bloodline of **Judah**) **becomes the King over His people Israel again and the whole world.** Shiloh fulfills the covenant promises of Genesis 49. His Davidic servant (also through Judah) prepares the way before Him (see Isaiah 40:10; 41:25; 42:1-2, 6-7; 49:1-7 & many others).

The great Prophet Isaiah addressed a special last-days "Davidic" servant (one in the bloodline of Israel's kings) to prepare the way before the LORD's Second Coming. All are substitutes for the LORD. God chose who led ancient Israel in the Bible, at least when the people allowed it to be so. At the beginning, He desired to lead His people and bless them. Moses offered this possibility to the Israelites at Sinai, but they were afraid of God's power, and because of their fear and unbelief, they chose Moses to lead them instead of God Himself. Joseph Smith tried to bring the early Saints to God at Kirtland, but they too were not ready for "the fullness" of the LORD and His ways. He and His "fullness" were rejected (chap. 7). The same occurred with the Prophet Samuel.

> "Then all the elders of Israel gathered themselves together, and came to Samuel unto Ramah, And said unto him, Behold, thou art old, and thy sons walk not in thy ways: now **make us a king to judge us like all the nations**. But the thing displeased Samuel, when they said, Give us a king to judge us. And Samuel prayed unto the LORD. And the LORD said unto Samuel, **Hearken unto the voice of the people** in all that they say unto thee: **for they have not rejected thee, but they have rejected me, that I should not reign over them**. According to all the works which they have done since the day that I brought them up out of Egypt even unto this day, wherewith **they have forsaken me, and served other gods,** so do they also unto thee. Now therefore hearken unto their voice… and shew them the manner of the king that shall reign over them" (2 Samuel 8:4-9).

There are some 44 scriptures addressing *the future* **Kingdom of God** on the Earth. In D&C 35:27, Jesus said, "The kingdom is yours **until I come**." In the LORD's prayer in Matthew 6:10, we read, "**thy kingdom come, thy will be done**, on earth as it is in heaven." John 15:20 states, "Verily, verily, I say unto you, The servant is not greater than his LORD; neither he that is **sent** greater than **he that sent him**." In Daniel 2:35, 44; 4:3 we read that God will set up **His** everlasting kingdom. It fills the whole earth, consuming all others. "The kingdoms of this world are become the kingdoms of our **LORD**, and his Christ . . ." (Revelation 11:15). In D&C 38:21-22, our LORD stated, "But, verily I say unto you that in time ye shall have no king nor ruler, for **I will be your king** and watch over you. Wherefore, hear my voice and follow **me**, and you shall be a free people, and ye shall have no laws but **my laws** when I come, for **I am your lawgiver**, and what can stay my hand?" (see also D&C 45:59). Last, D&C 76:107 tells us that in the end, "He [Christ] shall deliver up **the kingdom**, and present it unto **the Father**, spotless, saying: I have overcome and have trodden the wine-press alone, even the wine-press of the fierceness of the wrath of Almighty God."

A royal or **legitimate** *patriarchal bloodline* leads Israel. It is often taken for granted in the Old Testament, and is present in the monarchies of kings of many nations of this earth too. In scripture, (1) royal bloodline and (2) righteousness are the two primary traits necessary for leading Israel in the Bible and the Book of Mormon, along with (3) a legitmate anointing by one with proper authority to do so. Note the bloodline rule and reign of Abraham, Isaac, Jacob, and Joseph – the patriarchal fathers. At least three of them were "birthright" sons, destined to lead not only because of their **relationship** with God – which brought their **righteousness**, but because of their **royal bloodline**. One **anointed** them to lead. So too Moses and Aaron (brothers) and their sister Miriam. They led Israel during the forty years of wandering in the desert. And last, note the monarchies of David and Solomon and that of King Benjamin and his son Mosiah. Those who develop a **covenant relationship** with God are significantly **blessed spiritually, along with their posterity therafter**. This is the pattern of scripture. Jacob may be the best example, and his birthright son Joseph. The promises of the Book of Mormon are for us and others as the posterity of Joseph. Opposing those with royal right to lead, are the wicked ones throughout scripture who want power and take it.

King Benjamin, King David, and King Noah provide three good examples of earthly substitute kings versus the heavenly King to lead. The first of these was righteous. The second followed worldly ways for a time, including his multiple wives and concubine. He later repented, turning his heart to the LORD. The third oppressed the people and led them into idolatry and sexual perversion. He and his priests are a type for Brigham Young and the early Twelve.

The Tenet Rush: *The 1880's Push to Prove Polygamy was a "Tenet" of Mormonism*

As addressed briefly in chapter 3, it was in the late 19th century that some historians began producing false affidavits, statements, and stories, all tying the Prophet Joseph Smith to polygamy, and much of it through wives that were never his. This was done to avoid the forced removal of polygamy from the Utah Saints (mostly leaders) by the Federal Government. The false affidavits were manufactured to provide evidence that polygamy was an original "**tenet**" ("doctrine, belief, or practice") of the church brought forth by Joseph Smith. Brigham and other church leaders believed that the manufactured stories and modified history would help maintain their Constitutional, First Amendment rights to practice polygamy, without interference from the Government. The effort failed. Unbeknownst to most, polygamy was overthown by the combined efforts of Joseph Smith III and the Federal Government, while two unique court cases added additional important support to his leadership and mission. The bulk of the false affidavits, letters, and statements emerged in the 1880's, just prior to Wilford Woodruff's Manifesto in 1890.

While Young took control of the Brighamite faction of the church in unethical ways, a number of groups rejecting Young's leadership sought Joseph Smith III to lead their factions instead. Many were familiar with the scriptures that addressed this, and Joseph's blessing on his son. By age 27, and following three motivating experiences, Joseph Smith III finally accepted an invitation to lead the church later called the Reorganized Church of Jesus Christ of Latter Day Saints (RLDS) in Missouri. Today they call themsevles the Community of Christ. Serving as their President for 54 years, the firstborn son of Joseph and Emma Smith worked tirelessly for the first three decades of his leadership to eradicate Utah polygamy, and clear his father's name. Few are aware of it, and the fact that his work apparently fulfilled three prophecies. Two of them were in blessings by; (1) his grandfather, (2) his father, and a third was in a statement by (3) an unidentified visitor to Nauvoo. All three addressed Joseph Smith III's future completion of his father's work.

Joseph Smith III first attempted to help the Utah Saints through the missionary work of his two younger brothers, Alexander Hale Smith and David Hyrum Smith. They were sent to Utah on three occassions as missionaries to save the Utah Saints from the sin of polygamy and their unredeemed state. Eventually Pres. Joseph Smith III also made three trips there himself. He desired to win the people over to what he believed were the original **tenets** (doctrines) of Christ as taught by his father. Thus, **all three of Joseph and Emma's sons** attempted to **cleanse polygamy** from the Brighamite Saints. Leadership in Utah claimed Joseph had implemented this practice among them. It was the lie promoted by those leading the secret chamber at Nauvoo (Young, Kimball, Richards, and Taylor). It justified their practice of it as leaders over the people.

Reviewing the life of Joseph Smith III, we see that his mission was not to grow a new church, nor was he to be a revelator or seer to its people. Instead, his mission was to **complete** *his father's work* by (1) **publishing the JST version of the Bible in 1867**, and (2) by **cleansing** the Brighamite faction of the church through **removing polygamy** from them at the turn of the century. He did so in connection with a number of U.S. Government officials, including President Rutherford B. Hayes, Congressman George F. Edmunds of Vermont, and Governor Eli H. Murray of Utah Territory. Five events in the administration of Joseph Smith III reveal his achievements. The removal of polygamy occurred in the critical decade of the 1880's, when so many affidavits were created to stop its eventual demise. The five efforts below helped fulfill the three prophecies tied to him addressed earlier.

1. Creation of the 1863 RLDS church "**Declaration of Loyalty**" This document was sent to Congress and pledged strong support for the U.S. Government of Abraham Lincoln. It was meant to contrast the lack of support shown by the Utah church. It was attempting to create a theocracy tied to polygamy, disregarding federal authority.
2. Passing of the 1882 "**Edmunds Act**" by the U.S. Congress This law provided for the arrest and prosecution of those involved in polygamy or "unlawful cohabitation."
3. Passing of the 1887 "**Edmunds – Tucker Act**" by the U.S. Congress This law dis-incorporated the Utah church, allowing for seizure of any property valued over $25,000. It called for U.S. Marshalls to round up and imprison polygamists. This occurred, causing serious financial problems for the Utah church.
4. Success in the 1880 "**Kirtland Temple Suit**" in which the RLDS church gained ownership of the house of the Lord at Kirtland and was judged to be "the legal successor" church to the one founded by his father.
5. Success in the 1891-94 "**Temple Lot Case**" in which the RLDS church gained ownership of "the temple lot" for the future New Jerusalem Temple (temporarily), along with the same judgment that the RLDS church was again deemed to be "the legal successor" church to the one founded by his father. An 1895 appeal from the Church of

Christ Temple Lot returned "the temple lot" to the Hedrickite church on a technicality. The appellate court maintained the lower court's decision that the RLDS church was "the legal successor" church to the one founded by Smiths' father.

Joseph Smith III as Successor

God had his eye on the Smith family all along. Unknown to most Utah Saints, young Joseph Smith III was chosen to complete his father's mission, in fulfillment of three prophecies provided hereafter. He did so by, (1) **publishing his father's inspired re-translation of the Bible in 1867**, and by (2) **eliminating polygamy among the Utah Saints** (with help from the Federal Government). This stopped further cursings from coming upon them. The end of polygamy did not come until the turn of the century, marked by the 1890 *and* 1904 Manifestos. God knew that the Prophet Joseph and his brothers Hyrum and Samuel would be murdered because of a secret combination and their desire for gain (see D&C 38; 3 Ne. 16:10 & 30:2). He also knew that William Smith would live, but not be prepared to assume leadership at that point in time. The only choice left to fulfill God's word and will in scripture, was Joseph III. It was consistent with scripture in lineal bloodline succession to the firstborn son. It also fulfilled three prophecies.

Three Prophecies - *Joseph Smith III will complete His Father's Mission*

God said all things in His church are done according to His pattern (D&C 52:14), and that all truth is to be established in the mouth of two or three witnesses (2 Cor. 13:1; D&C 6:28). Three witnesses address succession of leadership from the Prophet Joseph to his firstborn son, and what that son would do.

1. According to Lucy Mack Smith (Joseph Smith III's grandmother), an early blessing was pronounced upon Joseph Smith III by his grandfather in connection with leadership **succession**. Joseph Smith Sr. was the first Patriarch over the church. He blessed young Joseph when he was only four years old, doing so in December of 1836. It provided a prophecy of what he would do in his later years. Joseph Smith Sr. stated, "**You shall have power to carry out all that your Father left undone** when you become of age" (blessing upon Joseph Smith III, recorded from memory at Kirtland Ohio by Lucy Mack Smith, grandmother in 1845).

2. Another **succession**-related blessing was given three years later in April of 1839, when his father Joseph Smith Jr. blessed young Joseph III. Lyman Wight assisted in it, stating, "Joseph called on me shortly after we came out of [Liberty] jail [1839] to lay hands with him on the head of the youth [Joseph Smith III], and [I] heard him cry aloud, '**You are my successor when I depart**,' and heard the blessing poured on his head." It was "one of Br Joseph's posterity" (letter, Lyman Wight to Cooper and Chidester, July 1855, Wight letterbook, 24, 26).

3. A third witness for Joseph Smith III's **succession** as leader, is provided in *two additional statements*, also serving as prophecy. The first was by his father two months later, and the second by a visitor who spoke to him at Nauvoo in 1853. It was on June 18 of 1839 that the Prophet Joseph made his first public reference to his firstborn son succeeding him in a **sermon** at the home of Anson Matthews. Having recently escaped from the jail, Joseph said, "that he sometimes thought he should be killed by his enemies, and if he should be, 'This boy' said he putting his hand on young Joseph's head, 'will carry on' or '**finish the work in my place**'" (William W. Blair diary, Mar. 9, 1863, RLDS archives, HC 3:777, 5:371-72).

Fourteen years later in the fall of 1853, an English convert to Mormonism in Nauvoo told young Joseph Smith III that God had given him a duty "*to unify and* **purify the church**," adding that Joseph was, "possibly doing a great wrong in allowing the years to go by unimproved." The visitor suggested that Smith prepare himself through study and prayer for this future work. This caused young Joseph to turn to God more seriously, and study the teachings of his father. This was the first of three events that led him to finally accept the leadership position of the RLDS church in 1860.[18] Evidence provided hereafter points to Joseph Smith III fulfilling these prophecies.

The Anointing and Blessing of Joseph Smith III

Just prior to the Smith murders, church Patriarch Hyrum Smith anointed 11-year Joseph Smith III to be the future leader over the church. Bishop Newell K. Whitney held the anointing oil in a horn for Hyrum's anointing. The horn was a symbol of power in antiquity (priesthood power). Sacrificial altars had a horn at each of their four corners. Following this anointing, his father - the Prophet Joseph Smith, then pronounced a blessing upon his oldest, firstborn son **to succeed him**, should he and his brothers not be available. These three men presided over the Aaronic, Melchizedek, and Patriarchal orders of the priesthood at Nauvoo. James Whitehead, Joseph Smith's private secretary at this time (and during the last two years of his life), provided the most detailed record of this important event. It has been swept under the rug by Brighamite leaders. Historians today say it took place in the upper Council Room of the Red Brick Store in the spring of 1844 (some say it was Wednesday, Jan. 17). This event is not found in our church history, for obvious reasons, but it was presented as evidence in Whitehead's court testimony in 1892, during the Temple Lot Case (see the verdicts, pages 122-23). This act became an important component of Josephite history (RLDS church records). Pres. Joseph Smith III addressed his anointing and blessing by his father and uncle in his own testimony in this same important court case.

The Legal, Legitimate Heir - versus the Usurper

The tradition employed in the LDS church today, to replace a church president who has died, utilizes **seniority**. The next president is the one with the longest tenure among the Twelve. God's word in D&C 43:3 addresses His way. It features three qualifications God put in place for one with **legitimate right** to lead. Young did not meet **any** of them. First, (1) no man could be "appointed" (chosen) to this calling, except it was through Joseph Smith, **God's mouthpiece**. Second, (2) not meeting this requirement would reveal *deception* or *false teaching* among the people. And third, (3) God said that His chosen leader must "*come in at the gate*," or be ordained to this calling by one with authority to do so. This is **God's law of succession** in leadership, as revealed in the eight modern scriptures listed on pages 116-17 (and those of the Bible there). They are clearly tied to blood lineage (father to son). On four different occasions the Prophet Joseph designated his son Joseph Smith III (his firstborn son) as his successor. They include:

1. Joseph's 1838 Liberty Jail statement about Joseph III, as recorded by Lyman Wight
2. Joseph's 1844 blessing upon young Joseph III on the 2nd floor of Red Brick Store in Nauvoo
3. Joseph's 1844 statement made just east of Temple Grove in Nauvoo, where in an assembly of some 3,000 Saints, the Prophet Joseph was asked who his successor would be. Turning around, he pointed to his firstborn son Joseph III seated behind him
4. And Joseph's statement the week of his murder, where before leaving home, Joseph again repeated that his son Joseph III would be his successor.

Note how Joseph's actions above are consistent with the clear pattern present in other scripture too.

(1) *Royal Patriarchal Bloodline* Joseph Smith III was the firstborn son of the Prophet Joseph Smith and his wife Emma, a royal patriarchal bloodline relationship. He was appointed by his father according to D&C 43:3.

(2) *Righteousness Before the LORD* Before assuming leadership over the RLDS church in 1860, Joseph Smith III demonstrated that he was a righteous man. He later succeeded in bringing forth more of God's word by publishing his father's inspired, re-translation of the Bible (the JST) in 1867. He also helped stamp out what the LORD called an "abomination" and a "whoredom" in the Book of Mormon (see chap. 1) among the Utah Saints, with the help of the Federal Government (as witnessed in the 1890 and 1904 Manifestos). By comparison, Brigham Young usurped leadership of the church and then corrupted it with polygamy and other new doctrines. He did not "**enter in at the gate**" (D&C 43:7; 2 Ne. 31:17), but attempted to climb up "**some other way**." God said such a one is "a thief and a robber" (see John 10:1; D&C 22:2).

(3) *A Legitimate Anointing / Blessing* A legitmate **anointing** to be Joseph's successor occurred at the hands of the Patriarch over the Church, Hyrum Smith (the highest office in the church was that of Patriarch). Newell K. Whitney, presiding church Bishop was present at this annointing as well. He held the horn of oil for Hyrum. The father of the firstborn son, the Prophet Joseph Smith Junior, then blessed young Joseph III to be his successor. Thus, the three presiding officers over the three priesthoods (Patriarchal, Melchizedek, and Aaronic) all participated in this important act. Joseph Smith III said in the Temple Lot Case (p. 79), "I was also present at a meeting in the grove near the temple, and I remember my father laying his hands on my head, and saying to the people that this was his successor, or was to be his successor." James Whitehead added his important testimony in the Temple Lot Case, stating there were many witnesses to this event which occurred in the upper floor of the Red Brick Store. Besides himself, they included Apostles John Taylor and Willard Richards, along with Reynolds Cahoon, Alpheus Cutler, Ebenezer Robinson, George J. Adams, W.W. Phelps, and John M. Bernhisel. Significantly, Whitehead also testified that a **vote** was also taken for this action by two bodies of Saints at Nauvoo; (a) those in the Nauvoo Stake High Council, and (b) some 3,000 Saints gathered east of the Nauvoo Temple. The specific date of the anointing and blessing is unknown, though Whitehead pointed to the winter of 1843 for it. Historian D. Michael Quinn believes it was Wednesday January 17 of 1844, or later in May or June, just before the murders of Joseph and Hyrum.

In ancient Israel a *prophet-priest* (authoritative *spiritual* leader) **anointed** the new **king** (the *civil* leader). In 1 Kings 16:34, we read, "And let Zadok the priest and Nathan the prophet **anoint** him [King Solomon] there [at the Gihon Spring, where he was first washed] king over Israel: and blow ye with the trumpet, and say, God save king Solomon." This new **king** was **the "firstborn" son** of the prior **king**. Those of *the priestly-prophetic line* were "**birthright**" sons, like Joseph of Egypt, the eleventh son of Jacob. He had *special prophetic gifts* (he was a dreamer with the gift of prophecy, etc.). His "**birthright**" status was revealed in his priesthood robe, with its many "marks" (not colors).

Believing Blood versus Unbelieving Blood

Those **born again** in Christ, receiving the baptism of fire and the Holy Ghost, have their blood purged spiritually and physically, according to Joseph Smith. Too few of the Brighamite Saints know what this is or how to receive it (see chap. 7). These blessed souls become the blood of Israel or Jacob, the birthright son of Isaac, who was the birthright son of Abraham. Such inherit the promised blessings of God. Joseph stated:

> "The Holy Ghost has no other effect than **pure intelligence**. It is more powerful in expanding the mind, enlightening the understanding, and storing the intellect with present knowledge, of a man who is of **the literal seed of Abraham**, than one that is a Gentile, though it may not have half as much visible effect upon the body; for as the Holy Ghost falls upon one of **the literal seed of Abraham**, it is calm and serene; and his whole soul and body are only exercised by the pure spirit of intelligence; while the effect of the Holy Ghost *upon a Gentile*, **is to purge out the old blood, and make him actually of the seed of Abraham**. That man that has none of the blood of Abraham (naturally) **must have a new creation by the Holy Ghost**. In such a case, there may be more of a powerful effect upon the body, and visible to the eye, than upon an Israelite, while the Israelite at first might be far before the Gentile in pure intelligence" (TPJS 149-50).

Christ said one cannot **see** nor **enter** the kingdom of God without being "**born again**" – meaning to receive both baptisms, one of water and one of fire (chap. 7). Those receiving "**the mighty change of heart**" become part of the church of Christ. God baptizes them into it via His fiery Holy Spirit. Nephi taught that there are save two churches only in 1 Nephi 14:10; one of the Lamb of God and one of the devil. Few are in the first one. Unbelieving blood corrupted the earth from the very beginning. In the book of Enoch we read about "the Watchers," some 200 fallen angels tempted by the beauty of mortal women. They descended to earth at Mount Hermon (north of Jerusalem) and mated with mortal women there. Their union resulted in a race of giants (see the many "giant" or Nephilim scriptures in the Bible and the book of Enoch). The great flood was sent to eliminate great wickedness which they helped introduce to the earth, including **a corrupt bloodline**. Joshua and his armies came into the Holy Land to cleanse it from this physical and spiritual corruption.

In JST Matthew chapters 21-23, Christ addressed the **wicked usurpers** of his day who had taken over leadership of the LORD's people in the Holy Land. They are the ones who killed John the Baptist, the ones who crucified Jesus Christ. The LORD called them a "**generation of vipers**." Some believe many of the Jewish leaders were Khazar Jews, those of Edomite ancestry who embraced cultural Judaism, but were not of the bloodline of Abraham through Jacob and his promised blessings. The Khazar Jews were attracted to the business skills and materialistic success of Jewish culture. Some today believe that these same Khazar Jews have used Freemasonry in western culture to infiltrate the banking, entertainment, and media industries, along with most Christian churches (chap. 5). Freemason church members completely dominated church leadership in Nauvoo.

Two Important Court Cases involving Joseph Smith III & Three Church Properties

The question of who should lead the church after the murder of the three Smith brothers, and why, has unique and informative ties to the Kirtland Temple, the Nauvoo Temple, and the temple lot for the future New Jerusalem Temple. All three historically important properties have a unique association to the right of **succession to lead** the church, and which church was, is, or will be the legal **successor church** to the one founded by Joseph Smith in 1830. Both court cases and their final verdicts involve Joseph's firstborn son, Joseph Smith III. Both cases were decided primarily upon evidence tied to **polygamy** within the Utah Brighamite church. They thus lost in both court cases.

The two court cases were; (1) the Kirtland Temple Suit of 1880 and (2) the Temple Lot Case of 1891-94. They provide verdicts stating that Joseph Smith III had legal right to **succeed** his father, and that he then led the legal **successor** church (he was President of the RLDS church at the time). Both decisions were determined by judges evaluating the **tenets** currently lived by three churches involved in the later Temple Lot Case. They were; (1) The RLDS church, which brought the suit to obtain the Temple lot for the future New Jerusalem Temple; (2) The Church of Christ Temple Lot (or Hedrickites), current owner of this lot in Independence Missouri; And (3) The Utah LDS church, which sided with the Hedrickites in order to again do battle with the RLDS church over important church property (they provided lawyers, money, and witnesses to aid the Hedrickite church). The Utah LDS church had lost in the 1880 Kirtland Temple Suit (they didn't show up), thus, the house of the LORD at Kirtland was awarded to the RLDS church – the legal successor church to the one founded by the Prophet Joseph Smith.

Pres. Joseph Smith III of the RLDS church brought suit in both court cases to claim ownership of; (1) the house of the LORD at Kirtland Ohio (the Kirtland Temple Suit, 1880), and (2) the lot (land) for the future New Jerusalem temple in Independence Missouri (the Temple Lot Case, 1894). Ownership of both properties was tied to who held clear title to them. The judges involved in both cases had to determine who merited ownership of the titles based on the current doctrines or "**tenets**" embraced by the churches involved (at the time of the court cases), versus the original tenets embraced by its founder, the Prophet Joseph Smith, in 1830. Since the Utah church had changed its "**tenets**" by embracing polygamy, and other new doctrines like Young's "blood atonement" and his "Adam-God theory," and because the Utah church implemented these changes in ways **not** consistent with original methods and doctrines laid out in their own scripture, the Utah church lost both cases and the opportunity to own the properties.

The judges verdicts in both cases say it all. They are especially enlightening and are included hereafter. They clearly address **succession** of both (1) who should **lead**, based on the **tenets** embraced (believed and lived), and (2) which church maintained the **tenets** of the original church founded by the Prophet Joseph Smith – thus becoming **the legal successor church**. In both cases the RLDS church was deemed to be **the legal successor church**, because it maintained these original **tenets**. The Utah LDS church was denied ownership of the properties involved because of changed doctrines (polygamy, blood atonement, the twelve taking the leadership role of the church, etc.). In the second case, Joseph Smith III was also determined to be the **legal successor** to the Prophet Joseph, his father, also because of the original "**tenets**" of the church founded by his father. Judge Philips stating that, "Brigham Young's assumed presidency was **a bold and bald usurpation**."

Both properties(the Kirtland Temple in Ohio and the Temple Lot in Independence Missouri) were thus granted to the RLDS church (then led by Pres. Joseph Smith III). In making his decision, the judge in the Temple Lot Case listened to all witnesses,[19] and then consulted the original lineal succession doctrine of the Doctrine and Covenants of Joseph Smith's early church. Brigham Young did not. Lawyers for the Church of Christ Temple Lot (or Hedrickites) appealed this decision in 1895, stating that unlike their partners (the Utah LDS church) in the lower court case, they did not embrace polygamy and other new doctrines as the Utah church did. The higher court thus reversed the lower court's decision, and the Temple Lot was returned to the Hedrickites in this 1895 appeal. This decision was based on a technicality; the Statute of Limitations had expired (time allowed to bring the suit to court), thus granting ownership of the temple lot back to the Hedrickites. Other parts of the lower court's verdict remained intact. Both of the properties at stake were and are significant. The "**house of the LORD**" built at Kirtland Ohio was the first of the Restoration movement, constructed by Joseph Smith (see his dedication prayer in D&C 109). Significant events occurred at its dedication in March of 1836 (chapters 5-7). The LORD accepted this structure in a personal visitation to Joseph Smith and Oliver Cowdery one week later (the day of Christ's resurrection). In addition, Moses, Abraham, and Elias/Elijah came to these two men there to provide specific keys of power (see D&C 110 & chap. 5).

The temple lot in the second case is also very significant. It is there (Independence Missouri) that the first temple of the Millennium will be constructed in what will become the city of New Jerusalem. Because polygamy and other doctrinal changes were embraced by the Utah church, and in ways not consistent with established doctrine, it lost in both suits for not following the "**tenets**" of the original church founded by the Prophet Joseph Smith. The verdicts rendered by judges in both cases are provided below. Important truths emerge in them.

1. *Legal Successor Church* The final verdicts of judges in both court cases hereafter ruled that the RLDS church was "the **legal successor**" to the church founded by the Prophet Joseph Smith, primarily because it was then following the "**tenets**" of the original or "primitive" church.

***Verdict #1 - 1880 Kirtland Temple Suit /** Judge Sherman ruled, "The...Plaintiff, the Reorganized Church of Jesus Christ of Latter Day Saints is a Religious Society, founded and organized upon the **same doctrines and tenets**, and having the same church organization, as the original Church of Jesus Christ of Latter Day Saints, organized in 1830, by Joseph Smith...That the church in Utah, the Defendant of which John Taylor is president, **has materially and largely departed from the faith, doctrines, laws, ordinances and usages** of said original Church of Jesus Christ of Latter Day Saints, and has incorporated into its system of faith the doctrines of **celestial marriage** and **a plurality of wives**, and **the doctrine of Adam-god worship**, contrary to the laws and constitution of said original Church. And the Court do further find that the Plaintiff, the Reorganized Church of Jesus Christ of Latter Day Saints, **is the True and Lawful continuation of, and successor** to the said original Church of Jesus Christ of Latter Day Saints, organized in 1830, and is **entitled in law to all its rights and property**."

*****_Verdict #2 - 1894 Temple Lot Case_ / Judge Phillips (representing a three-person panel of judges) ruled, "There can be no question of the fact that Brigham Young's assumed presidency was **a bold and bald usurpation**...The book [LDS Doctrine and Covenants] clearly taught that the **succession** should descend **lineally** and go to **the first-born**. Joseph Smith so taught, and . . . publicly proclaimed his son Joseph, the present head of Complainant Church, **his successor**, and he was so **anointed** . . . The Book of Mormon itself inveighed against **the sin of polygamy** . . . Conformably to the Book of Mormon, the Book of Doctrine and Covenants expressly declared 'that we believe that one man should have but one wife, and one woman but one husband.' And this declaration . . . reappeared in the Book of Doctrine and Covenants, editions of 1846 and 1856. **Its first appearance as a dogma of the church (the dogma of polygamy) was in the Utah Church in 1852** . . . Claim is made by the Utah Church that this doctrine is predicated of a revelation made to Joseph Smith in July, 1843. **No such revelation was ever made public during the life of Joseph Smith**, and **under the law of the church it could not become an article of faith and belief until submitted to and adopted [via a vote of appropriate parties] by the church. This was never done** . . . The Utah Church further departed from the principles and doctrines of the original church by changing in their teaching the first statement in the Article of Faith, which was, 'We believe in God, the Eternal Father, and in his Son, Jesus Christ, and in the Holy Ghost,' and in lieu thereof taught the doctrine of '**Adam-god worship**' . . . It has introduced societies of **a secret order**, and established **secret oaths and covenants**, contrary to the book of teachings of the old church. It has **changed the duties of the President, and of the Twelve, and established the doctrine to 'Obey Counsel**,' and has **changed the order of the 'Seventy, or Evangelists'** . . .

A considerable number of the officers and members of the church at Nauvoo did not ally themselves with any of the factions, and wherever they were they held onto the faith, refused to follow Brigham Young to Utah, and ever repudiated the doctrine of polygamy, which was **the great rock of offense on which the church split after the death of Joseph Smith** . . . In 1852 the scattered fragments of the church, the remnants of those who held to the fortunes of the present Joseph Smith, son of the so-called 'Martyr,' gathered together sufficiently for a nucleus of organization. They took the name of 'The Reorganized Church of Jesus Christ of Latter Day Saints,' and avowed their allegiance **to the teachings of the ancient church**; and their epitome of faith adopted, while containing differences in phraseology, in its essentials is but a **reproduction of that of the church as it existed from 1830 to 1844** . . .

It is charged by the Respondents, as an echo of the Utah Church, that Joseph Smith, 'the Martyr,' secretly taught and practiced polygamy; and the Utah contingent furnishes the evidence, and two of the women, to prove this fact"... "It perhaps would be uncharitable to say of these women that **they have borne false testimony** as to their connection with Joseph Smith; but, in view of all the evidence and circumstances surrounding the alleged intercourse, it is difficult to escape the conclusion that at most they were but sports in 'nest hiding.' In view of the contention of the Salt Lake party, that polygamy obtained at Nauvoo as early as 1841, **it must be a little embarrassing to President Woodruff** of that organization when he is confronted, as he was in the evidence in this case, with a published card **in the church organ at Nauvoo in October, 1843, certifying that he knew of no other rule or system of marriage than the one published in the Book of Doctrine and Covenants, and that the 'secret wife system**,' charged against the church, was a creature of invention by one Doctor Bennett, and that they knew of no such society. **That certificate was signed by the leading members of the church, including John Taylor the former President of the Utah Church**.

And **a similar certificate was published by the Ladies' Relief Society of the same place, signed by Emma Smith, the wife of Joseph Smith, and Phoebe Woodruff, wife of the present President Woodruff. No such marriage ever occurred under the rules of the church, and no offspring came from the imputed illicit intercourse**, although Joseph Smith was in the full vigor of young manhood, and his wife Emma, was giving birth to healthy children in regular order, and was _enciente_ at the time of Joseph's death. But if it were conceded that Joseph Smith, and Hyrum, his brother, did secretly practice concubinage, is the church to be charged with those liaisons, and the doctrine of polygamy to be predicated thereon of the church? If so, I suspect the doctrine of polygamy might be imputed to many of the Gentile churches. Certainly **it was never promulgated, taught, nor recognized, as a doctrine of the church prior to the assumption of Brigham Young**" (see endnote 23).

It should be noted that the **credibility of witnesses** in the Temple Lot Case was the single most important factor in determining the outcome of the case. Joseph Smith III developed credibility with the Court, especially when testifying at length on how purported revelations became law in the primitive church under his father (Abstract 50). *Lying* and *deception* (the first two sins addressed by the LORD in 3 Ne. 16:10 & 30:2) were part of the witness testimony supplied by the Utah church. Lyman O. Littlefield, President of the Quorum of Seventy (Utah church), openly evaded questions. Joseph C. Kingsbury (with ties to Section 132), refused to take the ordinary oath to '*tell the truth the whole truth and nothing but the truth*' of his knowledge of polygamy, and was thus *sworn* by '*affirmation*' only. He said, "I generally *affirm*, and I suppose it is because my understanding is that a man cannot be convicted of *perjury* on an *affirmation*, and he can if he is *sworn*" (Abstract 339). Mary Rachael Thompson (a witness presented as a supposed wife of the Prophet Joseph) was constantly prompted by Joseph Fielding Smith during her testimony.

2. *Legal Successor* Eleven-year old Joseph Smith III was anointed and blessed to be the **successor** of the Prophet Joseph Smith, consistent with God's word and will in the eight scriptures previously cited. Judge Phillips noted this to be consistent with the doctrine of the original church as read in his verdict. Joseph Smith III became President of the RLDS church in 1860 (the legal **successor** church in terms of "**tenets**" or doctrine at that time).

3. *James Whitehead Testimony* Additional testimony by James Whitehead revealed the following:

A. *D&C 132 Problems* The purported polygamy "revelation" that Brigham brought forth in 1852 in Utah, as presented to Whitehead by Bishop Newell K. Whitney at Winter Quarters in 1848, was **not** about polygamy, but instead about the **sealing of one man to one woman**. He testified that it was handwritten (perhaps by William Clayton) and was only **three pages** in length (much shorter than the current **eight** typewritten pages of D&C 132). He added that the handwritten document he saw at Winter Quarters was latter modified by the Brighamites to become pro-polygamy Section 132 of the Utah LDS Doctrine and Covenants (put there in 1876 without the vote of any priesthood body or the general membership of the church), where it was much longer in length.

B. *Apostasy* Whitehead also testified that the reason he left the church (joining the RLDS Church 17 years later in 1865) was because he saw the "corruption" of the "apostate" church, including polygamy and other changing doctrines brought in by Brigham Young. At Winter Quarters, he said he witnessed "drinking, wickedness, and carousing" by some of the Twelve. "That was not what Joseph Smith had taught, and so I left them, disgusted." He added that four of the Apostles left the church about this time, including John E. Page, Lyman Wight, William B. Smith, and Amasa Lyman. "They refused to follow his [Brigham Young's] leadership." Addressing polygamy, Whitehead said, "I have heard the doctrine of polygamy taught, and I hate and despise it. It is a doctrine of the Devil; there is no question about that. I do not believe in it, or countenance it in any way. I heard Brigham Young preach it at Nauvoo, after Joseph Smith was killed; that was one reason why I left the church. I saw enough to convince me that it was time for me to leave the church. They were preaching the doctrine of polygamy when they left Nauvoo in 1846. I do not know whether all that believed in the doctrine left or not. I expect they all did."

C. *Replacing William Clayton* Whitehead's testimony also revealed that he had replaced William Clayton as Joseph Smith's private secretary on June 11 of 1842. He then served Joseph in this capacity the last two year's of the Prophet's life. Whitehead stated that Joseph found Clayton was using church tithing funds inappropriately and had him then do other work. Historian D. Michael Quinn has verified that some of James Whitehead's stories are inconsistent, while others were outright lies. They are documented in D. Michael Quinn, *Joseph Smith III's 1844 Blessing and the Mormons of Utah*, Dialogue, Vol. 15, #2, pps. 71-73). Even with the lies (most likely to protect his standing in the RLDS church), Quinn believes his testimony about the anointing and blessing of Joseph Smith III is real. Quinn said, "I feel that we can safely accept Whitehead's testimony that the blessing did in fact occur during a private meeting in the council room of Joseph Smith's red brick store..." (see https://dialoguejournal.com/wp-content/uploads/sbi/articles/Dialogue_V15N02_71.pdf p. 79). Like many Brighamites, Whitehead's version of the facts were modified by him in places to appease those he chose to associate with. He was a Josephite.

4. *Joseph Did Not Teach Polygamy* The defendants (the Utah LDS church), through their chief witness Pres. Wilford Woodruff, alleged that Joseph Smith Jr. taught polygamy as early as 1842 [Abstract 302]. Woodruff's testimony was given to justify the practice. Pres. Joseph Smith III refuted this testimony in three ways:

Refutation #1 Pres. Joseph Smith III testified that in October of that same year (1842), John Bennett was excommunicated from the church because of spiritual wifery (later called "polygamy"). In addition, Smith cited the official church newspaper, the Time and Seasons (John Taylor editor), which ran an article, dated **1 Oct. 1842**, which stated, "We, the undersigned members of the Church of Jesus Christ of Latter Day Saints and residents of the city of Nauvoo, person and families, do hereby certify and declare that we know of no other rule or system of marriage then the one published from the Book of Doctrine and Covenants [of 1835 specifically Section 101, which provided for monogamous marriage], and we give this certificate to show that Dr. J. C. Bennett's "secret wife system" is a creation of his own make as we know of no such society in this place nor ever did. **This proclamation was signed by the entire Quorum of Twelve, including then Apostle Wilford Woodruff** [Abstract 303].

Refutation #2 The testimony of Joseph Smith III revealed that Brigham Young put forth the supposed revelation on polygamy to Joseph Smith at the General Conference of the LDS Church in Salt Lake City, Utah, in 1852 [Abstract 322]. Young stated that the revelation was given to Joseph Smith Jr. on July 12th of 1843, some eleven months before his death. Joseph Smith III revealed that the "revelation" had **not been brought before any priesthood quorum of the church, nor its regular membership** for approval via a **vote**, during Joseph Smith Jr.'s lifetime or thereafter in Utah (Abstract 322, see also the LORD's directives in D&C 107, and D&C 26:2). Smith stated that the first presentation of the so-called "revelation" to the public was at an LDS conference held in **1852**. Thus, this action was done by Young alone, and did not follow the law of common consent of the primitive church [in the LORD's directives in D&C 26:2, Mosiah 29:26, Alma 29:4, or 1 Sam. 8:7].

Refutation #3 Joseph Smith III also testified that there was no proper vote by priesthood quorums nor the general church membership for **the deletion of Section 101** in 1876. This Section featured an anti-polygamy statement and was part of the original 1835 Book of Commandments (which later became the Doctrine and Covenants). Smith testified that it was replaced with the pro-polygamy "revelation" on polygamy which later became D&C 132 in the canon of scripture of the Utah church. When questioned about this action by Brigham Young, Pres. Wilford Woodruff stated, "I do not know why it was done. It was done by the authority of whoever presided over the Church, I suppose. Brigham Young was the President then" (Abstract 309, this action went against God's directives in D&C 26:2; Mosiah 29:26; Alma 29:4; 1 Sam. 8:7).

5. *Usurped Power* The testimonies of Apostle Lorenzo Snow and Pres. Wilford Woodruff of the Utah LDS church revealed that Brigham Young and the Twelve had usurped leadership of the church from the First Presidency and three other priesthood quorums. The Quorum of the Twelve then held this power alone later in Utah Territory. Brigham Young led them as quorum President. The Utah church was judged as not following the original "tenets" of the faith in this matter (see D&C 107 for the LORD's instructions for four equal quorums to lead the church).

A Third Temple Property tied to Joseph Smith III – *The Nauvoo Temple burns*

There is one final temple property connection to Joseph Smith III to address with regard to **succession**. It too is about a clear title to the building and who owns it, thus revealing who is or is not a legal successor to lead the church. Stepping back in time some 50 years, we go to 1846 and Brigham Young's great difficulty in selling the Nauvoo Temple. It cost a lot to build and he was hoping to capitalize on its value. This property was originally in the hands of Joseph Smith as "Trustee in Trust" for the church. When he and his brothers were murdered, its care should have been passed down to Joseph Smith III as his legal successor, or to the First Presidency (which was dissolved upon the death of the Prophet). Instead, Brigham Young usurped control over the church and its physical assets. Young tried to sell the Nauvoo Temple thirteen times in three years after the Brighamite faction of the Saints left the city of Joseph for the mountain west. He hoped it would bring in many thousands of dollars, perhaps a half million dollars or more. All attempts failed because the important title to the building was in serious question (like those of the Kirtland Temple and the Temple Lot at Independence). James Strang, perhaps Young's primary rival to lead the church at this time in 1846-48 (and a lawyer by trade), wrote a piece that was published in the Nauvoo area. In it he warned of the title difficulties, stating that Young had no right to sell the temple, as he was **not the legal successor** for the church.

Strang not only protested Young's proposed sale of the house of the LORD at Nauvoo, but the one at Kirtland too (on two diferent occasions Strang possessed this Kirtland title). According to Hajicek, "Strang published…documents from the Hancock County 'Book of Mortgages and Bonds.' Those documents deeded the Nauvoo temple to Joseph Smith as the sole trustee for the Church of Jesus Christ of Latter Day Saints—and further required that **his successor as trustee would be the First Presidency of the church**. Young had not yet duplicated Strang's claim of the formal office of First President, instead claiming the right to lead by virtue of being president of **a lower body**, the quorum of twelve apostles."

Strang's articles and other efforts severly hampered Young's ability to acquire both the Kirtland structure and sell the Nauvoo Temple. These things followed a run-in that one of Strang's representatives, a Mr. Moses Smith, had with Brigham Young supporters in the Nauvoo Temple on Feb. 1 of 1846. It occurred as Moses Smith stood to address support for Strang to lead the church. A scuffle involving fighting with clubs ensued, apparently planned in advance by Brighamite supporters led by Hosea Stout (bodyguard for Brigham Young and Nauvoo's Chief of Police).

The competition with Strang was one of seven things motivating Young to destroy the Nauvoo Temple by fire on October 9 of 1848, that it might **not** fall into the hands of Strang or other "enemies." Hajicek quoted Young making nine statements tied to arson or burning property during his later years (before and after the Nauvoo Temple was burned by an arsonist). Six of these statements specifically reference **the burning of the Nauvoo Temple**! Young ordered property of the Saints burned on four occasions, rather than leaving it to others; (1) Dwellings at Winter Quarters, where the Tabernacle and 600 homes of the Saints were torched; (2) Fort Bridger and, (3) Fort Supply, both in what is now Wyoming. Young was also preparing to burn down, (4) Salt lake City, had Johnston's Army kept advancing in 1858. Looking back, Young said, "This year has made me think of the season that we were obliged to leave Nauvoo . . . Should we ever be obliged to leave our houses, the decree of my heart is that **there shall naught be left for our enemies** [Strang] **but the ashes of all that will burn**" (the congregation responded, 'Amen,'" JD 5:337; for all nine arson statements by Young and more on the burning of the Nauvoo Temple, see John Hajicek, *The Sale and Burning of the Nauvoo Temple*, a paper presented at the 25th annual meeting of the John Whitmer Historical Association, Kirtland Ohio). See http://www.strangite.org/Temple.htm

Fulfilling Prophecy

Reviewing the life of Joseph Smith III, we see that a significant part of his mission was to **complete a portion of his father's work** by (1) publishing the JST version of the Bible in 1867 and (2) **cleansing** the Brighamite faction of the church by removing polygamy from them at the transition from the 19th to the 20th century. This fulfilled the three prophecies addressed earlier. A portion of his mission may have been revealed to him in the first of three events that caused him to finally accept an invitation to lead the RLDS church in 1860. It occurred at Nauvoo in the fall of 1853, when an English convert to Mormonism sought him out, telling young Joseph that, "God had given him a duty to *unify* and **purify the church**," adding that Joseph was "possibly doing a great wrong in allowing the years to go by unimproved." He suggested that Smith prepare himself through study and prayer for the work of the LORD (endnote 18). This caused Joseph III to turn to the LORD more intensely, to study the work of his father and determine if he was a polygamist, as the Brighamites claimed. Instead, his research confirmed that his father was innocent, as all the Smith family had so testified. Notable contributions by Joseph Smith III, fulfilling the three prophecies, include:

1. *Published the JST Version of the Bible* God told the Prophet Joseph that the JST version of the Bible was to go to all the world bound together with the Book of Mormon. Joseph Smith III published his father's re-translation in 1867. Emma had kept the manuscript for this "re-translation" in safe keeping, hidden away from Brigham Young and others. Young wanted to take it west with all the other church documents he had gathered up in 1846, many of which were modified later in Utah. Emma transferred ownership of the JST to the RLDS Church in 1866. Both Emma and Joseph Smith III had previously joined the RLDS church (both did so without re-baptism).

2. *Eliminated Polygamy in Utah* Early efforts by Joseph Smith III to **cleanse** the Utah church of polygamy included an 1849 petition to Congress opposing the admission of the State of Deseret to the Federal Union, in the Mormon-controlled territory of the Great Basin. It then included the areas of Utah, Nevada, southern California, Idaho, western Colorado, northern Arizona, and New Mexico. Later he worked with Government officials to pass two new laws, the 1882 Edmunds Act, and the 1887 Edmunds – Tucker Act. Enforcement of both laws helped to end polygamy, resulting in the two Manifestos of 1890 and 1904. Both were official statements by church presidents, expressing that polygamy was ended in the church (they were **not** "thus saith the LORD" revelations).

Like the Utah Brighamite church, the RLDS church in Missouri (now called the Community of Christ) later departed from the original "**tenets**" of the Prophet Joseph's early church. This is revealed in four primary changes; (1) Women and gays later holding priesthood; (2) The Book of Mormon becoming a lesser, supportive book to the Bible; (3) Church Presidents were later selected outside the Joseph Smith bloodline; And (4) Administrative governance by Twelve Apostles, not the Smith bloodline, just like the Utah church. Both diminished the "traveling missionary" requirement of Twelve as described in D&C 107, along with the duty of "apostles" to come to **know** the LORD personally (Assumption #2, chap. 6). Both churches are also moving towards LGBTQ acceptance (see endnote 1).

Stay with the Smiths & Lineal Succession

There is one last tie to Joseph Smith III and succession worth addressing. In 1895, Katharine Smith Salisbury (age 83), the last remaining sibling of the Prophet Joseph Smith (his younger sister), spoke at an RLDS General Conference, stating, "I stand alone of my father's family and am here for the purpose of helping build this cause…" The cause was addressing the controversy brewing over who should lead the RLDS church, her nephew Pres. Joseph Smith III or one of the Twelve. This was the underlying battle between Brigham as President of the Twelve, and Joseph Smith III. She said, "My nephew…is the true and only successor of Joseph Smith, the martyr." In another later address at the same conference (Saturday, April 13), She stated that the night before her address, an angel came and gave her a message to be delivered to the people. She added, "Support the president, for he [is] truly the messenger of God. [I] was a witness of the Gospel in the first [place], and of the truth of the claim of Joseph [III] to the presidency and the rightful prerogatives of the position. Friday night an angel [came] to [me], [saying] the church had done wrong, and that unless the church shall follow the prophet in all things the Lord would certainly send His avenging angel and punish His undutiful and disobedient people."[20] It should be noted that the Prophet Joseph's third son, David Hyrum Smith, was also a candidate to lead the church for a time (see endnotes 2 and 20).

The Hyrum Smith Bloodline in Utah

While the prophetic mantle of the Joseph Smith bloodline led the RLDS church for a time in the Midwest, the last remnant of the patriarchal mantle in the Hyrum Smith bloodline was also short-lived among the Brighamite church. The Smith bloodline eventually lost power to the Quorum of the Twelve in both branches of the church, east and west. Men in the Quorum of the Twelve from both churches were to be "traveling missionaires," **not** administrators over local stakes and wards (see D&C 107), and yet both quorums took the Prophet mantle (east) and the Patriarch mantle (west) away from the Smith bloodline, incorporating these mantles into their own stewardships as members of the Quorum of the Twelve in their respective churches (LDS, then later RLDS). This occurred about 100 years apart. Katherine Smith (sister of the prophet Joseph) warned the RLDS Saints about such a change. The Twelve in the Utah church claim they are "Prophets, Seers, and Revelators." The LORD reserved these titles for Joseph and Hyrum.

According to the Prophet Joseph Smith, the office of Patriarch was once the highest office in the church, clearly ranking above the Twelve (see Times and Seasons, 6:904 [15 May, 1844]; Quinn, The Mormon Heirarchy, Signature Books, p. 216).[21] With Brigham Young later in charge, the office of Patriarch in the Smith bloodline was diminished in the Utah church. The Twelve first changed the title for it from "**Presiding Patriarch**," to "Patriarch **to** the Church," and then finally to "Emeritus Patriarch" with the last to hold this office, Eldred G. Smith. The Twelve in Utah eliminated the office of Patriarch to the Church entirely in 1979. Eldred G. Smith thus became the last Patriarch to the Church in the Smith bloodline. Quinn states, "For various reasons the First Presidency and Twelve were in conflict *with seven out of eight successors* of the original Presiding Patriarch, Joseph Smith, Sr. The hierarchy finally resolved the situation on 6 Oct 1979 by making Eldred G. Smith an "emeritus" general authority without replacing him. This permanently "discontinued" the office of Patriarch to the Church…Vacating the office in 1979 ended the conflicts" (Quinn, Extensions of Power, p. 131). It was one more battle won by the Brighamites over the Josephites, the removal of the last remnant of the Smith bloodline within the Utah faction of the church. The Twelve are now the sole powerful administrators in Utah. Today Stake Presidents oversee Patriarchs, even recommending blessing content. This has led to less inspiration and more sameness among the blessings generally (see endnote 21).

Part III: An Explosion of Polygamy & Other Changes

With the anti-polygamy Smiths out of the way, polygamy exploded in Nauvoo, though much of it was kept from the average Saint for a short while. In the six months following the murder of the three Smith brothers (from June to December of 1844), Brigham Young went from 4 wives to 14. Heber C Kimball went from 2 wives to 10. There were 56 new plural marriages in 1845 alone by church members. By 1846, the "spiritual wives" movement exploded 5-fold - to **255** plural wives (*Nauvoo Roots of Mormon Polygamy, 1841-46: A Preliminary Demographic Report*, p 32). As addressed earlier, the three men leading the secret chamber led the way. They ended up with 109 total wives as the First Presidency of the church in Utah. Young had 55 wives, Kimball had 43, and Richards had 11. In scripture, God said, "Neither shall he multiply wives to himself, that his heart turn not away" (Deut. 17:17).

Mansions began rising up in Nauvoo for Young, Kimball, Woodruff, and Snow. All were completed via increased tithing funds from the struggling Saints. Just weeks after the murder of the Smiths, Brigham and the Twelve increased the tithing amount to be paid from the beleagured Saints. Shortly thereafter, these same men exempted themselves from paying it. No revelation is cited for their changes. Young ended up with two more mansions in Utah (in Salt Lake City & St. George). Three universities were later named after him. None were named after Joseph Smith.

As we will see in ensuing chapters, history shows that neither the Nauvoo House nor the House of the LORD were ever finished, while the Masonic lodge building was completed and dedicated. The Saints were distracted by other priorities. These misplaced priorities resulted in curses upon the Saints as a whole, including innocent converts from the British Isles, many of whom were very poor. They gave all they had to come to the city of Joseph. Unknown to them, until they lived in Nauvoo for a time, they then found "spiritual wifery" was being practiced secretly among some leaders. They had a special priesthood for it. This news was especially traumatic for female converts, some of whom left their husbands in great zeal to come to Zion. Some of these women ended up marrying polygamous Apostles, becoming another wife for them. Polyandry was thus being practiced alongside polygamy. The spiritual wifery of the Cochranites featured both, along with adultery. Leaders justified it all using Joseph Smith's name.

Though many of the new converts from the British Isles were poor, they respected and trusted the Twelve. They had what Hugh Nibley called, "zeal without knowledge" - zeal for the new faith and its leaders, but without a saving knowledge of God and His will and ways. It wasn't long until many followed the Twelve into Brigham's form of spiritual wifery. The converts came to the Utah mountains using handcarts, pulling all they had. It was a terrible sacrifice for many. My ancestors were in the Willie Handcart Company. They were fortunate to not lose one family member on their rigorous journey westward. The new lifestyle of many in the Mountainwest cut them off from the rest of the country, and from heaven. This was especially true for those fully entrenched in the whoredom of polygamy. Pure revelation from the Rock had been severed by their choices. The gates of hell then prevailed, and for some four generations (D&C 10:69). William Smith did his best to expose what was happening in Nauvoo. He provides his perspective below in the following writings to the Saints.

The Ace in the Hole – *Apostle & Patriarch William Smith*

After the murder of his three brothers, William turned on the secret chamber, exposing their activities in Nauvoo. He did so in multiple statements made to the Nauvoo Saints, all during the succession crisis. Some of them were printed in various non-Nauvoo newspapers, and in public speeches both in and outside of the city of Joseph. Because William was revealing damaging information about the Twelve (like the Law Group), and about Brigham Young, and because he was a threat to Brigham's takeover of the church, Brigham had William excommunicated as part of an on-going effort to discredit him by John Taylor, editor of the two Nauvoo newspapers.

Today William's words are ignored by too many Latter-day Saints, primarily because he too was no "Saint." This made Taylor's job of discrediting him much easier. The Utah church today discredits William for his failings - to silence the powerful statements that follow. From time to time, William didn't see eye-to-eye with Joseph his brother. He even got into a physical altercation with Joseph at one point. Such is the nature of human relationships, including families. We also know that William practiced spiritual wifery on two different occasions, and by his own public admission. He also sought to be President of the church for a time following the death of his three brothers. William was also less than truthful in certain early matters. Later, he repented of these errors, but they would forever tarnish his reputation. These human errors should not keep us from exploring his writings, as he was once part of the secret chamber, with insights no other had.

His testimony of what was going on at Nauvoo is of great importance to us today in the following six documents. Had he not left Nauvoo, he and his statements may not have survived. They include: (1) His last public speech at Nauvoo, where he first began to expose the Twelve and their secret spiritual wifery, and his own; (2) A detailed "proclamation" to the Saints; (3) A letter to the Saints to help them awaken to their plight; (4) His testimony in the *Temple Lot Case*, where he gave his reason for leaving the Twelve; (5) A letter to Apostle Orson Pratt; And (6) A letter to Orson Hyde. A seventh document, a letter to his nephew, Joseph Smith III, then President of the RLDS Church was addressed previously. They speak volumes about what was really happening behind the scenes at Nauvoo.

1. William Begins to Expose the Secret Chamber After the murder of his brothers, William Smith spoke in public (his last as an Apostle) about his spiritual wifery in 1845 in Nauvoo. In it he revealed that he was secretly practicing spiritual wifery, along with other members of the Twelve at Nauvoo. The Law group also accused select members of the Twelve of this, just before the murders. William is the wild card played against Brigham Young and his followers. Once a part of Young's secret chamber and holding "the secret priesthood," he too practiced "spiritual wifery" secretly with them, but not under Young's control and direction. He was a wild one doing his own thing. Brigham Young and Heber C. Kimball were trying to manage the secrecy of it all and William was not cooperating. On August 17th of 1845, he spoke out publically against the secrecy surrounding his own practice of "spiritual wifery." He did so in a speech at the Grove, called, "*The gospel according to Saint William.*" In it he said:

> "...if a sister gives me her hand upon **the Spiritual Wife system**, to share with me the fate & destinies of time and eternity, I will not be ashamed of her before the public. That [which] I do in **the secret chamber** I would do in the broad daylight" (Aug. 17, 1845 speech in the Grove).

William's speech at the Grove was referenced by two members of secret brotherhood, both were English converts, and both secretaries to church leaders within it. One was George Watt (secretary to Brigham Young). He recorded William's entire speech in shorthand. The second was William Clayton (secretary of Joseph Smith and a spy for Heber C. Kimball). It is ironic that records kept by two men in the secret chamber, and by order of Brigham Young, are used here to expose it and Brigham Young as Master Mahan.

In all, six individuals used the term "**secret chamber**" to describe this secret combination at Nauvoo. They included, (1) the LORD in His 1831 prophecy (see D&C 38, verses 13 & 28); (2) Apostle William Smith here; (3) Emma Smith, wife of Joseph, and President of the Relief Society in Nauvoo; (4) Sidney Rigdon; (5) William Clayton; And (6) George Watt (Brigham Young's secretary). In William Clayton's Journal for the 17th of August 1845, we read:

> "At the stand to day Wm. Smith preached to the saints the first chapter of 'the gospel according to St Wm' as he termed it. It was just a full declaration of his belief in the doctrine of a plurality of wives &c. The people appeared disgusted and many left the ground. His object was evidently to raise an influence against the Twelve especially Brigham and Heber for he intimated in strong terms that **they were practicing such things in secret** but he was not afraid to do it openly. His course to day will evidently hurt him in the estimation of the saints more than any thing he has done before."

In this 1845 speech, William used the terms "spiritual wifery" and "secret chamber." Both terms fly in the face of doctored accounts today that were written later by Young, Richards, Clayton, and other historicans to claim that "plural marriage" was supposedly instituted by Joseph Smith in the doctored "revelation" said to be given him on July 12 of 1843. Young was instead practicing his version of Cochranite **spiritual wifery**. He later changed its name to the more acceptable, "plural marriage" and then "Celestial marriage" (see 13 names for the practice on p. 191).

William's use of the term "spiritual wifery" (and by others in their journals at Nauvoo) clearly shows its connection to the early Cochranite movement, which originally coined the phrase. In addition, the term "secret chamber" clearly reveals the secrecy surrounding this practice, both in Cochranite tradition, and in association with Danite coercion, the secret blood oaths of Freemasonry, and Young's new modified endowment (next chapter), wherein the secret priesthood and polygamy were central, related components. The term "plural marriage" was later inserted into historical documents after the fact to legitimize the practice, and to do so in connection with Joseph Smith, even though he spoke out against all such sexual sin right up until his murder. The new name was also tied to marriage, helping to further separate the Mormon practice of it from the Cochranites.

William Clayton's Journal entries record William's changed heart. Clayton was an English convert (brought into the new church by Heber C. Kimball). He became a scribe for Joseph Smith for a time. He was also a spy for Kimball (and Young) and a member of "the secret chamber." Like others in it, he was also a Mason. In this brotherhood, secret blood oaths were administered to protect one another in their sins (see Moses 5:29-31). His conversion to Heber and Brigham's version of Mormonism in England may have included plans to implement the practice of spiritual wifery later in Nauvoo. Four of the Twelve there eventually became Presidents of the church. All of them were polygamists, Masons, and members of the secret chamber at Nauvoo. These men were Brigham Young, John Taylor, Wilford Woodruff, and Lorenzo Snow. Few fruits originated in their leadership.

2. William Smith's Proclamation to the Saints This "Proclamation" was printed in the Warsaw Signal newspaper in 1845. It revealed the activities of Brigham Young and other members of the secret chamber and what they were doing behind the backs of Joseph and Hyrum. It was the only way William could reach the Saints, as secret chamber member John Taylor was the owner, editor, and printer for the church publication - The Times and Seasons, as well as the City of Nauvoo's newspaper, The Nauvoo Neighbor. Two months later, on October 19 of 1845, William Smith wrote a lengthy letter to the Saints. It is extraordinary in what it reveals. William's letter was published in the Warsaw Signal, which exposed many in "the secret chamber.

> "I will state unequivocally at the outset, that it is my firm and sincere conviction, that, since the murder of my two brothers, usurpation and anarchy, and spiritual wickedness in high places, have crept into the church, with the cognizance and acquiescence of those whose solemn duty it was to guardedly watch against such estate of things. Under the reign of one whom I may call a Pontius Pilate, under the reign I say of this B. Young, no greater tyranny ever existed since the days of Nero. He has no other justification than ignorance to cover the most cruel acts – acts disgraceful to anyone bearing the stamp of humanity; and this being has associated around him, men, bound by oaths and covenants, who are reckless enough to commit almost any crime, or fulfill any command that their self-crowned 'head' might give them."

Prior to this important letter, William had requested a private meeting with Brigham Young. He was given a meeting, but it was anything but private. It featured many men gathered at the Masonic Lodge to intimidate him. Feeling he was not safe in his return to Nauvoo, William stated:

> "I summoned my kind friends who watched over my safety for two or three weeks; The necessity of my doing this prompted me to write a letter to B. Young, stating to him that I did not feel safe in the hands of his police. The answer returned to me was from John Taylor, to the effect that I should meet the council the same day at six o'clock in the evening. Accordingly at the hour specified, I repaired to the place of meeting, not expecting, however, to find any one present save the 'Twelve,' or the Bishops. But on entering the room on the third story of the Masonic Hall, what was my surprize to find some fifty or sixty policemen all armed with their Bowie knives, pistols, and hickory clubs. How much more too, was my surprize, when after my entrance I found the door guarded, and the man whom I had supposed a particular friend of mine, chuckling with sparkling eyes to think he had me in his power. I was called upon by Brigham Young to make known my grievances...I told them that I considered my right to teach the church altogether unimpeachable...Further, that if the brethren did not want me or my councils, to announce such a sentiment and I would leave them. Let, said I, the Twelve say so -- Let the Bishops say so -- Let the police say so, and I am gone! But mark it, said I, where I go, there also the Smith family go, and with them also goes the Priesthood."
>
> "After I had spoken for nearly an hour to the foregoing purpose, Brigham Young arose, and although when he came into the room he had given me his hand, with a smiling countenance, launched forth in the following strain, with boisterous boldness: 'I will let William Smith know that he has no right to counsel this church, **for I am the man**! I will let William Smith know also, that he shall not counsel the police; furthermore, that where the Smith family goes the church will not go, nor the priesthood either! And I will let William Smith know that **I am the president and head of this church**' and strange to say all the police and the bishops, and the 'Twelve' who were present, said thereunto, 'amen.' The conclusion I drew from all this was, that it was an intentional hint to me that I had better leave... the brow-storm grew more palpable, not a smile, not a pleasant look greeted me, as I looked around on my old associates. Among those in the house I observed fifty or sixty of my well known brethren, but not one smile, amen, or consoling word reached me..."
>
> "In noticing the claims of Brigham Young to superior power and authority, I would here observe that I heard my brother Joseph declare before his death, that Brigham Young was a man, whose passions, if unrestrained, were calculated to make him the most licentious man in the world, and should the time ever come, said he, that this man should lead the church, he would certainly lead it to destruction. What, my brethren, I would ask you, are the claims of Brigham Young to the keys of the church, above the rest of the Twelve? **They are keys which Joseph never conferred on Brigham Young**, nor was power ever given to him to lead the church in his place as his **successor**. The church is hereby warned against any such pretensions, as **little Joseph, the son of Joseph Smith is the lawful heir to the office**, being the oldest son of the deceased prophet. I was present with Joseph at the last council that was held previous to the Twelve and others going on their electioneering campaign to the east and various other parts of the United States; it was at this time that I received my initiation **into the highest priesthood lodge**, was washed and anointed, and clad with the sacerdotal robe of pure white, and ordained to be

priest and king, and invested with all the power that any man on earth ever did possess; power entitling me to preach the gospel, to bind up the kingdom of God on earth, among all nations, and people of every tongue. In consequence of these endowments and ordination received from under the hands of Joseph, I hold as much power and as many keys to seal and bind on earth, as can possibly belong to Brigham Young; this power was **conferred equally on all the Twelve**, and not therefore bestowed on one. The brethren must understand, too, that Brigham Young holds the presidency over the eleven men by age merely, and not by any legitimate authority, neither has he any superior keys; and the saints will bear in mind that a presidency over twelve men, admitted out of courtesy to age, does not make a man president, prophet, seer revelator, and perpetual head of the church, over a whole dynasty of people, to the exclusion of **the lawful heir, the heir by blood and by lineage**. Brethren, let my true position be known to you; reflect and you will clearly see that Brigham Young is not lawfully or legally the prophet or head of the church, and that to claim such a right is usurpation and an act of tyranny; it is robbing the innocent -- the widow and the fatherless. Further, the saints are informed that the old pioneers, fathers and founders of this church of Christ in this last dispensation, namely the Smith family, must and will stand at the head, as leaders of this dispensation in time and in eternity. **According to our book of covenants, the priesthood must be handed down from father to son**."

"Again, the position of the 'Twelve' is defined in the same book, as merely a '**traveling high council'** to open and make known the kingdom abroad, and **not as a local presidency**. Since the death of Joseph and Hiram, the church has never been organized, although the materials have been all on hand. Its present condition is that of a headless body. It cannot be perfect until there are three presidents. It is just as needful that the church have all its members, with a head to govern it, now as in the days of Joseph, or many years ago. Temples therefore reared up, and endowments given, by usurpers, or by a headless body, can be no other than imperfect. And is not probable, I would ask, that Temples, Nauvoo Houses and other buildings, however richly wrought and gorgeously and sumptuously furnished, such palaces may be reared up in wickedness, by means of cheating and defrauding the poor, by keeping up secret combinations for robbing and plundering the Gentiles – a Gadianton Band -- altogether contrary to the book of Mormon, how, I would ask, can it be expected that the Almighty will bless or suffer to prosper. How, I would ask, can it be expected that Divine endowments can be given in such houses, or that God will ever bless such a priesthood or such a people…"

"It is astonishing indeed to see the religious chicanery and hypocrisy of those men. In the first place Adams comes on east, bearing letters from Willard Richards and the Council of Nauvoo, announcing the deaths of Hiram and Joseph Smith, to the scattering 'Twelve' with advice to me not to return at present to Nauvoo, for fear of increasing the excitement; thus by my absence enabling them to use all efforts, to get the Church bound up to Brigham Young, as its president; the rest of the Twelve resigning all their power into his hands, and thereby rendering themselves powerless. Thus they thought to get a dig at me, having the bishops ready to say 'amen!' with **a police bound by covenants and oaths to protect the said Brigham Young**, as the president and head of the church, and to carry out all his measures. While this Brigham Young was pampering the church with the idea that although little **Joseph was the rightful heir to the priesthood**, and office of his father as prophet, seer, and revelator, that it was not prudent to mention this for fear of the little child's life…"

"The impression that B. Young was the successor and had even more power than Joseph, that things prospered better, etc., etc., was spread about in all directions. -- And to complete this man's reign of power, there was adopted, as I have before alluded to, the system of spiritual wifery, which was entered into secretly: and directions given to John Taylor and others to proclaim on the stand that all saints should call on Brigham Young for counsel notwithstanding I was by right a counselor of the church. It was, my brethren, in this way, that the cords were drawn tighter and closer. Men's wives and daughters were secretly married at night-time to this Young, H. C. Kimball, William Richards, and others, and, in the dark night, were attending the **secret lodges**, until most of the 'Seventies' were thus sealed and bound under a cloak of adopting children into their kingdoms. **All these measures were profoundly secret**, and the actors **were bound to protect** the noble fathers and LORDs. In addition to this every exertion was made to ordain every one in the shape of man, and induce them to join the 'Seventies' and thus become adopted '**Brighamites**.' As soon as they had been induced to take the step, they soon found a reason for being no longer **Smithites**…"

"I call upon you, I say, to come out of this Brigham Young's power, and to denounce his claims and pretensions, for be assured, they are not of God. Discard, my friends, all such hypocrisy and secret works, all such deeds of darkness. For Gadianton Bands, secret combinations to murder, and plunder the gentiles, and trespass upon other men's rights, by discarding the marriage contract, can do nothing else than establish licentiousness, and corrupt the mortals of the rising generation. From all such abominations I proclaim myself free and independent, and I implore my friends again and again, especially those of the Smith family, to fly from this sink of iniquity and abomination, and assist in reorganizing the church of God on **the old and pure gospel of Mormonism**, and in accordance with the Book of Mormon, the Bible, and the Book of Doctrine and Covenants...Another matter may not be omitted, namely: that Brigham Young, John Taylor, and Willard Richards with the appointed bishops **have assumed the publishing of the Church Documents**, the Book of Covenants, and also Joseph's private history, as their own property entirely regardless of the rights of the Smith family as therewith connected."

"Again, in addition to all this assumption of power **they have combined themselves into secret lodges, councils**, etc., where they concoct all their plans unknown to the common people of the church, out of this have arisen **the whitling and whistling societies** for disposing of strangers, and **the beastly annointing** [Aunt Peggy's privy closet] of all who oppose their plans...I did not leave that place too soon, for the very day of my departure it was whispered to me that a secret plot was already concocted for taking away my life...All these things combine with their **secret combinations** I conceive to be ample cause to induce me to disfellowship such men, and to denounce all their measures. Joseph Smith inherited his priesthood by lineage, he being a descendant of Joseph, who was sold into Egypt, and the same priesthood is continued from father to son -- as was, also, my patriarchal office inherited from my father and brother Hyrum. And now, brethren, permit me to say, that so long as the sun, moon, and stars perform their successive revolutions, so long both on earth and hereafter, shall I have faith in the doctrine of **legal descent, lineage & blood**...The Twelve did not ordain me one of their number, nor decree my lineage in the Smith family, and I shall never suffer myself to be controlled by Brigham Young or any of his coadjutors. It was from a love of peace, my brethren and sisters, and from no other motive, that I have delayed the publication of these remarks...And now may the God of peace and abundant mercy abide with all the faithful . . . May He be present with all the honest in heart, and may He deliver the innocent from all fear, and prompt the pure-minded saint, to come out, and assist in building up the kingdom as it was at the beginning. That Zion may put on her beautiful garments, and see no more the wasting and destruction of her borders..." Young later excommunicated William for his remarks, see *http://olivercowdery.com/smithhome/BroBill/wmwrite.htm*

3. William's 2nd Warning to the Saints – *Printed in Two Newspapers* The following warning was printed in two newspapers in 1845; (1) the *Missouri Reporter*, St. Louis, Oct. 25, Vol. IV, #237, and (2) the Sangamo Journal, Springfield Illinios, Nov. 6, , vol. XV, No. 7. William wrote to the editor, "I wish to beg a place in your columns for the insertion of this article, as I am deprived of the privilege of speaking through the Mormon oracles (papers.) I do this, to correct the evils that now exist among that people denominated Saints in Nauvoo -- a place that for the last six months has been a resort for rogues and scoundrels, and a covert for thieves and murderers . . . my brethren, **the secret plans** and devices of those who have assured the leadership of the Church in that place . . . They have formed themselves into a **combination**, called a *city police*, with other *private councils*, &c., &c., by which to **suppress the liberty of speech** and endanger the lives of any who dare oppose their unhallowed purposes, or oppose their deep-laid plans to **fleece** the unwary and [more] faithful of the Mormon Church . . . At this important crisis of Mormon interests, when every exertion is being made by those eleven **wolves in** sheep's clothing, to continue the distress of their poor brethren, by **decoying them into the wilderness** [of the Mountain West], thereby the better enabling these ambitious tyrants to carry out their plans of robbery and murder to increase **their own wealth** and make the poor poorer -- at this crisis, I take the liberty to warn you, our brethren, in due time, that you may flee the awful vortex, and not be led by such men, or such false hopes as are held out in the circular of the so-called 'Mormon Twelve,' who, since the death of Joseph and Hiram, have contemplated the removal to the west, but not by the prophecy of Joseph or his counsel.

The name of Joseph is made use of, to carry out their plans, without the least authority; for Joseph taught no such doctrine. You must be cautious and believe no such things, and thus escape the devices of Satan! Save yourselves and property! You have only to look back a few short years or months, to see the sufferings of the Saints, many of whom during the past summer in Nauvoo have lived on potato tops and salt, and been constantly called upon by those men, until the last cent is gone. **When all is gone, they will tell you it is the Lord's -- you must sacrifice** -- that this is the only way to exalted glory. If you call for the return of money loaned, you are treated as

dissenters, *whittled* and driven from their midst as unworthy members of their society . . . And will you, brethren and sisters, still be guided and flattered by them into further troubles and ruin? What credulity! My God, I would ask you, can it be possible that the experience of the past is not enough to show you the bad counsel and the impolitic course of such a move as is now advised? Look at the distressed, the aged and the infirm -- again to settle in so large a body! I should think the folly of such wild and imaginary schemes had been too plainly told in the history of the past. Again, it is evident that the designs of those men will ruin all who follow them. This manifest in the self-righteous and so very christian epistle which they have addressed of late to the Churches. 'Israel,' they say, 'must be the head and not the tail.' To translate this into its true meaning, it should read 'Mormons must be the head,' which plainly shows the reason why there are so many broils and evils attending them, and why those assumed heads wish to leave a land of government and go to some more infant and weakened power, in order to hide themselves from their crimes and defy the authority of every land, wherever they settle -- that they may be the head and have the sole control and under their own assumption of power, shield themselves from the penalty of their brutal acts, by their tyranny and absolute rule.

So let me warn you again, my dear brethren, against these uncalled-for moves, and speculating plans to rob you of your gold, your house, your wives and children, and to **make you slaves** . . . If our religion is good, it will benefit our neighbors; and if it be of God, it will be a light not hid under a bushel, but put on a candle-stick to give light unto all men and love our neighbors as ourselves. To do this, we must settle where, in different bodies and parcels, we can teach them our doctrine, and like our neighbors and brethren according to the flesh, build comfortable houses for worship, and study the course of economy and the art to please by works of righteousness. Thus our neighbors will bless us, and we become a glorious people in the midst of the earth, filled with joy and peace, and **Josephites**, in deed and in truth; for it is thus the voice of the martyred Joseph speaks to all that respect his name or hold his memory sacred and dear; but not in favor of the wild and wicked plans of these apostate eleven, for their plans Joseph does not approve, nor do they have his approval. Ever and anon, you will hear from me again, dear brethren! With sentiments of esteem, I once more subscribe myself, Your friend and brother, And fellow-laborer in the Gospel of Jesus Christ, And Patriarch of the Church, William Smith. St. Louis, Oct. 25, 1845."

4. William's Testimony in the Temple Lot Case In 1893, William Smith provided testimony in the Temple Lot Case for the RLDS church. In it he provided reasons for why he left the changing church Young was putting in place. He stated, "The reason of the separation was that the church I had absolved myself from had changed the doctrine . . . in respect to several things, and especially in respect to the marriage relation. The first I ever noticed of the change in that regard was in 1845, at Nauvoo, Illinois; I refer to the practice of polygamy. The principal participants at that time were Brigham Young, Heber C. Kimball, John Taylor, Willard Richards, Orson Hyde, and Parley P. Pratt. They were the principal participants in that doctrine.

He added, "There were three or four propositions or doctrines that were introduced into the church after the death of my brother in June, 1844, under the council of a part of the Twelve. One point was—and it had never been taught previous to that time—that **Adam was God**, and also that Moses was a man-god. Another doctrine was that of '**blood atonement**,' meaning that if a man disobeyed the propositions of that council, meaning the remaining Twelve, he had to pay for it by the forfeiture of his life and atone for the sin by the shedding of his own blood, or allowing it to be shed by others. That was blood atonement for you, and it had never been taught in the old church, nor had the Adam-God doctrine ever been taught in the old church...Another point was the marriage question in regard to the **plurality of wives** that was taught after the death of Joseph and Hyrum Smith, my brothers. These new doctrines that I spoke of were what caused the separation between me and that body of people, and **neither of them were taught previous to 1844** nor for some time after 1844" (p. 93).

"I left Nauvoo in 1845 because my life was in danger if I remained there, because of my objections and protests against the doctrine of blood atonement and other new doctrines that were brought into the church. After I left I published an account of my separation from the church and the causes which led up to it. I think it occupied sixteen pages. It gave the cause of my separation from the church, and contained a statement of the **apostasy of the leaders** of the church at Nauvoo. I had five hundred of these pamphlets [Proclamation to the Saints] struck off" (p. 98). See Testimony of William Smith, Temple Lot Case, 1893, *http://olivercowdery.com/smithhome/BroBill/wmwrite.htm*

5. William's Letter to Apostle Orson Pratt On October 28, 1845, Apostle Orson Hyde of Nauvoo, wrote a letter to William Smith, who had fled from Nauvoo for his own safety and was in St. Louis. Orson called upon William to return to Nauvoo, "and abide in the council of your brethren"— which implied subjection to Brigham Young (see *Messenger and Advocate*, Pittsburgh, PA [December 1845], 413–414). On November 12, 1845, William replied, writing a strong letter of refusal. In part of it he stated, "My life and exertions will be in order to perpetuate the names of my father's family, and with honor to my noble martyred brothers Joseph and Hyrum wipe away the disgrace, the stain, the evils that, since their deaths have crept into the church. And by the too frequent use of their names, the twelve are carrying out the most wicked, base and unhallowed purposes that could be devised **under the cloak of Joseph and Hyrum's names**. Brethren! be assured that Joseph and Hyrum never would have sanctioned the present wicked plans of the twelve; their corruption their sink of iniquity, their removal to the wilderness, their doctrine of polygamy usurpation" (*Messenger and Advocate*, Pittsburgh, PA [Dec. 1845], 415–416).

6. William's Letter to Apostle Orson Hyde "I am now prepared openly and boldly, to expose every secret evil which is practiced by Brigham Young and his brother leaders at Nauvoo, and elsewhere. *I'm not now surrounded by an armed body of men, employed by the leaders of a Church to destroy the persons and property of those who honestly differ with them in religious opinion*, and are **bound by oaths** to murder indiscriminately whoever may oppose the secret and wicked plans and practices of the immaculate Brigham Young. As a specimen of the moral degradation existing among you, I will mention Parley P. Pratt as a fit subject to introduce. You are well aware that this unassuming and righteous apostle came from the East, a few days since, in company with a female whose appearance and conduct bear sufficient evidence of his utter disregard of virtue or religion. This is not the only crime he is guilty of. His iniquitous conduct is well known in the East and speaks for itself. It is needless for me to enlighten you further upon the character of B. Young, John Taylor, W. Richards, and many others who are continually preaching the doctrine, and openly practicing adultery; for this you know too well . . .

Scripture and reason teach us that *those who are led by wicked rulers must necessarily be astray*, and powerless as those who govern and direct them; for wicked rulers have neither Priesthood nor power . . . Your invitation to return to the quorum of the twelve, I treat with that calm and dignified scorn which such barefaced hypocrisy justly merits. No sir, I return no more to such a den of thieves and quorum of iniquity. I am fixed in my course and firm as the Rock of Gibraltar; and I protest against your proceedings and conduct. I know there are many friends now in Nauvoo who are afraid to express their opinion, but it will not always be so . . . And by too frequent use of their names, the twelve are carrying out the most wicked, base and unhallowed purposes that could be devised **under the cloak of Joseph and Hiram's names** . . ." (*see http://olivercowdery.com/smithhome/BroBill/wmwrite.htm*).

Letting the Cat Out of the Bag in Utah (1852)

Under Young's direction later in Utah, additional wives became commonplace for select, male Mormons, those utilizing the new special priesthood, all except those who were black. Only white males part of Young's priesthood could wield it to take more wives. Under Pres. Young, Utah was the only western territory where African-American slavery and slave-sales were protected by his territorial statute. Women were part of another kind of control.

It was in 1852 that President Brigham Young officially "let the cat out of the bag," informing the world of the fact that the Mormons were polygamists, a centrol component of his new, modified church put in place in the isolation of the west. Section 132 of the Doctrine and Covenants (Joseph's supposed pro-polygamy revelation from God) was announced publically to the world on August 29 of 1852 by President Young. It was published for the first time in the Millennial Star in its January 1853 issue. This was nearly a decade after the murder of the Prophet Joseph. With his 1852 announcement, Young admitted to secretly practicing polygamy for many years, finally "letting the cat out of the bag" officially. The secretive phrase, "letting the cat out of the bag" was used by both Young and Heber C. Kimball to describe their actions in finally revealing the practice to the world, while simultaneously keeping other lesser lies - "kittens" - secret. Note Brigham Young's condescending words to the Saints.

> "I will now say, not only to our delegate to Congress, but to the Elders who leave the body of the Church, that he thought that all the cats and kittens were let out of the bag when brother [Orson] Pratt went back last fall, and published the [132] Revelation [in The Seer] concerning the plurality of wives: it was thought there was no other cat to let out. But allow me to tell you, Elders of Israel, and delegates to Congress, you may expect an eternity of cats [lies and secrets] that have not yet escaped from the bag. Bless your souls, there is no end to them, for if there is not one thing, there will always be another" (JD 1:188, June 19, 1853).

The cat (lies tied to polygamy and murder) was kept secret by "masters of the secret" now in charge, Brigham Young, Heber C. Kimball, Willard Richards, John Taylor, and others. It was originally Cain who said:

"I am Mahan, the master [mind] of this great **secret**, that I may murder and get gain. Wherefore Cain was called Master Mahan, and he gloried in his wickedness" (Moses 5:31).

The footnote to the word "Mahan" in this scripture includes the clarifying words, "mind," (as in "mastermind") "destroyer," and "great one." Brigham Young and Heber had become "masters of the great secret" in England, then Nauvoo, and now Utah. Brigham later had Apostle Orson Pratt publish this great secret to the world in "The Seer," letting the cat out of the bag officially, and according to Young's timing (1853). Note Heber's later words.

"Dr. Bernhisel has just remarked, that he thought the cat was let out of the bag, when plurality was preached, but I suppose that he did not happen to think that **the cat might have kittens**, and the kittens grow to be cats, and thus increase to a vast number" (JD 3:263, Heber C. Kimball, June 10, 1855, see also JD 5:92, July 26, 1857).

The big lies (cats) always require more lies (kittens) to cover them up. Cyrus Wheelock, a prominent Brighamite elder in Utah, addressed Brigham, his polygamy, and his changing statements, stating, "He lived above the gospel law; had received **a higher endowment**, consequently had **a right to lie**"(*Address to the Saints in Utah and California: Polygamy Proven An Abomination*, Briggs and Attwood, 1869, p. 44). This is why some thirteen different terms emerged for spiritual wifery in Utah. In 1886, the Deseret News published them in an article (p. 191), showing how the Utah Saints used these deceptive phrases to keep the practice alive secretly (see also 3 Ne. 16:10 & 30:2).

Brigham Young's 1856-57 Rebaptizing Reformation

Four years after Young "let the cat out of the bag" with the Section 132 revelation, Pres. Young put in place a new Reformation. This was in September of 1856. It signaled a new commitment to **his** teachings and **his** version of the church, all in the remote valleys of Utah, away from government interference. Young used Alma's re-baptism model in the Book of Mormon as an important symbol of this re-commitment. Alma was the High Priest over the church in the Book of Mormon. He had his people re-baptized in a renewal of their commitment **to the LORD**. In Brigham's movement, the entire leadership of the LDS church was re-baptized along with a significant portion of the church membership. Young sought full acceptance of polygamy and other new doctrines he brought before the people.

The revivalist spirit tied to this movement resulted in **mass re-baptisms** in 1856-57. It should be noted that Young had many rebaptized earlier in August 6-8 of 1947 in Salt Lake City. Young's reformation effort through rebaptism was much more widespread ten years later. Not everything in it was rosy, however. Many saw the 1856-57 "reformation" as a forced recommitment to "the new order of things" in Brigham's theocracy. Two phrases often repeated by leaders in sermons at this time were, "**All who are not for us, are against us**," and "**It may be necessary to cleanse the platter**." These and other statements were inflamatory, especially when combined with Brigham's **blood atonement** doctrine. Many saw the zeal of Young's more widesspread reformation in 1856-57 turning into fanaticism.

Church leaders urgently promoted both **obedience to leaders** and **polygamy** during this time. Nelson Wheeler Whipple noted, "Among other teachings and instructions the plurality of wives was strongly urged and a great number of the men took more wives" (The History of Nelson Wheeler Whipple, Mormon File, Huntington Library, p. 56; see also Daniel H. Wells, JD 4:254 [March 1, 1857]). Frederick Loba (a Swiss emigrant who lost his wife crossing the plains in 1854) lived in Utah for three years, leaving in 1857. He referred to the "Reformation" as a dark and gloomy time of suspicion and accusation when "murder was openly advised in the public meetings . . . and persons whose faith in Mormonism was suspected were searched in the hope of finding evidence against them" (see Jean Frederick Loba, statement 4 in, *Utah and the Mormons*, New York Times, May 1, 1858, 4-5, also "Reminiscences," 1899, pps. 16-17, Kansas State Historical Society, Topeka).

Peter McAuslan (a handcart survivor from Scotland) said Young's blood atonement doctrine was taught in connection with the Reformation. He first heard of it in John Young's sermon preached in Utah Valley on September 27-29, 1856. "It was during the Reformation that the . . . doctrine known as 'blood atonement' was first preached in Utah. John Young [Brigham's older brother] . . . said there were hypocrites in Zion and that [they] were not fit to live and the time had come that **their blood would have to be shed** to save them and he continued, 'If you should find your fathers or your mothers by the way side with their **throats cut** go on about your business and say nothing about it for it would be all right. Zion must be purified'" (*History of George Armstrong Hicks, Written by Himself* [1878], Kent V. Marvin, Mary Anne Loveless, and Karen Kenison, chap. 10).

Recommittment with rebaptism was very different in Alma's day in the Book of Mormon. There, re-baptisms were done in love for the LORD and a choice to show it via an outward physical ordinance of rebirth. Alma's followers desired to be "born again" **in Christ**. Some believe Young's 1856 Reformation movement in Utah represented the end of the original covenant made **in the name of Jesus** as established between the early Saints and **the LORD** through the Prophet Joseph. The physical baptism under men's hand was and is to be followed by the greater spiritual baptism in God's fiery Spirit. Some believe "Brigham's reformation" was the start of a new corrupt covenant as part of His version of the church, with its new doctrines **not** approved by the LORD. These new doctrines included polygamy, blood atonement, the law of adoption, secret blood-oath penalties, exclusion of blacks from the priesthood, and other questionable doctrines Young put forth. A vote by members in support of Young was a vote for his "new order of things." Most of those remaining behind in Nauvoo did so because of new "Brighamite" changes. William Smith was one of the first to use the terms "Brighamite" and "Josephite" to separate the two belief systems. We know the LORD gave the church differing names at different points in time. At one point He removed His name entirely from the church, evident in the shorter name, "Church of the Latter-day Saints," seen on the exterior of the Kirtland House of the LORD (see endnote 2).

Under "strong recommendation" from President Young, the Reformation movement was carried to settlements and missions throughout Utah Territory and the world. Some of those who **refused** to be re-baptized lost their church membership. In Britain, zealous application of Reformation principles resulted in trimming down the church rolls of the less-committed. **Brigham's own son later called the Reformation "a reign of terror"** (Brigham Young Jr. diary, Dec. 15, 1862). Brigham's "Reformation" was characterized by coercion and fear. Thousands left Utah Territory and the faith at this time, disallusioned by the fear, control, polygamy, and poverty they experienced, along with the murders they became aware of in connection with Young's blood atonement doctrine (see chap. 5, pages 181-82, and Poly Aird's excellent 2004 paper published in *The Journal of Mormon History*, entitled, *You Nasty Apostates, Clear Out,* pps. 129-207available at *http://files.lib.byu.edu/mormonmigration/articles/YouNastyApostatesJMHVOL30_NO2.pdf*).

Killing Men to Save their souls

A portion of Young's "blood atonement" doctrine was focused upon **apostates**, those supposedly going against Brigham's view of things. Men **in the spirit of apostasy** were to be killed before they could commit further sin, **in order to save their soul.** Others already in apostasy were to have their blood shed, which entitled them to a new probation in eternity (see JD vol. I., pps 72-73, 82-83; vol. II, pps. 165-66; vol. III, pps 226, 236, 241, 246-47, 279, 337). Elder Jedediah M. Grant was a counselor in **the First Presidency** (after Willard Richards died). He was sometimes called "Brigham's sledgehammer" for his fiery speeches in the 1856 "Reformation" movement. He taught:

> "The Lord God commanded to not pity the person whom they **killed**, but to **execute the law of God** upon **persons worthy of death**. This should be done by the entire congregation, showing **no pity** [instead it was done by Brigham's hit men]. I wish we were in a situation to keep **God's law**, without any contaminating influence of Gentile laws; that the people of God might lay the ax to the root of the tree, and hew down every tree that did not bring forth good fruit...Putting to death the transgressors would **exhibit the law of God**...Do not traitors to earthly governments forfeit their life? But people will argue that we can try them on, but not for property or life. That makes the devil laugh, etc." (Jedediah M. Grant, Tabernacle sermon, March 12, 1854. His son was Heber J. Grant, a later church president).

One policy Young put in place at this time persists today, though in milder form. It featured two "home missionaries" (now called "home teachers") assigned to each ward. They were equipped with a 27-page questionnaire to judge the worthiness of the Saints interviewed. Its purpose was control. The questions addressed everything from hygiene and church attendance, to obeying the Ten Commandments, and of course one's support of **polygamy**.

Re-baptism marked the formal end of Young's 1856 Reformation movement, though its reform fervor continued through mid-1858. It was very much tied to Young's version of the church. There were and are a number of significant doctrines taught to the Saints that came from President Young. Some of them have since been repudiated by the modern LDS church and its leaders. Their removal negates the claim that mortal leaders – "the arm of flesh," "**can not and will not lead us astray**." Five of Young's early teachings now removed, include:

The Blood Atonement doctrine - leading to many murders (repudiated 1889)
Spiritual Wifery (the U.S. Government forced the LDS church to stop this practice in 1890)
The Adam-God theory (repudiated by 1902)
The ban on Blacks receiving the priesthood and participating in temple rites (removed in 1979)
Blood-oath penalties and other Freemasonry influences added to the Endowment (removed in 1990, p. 165)

By comparison, Alma's re-baptism efforts in the Book of Mormon signaled a re-commitment to Christ and His doctrine and gospel. It was "**baptism unto renewal**," versus "**baptism unto repentance**" for those not previously baptized. Those embracing Him and His ways became part of His church (see D&C 10:67). As High Priest over the church, Alma made re-baptism a **commandment** for members, while it was an *invitation* for non-members to come into the fold of God (see Alma 5:62). Men's dead works mean little in comparison to being "alive in Christ" (see 2 Ne. 25). The LORD said that those in His church "are begotten through me" (D&C 93:22). Those baptized into God's church, are baptized by Him in a fiery spiritual baptism that no man can imitate (see 3 Ne. 9:20; 12:1; JST Mat. 3:38; JST John 1:28; D&C 33:15 & chap. 3). It is a life-changing fiery event, preceded by one in water done by men on earth. A complete remission of sins occurs in it, and with this sanctification, potential receipt of the unspeakable gift and power of the Holy Ghost (see chap. 7). Those so blessed become His sons and daughters (see Mosiah 5).

Looking back to April 6, 1830, we see that Joseph Smith did something similar to Alma. Many had gathered to the Peter Whitmer farm in Fayette New York on this date. There, Joseph, Hyrum, and Samuel Smith, along with David, John, and Peter Whitmer Jr. were all **re-baptized**. They did so for five insightful reasons (see Assumption #9, Chap. 6). Many of the Saints today are also being re-baptized. They recognize the need for real faith **in the LORD Jesus Christ**, followed by sincere, heartfelt **repentance**. They are then are "**baptized unto repentance**" (Mosiah 26:22; Alma 5:62, 6:2, 7:14, 9:27, 48:19, 49:30; Helaman 3:24, 5:17; 3 Ne. 1:23, 7:26), making their covenant with the LORD, to remember Him and keep His commandments. Such seek the fiery baptism of the LORD, which must follow, if one is to be redeemed of the LORD, sanctified and made new in Him. The gift of the Holy Ghost can then follow.

Murder Continues In Utah

Like polygamy, Young's blood atonement doctrine survived until the turn of the century. It suggested that forgiveness for certain sins comes only through the sinner's shedding his blood. Many believe this led to many murders in Utah Territory and the Mountain Meadows Massacre, all under Young's direction. Pres. Young delighted in the fact that he had ruthless men that could carry out his wishes whenever violence was necessary. Addressing "blood atonement" sent upon his enemies, Young said:

> "And if the Gentiles wish to see a few tricks, we have 'Mormons' that can perform them. We have **the meanest devils on the earth in our midst**, and we intend to keep them, for we have use for them; and if the Devil does not look sharp, we will cheat him out of them at the last, for they will reform and go to heaven with us" (JD, 6, p. 176).

These enforcers, strikers, or hit men included former Danite and bodyguard to Joseph Smith, Orrin Porter Rockwell, Danite Hosea Stout (Chief of Police at Nauvoo), and Bill Hickman (Young's primary hit man in Utah). Hickman openly admitted to carrying out many murders for Brigham Young in Utah Territory. In 1871 a U.S. Marshall indicted Young for ordering one of many murders. No trial was ever held in connection with this indictment (see Wilford Woodruff's Journal, vol. 7, pages 45 & 52). Judge McKean wrote to U. S. Attorney General George H. Williams in the fall of 1873, complaining that he could neither convict the guilty in Utah Territory nor protect the innocent, and that the area had become a "**theocratic state**, under the vice regency of Brigham Young" (*Dialogue: A Journal of Mormon Thought*, Autumn 1966, p. 86-87). On September 21, 1856, Pres. Young said:

> "Now take a person in this congregation who has knowledge with regard to being saved... and suppose that he is overtaken in a gross fault, that he has committed a sin that he knows will deprive him of that exaltation which he desires, and that he cannot attain to it without the shedding of blood, and also knows that by **having his blood shed he will atone for that sin**, and be saved and exalted with the Gods, is there a man or woman in this house but what would say 'shed my blood that I may be saved and exalted with the Gods? (JD 4:219-20).

"There are sins that men commit for which they cannot receive forgiveness in this world, or in that which is to come, and if they had their eyes open to see their true condition, **they would be perfectly willing to have their blood spilt upon the ground,** that the smoke thereof might ascend to heaven as an offering for their sins; and the smoking incense would atone for their sins, whereas, if such is not the case, they will stick to them and remain upon them in the spirit world" (JD, 4:10).

"I was opposed to hanging, even if a man kill another, **I will shoot him, or cut off his head, spill his blood on the ground**, and let the smoke thereof ascend up to God; and if I ever have the privilege of **making a law on that subject, I will have it so**" (HC 5:296).

"I say, rather than that **apostates** flourish here, **I will unsheath my bowie knife**, and conquer or die. [Speaking to the congregation] Now you nasty apostates, clear out, or judgment will be put to the line, and righteousness to the plummet. If you say it is right, raise your hands [All hands go up]. *Let us call upon the Lord to assist us in this*, and every good work" (JD 4:375).

There are many other public statements by Young tied to his blood atonement doctrine. Young inserted another relative to this false doctrine in the early temple endowment. It later came to be known as **The Oath of Vengeance**. It was removed in the early 1930's. The blood-oath penalties (very similar to those in Freemasonry, p. 165) were removed in 1990. The Oath of Vengeance was focused on avenging the blood of Joseph and Hyrum. It stated:

"You and each of **you do covenant and promise** that you will pray and never cease to pray to Almighty God to *avenge the blood of the prophets upon this nation*, and that you will **teach the same to your children** and to your children's children unto the third and fourth generation."

The blood atonement doctrine, and Young's use of coercion, intimidation, and murder, cemented his power and lifestyle. He had become a powerful king in his own isolated kingdom outside of the United States border. The beginnings of this kingdom began much earlier in the spring of 1838 in Missouri. David Whitmer addressed the rising up of perhaps the first secret combination in the church. It is worth repeating:

"the heads of the church and many of the members had gone deep into error and blindness...In June, 1838, at Far West, Mo., a **secret** organization was formed, Doctor Avard being put in as the leader of the band; a certain oath was to be administered to all the brethren to bind them to **support the heads of the church in everything they should teach**. All who refused to take this **oath** were considered **dissenters** [apostates] from the church, and **certain things** were to be done concerning these **dissenter**s, by Dr. Avard's secret band... my persecutions, for trying to show them their errors, became of such a nature that I had to leave the Latter Day Saints..." (see David Whitmer, An Address To All Believers In Christ, 1887, pp. 27-28).

Bill Hickman: *Brigham Young's Primary Utah Hit Man*

The Prophet Joseph Smith employed Orrin Porter Rockwell as an early bodyguard. Later on Brigham Young put Rockwell to work for him in this capacity too. Young also used him, Hosea Stout, Bill Hickman, and other men to eliminate threats to his power. This often involved murder. All three men have been called "avenging angels," "destroying angels," "strikers," or members of "Brigham's posse." Rockwell and Stout were early Danite enforcers, but Hickman was Young's chief "hit man" in Utah Territory later on. Orrin Porter Rockwell did not keep a record of his work, but Hosea Stout and Bill Hickman did. They provide useful first-hand, contemporary evidence of the dark side of Brigham Young and the secret combination he led in Nauvoo and later on in Salt Lake City. These men kept King Brigham in power and wealth, surrounded by his many wives. They also shielded Young and others from justice. Like Young, Hickman never served prison time for murder. And all of them but Rockwell were polygamists too (Stout ended up with six wives, Hickman ten).

William Hickman's story is especially revealing. He wrote it himself, as a type of confession for his many murders in connection with his early devotion to Young's leadership, and his eventual realization that his zeal to support Young was misplaced (a form of idolatry). Young's murderous ways were closely tied to his "blood atonement" doctrine. Though Hickman devoted much of his life in serving Pres. Young as his enforcer, Young never paid him a cent. He also deserted Hickman in the end. William "Bill" Hickman eventually left Utah and the church, dying pennyless, sick, and alone. His confession reveals regret for his deception in blindly following Young. Select statements by Hickman hereafter reveal this and more. Editor John Beadle put them together in his book, *Bill Hickman: Brigham Young's Destroying Angel* (see also Hope A. Hilton, *Wild Bill Hickman and the Mormon Frontier*).

William (Bill) Hickman was a convert to Mormonism at Nauvoo. He had a sincere desire to follow church leaders early on. He was especially impressed with the Prophet Joseph Smith. Speaking of him, Hickman quoted the Prophet Joseph as saying, "Now brethren and friends, if any of you have anything against me, come and tell me, and I will make it right; do not be backward; come publicly or privately and see if I don't satisfy you or anyone that has anything against me" (p. 38-9). Hickman noted a significant difference between Joseph and Brigham. He continued, "In the fall Brigham Young assumed authority...but with many it was no go. They would say: 'He is no prophet; he was not called of God nor ordained by the prophet Joseph'...I became more personally acquainted with him afterwards, and soon became satisfied **he was no such man as Smith**, and really came to the conclusion that it [he] was a curse sent upon us, that we were not worthy to have so good a man as Smith to preside over us..." (p. 39-40).

Hickman later followed Brigham Young west. He said Young told him and other enforcers to, "Take the property [of those murdered] and divide it among yourselves, which we did...Here let me say that this is all I ever got for services rendered on Brigham Young's orders. Neither did I ever receive a present from him, not so much as one dollar. But from the cause of my former belief **I questioned nothing, supposing him right in all things, and it not only a duty, but highly necessary that I should obey his commands, and in the end it would prove both spiritual and temporal salvation to me, which situation thousands of others are now in, in this Territory**" (p. 87). Here Hickman admitted his deception tied to idolatry. Hickman was deceived and used. In the end, Young abandoned him.

Disillusioned after years of service to Young, and leaving behind Utah and the church, Hickman stated, "The night before I left, one of my boys, being out, was chased by this same gang [three men sent by Young to kill him, to prevent him from talking], thinking, I suppose, it was me. Now those watching me were men with whom I had never had any difficulty; but were of that kind that would kill father or son at the bidding of Brigham Young. This may seen strange, but there are plenty such in this country, that **believe they would be doing God's service to obey**, if Brigham told them to kill their own son, or the son to kill the father. For two reasons; One for obeying the great command of Brigham, and have nerve enough to do the deed; another, that **the man had done something that his blood should be shed to atone for his sins,** and it **thereby would be the means of salvation to the murdered man, and honor, and a promise of greater exaltation in the world to come to the slayer.**

In Hickman's statements, we see the same idolatry that led the Saints into polygamy, and the murderous blood atonement doctrine of Young. Faith and trust is better placed in the living God and His ways. Continuing, Hickman stated, "But let me here say that this is all Brigham Young's doctrine; I never heard of any such thing until I had been here several years. Those doctrines of shedding a man's blood to save, Adam being God, and several other abominable things of like character, have originated solely from Brigham; **obedience to the requirements of the Gospel**, as set forth, taught, and understood heretofore by the Mormons, **have almost entirely been set aside**, and the general teaching is, and has been, **to obey Brigham Young's counsel and that of his bishop**. Many is the time that at public meetings the people have been taught that the Bible, Testament, and other books of the former Mormon faith were of no use; that those things were good enough in the time of them; **but now we had the living oracles with us** [Brigham and the Twelve], and that all divine record was of no more use to us than an old newspaper. Brother Brigham was our Saviour, and would lead us to Heaven; he held the power of salvation for all in his own hands, and had his officers, who administered, such as bishops, etc. The great and all-important teaching to the people is: **Obey your bishops, and pay your tithings, and you are sure of being saved.** This may seem strange to those who have never heard of such things before; but I assure you there are hundreds in this Territory who are sanguine in this belief even now – and as for Mormonism, there is nothing in this country; it **is all Brighamism, and should be called so**" (pps. 176-178).

Looking back in regret, Hickman stated, "I would rather have died a dozen deaths than to pass through what I have, if I could only be alive again and see **right and justice triumph**...I think it right to come out and show the damnable course pursued by Brigham Young – guilty as I have made myself, and with no excuse to offer except **my fanatical belief**. Believe me or not, I was sincere. O my God! If any of my brethren (who used to be anyhow) in Utah think they can break the laws of heaven or this free Government, and Brigham will take care of them, let them come and see me here...lonely and no show to do anything for my family, and scarred all over my body, lame, and old, and poor, when I was once rich, and hated by man, and my life threatened if I stir away from this post...I might go into detail of family affairs – women in polygamy, property appropriations, thievings, and when, how, and by whom ordered, and the consequences when not ordered, and **many other atrocious deeds of murder done by the order of Brigham Young**, which I was not witness to – all of which would make a larger book than this...the day is coming fast – yes, in Utah! – that you will know the things set down in this book for truth" (pps. 195-96).

Book editor John Hanson Beadle recorded many of Hickman's most notable murders for Young in the Appendix of his book. Beadle stated, "I have . . . submitted to the reader only the most important, and smallest part, of the corroborative evidence [of murders by Hickman via Young]. As Utah affairs have been my study for years, a few may desire to know my opinion of Hickman's work. It is briefly this: I am convinced that what he has told is substantially true; but he has not told all the truth. There is good evidence of his having engaged in other matters of doubtful import, not alluded to in this work, particularly about Nauvoo...But the popular verdict will doubtless be that Hickman has **confessed** enough, in all conscience, and that if each of the other Danites has as much to tell, our worst opinions of Brigham Young have fallen far short of the bloody reality" (John Hanson Beadle editor, p. 221).

The Mountain Meadows Massacre

Some 120 people (men, women, and children) were murdered in Southern Utah on September 11 of 1847 in the Mountain Meadows Massacre. Many attribute it to Brigham Young and his blood atonement doctrine. Some believe the massacre was a form of revenge for the murder of Apostle Parley P. Pratt. John D. Lee was the only man brought to trial for this deed, in which Southern Utah Mormons, dressed up as Indians, murdered the immigrants passing through Utah Territory on their way to California. Many were from Arkansas. Pres. Young's blood atonement doctrine suggested that forgiveness for certain sins comes only through the shedding of the sinner's blood. This doctrine, and news that Apostle Pratt had been murdered by an Arkansas man on May 13, 1857, may have led to this massacre. Hector McLean killed Pratt. He was the estranged husband of Eleanor McComb, Pratt's 12th polygamous wife. Eleanor McLean portrayed Pratt as a martyr who had rescued her from her alcoholic, abusive husband. Less favorable national accounts said Pratt had seduced Eleanor away from her husband. Pratt and Eleanor met three years earlier when Pratt was living in San Francisco, presiding over a mission there. Eleanor embraced Mormon principles and was baptized into the church with her husband's consent.

In 1855, following a domestic dispute, Hector McLean secretly sent their children from San Francisco to New Orleans, Louisiana, to live with their maternal grandparents, whereupon Eleanor determined to leave him. She then traveled to New Orleans to get her children. Eleanor and Pratt had decided to meet at Fort Smith Arkansas, traveling back to Utah together. Hector got wind of this and beat them to Arkansas, where he filed charges against them and got warrants for their arrests. He then caught up with Eleanor and Pratt in Oklahoma and again took the children. Hours later, a state marshal arrested Eleanor, while a military escort apprehended Pratt. They were first taken to Fort Gibson and then to Van Buren. There, Eleanor was brought before Judge John Ogden. He released her without further charges. Pratt was kept overnight and secretly released early the next day. Hector McLean learned of Pratt's release, caught up with him, and then shot and stabbed him. Things done in secret don't bear good fruit.

Paul said, "For we wrestle not against flesh and blood, but against principalities, against powers, against the rulers of the darkness of this world, against **spiritual wickedness in high places**" (Ephesians 6:12).

God has added, "And the rebellious shall be pierced with much sorrow; for their **iniquities shall be spoken upon the housetops** and **their secret acts shall be revealed** (D&C 1:3).

This book is part of God's prophecy being fulfilled.

Chapter Five

The Nauvoo Masonic Temple

New Temple Theology

The "temple" plays a huge role in Latter-day Saint theology today. Portions of what is found in the current LDS temple endowment came from the LORD through the Prophet Joseph Smith. The primary purpose of the temple and of Joseph's endowment was instruction via pure revelation that assists us in returning to the LORD's presence. Other portions of the endowment have come to us from Brigham Young and his borrowing from sources like Freemasonry. They divert us from the more inspired path. Additional change has followed, moving us further from the Tree of Life. Like the spiritual wives doctrine, there is no canonized revelation from God to consult, or to turn to, with regard to our "endowment." It was conveniently absent for Young and his followers. This allowed the **secret chamber** to again claim that Joseph Smith brought it all forth, complete with Young's additions, his "sealings" of multiple wives to one man. And just like the false accusations of polygamy against Joseph, the murdered prophet could not counter Young's claims that he, as Prophet of the Restoration provided all of the new temple theology.

An important sign of early trouble, emerging after Joseph's murder, was that half of the Nauvoo Saints rejected the temple theology put in place by Young, along with his leadership, and his polygamy. They included the Smith family, William Marks (Nauvoo Stake President), four Apostles, and others later on, including the Nauvoo Temple architect William Weeks. He escaped Salt Lake City in 1848 after Brigham pushed him to take additional wives.

Hereafter we will see that Young and the Nauvoo **secret chamber** utilized Joseph Smith's name to *justify* the creation of a modified endowment to benefit them. Following Joseph's murder, Brigham and Heber took Joseph's new "sealing" doctrine and changed it to support marriages in the Nauvoo Temple, where multiple women were "sealed" to one man. Apostle Lorenzo Snow is one example. He had four women sealed to him in one day in the Nauvoo Temple in 1846. One of the greatest abmoninations before God is the practice of sexual perversion, *justified* by religious rites performed in God's holy name. It is "*spiritual wifery.*" This was the great sin of the Old Testament *Baal worshippers*, the New Testament Christians following Nicolas (*the Nicolaitans*), and *the Cochranites* of the early 19th century. It was the great Prophet Elijah that eliminated the filth and idolatry of Baal worship in 1 Kings 18 using fire from heaven, and it was this same Elijah that brought back the sealing power to Joseph and Oliver in the Kirtland Temple (see D&C 110). With Joseph gone, what Elijah brought back in priesthood power and authority was twisted to support the whoredom of polygamy, and within what was to become a temple **to the LORD's name**. Instead, it became something else with close ties to Freemasonry. Elijah's *sealing power* was never about polygamous marriage sealings, but about turning "the hearts of the children to <u>**the promises**</u> **made to the fathers**" (JSH 1:39). This *turning, sealing, binding*, or *remembering*, points us to the **covenant** <u>**promises God made**</u> to the ancient patriarchal fathers, promises tied to **salvation** in Christ the LORD, **not** polygamous marriage sealings of many wives to one man!

Satan succeeded in further corrupting the imporant truths Joseph had brought forth, fulfilling the LORD's prophecy in D&C 38:13 and 28. Desire for "gain" was Satan's weapon, desire for extra wives, power, money, and the honors of men. Joseph's inspired temple teachings were modified by Young to accomplish two goals; (1) To **prop up spiritual wifery**, And (2) To provide a **future financial funnel** for those in the **secret chamber**. Some of these changes remain. Others have been repudiated and removed. The question then is, what portions of the current temple endowment are of God through Joseph, and which ones are from Young, Kimball, and others? To have truth, we must turn again to God for answers, via His written word in scripture and in *pure* revelation. Some of the answers can only come from the latter, as there is great confusion in many opposing voices and our doctored history.

Hereafter, this chapter is divided into what could have been, and what resulted (and now remains), via four divisions. In *Part I: Joseph's Vision for a House of the LORD at Nauvoo*, Joseph Smith's vision of the exterior of the Nauvoo Temple is addressed. It coincides with John the Revelator's vision of the church of the Firstborn that will rise up in the Millennial day, as presented us in JST Revelation 12. In *Part II: An Endowment of Power From On High*, we turn to God's word and will learn what His "endowment of power from on high" was and is. In *Part III: The Salvation Focus of the Sealing Power*, scripture is used to reveal what God's definition of "the sealing power" really is, not what Young and Kimball have given us. Also addressed are Joseph's sealings of both women *and* men to him. They were part of an early proxy salvation rite for couples. And last, *Part IV: Transition from a House of the LORD to a Masonic Temple*, focuses on how Joseph's "house of the LORD" later transitioned to a hybrid Masonic Temple, after he was murdered. To create their modifed form of Joseph's endowment to support spiritual wifery, Young and Kimball appear to have borrowed from four different sources. Freemasonry was one of them. Each is explored as more is presented.

Part I: Joseph's Vision for the House of the LORD at Nauvoo

The Prophet Joseph was chosen by the LORD to bring forth the Restoration of the fullness of the gospel of Christ. Joseph had great love for the Saints. Like Moses, Joseph wanted to bring his people into the LORD's presence, if they would. In response to Joseph's pleas on the Saints behalf, the LORD gave the Nauvoo Saints a commandment to build another "house" **to His name**, one at Nauvoo.

It was yet another opportunity to unify and prove themselves worthy to God (as they had at Kirtland for a time), that they might receive more. They were to once again organize themselves, prepare every needful thing, and establish "a house, even a house of prayer, a house of fasting, a house of faith, a house of learning, a house of glory, a house of order, **a house of God**" (D&C 88:119, 109:8). It was to become a temple of His Spirit, built to His Name. If they followed God's clear directions, doing so in His time and His way, they would be greatly blessed. It did not happen. Instead, as we saw in chapter 3 and 4, a secret chamber rose up *to get gain* at Nauvoo (D&C 38:13 & 28). It was Satan's way to pollute the church from the inside. It was focused on the lusts of the flesh and the things of the world. After the Smiths were murdered, Brigham's "new order of things" transitioned the temple endowment to something else. The Temple Committee called it "the Nauvoo Masonic Temple," a description given us in the Joseph Smith Papers project. Cursings resulted.

Both the Israelites under Moses and the Saints under Joseph rejected the "fullness" the LORD had in store for His people. It began at Kirtland and intensified at Nauvoo. For many it continues today. It is a rejection of LORD Jesus as King and His higher ways (detailed in chapter 7). Christ is replaced with mortal leaders who are lifted up in His place. At Kirtland, the Saints could not live the higher law given in Section 42 of the D&C. It featured two primary conponents; (1) the higher law of real love for God *and* one another (the two great commandments) in "**the law of consecration**" (vs. 31-39), and for some (2) the higher law of **monogamy** (vs. 22-23). It was at Kirtland where the first Cochranite converts came from the Boston area. They planted the early seeds of spiritual wifery among the Saints. They took root at Nauvoo. The LORD gave the Saints a second chance to embrace the fullness at Nauvoo. It included *the fulness of the priesthood* that had been taken away earlier (see D&C 124:28), including rites made possible by keys of power brought back by Elijah, the sealing power. Its focus was **salvation**, including that for the dead – in baptism for the dead. Note the symbolic language in D&C 128:12-14. It has nothing to do with geneology, but with letting go of all our "dead works" of the flesh, our carnal nature, that we might put on the "new man" of holiness (Eph. 4: 24). Satan had plans to corrupt this work. Polygamy and Freemasonry were part of it.

When the original commandment was given to build a "**house of the LORD**" at Nauvoo, the Prophet Joseph knew very little about Freemasonry. This ancient brotherhood, known for its secrecy, would soon come to dominate the Nauvoo landscape, with four Masonic lodges and nearly 1,500 Mormon Masons. Besides polygamy, there were other secret things rising up at Nauvoo, including the secret signs and oaths of Masonry, the secret meetings of the Quorum of the Anointed (where the new "endowment" was first put in place), and the theocratic Council of Fifty (which Joseph had hoped to use against the polygamists). Joseph was made a king over all Israel in this Council.

The original purpose of both the "house of the LORD" at Kirtland and the new one to be built at Nauvoo, was the creation of a sacred school setting where the Saints could learn the path of ascension, or how to return to God in this life. In addition to washings and anointings and other rites performed at Kirtland - for the **salvation** of the living, the new "house" at Nauvoo was to feature additional rites for the **salvation** of the dead – in vicarious baptisms for them. Had Joseph remained alive, he would have revealed even more about what was to be part of the fuller Nauvoo endowment. In addressing the addition of the new baptism rites, Patriarch Hyrum Smith spoke of four kinds of baptisms utilized at Nauvoo at this time; two were performed inside the new structure using its unique baptismal font, and two more were to be done outside the building in the Mississippi River. Hyrum said:

> "Baptisms for [1] the dead, and for [2] the healing of the body [of the living] **must be in the font**, those [3] coming into the Church, and those [4] re-baptized [a recommitment] may be baptized in the river" (HC 4:586).

Joseph had a vision of the new house of the LORD at Nauvoo. Its exterior architecture was centered on the Bride of the Lamb. Inside the Saints were to be taught how to become **the bride of Christ**, or members of the church of the Firstborn (see D&C 76:54, 71 & 94). It required each saved soul to develop a loving, trusting relationship with our Redeemer, much like a good marriage. Marriage symbolism is found throughout scripture, pointing us to God's desire for this **relationship**. Satan wanted to stop the relationship from happening. Joseph envisioned the exterior of the building covered in Suns, moons, and stars. It would eventually have 432 stars on it, and in five varieties (4 types outside and a 5th inside). Collectively they illustrated those who are part of "the church of the Firstborn," the Bride of the Lamb. This church of **sanctified** believers was to rise forth from the darkness of the last days into the beautiful light of a second, needed reformation in the Millennium (chap. 8). Nauvoo resident Wandle Mace explained its eventual appearance, stating:

> "The order of the architecture was unlike anything else. It was a representation of the Church, **the Bride, the Lamb's wife**" (Wandle Mace autobiography, p. 207).

Two thousand years earlier, John the Revelator also saw this same Latter-day church in vision. He described it in JST Revelation 12. John compared it to, "a **great sign** in heaven, in the likeness of things on the earth; a woman clothed with the sun, and the moon under her feet, and upon her head a crown of twelve stars." This describes well the symbolic architecture of the Nauvoo Temple. John's "great sign" in heaven is believed to have appeared over Jerusalem at sundown on Sept. 22nd - 23rd of 2017. It was a harbinger of what is about to occur in our day; the coming forth of the Bride of the Lamb – a church of true believers – cleansed and prepared for her husband - the Bridegroom Jesus Christ. He is our Savior and Redeemer, our Rock and High Tower, our source of living waters. Isaiah 54 and portions of the Book of Mormon address a different bride - the *unfaithful bride*. She must be cleansed and prepared for her husband's return.

The **fullness** portion of the doctrine and gospel of Christ has been rejected by the Gentile Saints today. It is the second fiery or spiritual baptism, that of fire and the Holy Ghost (see chap. 7). Too few today know what it is or seek it. It is to be sanctified by the LORD Himself, afterwhich we can receive the Holy Ghost (chap. 7). The LORD addressed this rejection in a prophecy of our day in 3 Nephi 16:10. He later provided a description of what this **fullness** is in the later part of 3 Nephi 30:2. Joseph Smith's grand vision of the Nauvoo Temple exterior symbolized this new reformed, light-filled church, one that will rise up in our day among those who focus on **the LORD** and the **fullness** of His gospel, not men and their polluted churches (Mormon 8:38).

The church that both Joseph and John envisioned never rose up at Nauvoo. Instead, Joseph and two of his brothers were murdered, and the higher, fuller ways were then corrupted and diminished by those in the secret chamber. It is part of the awful situation we have inherited today. Hope is not lost, however. God saw it all coming in D&C 38 and other scriptures, like those of Isaiah and Jeremiah, and much of the Book of Mormon. Though the harvest is near and many souls not saved, all that is needed is to **turn** to the LORD. It is another word for **repent**. Alma made the change and turned to the LORD, becoming part of His church, the one Joseph and John saw in vision.

In attempting to place this vision on the stone walls of the temple at Nauvoo, the Prophet Joseph utilized the skills of architect William Weeks. Early on Weeks' attempted to modify Joseph's original plans for the building. The Prophet Joseph told him, "I wish you to carry out my designs. I have seen in vision the splendid appearance of that building illuminated, and will have it built according to the pattern shown me" (HC, 6:196). Joseph's "house of the LORD" at Nauvoo was to become a Temple to the LORD's **name**, illustrating the Bride of the Lamb rising up in the last days, but only if the Saints would devote themselves wholly to God and His ways, not their own. It is a choice addressed in the Bible and the Book of Mormon, known as the doctrine of **the two ways**. All must choose between "life or death, blessing or cursing." Moses said, "therefore choose life, that both thou and thy seed may live" (Deut. 30:19).

Part II: An Endowment of Power From On High

At the very beginning of the Restoration, God - because of love wanted to endow the Saints with **power** from on high – or from Him. Under Brigham Young later at Nauvoo, this endowment became something different. We have inherited his changes, and those of others after him. For truth's sake and for a more complete understanding of the original purposes of "the house of the LORD" and the original "endowment," we must again turn to God's word and will for answers first. The LORD commanded the Nauvoo Saints to build a "house" **two times** in D&C 124. It was to be built to **His name** (this was repeated 9 times). Both the new Temple and the "Nauvoo House" (a boarding house for visitors to Nauvoo) were to be built according to His **will** and His **timing, if** the Saints were to receive the great blessings He had in store for them.

As we will see hereafter, God's limited time frame was not adhered to, as neither building was ever completed. And because leaders began focusing on polygamy and other things following the Smith murders, neither structure was built to the **LORD's name**, with the focus being His **salvation** for the Saints, and more. Instead, personal businesses, Masonic lodges, their own homes, and spiritual wifery all became their higher priorities. Similar misplaced priorities were evident in the Israelites of Hagai, chapter one in the Old Testament. Thus, instead of blessings, both groups were cursed. And in the end, instead of a "house of the LORD" at Nauvoo, the Saints ended up with something else. Their building was hastily dedicated before it was finished. The Brighamite Saints then left Nauvoo for a salty land west (Jer. 17:6), known as Utah Territory. The cursing led to the destruction of what some called the Masonic temple.

Throughout scripture, the symbolic rites of the LORD's house point us to re-entering His presence. It is to be a house of learning, a school that teaches **"the way"** or path of *ascension.* There we are to receive pure revelation from God as part of the ceremonies that will prepare us for our *ascent return* to Him personally. The exterior architecture of the Nauvoo Temple expresses this pathway. We are to ascend up to God from the earth (which we are standing upon), passing by the moon, then the sun, and finally into the stars. It is the natural order of the heavens seen from our earthly perspective, as we stand upon the earth looking up.

Cleansing rites in connection with repentance were the focus of the Tabernacle of Moses in the wilderness, the House of the LORD built by Solomon in Jerusalem, and the "house" Joseph Smith built and dedicated earlier at Kirtland. Each was a place to prepare themselves for God's presence *and* His gifts. Because the Saints at Kirtland did as the LORD asked, they experienced a real "endowment of **power** from on high." It was centerd on cleansing rites using water, and God's sanctification of the Saints, whereby those prepared would receive the unspeakable gift of the Holy Ghost. Multiple times in the D&C, we read about the "**endowment of power from on high**." What is it?

To answer this important question we must go back to Kirtland, Ohio where the first "house of the LORD" of this dispensation was constructed. It remains standing. God did not destroy it. The Saints did something right and good there. It was finished and dedicated properly to the LORD, and to **His name**. Our LORD accepted it in a personal visition to Joseph and Oliver. There were many manisfestions of His Spirit there at its dedication in 1836, along with visitations by Moses, Elias, and Elijah (see D&C 110). The Kirtland Saints were blessed. The Nauvoo Saints were cursed, their building destroyed. The original purpose of Joseph's endowment was to fight the darkness not invite it.

Endowed with Power

Very early on in church history, God said that He wanted the Saints to receive an "endowment of **power** *from on high*" - or from **Him**. The Saints were to "tarry" or wait for it at Kirtland Ohio. The LORD told the New Testament Saints to also "tarry" - at Jerusalem. Both groups were to cleanse and prepare themselves that they might be endowed with real **power** from God Himself. This gift or endowment, which the Father had prepared for them, was **to counteract the evil one** and his plans to destroy Joseph, the Saints, and the early church. Note God's words below in 1831. He told Joseph and the Saints:

> "And now I show unto you a **mystery**, a thing which is had in **secret chambers**, *to bring to pass your destruction* in process of time, and ye knew it not… the enemy in the **secret chambers** seeketh your lives...**And that <u>ye might escape the power of the enemy</u>**, and be gathered unto me *a righteous people*, without spot and blameless — Wherefore, for this cause I gave unto you the commandment that ye should go to the Ohio; and there I will give unto you **my law** [the higher law in D&C 42 – the law of consecration *and* the law of marriage, one man and one woman]; and there you shall be **endowed with power from on high**…" (D&C 38:13, 28, 31-33).

Most references in scripture tied to the scriptural phrase, "**an endowment of power from on high**" refer specifically to God's gifting of **the Holy Ghost** to His people - after they are purified in the "born again" spiritual transformation (see chapter 7). It is to receive **the fuller** portion of the doctrine and gospel of Christ, not just the preparatory, symbolic water baptism only, but the greater spiritual baptism of fire and the Holy Ghost.

Like His disciples (followers) at Jerusalem, the LORD told the early Kirtland Saints to "tarry" there, or to wait on Him for His gifts, as **He** alone would provide them based on His timing. Those in the New Testament received their endowment - "**the gift and power of the Holy Ghost**" - on the Day of Pentecost (see Luke 24:49; Acts 1-2). It was "the promise of the Father," to be provided at a particular place *and* time of **His** choosing, and in a group *event*. It occurred for the Kirtland Saints during the dedication of "the house of the LORD" on March 27th of 1836. Nothing has occurred like it since in the church, as many things changed after Joseph's murder.

In early church history, the LORD placed His Spirit upon the Saints in a group event, just as He did throughout the Book of Mormon and the New Testament. He stated that if His "house" was not defiled, His glory would rest upon it. He added that "**the pure in heart** that shall come into it shall **see God**" (D&C 97:16). To see and experience God is the whole purpose of sacred space – or a "house of the LORD." God is **power**. Only He gives it and the gifts of the Spirit to those who love Him and humble themselves before Him via a broken heart and contrite spirit (3 Ne. 9:20). For far too many today, symbols at the temple - tied to entering God's presence - have replaced the real thing – God Himself and His **power**.

The promised "endowment of **power**" was to be especially useful for missionaries, in both the New Testament church and among the early Saints of the Restoration. It comes from "on high" or from God, not from other men in symbolic rites. The missionaries, and really all the Saints, needed to be cleansed and purified first (sanctification), before receiving this "unspeakable gift" tied to God's **power**. In the Lectures on Faith, part of the D&C until 1921, the Holy Ghost is defined as having access to "**the unified mind of the Father and the Son**" (see Lecture 5). Effective teachers of the gospel of Christ need to have access to God's mind and will (the Holy Ghost) so they could teach with real **convincing power**, or with God's influence upon them. Helaman's sons - Lehi and Nephi, did so in the Book of Mormon with great success.

A great outpouring of God's spiritual gifts, including the Holy Ghost, occurred at Kirtland on the dedication day of the House of the LORD – March 27, 1836. It was a fulfillment of "the promise of the Father" (Luke 24:49), that they might be endowed with real **power** from on high, comparable to the day of Pentecost in the New Testament. Angels were seen and heard at the dedication of this *completed structure*. A pillar of fire stood above the "house" (see **84:5**; 109:22, 35-38), and some were seen with cloven tongues of fire above their heads during the services. Many spoke in tongues, including babes, as many experienced a baptism of fire. The gift given became a significant aid in teaching thereafter. Chapter 7 explains how to receive this gift as part of embracing **the fullness** of the doctrine and gospel of Christ. Those who embrace this fullness, become part of His church, the one illustrated on the exterior of the Nauvoo Temple. In 1843, the Prophet Joseph stated:

> "Jesus Commanded them [the New Testament Saints] to tarry there [Jerusalem] until they were endowed with **power** from on high... for the Pentecost...The endowment was to prepare the disciples for their **mission** into the world" (Words of Joseph Smith, 22 Jan. 1843).

Missionaries are powerless to teach Christ's gospel without His influence, for it is His work. The Holy Ghost is what the disciples of Christ in 3 Nephi 19:9 wanted more than *any other thing* (3 Ne. 19:9). Today young missionaries are "endowed" at the temple before going out on their missions. For far too many of them today, however, it means sitting through a symbolic presentation and learning signs and gestures rather than receiving real **power** in the **gift of the Holy Ghost**; the unspeakable gift given of God Himself. It comes only after we are **sanctified** from all sin by Him. To receive it, we must repent, crying out to God for His mercy as did many in the Book of Mormon, like Alma. It is an *event*. Too many believe they already have this gift when they don't (see chapters 6 & 7). Remove all idols from your heart, and receive pure revelation from God. Then ask if you have this gift and what you must do to receive it.

Convincing others of the truthfulness of the Book of Mormon or the gospel of Christ does not come because one has sat through a temple endowment session, where symbolic signs and tokens are presented. Instead, it requires the LORD's cleansing blood to sanctify us - in connection with our own sincere, heartfelt **repentance**. Humility and a fiery cleansing from God then hastens our reception of "the gift and power of Holy Ghost" thereafter, having access to "the unified mind of the Father and the Son." Effective missionaries and all committed Saints must first develop strong **faith in Christ** the LORD, our Redeemer, as He is the supplier of this and all spiritual gifts. We can then receive the "the promise of the Father" (Luke 24:49). It is the real "endowment of **power** from on high" available to any believer in Christ, in or outside the LDS church. God says, "**repent** and **come unto me**." This five-word phrase is a concise summary of His doctrine and gospel. To do this, God says, "deny yourselves of all ungodliness" (Mor.10:32).

Symbols in the temple are useful for teaching purposes, but they only point us to the real thing – God and His gifts. As we will see hereafter, Brigham's additions to the endowment and the church in general, have diverted many from the truer path laid down in the Book of Mormon, a pathway focused on **redemption through Christ**, not the idolatry of worshipping leaders, the church, the temple with its "endless geneologies" (1 Tim. 1:4) and symbolic rites. A similar thing happened to the Israelites in Jerusalem. Their path became polluted too. They took pride in Herod's Temple, its rites, and their leaders, believing these things would save and protect them. Most of them rejected the living God Jesus Christ when He come among them - to save them. They valued "the deadness of the law" more than they did becoming "**alive in Christ**" (see 2 Nephi 25:26-27, and chapter 28).

Because of inherited lies and false traditions, many of the Saints have departed from, (1) an understanding of what the **endowment** is (and other parts of "**the fullness**"), and (2) **how** to receive it (see 1 Ne. 15:14, chap. 7). The Holy Ghost is to be given us to help us discern darkness from light, and to bring those who embrace truth back to Christ. The Holy Ghost is **oil** in the lamps of "**wise** virgins." It is the iron rod of *pure* revelation from God. In D&C 38, God implied that this "endowment" would help counteract the dark power present in **secret combinations** that would rise up among and around the Saints. It is given to "**escape the power of the enemy**" (v. 31), to discern the tares from the wheat, and the wolves dressed in sheep's clothing among us.

Because of idolatry, polygamy, and changes made by Brigham Young, we have inherited a modified "endowment" today. There is light and darkness in it. By reading all the seven references in scripture featuring the phrase, "**an endowment of power from on high**" listed below, we can note the differences between God's "endowment of **power**" versus Brigham's borrowed mix of concepts from four different sources that are addressed hereafter. God's word reveals that His original "endowment of **power** from on high," had two components:

(A) It was God's gifting of **power** in **the Holy Ghost** to those Saints gathered at Kirtland, at the dedication of the house of the LORD there (see D&C 33:15; 109:22, 35-37; 3 Ne. 9:20; 12:1; 2 Ne. 31:12; 3 Ne. 11:35; JST Mat. 3:38; JST Luke 3:16; JST John 1:28; 15:26). Additional scriptures point to a second gift.

(B) It was also an endowment of the greater Melchizedek priesthood **power** (June 1831), as promised to some men at the Morley Farm Conference at Kirtland. Both were planned events in space (a setting) and time by the LORD, where select groups of people prepared themselves for a great spiritual outpouring from Him.

In Jerusalem and at Kirtland, gifts of **power** were given of God at the specific place *and* time He chose. The future planned events provided **motivation** and **preparation time** for individuals to offer up the sacrifice the LORD had chosen, which in most cases was a "broken heart and a contrite spirit" (3 Ne. 9:20). We are to be on a divine nature. Note that an "endowment of **power**" occurred in four primary settings in scripture: (a) The base of Mt. Sinai, a natural mountain setting in the Old Testament, on the 50th day after leaving captivity in Egypt; (b) At Jerusalem on the Day of Pentecost in the New Testament (50 days after the LORD's resurrection; (c) At a number of different settings and points in time in the Book of Mormon; And (d) At the dedication of the House of the LORD at Kirtland Ohio (D&C 109, 110). The seven sets of scripture below are all tied to God's "**endowment of power from on high.**"[22]

1. Ex. 19:4-6, 8, 17-18; 20:18-20; JST Ex. 34:1-2; D&C 84:23-27, 49-59; Heb. 3 & 4 (most at Sinai)
2. Luke 24:49 & Acts 1 & 2 (gift and power of **the Holy Ghost**, Jerusalem) *
3. D&C 38:31-32, 38 (higher priesthood, Kirtland, 1831), see also 39:15, 18 & 23
4. D&C 43:15-16 (higher priesthood, Kirtland, 1831)
5. D&C 95:8-9 (gift and power of **the Holy Ghost**, Kirtland "House of the Lord," 1833) *
6. D&C 97:12-18 (gift and power of **the Holy Ghost**, Kirtland "House of the Lord," 1833) *
7. D&C 105:10-12 (gift and power of **the Holy Ghost**, Kirtland "House of the Lord," 1834) *

Two of the seven events above are tied to receiving power in the greater Melchizedek priesthood (#'s 3 & 4). Its potential gifting was preceded *first* by reception of the fullness of God's **word** (in the Book of Mormon and portions of the JST Bible), and then receiving the fullness of God's higher **law**, in the *law of consecration* and the *law of monogamy* (see D&C 42). Following the reception of the fuller **word** and **law**, the greater **priesthood** was then offered to 23 men called or invited to the Morley Farm Conference in 1831 (D&C 52). The men there had to demonstrate worthiness to be not just "*called*" but also become "*chosen*" by God to actually receive this *power* from Him in the greater priesthood. It required a strong *relationship* with God, cementing *trust*. It is no different today. Thus a very good definition for **power** in *the priesthood* today, is a *trusting, loving relationship with* God. We are to have faith and trust in Him, not men.

Four of the seven sets of scriptures above are tied to being "born again" in Christ, and receiving the gift or endowment of the Holy Ghost in connection with it (following a fiery cleansing in God's Spirit). Note that all portions of God's **fullness** were offered the Saints *before* there was a command by God in 1834 to build the Kirtland chapel or "house of the LORD" (completed in 1836). He invited the Saints to receive a fullness of, 1. His **word**, 2. His **law**, 3. His **priesthood**, 4. His **gospel**, and 5. His personal **rest** and **glory**. This is the "**fullness**" rejected by 1834 (see 3 Ne. 16:10; 30:2), necessitating a plan to help the Saints return to Him and His gifts - via *a second chance* at Nauvoo. More would also be presented there as well, in the sealing power brought back by Elijah. It would include **salvation** work for those on the other side of the veil too, that centered on *baptism for the dead.*

The goal of building a "house" dedicated to the LORD's name at Nauvoo, was designed to motivate and unify the Saints, bringing them together in love for this purpose (love for God and each other). God did the same thing with the ancient Israelites, **after** they rejected Him and His fullness at Sinai (a natural mountain temple). It is recorded in scripture as an important pattern for **us** today and is clearly presented in chapter 7, scripture by scripture. Too many ignore God's word and do not search it. Thus, they rely on mortal leaders, the arm of flesh, many of whom use them for gain (the wolves in sheep's clothing).

Power is Given in Various Settings

A careful review of scripture reveals that God has invited man to receive Him personally outside of a "house of the Lord" or a "temple," and that the *later* architectural constructions of men were often built to help the people return to Him, through symbolic teachings provided in these special settings. As stated earlier, this is exactly what happened at Mount Sinai and Kirtland. Sacred architecture and what goes on inside it, provides useful symbolic representations of what are to be **greater spiritual experiences or realities**, where we interface with God's Spirit and Him personally. It can happen in or outside a building. God said, "ye are the temple of the living God" (2 Cor. 6: 16-18).

Joseph never intended the temple and its symbolic ordinances to become an object of worship (a form of idolatry). When the Lord said he would raise up the temple (His own body) after His crucifixion and three days in the tomb, many misunderstood His statement. He as God had power over sin, death, and hell. In Revelation 21, we read that in heaven, there is no temple, as the Father and Son are the temple of it. They are the focus of all symbolic ordinances. God chose the Kirtland Temple and the time of its dedication to gift the Holy Ghost and other gifts of the Spirit to many of the Saints, those prepared for them. Signs of God's power followed the humble believers there, and in the New Testament on the "Day of Pentecost." They included the following signs:

Visual Signs Cloven tongues of fire were seen above the heads of some of the Saints.
A pillar of fire was seen above the Kirtland house of the LORD.
Angels were also seen (and heard).

Audible Signs Many spoke in tongues at this event. Others were able to interpret these tongues.
Many heard angels singing.

Felt Signs The baptism of fire and the Holy Ghost was experienced. It is when the Spirit of God was poured out in a warm – even hot sensation on the prepared. In them there was a great desire to praise and worship God, along with a feeling of incredible **joy** in God's **love**.

These and other gifts were and are available to all the humble and repentant, in or outside the LDS church. Latter-day Saints have the advantage of incredible scripture, in what the LORD calls, "*the fullness* of **my scriptures**" (the Book of Mormon and the full JST Bible). We are not being taught "*the fullness* in them today, however. It must be discovered on our own by diligently searching them, feasting upon them, and with revelation ("fruit of the Spirit," Gal. 5: 22-25).

Like the Jews of old, many Saints today take pride in having temples and a living Prophet. Grand architectural buildings and men don't save us. God does. The Israelites in Jesus' day had Herod's Temple, learned Rabbis, and the

High Priest, yet they rejected Christ. In scripture the LORD says we, the latter-day Gentile Saints will **deny** Him (2 Ne. 28:32), **reject** Him (2 Ne. 1:10), and **forsake** Him (Jer. 2:13), along with **the power of the Holy Ghost** (2 Ne. 28:26, 31). This is the rejection of **the fullness** He promised would occur (3 Ne. 16:10; 30:2). Many of our Christian brothers and sisters believe Mormons are not Christian, as many diminish Christ in favor of leaders, the church, or the temple. They see us turning to mortal leaders and our symbolic temples more than the living Christ. Hosea said:

> "For Israel [ancient *and* modern] hath **forgotten his Maker**, and buildeth temples; and Judah hath multiplied fenced cities: but I will send a fire upon his cities, and it shall devour the palaces thereof" (Hosea 8:14).

Like the Israelites of old, pride keeps many believing that we are the only ones who will be saved when trouble comes. Instead, we may be the ones in the great and spacious building pointing at others who are making their way to the Tree. They are holding onto the **iron rod**. In Jeremiah 7, similar pride and expectations for salvation were expressed.

> "Stand in the gate of the LORD's house, and proclaim there this word, and say, Hear the word of the LORD, all ye... that enter in at these gates to worship the LORD. Thus saith the LORD of hosts, the God of Israel, Amend your ways and your doings, and I will cause you to dwell in this place. Trust ye not in **lying words**, saying, The temple of the LORD, The temple of the LORD, The temple of the LORD, are these. For if ye throughly amend your ways and your doings; if ye throughly execute judgment between a man and his neighbor; If ye oppress not the stranger, the fatherless, and the widow, and shed not innocent blood in this place, neither walk after other gods to your hurt: Then will I cause you to dwell in this place...for ever and ever" (Jer. 7:2-7).

Architectural structures such as Moses' Tabernacle and "the House of the Lord" at Kirtland were useful in preparing believers to receive God and His gifts, especially if the things in them remain pure and undefiled. Other structures like Herod's Temple and the Nauvoo Masonic Temple became polluted. Inspired instruction in pure temples reminds believers to seek God, His presence, and His gifts – receiving **the real things from Him**. The LORD offered the Saints **the fullness** of all things early on in church history between 1830 and 1834. After the Saints failed to seek and receive **Him**, as Joseph had hoped, God then commanded that a house of the LORD be built at Kirtland later on that same year. It was a way to reclaim the people, after they first rejected His invitation to receive Him personally and His rest and glory (see chap. 7). His arms remain open to the unfaithful Bride.

Part III: The Salvation Focus of the Sealing Power

A second invitation was presented the Saints at Navuoo, in a new house there, and with the potential for more. Joseph had learned about the sealing power of Elijah. This great Old Testament Prophet came to return this power (D&C 110). New things tied to his "sealing" power were presented to the Saints in connection with **salvation** for the living *and* now the dead. We find the word "seal" or "sealing" used in the Book of Mormon in three basic ways. The most important are its (1) **salvation** ties, to both the living and the dead. There are also (2) those with the sealing power that are able to invite or command the elements (in God's name) to respond to their words. Such follow God's will on "earth as it is in heaven." A third use of the word "seal" is tied to (3) sealing up or closing a book. Moroni said he "sealed up" his precious record in the Book of Mormon to come forth in our day (Mor. 10:2).

God said we are under condemnation for not using and understanding what we already have – in the Book of Mormon and its covenant (see D&C 84:54-58). This is why there is a *sealed* portion of the Book of Mormon not yet given us - because of the "wickedness" and "abominations" of the people, those among us rejecting the fuller things (chap. 7). The "sealed portion" of the Book of Mormon will be given to those who value God's word, those who place their faith and trust in Him. His salvation is our most important sealing – a sealing to **Him**.

Salvation Sealing *to Christ – the Father of our Salvation*

King Benjamin taught that we are to be sealed to Christ directly as the father of our salvation (see Mosiah 5:15). It is to be sealed up to eternal life by Him personally in most cases (see Hel. 10:3-5; D&C 131:5). It is to receive "the more sure word of prophecy" (D&C 131:5) and directly from Him as THE Prophet, Jesus Christ (see 1 Ne. 22:20-28), telling us that we are in the "*blessed*" state of **salvation**, or that we are "**sealed up to eternal life.**" In this event, our LORD promises the faithful that they will inherit *eternal life*, His greatest gift. He seals up various individiuals to eternal life by His direct voice, or via select empowered servants like Joseph and Hyrum Smith. Both men had the sealing power. If moved upon by the Holy Ghost, they could, through the Spirit – seal up *living* individuals or groups to this blessed state of **salvation**. Note that in opposition to this, the wicked are sealed to Satan. They inherit damnation instead (see Alma 34:35).

King Benjamin did not seal his people together, nor did he seal them to himself as an intermediate man between his people and God! He (King Benjamin) wasn't part of a long chain of saved souls from him to God (the false "law of adoption" that came later with Brigham Young). Instead, he brought the people to God in a covenant with Him – "**the everlasting covenant**" tied to following God's will (endnote 31) into two baptisms, so that they might be sealed directly to Him as His sons and daughters. Christ then became the father of their **salvation**. This is the message of chapters 1 to 5 of Mosiah. Christ alone is the gate or mediator to the things of heaven. As a wise, humble King, and a holy, just man, King Benjamin brought his people together at the New Year that he might teach them from a great tower about the concept of being "born again" in Christ. The people of Mosiah chapter 5, said:

> "…we believe all the words which thou hast spoken unto us; and also, we know of their surety and truth, because of the **Spirit** of the Lord Omnipotent, which has wrought a **mighty change** in us, or in our **hearts**, that we have no more disposition to do evil, but to do good continually…And now, because of the *covenant* which ye have made ye shall be called the children of Christ, his sons, and his daughters; for behold, this day he hath **spiritually begotten you**; for ye say that your **hearts** are **changed** through faith on his name; therefore, ye are **born of him** and have become his sons and his daughters. And under this head ye are made free, and there is *no other head* whereby ye can be made free. There is *no other name* given whereby **salvation** cometh; therefore, I would that ye should take upon you the name of Christ, all you that have entered into the *covenant* with God that ye should be obedient unto the end of your lives…whosoever shall not take upon him **the name of Christ** must be called by some other name; therefore, he findeth himself on the left hand of God… hear and know the voice by which ye shall be called, and also, the name by which he shall call you…Therefore, I would that ye should be steadfast and immovable, always abounding in good works, that Christ, the Lord God Omnipotent, **may seal you his**, that *you may be brought to heaven* [while in this life] that ye may have everlasting salvation and eternal life, through the wisdom, and power, and justice, and mercy of him who created all things, in heaven and in earth, who is God above all. Amen" (Mosiah 5:2-15, select verses)

There are many key words in this and other portions of Mosiah, all associated with coming to Christ and being born again in Him – and then **sealed** to our LORD as His son or daughter. Some of these key words *include joy, prophecy, covenant, seal, eternal life, sons* and *daughters, mighty change,* and *born of him*. His is the father of our salvation (via His blood atonement). Each of us are to become the Bride of Christ, in a close marriage-like personal **relationship**. In 3rd Nephi we read about the disciples of Christ, and how they longed to have the Holy Ghost (3 Ne. 19:9). It was an endowment of power that came after they were born again in the LORD. We see that after they were baptized by water **and** by fire, they then prayed directly to Christ the LORD (see 3 Ne. 19:9-25). He had become the Father of their salvation. This is a significant overlooked transition point. He is our Mediator with the Father, and a "father" in His own right. We become **His** after we are born in Him. We then pray to Him and/or the Father. They reveal the Mother to us.

There are seven scriptures tied to a spiritual sealing mark placed in the foreheads of those sealed to Christ the LORD, those born again in Him (redeemed), or otherwise marked as "**His.**" These seven scriptures use the words, "seal," "mark," "name of the Father" or "forehead" in them, and include Ezekiel 9:4-7; Revelation 7:2-3, 9:3-4, 14:1, 22:4; Mosiah 5:15 and D&C 133:17-18. The LORD's servants have this mark on the forehead and perhaps their palms. It is seen by those on the other side of the veil (including enemies), and those permitted to see the marks here. It is believed to be the ancient Tau or Tav mark (a T or + cross). It is the last letter of the Hebrew alphabet, tied to judgment at the end (or that one has passed their judgment by Christ – He has chosen them). When their hand is held to the square, this seal is exposed, representing real authority in the name and power of God. The eighth scripture about "sealing" represents a sealing to "the evil one" (Alma 34:35), those who reject God and embrace darkness.

Salvation for the Dead

D&C 124 and 128 feature the doctrine of salvation for the dead in proxy baptism within the house of the LORD at Nauvoo. Salvation for the dead was part of the greater gift of God to be presented at the Navuoo Temple. The higher priesthood and specifically the sealing power in it, brought back to earth by Elijah (John the Baptist, Elias) is necessary to conduct baptism for the dead in temples. It is part of "turning the hearts of the children" to "**the** "**promises**" of eternal life – or real salvation – "**made to the fathers**" (like Abraham, Isaac, Jacob, and Joseph). Like them, we too are to receive the promise of eternal life ourselves **first** (salvation), then help others to receive it. Baptism in water must be performed on earth by men, physically, as a covenant sign to God (love and willingness to follow Him and keep His commandments). We help the dead with this ordinance here, via the power Elijah brought back to the earth (D&C 110). Note however, that the LORD specifically stated in D&C 24:31 that if the Saints did not build Him a house at Nauvoo *in the alloted time* that He would reject their baptisms for the dead and them and their church. He said:

> "But I command you, all ye my saints, to build a house unto me; and *I grant unto you a sufficient time* to build a house unto me; and during **this time** your baptisms shall be acceptable unto me. But behold, *at the end of this appointment* your baptisms for your dead shall not be acceptable unto me; and if you do not these things at the end of the appointment **ye shall be rejected as a church, with your dead**, saith the Lord your God" (D&C 124:32).

Were the Nauvoo Saints, their dead, and the church all rejected because of the sins God identified among them in 3 Ne. 16:10 and 30:2, in connection with polygamy and the secret things at Nauvoo? Was this cursing lifted for a time among the Saints thereafter? Brigham Young's focus on polygamy in his modified version of the temple endowment, after Joseph's murder, effectively diminished the knowledge of **the fullness** among the Saints. It was replaced with a polygamy focus. When it was outlawed by the Federal Government as the 20th century came in, saving our dead through proxy temple work then became a focus for many Saints, again diminishing the need to be **redeemed or saved** of the LORD (like King Benjamin's people).

The promise of eternal life or **Salvation** came to "fathers" like Abram (father of the faithful) and Sarai because they loved the LORD, developed a relationship with Him, and fulfilled their missions valiantly (JST Gen. 9:21-25; JST 14:40; Mosiah 5:15). With demonstrated faithfulness, God gave Abram and Sarai the new names "Abraham" and "Sarah." An "h" (tied to "life") was added to both their first names, signifying their receipt of "**eternal** *life*." Sarah in her old age and in her "barren" condition was then miraculously able to conceive and bare "*life*" in Isaac, her firstborn son. These "fathers" (and mothers) are now in heaven and will return with Christ at His second coming. The wicked shall burn. So says JSH1:37, "for **they** that come shall burn them." Our merciful, loving God prepared a way for His children to receive salvation through Christ, and for the dead too via the greater Melchizedek Priesthood and special "sealing" keys within it. This power was brought back to earth by great prophet Elijah (see D&C 110, 124, 128). He eliminated Baal worship and the sexual perversions tied to it in his day - by fire God sent down from heaven. The earth was cleansed by water earlier in the flood. It will be cleansed by fire, as we are to be, prior to our LORD's return. Only those sanctified will be able to stand in their fiery return.

Power Over the Elements

Beyond **salvation** sealing, a second type of sealing is found in scripture. It is evident in those granted the sealing power from God, providing power over the elements of nature. They respond in love and obedience (Abraham 4:18) to those who command in God's name. Such have become one with God, following His will completely. They are trusted individuals, using God's power only in accordance with His will. They are not only *called,* but *chosen, empowered,* and *sent* servants. They use this power to bring about God's will in "thus saith the LORD" blessings *and* cursings upon others. Often we see God's servants sealing the heavens shut, so that rain no longer falls. This leads to famine and real hunger, not just for food, but for the LORD and His living waters, both physical water and spiritual rain (revelation). This desire or "hunger" brings the people to humility and repentance. It is about to occur again in our day, that idolatry and other sins might be removed.

An example in the Book of Mormon of one so trusted was Nephi, son of Helaman in Helaman 10:7. What he did here "on earth" was a reflection of God's will, or that "which is done in heaven." The sealing power is also used to save those in desperate need of physical salvation from enemies, as when Moses parted the Red Sea to allow the Israelites to pass through. The same waters then came crashing down to destroy the Egyptian army. Joseph and Hyrum had the sealing power. Joseph's power was twisted to become part of Young's plural marriage sealings. To understand all this, we must first understand one clarifying scripture that Moroni gave Joseph Smith the night of his first visit to him on New Year's Day ("Rosh Hashanah" – meaning "head of the year" on the Bible calendar) of 1823.

The Promises God Made to the Fathers

The patriarchs or "fathers" in scripture, like Adam, Noah, Enoch, and Abraham had strong faith in the LORD, and came to know Him personally, wherein they were promised God's greatest gift – to have **eternal life**. The journey for each of us to receive this same promise begins as we heed the LORD's invitation to "**repent** and **come to me**." As we take it literally, we too can receive this promise. This is why the angel who visited Joseph Smith on Rosh Hashanah of 1823 quoted some forty scriptures to him that night (Oliver Cowdery recorded all of them, not just the five we currrently have in JSH 1). The first of these scriptures quoted was Malachi 3. In Joseph Smith History 1:39, we read that the angel quoted Malachi 4:6 *differently* than in the King James Version of our Bible (see also D&C 110:15), stating that **we** - the children must - *with our hearts*, **turn**, **seal**, **bind**, or **remember**, "**the promises** [God] **made to the fathers**," if we are to *abide* the great and dreadful day of the LORD's return. There will be much burning on this day.

These are some of the last verses of the Old Testament. Note that this isn't a physical *sealing* to "the fathers" themselves as we have been taught – but a *turning* to or **remembering the promises God made to them** and to **us** as their *bloodline* or *adopted* posterity. The same promises are to be **sealed** upon us too - and by our LORD who is "the Holy Spirit of Promise." Enoch, Abraham, and other early "fathers" (those who tried to bring their people to Salvation in Christ) made the same covenant we do at baptism – to *serve* God and obey **His will**. We have not been taught this concept (see JST Gen. 9:12; Mosiah 5:5, 8 & endnote 31). God has also made other promises to Enoch, Abraham, and Joseph of Egypt (father of Manasseh and Ephraim) that apply directly to us as their literal or spiritually adopted posterity. If we are obedient to the same covenant they made with God at baptism in "the New and Everlasting Covenant," for example, we inherit the same promises made to righteous men like Abraham (father of the faithful, to be given *the priesthood* to bless the entire earth with it through *service*), and Enoch and the rainbow covenant God made with him in JST Gen. 9, but only **if** we do as they did, by keeping our **covenants** with God. Keeping the same **covenant** results in inheriting the same **promises**, thus, we should know it and the other covenenat these "fathers" (Abraham, Isaac, Jacob, and Joseph sold into Egypt) made with God. Note Joseph Smith's clarifying words hereafter, relative to the Malachi verses Moroni quoted to him:

> "For behold, the day cometh that shall burn as an oven, and all the **proud**, yea, and all that do wickedly shall burn as stubble; for **they that come shall burn them** [Christ, and the "fathers" and other rightous ones God brings with Him at His return] saith the Lord of Hosts, that it shall leave them neither root nor branch." 'And again, he quoted the fifth verse thus: "Behold, I will reveal unto you the Priesthood, by the hand of **Elijah** the prophet [he came as John the Baptist in 1829 to Joseph and Oliver], before the coming of the great and dreadful day of the Lord. He also quoted the next verse differently: And he shall plant in the hearts of the children **the promises made to the fathers**, and **the hearts** of the children shall **turn** to their fathers. If it were not so, the whole earth would be utterly wasted at his coming" (JSH 1:39, Mal. 3:6 variation).

Turning has ties to **sealing** or **remembering.** We are to **turn** or **seal** our hearts as "children" - in remembering "**the promises** [God] **made to the Fathers**." It is **not** about being "sealed" *to them* or others as family members. The "fathers" were special servants who **brought their people to God** (like King Benjamin in the book of Mosiah). God's covenants with these "fathers" builds in a cumulative way for most all believers. **We are to remember them**. In this way our "hearts" are "sealed" or turned **to God** through the covenants He made with these "fathers." Brigham twisted this concept into *plural marriage sealings* in the endowment he modified. Especially relevant to us are those made to Enoch, Abraham, and **Joseph of Egypt** (through Manasseh and Ephraim his sons). **Their** promises are passed down to us through Lehi and his posterity, as we reside on the same inherited Promised Land west (see these specific promises in JST Gen. 48 & 50 & Gen. 37, 49, Duet. 33 & those made to the differing "Josephs" in 2 Ne. 3). One primary purpose of the Book of Mormon is to **reveal what these promises to the "fathers" are.**

1. Adam	Freedom to *choose* between the Tree of Life or the tree of knowledge of good and evil
2. Enoch	Helped *remove death* from his people by bringing them to God. They were translated.
3. Noah	Promise of no future destruction by water, instead the next cleansing will be by fire (the rainbow covenant). *Zion will return to Earth* when we do **God's will**, His commandments (JST Gen. 9:12).
4. Moses	Given the higher law, but *the people rejected it*. They were then given the lesser law (the Ten Commandments) along with the Holy Days calendar, and more… *We have done the same thing.*
5. Abraham	Promised numerous posterity (as the sands & stars), and that his posterity *will bless the whole earth through the priesthood* – which is service (**bringing others to Christ**), not sitting in the chief seats.
Isaac	He is a type for Christ, was *righteous* (did not get a new name), nearly *sacrificed* & had only *one wife*.

Jacob	The Earth is blessed through the covenant blessings given the house of Jacob (priesthood *service*).
Joseph	The house of Israel will look to Joseph's posterity for *spiritual* salvation in the last-days (Manasseh [firstborn son - kingship & Ephraim [birthright son - priest]). Joseph provided *physical* salvation for Jacob's house in Egypt. *See these promises in JST Gen. 48 & 50 & Gen. 37, 49; Duet. 33 & 2 Ne. 3.*
6. David	Kingship over Israel is eternal through David's posterity. *See 2 Samuel 7.*
7. **Christ**	Our Creator & King is **the father of our salvation**. He provides **salvation** and **resurrection.**
8. Joseph Smith	Restored "the plain and precious things" removed from the Bible in what the LORD called "the fullness of my scriptures" in the Book of Mormon & the whole JST Bible.

When "the fathers" come again *with* the LORD at His Second Coming, they will collectively "waste" or burn up the wicked, because of their great light and fiery glory. They will all have been born again in Christ. All had the promise of eternal life *sealed* upon them by Christ in His role as "the Holy Spirit of Promise" (see endnote 32). They are called "fathers" (with a small "s") because their primary missions involved bringing their people to **salvation** in Christ the LORD, that they might be **redeem**ed **by Him**, receiving the same promise of eternal life (which is *sealed* upon them **by Him** only). They preached *the fullness* of the doctrine and gospel of Christ (chap. 7), bringing their people to **salvation** at Christ's hands (like King Benjamin), thus becoming "fathers" to their people via unconditional **love** in their service. Too many today mirror the Brighamite **control method of obedience to leaders** *and* **their laws**, rather than God's better way, His *gentle persuasion* in an *invitation* to **repent** and **come to Him**. It results in receiving real **salvation from Him** through the **love** revealed in His blood **atonement**. Charitable, loving service provides **power** in "**the priesthood** *promised Abraham's posterity*" (see D&C 121:34-46). Christ-like **love** in that service is the key to *real* **power**, not control and coercion based on **fear** (Satan's way in blood oaths). Real love casts out all fear (1 John 4:18).

These and other "fathers" (and mothers) now dwell in heaven and are fully redeemed, having returned to the presence of God. We can be redeemed too, via the development of a direct relationship with Christ the LORD. It does not happen because of religion, men's dead works, or temple attendance, but only through **the grace and mercy of Jesus Christ**, "the Father" of our salvation. Build a trusting **relationship** with Him (Lecture on Faith 2:55). **Repent**, come to **Him** in real love. The LORD said He employs **no servant at the gate** to heaven (see 2 Ne. 9:41). He alone is our **Redeemer**. The lesser symbolic *physical* ordinances of men on earth point us to the greater reality of what God seals **spiritually** on us Himself. An "*anointing*" (or preparatory symbolic *ordinance* done by men on the earth) preceeds the actual sealing of that promised blessing upon us – by keeping the New and Everlasting Covenant with God – to willing *submit* to **God's** superior **will** and wisdom in *love*. Both things are necessary. Our lesser, preparatory, *physical* baptism in water by men on earth, preceeds the greater, fiery, spiritual baptism of fire and the Holy Ghost by the God of heaven. It is the same with the symbolic temple endowment, in both the initiatory washing ordinance and the parting of the veil to God. Both precede the real thing, done by God in His timing and wisdom, as we honor our covenant made at baptism with Him (not the church or men).

Misunderstood Sealings

Today's misunderstood "sealings" are done in connection with dead ancestors, via genealogy (along with marriage sealings). There is good intention involved with them, but this effort removes the important focus that sealing could have for us, in **our own redemption** or **salvation** first, through Jesus Christ, the father of our salvation, and the one who seals them on us in his role as the Holy Spirit of Promise (endnote 32). Satan has always tried to diminish Christ, and keep us from being saved by **Him**. *Distraction* via being *very busy* in callings is a significant part of this *diversion* from what really matters! To help God save others, we must **first be saved ourselves**. We are to first become the seed of Christ, the seed of The Righteous; a special name-title for Jesus Christ in Moses 7:45 and 47. This type of **salvation** sealing is the focus of King Benjamin's message to his people in Mosiah chapters 1-5. When we are spiritually born again in Christ, we become His seed and are "**sealed His**" (Mosiah 5:15). This is addressed in Isaiah 53:10 and Mosiah 14:10-14, and 15:10-12. In Mosiah 14:10 (Isaiah's words in 53:10), the Prophet Abinadi stated, "When thou shalt make his soul an offering for sin he shall see **his seed**." **His** sons and daughters are those who believe in **Him** and live **His** doctrine and gospel, not Brigham's corrupted version of it. They then become part of **His** church, not those of men. They are adopted into His great family through Abraham and the promises God made to Him as "the father of the faithful." Abinadi taught King Noah, Alma, and other priests in Noah's court. They had many wives.

> "Behold I say unto you that whosoever has heard the words of the prophets, yea, all the holy prophets who have prophesied concerning the coming of the LORD—I say unto you, that all those who have *hearkened unto their words*, and *believed* that the LORD would redeem his people, and have looked forward to **that day** for a

remission of their sins, I say unto you, that **these are his seed**, or **they are the <u>heirs</u> of the kingdom of God**. For these are they whose sins he has borne; these are they for whom he has died, to **redeem** them from their transgressions. And now, **are they not his seed**? Yea, and are not the prophets, every one that has opened his mouth to prophesy, that has not fallen into transgression, I mean all the holy prophets ever since the world began? I say unto you that **they are his seed**. And these are they who have published peace, who have brought good tidings of good, who have published **salvation**; and said unto Zion: The God reigneth!" (Mosiah 15:10-14; see also Gal. 3:14, 24-26; Eph. 1:5-6; John 1:12-13; Heb. 4:14, 6:20, 9:11-12).

Joseph Smith's Sealings

The LORD used the terms, "prophet, seer, and revelator" to describe only Joseph and Hyrum Smith at Nauvoo (see D&C 124:94 & 125, 1841), **not** others of the Twelve. This is significant. Hyrum was Patriarch over the church, serving with Joseph as the Prophet. At one later point, the two men became co-Presidents. Joseph and Hyrum were not just *called* of God, but they were also *chosen*, *empowered* and *sent* of Him (see D&C 121:34-40). They bore sweet fruit openly in their lives – via real love in their service. According to the LORD, both also held *the sealing power* (D&C 124:93-95, 124-25). This power was later twisted by Young and the secret chamber into marriage sealings of multiple women to one man. Canonized scripture does not support this change. God's word in scripture clearly defines the sealing power differently. It is tied to God's unconditional love for His children in the important concept of **Salvation** for them, and His *sealing* upon those who merit receipt of the blessings promised to them through the "fathers." Christ does this as "the Holy Spirit of Promise" (endnote 32). Turning to God's word, not men, provides these truths.

In 1842, Joseph received D&C 128. It and previous statements by Joseph were part of the introduction of proxy **salvation** for the dead to the Nauvoo Saints, through *baptism* and the associated covenant with it – *the New and Everlasting Coveannt*" (endnote 31). Joseph Smith extended this type of proxy **salvation**, by having *men* and women (some marrried) receive God's *sealing*, Joseph acting as God symbolically at Nauvoo. It was not marriage, but only a symbolic salvation rite intended to be part of the endowment, where couples were sealed up to eternal life symbolically by Christ – Father of their salvation through His blood atonement. This type of *preparatory symbolic sealing done by men on earth* (as a teaching tool), is seen with Israel at Mt. Sinai. The children of Israel refused to personally meet with God there and be sealed to Him as the Bridegroom. Moses became God's representative to symbolically betroth Israel to Him. This type of symbolic sealing of the children to the Father was changed by Young in two ways;

(1) First, Young turned Joseph's proxy **salvation** sealings of a couple to Christ (a teaching tool), into **plural marriage sealings** of multiple women to one man in marriage. It was the perfect cover for his spiritual wifery, where Elijah's returned sealing power, in Young's "*secret priesthood*," was used to *seal* multiple women to one man in the temple. Lorenzo Snow is a good example. He had four women sealed to Snow in plural marriage in one day in 1846. Young later used Udney Jacob's publication, *The Peacemaker* (addressed later) to further bolster his new doctrine, along with other things. Young's changes to God's **doctrine**, mixed with sexual sin, made it an "abomination."

(2) Second, Young implemented more new doctrine, "**the law of adoption**" (1846-1894), or the sealing of men and women **to other men** *of stature* – to the apostles (raising men up in **idolatry**). He twisted Joseph's symbolic *sealings* of God's children to **Him** (Joseph standing in His place) - to a process where men and women were sealed to God in a long chain **through Joseph**, and **now the apostles**. It then extended through other "fathers" above them, forming a long line of "sealed" individuals going all the way back to Christ and then God the Father. Similar sealings of men to Brigham, Joseph, and others in the Twelve were done for a time in Nauvoo, and later on (until 1894 when it stopped).

Brigham Young **was the first** to seal men and women **to Joseph, to him, and to the Twelve** inside the Nauvoo Temple in His new "law of adoption" rite. Thirty-eight men were sealed to Brigham Young in 1946 in the Nauvoo Temple before leaving for Utah. Later in Utah in 1885, Wilford Woodruff had 45 men sealed to him. Many Saints wanted to be sealed to a specific leader (their favorite Apostle) in this idolatrous fashion. The Twelve lifted themselves up as substitute saviors, standing between Christ and other men. It came with pride and seeking the honors of men.

King Benjamin taught that **Christ seals us to Him** (Mosiah 5:15) as the father of our salvation. **We don't do the sealing.** Joseph may not have undserstood this well. Certainly Brigham Young didn't, or he changed it for his own purposes. Young's modified definition of the endowment (given the Saints in the temple today, see pps. 167-71) utilizes **intermediate** angels and sentinels who accept signs and tokens from us before we can pass on into God's presence. It is a false doctrine, a form of idolatry where men are placed between God and us. Such want our devotion, our loyality, and our money. The LORD just wants our **love**, our **heart**, our **will** swallowed up in **His**. This is the real **focus** of "the New and Everlasting Covenant," made with God in a *legitmate* baptism done in **His name** (Chap. 7).

Pres. Woodruff did away with "the law of adoption" in 1894. In place of it, he encouraged the Saints to **seal their own past family members to them**, not have themselves sealed to **church leaders**. This is our false tradition today. King Benjamin in the Book of Mormon provides doctrinal clarity for what God's "sealing" is. "Save" family members *ourselves* through Woodruff's "law of adoption" sealing is now a primary focus for many Saints inside LDS temples. It is based on Woodruff's *modification* of Brigham's *modification* of Joseph's symbolic Nauvoo teachings, best illustrated in Mosiah 5. All things in the temple are symbolic, meant to be realized in a personal **relationship** with Christ the LORD, father of our salvation. He does the real sealing, not men.

Christ is **the gate** and **door** to heaven, the Father who seals us to **Him** (as King Benjamin taught). We are to become His bride (symbolized in the exterior architecture of the Nauvoo Temple), implying a good **relationship** with Him, honoring His love and service to us. Young made the endowment about plural marriage sealings between many women *and* one man. Later in Utah, Young introduced additional temple work for the dead, including the entire endowment for the dead as we know it today. There is no revelation from God supporting this, though Joseph Smith *appears to have taught* that other proxy work for the dead would be forth coming (we don't know if these were modified statements). These rites would involve both baptism and ordinantion to the priesthood, but not an entire endowment for the dead (see TPJS, pps. 362-63, 1976 version). Idolatrous worship of **eternal families** in the modern endowment has replaced worship of God, where He seals us up to eternal life through Him as author or Father of our salvation. Our dead works (2 Ne. 25) in sealing family units together into eternity dominates our focus today.

Joseph Smith was learning many new things at Nauvoo from the LORD, and with time would have clarified these and other endowment rites for the Saints. Brigham Young mingled the philosophies of men like Udney Jacob in *The Peacemaker*, with Freemasonry, and the truths Joseph was bringing forth, to create his version of God's endowment. He used these and other things to create a bulwark for his own vision of a new kingdom, one that he could be king over, holding all power there. As President of the church and Governor over the Territory, he also claimed he was the lone man on the earth to wield "**the sealing power**" of Elijah (D&C 132:7). **Only he** could approve polygamous marriage sealings. He then called others to be part of this abmoninable practice (including some of my distant relatives). Satan places these things into Brigham's heart as a way to support his belief in polygamy, and further sustain the **power** he had *usurped* from Joseph. Brigham spoke highly of Joseph in public, but in his heart, he felt jealousy and disdain for his opposition to the spiritual wives doctrine he held onto in his heart.

William Clayton (Joseph Smith's scribe) was part of the secret chamber in Nauvoo, altering many documents later on for Young. He claimed that Joseph said there were *two seals* placed on those **in polygamous marriages**, one was –

> "placed upon a man and woman when they make the covenant [of **marriage**] and the other was the seal which allotted to them their particular **mansion**" [or exaltation], William Clayton Journal, October 20, 1843).

Neither is correct. Clayton's writings are often suspect, reflecting Young's pro-polygamy stance and his modifications. Clayton served as a planted spy and editor for Brigham and Heber. Like them, Clayton also practiced "spiritual wifery" and as early as 1839 in England. Although he was married *and* on a church mission, he had a **mistress** there in Sarah Crooks, as his journal reveals (see chap. 4 and endnote 12). In it he revealed his love for Crooks and how his feet were washed by her prior to sex (typical of the Cochranites). Note that the first supposed seal Clayton addressed above is that tied to **a marriage sealing**. The second addresses **exaltation** - or inheriting **grand mansions** in the hereafter. **Plural marriage** in connection with **exaltation** are both emphasized by Brigham Young in D&C 132. King Benjamin, the Book of Mormon, and the JST version of the Bible provide **no** support at all for these things.

Part IV: Transition from a House of the LORD to a Masonic Temple

Joseph, the Saints, and the new church he led were the target of Satan early on. This is evident in God's prophecy in D&C 38 and His solution for it in its later verses. To combat Satan's darkness, the Saints then and today need only to **turn** to God. If they do so completely, in full submission, with a broken heart and contritie spirit, all can receive the "mighty change of heart" and the gift or "endowment of the Holy Ghost (see chap. 7). It is the needed oil in the lamps of wise, discerning virgins, helping them receive revelation directly from God to separate light from darkness.

Satan and evil men used **secrecy** at Nauvoo to spread darkness. **Secrecy** is a primary tool of Satan and **secret** societies generally. God doesn't hold secrets, only mysteries. They are truths to be realized and lived. **Secrecy** was and is a central component of Freemasonry at it highest levels. By 1844, 1,492 men embraced this brotherhood in Nauvoo. Many of the early Danites in Missouri were Masons (1838). They used its **secret oaths** and related penalties for coercion and control, and to protect one another (see pps. 83-5, 164-65, 178-79, 182-83). This is the message of Moses 5:29-59 (Joseph's inspirired re-translation of Genesis) and the book of Enoch, now removed from the Bible. In both books evil is perpetuated among those involved via **secret oaths** to protect one another in their sins. The Danite order was one of the first **secret combinations** in the church. Those in the secret chamber were protected *in their actions* with these oaths, regardless of whether their actions were in line with God's will or not. Brigham Young capitalized upon this feature of Freemasonry once Joseph was gone. Control and obedience became a hallmark of Young's administration. Hit man Bill Hickman followed Young's directions, assuming that his desires as a leader over the church were in line with God. As we saw in the last chapter, Hickman came to understand that his trust was misplaced. It was a dangerous, false assumption, an iniquity based on idolatry.

Modifying Joseph's Endowment

Following Joseph's murder, the secret chamber, led by Young and Kimball, modified Joseph's temple endowment to support polygamy *and* provide "gain" for the secret chamber. They borrowed from three primary sources to create their new temple theology; (1) Joseph's early endowment, (2) The concept of multiple wives, first seen in Cochranite spiritual wifery in the Boston and Saco Maine areas, including two influential publications that promoted polygamy; (A) The Peacemaker, and (B) The Testimony of the Twelve Patriarchs. The third influence was (3) Freemasonry.

1. Joseph Original Endowment Joseph's early endowment at Nauvoo was focused on early teachings in the Book of Moses and Abraham. They were taught to a small group of people early on. Latter this expanded greatly under Brigham Young. Joseph's early instructions were centered on returning to God and fellowship with Him, as addressed throughout scripture in its marriage symbolism. Without a relationship with God, there is little revelation. The temple was to be a tool in learning to receive it. The Nauvoo Temple exterior architecture supported marriage symbolism in its portrayal of JST Revelation 12, John's vision of the Bride of the Lamb. D&C 88:119 and 109:8 invite the Saints to organize themselves and "prepare every needful thing; and establish a house, even a house of prayer, a house of fasting, a house of faith, a house of learning, a house of glory, a house of order, a **house of God**." To do this effectively, the ordinances of Joseph's "endowment" featured; (a) the Creation story, (b) the experiences of Adam and Eve and their necessary temptation by Satan, that they might gain experience and knowledge, (c) the early washing and anointing rites of Kirtland, (d) "sealing" doctrine tied to **salvation** in Christ, and (e) new baptism for the dead rites with priesthood ordination. Many see it as a merciful extension of Christ's **salvation** to those on the other side of the veil. Others believe baptism for the dead symbolically points to our "dead works."

2. Spiritual Wifery This two-word phrase effectively defines the age old mix of religion with sex; the first used to justify the second. Cochranite converts to the church in 1832 brought the practice with them. Brigham Young and others in the secret chamber were influenced by it, making it part of church doctrine after Joseph's murder. The new temple doctrine of Young helped cement it in place.

A. The Peacemaker: *New Plural-Marriage Sealings* The Peacemaker was a very important influence upon Brigham Young and his new emerging temple doctrine at Navuoo. It was published there in 1842 by Udney Hay Jacob - on *The Times and Seasons* press. It made use of Udney Jacob's interpretation of Elijah's **sealing** doctrine to justify polygamy using Malachi 3 and 4. It was mixed with Joseph's "spirit of Eljiah" doctrine and his sealing of men and women to him in Nauvoo, to create a new false endowment that supported polygamy. The secret chamber claimed Joseph sealed men to him in "**the law of adoption**," whereas he was sealing many women to him in "**the new and everlasting covenant**" **of plural marriage**. Neither is true. Both are false doctrines. Both are thought to have originated mainly from *The Peacemaker*.

Four borrowed teachings from *The Peacemaker* are addressed below, each used by Young and the secret chamber to promote polygamy. It all began in 1842 when a new lie was spread around Nauvoo, that the Prophet Joseph Smith printed the pro-polygamy pamphlet entitled *The Peacemaker* on *The Times and Seasons* press as a test to see how people would react to his new doctrine. This is a false narrative. On its cover were the words, "J. Smith Printer." They were placed there by those in the secret chamber without Joseph's knowledge or approval! *The Peacemaker* was a two-chapter version of a larger book manuscript on the subject of polygamy by Udney Hay Jacob. He had come to

Nauvoo to have it printed on the press nearest his home, *The Times and Seasons.* Though Joseph Smith was editor of *The Times and Seasons* at this time, he was very busy, hiding from capture by the Missourians, running the church and the city of Nauvoo, and battling John Bennett's accusations in court. Joseph turned the editing, publishing, and printing duties over to the Twelve, and specifically to John Taylor, Willard Richards, and Wilford Woodruff (secret chamber members). Taylor eventually become editor of *The Times and Seasons*, along with the *Nauvoo Neighbor*, a press he owned. Four primary things were taught in *The Peacemaker*, things Brigham borrowed.

1 . *New Spirit of Elijah Doctrine* The "**everlasting covenant**" of Malachi 3 & 4 (following God's **will** – endnote 31), was used by Young to justify a new marriage covenant involving many wives sealed to one man. Because it was tied to Elijah's sealing power, the marriages were not just for time, but for eternity as well. They were "everlasting." Young's "new and everlasting covenant" of plural marriage replaced the original "everlasting covenant," which in scripture is the fullness of the gospel of Christ (D&C 66:2, or the two baptisms with the gift of the Holy Ghost). This "**whoredom**" involving *sexual sin*, thus also became an "**abomination**" because it involved *changed doctrine.*

John D. Lee was the adopted son of Brigham Young. His biography reveals that a new "Elijah" doctrine was introduced to the Saints by the apostles in Nauvoo in 1845 (the year after Joseph's murder). Lee stated, "In the Winter of 1845 meetings were held all over the city of Nauvoo, and the spirit of Elijah was taught in the different families as a foundation to the order of **celestial marriage**, as well as the **law of adoption**. Many families entered into covenants with each other—the man to stand by his wife and the woman to cleave unto her husband, and the children to be adopted to the parents. I was one of those who entered into covenants to stand by my family, to cleave to them through **time** and **eternity**...Others refused to enter into these obligations, but agreed to separate from each other, dividing their substance, and mutually dissolving their former relations [marriages] on friendly terms.

Some have mutually agreed to **exchange wives** and have been **sealed** to each other as husband and wife by virtue and authority of the holy priesthood [through Brigham]. One of Brigham's brothers, Lorenzo Young, now a bishop, made an **exchange of wives** with Mr. [Isaac] Decker . . . They both seemed happy in the exchange of wives . . . All persons are required to be **adopted to some of the leading men of the Church**. In this, however, they have the right of choice, thus forming the links of the chain of priesthood back to the father, Adam, and so on to the second coming of the Messiah...The ordinance of **celestial marriage** was extensively practiced by men and women who had covenanted to live together, and a few men had dispensations [permissions] granted them [by Brigham Young] to enter into plural marriages, which were taught to be the stepping-stone to **celestial exaltation**. Without plural marriage a man could not attain to the fullness of the holy priesthood and be made equal to our Saviour . . . My second wife, Nancy Bean... was **sealed** to me in the Winter of 1845.... Plural marriages were not made public. They had to be kept still . . . In the spring of 1845 Rachel Andora was **sealed** to me" (John D. Lee, *Mormonism Unveiled or The Life and Confessions of the Late Mormon Bishop, John D. Lee* [Bryan, Brand and Company, 1887], p. 165-67).

2. *Male Dominance* *The Peacemaker* stressed the divine and absolute authority of the husband *over* the wife, requiring full submission to him and his patiarchal priesthood authority. *The Peacemaker* interpretation of Elijah's doctrine reflected a need for "**obedience to the fathers**" those wise, authoritative patriarchs over the family. This control counteracts the love aspect of D&C 121:34-46. It is a hallmark of Young's administrative style. Second in command later in Utah, Heber C. Kimball (43 wives), stated, "What power has any one of my wives to act independently; she has not a particle of power. She must act in connection with me as the limb acts in connection with the tree from which it springs. If not she is a dead limb; will they ever come to life again after they are dead? No! They must be cut off and thrown back into the earth to return to their mother element" (JD 6:67).

3. *The Difference Between Fornication & Adultery* *The Peacemaker* also featured a lengthy discourse on the difference between fornication and adultery. Note the following statement from it; "the wife was bound to yield obedience and submission to her husband in all things, as well as the body, by the spiritual nature of that covenant. And again, when a woman *apostatizes in spirit* from her husband she then commits *fornication* against *the spiritual law of marriage*, and in no other way can a married woman commit fornication." Udney Jacob appears to have left for Utah with his new wife Lousia L. Jacob in 1846, leaving behind his wife Elizabeth of forty years and their seven children. Elizabeth refused to be part of Udney's polygamy, and thus had spiritually "apostatized," according to Udney Jacob.

4. *Peace* *The Peacemaker* claimed that polygamy was the real way to peace in America. Udney Jacob was a non-Mormon Jewish man who supported polygamy. He joined the church a year later in 1843. Taylor and others in the secret chamber became aware of the contents of *The Peacemaker* and secretly printed it **without Joseph Smith's knowledge or approval**, placing Joseph's name on its front cover. Joseph did not know Udney Jacob at this time and

was upset that the pamphlet was printed, and with his name upon it. Joseph disavowed all ties to the publication. In a notice in the *Times and Seasons* on December 1st of 1842, he said:

> "There was a book printed at my office a short time since, written by Udney H. Jacobs, on marriage, without my knowledge; and had I been apprised of it, I would not have printed it; not that I am opposed to any man enjoying his privileges; but I do not wish to have my name associated with the authors in such an unmeaning rigmarole of **nonsense, folly, and trash**."

Udney Jacob believed he was the re-incarnated Elijah. A comparison of the doctrines in *The Peacemaker* with those of the Brighamite polygamists of 1845 and beyond shows clear borrowing by Young and the secret chamber. Especially useful for Young were the Elijah teachings tied to Malachi 3 and 4, which he twisted to justify polygamy. Elijah had nothing to do with polygamy. He fought against all sin as seen with the 450 priests of Baal in 1 Kings 18, bringing down fire from heaven to destroy them. These wicked priests were practicing idolatry, sexual perversion, and child sacrifice, and getting the people involved with it too. Brigham Young, like King Noah, led his priests (the Twelve) and the Saints into polygamy using *The Peacemaker* and its corrupt Elijah doctrine. It replaced knowledge of salvation within polluted Elijah's teachings, with the whoredom of "spiritual wifery."

The attraction of Brigham's new marriage covenant to some, a covenant **sealed** or cemented in his new Nauvoo Masonic Temple rite with the blood-oaths found in Moses 5, wasn't just more wives for the men, but a new kind of marriage, one that lasted **not only for time, but through eternity**. It was "**everlasting**." This clearly came from Udney Jacob's teachings in *The Peacemaker*.

The Peacemaker was also responsible for other false doctrines, including "**the law of adoption**," where men or women were "sealed to those leading the church - the Twelve. This was an idolatrous rejection of Christ, another way to diminish His saving mission by lifting up men (the Twelve) between the LORD and the people. Later it became a popularity contest for some of the Saints to choose who to be sealed to - Young, Heber, Taylor, or another.

Young's crafty move in borrowing Joseph's and Elijah's doctrine helped him promote the same evils of old. Young would eventually take all power later in Utah, serving as church President, governor over the territory, head of the militia, the Indian Agent for the Federal Government, and perhaps most important to him - **the sole man on the earth** that could sanction polygamous marriages via his supposed "**sealing power**" (see D&C 132:7). He then called other men to practice it. One of my relatives was one of them. Young made "the spritual wives" doctrine of the Cochranites more palatable by associating it with marriage and with his temple rites, calling it "**the new and everlasting covenant of marriage**," a covenant necessary to receive exaltation in his new kingdom out west. It was put in place with covenant signs and blood-oaths used by Cain and Lamech, oaths made with Satan. Young said, "The only men who become Gods, even the Sons of God, are those who enter into polygamy" (JD 11:269).

Mary Page Eaton, widow of Apostle John E. Page (who served from 1838-46), read *The Peace Maker* in 1846 at Nauvoo. She suggested that others compare *The Peace Maker* to D&C 132, stating that, "they will see the sameness of the two . . . Both teach much cruelty to women who do not obey their husbands' mandates, and say they 'shall be destroyed' for an offense which the man has no punishment for, only that his wife shall be given to another man! They teach concubinage by saying the Lord gave wives and concubines to David and Solomon" (*The Saints' Advocate* 6 [June 1884]: 450).

It is important to note that knowledge of the visitation of Elijah and his transfer of priesthood keys to Joseph Smith and Oliver Cowdery inside the Kirtland Temple on Sunday April 3rd, 1836, **had not yet come forth at this time in the church**. Apparently the LORD wanted it this way for a time. Elijah's visit to the two men wouldn't be made public until **1876**. Besides Joseph's early teachings of Elijah, much of Young's understanding of Elijah's doctrine was obtained via *The Peacemaker*. This becomes obvious when one compares his teachings side-by-side with those of Udney Jacob. Similarities appear with the 1845–46 *Times and Seasons*, parts of the *Journal of Discourses*, and Orson Pratt's publication on polygamy entitled, *The Seer*. A detailed overview of the importance of the Peacemaker is found in chapters 8-11 of the Restoration Bookstore, http://restorationbookstore.org/articles/nopolygamy/jsfp-vol2/2chp10.htm

B. The Testament of the Twelve Patriarchs, the Sons of Jacob This pro-polygamy book was influential upon the apostles while in England. It was printed by a British elder in the church. He made 100 copies available for sale in the Millennial Star office of the church in Liverpool in 1843.[23] This was just after many of the Twelve served missions together in the British Isles (1839-41). This was one year after *The Peacemaker* was printed on the *Times and Seasons* press in Nauvoo (1842). Many of the Apostles were exposed to both publications. They both addressed the legitimacy of polygamy among the ancient patriarchal fathers, men who held a special "patriarchal" priesthood to practice it. Young and the secret chamber tapped into this priesthood to justify their spiritual wifery.

3. Freemasonry Brigham and Heber borrowed a number of things from early American Freemasonry (and from ancient Egyptain and Jewish sources) to modify portions of the endowment. The "*craft*" of Freemaonry in Joseph's day was an ancient English brotherhood centered on *secretive* fellowship between men. It borrowed many things from ancient sources. By this time Masonry had highly organized rites with related symbols. They were used to advance a candidate through three degrees; 1. Apprentice, 2. Fellow, and 3. Master. Heber C. Kimball had full documentation for these rites. Advancement through them utilized stories, covenants, and accompanying signs and symbols. Especially useful for Young and the secret chamber were the secret blood-oaths of Masonry. They were useful in keeping polygamy under wraps until Young and Kimball finally "**let the cat out of the bag**" in Utah in 1852.

Under Young the blood-oaths were tied to severe **penalties**, used in the endowment until 1990. Originally – in scripture - they were part of *free-will* offerings made to God, a representation of willingly giving one's life out of love, if necessary. Young utilized a more severe, penalizing version of them to protect the **secrecy** of *spiritual wifery* and other acts, like hiding the embezzlement of donations by the Twelve from the Saints for the Nauvoo House and the Temple. In addition to Joseph, those printing the Expositor claimed that the Twelve were using the blood-oaths to hide the embezzlement of funds. Instead of **willingly** offering to have one life's taken (rather than breaking a covenant with the LORD), Young made the penalties in the endowment a type of retribution or "**blood atonement**," an act worthy of death (see p. 165). This doctrine later became a hallmark of Young's administration, one where fear and coercion lay beneath the surface of his preaching for obedience to the Twelve or "the Brethren."

Young's definition of "the endowment" states that one is enabled to walk back into the presence of God, by passing angels who stand as sentinels. By giving them **the key words, the signs and tokens**, pertaining to the holy Priesthood, these individuals are able to gain their eternal **exaltation** in spite of earth and hell" (Brigham Young, JD 2:31 Apr 6, 1853). Nowhere in scripture is there support for this. Young's definition of the endowment differs from that of the LORD and Joseph Smith as addressed hereafter (p. 164). Some of the key words, *signs*, and *tokens* of Masonry may *have* had light in them, originating in more ancient things tied to *marks* of the LORD's atonement ("*the infallible proofs*" of His love for us in His body, Acts 1:3). Evil men use them and change them for their own purposes.

> "And it came to pass that they did have their **signs**, yea, their **secret signs**, and their **secret words**; and this that they might **distinguish a brother who had entered into the covenant,** that whatsoever **wickedness** *his brother should do he should not be injured by his brother, nor by those who did belong to his band*, **who had taken this covenant**. And thus they might **murder**, and **plunder**, and **steal,** and **commit whoredoms** *and all manner of wickedness*, contrary to the laws of their country and also the laws of their God…Now behold, it is these **secret oaths** and **covenants** which Alma commanded his son should **not** go forth unto the world, *lest they should be a means* of *bringing down the people unto destruction*" (Helaman 6:22-23, 25)

Strong's Concordance #226 unites the word "*mark*" with "*sign, token*," and "*oth*" or "**oath**" as part of the **oath** Cain made with Satan and evil men to "murder and get gain." It is a part of the corrupted mark of cain *and* the beast. An overview of the penalties, hand *gestures*, *signs, names*, and associated meanings of each of the three primary stages of progression in the Freemasonry ritual, reveals much about the early endowment at Nauvoo, as there are many clear **similarities** between them both (see http://www.ephesians5-11.org/handshakes.htm).

The evil at the top of this organization is not apparent *at its lower levels*. Those at its highest levels use the *oath* to hide lying, deception, murder, and other dark purposes. **Blood-oaths** and their related **penalities** have been a favorite tool of all **secret combinations** since the very beginning. They are inspired of Satan and are used to murder (an exchange of life) and get gain (see pps. 83-5, 164-65, 178-79, 182-83 & Moses 5:29-31). The 200 Watchers in the book of Enoch (special "sons of God" or angels who watched over mankind), *lusted* after mortal women on earth and descended here, making **secret oaths** with each other atop Mt. Hermon (its ancient name "*Mt Armon*" has ties to this *covenant*). They took *multiple wives*, bearing children with them that resulted in the "giants" of the Old Testament. It led to terrible corruption of the earth (including DNA) and oppression of men (Moses 7). The Flood in Noah's day was brought on to eliminate this oppression, wickedness, and polluted DNA. *Love* and *invitation*, not **secrecy**, *fear*, and *control*, are the only way to bind men together in a real unified brotherhood (see the opposing **oaths** of D&C 88:133 versus those of Moses 5:29-31).

Brigham also borrowed various symbols used by the Masons. These include two pillars, the compass and the square, the beehive, the all-seeing eye, *and* clasped hands in a covenant. These were not found on the Nauvoo Temple but did appear on the Salt Lake Temple designed by Young. He had plans to put actual *compass* and *square* symbols on the exterior of the Salt Lake Temple, but John Taylor nixed this idea after Young died. The Masons *borrowed* these and other symbols from various sources themselves, like ancient Israel and Egypt. Today, ancient inspired symbols like the *rainbow, the swastika, the pentagram,* and *numbers 13* and *911*, are borrowed and twisted by Satan for his evil purposes.

A Short Summary of Mormonism & Freemasonry

Current Mormon history suggests the Saints at Nauvoo quickly embraced Freemasonry because Joseph Smith did. Today it is taught that Joseph fully embraced "*the craft*" when very little evidence exists to support it. Like the claim that Joseph practiced polygamy, Joseph's name is and has been used in connection with "*Freemasonry*" at Nauvoo to give it instant credibility at that time. We know many Mormon leaders were Freemasons prior to embracing the gospel, including Brigham Young, Heber C. Kimball, and Newell K. Whitney. Some also point to Joseph's father and brother Hyrum as being Masons early on to add further credibility to "*the craft*" at Nauvoo. The involvement of the Smiths with Masonry appears to be limited and short lived. Records today suggest that by 1845 there were 1,492 men in the Nauvoo area that were part of five Masonic lodges. This was triple the total number of Masons in all of Illinois (some 400 total men).

Those suggesting Joseph was a polygamist also suggest he was granted Master Mason status in one day because of (1) his knowledge of the mysteries, and (2) his influence among the Saints. They suggest his rapid advancement through the first three levels of Freemasonry caused great concern among Masons away from Nauvoo and this was part of the reason for his latter muder. This accusation is also important because of what occurs when one is made a **Master Mason**. In this rite, the death and resurrection of "Hiram Abiff" occurs (see 2 Chron. 4:16: Huram Abiv, "Hiram, his father"). Hiram Abiff is the "resurrected dead **Master**," the one who discloses the great **secret** or mystery to others in the Masonic Temple rites, granting them eternal life. Some try to tie Joseph Smith to Hiram Abiff in a similar role with the Saints. It is the LORD Jesus Christ who conquered death and now grants "life" and "eternal life" to those who love and follow Him and the Father, not men like Hiram Abiff, Joseph Smith, or any man.

In Joseph's day men advanced through three early degrees, from (1) Entered Apprentice to (2) Fellow in the Craft to (3) Master Mason, using secretive gestures and words, along with ritual clothing (the apron tied to Lucifer's "priesthoods"). The LDS temple endowment, put in place by Young and Kimball was purposely very similar to these rites (see *http://www.ephesians5-11.org/handshakes.htm*). Continual changes since then (especially the changes made in 1990), removed many of them, though others still remain in place. The Masonic rituals are centered on developing a coersive *secret* covenant relationship with fellow craft members and with the lord of this world. They are a corrupted version of the true covenant relationship we are to make **with God** alone, doing so openly and willingly in love, not fear and coercion. The Book of Mormon clearly teaches us that this new covenant is to **do God's will**, as addressed in **Mosiah 5:5** and many other scriptures. The Masonic oath, on the other hand, has much more in common with Cain's oath with Satan or Lucifer in Moses 5, that one might "*murder and get gain.*" The three-part Masonic advancement into the presence of a false lord is a corrupted copy of advancing into God's holy presence in the three tiers of sacred space of the Tabernacle of Moses or Solomon's Temple. In both structures, the High Priest advanced using various rites and symbols tied to our LORD and His merciful atonement, from the outer court, to the Holy Place, and finally into God's symbolic presence in the Holy of Holies.

Various symbols and rites in Freemasonry are said to originate in traditions much older than the beginning of 17th century "Speculative Freemasonry." Some claim that the Prophet Joseph recognized a generic relationship between ancient Egyptian and Jewish [Kaballah] sources with those of Freemasonry, and that Joseph used portions of Freemasonry to help him formulate the endowment. We should be very careful making these connections, as Freemasonry was as a major corrupting influence in Nauvoo along with polygamy. Young put Heber C. Kimball to work in establishing five Masonic lodges in the Nauvoo area, all to promote polygamy and control among the Saints early on. The craft was latter abandoned in Utah, but the desire for control remains in portions of the endowment.

Taking a larger view of things, we see that although our nation was founded on Christian principles, Satan used the secret blood oaths of Freemasonry to effectively corrupt both our nation and the gospel of Christ within Mormonism. A number of our founding fathers were Freemasons, as were those that put our commerce system in place, now dominated by the Federal Reserve. It was put in place secretly in 1913 and is controlled by international bankers (the Illuminati) that are tied into Freemasonry. The Masonic symbols dominating our Nation's capital (such as the compass and square, the inverted pentagram, and the Washingtom Monument) point to the false lord of this land and to idolatrous Baal worship generally (endnote 1). Idolatry, darkness, secrecy, and sin will all be removed before the LORD Jesus returns.

House to Temple

Freemasonry is said to have ancient ties to building important places of worship, like the striking Cathedrals of Europe. Some Masons even claim that "*the craft*" was part of the construction of Solomon's Temple. Many "temples" around the world and throughout history are tied to idolatrous worship, however, like the temples of Baal, Diana, and Zeus (see D&C 93:1 and 19-20). Many corrupt, powerful men throughout history (like King Noah in the Book of Mormon) were focused on building many elaborate and expensive structures, all at the expense of the people and especially the poor. Some believe this continues today with the very elaborate and expensive new LDS Temple in Rome. A better definition of the "**house**" of the LORD is found in 2 Cor. 5:1. "For we know that if our earthy **house** of this tabernacle were dissolved, we have a building of God, an **house** not made with hands, eternal in the heavens." The Prophet Joseph most likely understood this well. It is a mystery for those who hunger and thirst for truth. He wanted the Saints to experience the living God as he had. He prayed on their behalf and as a result was given the commandment to raise a "**house**" **to the Lord's name** in Nauvoo. The "**house**" was to *become* a "temple to the LORD's name." God mentioned this phrase in connection with **His name** *nine* times in D&C 124. It was critical that the Saints build it in **the LORD's way and timing**, *and* that it be completed and dedicated **to Him**.

> "And inasmuch as my people build a **house** unto me **in the name of the Lord**, and do not suffer any unclean thing to come into it, that it be not defiled, *my glory* shall rest upon it; Yea, and *my presence* shall be there, for **I will come into it,** and **all the pure in heart that shall come into it shall see God**. But if it be defiled **I will not come into it**, and *my glory* shall not be there; for **I will not come into unholy temples**" (D&C 97:15-17).

In unmodified scripture, God uses words carefully to communicate specific truths. His use of the word "**house**" versus "**temple**" is noteworthy in all of scripture, but especially so in the D&C. Note, for example, the words He gave King Solomon *and* the Prophet Joseph Smith in their *inspired dedicatory prayers* for the special "**houses**" they built. Both men used the word "**house**" 100% of the time, **not** the word "**temple**." Solomon used "**house**" 12 times in his prayer, Joseph 31 times. The word "**temple**" is **not** found in either prayer! Note too that **the LORD** used the word "**house**" 100% of the time in Sections 95, 105, 109, 110, and 124 of the Doctrine and Covenants to address the Kirtland and Nauvoo "**houses** of the LORD," not **temple**. The word "**house**" is used 231 times in the D&C, whereas "**temple**" is used 49 times, and 30 of these references are supplied by *men* – not God, *in the introductory statements* to God's words in the revelations to Joseph that followed. The word "**house**" may refer to God's people too, as in the "**house** of Israel," or to a home, or sacred structure. For a "**house**" to become a "*temple* to **the LORD's name**," much is required, primarily purity of the heart. Because men call a structure a "**temple**," does not make them one in the LORD's mind.[24]

According to the LORD's own words - in a decree, the Brighamite Saints at Nauvoo were apparently "rejected as a church with their dead," and then cursed and moved out of their place (see D&C 124:32, 45 & 48). Why? The reasons are straightforward. After Joseph was murdered, Brigham and other leaders did not do as the LORD directed (see vs. 47 & 55). Those whom God had appointed to lead the people (v. 45) were murdered by those in the secret chamber, that others might usurp power and get gain (see 3 Nephi 16:10; 30:2). The two buildings the LORD commanded to be built "**to the LORD's name**" (v. 32) were never completed. The Saints at Nauvoo never completed what they called "the temple" nor "the Nauvoo House" (a boarding house for visitors), yet they did complete mansions for the Twelve, businesses, and five Masonic Lodges. Leaders turned their hearts *away* from God, embracing worldly ways.

God requires purity from His people. The LORD Jesus cleansed Herod's Temple of its impurity two times in the Bible, the first at the start of his mission in John 2:23, and the second at it end in JST Matthew 21. His words in JST Matthew 21 are especially telling. He spoke to those who *took power* in His day at Jerusalem. It is a type for those taking power at Nauvoo. In verses 12-14, Jesus first cast out the money changers from the corrupted temple. He then healed the blind and lame. Both events made the wicked leaders angry. In verse 11, Christ told them, "It is written, **My house** shall be called the **house of prayer**; but **ye have made it a den of thieves**." He added in later verses, "those wicked ones **reject me**...And the kingdom of God shall be taken from them, and shall be given to a nation bringing forth the fruits thereof (meaning the Gentiles [the Saints for a time])...And when the LORD therefore of the vineyard cometh [at His Second Coming], he will destroy those miserable, wicked men, and will let again his vineyard unto other husbandmen, even **in the last days**, who shall render him the fruits in their season [see D&C 84:58]. And then understood they the parable which he spake unto them, that **the Gentiles should be destroyed also**, when the LORD should descend out of heaven to reign in his vineyard, which is the earth and the inhabitants thereof." Hope remains for those Gentile Saints among the unfaithful bride - those who turn to the LORD, as His arms remain stretched out still in mercy to her, and in judgment upon the prideful and ungodly. This is the message of Isaiah 54. The Bride must be cleansed first, by repentance and by putting her faith and trust in the living God.

The Endowment We Have Inherited

The Saints today have inherited Brigham's modified endowment. There are three different definitions for it given us by, (1) the LORD in D&C 124 (1841), (2) the Prophet Joseph (1835), and (3) President Brigham Young in Utah.

1. *God's Definition* When God spoke of an "endowment of power from on high," it was most frequently tied to the gift and power of the Holy Ghost (see Assumption #5, chap. 6 & D&C 33:15; 109:22, 35-37; 3 Ne. 9:20; 12:1; 2 Ne. 31:12; 3 Ne. 11:35; JST Mat. 3:38; JST Luke 3:16; JST John 1:28; 15:26). We also have D&C 124:39 (1841), where God addresses the new Nauvoo endowment; "Therefore, verily I say unto you, that your **anointings**, and your **washings**, and your **baptisms for the dead**, and your **solemn assemblies**, and your **memorials for your sacrifices** by the sons of Levi, and for your **oracles** [revelations] in your most holy places wherein you receive conversations, and your statutes and judgments, for the beginning of the revelations and foundation of Zion, and for the glory, honor, and endowment of all her municipals [those belonging to His church], are ordained by the ordinance of my holy **house**, which my people are always commanded to build unto my holy name."

Note what is present *and* not present in God's definition. It features no reference to (1) marriage sealings (polygamous or otherwise), no (2) secret signs, tokens, or penalties, (3) no proxy work for the dead beyond baptism, and (4) no use of the word "temple." What does "endowment of all her municipals" mean? The 1828 Webster's Dictionary defines "municipal" as "one who enjoys the rights of a free citizen," or potentially the rights of belonging to the LORD's kingdom. We do not know how accurate this statement is and whether it has been modified.

2. *Joseph's Definition* On Nov. 12, 1835, the Prophet Joseph stated: "You need an Endowment brethren in order that you may be prepared and **able to over come all things**. Those that reject your testimony will be damned. The sick will be healed, the lame made to walk, the deaf to hear and the blind to see through your instrumentality [gifts of the Spirit following real believers] . . . But when you are **endowed** and prepared to **preach the gospel** to all nations, kindred and tongues in their own languages you must **faithfully warn** all and bind up the testimony and seal up the law" (Joseph Smith Diary, 12 Nov 1835). Effective missionary work means having God's Spirit with us, especially in the Holy Ghost - access to the unified mind of the Father and the Son (see Lecture of Faith 5). Joseph's endowment definition here is consistent with the LORD's statements on p. 164, those tied to the gift of the Holy Ghost. Young's defintion below is different.

3. *Brigham's Definition* President Young stated, "Your endowment is, to receive all those ordinances in the house of the Lord, which are necessary for you, after you have departed this life, to enable you to walk back to the presence of the Father, passing the angels who stand as sentinels, being enabled to give them **the key words, the signs and tokens**, pertaining to the holy Priesthood, and gain your eternal **exaltation** in spite of earth and hell" (Brigham Young, JD 2:31 Apr 6, 1853). This is the definition used today in LDS temples.

Contrast Young's definition with Nephi's statement in 2 Nephi 9:41, that, "**The keeper of the gate is the Holy One of Israel; and he employeth no servant there**." Christ alone is our Judge, Mediator, and Redeemer. We can approach Him personally through personal prayer and repentance, as Joseph did in the grove in 1820. There is no account in scripture of those coming into our LORD's presence that mentions secret signs and tokens as a requirement for doing so. The experiences of Enoch, Moses, Abraham, Isaiah, John the Beloved, Lehi, Joseph Smith, and others, reveals that all of them made it to God or the Tree of Life (doing so spiritually in an ascent-vision) without an intermediate individual accepting symbolic secret signs or tokens from them, prior to entrance into God's presence. Putting men between us and God can lead to idolatry and our own unredeemed state. It is a primary message in this book and the Book of Mormon.

A second purpose for Joseph's "house of the LORD" at Nauvoo, was additional baptism for the dead. Pres. Young added more symbolic ordinance work for the dead later on, including the entire endowment. No revelation is cited for this. For many of the Saints, this has come to dominate their temple focus. The living are to be "saved" or "redeemed" by God first - in a direct sealing to Him (see Mosiah 5:15), before reaching out to others beyond the grave. Symbolic ordinances can be useful, but do not insure salvation. God's redeeming blood does. The Josephite Saints that rejected Brigham Young and his polygamy, rejected many of his new things tied to the temple too. The washings and anointings, the instruction about Adam and Eve, and baptism for the dead were useful rites at Nauvoo. Some other additions were not. Moroni saw our day and warned us about embracing the "evil gift" (see Moroni 10:30). Pondering and prayer upon this is the only way to know God's purpose behind this phrase.

The Infallible Proofs versus Symbols Only

The whole purpose of the temple is to encourage us to part the veil of our **unbelief** and return to God's presence, like the Brother of Jared. The symbols and rites of the temple (some of which are of ancient origin) are to remind us to seek for, and partake of, the *real signs* and *tokens* of God's love for us, by seeing and feeling the marks of our LORD's Atonement in His side, feet, hands, and wrists. They are "**the infallible proofs**" of His **love** for us (see Acts 1:3). God demonstrated His great love for us in His great suffering at the scourging, in Gethsemane, and upon the cross. All Christians everywhere are invited to bear witness of these marks of love - personally, along with the reality of our LORD's resurrection. In third Nephi, 2,500 people at Bountiful partook of these real signs and tokens of God's love for us. We can too, and then bear testimony to others with power and real knowledge – that Jesus is the Christ. Each of us can have this life-changing experience here and now. It is to know God and receive Him personally as "the heavenly gift," the greatest gift or endowment we can receive in this life (see Lectures on Faith 2:55)!

Brigham's Modifications to the Endowment

Twelve of Brigham Young's additions to Joseph's "endowment" are provided hereafter. We continue to utilize some of them, while others have been repudiated and removed. No revelation from God is cited for them, nor the additions or deletions that came after him by individuals or committees.

1. *Young's New & Everlasting Covenant – New Sealing Doctrine* Brigham Young replaced the original "New and Everlasting Covenant," which is **the fullness** of the gospel of Christ (D&C 66:2) in following **God's will** (JST Gen. 9:12; Mosiah 5:5, 8), with his "New and Everlasting Covenant" of plural marriage (D&C 132). He replaced Christ's **salvation** with what the Book of Mormon calls a "grosser crime "a whoredom," and an "abomination" (Jacob 2). In scripture the word "abomination" is tied to things that are exceptionally "disgusting," "loathsome" or shameful," or "absolutely intolerable." It can be arrogant pride in ignoring God's law and will by participating in evil, idolatrous, immoral practices like homosexuality or polygamy. Saving doctrine in following **God's will** was replaced by Young and his ways. God and Isaiah said we have **broken the everlasting covenant** (see chap. 7). This is the message of the *first* Section of the Doctrine and Covenants (see D&C 1:15-16; Isa. 23:5).

> "For they [the Gentile Latter-day Saints and others] have **strayed from mine ordinances**, and have **broken mine everlasting covenant**; They seek **not the Lord** to establish **his righteousness**, but every man walketh in **<u>his own way</u>**, and after the image of **<u>his own god</u>**, whose image is in the likeness of the world, and whose substance is that of an **<u>idol</u>**, which waxeth old and shall perish in Babylon, even Babylon the great, which shall fall" (D&C 1:15-16).

If we do not understand the everlasting covenant (seeking **God's will**) it is harder to *embrace* this second greater (or fuller) baptism that is part of it - the spiritual baptism that is done by God Himself (see 3 Ne. 9:20, 11:35, 12:1; 2 Ne. 31:12; 3 Ne. 11:35; JST Mat. 3:38; JST Luke 3:16; JST John 1:28; 15:26; D&C 33:15); And (2) by *changing* what this covenant is. The second fiery baptism "cleanses us from all sin." It is when our sins are fully remitted via God's fiery Spirit (2 Ne. 31:17-18, 20-21; Joseph Smith HC 6:316). To experience this is to be "born again" (Mosiah 5:7; 27:24-28; Moses 6:59, 65), receiving "the mighty change of heart" (Alma 5:12-13), or receiving "the baptism of fire and the Holy Ghost" (2 Ne. 31:17-18). With it we finally obtain **the Holy Ghost**, or receive "an endowment of [real] **power** from on high" (Luke 24:49 & Acts 1 & 2; D&C 38:31-32, 38; 95:8-9; 39:15, 18, 23; 97:12-18; 105:10-12).

To be saved or **redeemed**, all people (and the earth herself) must receive both baptisms; *the lesser* water baptism, and *the greater* or fuller spiritual baptism (see John 3:3-5, 5:24; D&C 5:16, 33:11-15, 39:6; Mosiah 27:25; Alma 5:6-16, 26-28, 49; 3 Ne. 30:2). The first of the two baptisms is carried out by one with the lesser (Aaronic), the second by one with the greater or fuller (Melchizedek) priesthood. John the Baptism addressed one greater than him (Christ) who would come after him, saying, "he shall baptize you with fire and the Holy Ghost" (JST Mat. 3:38-40). Joseph's firstborn son, Joseph Smith III, brought this scripture and other JST scriptures forth for us in 1867, as part of what God called, "the **fullness of my scriptures**" in D&C 42:12, 15, 56-59.

Even though the U.S. Government forced the Saints to give up polygamy at the end of the 19th century, Young's change in the "everlasting covenant" is still with us. Today temple marriage sealings are between one man and one *or more women*. Men today can be sealed to more than one wife, via death of an earlier wife, whereas women **can only be sealed to one man**. Elders Nelson and Oaks of the First Presidency today, are sealed to two women each.

2. *Blood-Oaths with Penalties* God invites with love, Satan uses fear, force, and revenge. The LORD accepts our **free-will** offerings, given willingly to Him and to one another because of our *unconditional* **love**. Covenants with God were taken very serious anciently, and were thus accompanied by a token or symbol of **giving one's life willingly** if the covenant with **HIM** wasn't kept (Gen. 15:9; Alma 46:20-22). In Young's version of the temple penality, the Freemasonry cutting gesture at the neck, the breast, and the bowels became **retribution** and **punishment** upon the wicked, those needing cleansing via **blood atonement** at the hands of other men as their executioner. The Freemasonry penalties punish those who break covenants with their brothers - to keep things secret, in order to protect them in their secret acts of darkness and sin, typically in getting gain (see http://www.ephesians5-11.org/handshakes.htm). At Nauvoo, this also involved the secrecy of spiritual wifery (see also pps. 82-84).

Brigham Young's changes were tied to *conditional love*, with vengeful **penalties** forced upon one within his new "blood atonement" doctrine. He and others following him believed some sins required the death of the perpetrator to atone for them. It became a hallmark of his "new order of things," in the fear and coercion underlying his demands for obedience within his new western kingdom. It resulted in many murders by his enforcers, and perhaps the Mountain Meadows Massacre. Such things are inspired by Satan, as laid out in Moses 5. Young's version of covenant-based penalties in the temple were removed in 1990 for two reasons; (1) First, they apparently triggered SRA flashbacks for some attending the temple for the first time. This occurred during the penality portion of the pre-1990 endowment. And (2) The removal of Young's version of the penalties was also tied to political correctness, as their removal came after surveys were sent out to the Saints, seeking their imput on various temple concerns, one being the penalties. Christ's sacrifice for us was a loving, **free-will offering**, made in Gethsemane. The crucifixion the next day was a forced torture and execution by Jewish leaders (carried out by the Romans), which the LORD also endured, but at the hands of wicked men leaders who had taken control of the church (the high priest Caiaphas). Young's version of the penalities mirrored the execution pattern in his blood atonement doctrine, not a love-based free will offering.

3. *The Oath of Vengeance* Brigham also added "the oath of vengeance" to the early temple endowment to avenge the murder of Joseph and Hyrum Smith. It too was tied to Young's "blood atonement" doctrine. It has since been repudiated. Many believe both had ties to the many murders committed by Rockwell, Stout, and Hickman (all for Young), along with the Mountain Meadows Massacre. God said revenge is mine (Rom. 12:17-19). All judgment is His alone (John 5:22), not any man.

4. *The Law of Adoption* Young modified Elijah's sealing doctrine to include adoption. Men and women were sealed to proxy saviors above them, men like Joseph Smith and the Twelve. They were part of a line of saviors extending back to other "fathers" and to the LORD and the Father. Wilford Woodruff did away with the "law of adoption." Men often lift themselves up before other men for gain. Christ said He is the light we are to lift up before men, and the things he does (3 Ne. 18:24).

5. *Expanding Work for the Dead* Young added more vicarious work for the dead today, including the entire endowment, going beyond baptism for the dead, ordinations, washings and anointings, etc., as introduced by Joseph Smith. This additional vicarious work today can become a primary focus (a distraction and diversion) for many Saints, instead of (1) receiving salvation, and (2) obtaining the gift of the Holy Ghost, (3) real power in the priesthood, (4) more of the gifts of the Spirit, (5) serving the living, and (6) entering the LORD's presence.

6. *Protestant Minister* Young added a Protestant minister to the endowment, paid by Lucifer to preach false doctrine to the people. In some ways he fulfilled this role himself. This minister was also eventually removed.

7. *Peter, James & John* Young replaced "messengers" with these three specific leaders of the Twelve.

8. *Consecrating All to the Church* An estimated 40% of the Saints deeded all their possessions to the church in 1855-56. Brigham Young added this endowment covenant where participants consecrated **all they have** to his version of the church. It was originally a covenant to give one's all to the LORD. The Law of Consecration (D&C 42) is how we are to care for the poor, along with tithes and offerings; a representation of real, unconditional love for God and

others. Note Young's statement tied to those wanting to leave Utah after finding it was not the Zion they hoped for. Speaking in Parowan one year after he reinstituted the Law of Consecration, he said, "If the people had done **their duty** and consecrated **all their property** to the Church . . . they could not have gone away and lost their souls [necessitating blood atonement]. If any man will say, 'I am going to apostatize,' I will advise him to **consecrate all he has** that he might be kept with the Saints and saved, so that if you are tempted to go away, you may feel it best to stay where your treasure is" (John G. Turner, *Brigham Young: Pioneer Prophet*, Harvard College, p. 248).

9. *Veil Lecture* Young added a lengthy lecture at the veil, one tied to his Adam-God doctrine. It was originally a question and answer session. Both things were later removed from the endowment.

10. *Blacks Barred from the Priesthood* President Young barred black men from holding the priesthood because of an ancient curse he believed God placed upon them. Thus, they could not enter the temple, nor participate in various priesthood ordinances outside it. Under Young, Utah was the **only** western Territory where African-American slavery and slave-sales were protected by Territorial statute! Young said, "Shall I tell you the law of God in regard to the African race? If the white man who belongs to the chosen seed mixes his blood with the seed of Cain, the penalty, under the law of God is **death on the spot**. This will always be so" (JD 10:110). These views were reversed offically during Pres. Kimball's administration (see Asssumption #3, chap. 6 & p. 165, temple penalties).

11. *No Evil Spoken of the LORD's Anointed* Brigham Young added a statement to the endowment ritual that there should be "no evil spoken of the LORD's anointed." He didn't want his authority to be questioned. This false doctrine remains with us today (a form of idolatry). We are to all practice righteous judgment (with oil in our lamps) to discern light from darkness, and false shepherds from true ones, the "wolves in sheeps clothing."

Abinadi was sent of the LORD to call King Noah and the priests of his new church to repentance. It was very sharp criticism. Abinadi was speaking "ill" of a supposed anointed King in Noah, who along with his priests taxed the people heavily to support their luxurious lifestyle and their many wives and concubines (Mosiah 11). Joseph Smith taught that a prophet is only speaking as a prophet when the spirit of prophecy (a gift from God) descends upon him. Otherwise that person is giving their personal opinion or even false doctrine.

Brigham Young taught that everything in his sermons was worthy of being called scripture. Very few men are actually "anointed by God Himself." Many men are anointed by other men in temples (see "The Second Anointing" below). As we saw in the previous chapter, Young did "not enter in at the gate," either spiritually (by being born again in Christ), or physically (by being appointed by Joseph to be his successor, or by God). Elder Dallin Oaks said, "Evil speaking of the LORD's anointed is in a class by itself. It is one thing to depreciate a person who exercises corporate power or even government power. It is quite another thing to criticize or depreciate a person for the performance of an office to which he or she has been called of God...It does not matter that the criticism is true" (Dallin Oaks, Criticism, May 4, 1986; see Assumption #3, Chap. 6). It is important, however to make sure that a person is actually "called of God." Many are *called* by other men, but few are **chosen**, *empowered,* and *sent* **of the LORD**, as "their hearts are set on the things of the world and the honors of men" ("gain," D&C 121:34-46).

12. *The Second Anointing: Reward for Leaders* Today's apostles regularly administer the "second anointing" ordinance to *other leaders* and their wives as a reward to those who faithfully serve the Brethren, proving loyal to them. It is a symbol, not real salvation. Only God pronounces that upon us, because of the His atonement.

Brigham Young was the first to provide this symbolic ordinance upon *other leaders* inside the non-completed Nauvoo Temple (others also participated in the rite before it was offered inside the structure). It is done today on Sundays in our Temples. Those receiving this symbolic ordinance are said to have their "calling and election made sure," **a guaranteed place** in the Celestial Kingdom. Men are thus pronouncing other men "saved," because of loyality to them – in their works. Without the Spirit to guide them, it is meaningless, as only our Redeemer can pronounce individuals saved, because of His atonement and His grace, "lest we boast in our works." Like everything else in the temple, the symbolic rites there point to greater spiritual realities, ones that only God himself can perform on us, and in His time and way, as we turn to HIM. He says, "repent" and "come unto me."

The average Latter-day Saint knows nearly nothing about this private rite and will likely not receive it from an apostle. They typically give it to other General Authorities (Seventies and new apostles) and to Mission Presidents, Temple Presidents, and some Stake Presidents, along with their wives. The apostle washes the feet of the lesser leader and his wife in the temple, anointing their head with oil. They are anointed as a "priest and priestess" and a "king and queen," and are supposedly sealed up to eternal life by the apostle (because of his supposed "sealing power"). Such are said to receive "the fullness of the priesthood." The leader and his wife are then invited to retreat to a room in the temple, wherein the wife is encouraged to privately wash her husband's feet. She lays her hands on his head to give him a blessing, making him a King and a Priest to God.

There is no record of this occurring in Christ's day or the Book of Mormon, though certainly Mary washed Christ's feet prior to His "treading the winepress alone." Joseph Smith also washed the feet of those in the School of the Prophets. In the single issue of the Expositor (June 7, 1844), the Law group cited **men** "sealing" up **other men** "to eternal life" one false, heretical doctrine, along with polygamy. It is tied to "receiving the honors of men," rather than that of God. Scripture tells us that the Father has committed **all judgment** into the hands of His Son (John 5:22), not imperfect men. Because Christ alone spilled His blood for us in the Atonement, He alone can pronounce us saved. Scripture says our LORD is "no respector of persons" (D&C 38:16; Acts 10:34), and thus He does not favor the shepherds who sit in the chief seats over the sheep. God is fair, merciful, and just to all. He provides the blessings of real worth, including salvation via His grace, not our works – or our loyalty to the Brethren. Paul wrote, "For by grace are ye saved through faith; and that not of yourselves: it is the gift of God: Not of works, lest any man should boast" (Eph. 2:8-9; 2 Ne. 25:23; 2 Ne. 10:24; Psalm 10:3; Isa. 61:6).

God knows our hearts. He seals us up to eternal life, doing so as "THE Prophet" (1 Ne. 21:20-23), when He provides "the more sure word of prophecy," stating that we will inherit eternal life. It may occur in the privacy of one's home, and it is given to only those **HE CHOOSES**, acting in the capacity as "the Holy Spirit of Promise." The prideful and the elite honor each other symbolically. They "have their reward" (3 Ne. 13:2). Brigham Young conducted the rites below in the Nauvoo Temple in 1846, two years after Joseph's murder.

Jan. 1, 1846 / Young did the **first LDS temple sealing of a couple** for "time and eternity" in the Nauvoo Temple.
Jan. 8, 1846 / Young performed the **first LDS temple "second anointing"** ordinance on his close friend and fellow leader Heber C. Kimball and his first wife Violate.
Jan. 25, 1846 / Young did the **first law of adoption sealing of one man to another**. Rank and file male members of the Church scrambled to be "sealed" to the Apostle of their choice (see Quinn, Mormon Hierarchy, p. 655). King Benjamin informed us that his people were sealed directly to God. They took **His** name upon them.

Apostle Page's Temple Endowment

John E. Page served in the Quorum of the Twelve for eight years, from 1838 to 1846, baptizing over 600 people in two of those years. He also experienced the great spiritual outpouring at Kirtland, "the endowment of power" in the Holy Ghost at the temple's dedication. Following his Nauvoo Temple experience, Apostle Page denounced Brigham Young and the Twelve for teaching false doctrine. *The Nauvoo Temple Endowment Register* for Dec. 10, 1845, shows that John and Mary Page went to the Temple on that date, and received the "ordinance" of "washing and anointing" and an "endowment." His wife Mary remarried after his death and was questioned in in the Temple Lot Case of 1894 about "the endowment" given inside the Nauvoo Temple. She stated:

> "By endowments in the church I understand as endowments in the Bible is spoken of [as the] **endowment of the Holy Spirit** . . . My husband . . . said it was of the Devil, and so we rejected it. I never went through all of it, and that was after Joseph Smith died . . . There was nothing of the kind in the church in 1840, but in 1846 there was a kind of sham curiosity of an endowment there . . . My husband publicly denounced them for teaching falsehoods" (testimony of Mary Page Eaton, Temple Lot Case, pps. 272–273).

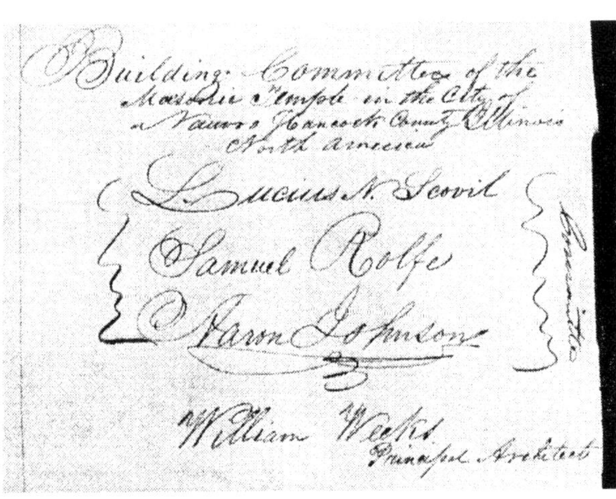
Building Committee of the Masonic Temple in the City of Nauvoo Hancock County Illinois North America
Lucius N. Scovil
Samuel Rolfe
Aaron Johnson
Committee
William Weeks
Principal Architect

Apostle Page's claim of false doctrine brought immediate action by the Quorum of Twelve. They met on February 9, 1846, where "Elder Page was disfellowshipped from that quorum." Four months later on June 26, he was excommunicated (see *Latter-Day Saint Biographical Encyclopedia* 1:92–93).

Masonic Lodge & Temple*: Two Buildings, Two Architects*

Few know that the Temple Committee at Nauvoo called the new structure to be on the hill east, a "Masonic Temple"? Mormons who were also Freemasons on the temple committee may have seen the new building as "Masonic" in many ways from the very beginning. The lines between the two organizations was gray in Nauvoo. They knew that

Mormonism and Masonry had ties to one another within Joseph's new temple ordinances. The current church history put forth claims that the first endowment ceremonies in Nauvoo (at the Red Brick Store) came forth only seven weeks after Joseph Smith was inducted into Freemasonry. This narrative may be suspect.

Today, adult missionaries for the church in old reconstructed Nauvoo have been instructed to tell tourists that what is now called the "Cultural Hall," once housed the Masonic Temple rites on its third floor, and that other portions of the building were used for a variety of cultural events. The current narrative is that the top floor of the Nauvoo Lodge building **was** the early "Masonic Temple." In reality, the whole building was a Masonic Lodge put in place by Heber C. Kimball. The lodge building (at White Street and Main) was also used for various cultural events. It was dedicated on April 5th, 1844 as a Masonic Lodge just two months before the murder of Joseph and Hyrum. This building was too small for the growing population of Masons in Nauvoo (some 1,500 men), and thus earlier in February of **1843**, plans were put in place by Mormon Masons to build a much larger "Masonic Temple." The Nauvoo Lodge minute book #2 for Feb. 16, 1843 reveals these plans, stating:

> "On February 16, **1843**, **members of the Nauvoo Lodge** discussed and unanimously approved the building of a **Masonic temple** in Nauvoo to better accommodate the needs of the lodge...Navuoo Masons and their guests met on **June 24** for the cornerstone laying [for the building]...Following the song, the group marched to a grove in the city where they heard an address from **Mormon apostle** and **Master Mason** John Taylor" (Nauvoo Masonic Lodge Minute Book 2, 16 February; 15, 19, 24 June 1843, and 5 April 1844, CHL; "Freemasons,"Nauvoo Neighbor, June 28, 1843). John Taylor was "the Worshipful Master of the Nauvoo Masonic Lodge.

Research in the Joseph Smith Paper's Project reveals that the "Principal Architect" hired to design this new "**Masonic Temple** on the hill was William Weeks. Official LDS church publications and websites today state that the architect for "the Nauvoo Temple" was also William Weeks (see below left). They are one and the same building.

Although the current narrative today is that the third floor of the Nauvoo Lodge building was the Masonic temple, historical documents like the one at the left show that architect William Weeks was designing a Masonic Temple. This is supported by the fact that three different architects at Nauvoo were employed for three different Nauvoo buildings. Two of them were Masonic structures; (1) the Masonic lodge at Main and White streets - with architect Lucious Scovil, and (2) the Masonic temple up on the hill - with architect William Weeks. A third building, (3) the Nauvoo House across from Joseph and Emma's older homestead - was designed by architect Lucian Woodworth. All three designers were Mormons *and* Freemasons.

The LDS Church Purchased Two Masonic Buildings in Nauvoo

In 1967 the LDS church purchased the old Nauvoo Masonic Lodge building (at Main and White streets), changing its name to the "Cultural Hall." Thirteen years earlier, in 1954, President David O. McKay purchased the ruins and land tied to the original "Nauvoo Masonic Temple" up on the hill to the east. Pres. McKay may have purchased the remains of this building for three reasons.

(1) The first may be that the church wanted to obtain the contents of its sealed copper box, inside the northeast cornerstone (it was sealed up at the dedication ceremony for this "temple" on **June 24**, 1843). This cornerstone box held 44 torn-out pages from the original Nauvoo Lodge minute book #1. They are now in the vault of the First Presidency in Salt Lake. What do they say?

(2) A second reason for the misdirection may be that Joseph Smith had a luke-warm relationship with Freemasonry. Though he was advanced to Master status in a single day, his Nauvoo statements reveal little commitment of any to the brotherhood, especially in comparison to men like Kimball. Joseph simply borrowed portions of Masonry and other influences to help him construct portions of the endowment. His single known statement about Masonry was that the craft was tied to keeping secrets. Joseph's research into Masonry and other things generated questions that he took to the LORD, all to determine what to put into the new endowment and how.

(3) A third reason for the misdirection may be the close relationship between early Mormonism and Freemasonry. Many Mormon men were Masons at Nauvoo (1,492) and may have seen the structure as Masonic from the beginning. Heber C. Kimball, second in command to Brigham Young in Nauvoo and later in Utah in the First Presidency, stated:

> "We have the **true Masonry**. The Masonry of today is received *from the apostasy* which took place in the days of Solomon, and David. They have now and then a thing that is correct, but **we have the real thing**" (Stanley B. Kimball, The NauvooYears', https://scholarsarchive.byu.edu/cgi/viewcontent.cgi?article=1737&context=byusq).

From 1844-46, Young and Kimball used the secrecy and rites of Freemasonry at Nauvoo in modified form to help them hide their spiritual wifery. They used Freemasonry just as they used Joseph Smith's name and various elements of Mormonism, all for their own purposes.

The Legacy of Secrecy

The Prophet Joseph spoke out against **secret** things generally, and yet Brigham and Heber claim it was Joseph that came up with many of the **secret** things at Nauvoo. A number of the secret ways of Masonry were imported into Mormonism via Young's modified temple theology. **Secrecy** leads to *lies* and *deception* (see 3 Ne. 16:10, 21:19, 30:2, and Book of Commandments 5:5-6). Addressing the **secret oaths** of the Danites while in Liberty Jail, Joseph stated:

> "And again, I would further suggest the impropriety of the organization of bands or companies, by **covenant** or **oaths**, by **penalties** or **secrecies** . . . Pure friendship always becomes weakened the very moment you undertake to make it stronger be **penal oaths** and **secrecy**" (HC, vol. 3, p. 303).

He later added:

> "there has been frauds and **secret abominations** and evil works of darkness going on leading the minds of the weak and unwary into confusion and distraction, and palming it all the time upon the presidency while mean time the presidency were **ignorant** as well as **innocen**t of these things, which were practicing in the church in our name" (Joseph Smith, Dec. 1838, Times and Seasons, vol. 1, no. 6, April **1840**).

As addressed earlier, just before he was murdered, Joseph went to William Marks (Stake President) stating that he had regretted some things (see p. 104). One was not taking action sooner to eliminate polygamy among the Saints. We know Joseph removed his garment on June 20th of 1844, seven days before his murder. He asked *all* of the Twelve to do the same. Was this a repudiation of the darker things in Masonry and the growing secrecy it supported at Nauvoo? After the Smith murders, the **secret** tactics tied to coercion and fear increased at Nauvoo under Brigham Young. They were used by (1) the police force there (many former Danites), (2) the "whistling and whittling brigade," and those intimidating others via the actions of (3) "Aunt Peggy." Much of this secrecy and coercion was used to support polygamy and to get gain. These efforts continued in Utah Territory for decades under Pres. Young. Hosea Stout and Bill Hickman attest to various enforcement techniques for Young in their journals.

The rise in secrecy coincided with the rise in polygamy. Involvement in it increased dramatically following the Smith murders. It exploded once the Smiths were out of the way. There were **56** new plural marriages in 1845 among church members, mostly leaders. Brigham Young went from 4 wives to 14. Heber C Kimball went from 2 wives to 10. By 1846, the "spiritual wives" movement increased five-fold to **255** plural wives (see Nauvoo Roots of Mormon Polygamy, 1841-46: A Preliminary Demographic Report, p 32).

Emma Smith said "the secret things" at Nauvoo led to her husband's murder. Chief among the Masonic influences brought into the Nauvoo endowment were its modified **secret** blood-oaths and the severe penalites tied to them. They were used to protect Brigham's "new order of things." Freemasons have been the masters and keepers of secrets throughout history. Joseph said, "The secrets of Masonry is to keep a secret" (Joseph Smith journal, Sunday Oct. 15, 1843). The penalties made use of ritual mutilation (or cutting) gestures at the neck, the chest, and the lower abdomen as a fear-based tactic to keep the secrets in place. On LDS church websites today, the secret actions of those in the secret chamber are made more palitable via subtle word changes.

> "Plural marriage was introduced among the early Saints [the leaders] incrementally, and participants were asked to keep their actions **confidential**" (LDS.org, Plural Marriage in Kirtland and Nauvoo, 2014).

Besides polygamy, a second purpose of the secret chamber and modifications to Joseph's endowment was finanacial gain. After the murder of the Smiths, mansions were built for Brigham and other members of the Twelve. The secret oaths were useful for concealing the embezzlement of donations by many of the Twelve. These were funds collected from the Saints for the Nauvoo House and the new Temple. Joseph called out Brigham and others for his discovery of some $200 a day that was disappearing. Those printing the single issue of the Expositor were fully aware of the embezzlement *and* of the secret practice of polygamy by members of the Twelve. The editors of the Expositor claimed that the Twelve believed they were **justified** in their embezzling scheme for any one of three reasons:

1. If the money taken was from non-church members (by Mormon leaders who were Masons)
2. If a portion of it was given to the Nauvoo Masonic Temple fund
3. If the practice was safeguarded via a Masonic secret blood-oath

Just weeks after the murder of the Smiths, Brigham Young and the Twelve increased the tithing amount the Saints were required to pay. Shortly thereafter they then saw to it that the Twelve and the temple committee were exempt from paying it. Tithing became a profitable financial funnel for those in the secret chamber after Joseph's death. Later in Utah, shrewd businessman Heber J. Grant, President of the church, implemented "the temple recommend" as a requirement to enter a temple. It utilized questions tied to full payment of tithing for participation in what are now called the "**saving**" ordinances of the temple. In 1923, Grant made the church a 501c3 corporation. God said salvation is available without money or price, requiring only a broken heart and a contrite spirit (3 Ne. 9:20). Three witnesses bear out this truth (2 Ne. 9:50; 26:25; Alma 1:20). Bill Hickman said Young demanded two things of the Saints; their obedience and their tithing.

Other Ties to Freemasonry

Satan corrupts the things of God by taking away the light God provides (see D&C 93:39). Secret combinations do this from within. Many at the top of Freemasonry (30 to 33rd degree) have used its secrecy and oaths for dark purposes in the other organizations they lead. Powerful men the world over use the upper levels of this secret brotherhood to build a great worldwide secret combination focused on putting the New World Order in place, one led by the dark lord of this world. Besides the typical characteristics of "gain" (sex, power, money, control, etc.), many among them desire to replace the Christian God Jesus Christ (or Adonai) with Lucifer (a name meaning "light bearer").[25] Many in positions of power – the illuminated elite or "Illuminati"- genuinely believe he is more benevolent than Adonai and have turned to him for the things of the world and the pleasures of the flesh. They believe he will bring in a golden age of enlightenment, as illustrated on the back of our Masonic inspired one-dollar bill.

Those supporting the creation of this New World Order believe that their new millennial age of enlightenment will be brought in by a third great world crisis, creating an environment where everyday people will be so desperate, they will give up many things they hold dear. The illuminated elite are hopeful that the uneducated masses (the sheep) will welcome in a controlled path to world peace via world dominance by the One World Order and its dark lord. Christians supporting Adonai will be put down. World War III will provide them this necesssary crisis, a battle originating in religion - the struggle between Muslims and Jews. The traditional Christian belief system will be classified with the enemy by those in power. For the elite, World War III will be the final necessary struggle to bring in the kingdom of the dark lord. Nimrod and his great tower at Babel was an early attempt to do the same thing early in world history. Its tower was reaching for the God of heaven – to destroy Him. One like him will rise up to attempt it again. Isaiah's "servant" will do battle with him. The darkened path to take away all freedom is provided by war.

World War I	The creation of **the League of Nations** (with wisdom, U.S. leaders would not participate at this time)
World War II	The creation of **the United Nations** (the U.S. houses this world government in NYC, paying for it)
World War III	The anticipacted creation of **the New World Order** (with Lucifer at the top of it all)

Contrasting this is the real God of light, Christ the LORD. He will deliver the faithful. He invites with love, whereas Satan uses fear and force to take away man's will and agency. The early Saints of Europe were brought into the gospel by Young and the Twelve at Nauvoo, following them west to Utah. Many of the poor European Saints were familiar with the centralized power of a "king." Evil men have used secrecy to corrupt governments, institutions, and churches for thousands of years. In a 1987 Jeffrey Hadden survey, questions were sent to some 10,000 Protestant clergymen in America, 7,441 replied. Their answers were shocking. A huge percentage of the Christian Pastors did **not** believe (1) Christ was resurrected, that (2) he was born of a virgin birth, that (3) demons exist in the world today, and (4) that scripture was and is the inspired Word of God in faith, history, and secular matters. Another survey published in August 1988 by *the Association of North American Missions* revealed that selfishness and indifference was flourishing among many churches because most Christian denominations had been penetrated by the materialism of Masonry.

Tom C. McKenney, coauthor of *The Deadly Deception*, revealed that of the two largest Protestant denominations in the United States, "90 percent of one and 70 percent of the other have pastors who are members of the Masonic Lodge."

According to Day, **Masonic penetration of Christian churches** began at the turn of the 20th century. Myron Fagan, a well-known Jewish-American playwright on Broadway and Hollywood (who became a Christian) published a series of audiotapes released in 1967 entitled, *The Illuminati*. In them, Fagan revealed how the **takeover of Christianity** was to be accomplished. Jacob Schiff (son of a Jewish Reform Rabbi born in Frankfurt, Germany) was sent to the United States to carry out four specific assignments in connection with Freemasonry, and the **pollution** of Christianity.

(1) The first was to control America's money system via the Federal Reserve System. Fagan detailed how Masonic money and power backed Jacob Schiff and his establishment of the German House of Warburg a banking system in America, with J.P. Morgan and John D. Rockefeller as front men.
(2) The second was to find men who, for a price, who would willingly serve as stooges for a great conspiracy. They were then promoted to various Federal positions in Congress, the U.S. Supreme Court, and many Federal agencies. The same men were groomed for the Council on Foreign Relations, part of the New World Order.
(3) The third was to create minority group strife across the nation, particularly between races. The NAACP was created for this purpose (the National Association for the Advancement of Colored People).
(4) The fourth was to **destroy religion** in the United States, **Christianity** (and Adonai) being the chief target. This goal became the task of the National Council of Churches, along with the Rothschilds.

According to Day, Adam Weishaupt, a cultural Jew who was raised a Catholic, started the Lucifer-worshiping occult organization known as the *Illuminati*. He was also a Freemason and used it to further the Illuminati's goal of world control via a One World Government. Jacob Schiff later selected John D. Rockefeller to finance and direct an institution to that end. Fagan told how young men were selected for the ministry and then taught how to dilute the Christian message. The Jews Fagan spoke of were not those descended from Abraham through Jacob, but through another line. As the *Jewish Almanac* points, "Strictly speaking it is incorrect to call an Ancient Israelite a 'Jew" or to call a contemporary Jew an Israelite or a Hebrew" (1980 *Jewish Almanac*, p.). Additional authorized sources such as *Encyclopedia Judaica, The Universal Jewish Encyclopedia*, and others concur. Jewish historian Aurthur Koestler stated that some of the people known as Jews today "are descendants of Abraham, but not of Isaac and Jacob. History reveals that they originate in the fierce Turkish, Khazar tribes who once roamed southern Russia. They adopted Judaism between the 7th and 9th centuries AD. Today, the Khazars are known as 'Jews" not because of any racial [bloodline] question, but because of their religion" (Aurther Koestler, The Thirteenth Tribe, Random House). The Khazars embraced Judaism (the deadness of "the law" – 2 Ne. 25) to be part of what was perceived as a unified culture that was very successful in **business** matters. These people often lead America's banking and film industries, and also occupy many leadership positions in the government. Jewish historian.

Day added that many Christian Pastors are being trained by FEMA representatives to help round up dissidents (freedom loving Christians and others) when martial law by the NWO is put in place. The Brighamite Saints are a useful target for them. They have been trained to follow leaders obediently. Because of the Saints trust in men at the top, it is believed many will gladly turn over their food storage to local leaders and then be rounded up and put in "community centers" (a code name for FEMA camps). See Lorraine Day, *How the New World Order is Using the Christian Churches and their Pastors to Destroy Christianity*.

Daniel of the Old Testament refused to obey the law of the land when it went against God's law. He continued to pray three times a day to the God of heaven. The LORD didn't stop Daniel from going into the Lions' den. Instead, He miraculously delivered Daniel by closing the mouths of the lions. It required Daniel's faith and trust in Him, not trust in the King. Paul said, "We ought to obey God rather than man" (Acts 5:29). After putting away his additional wives, a repentant King David said, "It is better to trust in the LORD than to put confidence in man" (Psalm 118:8).

Two Lords, Two Ways

Moroni, Mormon, Isaiah, Jeremiah, and other inspired Prophets have seen our day, suggesting there are really only two ways to live. Nephi spoke of only **two churches** (1 Ne. 14:10). Moses addressed the doctrine of the **two ways** in Deuteromony 30:16-19, leading to *blessing* or *cursing*. Able was blessed, Cain cursed. They represent two classes of people on Earth. Paul called those who follow God and **His will** em "the children of obedience," and the disobedient who mix **their own will** with the things of God "the children of disobedience" or "*wrath*" (see Ephesians 2:2-3). Perhaps addressing the current modified temple endowment in the last book of the Book of Mormon, Moroni stated:

> "And again I would exhort you that ye would **come unto Christ**, and lay hold upon every **good gift**, and touch not the **evil gift**, nor the unclean thing. And awake, and arise from the dust, O Jerusalem; yea, and put on thy beautiful garments, **O daughter of Zion** [the unfaithful bride of Isaiah 54 - us]; and strengthen thy stakes and enlarge thy borders forever, that thou mayest no more be confounded, that the covenants of the Eternal Father which he hath made unto thee, O house of Israel, may be fulfilled" (Mor. 10:30-31).

> Paul also addresses the "unclean thing," stating, "And what agreement hath the temple of God with idols? for **ye are <u>the temple</u>** of the living God; as God hath said, **<u>I will dwell in them</u>**, and walk in *them;* and **I will be their God**, and they shall be **my people**. Wherefore come out from among them, and be ye **separate**, saith the Lord, and **touch not the unclean thing**; and **I will receive you**, And will be **a Father** unto you, and ye shall be **my sons and daughters**, saith the Lord Almighty" (2 Cor. 6:16 – 18).

An endowment is a **gift**. Chapters 6 and 7 address the *spiritual* endowment God intends us to receive, one supportd by His holy word in scripture. The purpose for Joseph Smith's "house" at Nauvoo and his early version of the endowment, was that the house men were building would *become* a temple "to **the LORD's name**." One where a pillar of fire would be seen and established over it, revealing its approval by God. Its purpose was to help believers return to His presence, He who is the God of love, light, and hope. He is Jesus Christ, the Son of the Father and our Advocate with Him. He is also God, the Creator of heaven and earth, and our beloved Savior! Joseph had the exterior of the "house" at Nauvoo illustrate the bride of the Lamb, a *faithful* bride full of light. It became something else. It was destroyed, struck by lighting, a tornado, and then burned down by an arsonist.

The Gift at the Veil

At the conclusion of the temple ritual all participants approach the lord at the veil to receive an endowment from him. Prior to 1990, ritual covenants with this lord were made prior to the enactment of **three mutilation penalties** for revealing the secret blood oath (and its signs, tokens, and penalties) to others. Related warnings were added followed by a ritual embrace with this lord. He symbolically stands behind the temple veil yet today. There, participants make physical contact with him. It once had five points of contact on the body, all to create "*fellowship*" (it was called "the five points of *fellowship*" by both Mormons and Masons, see Eph. 5:11). It is during this ritual embrace that the words of the gift, blessing, or endowment are given secretly, in a whisper from mouth to ear, and repeated back to him.

The words reveal much to us. There is **no** Christ-centeredness in them. They feature the bestowal of three *physical* or "*carnal*" *blessings* instead; **power**, **health**, and **strength**. There is **no** mention of a purified heart, increased love or charity, nor the gifts and fruits of the Spirit (D&C 46; 1 Cor. 12; Gal. 5). Instead, they represent three earth-bound rewards of a false, carnal one who seeks to reign over us. He promises *physical* **health**, tied to the *navel* and *marrow in the bones.* **Strength** is also promised and in "*the loins*." In the Bible *the loins* are associated with *sexual organs* and posterity. The promise of **power** *in the priesthood* is also made, lasting throughout time and eternity. This priesthood is symbolized in the *green apron*. It is during the endowment that **Satan** tells all those seated that the apron is an emblem of "**his priesthoods**." We know that Adam and Eve worn an apron they made of fig leaves in Genesis 3:7 (tied to the temptation of Satan). In the Book of Mormon we read of the lambskin apron covering the loins of those making secret blood oaths within secret combinations. The Gadianton robbers dyed this lambskin red with blood (3 Ne. 4:7). Its placement **over the top** of all other clothing there is significant.

In D&C 18:3 we are told by God "to **rely** on that which has been written" to guide us in all things. John 8 states, "If ye continue in **my word**, then are ye **my disciples** indeed; And **ye shall know the truth, and the truth shall make you free**" (John 8:31-32). A word search of "**loins**" in scripture leads us to three words found in the veil blessing, "**strength, navel**," and "**sinews**." They are found in two verses in Job, perhaps the oldest book in the Bible.

> "Behold now behemoth, which I made with thee; he eateth grass as an ox. Lo now, his **strength** is in his **loins**, and his *force* is in the **navel** of his belly. He moveth his *tail* like a cedar: the **sinews** of *his stones* are wrapped together. His bones are as strong pieces of brass; his *bones* are like bars of iron" (Job 40:15-18).

Behemoth and *Leviathan* are two great beasts in the book of Job (one of land, one of the sea) that both symbolize **the power of evil connected with Satan**, who is mentioned in the first chapters of the book. God addressed these things to Job that He might humble him, and reveal that He (God) has all power over the strong things of this world. Some suggest that the word "move" is "extend" in connection with male genitals, as the verse also addresses the sinew around "his stones," an interpretation supported by the Vulgate Bible which uses the word "*testiculorum.*" God's precious word in scripture tells us that the natural man is *carnal, sensual,* and *devilish*, and that he is an enemy to God, and that thus must be rooted out of us. It is only possible in the mighty change of heart, made possible when the true LORD Jesus baptizes us in His fiery Spirit. It comes with the sacrifice He desires; a broken heart and a contrite spirit. He did away with the bloody sacrifices of terrified animals and innocent children given to Baal. The word "carnal" all throughout scripture means something that is not spiritual. It is tied to mortal, worldly things (D&C 67:10) and to all things sensual (Mosiah 16:10–12). The collection of scriptures below tells us a lot more.

> To be carnally-minded is death (2 Ne. 9:39). Men are naturally carnal, sensual, and devilish (Moses 5:13, 6:49; Alma 42:10). This natural man is an enemy to God and should be put off (Mosiah 3:19). The natural man receiveth not the things of the Spirit (1 Cor. 2:14). He that persists in his own carnal nature remaineth in his fallen state (Mosiah 16:5; Alma 42:7–24; D&C 20:20). Natural or carnal men are without God in the world (Alma 41:11). Because of his transgression, man became spiritually dead (D&C 29:41). Neither can any natural man abide the presence of God (D&C 67:12). He that persists in his own carnal nature remains in his fallen state (Mosiah 16:5). Those who follow after Satan's will or their own will and carnal desires must fall (D&C 3:4). To change and be made new, all must be born of God, changed from their carnal and fallen state (Mosiah 27:25).

The false lord of this earth and those following him in the upper levels of Masonry, the Illuminati, and many secret combinations the world over, including churches – oppose Christ and are attempting to secretly raise up Lucifer. They hate Christ and call Him Adonai. They diminish Him at every turn. It must not be so for the Saints and other believing Christians today. The choice for all involves **two ways only**. We can be part of the church of the Lamb or the Firstborn (see "how" in chapter 7), or the great and abominable church of the devil (see 1 Ne. 14:10). Wise virgins choose "**the way** of salvation of our God." Note just three related scriptures.

1. *John 14:6* – "**I am the way**, the truth, and the life: no man cometh unto the Father, but by me."
2. *D&C 1:16* – "They seek not the Lord to establish his righteousness, but **every man walketh in his own way**, and after the image of his own god, whose image is in the likeness of the world, and whose substance is that of an idol, which waxeth old and shall perish in Babylon, even Babylon the great, which shall fall."
3. *D&C 82:6* – "And the anger of God kindleth against the inhabitants of the earth; and none doeth good, **for all have gone out of the way**" (see also 2 Ne. 28:11).

Especially dangerous are **the binding oaths** of Satan and evil, designing men, whether in places called "temples" or in church meetings. They are *legally binding* in the courts in heaven, as God recognizes covenants. Satan is our accuser relative to them, whereas our merciful LORD is our advocate with the Father there. In the October General Conference of 2014, Elder Nelson (now President over the Church) said, "Our sustaining of prophets [men calling themselves, "prophets, seers, and revelators"] *is a personal commitment* that we will do our utmost to uphold **their prophetic priorities**. *Our sustaining* is an **oath**-like indication that we recognize their calling as a prophet to be *legitimate and* **binding upon us**" (Russell M. Nelson, 2014, *Sustaining the Prophets*, General Conference Address). I choose to take Christ's yoke upon me, not the binding oaths of men. I desire to be washed clean in His blood, not be bound down by **the chains of hell**. Only our LORD's blood and His word have power to break them and remove them, that we might avoid "the second [spiritual] death." Nephi and Alma were clear about these **binding chains** and **cords**.

> "O that **ye would awake**; **awake from a deep sleep**, yea, even from **the sleep of hell**, and **shake off the awful chains by which ye are bound**, which are **the chains which bind the children of men**, that they are carried away captive down to the eternal gulf of misery and woe" (2 Ne. 1:13; see also Moroni 10:30).
>
> "O, my beloved brethren, turn away from your sins; **shake off the chains of him that would bind you fast; come** unto that **God who is the rock of your salvation**" (2 Ne. 9:45; see also 2 Ne. 28:19).

"And may the Lord grant unto you repentance, that ye may not bring down his wrath upon you, that **ye may not** be **bound down by the chains of hell**, that *ye may not suffer the second death*" (Alma 13:30; see also Alma 5:7).

When Mitt Romney ran for President of the United States many were concerned that his LDS temple covenants would take precedence over his oath of office of President. The concern *was* confirmed in the words of U.S. Senator Gordon Smith, a two-term Republican Senator from Oregon. Speaking behind closed doors to the Twelve, Smith spoke of elected LDS Senators and Congressmen and the good that they can do there, stating "Having them in there and knowing that their temple recommend **is more important** *than their election certificate* is of *inestimable value* in terms of what I have seen" (Feb. 18, 2009 statement by Senator Gordon Smith to top church leaders, see https://www.youtube.com/watch?v=4TuCWXBRX9g&feature=youtu.be). Freemasonry and Brigham Young have given us a new endowment. Participants in the temple ritual willingly agree to place themselves under the power of "the man of sin" if they fail - in any way - to keep all covenants made in the temple. This puts them under the older, lesser "**law**" (with its fear and retribution) rather than the **love** and **grace** of Christ. They are thus **bound** by the **chains** (of the one giving us the apron) when any covenant is violated in any way, something most of us are sure to do. Following one's willing entrance into this covenant, participants then *seal* it by taking the unseen hand of one behind a curtain and giving him *secret signs* and *tokens*. He appears to be the one "Who opposeth and exalteth himself above all that is called God, or that is worshipped; so that he as God sitteth in the temple of God shewing himself that he is God" (2 Thess. 2:4). Jesus said, "I am come in my Father's name, and ye receive me not: if another shall come in his own name, him ye will receive" (John 5:43).

The angel who first visited Joseph Smith on Rosh Hashanah of 1823, quoted forty scriptures to him (see www.7witnesses.com). The first two of these may have a direct tie to this deceptive, replacement temple covenant. The first scripture quoted Joseph was Malachi 3. In the two Malachi chapters preceding it we are given context as we read about the unfaithfulness of the Bride Israel (anciently and today). She is in a fallen state and is delighting in a false covenant with a false Lord. The priests are offering polluted bread upon the altar. It is not accepted. Chapter 3 then addresses (1) a coming **special servant** to help a people in dire trouble; (2) **a false lord** whom the people are seeking and delighting in; And (3) a warning that they are straying dangerously from the pure ordinances of the **true LORD**.

The King James Bible uses the word "Lord" in two ways. One has all capital letters and refers to the true LORD Jesus or JEHOVAH of the Old Testament, whereas the "Lord" in Malachi 3:1 has only the first letter L capitalized. It does not necessarily mean JEHOVAH, but one desiring to be called "Lord." Sometimes this is in reference to wicked mortal rulers who **want** to be worshiped by others, ones like Lucifer or King Noah of the Book of Mormon. Adding words to Malachi 3:1 – the first scripture given Joseph Smith in 1823 – helps us see this verse in a new light.

"and the [false] Lord, whom ye [currently] seek, shall suddenly come to his temple, even the messenger of the [false] covenant, whom ye [currently] delight in."

Chapter 4 of Malachi then addresses a great burning soon to cleanse the wicked and prideful from off the earth at the LORD's second coming. Those who fear (love and honor) Him who is the true LORD will enjoy healing in **His** wings (Mal. 4:1-2). John tells us in Revelation that he is given keys to open the gate for "the man of sin" and others to come through and then afflict those who have taken **the mark of the Beast** upon them (John 20:1). They are tormented by dark forces for 5 months. The false covenant embraced in Brigham's temple "endowment" appears to be a substitute for the simple *baptismal covenant* taught us in the Book of Mormon, where King Benjamin's people all agreed to do **the will** of the True LORD (Mosiah 5:5). It is "the New and Everlasting Covenant." Instead of the saving *spiritual* endowment known as the baptism of fire and the gift of the Holy Ghost (requiring a broken heart and contrite spirit), with the gift of the Holy Ghost following, many have willingly made a false, outward ceremonial covenant to a false Lord and using *secret signs* and *tokens* while wearing a *green apron* over all other clothing. Half the Saints at Nauvoo embraced this replacement covenant along with Brigham Young's spiritual wifery. Curses have followed for four generations. D&C 113 tells us that "...the **bands of her neck** are the *curses* of God upon her, or the scattered remnants of Israel in their scattered condition among the Gentiles" (D&C 113).

Purposeful Lies and deception

Many "are **deceived** today by the *craftiness* of men" (D&C 76:75; 123:12; Job 5:13; Luke 20:23; 1 Cor. 3:19; 2 Cor. 4:2; Eph. 4:14; Psalm 83:1-4). The LORD addressed the "*craft*" (from the Hebrew "*aram*" meaning "*serpent, subtlety, shrewd*") of **lying** and **deception** in *seven* scriptures. They are about "*secret*" or "*hidden*" things (from the Hebrew "*sod*"). God has listed "**lies**" and "**deception**" *first* and *second five* times **for us** in 3 Nephi 16:10, 21:19, 30:2 (the third sin there is **whoredoms**), Book of Commandments 4:5-6 (p. 249), and D&C 123:12-13 (also D&C 45:57; Moses 4:4). God commanded all "*wise*" virgins to *diligently search Isaiah*, as its underlying message, like that of Jeremiah, is *abuse of the sheep* **by the shepherds**. They **lie** and **deceive** for **gain** (which includes *whoredoms*). The following scriptures address "watchmen," those who are asleep or worse, those turning to darkness, using the sheep for gain. The enemy then advances. In chapter 34 of Ezekiel we read; "Son of man, prophesy **against the shepherds** of Israel…neither did my shepherds search for my flock, **but the shepherds fed themselves**, and fed **not** the flock…**Therefore will I save my flock**, and they shall no more be a prey; and I will Judge between cattle and cattle…*I have broken the bands of their yoke*, and *delivered them out of the hand of those that* **served themselves of them**." Scriptures addressing our shepherds negatively are plentiful in Isaiah, Jeremiah (chapters 1-23), and other books of scripture. See Isaiah 1:5, 3:12, 9:16, 22:15-25, 28:1, 3, 7, 15; 19:14 29:10, 56:10, 62:6; Jeremiah 2:8, 13; 5:11-13, 26-31; 10:21; 13:13; 14:14-15; 23:1-32; Ezek. 34:1-3, 8, 22-24, 27; 37:22-28; Hosea 2:16-17, 3:4-5; JST Luke 12:54; JST Matthew 21:55; 2 Nephi 2 Ne. 26:29; 28:3-4, 2, 11-15, 21, 24-25, 31, and D&C 64:38-43; 85:7-9; 89-95; 101:44-61, 90; 124:24-26 101:44-61, 90.

Third Nephi chapter 6 addresses the *secret combination* existing between *lawyers*, *judges*, and **high priests** (3 Ne. 6:21 & 27), and the blood oaths they made with each other and with Satan (3 Ne. 4:28-30). Thus was just before the great destruction came, cleansing the Book of Mormon lands prior to our LORD's visit to the righteous gathered at Bountiful. The best scriptures addressing *secret combinations* and their *blood-oaths* include: (1) *The Book of Enoch* – 1:1-2, 4:1-8, 69:12-13; (2) *The Book of Moses* – chapters 1 and 5; (3) *The Book of Mormon* – Alma 37:21-33, 45-47; Hel. 6:16-40; 3 Ne. 6:21, 27-30; Morm. 826-41; Ether 87-26; And (4) *The Doctrine and Covenants* – All of Section 38; 42:64; 117:11; 123:7-17. Scriptures addressing the removal of these particular "plain and precious things" include, Moses 1:23, 41; 4:4; 1 Ne. 13:32; 2 Ne. 3:9, 9:21, 27-29; JST Luke 11:53; D&C 18:3.

Pres. Ezra Taft Benson led the church during the period of its greatest missionary success (1989). It is clear why. He continually preached three things; Our need to (1) study **the Book of Mormon**, (2) **remove pride** in our lives, and (3) **repent.** He also addessed the spread of *secret combinations* among us. His actions mirror those of true prophets throughout scripture, and like them, he wasn't popular with all the people. Missionary success in the LDS church is now at is lowest recorded levels (endnote 4). Pres. Benson taught that false prophets pacify and lull people into carnal security (2 Ne. 28:21). Many turn to leaders when they should be turning to God (see Ezek. chap. 14). He stated, "As watchmen on the tower of Zion, it is our obligation and right as leaders to speak out against current evils – evils that strike at the very foundation of all we hold dear…In times as serious as these, we must **not permit fear of criticism** to keep us from doing our duty, even at the risk of our counsel being tabbed as political, as government becomes more and more entwined in our daily lives…Speaking out against immoral or unjust actions has been the burden of prophets and disciples of God from time immemorial. It was for this very reason that many of them were persecuted. Nevertheless, it was their God-given task, as watchmen on the tower, **to warn the people**" (Ezra Taft Benson, Conference Report, April 1973). Watchmen that will be replaced are addressed in JST Matthew 21; D&C 85:7-9, 101:44-61, 89-95, 101:90; 124:24-26; Isa. 22:15-25. *Inspired* Prophets prophecy, *real* Seers see visions, and *true* Revelators reveal truths and are never silent regarding those events that are coming.

One of the stated goals of two men at the top of Freemasonry, is keeping those at its lower levels **ignorant** (**lies** and **deception**) of what is *really* going in. This keeps the underlings mostly unaware of who those at the top are. The ignorance and deception quietly provides *gain* for the top tier. The lower levels provide the innocent *foundational face* to the public. This two tier system is the model of many organizations, including Freemasonry, Catholicism, and modern Mormonism. The Prophet Mormon saw that all churches today are polluted (Morm. 8:36). Albert Pike stated:

> "Masonry, like all the **Religions**, all the Mysteries, Hermeticism, and Alchemy, conceals its **secrets** from all except the Adepts and Sages, or the Elect, and uses false explanations and misinterpretations of its symbols to mislead those who *deserve* only to be *mislead*; **to conceal the Truth**, which it calls light, and draw them away from it" (Albert Pike, *Morals and Dogma*, pps. 104-5).

Pike wrote for the Southern Jurisdiction of Scottish Rite Masonry. He was the Sovereign Grand Commander of that Masonic body from 1859 until his death in 1891. Though his statement is 120 years old, his words reflect the majority of those committed to the New World Order today. Manly P. Hall added:

"Freemasonry is a fraternity *within* a fraternity -- an outer organization **concealing** an *inner brotherhood* of the elect . . . it is necessary to establish the existence of these *two separate* and yet *interdependent orders*, the one visible and the other **invisible**. The visible society is a splendid camaraderie of 'free and accepted' men enjoined to devote themselves to ethical, educational, fraternal, patriotic, and humanitarian concerns. The **invisible** society is a **secret** and most August [defined as 'of majestic dignity, grandeur'] fraternity whose members are dedicated to the service of a *mysterious* arcannumarcandrum [defined as 'a **secret**, a mystery' or **the secret of secrets**"]."
(Hall, Lectures on Ancient Philosophy, p. 433) ("the secret of secrets").

Those in the "outer" organization are typically unaware of the inner **secret** brotherhood, which is protected by the degree system (approval process, loyality) that initiates must pass through to gain further "light" about the true nature of their *craft* of **deception**. At its head, in the highest degrees are those who often look to the "light bearer" (Lucifer). Many of them love Satan more than God, like Cain and Lamech in Moses 5. Besides using the masses for gain, the two-tiered secretive organizations are also used to help bring in the New World Order and its leader, the dark lord of this world. Albert Pike, speaking at a conference of the **secret**, second tier leaders in 1889, stated:

"What we must say to the crowd is—We worship **a** God...To you, Sovereign Grand Inspectors General, we say, so that you can repeat it to the Brethren of the 32nd, 31st and 30th degrees:—The **Masonic religion** must be, by all of us initiates *of the high grades*, maintained in the purity of **the Luciferian doctrine**. If Lucifer were not God, Adonai (the God of the Christians) whose deeds [Old Testament stories] prove his cruelty, perfidy and hatred of man, his barbarism and repulsion of science—if Lucifer were not God, would Adonai and His priests slander him? Yes, Lucifer is God, and unfortunately so is Adonai. For the eternal law is that there is no splendor without shadow, no beauty without ugliness, no white without black, because the absolute can only exist as two, because darkness is necessary to light to serve as its compliment . . . The true and pure philosophical religion is the belief in Lucifer, equal to Adonai, but Lucifer, God of Light and God of Good, is fighting for humanity against Adonai, God of Darkness and God of Evil" (Albert Pike, *address to the 23 Confederated Supreme Councils of the World*, 14 July 1889). For more on Lucifer as "the light bearer," a fallen angel, see endnote 25.

In a circular published on March 18, **1775**, by the Grand Orient of France, reference is made to two divisions of Freemasonry. This is further support by Albert Pike and Albert Mackey, both 33rd Degree Masons and authors. Pike published *Morals and Dogma* (1872) and Mackey, "*The Encyclopaedia of Freemasonry*" (1873). Both books reveal much about the Lucifer focus of "**the craft**." Those in upper level invisible Masonry lead a cooperative group of men on a global scale for the Great Architect (Lucifer), that they together might bring in the New World Order.

If a man reveres Jesus Christ at the beginning of his membership in Masonry, he is immediately placed in the lower level visible society and rarely learns the truth about the organization. He would not become an Adept, a Sage, or one of the Elect; terms reserved only for those of the invisible society. He would be deliberately lied to concerning the reality of the Masonic doctrines. He would be given deliberate misinterpretations of its symbols, so that he would think he knew the truth. Pike stated, "Fictions are necessary to the people, and the Truth becomes deadly to those who are not strong enough to contemplate it in all its brilliance . . . So Masonry jealously conceals its secrets and intentionally leads conceited interpreters astray" (Morals and Dogma, pps. 103- 105). "Fictions are necessary" so that lower level, visible Masons are not devastated by the reality of Lucifer worship at the highest levels, leaving "the craft" and exposing its secrets. Liars use this two-tier method of deception to seize control of nearly all things.

Idolatry and sexual obsession and perversion go hand in hand. The obelisk is the major symbol for ancient Baal worship along with modern Satan or Lucifer worship today. This is the reason why obelisks are associated with Freemasonry. It represents an obsession with sex and the erect phallus. Albert Pike stated, "Hence the significancy of the phallus, or of its inoffensive substitute, the obelisk, rising as an emblem of the resurrection by the tomb of buried Deity ..." (Morals and Dogma, p. 393). Today obelisks stand atop the graves of many Freemasons. They are emblems of the future resurrection of a "buried Deity" in the minds of many Masons. The "invisible Mason" believes he is becoming a god via devotion to the "antichrist." In 1898, Congress approved the raising of the Albert Pike memorial in Washington D.C. Our tax dollars were used to raise up a memorial to one of America's top worshippers of Lucifer.

Obelisks were originally created by Egyptian Pharaohs. In the Bible we read, "King Jehu said to the guards and to the officers, 'Go in and slay them; let none escape'. "And they smote them with the sword; and the guards before the king threw their bodies out, and went into the inner dwelling of the house of Baal. They brought out the obelisks of the house of Baal and burned them" (2 Kings 10:26, *Amplified Bible*). God ordered such obelisks burned, but only after He ordered King Jehu to slaughter the worshippers of the obelisk, the Baal worshippers. Modern Israel must put away "sacred pillars" and "Asherah poles" dedicated to Baal. The Washington Monument, the obelisk at Vatican city, and some church steeples represent three incarnations of this idolatry (see 1 Kings 14:23, 16:32, 2 Kings 3:2, 10:26, 11:18). Lucifer is the false *lord* of this earth. Much of modern Freemasonry, the New Age movement, Theosophy, witchcraft, and Satan worship are inseparable in honoring him. They are united in their commitment to a One-World Order and the Beast system of the coming Antichrist.

Masonry, Catholicism & Modern Mormonism

There is much in common among these three organizations today. Each has a false public face and greater and dark reality at their highest levels. The top leaders in all three are focused upon gain. Albert Pike, the Pope, and Pres. Nelson are lifted up as lights before those they lead, all three men replacing the LORD Jesus as the real light. The dedication of the new LDS Temple in the capital of Roman Catholicism is symbol of unification among those part of the Great Whore Babylon – the Great and Abominable Church, those focused on what Cain, the Watchers, the Nicolaitans, and those in the secret chamber at Nauvoo all desired; sex, power, money, and the honors of men. The top Masons shepherd nearly everything in our government. And these two religious leaders shepherd many people, but into what? **All three use the sheep** rather than feeding them. The secrecy of blood oaths with Satan and each other keeps child sexual abuse, pedophilia, abortion, human sacrifice, and SRA all in place at their higher levels. Their oaths are the mark of Cain, the beast, and the false prophet (Rev. 17 & 19). The deceived, ignorant, and innocent remain aloof of it all. Note the words of those in control of the New World order, the Jusuits of the Catholic Church.

Alice Bailey, wife of 33rd degree Foster Bailey stated, "There is no dissociation between the One Universal Church, the sacred inner Lodge of all true Masons, and the inner-most circles of the esoteric societies . . . Once you get into the Inner, Invisible part of Freemasonry, there is no distinction possible between the true Universal Church [the church of Antichrist], and similar inner-most circles of the other secret societies throughout the world . . . In this way, the goals and work of **the United Nations** shall be solidified and a new Church of God, **led by all the religions** and by **all of the spiritual groups**, shall put an end to the great heresy of *separateness*" (statement by Alice Bailey, The Church in Eclipse, in *Toward the Marriage of the Cross and the Triangle*, p. 476). She added, "The Masonic Movement ... is the custodian of the law; it is the home of the Mysteries, and the seat of initiation. It holds in it symbolism the ritual of Deity, and the way of salvation is pictorially preserved in its work. The methods of Deity are demonstrated in its Temples, and under the All-seeing Eye the work can go forward. It is a far more occult organisation than can be realised, and it is intended to be the training school for the coming advanced occultists" (Alice Bailey, *Externalisation of the Hierarchy*, pps. 511-13).

Pope John XXIII said, "The mark of Cain is stamped upon our foreheads. Across the centuries, our brother Abel was slain in blood which we drew, and shed tears we caused by forgetting Thy love. Forgive us, Lord, for the curse we falsely attributed to their name as Jews. Forgive us for crucifying Thee a second time in their flesh. For we knew not what we did" (see http://www.goodreads.com/quotes/106953-the-mark-of-cain-is-stamped-upon-our-foreheads-across). The "Cain" *principle* or "**mark**" is to mix *religion* with **one's own will**, not God's will. Abel sought God's will.

According to former Roman Catholic Bishop Gerard Bouffard, the Vatican is "the real spiritual controller" of the Illuminati and New World Order while the Jesuits, through the Black Pope, Jesuit Gen. Fr. Peter Hans Kolvenbach, actually control the Vatican hierarchy and the Roman Catholic Church. "The man known as the Black Pope controls all major decisions made by the [White] Pope and he in turn controls the Illuminati. I know this to be true since I worked for years in the Vatican and traveled with Pope John Paul II. The [White] Pope takes his marching orders from the Black Pope as the Jesuits also are leaders of the New World Order, with the task of **infiltrating other religions** and **governments** of the world in order to bring about **a one world fascist government** and a **one world religion** based on **Satanism** and **Lucifer**. People can't imagine how evil and how much destruction they have caused and will cause while, at the same time using the perfect cover of hiding behind black robes and professing to be men of God." Bishop Bouffard left the Catholic Church, becoming a born againt Christian, now living in Canada. He worked for six years as a Vatican priest and passed sensitive daily correspondence between the White Pope and the leaders of the Jesuit Order residing at Borgo Santo Spirito 5, near St. Peter's Square" (Bouffard's statements were made on Greg Szymanski's radio show, The Investigative Journal, see archives, www.gcnlive.com).

"God's Word has given warning of the impending danger; let this be unheeded, and the Protestant world will learn what the purposes of Rome really are, only when it is too late to escape the snare. She is silently growing into power. Her doctrines are exerting their influence **in legislative halls, in the churches**, and in the *hearts* of men. She is piling up her lofty and massive structures, in the *secret* recesses of which her former persecutions will be repeated. Stealthily and unsuspectedly she is strengthening her forces to further her own ends when the time shall come for her to strike. All that she desires is vantage-ground, and this is already being given her. We shall soon see and shall feel what the purpose of the Roman element is. Whoever shall believe and obey the Word of God will thereby incur **reproach** and **persecution**" (statement from the Vatican website, Roman Catholic Church, GC88 581.1).

"The truth is, the Jesuits of Rome have perfected Freemasonry to be their most magnificent and **effective tool**, accomplishing their purposes among protestants" (John Daniel, *The Grand Design Exposed*, CHJ Pub., 1999, p. 302).

Albert Pike looked towards three world wars (letter to Mazzini, Aug. 15, 1871), stating, "We shall unleash the nihilist and the atheists, and we shall provoke a formidable social cataclysm which in its horror will show clearly to the nations the effect of absolute atheism, origin of savagery and the most bloodly turmoil. Then everywhere, the citizens, obliged to defend themselves against the minority of revolutionaries, will exterminate those destroyers of civilization, and **the multitude, disillusioned with** *[corrupted]* **Christianity** . . . will receive the pure light through the universal manifestation of **the pure doctrine of Lucifer** . . . *the destruction of Christianity and atheism.* Both conquered and exterminated at the same time (Albert Pike in Griffin, *Fourth Reich of the Rich*, pps. 71-72). See also Walter Veith, https://www.youtube.com/watch?v=4OdGXCYVtag&feature=youtu.be "The Mark of Cain and The Origin of Freemasonry."

Light Will Shine Upon the Darkness

Opposing the darkness is the saving gospel of Christ, **the gospel of the Kingdom** that **He** will bring to us. God's judgments are coming before this time. Darkness will be revealed openly upon the housetops in the last days, part of His "strange act" (Isa. 28:21; D&C 95:4, 101:95), His "marvelous work and wonder" (1 Ne. 22:8, 2 Ne. 25:17; 29:1, 3 Ne. 29:9). **His word** (in scripture and from His mouth) will by a powerful sword, dividing light from darkness!

> "And the rebellious shall be pierced with much sorrow; for their **iniquities** shall be spoken upon the housetops and **their secret acts shall be revealed**" (D&C 1:3; Matt. 10:27; Luke 12:3).

> "**I** must needs destroy **the secret works of darkness**, and of *murders*, and of *abominations*" (2 Ne. 15:10).

> "And the Lord said: I will prepare unto my servant Gazelem, a stone, which shall shine forth in darkness unto light, that I may discover unto **my people who serve me**, that I may discover unto them **the works of their brethren**, yea, their **secret works**, their works of darkness, and their wickedness and abominations . . . **I** will bring forth **out of darkness unto light all their secret works and their abominations**; and except they **repent** I will destroy them from off the face of the earth; and **I will bring to light all their secrets and abominations**, unto every nation that shall hereafter possess the land" (Alma 37:23, 25).

The Nauvoo and Later Cursings: *Darkness precedes Light*

The LORD excused the Saints in Missouri for not completing the temple in Jackson County, but like the Israelites of Hagai chapter 1, the Saints were cursed for failing to complete the house of the LORD at Nauvoo. They rejected God and His ways in favor of men and their polygamy. William Clayton stated that Joseph "spake on the importance of building the Nauvoo House stressing that the time had come to build it, and the church must either do it or suffer **the condemnation** of not fulfilling the commandments of God" (William Clayton journal, 1842-46). Neither the Nauvoo House nor the Temple were ever completed, for leaders had other priorities. The Saints were thus "**rejected** as a church with their dead" as God said (see D&C 124:31-33, 43-49).

Led by Young and the secret chamber, the cursing of the Brighamite faction of the church came because of **idolatry**, **polygamy**, and other sins, including *priestcraft* and *murder* (see the sins listed in 3 Ne. 16:10 and 30:2). Many wonderful, innocent people, good Latter-day Saints, *suffered* because of the sins of those leading them. Rather than focusing on the living God, His Name, and His "house," leaders and thus the people, like the Israelites under Zerubabbel (Haggai 1:7-11), became focused on other things. The secret chamber **did finish** and dedicate a Masonic Lodge before Joseph was murdered. Young, Kimball, and other brothers in Freemasonry put new things in place inside the Nauvoo Masonic Temple. Though this building wasn't fully completed, leaders were successful in changing "the everlasting covenant" (to do **God's will**, Mosiah 5;5) to a covenant tied to plural marriage. Lorenzo Snow took advantage of it and had four wives sealed to him in one day inside the structure.

Following the murders of the Smith brothers, Young, Kimball, Richards, and Taylor built mansions for themselves with the tithing funds of the struggling Saints. This too is another Young legacy; comfort and honors for those at the top, just like King Noah and his replacement priests. Many suffering Saints coming to Nauvoo from Europe had little by comparison. My relatives were among them. They crossed the plains in 1847 with all they had on one handcart. In Luke 19:46, our LORD said He wanted His "house" to be a "house of prayer," **not** a den of thieves.

The LORD's command to build a "house" (2 times) "to **His Name**" (used 9 times) is found in D&C 124. He provided clear parameters for how this was to procede. Following rejection of Him and the fullness, a cursing followed that has continued for four generations, a **natural result** of the actions of wolves among the sheep (see 3 Ne. 16:10 and 30:2), **not** that of a venegeful, unkind God. We **reap** what we and those who lead us - **sow**. God gave the Nauvoo Saints a second chance after the rejection of His "fullness" earlier at Kirtland (chap. 7). He is waiting with arms strectched out **still**. We read in just eight of the many verses of D&C 124:

> "For there is not a place found on earth that he may come to and **restore again** that which was lost unto you, or which he hath taken away, even **the fulness of the priesthood**...But I command you, all ye *my saints*, to **build a house unto me**; and I grant unto you a **sufficient time to build a house unto me**; and during this time your baptisms shall be acceptable unto me. But behold, at the end of this appointment your baptisms for your dead shall **not** be acceptable unto me; and if you do not these things **at the end of the appointment ye shall be rejected as a church, with your dead**, saith the Lord your God...**If ye labor with all your might**, I will consecrate that spot that **it shall be made holy**. And if *my people* will hearken unto my voice, and unto the voice of my servants [Joseph & Hyrum Smith] whom **I have appointed** to lead *my people* behold, verily I say unto you, **they shall not be moved out of their place**...And it shall come to pass that if you build a house unto **my name**, and **do not do the things** that I say, I will **not** perform the oath which I make unto you, neither fulfill the promises which ye expect at my hands, saith the Lord. For instead of blessings, ye, by your own works, bring **cursings**, *wrath, indignation, and judgments* upon your own heads, by your follies, and by all your **abominations, which you practice before me**...And again...I command you again to build a house to my name...that you may **prove yourselves unto me that ye are faithful in all things whatsoever I command you**, that I may bless you, and crown you with honor, immortality, and eternal life" (see D&C 124:28, 31-32, 44-45, 47-48 & 55).

Following a church conference in 1845 in which Brigham and Heber said the Gentiles **were** being cut off by God for *their* supposed murder of the Smiths, the Josephite detractors of Brigham and his "new order of things" believed **they** (the Brighamites) were the ones being "**cut off**" by God. Joseph Smith III, James Strang, Lyman Wight, Alpheus Cutler, and Charles B. Thompson all made statements accusing the Brighamite faction of the church of being rejected by God, "with their dead," because of Young's polygamy and new doctrines, like his "blood atonement" and "Adam-God theory." They also pointed to the fact that the Nauvoo Temple had **never** been finished (D&C 124:32). Brigham Young made **four** statements clearly showing that he knew the Nauvoo Temple was **never** completed. In just one of them in 1853, Brigham said, "We shall *attempt* to build a temple to the name of our God. This has been *attempted* several times, but we have **never** yet had the privilege of **completing** and enjoying one" (JD 1:277). The other references include JD 4:42, 18:303-04, and 19:220. Joseph had envisioned a "house of the LORD" raised up to the living God. In 1846, just prior to departure of the Brighamite Saints from Nauvoo, thousands of ordinances were performed in the Nauvoo Masonic Temple. Many featured multiple wives being sealed to a single man.

William Week's Untold Story

Although Nauvoo Masonic Temple architect Willaim Weeks and his family were among the 1847 pioneers, entering the Salt Lake Valley in the Jedediah M. Grant Company, Weeks could no longer endure Young's version of Mormonism. History shows that he eventually left Brigham's version of the church in Utah Territory, because he didn't support polygamy and because Young was exerting too much control over him, including pushing him into the practice. By 1848, he left Utah Territory with many other disillusioned families. A party of nine men (Brigham's enforcers) was sent out to bring them all back. Young wanted Weeks to build the first Utah temple, but history shows that he became openly disaffected with Young. Week's nephew said he left the church because, "he did not believe in polygamy," adding also that he "did not like so much *bondage*" under Young's leadership.

The **control** and **conformity expected** under Young's leadership (another Mormon legacy from Young) is visible in a report sent to Young. Those leaving had to have Young's *approval* first. "We take this opportunity to inform you [Pres.

Young] that Brother William Weeks and three other men . . . with their families and teams started for Goodyear's *without* your **knowledge** or **consent**. As soon as we learned this fact we wrote them a brief letter, requesting them to return to this place **immediately** and dispatched it by Brother John Van Cott, our **marshal**, who delivered the same...Their minds are somewhat embittered and we shall do all we can to save them." A ten-day wait brought no results, so on 24 October, "John Van Cott was instructed to take nine men and **bring in** Weeks and company."

On 21 June, John Smith wrote to President Young stating, "William Weeks, William Fields, Brother Sears and families have left the valley **without consent** to return to the [Eastern] states." In the conversation that ensued, President Young told Field to tell Weeks, when he saw him, "that he should have no peace of mind until he came to the valley and **made restitution** for **the wickedness** he had committed." Later, on July 8, Brigham Young sent a message to William, "that the Saints could build a temple without his assistance, although he [Weeks] said they could not." At the October general conference of the church that year, William and his wife Caroline were **excommunicated** by Young from **his** church. Week's daughter Caroline said that the Weeks family eventually went to San Bernardino in 1857. She said her father remained a great admirer of Joseph Smith. "Father always believed in Joseph Smith's church." RLDS records show that a William Weeks, "joined the [Josephite] reorganization in its early days," but "was not prominent in church history" (see J. Earl Arrington, William Weeks, Architect of the Nauvoo Temple, BYU Studies, 1979).

Thousands Flee Utah in the Late 1850's (see also pps. 83-86)

Many of the those *coming* to Utah in the handcart companies and wagon trains were met by those *leaving* the valley, those Brigham Young called "**dissenters**" or "**apostates**." The Salt Lake Valley was *supposed* to be a spiritual utopia. The *Weekly California Express* in Marysville, California announced, "Many dissatisfied persons are leaving the country, and it is estimated that Brigham has lost not less than *five thousand followers* . . . A general stampede seems to have seized the sojourners, and they are leaving the Territory in all directions" (Salt Lake Correspondence, *Weekly California Express,* Aug. 6,1859, 4). Theirs is an untold story. They left Brigham's new kingdom because of **fear**, **control**, **polygamy**, **poverty**, and general **disallusionment** with Young and other things. Many enthusiastic Saints (some 40% of the Saints) had deeded their property to the church, all under the direction of Brigham Young (and part of temple *oaths*). It wasn't enough though. On January 20, 1854 he convinced the territorial legislature to enact a bill that empowered probate judges to **seize property** "left by any deceased or *abscondent persons*" and to give it to the PEF (Perpetual Emigrating Fund). John Hyde, an early European convert and handcart survivor, wrote that this new law was all about **control**. He said, "the object of this policy at the [1854] conference was to prevent Gentiles from purchasing any property *without ecclesiastical sanction*; to hinder departing apostates from taking *any property* from the Territory; to make it the interest of every man to be **submissive**, and thus to more completely **rule** the people . . . Men love riches, and can't leave without means; now, if you tie up the calf the cow will stay"(quote of John Hyde by Mary Powell Sabin, Autobiography, 1926, pps. 10–14, LDS Church Library, in Will Bagley, *One Long Funeral March: A Revisionist's View of the Mormon Handcart Disasters*, p. 71).

As early as March 27, 1853, Brigham Young **ordered** those unhappy in Utah to leave. He stated, "**You nasty apostates, clear out** . . . The moment a person decides to leave this people, he is **cut off** from every object that is durable for time and eternity . . . *Every possession* and object of affection **will be taken** from those who forsake [his version of] the truth, and **their identity** and **existence** will eventually **cease**" (JD 1:83). **Fear** tied to Young's blood atonement doctrine and **how** it was carried out became one of many tools he used to control the Saints in his new kingdom. Blood atonement had close ties to the secret blood-oaths made in Young's modified temple endowment. The first of three penalties tied to breaking this oath was *slitting the throat.* Those who knew "the mysteries," the secrets of the Nauvoo endowment, were particularly suspect. Some knew that leaving Young's kingdom put them in peril.

According to Hicks, It was during Young's 1856-57 Reformation movement that that the doctrine known as "blood atonement" was first preached in Utah Valley by Brigham's older brother John. Hicks stated, "John Young . . . said there were hypocrites in Zion and that [they] were **not fit to live** and the time had come that **their blood would have to be shed** *to save them* and he continued, 'If you should find your fathers or your mothers by the way side with **their <u>throats cut</u>** [as a sign] go on about your business and say nothing about it for it would be all right. **Zion must be purified**'" (*History of George A. Hicks*, [1878], Kent V. Marvin, Mary Anne Loveless & Karen Kenison, in Will Bagley, *One Long Funeral March: A Revisionist's View of the Mormon Handcart Disasters*). This great wickednes points back to Cain's **oath** (see pps. 83-84). It is the "mark of Cain," the "mark of the beast" (Rev. 16-17). Strong's Concordance #226 unites the word "*mark*" with "*sign, token*," and "*oth*" or "<u>**oath**</u>" – the **oath** Cain made with Satan and evil men!

The inflammatory language directed to those who would **not** obey church leaders, by the Young brothers and some Stake Presidents and Bishops, led to a number of **murders** in Utah, like the Potter-Parrish murders in Springville in 1857. Various members of the Parrish and Potter families were outspoken about the abuses they saw in Utah and wanted to leave. Just before their departure, three of the men were **murdered**. One had his **throat cut** (the other two were shot). One escaped to tell about it. The niece of William Parrish (the older man who had his throat cut) said that the people who left Utah, "were mostly a good people, honest, and sincere in their religion, *until*, they saw the wickedness that was being practiced [by leaders]. Many knew nothing of polygamy, until they came there and saw it practiced, and when they were there, there was no way for them to get away. They were too poor . . . and they must **obey the laws of the Church**, and do as they were told and ask no questions" (240 Keir Parrish, Memoir, she moved to San Bernardino after the Mountain Meadows Massacre). Addressing blood atonement, Brigham Young stated:

> "I could refer you to **plenty of instances** where men have been **righteously slain, in order to atone for their sins**. I have seen scores and hundreds of people for whom there would have been a chance (in the last resurrection there will be) if their lives had been taken and **their blood spilled** on the ground as a smoking incense to the Almighty, but who are now angels to the devil... I have known a great many men **who left this Church** for whom there is no chance whatever for **exaltation**, but **if their blood had been spilled**, it would have been better for them, the wickedness and ignorance of the nations forbids this principle's being in full force, but the time will come when the law of [Young's false] God will be in full force." . . .
>
> "All mankind love themselves, and let these principles be known by an individual, and he would be **glad to have his blood shed**. That would be loving themselves, even unto an eternal exaltation. Will you love your brothers and sisters likewise, when they **have committed a sin that cannot be atoned for without the shedding of their blood? Will you love that man or woman well enough to shed their blood?**" . . .
>
> "**This is loving our neighbor as ourselves**; if he needs help, **help him**; and if he wants salvation and it is necessary **to spill his blood** on the earth in order that he may be saved, **spill it**. Any of you who understand the principles of eternity, if you have sinned a sin requiring the shedding of blood, except the sin unto death, would not be satisfied nor rest until **your blood should be spilled**, that you might gain that salvation you desire. That is **the way to love mankind**" (*Deseret News*, Feb. 18, 1857, JD 4:219-20)

Stephen Forsdick, an early handcart company survivor, mentioned the danger of breaking his endowment covenants twice in his journal. "At that time, the Temple [in Utah] had not been built, but all the **secret work** was done in the Endowment House [in Salt Lake City], with **oaths** and **vows of secrecy**. They had [Young's] Destroying Angels to **enforce the penalty** for violating such **oaths**" (Stephen Forsdick, Autobiography, p. 30, LDS Church Archives"). John Hyde, another handcart survivor, stated, "remembering that Margetts and Cowdy were both **'covenant-breaking'** *apostates*; that they were returning to their native country; that they could make many terrible disclosures, and do [Young's] Mormonism much injury in England; that it was Mormon law that **they should die**, and Mormon interest to **kill them**." He added, "Some of the leading spirits of that band [the Danites] are still in Salt Lake City. Although they do not maintain their organization, being generally merged into 'Brigham's **Life** Guards,' yet without the same name, they have performed the same deeds . . .They never threaten what they will not perform, and **fear of risking the penalty** withholds many from apostasy" (John Hyde Jr., *Mormonism,* 102-6 *Mormonism,* see also D&C 64:35-36). Charles Derry, a stalwart Latter-day Saint from England stated that, "there were **oaths** to take that I could not conscientiously subscribe to . . . "I know that polygamy, blood atonement, and their *oppressing* system of tithing, together with the necessity of **honoring** the 'file leaders'... as the Lord's anointed, were **the burden of their teaching**" Charles Derry, *Autobiography of Elder Charles Derry*, Price Publishing Company, pps. 35-42).

Summarizing the reasons why thousands left Utah Territory in the late 1850's, author Polly Aird stated that they included, "**the demands of obedience**, the [false] tenet and practice of **polygamy**, the excesses of **the Reformation**, the perceived **failure of Brigham Young** and other Church **leaders** to set and live up to a high moral standard, and the **insidious** atmosphere of **fear**. It is not surprising that some took the road out of Zion" (see Polly Aird, "*You Nasty Apostates. Clear out*": *Reasons for Disaffection in the Late 1850's*, p. 82, in Journal of Mormon History, vol. 30, issue 2, article 1). Available at http://files.lib.byu.edu/mormonmigration/articles/YouNastyApostatesJMHVOL30_NO2.pdf

Destruction of the Nauvoo Masonic Temple

Joseph and the Saints sacrificed much at Kirtland. They were rewarded with a great outpouring of the LORD's Spirit at the dedication of the house of the LORD at Kirtland. God accepted this house. It was built to **His Name**. He visited Joseph and Oliver inside it a week after its dedication, doing so on Sunday April 3rd, the day of the LORD's resurrection 2,000 years earlier. The "house" at Kirtland remains standing, a monument to a dedicated people and their **love** for God. The building at Nauvoo was cursed, as were the Saints for four generations from Joseph's murder. We are at the end of this cursing, the one addressed in D&C 124, verses 32, 46-48, and D&C 84:49-58. My relatives endured many trials at Nauvoo and later on as a result of decisions made by those leading the church at that time. The Nauvoo (*Masonic?*) Temple was **destroyed** in this *curse*! Early on its roof caught on *fire* (Feb. 1846). Latter its tower was struck by *lightning* (Sept. 1848). One month later an *arsonist* (most likely under Brigham Young's own orders, see pps. 131-32) then *torched* the structure (Oct. 1848). Two years later a *tornado* cast down down three of its walls (1850). And finally, in 1865, the last wall standing was *torn down* by Nauvoo residents. Its stones were then used for other purposes, just like those of Solomon's Temple and Herod's Temple in Jerusalem. All three structures were **destroyed** because of the **idolatry** and other **sins** among the people (this is documented by the LORD in 3 Ne. 16:10, 21:19, and 30:2). It was a sad ending to the "house" Joseph envisioned as "the bride of the Lamb" in JST Revelation 12. Its destruction is perhaps better illustrated by "the *unfaithful* bride" of Isaiah 54.

As we saw in the previous chapter, Brigham Young tried to sell this structure thirteen different times without success! He did not have clear legal title to it as "the Trustee in Trust," simply because he was **not** a legitmate successor via bloodline to the Prophet Joseph, as confirmed in a number of ways, including the judges verdict in the Temple Lot Case. If Young couldn't have the money tied to its sale, then neither would anyone else! And he certainly didn't want it to fall into the hands of James Strang, his primary opponent to lead the church from 1846-48. Evidence clearly shows that Young *torched* the building. It was **defiled** long before he *burned* it down (1 Cor. 3:17; D&C 93:35, 97:17).

Fighting broke out inside the temple when James Strang sent his representative to Nauvoo to raise supporters for him as a possible successor to Joseph. Young sent his supporters to stop the speech, using Chief of Police Hosea Stout (Young's body guard and enforcer) to do it. Earlier Stout struck a man with a rock inside the temple, nearly killing him, as He was a suspected spy - a supporter for someone *other than* Young (perhaps Strang). U.S. Marshalls also entered the temple (including its top floor where the endowment rituals were conducted) to arrest Young and others of the Twelve. They were suspected of *counterfeiting* coins. Perhaps most offensive to the LORD were the many **polygamous** marriages inside it, in rites *falsely* associated with Elijah's sealing power. Elijah used his God-given power to **destroy** Baal worshippers by *fire from heaven* in 1 Kings 18. Baal worship involved *sexual perversion* and child sacrifice. Elijah's "sealing power" was ultimately tied to **salvation** in Christ, not the abomination of polygamy! *Fire* is coming again in our day to cleanse the earth. The bride of the Lamb will also be cleansed and prepared for her husband, or she shall not stand at that day. Ask to know how you can prepare.

When designing the LORD's house at Nauvoo, the Prophet Joseph is said to have first rejected a lightning rod that was to sit atop it. He said, "if God, who now holds the *lightnings* in his hands chooses to direct a thunderbolt against those solid walls and demolish the building, it is his affair" (*Nauvoo Rustler*, 10 March 1891; see Colvin, "Mormon Temple at Nauvoo," p. 2). This was a prophecy from Joseph. A unique weathervane did sit atop the Nauvoo Masonic Temple, featuring an angel in long robes flying horizontally, with a trumpet to his mouth. Above it was a traditional **Masonic** compass and square motif. It was a capstone for the whole structure, marking its focus and the false lord it later came to respresent under Young. Again God decreed, "...whatsoever temple is defiled, **God shall destroy that temple**" (1 Cor. 3:17; D&C 93:35, see also 97:15). The LORD made sure that the Nauvoo Masonic Temple was destroyed, and to every stone, just like the temples of Jerusalem, once they had been defiled by idolatry and other sin.

Inherited Curses – to the 4th Generation

Bishop Glenn L. Pace, counselor in the Presiding Bishopric of the LDS church addressed the growing problem of **secrecy** in Satanic ritual abuse (or SRA) among Mormons along the Wasatch Front. He did so in his "Memorandum" of July 19, 1990, sent to the "Strengthening Members Committee." In it Pace detailed the purposes behind SRA and its mind **control**, **fear**, and **coercion**, all used to **keep secrets** – those tied to Satanism and other **secretive** acts useful for those seeking "**gain.**" The MK Ultra program within the U.S. Government uses similar *programming* for special military personnel, and for covert operatives (like those of the CIA), but without the clear and very real **Satanic** connections. The information Pace brought forth is believed to have led to the removal of **the secret blood-oath**

penalties from the LDS temple endowment later that same year (1990). These **penalites** were borrowed from Freemasonry early on, as the two rites are nearly identical. The **penalties** followed instruction on the masonic *signs* and *tokens* prior to their removal. Originally tied to the marks of the atonement in the LORD's body, these *signs* were *originally* tied to *real unconditional, unfeigned* **love**. Satan took them and perverted them in his way.

In his 1990 memo, Pace first addressed genuine concern for those who were experiencing SRA along the Wasatch Front and elsewhere, and those leaders who had to deal with it without direction from the church. He cited kowledge obtained from sixty Latter-day Saints he had interviewed from 1989-90 that were personally involved in SRA, stating that perhaps *three times* as many could have been interviewed as part of his report, had he not limited his interviews to one per week. Of the 60 victims interviewed, 53 were female, 8 of them children (most were children when the abuse first occurred). The victims were mostly abused by relatives, often their parents. He found that 53 were currently living in Utah, and that 45 of them had witnessed or participated in **human sacrifice**. All witnessed **torture**. Most were diagnosed with Multiple Personality Disorder or some other form of dissociative disorder that helped them deal with their trauma. They were from all layers of Latter-day Saint culture, lay members to various leaders. Portions of his memo are provided hereafter. It is another legacy of our early turning away from God as a people in **idolatry**!

According to Pace, "One of the objectives of the occult is **to create multiple personalities** within the children in order to **keep the secrets**." They live in a society within a society [just like Masonry] and compartmentalize layer upon layer to function normally where possible. Much like the mind-control techniques of various government programs involving *brainwashing*, Pace said children in SRA are, "put in a situation [**fear**] where they believe they are going to die – such as being *buried alive or being placed in a plastic bag and immersed in water.* Prior to doing so, the abuser tells the child to pray to Jesus to save her *and nothing happens* – then at this last moment she is *rescued*, but the person saving her is a representative of **Satan**. He uses this experience to convince her that *the only person who really cares about her is* **Satan**, she is Satan's child and *she might as well become loyal to him.* Just before or shortly after their baptism into the Church, children are baptized **by blood** into the satanic order, which is meant to *cancel out their baptism into the Church.* They will be asked if they understand or have ever felt the Holy Ghost. When they reply that they have, they will be reminded of the horrible things they have participated in and will be told that they have become a son (or daughter) of perdition and . . . have *no chance* of being saved or loved by our Father in heaven or Jesus [hopelessness].

All of this **indoctrination** takes place with whichever personality has emmerged to endure the physical, mental, and spiritual pain. Consequently, there develops within each of these individuals the makings of what I call a civil war. As the memories surface, there are personalities who feel they have given themselves to Satan, and there is no hope for forgiveness. The core person is an active member of the Church, often with a temple recommend. As integration takes place, the civil war begins. Most victims are suicidal. They have been *brainwashed* with drugs, hypnosis, and other means to become suicidal as soon **as they start to tell the secrets**." Continuing threats strengthen this belief...Pace then added, "I'm sorry to say that many of the victims have had **their first flashbacks while attending the temple for the first time**. The occult along the Wasatch Front uses the doctrine of the Church to their advantage. For example, the verbiage and gestures are used in a ritualistic ceremony in a very debased and often bloody manner. When the victim goes to the temple and hears **the exact words**, horrible memories are triggered." The Memorandum asks for advice in how church leaders (Bishops and Stake Presidents) might deal with this complex issue. Pace then concluded, quoting many relevant scriptures, beginning with **Moses 5:29-31**. He said that all of his experiences with the victims of SRA dealt with **secrecy, swearing not to tell, murdering to get gain**, and **power.** He then quoted Moses 5:50-51, addressing how **the secret works of darkness** were spreading throughout the earth in 6:15, adding that they will always be with us in 2 Nephi 9:9, 10:15, and 26:22. Pace also quoted Alma, where God commanded some to not reveal the wording of the **secret blood oaths** in Alma 37:21, 25-28. He addressed Helaman 2:3-4, 8 and the spread of **secret** things within the government (Hel. 3:23). Then, using Helaman 6, he stated that Satan makes these things known to his followers, regardless of what the Prophets do or don't do (Helaman 6:18, 21-26, 39-30).

Pace said, "In light of this scripture, it is **naïve** for us to think these things would **not** exist in our own generation...Surely Satan would not 'pass" on this most important dispensation. In Helaman 8:1 we learn that people in **high places** were members of the Gadianton band and **secret combinations**...We have allegations to indicate that this is true of people **in high places today** (1990, 29 years ago) **in both the Church and the government** who are leading this **dual life**." Pace then quoted Mormon 1:18-19, Mormon 8:27, and Moroni 9:10. Note 3 Nephi 6:27-

29, with similarities to D&C 38. What is described, is the corruption present before the destruction of third Nephi came, and then great light in Jesus Christ. He is our only hope!

> "Now it came to pass that those **judges** had many friends and kindreds; and the remainder, yea, even *almost all* the **lawyers** and the **high priests**, did gather themselves together, and unite with the kindreds of those **judges** who were to be tried according to the law. And they did **enter into a covenant one with another**, yea, even into that **covenant** which was given by them of old, which covenant was given and administered by **the devil, to combine against all righteousness**. Therefore they did combine against the people of the Lord, and enter into a **covenant** to **destroy** them [see D&C 38], and to deliver those who were guilty of murder **from** the grasp of justice, which *was* about to be administered according to **the law**" (3 Ne. 6:27-29).

Pace then added "that we should do something about it," citing Ether 8:20-24 (see Joseph's strong words in D&C 123:7-17). He concluded his memorandum stating, "Over the last eighteen months I have acquired a compassionate love and respect for the victims who are fighting for the Safety of their physical lives and, more importantly, their souls" (Bishop Glenn L. Pace, Pace, portions of his *Memorandum to the Strengthening Members Committee*, July 19, 1990). Two things of note resulted from the Pace Memorandum; (1) There were many changes made to the endowment, including remmoval of the sacred embrace at the veil and **the mutilation penalties** associated with *revealing* the signs, tokens, and oaths; And (2) Bishop Pace was reassigned outside the United States. Little has been done for victims. Some suggest there may be a relationship between the ritual abuse Pace revealed and a special altar spoken of by President Wilford Woodruff in the Salt Lake Temple. Woodruff said Brigham Young told him that "under the pulpit in the west End [of the SLC Temple basement] will be a place to Offer Sacrafizes. [sp] There will be an Altar prepared for that purposes [sp] so that when any sacrifices are to be offered they should be offered there" (Wilford Woodruff's Journal: 1833-1898, December 18, 1857, vol. 5, p. 140). What was the purpose of this special altar?

Chapter Five Summary

It has been 29 years since the Glenn Pace memo. Where are we today? A quick review is useful. In 1831 the LORD prophesied that a **secret chamber** that would rise up in the church. A year later in June of 1832, the first Cochranite converts were brought to Kirtland, bringing their *spiritual wifery* with them. Twelve years later in 1844, Brigham Young and other leaders in the Twelve were practicing it **secretly** in Nauvoo. They utilized the secrecy and oaths of Freemasonry to protect the practice, their positions of power, and create opportunities for other "gain." Joseph and two of his brothers were murdered that the takeover would be complete. Just before his murder Joseph removed his garment and asked the Twelve to do the same (see endnote 16). Forty years later in 1890, the Prophet's firstborn Son, Joseph Smith III, with the help of the Federal Government, helped put legislation in place, leading church President Wilford Woodruff to issue the 1890 Manifesto. Polygamy was beginning to disappear, but much of the pure gospel of Christ, the fuller parts had already been **rejected**, and are now mostly forgotten (chap. 7).

Nine years later in 1898, Pres. Woodruff, troubled by the financial collapse of the church went to bankers gathered at the Bohemian Grove in San Francisco for help. Days later he was dead. Then later in 1923, Pres. Grant (a successful businessman) mortgaged Temple Square with the help of more bankers for additional help (see chap. 6). It was then that Grant made the church a 501c3 "**corporation**," one modeled after the Catholic church and the ancient "corporation sole" were the man at the top makes all decisions without the consent of the people (see p. 204). He also put in place a new "temple recommend" in order for one to participate in the "saving ordinances" of temple. It became an effective financial funnel for the church. The modern temple has diminished the saving role of the blood atonement of Christ, a gift that is free and available to all. His sacrifice is what parted the veil at the crucifixion, allowing us through repentance to return to the Father's presence. This was the whole focus of the ancient Tabernacle and Solomon's Temple; step-by-step progression back into **God's presence**. The Saints today are diverted from this path to light by a substituted focus upon genealogy, work for the dead, and sealing to one another, instead of our sealing to God (Mosiah 5:15) *and* a return to His "rest."

Today (2019) there is now great wealth in the "The Corporation of the President of the Church of Jesus Christ of Latter-day Sainits." Brigham Young's modified endowment as a "**financial funnel**" has been realized. This is contrary to the false statement by Pres. Monson that the church is **not** *wealthy* (and has **no** *paid ministry*, see https://www.youtube.com/watch?v=x39QxMcMpGQ and chap. 6). We learn from Mormonleaks that thirteen of the church's associated LLCs are worth an estimated **32 billion dollars** (2017). In April General Conference of 2018, seven new temples were announced by Pres. Nelson, each costing many millions of dollars. No orphanages or soup kitchens were announced.

In January of 2019 Pres. Nelson and the Twelve made sweeping changes to the temple endowment. I list only five of them; (1) The dramatic changes for women are all tied to political correctness, done to stop the exit of so many from the church, leading to the concern of its future financial stablility; (2) Reference to "the Law of Consecration" [real love for one another] and receiving it "by covenant" has been removed. The Saints are now left with a covenant to give all their time, talents, and resources **to the church**, not to God and those in need; (3) Wording tied to the marriage relationship has been modified, allowing for a potential future false "revelation" on gay marriage (see also endnote 1). It states, "the women of God's kingdom and the men of God's kingdom shall have no sexual relations *except* with those to whom they are legally and lawfully wedded according to His law" (gender was removed); (4) Reference to Satan's "apron as an emblem of my [his] power and Priesthoods" was removed; (5) Reference to finding Satan in this world "striving to lead the posterity of Adam astray with all manner of false doctrine" was also removed. These most recent changes reflect a focus on money, political correctness, and the secrecy of which lord is being worshipped and whose law we are under.

Then in March of 2019 Pres. Nelson made some kind of alliance with Jesuit Pope Francis and the Catholic church just prior to the dedication of the new Rome Temple. Did he bring the church and its members into the "beast" system John spoke of in Revelation chapters 13 and 17? If so, the Saints could be under two binding covenants; (1) The first is to the lord of the green apron and his power and priesthoods; And (2), the second to honor the "**priorities**" of our leaders, those potentially made with the Jesuit Pope Francis and others. Note again Pres. Nelson's words in 2014.

> "Our sustaining of prophets [men calling themselves, "prophets, seers, and revelators"] *is a personal commitment* that we will do our utmost to uphold **their prophetic priorities**. *Our sustaining* is an **oath**-like indication that we recognize their calling as a prophet to be *legitimate and* **binding upon us**" (Russell M. Nelson, 2014, *Sustaining the Prophets*, General Conference Address).

Many believe Pope Francis is the "false prophet" of Revelation 13 and 17. His focus is creating a one world church as part of a new world order. It is a resurrection of the all powerful church of the Middle Ages, one were church and state are combined, and under the false lord who wishes to have dominon over this earth and its people. Robert Muller, the former Assistant Secretary General of the United Nations (and a German new age believer) made the following statement.

> "We have brought the world together as far as we can *politically*. To bring about a **true world government**, the world must be brought together *spiritually*. What we need is a **United Nations of Religions**."

This will be fulfillment of Revelation 13:11-14, tied to the false worship of Lucifer, the anti-Christ and those following him. Those who refuse will be beheaded (Rev. 13:15; 20:4). This path will lead to "the abomination of desolation" and the anti-Christ claiming he is God in the temple at Jerusalem. Recent Popes, but especially Jesuit Pope Francis have been meeting with the heads of men's churches, those part of the great and abominable church, including Muslims, the Christian "Hillsong church, and now the Mormons (recall the "Be One" conference in Salt Lake in June of 2018).

Nephi said there are "**two churches** only" (1 Ne. 14:10), one focused on Christ the Lamb and liberty, and one focused on gain and total control. The "corporation sole" of both the Catholic and LDS church originates in ancient Roman law. It and covenants the Saints make are effective tools to get "gain" an maintain control (see Moses 5:40, Alma 34:35 & Rev. 9:3-4 *versus* Ezek. 9:4, Mosiah 5:15, Rev. 7:2-3, 14:1, 22:4 & D&C 133:17-18). Isaiah spoke boldly of "the drunkards of Ephraim" in the last-days who make **lies** *their false refuge*. He said they "have made a **covenant with death**" (Isa. 28:15), resulting in the binding chains and cords of hell spoken of in 2 Nephi 1:13 and 9:45?

All is not well. The growth rate of the church today is at an all-time low. Many are resigning from the faith in ever increasing numbers. The highest conversion years were during Pres. Benson's leadership. He spoke out boldly against *secret combinations* in saw in Washington D.C. and elsewhere, advocating that **the Saints repent**, get rid of **pride**, and focus on the **the Book of Mormon message** – which is coming to Christ the LORD. President Benson's time in office was cut short, because of his focus on the things of God.

Too many today are throwing out the baby with the bathwater. He is Christ the LORD and His path to the Father. Too many are throwing out the Book of Mormon too, because they believe Joseph Smith was a secretive polygamist. This **lie** has caused many to abandon the message of this important book and its focus upon our LORD. Satan laughs as Christ is diminished as the "saving ordinances" of the temple replace Him. The LORD Himself said He would be *denied, rejected,* and *forsaken.* Mormon added that we would be *ashamed* of Him. Paul taught that **we** are the "temple of the living God" (2 Cor. 6:16-18) and that the "kingdom of God is within you [us]" (Luke 17:21; 1 Cor. 6:15). We can enjoy the gifts and fruits of the Spirit (Eph. 5) in our body, "the temple of the Holy Ghost" (1 Cor. 6:19-20). Seeing our day, Isaiah stated:

> "Woe to the rebellious children, saith the LORD, that take counsel, **but not of me**; and that **cover with a covering**, *but not of* **my spirit**, that they may add sin to sin" (Isa. 30:1). Hosea added:

> "They will not frame their doings to turn unto their God: for **the spirit of whoredoms** is in the midst of them, and they have not **known the LORD**" (Hosea 5:4).

Invite God's **light** and **truth** to be your covering, one of **His Spirit**. God's light is what the symbolic garment points to. All men and women come to the earth with "the light of Christ." It can and should be increased. Sodom and Gomorrah embraced a new corrupt morality. Both cities were destroyed by *fiery* hail raining down from the heavens - for *two* reasons; (1) *sexual perversion* taking hold of the people, and (2) ignoring *the plight of the poor.* Real love for God and one another is what is required to bring about the Zion we long for. The *law of consecration* and *monogamy* are the two higher laws address in D&C 42, entitled "The Law." Both are often rejected. Real love for God and one another must replace all the idols in our hearts. Some 150 million children remain in orphanages today. Sixty million have been killed by abortion since Roe Versus Wade.

The seven new temples announed in 2018 and the dedication of the very expensive Rome Italy Temple (March 10-12, 2019) may be a modern fulfillment of Hosea's ancient prophecy. "For Israel [ancient and modern] hath **forgotten his Maker**, and **buildeth temples**; and Judah hath multiplied fenced cities: but I will send a **fire** *upon his cities*, and it shall devour the palaces thereof" (Hosea 8:14). In March of 2019, President Nelson made an alliance with Pope Francis, calling him "His Holiness." This Jesuit Pointiff leads 1.2 billion Catholics. He, along with the United Nations is seeking a one world religion, the great "beast" of Revelation 13 and 17. **Fire** will be coming again, like that used by Elijah to cleanse the earth of the 450 priests of Baal, in **fire** sent down from heaven. Baal worship in the Bible repeatedly plagued ancient Israel. It has risen up strongly among us today. Baal was lord of thunder, **fertility**, and **gain**. His worship involved **sexual immorality**, the confusion of gender, and **the offering up of innocent children**, in *the exchange of life portion* of *secret blood-oaths* with Satan. The illuminated elite have sacrificed children for millennia, drinking blood that is full of fear-induced hormones that are thought to extend life.

In 2016, when the battle over America's future ensued between Donald Trump and Hillary Clinton, the ancient sign of Baal re-appeared in New York City, one month before the election. This is the same city that in January of 2019 celebrated a new state law allowing for abortions to occur into the end of third trimester, or the 9th month! Buildings were lit up with pink light to celebrate this, similar to when the Supreme Court forced all 50 states to marry same-sex couples in 2015. The sign was erection of the "Arch of Baal" in New York City, through which ancient worshippers passed. Later in 2018, another battle ensued over nomination of conservative Brett Kavanaugh to the Supreme Court. The day before accusations began against him, the same sign appeared again, the erection of another "Arch of Baal," this time at the Washington Mall – directly facing the Capitol building where the battle between light and darkness continues. Our leader must be God, not the arm of flesh. Jeremiah 23, Ezekiel 34, and Isiaiah 1 and 28 reveal that leaders frequently lead the people into idolatry, sexual perversion, and other evils. Let us be wise, discerning "virgins."

In Gary Beaton's "Liberty Charter," he sought to remove the binding chains of hell that at least nine of our founding fathers appear to have put our new country under as Freemasons. This crack in our nation's early foundation was symbolized by the crack of the Liberty Bell. Mr. Beaton's Liberty Charter PDF and his youtube video on this subject are worth your time (https://www.youtube.com/watch?v=gjk10zEMmCY). He and all wise virgins with oil in their lamps recognize light from darkness. They know that our only hope is to hunger and thirst *after* **Righteousness** (Moses 7:45 & 47) and his wise and loving guidance.

Chapter Six

Our Awful Situation

Today's Doctrines

There are many things we *assume* to be true because of *pride*, and because we have placed our *trust* in men, the arm of flesh. WHO we believe determines WHAT we believe. Our idolatry, in making men and the church **our head**, rather than God, has led to blindness and curses (2 Ne. 4:34, 28:31; Jer. 17:5). The Book of Mormon prophets saw our day, and because of their **love of God**, one another, and us, they were granted a view of us in our "**awful situation.**" They wrote about it for our sakes. And that "awful situation" is two-fold in the Book of Mormon; (1) It is to be surrounded by secret combinations that *lie* and *deceive* for gain (Ether 8:24). This then results in another "awful situation"; ignorance of our own **unsaved condition** (Mosiah 2:36-41), and when *the great harvest of souls* is right around the corner. There will be great lamentation in that great and dreadful day.

> "This shall be your *lamentation* in the day of *visitation*, and of *judgment*, and of *indignation* [for]: **The harvest is past**, the summer is ended, and **my soul is not saved**"(D&C 56:16, see also D&C 45:2 & Jer. 17:11).

The LORD has repeatedly invited us to "*awake* and *arise,*" by coming out of Babylon and its idolatry, that we might turn to Him instead. The "**awful situtation**" phrase is used two times in the Book of Mormon as addressed above. Ties to secret combinations are addressed **83** times in the book, more than any other book of scripture. They are not just in governments, but nearly everywhere, including schools *and* churches. Nephi and Mormon said **all** our churches are *corrupted* or *polluted* (2 Ne. 28:11; Morm. 8:36), having *all* gone out of "**the way,**" the LORD's way. Mormon added that too many of us are *ashamed* of Christ.

Lies and Deceptions Given All, Including the Saints

As we saw in chapter 3 (pages 88-89) there are *seven* scriptures where our LORD and others address the sins among us as LATTER-DAY SAINTS. God wants the "**wise**" virgins to "awake and arise and go forth," that more might come out of Babylon to meet **Him**. The sins of our day are listed in all of them with "**lies**" presesent *first* followed by "**deception**" *second* in each of them! They include (1) 3 Ne. 16:10; (2) 3 Ne. 21:18-20; (3) 3 Ne. 30:1-2; (4) Chapter 4, verses 5-6 in the 1833 Book of Commandments; (5) D&C 123:7-17; (6) Ephesians 4:10-14; And (7) D&C 45:57.

The order of the listing reveals that we have been **lied** to and **deceived** by *false shepherds* in governments, schools, *and* churches. Many sheep have been fleeced, others left to wander in forbidden paths. The LORD Jesus is the good Shepherd (see John 14). The sheep enter into His sheepfold only by the door or gate – which is **Him**. He employs no servant there (2 Ne. 9:41). They hear His voice and follow Him. In the seventh scripture below our LORD has given us a *5-part* scripture on how to return to His holy presence. The number 5 is a *covenant* number tied to *life*, *eternal life*, and His "**grace.**" There are many other 5-part sctiptures like it, including D&C 93:1 (perhaps the clearest). D&C 45:7 is about **not being deceived** by *crafty* men who use us. "Children of light" have oil in their lamps.

> "For they [1] that are **wise** [virgins – who "*repent* and *come unto* me"] and [2] have received **the truth** [Jesus Christ as their light], and [3] have taken **the Holy Spirit** for their guide [been "born again" in Christ, receiving the gift and power of the Holy Ghost – "*the endowment of power from on high*" – to guide them], and [4] have **not been deceived** [by the lies, deceptions of those in the secret combinations surrounding us] - verily I say unto you, [5] **they** shall **not be hewn down and cast into the fire**, but shall **abide the day**" (D&C 45:57) of God's return.

Churches Built Up to Get Gain

In 1828 the LORD provided us a simple 5-word summary definition of what His doctrine, gospel, and **church is**; a definition coming prior to April 6, 1830. God's definition of His church is not a financially successful, large corporation, but those wise virgins who have heeded His invitation to "**repent and come unto me**" (D&C 10:67-68, 93:1; 1 Ne. 10:18-19; 2 Ne. 9:23-24; 28:31-32; Jacob 1:7; Alma 5:33-34; Ether 4:7-19; Mor. 7:34; 3 Ne. 9:14, 22, 51; 11:14; 12:19-20, 23-24; 27:5-21; 30:1-2). **His** church is made up of the humble few who love Him with all their heart. They seek **His** will, and obey **His** commandments (see Mosiah 5:5; D&C 10:56). He said those who *don't* repent and come unto me are "**under the bondage of sin**" (D&C 84:50-51). Most churches are "**built up to get gain**" – and "**not unto me.**" The verses before and after the following scriptures provide additional context for them.

1. "For the time speedily shall come that [1] **all churches which are built up to get gain**, and [2] all those who are built up to get **power** over the flesh, and [3] those who are built up to become **popular** in the eyes of the world, and [4] those who seek the **lusts of the flesh** and [5] the **things of the world**, and [6] to do all manner of **iniquity**; yea, in fine, [7] all those who belong to **the kingdom of the devil** are they who need fear, and tremble, and quake; they are those who **must be brought low** in the dust; they are those who must be **consumed as stubble;** and *this is according to the words of* **the prophet**" (1 Ne. 22:23). The Law and the Prophets (the Bible) spoke repeatedly of the coming of a great **Prophet** to the earth. **He is Christ**. Seven times in this same chapter Nephi reveals that Christ is **The PROPHET** we are to follow. See verses 2, 15, 17, 20 (2x), 21, 23. See also John 4:44, 6:14, 7:40 and JSH 1:40.

2. "For it shall come to pass in that day that **the churches which are built up**, and **not unto the Lord**, when the one shall say unto the other: Behold, I, I am the Lord's; and the others shall say: I, I am the Lord's; and thus shall every one say that hath **built up churches**, and **not unto the Lord**" (2 Ne. 28:3).

3. "O ye wicked and perverse and stiffnecked people, **why have ye built up churches unto yourselves to get gain**? Why have ye transfigured the holy word of God, that ye might bring damnationupon your souls? Behold, look ye unto the revelations of God; for behold, the time cometh at that day when all these things must be fulfilled" (Mormon 8:33).

4. "And the Gentiles are lifted up in the pride of their eyes, and have stumbled, because of the greatness of their stumbling block, that they have **built up many churches**; nevertheless, they *put down the power and miracles of God*, and preach up unto themselves *their own wisdom* and *their own learning*, that they may **get gain** and grind upon the face of the poor. And there are many churches built up which cause envyings, and strifes, and malice. And there are also **secret combinations**, even as in times of old, according to the combinations of the devil, for he is the founder of all these things; yea, the founder of murder, and works of darkness; yea, and he *leadeth them by the neck* with a flaxen cord, until he *bindeth* them with his *strong cords* forever. For behold, my beloved brethren, I say unto you that the Lord God worketh not in darkness" (2 Ne. 26:20-23).

5. If *this generation* harden not their hearts, I will establish **my church** among them . . . whosoever belongeth to **my church** need not fear, for such shall inherit the kingdom of heaven. But it is they who do not fear me, neither keep my commandments but **build up churches unto themselves to get gain**, yea, and all those that do wickedly and *build up the kingdom of the devil*—yea, verily, verily, I say unto you, that it is they that I will disturb, and cause to tremble and shake to the center. Behold, I am Jesus Christ, the Son of God. I came unto mine own, and *mine own received me not.* **I am the light** which shineth in darkness, and the darkness comprehendeth it not . . . I will also bring to light **my gospel** which was ministered unto them, and, behold, they shall not deny that which you have received, but they shall build it up, and shall bring to light the true points of **my doctrine**, yea, and the only doctrine which is in **me** . . . Behold, this is **my doctrine**—whosoever **repenteth** and **cometh unto me**, the same is **my church**. Whosoever declareth more or less than this, the same is not of **me,** but is against me; therefore he is not of **my church**. And now, behold, whosoever is of **my church**, and endureth of **my church** to the end, him will I establish upon **my rock**, and the gates of hell shall **not** prevail against them" (portions of D&C 10:46-70).

Look below at the path to destruction. It begins with idolatry and the sins tied to it among us.

The Ten Events Leading to Coming Judgment

1. The people wax strong in **Pride**	Helaman 11:37
2. The voice of the people makes Evil their choice	Mosiah 29:27
3. The people corrupt the laws of Jesus Christ	Helaman 5:2
4. The people cast out the Righteous	Helaman 13:13-14
5. Murder, fornication and other wickedness is pervasive	Helaman 8:26
6. Judges murder the inspired men of Jesus Christ	3 Nephi 6:21,23
7. The wicked seek to establish their king of Lies	3 Nephi 6:30
8. Lawyers, judges & **high priests** make *oaths* with one another & the Devil	3 Nephi 6:21, 27-30
9. Secret combinations manage the Government & Churches	Helaman 6:38-40
10. God destroys corrupt governments and churches	3 Nephi 7:6

King Benjamin said Christ is to be our **head** (see Mosiah 5:8). He lifted the LORD up as his light (3 Ne. 18:24), **not** himself before the people (2 Ne. 26:29). The Saints today are *the unfaithful bride* in Isaiah and other scriptures. Speaking of the day He comes to get His Bride, Jesus said:

> "And at that day, when I shall come in my glory, shall the parable be fulfilled which I spake concerning the **ten virgins**. For they that [1] are **wise** and [2] have received **the truth** [though difficult] and [3] have taken **the Holy Spirit for their guide** [by being born again in me and receiving the Holy Ghost], and [4] have **not been deceived** [by Satan and crafty men]—verily I say unto you, **they** [5] **shall not be hewn down** and **cast into the fire**[with the unfruitful trees of the vineyard] **but** [6] **shall abide the day** [the great and dreadful day of coming judgment upon Babylon]. And [7] **the earth shall be given unto them** for an inheritance…" (D&C 45:56-58).

King Benjamin overcame many obstacles before he established peace among his people. Mormon tells us that using the sword of Laban, he went in "the strength of the LORD" to contend against all the enemies of the people. Significantly, before he could teach "**the way** of salvation of our God," he had to overcome "**false Christs, false prophets, false preachers**," and "**false teachers**." They are the enemy. He was assisted by all "the **holy** prophets who were among his people" (Words of Mormon 1:15-17). The holy ones did not seek acclaim, money, nor power. They quietly sought God, truth, and *the welfare of Zion* generally. They were persecuted by **the false teachers.**

Contrast God's people (below left) with the seven characteristics of the great and abominable church (below right) as found in 1 Nephi 22:23. Note how the LORD defines **His** "doctrine, gospel, and church" (left) in just *five words.* Those embracing His pathway are led to Him - the Tree of Life. King Benjamin wanted his people to embrace **the fullness** of **the way** of salvation, that they might all be **redeemed** of God as he was. They were wise virgins. They looked to Christ for redemption – knowing that He was the father of it. Foolish virgins follow men, those dressed in white (tares among the wheat). They lead others into darkness. Lehi learned this the hard way via experience. Only when he cried out to God for **His mercy** was he delivered from the dreary wasteland (see 1 Ne. 8:5-8). Alma learned the same lesson (Alma chapters 5 & 36). Nephi saw the Tree of Life vision too. He spoke to us, saying, "Behold…

"There are save **two churches** only" (1 Ne. 14:10). Which one are you in?

Moses addressed *Two Ways*" leading to "*blessing* or *cursing,*" *life* or *death* (Deut. 30:1, 15, 19).

The Church of Christ – *built on* **the Rock** (D&C 10:67)

1. **Repent** *and*
2. **Come unto Me**

The Churches of Men & Satan – *built on sand* (1 Ne. 22:23)

1. Seek gain *selfishly*, often at the expense of the people
2. Seek power *over the flesh*
3. Seek to be popular *in the eyes of the world*
4. Seek the lusts *of the flesh*
5. Seek the things *of the world*
6. Seek *to do all manner of* iniquity
7. *Such belong to the kingdom of the devil*

Those under the **bondage of sin** reject God's invitation to come to Him (D&C 84:50-53; 3 Ne. 18:25, 21:20; JST John 6:35, 44 – 45)

Names for God's Church

The Church of the Firstborn or Lamb (1 Ne. 14:10; D&C 76:54; Heb. 12:23)
The Virgin Bride of the Lamb, His wife (Rev. 19:7)
The Kingdom of God (Jacob 2:18)
The Church of Christ (3 Ne. 27:8; 4 Ne. 26)
Holy Church of God (Morm. 8:38)
The True Faith (3 Ne. 6:14) & Fold of God (1 Ne. 15:15)

Names for the other Church

The Great and Abominable Church (1 Ne. 22:23)
The Whore, The Whore of Babylon (Rev. 14:15)
The Kingdom of the Devil (2 Ne. 28:21)
MYSTERY, BABYLON THE GREAT, THE MOTHER OF HARLOTS AND ABOMINATIONS OF THE EARTH (Rev. 17:3)
The Great Harlot (Rev. 17:1-2)

Primary Scriptures

D&C 10:67-68; 1 Ne. 10:18-19; 2 Ne. 28:32; Jacob 1:7; Alma 5:33-34; 3 Ne. 9:14, 20-22; 3 Ne. 12:19-20, 23-24; 30:2; D&C 93:1; Mos. 5:15

Primary Scriptures

1 Nephi 14:10 & 1 Nephi 22:23
Alma 5:38-39 & 34:35

The Way of Life and Salvation
"the doctrine of Christ"

The way of (spiritual) **death**
doctrine of men and devils

God's Word: *Scripture & Pure Revelation from Him*	**Man's word & religion**
The Joseph Smith Way	**The Brigham Young Way**
"**Repent** *and* **come unto Me**" (God) "**I am** the way, the truth, and the life"	"Follow the Prophet" (a man) "We cannot and will not lead you astray"
1. Faith in the LORD Jesus Christ 2. Repentance (confess and forsake sin to God) 3. Baptism in water to bury the old man, a new one arises 4. Baptism by fire to receive the gift of the Holy Ghost 5. Hold on to the rod & partake of the Tree – God & His Love	1. Faith in leaders, the church, and its programs 2. Pride, the church is true, all is well, confess to leaders 3. Baptism in water to join a church 4. To receive a temple endowment one must pay tithing 5. Obtain leadership callings and the honors of men, including a Second Anointing from other men
Focus on God, *His love & a relationship with Him*	*Idolatrous* **Focus on men & their religion:** *churches, leaders, temples*

As we saw in the prior chapters, many lies were inserted into our history to make the Prophet Joseph out to be polygamist. **Lies** and **deception** have been tied to the **whoredom** of spiritual wifery since its first inception among the Saints in Kirtland. These three sins, listed in this order in 3 Nephi 30:2, bore bitter fruit in the Nauvoo era. For a time the polygamists were kept from legal trouble by removing themselves from the United States, until laws of the Federal Government and two Manifestos led to its end. Even then, many continued the practice, lying to cover it up.

One 1886 *Deseret News* story freely admited to the purposeful institutional practice of **lying** among the Saints to protect polygamy. It reveals thirteen different names created to hide the practice. Many of the Saints parsed their words carefully (as lawyers do) to hide what they were doing, as guilty parties were arrested and imprisoned for "unlawful cohabitation" after Woodruff's first Manifesto (1890). **Lying** became **acceptable** to protect what most believed was a higher, "sacred" practice. This **whoredom** was first called (1) "spiritual wifery" at Nauvoo. Later it came to be called (2) Brigham's "new order of things" in Utah. It was also called (3) "the order of the priesthood," (4) "eternal marriage," (5) "the divine order of marriage," (6) "the Holy order of marriage," (7) "living up to your privileges," and (8) "a different view of things." Most of the Saints referred to it as (9) "the plurality of wives," (10) "plural marriage," (11) "celestial marriage" or (12) "the New and Everlasting Covenant." The term "polygamy" (13) was seen as a corrupted form of this doctrine, not the "inspired" practice of the Saints. God and the Prophet Jacob said that many were *excusing themselves* in this "**thing**" because of that which was written of David and Solomon, when in reality it was a "**grosser crime**," an "**iniquity**" a "**whoredom**," and an "**abomination**" (see Richard Van Wagoner, Mormon Polygamy: A History, Second Edition).

Brigham and others convinced the Saints that God had put it all in place first through the Prophet Joseph. Joseph's name was used to **justify** this **strong delusion**. Lies are believed by those holding **idols** in their hearts – when one wants a *thing*. Seeking truth and God's will (rather than our own) helps us receive **truth** in *pure* revelation from Him.

> "And for this cause God shall send them **strong delusion**, that **they should believe a lie**" (2 Thess. 2:11). "A faithful witness will not lie; but a false witness will utter lies" (Prov. 14:5). "The prophets prophesy falsely, and the priests bear rule by their means; and *my people* love to have it so . . . " (Jer. 5:31).

The Joseph Smith re-translation of Ezekiel 14 makes an important change in addressing these idols in our hearts, and the deception that can come from leaders, stating that *when a prophet is* **deceived**, "I the LORD have **not** deceived that prophet . . . they shall bear punishment of their **iniquity**" (JST Ezek 14:9-10). It is a great **lie** that prophets *cannot* lead us astray. Men sin. Men are falliable. God is not. When men speak under the Holy Ghost, there is truth.

Today, many use lies and deception, *or* allow falsehoods to exist without correction. Some do so to avoid damaging truths that might hurt their standing among men, or the image of the church and its leaders. **Loyalty to leaders** and their narrative remains more important today for too many, rather than honesty. Blind loyalty and obedience is the hallmark of idolatry, typical of the Brighamite way we have inherited. It is not God's way of "**persuasion, long-suffering**, and **love unfeigned**," the way leading to real power in **priesthood** (see D&C 121:34-46). Demand by leaders for obedience and conformity from the Saints is an inherited **iniquity** from the days of Brigham Young. God does not work this way. It cuts leaders off from God, and those following these leaders. Brigham Young demanded obedience from the Saints - *and* their tithing. Inspired servants like King Benjamin were focused on God and His love and love for one another. His people were **redeemed** of the LORD.

One former CES employee stated, "In my effort to defend the church from detractors I learned that members get excommunicated *precisely because they publish* **the truth**, *and refuse to adopt lying, deception, or suppression of facts as an ethical standard.* **Loyalty** [to those in charge] **is more important in the LDS church than honesty**. I found this out the hard way while teaching for the Church Education System. Honesty was referred to as undermining the testimonies of the youth, or undermining the authority of the prophets." Such are false prophets (Ken Clark, "lying for the LORD, http://www.mormonthink.com/files/lying-for-lord-ken-clark.pdf).

A war of light versus darkness has raged since the very beginning. Those in the church today who seek truth and share it face an uphill battle. In scripture the list of these courageous ones who spoke out against darkness, calling for repentance, included Jesus Christ, John the baptist, Enoch, Abraham, Noah, Lehi, Nephi, Mormon, Moroni, Alma, Abinadi, Samuel the Lamanite, and Joseph Smith. When the Nephite civilization reached its peak of wickedness just before their great destruction, **the civil leaders** (lawyers and judges) *combined* with the **religious leaders** (the high priests) **against all righteousness**.

> "those **judges** had many friends and kindreds . . . almost all the **lawyers** and the **high priests** did gather themselves together, and unite with the kindreds of those **judges** . . . and they did enter into a **covenant** one with another . . . that **covenant** which was given by them of old . . . **administered by the devil**, to **combine against all righteousness** . . . they did combine against the people of the LORD . . . to destroy them, and to deliver those who were guilty of murder from the grasp of justice . . . and they did **covenant** one with another to destroy the governor, and to establish a **king** over the land, that the land should **no more be at liberty**" (3 Ne. 6:27-30).

Brigham was that king at Nauvoo and in later Utah (see Mosiah 11:1-8). Today the wolves in sheep's clothing are more *subtle* (a word tied to *lying, deception*, or being *crafty*). Many are blind to it. Others want to remain in wonderland. The LORD and His sent prophets saw our plight. God will not suffer that we the Gentile Saints "shall forever remain in that **awful state of blindness**." Through Joseph Smith, He brought forth "*the plain and precious parts of the gospel of the Lamb* which have been *kept back* by that **abominable church**" (see 1 Ne. 13:32). The secret combination keeping this "fullness" back is all about **gain**. They keep the people in darkness and ignorance so that the gain continues coming in. It is a type of slavery. Early on, Alma said, "I did harden my heart, for **I was called many times** and **I would not hear** . . . I went on rebelling against God" (Alma 10:6). Paul said that many in the last-day would **not endure sound doctrine** (2 Thess. 4:2-4; 3:15-16), and that many "will depart from the faith, giving heed to seducing spirits, and **doctrines of devils**." They speak "lies in hypocrisy" (1 Tim. 4:1-2). When the voice of the people chooses ignorance instead of truth, and iniquity collectively, they are ripe for destruction (see verses 19, 27, 32). The great and spacious building they lift themselves up in - will fall. Such follow "the father of lies" (2 Ne. 2:18). The **few** they make fun of below, those holding tightly to the rod – **the word** of God (our LORD, His written word, and pure revelation from **Him**), are the few that will be saved. Their courageous path is marked out by faith and trust in Him.

Jesus commanded us to "**diligently search**" Isaiah in 3 Ne. 23:1-3. Those with the Spirit understand its sobering message is for us, not just ancient Israel. This is why Nephi, Mormon, and Moroni put Isaiah's message in the book. They saw it was focused upon us. Note what just a portion of it says below. God spoke to *the Ephramite Saints of today*:

> "And *all the people shall know*, even **Ephraim** . . . that say in the **pride** and *stoutness of heart*: The bricks are fallen down [the 911 tragedy], but we will build with hewn stones; the sycamores are cut down, but we will change them into cedars. Therefore the Lord shall *set up the adversaries* of Rezin *against him*, and *join his enemies together*; The Syrians *before* and the Philistines *behind* [the enemies of Israel] and **they shall devour Israel** with open mouth. *For all this his anger is not turned away, but his hand is stretched out still.* For **the people turneth not unto him** that smiteth them, **neither do they seek the Lord of Hosts**. *Therefore will the Lord cut off from Israel* **head** and **tail**, branch and rush in one day. The *ancient, he is the head*; and **the prophet that teacheth lies**, he is the tail. For **the leaders** [both *civil* and *religious*] **of this people cause them to err**; *and* **they that are led of them are destroyed** [idolatry]. Therefore the Lord shall have no joy in their young men, neither shall have mercy on their fatherless and widows; for every one of them is a hypocrite and an evildoer, and every mouth speaketh folly. *For all this his anger is not turned away, but* his hand is stretched out still (2 Ne. 19:9-17).

The LORD knows the works of those who turn things **upside-down**, making evil – good, and good – evil (2 Ne. 27:27). We live in such a day. What follows hereafter is a top ten listing of the **lies** we have inherited as Brighamite Saints, **lies** which many have chosen to believe. They are **strong delusion**. In them we see the frailties of men, and the reasons we must **turn** to God, instead of men dressed in white. I love the gospel of Christ set up by Joseph Smith, and the word he brought forth in our incredible scriptures. The changes introduced after Joseph's murder are the problem. For too long we have **assumed** that the changes are good, primarily because we have **trusted in the arm of flesh**. Hereafter, a top-ten list of these **lies** is presented. Pray for truth and understanding, as salvation rests upon it.

The Top Ten Assumptions as Questions

1. Are we as Latter-day Saints saved?
2. Do the "apostles" have a witness of Christ?
3. Do our leaders receive frequent revelation?
4. Are leaders paid for their priesthood service?
5. Is correct doctrine taught in the church?
6. Do changes in ordinances reflect God's will?
7. Is church history accurate? Are we being told the truth?
8. Was all the law of Moses fulfilled?
9. Is the Church True? What is God's definition of His church?
10. Will the Saints be spared in the coming judgment?

Assumption 1: *Are we as Latter-day Saints Saved or Redeemed?*

Too few Saints know what redemption is. I know as I was one of them. Because of pride, I assumed I already had it, as I was baptized, served in many callings, and went to the temple regularly. My works were dead, however. I had not become alive in Christ, in relationship with Him. Without His redemption we do not have the Holy Ghost on a more permanent basis. God provides sanctification that can lead to this gift, not other men and churches. Salvation does not come from works, the church, or temple attendance (2 Ne. 25:23; Eph. 2:8-9), but only by turning our whole heart to God, seeking His mercy, grace, and love. This pathway is laid out in detail in chapter 7.

Assumption 2: *Do the 15 men called "apostles" have a witness of Christ?*

Unlike the early teachings of the Prophet Joseph and Oliver Cowdery, statements by leaders today actually downplay their need to **see**, **know**, and be **empowered** and **sent** by Christ in this life. Thus are they witnesses **of Him**, **for Him**, and **by Him**? Have they put into practice the "**apostolic charge**" of Joseph and Oliver given, the same charge given the first early members of the Quorum of the Twelve, to become actual or "**special**" witnesses of the LORD Jesus Christ while here in the flesh? This "charge" is presented farther below. To receive truth, we must rely *first* on God's holy word in canonized scripture, and that given of Him in *pure* revelation. In an important revelation given to Joseph Smith, Oliver Cowdery, and David Whitmer in June of 1829 - on calling the Twelve disciples of Christ for the first time in this dispensation (Section 18), the LORD said to these three witnesses *and* to us as the Saints:

> "I give unto you a **commandment**, that **you rely upon the things which are written**. For **in them** are **all things** written concerning the *foundation* of **my church**, **my gospel**, and **my rock**. Wherefore, *if* you shall build up **my church**, upon the *foundation* of **my gospel** and **my rock**, the gates of hell shall **not** prevail against you" (D&C 18:3-5).

This is a clear charge from the LORD to rely on His **words** as recorded in *canonized scripture* (approved and voted on [D&C 132 was not approved or voted on]), otherwise hell will rage against them. The LORD next stated that Joseph Smith has been **called** of Him. He follows that by stating, "I command all men everywhere to **repent**." Next He says that Oliver and David (with Joseph) are **called** with the same **calling** as was Paul the apostle (vs. 8 and 9). He then reminds them that He "suffered the pain of all men, that all men might **repent** and **come unto him**," and that coming to Him means doing so in **repentance** (vs. 11 -12). Great **joy** is the result of being forgiven, as expressed by Alma in Alma 36:12 – 30 (where "joy" is mentioned five times, the number for "grace"). Next, God said, "You are **called** to cry **repentance** unto this people" (vs. 14). Bringing just one soul to Christ brings **joy**. Imagine then the great joy of bringing many souls to Him (vs. 15-16). Christ said, "Behold, you have **my gospel** before you, and **my rock**, and **my salvation**" (v. 17). Use it. Verses 18 to 25 clarify other important responsibilities.

Disciples versus Apostles In verses 26 - 27 and 37 - 38, God said that others were to be **called** to "declare **my gospel**" to Gentiles and Jews, and as His "**disciples**" **not** "apostles," as this is a title reserved for those Twelve that God Himself called in the Holy Land 2,000 years earlier. This is apparent with the twelve men Christ called at Bountiful in the Book of Mormon. He called them "disciples" ("followers") **not** "apostles" ("sent ones"). See 1 Ne. 12:9-10, 3 Ne.

19:4, 28:4-10, and John 8:32. The word "apostle" is Greek for a "messenger" or a "**sent one**." After choosing them to be **witnesses of him** spiritually and literally, Jesus said to those to be served of them, "I have **chosen** from among you to minister unto you, and to be your **servants**" (3 Ne. 12:1). Many want the honors of men and to sit in the chief seats. Humble **servants** of the Master, **called** (under's God's Spirit and influence) are to become **chosen** by Christ, and then **empowered** and **sent** by Him too. They are to bear witness that they **know** Him – literally. His humble servants always point others to Him, the light we are to hold up before men (see 3 Ne. 18:24).

In verses 37 to 38, Oliver and David were told by the LORD to "search out the Twelve, who shall have **the desires** of which I have spoken; And by *their* **desires** and *their* **works** you shall know them." As addressed in verses 26 and 27 – their "desire" must be the "desire" to take upon them Christ's **name** with "**full purpose of heart.**" After finding them, Oliver and David were to "fall down and worship the Father in my name" (v. 40). The LORD then provided what qualifies the Twelve, that state of their heart.

> "The twelve are they who **shall *desire* to take upon them my name with full purpose of *heart*"** (v. 27).

This is repeated three times. God says that if they have "this **full purpose of heart**, they are **called** to go into all the world to preach **my gospel** unto every creature. And they are they who are **ordained of me** to baptize in **my name**, according to **that which is written**" (v. 28 - 29). A third time the LORD reminds them to trust in the **written word**.

> "And you have that which is written before; wherefore, **you must perform it** according to **the words which are written**" (v. 30).

Here we see that God's **word** is the standard and foundation for all that is done in His doctrine, gospel, and church! God then speaking to the Twelve, tells them, "Behold, **my grace** is sufficient for you; you must **walk uprightly before me and sin not**." He then added specific duties for the Twelve. They include:

1. "ordain priests and teachers to **declare my gospel**, according to the power of the Holy Ghost, which is in you and according to the callings and gifts of God unto men" (D&C 18:32).
2. "And you must preach unto the world, saying: You must repent and be baptized, in the **name** of Jesus Christ." And then tell them, "you must keep **my commandments** in all things (vs. 41-43). "After you have received this, if you keep not my commandments you cannot be saved in the kingdom of my Father" (v. 46).

In additional scripture, God provided more duties for the Twelve. Some are for the Seventy too, as both are to serve as "traveling missionaries" sent out into the world. Those with an asterisk are addressed in Acts 1-8. They are to be:

3. They are traveling missionaries, proclaiming the gospel, preaching **my word** (D&C 107:23, 35, 38; 124:127, 139-40).
4. They are sent out to open the door of **missionary** labor (D&C 107:35; 124:127; Acts 4:4; 6:7).
5. They are to be **special witnesses** of the LORD's name in all the World (D&C 124:23), revealing His attributes and character, teaching us to "seek His face" (Lectures on Faith 1-7; Acts 1:3-4, 8; 2:32; 3:15; 5:32).
6. They are to **baptize** with water (3 Ne. 12:1, 19:9, 13-14, 20; D&C 20:38-43).
7. They are to lay on hands, inviting others to receive the **fiery baptism** & the Holy Ghost (Mor. 2:2; D&C 20:38-43).
8. They are to **ordain** others (D&C 20:38-43; Acts 2:38; 8:17-18).
9. They are to administer the **Sacrament** (D&C 20:38-43).
10. **Miracles** are to follow the Apostles as a **sign** of the **power** God gave them to, "**heal the sick, cleanse the lepers, raise the dead, cast out devils**" (Mat. 10:8). They aren't just called, but "chosen," "**empowered**" and "sent" out into the world **by God** (not men) to model the behavior of Christ. God said, "**By their fruits ye know them**" (Mat. 7:16; 3 Ne. 14:15-16). Is this occurring today? See Acts 2:1-4, 43; 3:6; 4:31; 5:12, 16; 8:17, 39.

The Important Apostolic Charge

Joseph Smith and Oliver Cowdery "charged" the newly chosen Twelve disciples of their day to become **actual witnesses of Christ**. The apostles in Jerusalem and the disciples in Third Nephi were given the blessing of seeing and touching the marks of the atonement in our LORD's body. They are the "**infallible proofs**" (Acts 1:3) of His love for us. The tokens of the temple are only symbols pointing to them. Speaking to the Twelve, Oliver Cowdery stated:

> "It is <u>necessary</u> that you receive **a testimony <u>from heaven</u> to yourselves**; so that you can bear testimony to the

truth of the Book of Mormon, and **that you have seen the face of God**. That is more than the testimony of an angel. When the proper time arrives, you shall be able to bear this testimony to the world. **When you bear testimony that you have seen God**, this testimony of God will never suffer to fall, but will bear you out; although many will not give heed, yet others will. You will therefore see **the necessity of getting this testimony from heaven**. **Never cease striving until you have seen God face to face**. Strengthen your faith; cast off your doubts, your sins, and all your unbelief; and nothing can prevent you from **coming to God**. Your ordination **is not full and complete till God has laid his hand upon you** [and empowered you]. **We require as much to qualify us** as did those who have gone before us; God is the same. If the Savior in former days laid his hands upon his disciples, why not in latter days? . . . The time is coming when you will be perfectly familiar with the things of God . . . You have our best wishes, you have our most fervent prayers, **that you may be able to bear this testimony, that you have seen the face of God**. Therefore **call upon him in faith in mighty prayer till you prevail**, for **it is your duty and your privilege to bear such a testimony** for yourselves" (HC, 2:192-98).

Fifteen men leading the Brighamite church today *call themselves* "apostles" and "prophets, seers, and revelators" when the LORD did not use any of these terms to describe them. They do not claim to have seen Him, yet they call themselves "sent ones" of the LORD or "apostles." Christ called the first Twelve chosen by Oliver and David "disciples," meaning "followers." God's words in D&C 121:34-35 answers this question.

"Behold, there are many *called* but few are **chosen**. And why are they *not chosen*? Because **their hearts are set so much upon the things of this world**, and **aspire to the honors of men**…" (D&C 121:34-35).

Joseph and Oliver "charged" the new twelve "disciples" to become *actual witnesses* of Christ. In later portions of the D&C, the word "disciple" (in the 1833 Book of commandments) was changed to "apostle" in the later 1835 edition of the Doctrine and Covenants (see http://www.josephsmithpapers.org/paper-summary/discourse-2-july-1839-as-reported-by-willard-richards/1). Men want honor and other gain. God wants men with pure hearts and clean hands, those who will sacrifice their own desires and will to know **His will**, that they might serve Him and others effectively.

The Apostolic "charge" is ignored today as we see in the words of those that call themselves "apostles" hereafter. It is the duty of all "**called**" "disciples" (followers) of Christ everywhere (especially leaders) to become "**chosen**" by Him to receive a witness of His reality. Too many Saints don't believe it is possible for them, or that it is even necessary in this life. This represents a lack of faith in the LORD Jesus and an understanding of the purposes of the gospel. The book of Ether addresses our need to have more faith in Christ. Our LORD IS mighty to save. He can do it, IF WE BELIEVE. To have **unbelief** is a great sin in the Book of Mormon. Unbelief is also believing things that are **not** true.

To be **called** is simply the first step on the ladder to the greater things, **the fullness**. To seek and receive Christ in this life is our calling and birthright. To receive Him (the first gift listed by Him in His listing of the gifts of the Spirit in D&C 46), is to receive Him as "**the heavenly gift**" (Ether 12:8). Many non-Latter-day Saint Christians, Jews, and Muslims are seeing Christ the LORD and coming to **know** Him. Too many Latter-day Saints are in unbelief and are missing out on the whole purpose of religion – to **know** God personally and receive of His love and gifts. Church leaders are in this same category. Too many of them are **not** heeding the Lord's invitation throughout scripture to "**repent** and **come unto me**." He has said that those who do not respond to His invitation **are under the bondage of sin** (see D&C 84:49-52; see also 3 Ne. 18:25; 21:20; JST John 6:35, 44-45). It is a simple and direct statement.

In Moroni 7:31, we read that "**chosen vessels**" of the LORD bear witness of Him. They are "**blessed**" individuals who have obtained "**the testimony of Jesus**" (see Rev. 12:17, 19:10; D&C 46:13-14; 76:51, 101 & 88:4, 74-75). Such have seen Him, felt the marks of the atonement in His body, and have been promised eternal life. In this way they become actual "*special*" witnesses of His reality – **that He lives**! Such have come to **know** the Lord. We all can. Have you? The Prophet Joseph Smith said, "It is not the multitude of preachers that is to bring about the glorious millennium! But it is those who are "**called**, and **chosen**, and **faithful**" (TPJS p. 42).

The Lord's people, and especially those who lead, are to be more than just *called*. They are to become **chosen**, **empowered**, and **sent** by the LORD personally. Too many today are *called* by other men into positions of authority, taking upon themselves various titles to have the honors of men. Few actually become **chosen by God** to obtain more. God addressed being "**chosen**" **by Him** in D&C 95:2-5, 105:33-37, and 121:34-46. The LORD said:

"I design to prepare **mine apostles** to prune my vineyard for the last time, that I may bring to pass *my strange act*, that I may pour out **my Spirit** upon all flesh. But behold, verily I say unto you, that there are **many who have been ordained among you, whom I have called but few of them are chosen. They who are not chosen have sinned a very grievous sin**, in that **they are walking in darkness at noon-day**" (D&C 95:4-6).

Those who reject God's invitation to **repent** and literally **come unto him** are walking in **darkness** and are under **the bondage of sin** (see D&C 84:50-53; 3 Ne. 18:25; 21:20; JST John 6:35, 44-45). They could have "the light of the world" to guide them personally. **True shepherds** seek God, becoming "**chosen**" actual witnesses of His reality.

"There has been a day of *calling*, but the time has come for a day of **choosing**; and let those be **chosen** that are are *worthy*. And it shall be manifest unto **my servant**, *by the voice of the Spirit*, those that are *chosen*; and they shall be **sanctified** [the fiery baptism]. And inasmuch as they follow the counsel which they receive, they shall have **power** after many days to accomplish *all things pertaining to Zion*" (D&C 105:35-37).

Servants of the living God are to be (1) **called**, (2) **chosen**, (3) **empowered**, and (4) **sent** of the LORD Jesus. They are to become **productive trees** in the LORD's vineyard. Such can then (5) "**bear fruit meet for the Father's** [Celestial] **kingdom**" (D&C 84:58). Because too few are coming to the Tree and tasting of its fruit, there is little teaching of how to do it. It is becoming a forgotten doctrine. The same thing occurred in Christ's day. Humble yourself before God, repent, and ask Him specific questions about the sancitification of your own soul.

Brigham Young never claimed to have seen Christ. "I don't profess to be such a Prophet as were Joseph Smith and Daniel; but I am a Yankee guesser" (JD 5:77). Many in the Book of Mormon, however, claimed this witness (see the list on pps. 190-91). Their witnesses were given validity and authority by it. It gives us hope and an example for how we too might obtain the same thing. There is little reason to follow one without this witness. Anciently one followed a true servant of God because they demonstrated "the gifts and fruits of the Spirit." And they openly testified of many of their experiences with the LORD, as did their personal lives. The Twelve today are to bear witness of the reality of Christ, and His love, having experienced it themselves. They are then to reveal their witness openly or as the Spirit directs in teaching others "the way of salvation" of our God. What do our leaders say today?

Statements by Modern Leaders

Elder Boyd K. Packer Pres. Boyd K. Packer of the Twelve was called to the Twelve, first as an Assistant to them. He was surprised by the testimonies of those who called him. He stated, "President McKay explained that one of the responsibilities of an Assistant to the Twelve was to stand with the Quorum of the Twelve Apostles as a special witness and to bear testimony that Jesus is the Christ. What he said next overwhelmed me: "Before we proceed to set you apart, I ask you to bear your testimony to us. We want to know if you have that witness." I did the best I could. I bore my testimony **the same as I might have in a fast and testimony meeting** in my ward. *To my surprise, the Brethren of the Presidency seemed pleased and proceeded to confer the office upon me.* That puzzled me greatly, for I had **supposed** that someone called to such an office would have an *unusual, different, and greatly enlarged testimony and spiritual power.*"

"It puzzled me for a long time until finally I could see that I already had what was required: an abiding testimony in my heart of the Restoration of the Fullness of the gospel through the Prophet Joseph Smith, that we have a Heavenly Father, and that Jesus Christ is our Redeemer...Some years ago, I was with President Marion G. Romney...He told them that 50 years before, as a missionary boy in Australia, late one afternoon he had gone to a library to study. When he walked out, it was night. He looked up into the starry sky, and it happened. The Spirit touched him, and a certain witness was born in his soul. He told those mission presidents that he did not know any more surely then as a member of the First Presidency that God the Father lives; that Jesus is the Christ, the Son of God, the Only Begotten of the Father; and that the Fullness of the gospel had been restored than he did as a missionary boy 50 years before in Australia. He said that his testimony had changed in that it was much easier to get an answer from the LORD. The LORD's presence was nearer, and he knew the LORD much better than he had 50 years before. There is the natural tendency to look at those who are sustained to presiding positions, to consider them to be higher and of more value in the Church or to their families than an ordinary member. Somehow we feel they are worth more to the LORD than are we. It just does not work that way!" (The Weak and the Simple of the Church, Oct. 2007 General Conference.)

Elder Dieter Uchtdorf Elder Dieter Uchtdorf of the prior First Presidency stated, "**You do not need to see the Savior, as the** [ancient] **Apostles did**, to experience the same transformation" (Dieter F. Uchtdorf, "Grateful in Any Circumstance," General Conference, 6 April 2014).

Pres. Dallin Oaks Confronted by one individual with the claim that, "current apostles have no right to run the affairs of the church since they do not meet the New Testament standard of Apostles because they do not testify of having seen Christ," Elder Dallin Oaks responded by saying, "The first answer to this claim is that modern apostles are called to be witnesses of the name of Christ in all the world, Doctrine and Covenants 107:23. **This is not to witness of a personal manifestation**. To witness of the name is to witness of the plan, the work, or mission such as the atonement and the authority or priesthood of the LORD Jesus Christ, which an apostle who holds the keys is uniquely responsible to do" (Elder Dallin H. Oaks, Boise, Idaho, June 17, 2105). Elder Oaks reveals here, that in his view, what is special about his witness - is his assignment within the church – *his calling, not his experience with God or being chosen by Him to receive Him*!

One young person asked Elder Oaks about being "born again' in Christ, like Alma. She asked, "What should we pray for to receive the same testimony if not conversion that Alma the Younger experienced?" Elder Oaks answered, "**I don't think you are likely to have the kind of experience that Alma the Younger had**. Remember he had a miraculous appearance of an angel and really got hit over the head, spiritually. Most of us don't have that kind of experience, but I interpret your question, Heather, as being 'how can we get the kind of testimony that he received.' I don't think we will get it like Paul did on the road to [Damascus] where an angel appeared to him, where Alma the younger had that startling experience. The Lord gives a few of those kinds of experiences and they are recorded in the scriptures to catch our attention and teach us the answer. I've never had an experience like that and **I don't know anyone among the 1st Presidency or Quorum of the 12 who've had that kind of experience**. Yet everyone of us knows of a certainty the things that Alma knew. But it's just that unless the Lord chooses to do it another way, as he sometimes does; for millions . . . of His children the testimony settles upon us gradually. Like so much dust on the windowsill or so much dew on the grass. One day you didnt have it and another day you did and you don't know which day it happened. That's the way I got my testimony. And then I knew it was true when it continued to grow."

The trend away from expectation to have an actual witness of Christ started earlier in 1900, when Pres. Lorenzo Snow exempted a newly called "Apostle" from the "Apostolic Charge," effectively canceling it. This was when businessman Reed Smoot was called to be an "Apostle." He was long regarded as "reliable in business, but [he] has little or no faith" (see Francis M. Lyman to Joseph F. Smith, 17 Apr. 1888, fd 7, box 6, Scott G. Kenny papers, Marriott Library). President Snow blessed him to receive, "the light of the Holy Ghost" so that he could bear testimony of Jesus Christ and Joseph Smith via the Holy Ghost, something all of us are to have. This is not a "**special** witnesses."

Moroni encouraged us to part the veil of our own unbelief, as did the brother of Jared (see Ether 3:13-17, 4:7-8; 12:8 & 12). In God's word (D&C 107 and elsewhere), the Twelve Apostles were and are called to to be continually traveling missionaries, sent out into the world as special witnesses of the reality of the LORD. They were and are to proclaim and teach Christ and His gospel, like the Apostle Paul, baptizing others and laying their hands upon them thereafter, inviting them with power to receive the baptism of fire and the Holy Ghost; an ordinance the LORD Himself then completes (see 3 Ne. 9:20; 12:1; JST Mat. 3:38; JST John 1:28; D&C 33:15).

The last modern leader to publically claim he saw Christ was Elder George Q. Canon. The Book of Mormon prophets, on the other hand, all stated that they saw Christ, so that the people they served would have confidence in their ability to lead them. Why else would or should they follow them? It also provided hope to them - that they too could part the veil to God. Those in the Book of Mormon who stated that they had seen Christ include, Lehi in 1 Nephi 1:9, Nephi in 2 Nephi 11:2, Jacob in 2 Nephi 2:4; 11:3, Lamoni in Alma 19:13, Alma the younger in Alma 27:28 & Alma 36:22, Mormon in Mormon 1:15, the brother of Jared in Ether 3:14, and Moroni in Ether 12:39, along with the multitude and the LORD's disciples in 3 Nephi, some 2,500 people. This is the pattern among the LORD's trusted servants in the Book of Mormon - the foundational document of our faith!

Discerning True Shepherds from Wolves in Sheeps Clothing (wool suits)

As followers of Christ, the average Latter-day Saint has every right, and even a duty, to know if leaders have been "**chosen**" **by God** to receive a **special** witness of him. Instead, some leaders get mad when they are asked this question. Why is this useful? (1) It gives us a reason to listen to them and support them as leaders, as first-hand experience is always the best teacher. It reveals that they know "**the way**." And (2) it strengthens our resolve to experience the LORD and His love ourselves. It would be wonderful to hear them say, "I have seen the LORD Jesus. I know He is real for He has embraced me. I have seen and felt the marks of the atonement in His side, His feet, His hands and wrists. He has sent me to bear this testimony and witness to you, for He lives!" Joseph Smith and Sidney Rigdon bore a similar testimony to us in D&C 76:22-25.

One of the core responsibilities of an apostle is to **lay on hands** – to authoritatively invite others to receive the gift of the Holy Ghost. To do so, they must have first received this gift themselves. Men do not give this gift. Qualified, empowered servants provide an authorized invitation to receive it, via the authority God has given them – through the inspiration of the Holy Ghost. The Lord has revealed how we can know if our leaders are humble followers of Christ (having been "chosen," or at least on this pathway), or if they are wolves in sheeps clothing. The following five scriptures are instructive:

> "...**trust no one to be your teacher** nor your minister, except he be a man of God, **walking in his ways** and **keeping his commandments**" (Mosiah 13:14).
>
> "Beware of false prophets, which come to you in sheep's clothing, but inwardly they are ravening wolves. Ye shall **know them by their fruits**" (Mat. 7:15-16; see also D&C 84:58).
>
> "For it shall come to pass that **the inhabitants of Zion shall judge all things pertaining to Zion**. And liars and hypocrites shall be proved by them, and they who are **not** apostles and prophets shall be known" (D&C 64:38-39).
>
> "But I fear, lest by any means, as the serpent beguiled Eve through his subtilty, so your minds should be corrupted from the simplicity that is in Christ. For if he that cometh preacheth **another Jesus**, whom we have not preached, or if ye receive **another spirit**, which ye have not received, or **another gospel**, which ye have not accepted, ye might well bear with him. For such are false apostles, deceitful workers, transforming themselves into the apostles of Christ. And no marvel; for Satan himself is transformed into an angel of light. Therefore it is no great thing if his ministers also be transformed as the ministers of righteousness; whose end shall be according to their works" (2 Cor. 11:3-4, 13-15; see also Deut. 4:2, 13:5, 18:20; 1 Kings 12:31; Isa. 9:15, 28:7, 30:10; Jer. 2:8, 14:14, 23:11, 16, 28:15; Lam. 2:14, Micah 3:5, 11; Gal. 1:9; 1 Ne. 13:26, 2 Pet. 2:1; 2 Ne. 28:9, Jacob 7:2, Mosiah 11:5, 3 Ne. 18:25, 21:20; Mat. 7:15, 24:24; Titus 1:16, JST John 6:35, 44-45; D&C 10:28, 33:4, 76:98-107).
>
> "And by this **you may know they are under the bondage of sin**, because they **come not unto me**. For whoso **cometh not unto me is under the bondage of sin**. And whoso receiveth not my voice is not acquainted with my voice, and is not of me. And by this you may know the righteous from the wicked..." (D&C 84:50-53; 86:2-3).

Additional Prophet Tests in Scripture

The Bible provides four Prophet tests to determine if a professed prophet is legitimate. They are:

1. Do their prophecies come true? (Deut. 18:15-22)
2. Is their message consistent with God's messages in scripture (Deut. 13:1-5)
3. Do we obey a man of God - a Prophet, or God? (1 Kings 13)
4. Do they seek the LORD and come to Him? Three invitations to come to him include:
   A. "**Awake & Arise** (Mor. 10:31; D&C 117:2; 133:10; Jud. 5:12; Isa. 51:9, 52:1; Eph. 5:14; Prov. 6:9; Hab. 2:19
   B. "**Come follow me**" (2 Ne. 31:12; Luke 9:23, 59; John 10:27, 12:26; D&C 38:22, 100:2).
   C. "**Repent and come unto me**" (1 Ne. 10:18-19; 2 Ne. 9:23-24; 28:31-32; Jacob 1:7; Mos. 26:22-24; Alma 5:33-34; Ether 4:7-19;Mor. 7:34; 3 Ne. 9:14, 22, 51; 11:14; 12:19-20, 23-24; 27:5-21; 30:1-2; D&C 93:1; D&C 10:67-68), and "deny yourselves of all ungodliness" (Moroni 10:30). All must "come unto Christ." It is the whole purpose of any Christian church, and is one of the first statements in LDS Church Handbook of Instructions that I had for a time (there is another more secretive "Handbook" for leaders up the chain).

The LORD spoke to hypocritical Pharisees in His day as those who outwardly kept the law, those who spoke eloquently of God, but had hearts far from Him. This sentiment was addressed to Joseph Smith in the First Vision. They "teach for doctrines the commandments of men" instead of His doctrine. Such are wolves among the sheep, seeking to control them for gain (1 Nephi 22:23). Some have fallen asleep (D&C 86:2-3). The Master said to them:

> "But woe unto you, scribes and Pharisees, hypocrites! for ye shut up the kingdom of heaven against men: **for ye neither go in yourselves,** neither suffer ye them that are entering to go in" (Mat. 23:13).

"Woe unto you, lawyers! For ye have taken away the key of knowledge, the fullness of the scriptures; **ye enter not in yourselves into the kingdom**; and those who were entering in, ye hindered" (JST Luke 11:53).

The LORD spoke of many who speak in His name **in vain** in the latter days, stating:

"And many will say unto me in that day, LORD, LORD, have we not prophesied in thy name; and in thy name cast out devils; and in thy name done many wonderful works? And then will I say, **Ye never knew me**; depart from me ye that work iniquity (JST Mat. 7:22-23, the non JST verse states, "*I never knew you…*").

Coming to **know** the LORD is the reward of the five "wise virgins," those allowed to enter into the bridal chamber with the Bridegroom in JST Matthew 25:10-11 (see also JST Mat. 7:33). The unwise virgins have no oil in their lamps. In the JST versions of these verses, the LORD declares that the unwise virgins had not come to "**know**" Him.

"Afterward came also the other virgins, saying, LORD, LORD, open unto us. But he [the LORD] answered and said, Verily I say unto you, **Ye know me not**" (JST Mat. 25:10-11).

Christ addressed the leaders of the people in the meridian of time as "blind guides," the blind leading the blind into pits (Mat. 15:1). In D&C 86:2-3, the LORD said "the apostles…sowers of the seed…have fallen asleep." The Book of Mormon tells us that the heads of "the seers" have been covered because of the iniquities of the people" (2 Ne. 27:5). Polygamy was clearly one of these "iniquities" in early on. Idolatry, formalism (adherance to the dead works of the law alone), and seeking gain and the honors of men are the focus of too many today (D&C 121:34-35). Isaiah said:

"Hear the word of Jehovah, you who are vigilant for **his word**; your brethren who abhor you, and exclude you because of **my name**, say, Let Jehovah manifest his glory, that we may see cause for your joy! But it is they who shall suffer shame" (Isa. 66:5).

Gileadi's commentary on this third verse is noteworthy. He stated, "Jehovah's servants – "who are of a humble and contrite spirit and who are vigilant for my word" (v. 2) – come under censure by ecclesiastical authorities who feel threatened by their zeal for Jehovah. Such self-righteous "brethren" "abhor" or "hate" their zealous counterparts and "exclude" or "thrust" [them] out" from among them, humiliating them [see also Mormon 8:28]. In the end, however – after it has served Jehovah's purpose of refining his servants and testing their loyalties – their momentary shame (Isa. 61:7) turns into their persecutors' everlasting shame (Isa. 41:11; 65:15). The descent phase of those who are ostracized by abusive authorities thus resembles that of Jehovah's servant, who they similarly "abhor" and accuse (Isa. 49:7; 50:8-9). Both, moreover, follow the pattern of Jehovah himself, who descent phase includes prosecution by unrighteous authorities (Isa. 53:7-9; see Avraham Gileadi, Apocalyptic Commentary of the Book of Isaiah, Hebraeus Press, pps. 422-23). This is exactly what is happening to many good people who love the LORD today. As they choose to follow Him, some are being thrust out. We can "collectively" (as a church) remove the "condemnation" upon us, but it much occur first "individually." Each individual (follower and leader) has the responsibility to "act upon" righteous principles put forth in the divine "pattern" present in scripture and outlined in Article of Faith #13. It must be personalized first, then collectively if we are to become one in Christ and have godliness in our character.

Assumption 3: *Do our leaders receive frequent revelation from God?*

Without pure revelation from our **rock**, our sure foundation Jesus Christ, to guide leaders and regular members of the church, the gates of hell prevail. So says our LORD. He warned us about this in Matthew chapter 16, D&C 10, and other scripture. Speaking to His disciples at Jerusalem, God asked:

"But whom say ye that I am? And Simon Peter answered and said, Thou art the Christ, the Son of the living God. And Jesus answered and said unto him, Blessed art thou, Simon Bar-jona: for flesh and blood hath not revealed it unto thee, but my Father which is in heaven. And I say also unto thee, That thou art Peter, and upon **this rock** [pure revelation from God] I will build my church; and the gates of hell shall not prevail against it" (Mat. 16:15-18).

The fifteen called "disciples" (followers) today are not the foundation of the church, Christ is. They are to be **built upon Him** and **His** principles of righteousness, as is all the body of Christ (Eph. 2:20). God said:

"Behold, this is my doctrine—**whosoever repenteth and cometh unto me, the same is my church**. Whosoever declareth more or less than this, the same is not of me, but is against me; therefore he is not of **my church**. And now, behold, whosoever is of **my church**, and endureth of **my church** to the end, him will I establish upon **my rock** [direct, pure revelation from me], and the gates of hell shall not prevail against them" (D&C 10:67-69).

Silence

Revelation from the LORD is not cited for most changes made in the church since the days of the Prophet Joseph Smith, the early days when revelation from God was common through Joseph. Second Nephi 27:5 says *the heads of the seers are covered* because of the **iniquities** of the people. Though there has been some revelation - because of the LORD's love for his needy people, it could and should be be much more common. It should also be shared with the Saints openly if it has come. Sins like polygamy, idolatry, and unbelief have cut off those who are not seeking God - from His guidance (Psalm 66:18; Isa. 59:2). Thus the gates of hell have prevailed for some four generations.

The first six Presidents of the church following Joseph Smith practiced polygamy. The fifth of these was Joseph F. Smith (Heber J. Grant was the last). He married Levira Annette Clark when she was 16 (the daughter of Samuel Smith [Joseph's brother]). She divorced him seven years later, after Brigham Young directed Joseph F. Smith to take additional wives (he would take six total). As presented below, later as church President, Joseph F. Smith testified before U.S. Congress that he did not receive revelation, adding that the original Twelve were chosen in Joseph Smith's day *by revelation*, whereas those chosen later in his [Joseph F. Smith's] administration, *were chosen by other men in committee.* Moroni saw our day and our "awful situation." Speaking of the powers of darkness prevailing on the earth, causing silence to reign, God provided a prophecy to the Prophet Joseph in 1831. It is tied to the secret chamber rising up in Nauvoo and how to combat it.

> "For all flesh is corrupted before me; and the powers of darkness prevail upon the earth, among the children of men, in the presence of all the hosts of heaven— Which causeth **silence to reign**, and all eternity is pained, and the angels are waiting the great command to reap down the earth, to gather the tares that they may be burned; and, behold, the enemy is combined. And now I show unto you a *mystery*, a **thing** which is had in secret chambers, to bring to pass even your destruction in process of time, and ye knew it not...I say unto you that the enemy in the secret chambers seeketh your lives...but ye know not the hearts of men in your own land" (D&C 38:11-13, 28-29, see also D&C 5:33, 10:6, and 45:57).

Matthew 24:24-26 also addresses secret chambers of darkness. There the LORD addressed **false prophets deceiving** "the very elect" in the last-days, and in places where Christ the LORD "is not" (see also D&C 123:12-15). Because of the choices made, darkness has prevailed for four generations. Fortunately, the veil of darkness is being lifted for those who love God and seek **Him**, both in and outside the LDS church.

Cut Off From God: *Statements on Revelation by Modern Leaders*

Sin cuts us off from God, including idolatry and unbelief. Pure revelation from God, real power in the priesthood, and the gifts and fruits of the Spirit then disappear. Note seven things in scripture that cut us off from God. My favorite is the first; (1) **Not seeking**, **hearing**, and **following** **"THE Prophet,"** who is **Christ** (see 1 Ne. 22:17-25; JSH 1:40); (2) Breaking commandments without **repenting** (2 Ne. 4:4; D&C 56:3; Morm. 3:15; D&C 63:63); (3) **Lust** for one another (Ether 10:11; D&C 42:22-23; 63:13-16); (4) seeking **power** and control over others (D&C 121:34-35); (5) Focusing on **money** (Mosiah 18:24-26, 27:5); (6) Seeking "the **things of the world**, and (7) "the **honors of men**" (D&C 121:34-46). The gates of hell then prevail against us. Being "cut off" from God is an awful situation.

The Prophet Joseph said, "I cannot believe in any of the Creeds of the different denominations, I want to come up **into the presence of God** and learn all things [from Him directly], but the Creeds **set up limits**" (HC 6:57). Joseph added, "The best way to obtain **truth** and wisdom is not to ask from books, but to **go to God in prayer, and obtain divine teaching**" (TPJS, p. 191). The LORD said:

> "I have spread out my hands all the day *to a people who walketh* **not** *in* **my ways**; and their works are evil and not good, and **they walk after their own thoughts**" (JST Isa. 65:2).

Men in the midst of sin, like polygamy, cut themselves off from God. Pres. Joseph F. Smith (polygamist and 6th church president) stated that polygamy was brought into the Utah LDS church by a *revelation* from God (the supposed July 12, 1843, "*revelation*" to the Prophet Joseph). He added that a *revelation* from God also ended it (the 1890

Manifesto of Wilford Woodruff). Neither statement is accurate, reflecting the deception that has accompanied the whoredom of polygamy since its inception among the Saints. Like Willford Woodruff, Joseph F. Smith also provided a "Manifesto" in 1904. Both were "statements," **not** a "thus saith the LORD" *revelation.* Smith's second Manifesto was given just before the congressional hearings began on Reed Smoot, U.S. Senator from Utah, to determine whether he should be seated representing Utah, a state with polygamy. Seeing the Saints and their whoredoms, God listed *lies, deception*, and *whoredoms* in a 1, 2, 3 order in His "top ten" listing of the sins of our day (see 3 Ne. 30:2; see also 16:10).

During questioning about polygamy among the Mormons in 1904 in the Reed Smoot Hearings (Vol.1, p. 483 – just after the second "Manifesto" of Smith was issued), we read various questions directed to President Joseph F. Smith by U.S. Senators, with Pres. Smith's answers following. In response to one of their questions, Pres. Joseph F. Smith said:

> "**I have never pretended nor do I profess to have received revelations**. I never said I had a revelation except so far as God has shown to me that so called Mormonism is God's divine truth; that is all."

Note also below how President Smith described the method for calling new "apostles." It was by the committee decision of men - or "the body," **not** by a "thus saith the LORD" revelation.

Q. Senator McComas: "When vacancies occurred thereafter, by what body were the vacancies in the twelve apostles filled? A. Pres. Smith: "Perhaps I may say in this way: **Chosen by the body**, the twelve themselves, by and with the consent and approval of the first presidency."

Q. Senator Hoar: "**Was there a revelation** in regard to each of them?" A. Smith: **No**, sir; not in regard to each of them. Do you mean in the beginning?" [with the Prophet Joseph Smith]

Q. Senator Hoar: "I understand you to say that the original twelve apostles [time of the Prophet Joseph Smith] were selected by revelation?" A. Pres. Smith: "**Yes**, sir."

Q. Senator Hoar: "Through Joseph Smith?" A. Pres. Smith: "**Yes**, sir; that is right."

Q. Senator Hoar: "**Is there any revelation** in regard to the subsequent ones? A. Pres. Smith: "**No**, sir; **it has been the choice of the body**" [chosen by men ever since].

Q. Senator McComas: "Th**en the apostles are perpetuated in succession by their own act** and the approval of the first presidency? A. Pres. Smith: "**That is right**."

Seniority in the Quorum of the Twelve is now used to determine the next president of the church, **not** revelation from God. God told Jeremiah:

> "For **my people** have committed two evils; **they have forsaken me** the fountain of living waters, and hewed them out cisterns, broken cisterns [imperfect sinful mortal men], that can hold no water" (Jer. 2:13).

Hinckley Interview In a 1997 radio interview, Pres. Gordon Hinckley stated, "Let me say first that we have a great body of revelation, the vast majority of which came from the Prophet Joseph Smith. **We don't need much revelation**. We need to pay more attention to the revelation we've already received" (Pres. Gordon B. Hinckley, "Sunday Interview, Musings of the Main Mormon," Don Lattin, Chronicle Religion Writer, April 13, 1997). God said:

> "...wo unto him that shall **deny the revelations of the Lord**, and that shall say **the Lord no longer worketh by revelation** . . . prophecy . . . gifts . . . tongues . . . healings, or by the power of the Holy Ghost" (3 Ne. Ne. 29:6).

Pres. Kimball's Non-revelation on Blacks & the Priesthood In a 2008 BYU Studies article, we read that the "revelation" on the blacks receiving the priesthood was technically **a non-revelation action**, taken by Pres. Kimball and the Twelve – one they pursued **if they did not receive any direction from the LORD**. And that is what happened, as according to their own words, there was no revelation from God on this matter. In reading the words of this good, sincere man, we see that Pres. Kimball and the Twelve asked God to intervene with a revelation **if they were wrong - in their action that included lifting the ban on blacks having the priesthood**. "He [Pres. Kimball] had reached a decision after great struggle, and he wanted the LORD's confirmation, **if it would come**. They surrounded the altar in a prayer circle. President Kimball told the LORD at length that **if extending the priesthood was not right**, if the LORD did **not** want this change to come in the Church, he would fight the world's opposition" (Spencer W. Kimball and the Revelation on the Priesthood, BYU Studies 47:2, pps. 54-56). Weeks after the priesthood "revelation" U.S. President Jimmy Carter signed a civil rights executive order elimanting tax-exempt status for any organization discriminating against individuals because of race. In Joseph's day Elijah Abel (a black man in Nauvoo) held the priesthood. He was a Seventy. Brigham Young later put in place a ban on blacks holding the priesthood. In 1847, when Brigham Young was informed that a black man in Boston married a white woman, he told the Apostles that *he would have killed both of them if he could* (Quinn, *The Mormon Hierarchy*, Signature Books, p. 660). The Saints and blacks in the church endured much between Brigham's day and 1978, the year the ban was lifted **without** a cited revelation.

Reliance on Scholars According to Elder Ballard, the Twelve and other leaders turn to scholars at BYU and elsewhere when difficult questions arise. In comparison to God's word in pure revelation and scripture, the words of scholars are a sandy foundation. He stated, "When I have a question that I cannot answer, I turn to those who can help me. The Church is blessed with **trained scholars** and who have devoted a lifetime of study, who have come to know our history and the scriptures. These thoughtful men and women provide context and background so we can better understand our sacred past and our current practices" (M. Russel Ballard, Southern Utah Conference, Sept. 2015). Compare this to 2 Ne. 4:34; 2 Ne. 28:31; Jer. 17:5 & Psalm 118:8. Turning to God rather than scholars is a better plan. The ancient Jews held up their Rabbis as their source of knowledge. Joseph Smith said we should go to God for knowledge directly.

Sadly, when one young woman asked Elders Holland and Eyring in March of 2017 about how she might develop a better relationship with God through her prayers, she was told that she should "be modest in her expectations," and that it is "a little bit of a lofty goal" (see minute 38, https://www.youtube.com/watch?v=VZXEtcdVcRA). Their comments reveal the sad reality that *few leaders have sufficient faith to part the veil, or to encourage the Saints to the do the same.* Instead, God's word tells us to look to Him in all things, and to strengthen our Faith in the LORD. In the Book of Mormon we have many examples of those who parted the veil to God because of their **strong faith in Christ**. Their hearts were open and soft, not hard. One of many examples is the Brother of Jared (Ether chapters 3 and 12). When we part the veil to God, it is because of our **faith in Him** (not leaders), followed by His pure revelation to us. The Prophet Joseph stated:

> "Salvation cannot come without revelation; **it is in vain for anyone to minister without it**. No man is a minister of Jesus Christ **without being a prophet**. No man can be a [true] minister of Jesus Christ except he has the testimony of Jesus; **and this is the spirit of prophecy**" (TPJS p. 160).

The LORD lifts the covering over the heads of those that love Him. He desires us to learn how to receive guidance directly from Him, not other men. Too many rely on leaders so they don't have to think and work for these things.

Seeking Gain

Many preach for "filthy lucre" (Titus 1:11), thus God's grace or Spirit does not attend them. When there is priestcraft (2 Ne. 26:29), we are cut off from God. If we shun payment for preaching God's word, the LORD said we can instead, "**wax strong in the Spirit**, having the knowledge of God, that they might teach with power and authority from God" (Mosiah 18:26; Alma 30:32-35). It requires serving from the heart, rather than "for gain" (1 Ne. 22:23). In most scripture, it is clear that payment should not accompany preaching (see 2 Nephi 26:20, 25, 27, 29-31; Jacob 2:13-19; Mosiah 2:14, 18:24-26, 27:5; Alma 1:3, 4:8-12, 30:32-35, 60:36; Hel. 13:28-29; Mormon 8:32-33, 36-41; D&C 38:25-27; 42:29-31; 52:40; 70:14; 83:6; 84:78-86, 103; 105:1-5; Acts 20:34; 1 Cor. 9:18; Jer. 7:6, all of chapter 23; Ezek. 22:25-29; all of chapter 34; Amos 6:1-6; and Micah 3:1-12).

> Mormon said, "...yo**ur churches, yea, every one, have become polluted** because of the pride of your hearts... Why have ye polluted the holy church of God...Why are ye **ashamed** to take upon you **the name of** Christ" (Morm. 8:36-38)? The gates of hell then prevail against us, and unto the fourth generation (see JST Mat. 16:16-19; D&C 10:69, 18:3-6; 2 Ne. 4:32-35; 9:41; Hel. 3:28).

Scripture shows that "watchmen" have often kept the people in the "dark" for the purpose of **gain** of all kinds. They then feed themselves rather than the sheep. Ezekiel 34 and Jeremiah 23 address such shepherds very well. Without revelation from God and the voice of alert watchmen, there is captivity and destruction (see Hosea 4:6; Isaiah 5:13). When watchmen are silent or asleep, the enemy advances. In chapter 34 of Ezekiel we read;

> "Son of man, prophesy against the shepherds of Israel...neither did my shepherds search for my flock, but the shepherds fed themselves, and fed not the flock...Therefore will I save my flock, and they shall no more be a prey;

and I will Judge between cattle and cattle. And I will set up one shepherd over them, and he shall feed them…I the Lord have spoken it…I have broken the bands of their yoke, and delivered them out of the hand of those that served themselves of them."

Scriptures addressing this situation are found throughout Isaiah (chaps. 1 & 28), Jeremiah (chapters 1-23), and other books. They include: Isaiah 1:5, 3:12, 9:16, 22:15-25, 28:1, 3, 7, 15; 19:14 29:10, 56:10, 62:6; Jeremiah 2:8, 13; 5:11-13, 26-31; 10:21; 13:13; 14:14-15; 23:1-32; Ezek. 34:1-3, 8, 22-24, 27; 37:22-28; Hosea 2:16-17, 3:4-5; JST Luke 12:54; JST Matthew 21:55; 2 Nephi 2 Ne. 26:29; 28:3-4, 2, 11-15, 21, 24-25, 31, and D&C 64:38-43; 85:7-9; 89-95; 101:44-61, 90; 124:24-26 101:44-61, 90. Pres. Ezra Taft Benson taught that false prophets pacify and lull people into carnal security (2 Ne. 28:21). Instead of turning to them, we should be turning to God (see Ezek. chap. 14). Pres. Benson added:

> "As watchmen on the tower of Zion, it is our obligation and right as leaders to speak out against current evils – evils that strike at the very foundation of all we hold dear . . . Nevertheless, it was their God-given task, as watchmen on the tower, to warn the people" (Ezra Taft Benson, Conference Report, April 1973, Benson was a President of the LDS Church). Scriptures where watchmen are replaced include JST Matthew 21; D&C 85:7-9, 101:44-61, 89-95, 101:90; 124:24-26; Isa. 22:15-25.

Note our first seven church Presidents and their number of wives. The six following Joseph were all *polygamists.* The first four were members of the secret chamber. The first five were Freemasons.

Joseph Smith, 1	Joseph was a gifted Prophet, Seer, and Revelator, brought forth much scripture, was *anti-polygamy*
Brigham Young, 55	Brigham took power, *made polygamy official church doctrine*, changed other doctrine, etc.
John Taylor, 16	Edited 2 Nauvoo newspapers with five anti-Smith articles, had a *pro-polygamy "revelation"* in 1886
Wilford Woodruff, 10	False Founding Fathers story (St. George Temple), Bohemian Grove visit with death following
Lorenzo Snow, 11	Like Brigham, claimed he had a *pro-polygamy revelation* while on his English mission in 1840's
Joseph F. Smith, 6	Testified before Congress that he was not receiving revelation, the Twelve were chosen by men
Heber J. Grant, 3	A businessman who mortgaged church property without a vote of the church. He incorporated the church in 1923, eliminated the "Apostolic charge" and the Lectures on Faith from the D&C, removed rebaptism and wine in the sacrament, eliminated D&C 132 then put it back in.

The veil of darkness causing silence to reign will soon be thrown down, at least for the righteous and humble. Inspired prophets will prophesy, seers will see visions, and revelators will reveal truths. So says Joel 2:28-32.

Assumption 4: *Are priesthood leaders paid for their service?*

Speaking to His disciples, the LORD Jesus taught, "Take nothing for your journey, neither staves, nor scrip, neither bread, neither money; neither have two coats apiece" (Luke 9:3; 10:4; Mark 6:8; D&C 84:86-87). In one LDS church Pamphlet, we read, "**The true church must have <u>no paid ministry</u>**" (17 Points of the True Church). God commanded that, "there shall be **no priestcrafts**; for, behold, priestcrafts are that men preach and set themselves up for a light unto the world, **that they may <u>get gain</u>** and **<u>praise</u>** of the world, but **they seek <u>not</u> the welfare of Zion…But the laborer in Zion shall <u>labor for Zion</u>**; for **if they labor for money** they shall perish" (2 Ne. 26:25-31). "…all their priests and teachers **should labor with their own hands for their support**" (Mos. 27:4). "And my vineyard has become **corrupt every whit**; and there is none which doeth good save it be a few; and they err in many instances because of **priestcrafts**, all have corrupt minds (D&C 33:4). Especially insightful is Mosiah 18:26. In it we read that God's grace and Spirit are poured out upon those **sacrificing** for God and others in their service.

> "And the priests were **<u>not</u> to depend upon the people for their support**; but for their labor they were to receive the **grace** of God, that they might **<u>wax strong in the Spirit</u>**, having the knowledge of God, that they might teach with **power** and **authority** from God" (Mosiah 18:26).

Though Joseph Fielding Smith, Elder Packer, Pres. Monson, and others have *claimed* that there is no paid ministry in the LDS Church in their speaches, this false claim applies only to low-level church leadership, such as Bishops and Stake Presidents and those in local Wards and Stakes. Pres. Monson mislead the Saints saying, "…**our church has no paid ministry**" (Our Sacred Priesthood Trust, April Conf. 2006). Bishops and Stake Presidents are the lesser face of the institution to the world. Pres. Hinckley stated that living allowances for general authorities "come from…business income and not from the tithing of the people." Business income began, however, with tithing and its interest, thus it too belongs to the LORD (Mat. 25:26-30). Top leaders (General Authorities) **are paid** for preaching, teaching, and other service, via tithing and *the many for-profit businesses* of the LDS church. They also receive other benefits (cars, housing, travel expenses, servants, etc.). Salaries are given the First Presidency, the Twelve, and the Seventy, and most Mission Presidents. It is *called* "a living allowance" (see http://puremormonism.blogspot.com/2014/02/bare-necessities-how-to-calculate-what.html).

The LORD's word in scripture (especially the Book of Mormon) provides much enlightenment on **not** receiving payment for preaching and other service to God (see 2 Nephi 26:20, 25, 27, 29-31; Jacob 2:13-19; Mosiah 2:14, 18:24-26, 27:5; Alma 1: 3, 30:32; Hel. 13:28-29; Morm. 8:32-33, 36-41; D&C 38:25-27; 42:29-31; 52:40; 70:14; 83:6; 84:78-86, 103; 105:1-5; Jer. 7:6, all of chap. 23; Ezek. 22:25-29; all of chap. 34; Amos 6:1-6; and Micah 3:1-12). King Benjamin and Alma the High Priest over the church are two very good examples in the Book of Mormon. Both men **did <u>not</u> depend upon the people for their support**. They spoke out against priests living off of the people or the church. With God's grace, these men were told that they would "**wax strong in the Spirit**, having the knowledge of God, that they might *teach with power* and *authority* from God" (Mosiah 18:26; see also Alma 30:32-35). God's grace and Spirit is withdrawn when there is iniquity and sin among us (as in moral sins like polygamy, see the list p. 193).

Estimated salaries for General Authorities are thought to be $70-100,000 for the members of the Seventy, $200,000 + for the Twelve, and $400,000 + for the First Presidency. In Brigham Young's day, Young and the Twelve **exempted themselves** from paying tithing (while living off it), an exemption remaining in place today. Pres. Hinckley referred to General Authority salaries as a "living allowance." He stated, "I should like to add, parenthetically for your information, that the living allowances given the General Authorities, which are very modest in comparison with executive compensation in industry and the professions, come from this business income [see **for profit** businesses list, p. 6] and not from the tithing of the people" (Pres. Gordon B. Hinckley, Second Counselor in the First Pres., Questions and Answers, October 1985 General Conference, https://www.lds.org/general-conference/1985/10/questions-and-answers?lang=eng The "allowance" for Mission Presidents is generous and includes all living expenses, including funding for family trips, gifts on holidays, maids, cooks, and activities.

Turning to the World - the Bohemian Grove

With the church in deep debt in 1898 (following the Manifesto of 1890), church President Wilford Woodruff turned to outside financial help from the Bohemian Club near San Francisco. Seeking assistance from these powerful financiers, Woodruff served as the main speaker one evening. He died suddenly days later.[26]

Incorporation - *into the Corporation Sole*

The LDS church was incorporated in 1923 during the Administration of President Heber J. Grant. As noted earlier, he changed the status of the church form a "*religious society*" to a 501(c)(3) **corporation** in 1923, making the new organization subservient to the IRS. In its Articles of Incorporation, we read the new name for the church is, "The Corporation of the President of the Church of Jesus Christ of Latter-Day-Saints." This "church" has been officially under the control of the federal government since 1923, a huge secret combination, some calling it "the deep state." In order to protect its tax-free status, church leaders do not speak out on politics or moral issues, nor are they calling the people to repentance (like Abinadi did). Hence there was silence on the 2015 Supreme Court decision forcing all states to now marry gay and lesbian couples. It also explains why the church continues to align itself with LGBTQ issues (three moves in June of 2018 alone, see endnote 1).

Few Latter-day Saints know that the president of this corporation now owns, personally and completely, all the property and assets of "The Corporation of the President." He can sell them or mortgage them anytime he desires, *without* the knowledge or **vote** of "church" membership! Wording in *the Corporation Sole contract* states, "Such real and personal property may be situated, either within the State of Utah, or elsewhere, and *this corporation* shall have power, **<u>without</u> any authority or authorization <u>from the members</u> of said Church** or **religious society**, to grant, sell, convey, rent, mortgage, exchange, or otherwise dispose of any part or all of such property." The LORD said exactly the opposite, "And there shall **not** any part of it [funds] be used, or taken out of the treasury, **<u>only by the voice and common consent</u>**" (D&C 104:71). It is an "awful situation" (Ether 8:24).

The LDS church makes use of a rare mode of incorporation known as "**The Corporation Sole**." It can be traced to ancient Roman law, where the Corporation Sole **was <u>the way to vast riches</u>** for the Holy Catholic Church, which was protected under Emperor Constantine. All financial and other powers were vested in **one man**—the Pope (or in our case, the mortal man many call "the Prophet" or president of the corporation sole). Of necessity or convenience, in that same year (1923), President Grant and his associates took out a $30 million loan [presumably against the tithing income stream], **without** knowledge of the Saints or a vote using the entire temple block in Salt Lake City as collateral. In this secret move, the Tabernacle, the Salt Lake Temple, the Deseret Gymnasium, the Beehive House, and related lands were mortgaged to finance various "business ventures" that today bring in billions of dollars per year. This mortgage lasted into the 1970s. One of the chief financiers of this venture was Chase National Bank.

The shorter public name, "The Church of Jesus Christ of Latter-day Saints" is **merely** a *trademark* name. A trademark is an intellectual property owned by a company; it functions as a commodity that only the owner can legally use. Since 1996 the name "The Church of Jesus Christ of Latter-day Saints" has been **owned** by the corporation's subsidary – "Intellectual Reserve, Inc." In his attempt to bring transparency to and expose the Church's relationship with a certain company to its members, President Harold B. Lee, under his authority as corporation president, amended the Articles of Incorporation in 1973. On December 26 of the same year, 1973, Harold B. Lee **died** of a massive heart attack. Many believe he and President Benson were "removed" as were Joseph, Hyrum, and Samuel (see 3 Ne. 16:10, 30:1-2).

It is well documented that Pres. Grant was more interested in the business matters of the church than developing spirituality in his own life and that of the Saints. Eight years after being ordained an apostle, He stated, "I am greatly deficient in spiritual gifts" (*The Diaries of Heber J. Grant*, 1880-1945, p. 5). Nine years after that, he expressed guilt over his obsessive *business* interests, stating, "I felt that I had been neglectful too much of my time to *business* affairs" (diary entry, Nov. 4, 1889). Pres. Grant's own mother informed him of his reputation among the Saints. He recorded this in his diary, "Mother called this morning and we had a long talk. I learned that it was the opinion of a great many of the Latter-day saints that I was filled with pride and that there was nothing in this [life] that I cared about so much as I did about **making money**. It was the opinion of some that the Lord should remove me out of my place as I was so worldly minded and so full of pride. I had no respect for the poor among the people" (diary entry, July 19, 1889). Note the words of his secretary, the secretary to the First Presidency (John Nuttall). He stated, "Financial matters have more weight with...Heber J. Grant than the things of the Kingdom" (*In the President's Office: The Diaries of L. John Nuttall*, 1879-1892, Signature Books, p. 268). Pres. Grant freely admitted, "I have never prayed to see the Savior" (*The Diaries of Heber J. Grant*, p. 468).

Today the church has many salaried employees beyond the General Authorities, part of many **for-profit** businesses owned by the church. There are some some *thirty* distinct entities; Deseret Management Corporation, Beneficial Financial Group, Bonneville International, Bonneville Communications, Bonneville Interactive Services, Bonneville Satellite, 35 different radio stations, KSL Television Station, Deseret Book, Excel Entertainment, Deseret Morning News, Hawaii Reserves, Polynesian Cultural Center, Laie Shopping Center, Laie Water Company, Laie Treatment Works, Temple Square Hospitality and Temple Square restaurants, Zions Securities Corporation, Ensign Peak Advisors, Farm Management Corporation, Deseret Land and Livestock, Sun Ranch, Deseret Ranches of Florida, Deseret Farms of California, West Hills Orchards, Cactus Lane Ranch, Deseret Trust Company, LDS Family Services, Property Reserves Inc., and Deseret Mutual Benefit Administrators (DMBA).

On May 22, 2018 the church issued a press release through the Mormon Newsroom titled "Church Finances and a Growing Global Faith" in which they state a portion of the church's reserve funds are held in the stock market. MormonLeaks™ uncovered thirteen LLCs that appear to have ties to the church. All of these companies save one filed an SEC Form 13F for year ending December 31, 2017, revealing their holdings in the United States stock market. The most recent Form 13F filing for the other company — Clifton Park Capital Management, LLC (CPCM) — was filed for year ending December 31, 2015. The combined value of each company at the filing of their most recent year end 13F is approximately $32,769,914,00, ot **32 billion dollars**. Gain is centerstage, just like Moses 5:31. See https://mormonleaks.io/wiki/index.php?title=Investment_Portfolios_Connected_to_the_Mormon_Church

Nephi informed us that the churches of men in *our day* are established to "**get gain**" (1 Ne. 22:23). This is the great purpose of secret combinations as addressed in Moses 5 and the Book of Mormon (see Alma 37:21-33, 3 Ne. 6:10-30 & Morm. 8:27-41). God promised that in the last-days, the wrath of God will "be poured out upon the mother of harlots, which is the great and abominable church . . . at that day, the work of the Father shall commence, in preparing the way for the fulfilling of his covenants, which he hath made to his people who are of the house of Israel" (1 Ne.

14:17). Nephi then addressed John the Revelator, who wrote of our day. John's words are "sealed up to come forth in their purity…in the own due time of the LORD, unto the house of Israel" (v. 26). The words of John the Baptist will also come forth to the righteous (see D&C 93). Note also Alma 37:23. There, one with the special name-title Gazelem will rise up in our day. He will use a stone to reveal the secret acts of darkness among us, those among our "brethren." They will be revealed unto the LORD's "servants." Abinadi was such a man. His words inspired Alma to leave the secret combination of King Noah, that he might come to know the LORD (see also Ether 1:1-4). Scripture encourages us to "awake and arise," as the Bridegroom is coming (D&C 133:10). His judgment will come first.

Tithing *& Other Financial Matters*

The purpose of tithing is clearly given us in JST Genesis 14, where Abraham paid tithing to Melchizedek for **one** clear purpose – **to help the poor.** No other purpose (like temples and other buildings) is listed there.

> "And he [Melchizedek] lifted up his voice, and he blessed Abram, being the high priest, and the keeper of the storehouse of God; Him whom God had appointed to receive **tithes for the poor**. Wherefore, Abram paid unto him tithes of all that he had, of all the riches which he possessed, which God had given him more than that which he had need" (JST Gen. 14:37-39).

Of the estimated seven billion dollars collected in tithing *and* profits from the *for-profit* business interests of the church each year, only 3/4 of 1 percent of it goes to humanitarian aid. A number of other Christian churches utilize a higher percentage of their profits to care for the poor. President Monson once explained that money spent on the poor in the church comes completely from **fast offerings**. The portion of tithing spent on the poor comes in the form of the humanitarian aid fund. In 2011, the church disclosed exactly how much money was spent in the preceding **26 years** on humanitarian aid: $1.4 billion. This amounts to $53.8 million per year, or 0.76% of tithing per year. Where does the **seven billion** dollars a year go that comes from tithing and the *for-profit* business interests of the Church (numbers no longer revealed to regular members)? Smith estimates that, "29% of tithing goes to CES, 21% in ecclesiastic and administrative salaries, 14% to temple construction and operation, 11% to chapel construction and maintenance, and 0.76% to humanitarian aid" (see Robert Smith, *Teaching for Doctrines the Commandments of Men*, pps. 72-121, free on-line PDF). One GA has revealed that monthly payments have been made and are being made to the Roman Catholic Church, at or near the top of the beast system of this world for some time (see p. 230 and Revelation 13).

Malachi is the last book of the Old Testament. Our leaders often quote Malachi 3:8 to remind us to pay a full tithing. Too few understand Malachi's real message. Its four chapters are about **the leaders of Israel abandoning God.** They were not offering an acceptable offering to God, a reflection of the state of their hearts. They, as unfaithful priests and leaders of Israel are the bride that becomes unfaithful to her Husband, the Bridegroom Christ. Note the summary below of the four chapters of Malachi. He was the first prophet quoted to young Joseph Smith on the night of the angel's first visit to him on Rosh Hashanah (Sept. 22-23) of 1823.

Chap. 1 The priests practice **idolatry**, the son rejecting his father, **the servant his master** (vs. 6, 10-11).

Chap. 2 **The priests do not provide an acceptable offering** to the LORD of hosts. They have departed out of **the way**, leaving their husband (Christ). The Nauvoo leaders left their first wife for polygamy (vs. 1, 7-8, 14-16).

Chap. 3 God is coming, preceded by the messenger of His covenant. **Who will abide the day**? The priests rob God **by departing from His ordinances, offerings, and Holy Da**ys (vs. 1-3, 7-9, 14-18, Ezek. 22:26).

Chap. 4 **A day of burning** judgment is coming. The Son of Righteousness will come with healing in His wings after the burning. Elijah is sent before this great and terrible day of the LORD, that the hearts of the children may turn to the **promises made to the fathe**rs (1-6, JSH1:37-39; Isa. 11:1, 11-13). See "sealing" chapter 5.

Besides making the church a corporation in 1923, Pres. Grant put temple recommend interviews in place to control who could go to the temple. He then made payment of a full tithe necessary to get a recommend. Brigham Young began this trend earlier, when he increased tithing and exempted leaders from paying it. He also added **total consecration to the church**, as part of the covenant the Saints make in the endowment ceremony, a modification of God's **Law of Consecration**, where we **are to care for the poor among us** and have love one another (clear reference to this law was removed in the January 2019 changes to the endowment). In Mosiah 11 we read about King Noah. Pres. Grant and Pres. Brigham Young are comparable to him. When King Noah and Brigham Young came to power, they immediately raised taxes upon the people. In Brigham's case, it was once the Smiths were gone.

> "And he [Noah] laid a tax of one fifth part [20%] of all they possessed, a fifth part of their gold and of their silver, and a fifth part of their ziff. . .copper. . .brass. . .iron. . .their fatlings. . . and. . . all their grain" (Mos. 11:3).

One month after the Smith's were murdered, Brigham Young and the Twelve changed the law of tithing from 10% or "one tenth of their interest annually" (D&C 119:3-4, 1838) to their new higher standard - "a tenth of all their property and money **[given at conversion]**...and then let them continue to pay a tenth of their income from that time forth." The Twelve didn't pretend this was a revelation from God, only that there was greater need. History shows that tithing coming in from the Saints then fell dramatically. *Punishments* were then put in place to counter this. Sadly, there was no exemption for those who had already paid one-tenth of all their property upon entering the new church.

Note that this combined burden adds up to the 20% "tax" of King Noah (see Mosiah 11). By January of 1845, **the Twelve** re-emphasized "**the duty of all saints to tithe themselves one-tenth of all they possess when they enter into the new and everlasting covenant: and then one-tenth of their interest, or income, yearly afterwards.**" However, **two weeks later**, the Twelve, along with bishops Newel K. Whitney and George Miller, and the Temple Committee, voted to **exempt themselves** from paying tithing at all. This was due to their services to the church. Widows, the fatherless, strangers and Levites (unpaid servants) were the only ones exempt from paying tithing in scripture (Deut. 26:12-13). **Nowhere** in scripture does it say that leaders should be exempt in this sacrifice.

According to Charles Derry (a stalwart English convert who brought his family to Utah Territory in one of the ten handcart companies in the late 1850's) said that the tithing policy of the church was a means of keeping the people poor. He called it *oppression,* stating, "The man that has not sufficient means to provide himself with the absolute necessaries of life, much less having a surplus, is [1] tithed one-tenth of his time and [2] one-tenth of what he raises; also [3] one-tenth of what property he has when he arrives there. Now, I ask every candid mind if this is not the heaviest kind of oppression? Nay, is it not robbery to take the bread from the mouths of those half-naked children, and especially when we understand that this is no voluntary contribution?" He added, "I had spent six years in preaching the gospel without remuneration, and had come to Utah in obedience to the counsel of the authorities." When his bishop learned that Derry wanted to leave Utah, he confiscated Derry's oxen and wagon gears to pay his PEF (Perpetual Emigration Fund) debt. He believed his debt was a tool used to prevent him from leaving. Those wanting to leave had to have a certificate signed by Brigham Young saying he had made settlement on all debt. See Charles Derry, *Autobiography*, pps. 27-28, 45-54, Price Publishing Company, in Polly Aird, *You Nasty Apostates. Clear out: Reasons for Disaffection in the Late 1850's*).

Alma desired to repent of his sins and *iniquities* after Abinadi called all to repentance. He spoke out against payment for leaders, those who preach the gospel of Christ (see Mos. 18:24, 26). Iniquity is defined as serious, premeditated moral sin worthy of punishment, one opposite morality, purity, and goodness. Some say this word is also tied to "lacking equity" due to injustice. In it, one group benefits at the expense of others under their control. The definition of Zion is unity among God's people, those who are pure in heart. There is no poor among them. In Noah's day and today, one group was superior, more worthy, more entitled, and deserving of "the honors of men" (see 1 Ne. 22:23; D&C 121:35; 2 Ne. 28:12-13). They sat in the chief seats. God provided a better way. His Prophet Nephi said:

> "Come unto me all ye ends of the earth, buy milk and honey without money and **without price.** Behold, hath he commanded any that they should depart out of the synagogues, or out of the houses of worship? Behold, I say unto you, nay...None are forbidden. He commandeth that there shall be n**o priestcrafts**; for, behold, priestcrafts are that **men preach and set themselves up for a light** unto the world, that they may **get gain** and praise of the world; but **they seek not the welfare of Zion**...all men should have charity...But **the laborer in Zion shall labor for Zion**; for if they labor for money they shall perish" (2 Ne. 26:25, 28-29, 31).

Tithing is applied differently today than it was in the earliest days of the LDS church (see the two requirements of D&C 119, "a standing law forever" according to the LORD). Originally it was 10% of our excess or interest, after all bills and living expenses were calculated for a family. Today it is assumed to be 10% of our gross or net. The Saints today meet once a year with their Bishops. It is to determine if they are paying their fair share. Pres. Grant implemented temple recommends as a requirement to enter the temple. It revealed if the Saints were paying a full tithing, a way to insure more funding for the church. A better reason to meet with a Bishop once a year would be to determine if one is making spiritual progress on "the way of salvation," especially with regard to implementing the doctrine of Christ in the lives of the Saints. Salvation is the core purpose of Christ's church, as stated in one of the first statements in the Handbook of Instructions.

Obtaining the Things of the World

In the Middle Ages the Catholic church required money to get an ancestor out of purgatory. Today Latter-day Saints must pay a full tithing to go to the temple and do ordinance work to potentially save a dead ancestor. In the Book of Mormon, Christ said salvation is available without money or price (2 Ne. 26:27-29). And rather than orphanages and other aid for the world's 150 million orphans, an elaborate and expensive mall was built in downtown Salt Lake City. It is an embarrassment to many of the Saints, while others love it. At its dedication, all three members of the First Presidency shouted, "Let's go shopping!" The 501-(c)3 tax exempt status of nearly all Christian churches today is thought to be both a carrot and a stick simultaneously, held over leaders of churches. It insures conformity to numerous U.S. Government rulings, including those tied to our continual decline in morality via various Supreme Court decisions. One of the most recent ones forced all 50 states to sanction gay marriage. This important decision was made on **June 26** of 2015, a specific day tied to other important moral decisions in our land, and most of them on this same day. It was the day in antiquity when the "walls" surrounding Jerusalem were "torn down" – representing our walls of morality today. They have come down that the worship of Baal might rise up (endnote 1). It involved idolatry and sexual sin, with child sacrifice. All three are rampant today. See the following:

> http://lds-church-history.blogspot.com/2010/12/lds-history-summary.html
> http://puremormonism.blogspot.com/2012/12/are-we-paying-too-much-tithing.html
> D. Michael Quinn, *The Mormon Hierarchy: Extensions of Power*, chapter 6.

Ancient Israel is a type for modern Israel. The LORD told Ezekiel:

> "Son of man, **prophesy against the shepherds of Israel**, prophesy, and say unto them, Thus saith the Lord GOD unto the shepherds; Woe be to the shepherds of Israel that do **feed themselves**! should not the shepherds **feed the flocks**? Ye eat the fat, and ye clothe you with the wool, ye kill them that are fed: but ye feed not the flock. The diseased have ye not strengthened, neither have ye healed that which was sick, neither have ye bound up that which was broken, neither have ye brought again that which was driven away, neither have ye sought that which was lost; but with force and with cruelty have ye ruled them...As I live, saith the Lord GOD, surely because **my flock became a prey**, and my flock became meat to every beast of the field, because **there was no shepherd,** neither did my shepherds search for my flock, but **the shepherds fed themselves**, and fed **not my flock...** Therefore **will I save my flock**, and they shall no more be a prey; and I will judge between cattle and cattle. And I will set up one shepherd over them, and he shall feed them...And I the LORD will be their God...they shall be safe in their land, and shall know that I am the LORD, when I have broken the bands of their yoke, and delivered them out of the hand of those that **served themselves** of them" (Ezek. 34:2-4, 8, 22-24, 27).

Assumption 5: *Is correct doctrine is taught? Two examples; (1) How do men obtain priesthood? (2) Do we have the Holy Ghost?*

God told his disciples in Jerusalem, and Joseph Smith in the First Vision, that hypocrites and deceivers, "teach for doctrines the commandments of men" and mingle them with scripture (Mat. 15:9; JSH 1). God added that such men deny "**the power** thereof." Two ways we deny the **power** of God is to **not seek God's Spirit, will,** and **influence** in the things we do. This is apparent in (1) how boys and men obtain priesthood today, and (2) and our false beliefs about the Holy Ghost and how it is obtained. Both reveal our current "awful situation."

1. How is Priesthood obtained today? Men in good standing *with leaders* (rather than God), and who reach a certain age (like 12), are *automatically* given the priesthood in the LDS church today, by one who is said to have "priesthood" (it was done by a calling only in the RLDS church). Our "standing" with God, best illustrated by a *loving* **relationship** with Him, is tied to His *trust* in us, via His *foreknowledge* of us and our talents, abilities, and mission. These things are much more important than age or one's standing with a mortal leader. Any "calling" to God's priesthood is by Him via the Holy Spirit in revelation! And any **power** apparent in one's priesthood (healing, raising the dead, casting out evil, etc.) is a gift given only by God. Priesthood power can only be apparent within a **living, spirit-guided ministry**, not one that utilizes age, seniority, a handbook of instructions, or some other order administered by men. The subject of priesthood and its God-given **power** deserves further study (see JST Gen 14 and Alma 13).

2. What is the Holy Ghost and how do we obtain it? All can receive this special special gift of **power**, also called "the endowment of **power** *from on high*," but ONLY from God Himself. This occurs when we are **sanctified** by Him – or when we are "born again" in Christ. There is no other way. Too many today believe they already have this gift when they do not, at least in a more permanent way. Elder Bruce R. McConkie stated that false doctrines are often taught in the church, partly as a test, and partly because of men's weaknesses.

> "I do not know all of the providences of the Lord, but I do know that he **permits false doctrine to be taught in and out of the Church** and that such teaching is part of the sifting process of mortality... True religion is found only where men worship the true and living God. False religion always results from the worship of false gods . . . as Joseph Smith . . . taught, **a prophet is not always a prophet**, only when he is acting as such. **Prophets are men and they make mistakes**. Sometimes they err in doctrine. This is one of the reasons the Lord has given us the Standard Works. They become the standards and rules that govern where doctrine and philosophy are concerned. If this were not so, we would believe one thing when one man was president of the Church and another thing in the days of his successors. **Truth is eternal and does not vary**. Sometimes even wise and good men fall short in the accurate presentation of what is truth. Sometimes a prophet gives personal views which are not endorsed and approved by the Lord...We are all mortal. We are all fallible. We all make mistakes. No single individual all the time is in tune with the Holy Spirit. Wise gospel students do not build their philosophies of life on quotations of individuals, even though those quotations come from presidents of the Church. **Wise people anchor their doctrine on the Standard Works**...[and on Christ]. We do not solve our problems by getting a statement from the president of the Church or from someone else on a subject . . . we have the Standard Works and it is our responsibility to get in tune and understand properly what the Lord has revealed and has had us canonize...**the heads of the Church have the obligation to teach that which is in harmony with the Standard Works**" (letter from Elder Bruce R. McConkie to BYU professor Eugene England, Feb.19, 1981).

It is good to show respect to honorable church leaders. Two of my favorites were Spencer W. Kimball (he attempted to take the gospel to our Native American brothers and sisters) and Ezra Taft Benson (he encouraged us to repent, use the Book of Mormon, and be wary of pride and secret combinations). Like all men, they too were imperfect, but when under the influence of the Holy Ghost, they shared important truths with us. President Spencer W. Kimball pointed out errors in one of Elder Benson's addresses when he (Elder Benson) was part of the Twelve (he later became church President). Pres. Kimball stated that Elder Benson's talk on the "Fourteen Fundamentals of Following the Prophet" was full of **false doctrine** (*it continues to be taught today*). Pres. Kimball refuted it just after Elder Benson delivered it in a BYU Devotional. He was, "concerned about Elder Benson's February 1980 talk" there, and wanted "to protect the Church against being misunderstood as espousing . . . an *unthinking* '**follow the leader**' mentality." Pres. Kimball later required Elder Benson to explain himself to a combined meeting of all general authorities the following week. Additionally, Pres. Kimball asked Elder Benson to apologize to the Quorum of the Twelve Apostles, but they "were dissatisfied with his response." Elder Benson had apparently just bestowed on President Kimball - the thorny crown of **infallibility**. Pres. Kimball was refuting the idolatry tied to the concept that **no man is infallible**.

Receiving the Holy Ghost – *the Promise of the Father*

We must be purified in two baptisms to receive the priceless gift of guidance, known as "the promise of the Father," the "record of heaven," "the unspeakable gift," or "the first comforter." It was the most coveted gift of the twelve disciples of Christ in 3 Nephi 19:9. Satan does not want us to have this or any other spiritual gift, as it is very useful in providing truth, in revealing darkness, false spirits, false prophets, and deception generally. This is why God spoke of the "endowment of **power** from on high" in 1831 in the same Section of the D&C (38) where He addressed "the secret chamber" that would rise up at Nauvoo ten years later (chap. 5). Satan wants us to remain in ignornce and darkness. In most scriptures using the phrase "an endowment of **power** *from on high*," they are addressing the unspeakable *gift* and **power** of the Holy Ghost (see Luke 24:49; Acts 1:4; D&C 43:15-16; 95:8-9 & 105:10-12).

Only those cleansed from all sin in the holy blood of Christ receive this unspeakable gift. Few eight-year olds exhibit sincere remorse for sins committed, and specifically the *broken heart* and *contrite spirit* the LORD has asked us to offer Him as our sacrifice. Most often 8-year olds are baptized for the purpose of joining the church, rather than **coming unto Christ in sincere repentance**. This is one reason why having the Holy Ghost is so rare. It is gifted by God as part of entering His church. And note that only God actually gives this gift to us, not man (see D&C 33:15; 3 Ne. 9:20; 12:1; 2 Ne. 31:12; 3 Ne. 11:35; JST Mat. 3:38; JST Luke 3:16; JST John 1:28; 15:26). Those performing the confirmation with priesthood authority invite others to receive it. The authorized diciples of Christ in Third Nephi were "called," "chosen" and "empowered" by Him to invite the baptism of fire and Holy Ghost to come upon others who were prepared to receive it. They did so with real authority and power. It is lacking today (see chap. 7). Teaching on the Holy Ghost was originally provided by the Prophet Joseph Smith in the School of the Prophets, and specifically in Lecture on Faith #5. Confirmation is a symbolic "inviting" ordinance done by imperfect men on earth, to symbolize the real gifting of power in the Holy Ghost by God after **He** baptizes us in His fiery Spirit – to cleanse us from all sin. Our sins are thus remitted. This makes us sufficiently clean to receive a greater portion of His influence, His mind, and His Spirit, along with that of the Father, as they are **One**. The Holy Ghost or Spirit is an intermediate transmitter of their light and influence. It is the center post of the "Tree" (of Life and Spirit) or Menorrah in the ancient Tabernacle and Temple Solomon built.

According to Lecture on Faith 5, the Holy Ghost or more specifically "the Holy Spirit" is **the unified mind of the Father and the Son**. False ideas about the Holy Ghost taught today originated in a public statement by Apostle Orson Hyde, as quoted in D&C 130:22 (addressed hereafter). It has since become the official doctrine of the Holy Ghost in the church. God alone provides access "to the unified mind of the Father and the Son," through the transmission of the Holy Ghost or Holy Spirit, after one is first cleansed and purified from all sin in God's fiery baptism of us (3 Ne. 9:20, 12:1; D&C 33:15). It is a precious, priceless, unspeakable gift - to have access to the unified mind of both the Father and the Son. They are One. They are God (along with Mother). We desperately need this pure form of revelation from them today. The LORD told Peter, "upon this rock [Christ the LORD] I will build my church, and the gates of hell shall not prevail against it" (JST Mat. 16:16-19). We are to rely on Him as "the stone of Israel" (Gen. 49:24; D&C 50:44), the "chief cornerstone" (Eph. 2:20), the "stone the builders refused [rejected]" (Psalm 118:22). The same is become "the head of the corner" (Mat. 21:42). We are to rely on Christ and the Father for revelation through the Holy Spirit or Holy Ghost. Jesus is the Light of the World, providing direction, counsel, light and knowledge via direct revelation to each of us, if we will seek **Him** and **His will**. He as our Savior is the power behind all things of note in His church. Helaman, father of the great missionaries Nephi and Lehi, taught:

> "And now, my sons, remember, remember that it is upon **the rock** of our Redeemer, who is Christ, the Son of God, that ye must **build your foundation**; that when the devil shall send forth his mighty winds, yea, his shafts in the whirlwind, yea, when all his hail and his mighty storms shall beat upon you, it shall have no power over you to drag you down to the gulf of misery and endless wo, because of **the rock** upon which ye are built, which is a sure foundation, a foundation whereon if men build they cannot fall" (Helaman 5:12).

Our God also provides us "**living waters**," a symbol for the Spirit. Broken, imperfect men provide stagnant water by comparison, for we are broken, imperfect cisterns. Jeremiah, speaking on behalf of the Lord, said:

> "For **my people** have committed two evils; **they have forsaken me** the fountain of living waters, and hewed them out cisterns, broken cisterns, that can hold no water" (Jer. 2:13). Man is that broken cistern.

Seeking God's word above that of men helps us avoid deception. Three scriptures are worth repeating here:

> "For you shall live by every word that proceedeth forth from **the mouth of God** [not man]. For the word of the Lord is truth, and whatsoever is truth is light, and whatsoever is light is Spirit, even the Spirit of Jesus Christ. And the Spirit giveth light to every man that cometh into the world; and the Spirit enlighteneth every man through the world, that hearkeneth to the voice of the Spirit. And every one that hearkeneth to the voice of the Spirit cometh unto God, even the Father" (D&C 84:44-47; see also Mat. 4:4; 2 Ne. 32:1-6).

> "And w**hoso treasureth up my word**, shall **not be deceived**" (JST Mat. 1:37). He added, "If ye continue in my word, then are ye my disciples indeed; And ye shall know the truth, and the truth shall make you free" (John 8:32).

When men seek the desires of their hearts, rather than God's will, they often get what they desire, and often this is deception within false revelation (see Prov. 23:7, Isa. 66:2-4, Ezek. 14:1-11, 2 Thess. 2:10-12, James 4:3, Jacob 4:14, Alma 29:4, and Morm. 9:28). Pure revelation from God is the iron rod we must individually hold on to. Scripture repeatedly reveals that men who depend upon their own wisdom, and the desires of their hearts - are lead astray. They are then given "**strong delusion**," especially if carnal desires within rule us (2 Thes. 2:10-12). This is what happened to Nicholas and the Nicolaitans, and Brigham Young and those following him.

Origin of Current Holy Ghost Doctrine

Research in the Joseph Smith Papers Project (BYU) reveals that our incorrect definition for the Holy Ghost today comes from D&C 130:22. Verse 22 is not scripture in the traditional sense (not a revelation from God through Joseph Smith), but instead a record of incorrect teaching by Elder Orson Hyde. It was added to our canon of scripture in 1876, **35 years after** Joseph Smith placed the Lectures on Faith in the Doctrine and Covenants. Research reveals that the Prophet Joseph was uncomfortable with Elder Hyde's summary of his teachings when he first heard them. Joseph corrected him in private afterwards. Sadly, Hyde's summary has become the **definition** of the Father, Son, and Holy Ghost in the LDS church today, pre-empting and negating other verses of scripture in our canon and other teachings by Joseph Smith. It reads.

> "The Father has a body of flesh and bone as tangible as man's; the Son also; but the Holy Ghost has not a body of flesh and bones, but is a personage of Spirit. Were it not so, the Holy Ghost could not dwell in us" (D&C 130:22, incorrect teaching by Elder Orson Hyde).

Nowhere in D&C 130 is there a statement by God or Joseph that this verse is **the** definition of the Godhead, whereas Lecture 5 of *The Lectures on Faith* lay out what the Godhead is (*The Lectures on Faith* were taken out of the D&C in 1921). A better, more accurate scriptural definition of the Holy Ghost is easily obtained by scanning all references for the Holy Ghost in the Index at the back of the D&C. Verse 22 of D&C 130 is very different from all others, and the only one expressing what it does. It is an inaccurate citing of Joseph's instruction, repeated by Elder Hyde, according to Joseph Smith's own words in his journal (kept by Willard Richards). There Joseph (via Richards) noted a mistake in Elder Orson Hyde's definition of both the Father *and* the Holy Ghost. Writing for Joseph, Willard Richards stated that Elder Hyde, "again revertd to mistake. &c [meaning etc. – following -] the Father has a body of flesh & bones as tangible as mans, the Son also, but the Holy Ghost is a personage of spirit" (see Joseph Smith Papers Project http://www.josephsmithpapers.org/paper-summary/journal-december-1842-june-1844-book-2-10-march-1843-14-july-1843/50).

It is generally believed that the Father has a body, but one not tangible *in the same way* as the body of men, or we would not read that the Son differs from Him being a "personage of tabernacle" in Lecture on Faith 5. The Father's body is apparently much more refined - a purer form of matter with great intensity of light and power, so much so that we would be destroyed in His presence if we were not first transfigured by Him to endure His fiery presence.

Elder Hyde's instruction suggests that the Holy Ghost is an individual – a male personage (like the Father and Son), but without a body, that He might dwell within us. The fifth Lecture on Faith counteracts this, providing an **officially approved** and **voted on** definition of what the Holy Spirit is, as provided by the first prophetic leader of the church, Joseph Smith. He had individual priesthood quorums vote to have the Lectures on Faith put into our Canon of Scriptures, followed by a vote of regular Church membership. These lectures, the "doctrine" portion of the Doctrine and Covenants, were removed in 1921 by a committee, led by academic James E. Talmage (without a vote by priesthood quorums or the church). His replacement book, Articles of Faith, became a classic best-seller among the Saints, along with the book, *Jesus the Christ*. False things are taught in both of them, along with truth. The "covenants" portion of the D&C are the revelations or oracles given to the Prophet Joseph by God.

Lecture 5 informs us that Holy Spirit is the unified mind of the Father and the Son. The gift or endowment of having access to the mind of God is granted only after we are sanctified from all sin – in the baptism of fire and Holy Ghost event. The Holy Spirit or Holy Ghost is the connecting point between the Father and the Son and us, the shaft of the Menorrah in the ancient Tabernacle. Once we are cleansed from all sin by our sincere repentance, and by God's fiery Spirit - our spirit or "ghost" has access to or may abide in or with the unified mind of the Father and Son (and eventually Mother). We can then become "one" with them. Lecture 5 states:

> "There are **two personages** who constitute the great, matchless, governing and supreme power over all things. They are the Father and the Son: **the Father being a personage of spirit**, glory, and power, possessing all perfection and Fullness. The Son, who was in the bosom of the Father, **a personage of tabernacle**, made, or fashioned like unto man, or being in the form and likeness of man . . . And he being the only begotten of the Father, full of grace and truth, and having overcome, received a Fullness of the glory of the Father—**possessing the same mind with the Father, which mind is the Holy Spirit** . . . being filled with the Fullness of the Mind

of the Father, or, in other words, the Spirit of the Father: which Spirit is shed forth upon all who believe On his name and keep his commandments: and all those who keep his commandments shall grow up from grace to grace, and become heirs of the heavenly kingdom, and joint heirs with Jesus Christ; possessing **the same mind**, being transformed into the same image or likeness, even the express image of him who fills all in all: being filled with the Fullness of his glory, and **become one in him, even as the Father, Son and Holy Spirit are one**" (a portion of Lecture 5, *Lectures on Faith*, see also John 13, being "one" with the True Vine).

Additional Joseph Smith Statements on the Holy Ghost

The Holy Ghost [connecting Spirit to the mind of God – Father and Son] knows all things (D&C 35:19). It brings all things to our remembrance (John 14:26). It bears record of all things, and especially of the Father and the Son (D&C 20:26-27; Moses 6:66). **It shows us all things that we should do to return us to their presence** (2 Ne. 32:5-6). Those empowered by it, teach with convincing power (2 Ne. 33:1; Hel. 5:45-51). The word of God in scripture unfolds to those with access to the mind of God. Having received a portion of greater access to God after the fiery baptism, the Prophet Joseph Smith stated:

> "Immediately on our coming up out of the water after we had been baptized, we experienced great and glorious blessings from our Heavenly Father. No sooner had I baptized Oliver Cowdery, than the Holy Ghost fell upon him, and he stood up and **prophesied** many things which should shortly come to pass. And again, so soon as I had been baptized by him, I also had the **spirit of prophecy**, when, standing up, I **prophesied** concerning the rise of this Church, and many other things connected with the Church, and this generation of the children of men. We were filled with the Holy Ghost, and rejoiced in the God of our salvation. Our **minds being now enlightened**, we began to have **the scriptures laid open to our understandings**, and the **true meaning and intention** of their **more mysterious passages revealed unto us** in a manner which we never could attain to previously, nor ever before had thought of" (Joseph Smith History 1:73-74).

The Prophet Joseph later added:

> "A person may profit by noticing the first intimation of the spirit of revelation; for instance, when you feel **pure intelligence** flowing into you, it may give you s**udden strokes of ideas**, so that by noticing it, you may find it fulfilled the same day or soon; (i.e.) those things that were presented unto your minds by the Spirit of God, will come to pass; and thus by learning the Spirit of God and understanding it, you may grow into **the principle of revelation**, until you become perfect in Christ Jesus" (Joseph Smith, HC, p. 381).

> "The Holy Ghost has no other effect than **pure intelligence**. It is more powerful in **expanding the mind**, **enlightening the understanding**, and **storing the intellect** with present knowledge, of a man who is of the literal seed of Abraham, than one that is a Gentile, though it may not have half as much visible effect upon the body; for as the Holy Ghost falls upon one of the literal seed of Abraham, it is calm and serene; and his whole soul and body are only exercised by **the pure spirit of intelligence**; while the effect of the Holy Ghost upon a *Gentile*, is **to purge out the old blood, and make him actually of the seed of Abraham**. That man that has none of the blood of Abraham (naturally) must have **a new creation by the Holy Ghost**. In such a case, there may be more of a powerful effect upon the body, and visible to the eye, than upon an Israelite, while the Israelite at first might be far before the Gentile in **pure intelligence**" (TPJS 149-50).

For these and other reasons the Holy Ghost is sometimes called the "comforter" (a "first comforter," John 14:26) or "the record of heaven" (Moses 6:61). Latter-day Saints simply call it "the Holy Ghost." Most other Christians refer to it as the Holy Spirit - as does Joseph Smith's Lectures on Faith. Many believe our spirit or "ghost" is cleansed or sanctified in the "born again" experience and thus able to interact with God via the Holy Spirit. Some believe we are also able to tap into our "higher self " better as well, the "higher self" being a portion of our Spirit left in the spirit world before descending here.

One final point should be addressed. Mother in Heaven plays an important and essential role in comforting us – as mothers are nurturers. She is part of the Godhead as well, as she and Father and our Savior – the Son – are all one. She is often tied to the Holy Spirit, as she, the Spirit of Christ or God, and the Holy Ghost are different. Note some of the other things embraced today (below right) that differ from teachings in the earliest days of the church (left). God's two witnesses in His word in scripture *and* pure revelation bring us to the truth.

God is eternal and unchanging	*God was once a man and we can become like Him*
The Holy Ghost connects us to the mind of God	*The Holy Ghost is a separate male personage of Spirit*
The Everlasting Cov. is baptism of water & fire	*The New and Everlasting Covenant of Marriage (plural)*
Trusting in man, the arm of flesh, leads to cursing	*Our mortal leaders are infallible and cannot lead us astray*
We are sealed to Christ	*Family members are sealed to each other & dead ancestors*
We are saved by the blood of Christ	*We and our dead are saved via temple ordinances*

Assumption 6: *Do changes in ordinances & doctrine reflect God's will?*

Rather than revelation from God, changed ordinances (like those at the House of the LORD) most often reflect the administrative will of a single person, or a committee and their decisions, based on convenience, speed, efficiency, political correctness, etc. This is apparent in the words of leaders. In Section One of the D&C, the LORD said:

> "For they have **strayed from mine ordinances**, and have broken mine everlasting covenant; They seek not the LORD to establish **his** righteousness, but every man *walketh in his own way*, and after the image of his *own god*, whose image is in the likeness of the world, and whose substance is that of an idol, which waxeth old and shall perish in Babylon, even Babylon the great, which shall fall" (D&C 1:15-16; see also Isa. 23:5).

The Prophet Joseph Smith said, "Ordinances instituted in the heavens before the foundation of the world, in the priesthood, for the salvation of men, **are not to be altered or changed**" (TPJS p. 308). Brigham Young redefined "the everlasting covenant" as "the new and everlasting covenant of [plural] marriage." God's order of things ("ordinances"), like the Holy Days, the doctrine of Christ, the Sacrament, and the ordinances of the House of the LORD have all been modified by **men** to make them more palatable, convenient, faster, and cheaper. As stated in chap. 4, vast changes were made to the endowment in 1990, including removal of *the penalties* in connection with SRA flashbacks (see the Pace Memorandom). In January of 2019, Pres. Nelson made more sweeping changes to the endowment, most affecting *women's issues*. In addressing the many changes to the endowment he saw in his day, Hugh Nibley stated, "So, I say that in all my years of going through the temple, I have marked a growing list of changes, a steady subsiding towards what is easier to do, and especially easier to accept, in our busy, telestial business world, to accommodate to greater convenience, comfort, efficiency and complacency" (Hugh Nibley, "The Vital Link" [title of the FARMS-issued audio tape] also titled "A House of Glory," in the FARMS volume Temple of the Ancient World, 1994, delivered at BYU, April 6, 1993, typescript from the audio tape, pps. 8-9;16-17). He added, "In ancient times, apostasy never came by renouncing the gospel *but always by* **corrupting** *it*...(Hugh Nibley, One Eternal Round: The Hermetic Tradition, Temple and Cosmos, FARMS – Deseret Book, p. 395).

President Heber J. Grant was the last President of the church to practice polygamy. God said that iniquities cut us off from God's presence (2 Ne. 27:5). Grant was a practical-minded businessman. He believed **fidelity to church leaders** was more important than **spiritual things** in the kingdom, including having a sure witness of the LORD. This widespread attitude persists today. Earlier his business minded approach in leading the church was addressed. His mother, his personal secretary, and others felt his spirituality was lacking (see Assumption #6, chap. 6). A list of nine changes he made during his administration is provided hereafter. Revelation is **not** cited for **any** of them.

(1) *The Lectures on Faith* were removed from our canon scriptures (the D&C) in 1921 without a vote of the Saints, further diminishing instruction on the **faith** required to part the veil to God. They were put into our canon of scripture by a vote of preisthood quorums and the whole church – as "all things" are be done by common consent (D&C 26:2). The committee removing them without a vote was headed up by James E. Talmage, an academic from the Univ. of Utah who later became an "apostle." His best selling book, *The Articles of Faith*, replaced *The Lectures on Faith* (which were compiled and approved by Joseph Smith). They were considered the "doctrine" portion of the Doctrine and Covenants. Joseph's revelations or oracles where considered the "covenants."

(2) Two years later on November 26th of 1923, President Grant had the Church incorporated. It is now called, "The Corporation of the President of the Church of Jesus Christ of Latter-day Saints." Church Presidents now hold all power (this goes against the LORD's direction for four equal quorums to lead the Church in D&C 107). With them the Twelve oversee many for-profit businesses. See *http://mormondisclosures.blogspot.com/2012/09/boogie-on-down-corporation-with-sole.html,* rather than serving as traveling missionaries sent out into the world to bear testimony of the LORD Jesus. The President is the sole leader over the church in all matters.

(3) Pres. Grant (*as* "Trustee in Trust of the church) **sold the entire temple block** (all buildings and property) to Anthony Ivins, and then had him sell it back to him *as* President of the Corporation of the President of the Church of Jesus Christ of Latter-day Saints for $1.00. He did this so that he as the corporation president could then mortgage the Salt Lake Temple and all other buildings and property of Temple Square (which were built by and dedicated to the LORD in the sacrifice of the Saints via their tithing) to the Chase National Bank and others in New York, thus to secure a $3,500,000.00 loan. Full records of these and other related transactions were verified by three men (M. Peterson, Alonzo Cole, and Clyde Neilson, all residents of Salt Lake County) who made copies of three "Bargain and Sales" deeds (#'s 501,787 and 501,790 and 502,184, all in 1923), along with two Mortgages (in 1931 and 1936), held by Recorders in the Salt Lake County and Box Elder County offices. This knowledge was brought forward in 1936. Pres. Grant lied to cover it up in a Deseret News article on April 4, 1936. In addition to deceiving the Saints, Pres. Grant broke two laws in doing so; (1) He did not obtain a vote from the Saints as God stipulated in D&C 26:2, and he broke the law governing "not-profit corporations" which states that notification must be made to those in their membership 15 days in advance of any vote on issues affecting them. No notification was made, nor a vote held.

(4) Pres. Grant removed **wine** from the Sacrament ordinance in 1906. He also canceled **kneeling** (an expression of humility and gratitude) by the congregation (3 Ne. 19:6). The Savior set the example for both, instituting the Sacrament using wine *and* kneeling among three groups of people at the Last Supper in Jerusalem (Mat. 26:26-29), at Bountiful in 3rd Nephi (3 Ne. 18 & 19), and in Joseph Smith's Restoration (D&C 20, 27, 89 & Mor. 4 & 5).

(5) Pres. Grant made adherence to the **word of wisdom** a requirement to enter the temple in 1933, via a "**recommend**," provided by mortal leaders. The interview process controlled who was permitted to enter into the temple. The process served as a *financial funnel* for the struggling church. Pres. Grant then made full payment of tithing a requirement to enter the temple thereafter. The state of our *heart* is the LORD's measure of worthiness, not money.

(6) Administration and committee recommendations took on a greater role than **revelation** during Grant's administration. He was not considered a spiritual man by all those around him, but rather a *shrewd* business man. God said revelation from Him is the "rock" that keeps "the gates of hell" from prevailing against the kingdom of God (see JST Mat. 16:16-18).

(7) For some 22 years of Pres. Grant's administration, ordinations did not confer priesthood. Men were ordained to offices in the church without conferral of priesthood first.

(8) Pres. Grant stopped **re-baptisms** *in temples* in 1922. They were discontinued *outside* of temples earlier with Pres. Woodruff in 1897. No revelation from God was cited for either change. Temple records from four early Utah temples from 1877 to 1893 reveal that there were 7,788 re-baptisms done in them to *renew covenants*, and 22,403 re-baptisms done for *improved health*. This was in addition to baptisms for the dead (see endnote 27).

(9) Though once a polygamist, Pres. Grant removed Section 132 from the D&C in 1930, until pro-polygamists complained. He then put it back in the Doctrine and Covenants (James E. Talmage did not see it as having "*enduring value*," see chap. 2). No vote was sought from the Saints by either of Pres. Grant's decisions regarding Section 132.

Baptism and Temple Worthiness Questions

Question 3 of 6 of the baptism worthiness interview, and questions 4 and 14 (of 15 total) for a temple recommend, encourage the Saints to put faith and trust in church leaders more than God (see Mos. 18:7-10). Questions include:

#3. "Do you believe that [current Church President] is a prophet of God? What does this mean to you?"

#4. "Do you sustain the President of the Church of Jesus Christ of Latter-day Saints as the Prophet, Seer, and Revelator and as the only person on the earth who possesses and is authorized to exercise all priesthood keys? Do you sustain members of the First Presidency and the Quorum of the Twelve Apostles as prophets, seers, and revelators? Do you sustain the other General Authorities and local authorities of the Church?"

#14. "Have there been any sins or misdeeds in your life that should have been resolved with priesthood authorities but have not been?"

Changes in Washings

The initiatory washing and anointing ordinance once required three separate bathtubs insde the Kirtland house of the LORD (this continued through the Salt Lake Temple). The first tub was for, (1) a complete washing; The second tub was for (2) a complete rinsing; And the third tub was for (3) the pouring of oil over the entire body. Years later this was changed to applying water and oil to select body areas. Today a touch of water and oil is placed on the forehead. A second example tied to washing is useful. George F. Richards made many temple ordinance changes, without citing revelations for them. This did not stop him from criticizing the Catholic church for their evolving mode of baptism, from immersion to finally sprinkling. He stated, "For a century we have tried to show to the world from the scriptures that baptism is necessary to man's salvation; that baptism signifies immersion and that immersion was the only form of baptism known and practiced in the primitive Church until several centuries A. D., and that the changing of the mode of baptism from immersion to pouring or sprinkling is *apostasy* and fulfills the prediction of Isaiah with respect to the last times, 'The earth, also, is defiled under the inhabitants thereof, because they have transgressed the laws, **changed the ordinance**, broken the everlasting covenant'" (George F. Richards, Conf. Report, April 1930, p.76).

Joseph's Articles of Faith Changed in 2018 New 2018 Articles of Faith actually reveal our **lack** of faith. Article of Faith 5, for example, removes words suggesting faith in "the gift of tongues, prophecy, visions, etc." No vote was taken.

Assumption 7: *Is church history accurate?* Fifteen example **lies** are presented hereafter. Many of them were produced in affidavits in the 1870's and 1880's to try and prove that polygamy was an original **tenet** or **doctrine** of the faith. Some of these were disproved in the 1894 Temple Lot Case. With the urging of Joseph Smith III, the Federal Government enacted laws leading to the two Manifestos #1 (Wilford Woodruff) and #2 (Joseph F. Smith), to stop the Saints from practicing polygamy. His work helped fulfill three prophecies tied to completion of his father's mission, the cleansing of the church of this whoredom, and the clearing of Joseph's name to some degree (see JS History 1:33). The **lies** originally justified polygamy. Today they are used to maintain power and retain other gain.

1. The first lie – that Joseph was a polygamist (see 3 Ne. 16:10, 21:19, 30:2) - then led to fourteen more.

2. Numerous false affidavits and stories were produced in the 1880's to support polygamy. They suggested that Joseph taught polygamy and included affidavits from many of Joseph's "so called" polygamous wives. Judge Phillips in the Temple Lot Case called three supposed wives of Joseph giving testimony there "liars." See chap. 2.

3. The Angel with Sword story was a fabrication (see chap. 1).

4. The story of the Transfiguration of Brigham Young as Joseph is false, brought forth years after the fact to support Young's leadership. See https://www.dialoguejournal.com/wpcontent/uploads/sbi/articles/Dialogue_V34N0102_171.pdf

5. The Founding Fathers coming to the St. George Temple (false polygamous marriage and law of adoption sealings) has proven to be false (see http://puremormonism.blogspot.com/2013/04/wilford-woodruffs-pants-are-on-fire.html).

6. The "**last charge**" by Joseph was not to the Twelve but to the Council of Fifty. He charged them to clean up the the mess caused by polygamy among the Twelve. Joseph "shook his garment" free of the blood, sins, and iniquities of those among him, as did Paul (Acts 18:6) and Jacob (2 Ne. 9:44-45; Jacob 1:19, 2:2). This event is now falsely portrayed as a transfer of all **power** from Joseph to the Twelve, including the sealing power upon Brigham. It was instead a transfer of responsibility to those guilty at this meeting. See p. 116 and endnote 16.

7. Brigham's 1856-57 Reformation (with re-baptism) was a control mechanism put upon the Saints based on fear. The blood atonement doctrine spread at this time (throat cutting ties to the temple oaths). Many Saints (as many as 5,000) left the Salt Lake Valley in the late 1850's. It is one of many untold stories we should become aware of. The most common reasons for the exodus by early emigrants (most arriving by handcart companies), included fear, Young's control tactics, poverty reinforced by excessive tithing, polygamy, and a lack of spirituality. Many who tried to leave were coerced into returning by Young's "enforcers," at least until they paid back their PEF (Perpetual Emigration Fund) loans. Young was glad to see the apostates leave, stating, "You Nasty Apostates. Clear out." The journal entries of many Saints paints a sad tale, one laying the foundation for the current atmosphere of obedience and control, one continuing today. They parrallel heroic tales of many who survived the handcart experiment, called by Young "my old plan." Others referred to it as "a funeral march." Most chose to never speak of it, not only because of fear, but because of the memories. For more on these fascinating stories, see Polly Aird, *You Nasty Apostates. Clear out: Reasons for Disaffection in the Late 1850's*, and Will Bagley, *One Long Funeral March: A Revisionist's View of the Mormon Handcart Disasters.*

8. Brigham called his handcart scheme "my old plan." It was a willing sacrifice by the Saints, but some among them called it "a funeral march." Brigham diverted some of the rescuers to recover his merchandise from a 22-wagon train seen by those in the Willie Handcart Company (my relatives were in it). Brigham had some 6 tons of liquor, tobacco, etc., for his Salt Lake Store, overseen by Heber C. Kimball (see Will Bagley, *One Long Funeral March: A Revisionist's View of the Mormon Handcart Disasters*).

9. The Brighamite Saints in Utah were cursed with droughts, heavy snows, insect infestations (the Seagull Salvation story), and Indian trouble, and more.

10. Things claimed to be "revelations from the LORD" which were not. These include the two manifestos, the revelation on blacks and the Priesthood, etc.

11. The Brighamites are the Good Guys & the Josephites are the Bad Guys.

12. The Brighamite Saints were not forced out of Nauvoo due to persecution tied to freedom of religion. The real reason leaders led half the Saints west was to practice polygamy outside of the U.S. borders in Utah Territory. Those left behind (the Josephites and others) were unmolested.

13. Emma Smith was not an evil, cursed woman as Brigham said, but one who stood up against him.

14. Joseph and Hyrum Smith were killed by traitors from within at Carthage Jail (see chap. 4).

15. The church wasn't organized on April 6, 1830. It was already in place, functioning well. There were five other purposes for the meeting that day, one being official licensing for "elders" in New York State (Assumption #9).

Assumption 8: *Was all the law of Moses fulfilled in Christ?*

During the 2018 Spring General Conference, Pres. Nelson announced *seven new temples.* Love for God and one another was spoken of along with more ministering among the Saints. The priesthood changes made at this Conference were **not** accompanied by "thus saith the LORD" revelation from God. Decisions were made by men *for* the Saints, **not** with our **input** or our **vote**. This was Brigham's way, but **not** the LORD's way. **No** opportunity to discuss them beforehand was provided, and **no** vote was sought from priesthood quorums or church membership to approve them. God designed his church government differently, with four equal groups who had to **unanimously approve** new scripture or **changes** in the church. They were; (1) First Presidency & (2) general membership [local government], along with (3) the Twelve, and (4) the Seventy [government out in the mission field], see D&C 107). Brigham Young used the same kind of *strongarm control* with polygamy. Too few Saints today read God's word to compare it to what is happening. God spoke out against top down dictatorial or corporate decision-making. He gave us the law of "**common consent**," stating that **<u>all things</u>** were to be done "by **common consent** in the Church and by **much prayer** and **faith**" (D&C 26:2). All of the body of Christ are to be involved in such things. Top-down decision making is how corporations are run, and by the corporation president. The supreme power of one man in the corporation sole was developed in ancient Rome and now resides in both the Catholic Church and the modified church now in place in Utah. The Pope today wants a one world government and a one world church. If the sleeping sheep aren't careful, we will have it. Nephi described this future church as one centered on gain (1 Ne. 14:10; 22:23).

Many smooth words were spoken at the 2018 General Conference. What wasn't said on Saturday, the first day of spring 2018 General Conference, spoke just as loudly, however. There was no information on finances or missionary efforts. Their numbers are opposite. Billions of dollars are coming into church coffers, while membership via missionary work is at an all time low (endnote 4). The reason for the increased gain and the decreasing baptisms are easily identified by our modern focus, seen in our calendar, for example. On day one of this Spring General Conference - Saturday March 31st - there was much adulation for Elder Nelson, a new church president. There was **no mention** that this special day was **Passover**, the day of **Christ's Atonement**, the day He was crucified for each of us – providing our **spiritual deliverance**! It was also the day the ancient Israelites were **delivered by Him** *physically* from Egypt in the first Passover. They had been in captivity for 400 years. Both forms of deliverance were made possible by our LORD's miraculous power, symbolized in the blood of the Lamb placed on the doors of all those delivered in Egypt. It was an expression of His great love for those turning to Him in repentance. His saving mission in connection with Passover was not mentioned at General Conference this day. Was this ignorance, indifference, or worse? The LORD said He would be "denied" (2 Ne. 28:32), "rejected" (2 Ne. 1:10, and "forsaken" (Jer. 2:13), by His own people. Mormon said we would be "ashamed" of Him (Morm. 8:36).

The next day of conference, the word "Easter" was used a number of times in connection with "Sunday." Both the words "Easter" and "Sunday" represent pagan substitutions for the LORD's deliverance of His people on the Holy Day of Passover by the Roman Emperor Constantine. This Emperor was supposedly converted to Christianity on his deathbed. He made many changes to the Christian church he led (as a civil leader). Constantine said that his changes were made for the sake of convenience. They also allowed his idolatrous worship practices to become part of a new calendar and church. We have embraced both. The worship of the sun, which he brought into the Gregorian calendar (now used throughout the Christian world) was on **the first day** of the week (now called "Sunday"), **not the seventh** or Sabbath day of the LORD, tied to **rest** after God's six days of creation. In addition, Constantine's new Easter holiday cancelled out Passover, the LORD's holy day instituted that we might **remember Him**. Easter is tied to Ishtar and idolatry. Constantine hated the Jews and the calendar Moses put in place to remember and honor God.

Another change to our calendar began with academic James E. Talmage (later of the Twelve). In his book *Jesus The Christ*, he expressed *his personal opinion* that April 6th was the brithday of the LORD. This has since become an LDS tradition, just as Christmas on December 25th became the tradition of Catholics and now the whole Christian world. Nost of the Saints today believe April 6 is Christ's birthday. This has been proven false in the Joseph Smith Papers project. Researchers there show that it was based on the limited understanding of Talmage at the time. He thought the added words of John Whitmer in the first few verses of D&C 20 (especially verse 1) were the actual words of the LORD to Joseph Smith in a revelation to Him. In reality, they are the added words of John Whitmer, who wrote them *as a preface* to the actual, later revelation. Other LDS church leaders took Talmages' words as gospel and soon the tradition became doctrine. April 6 is close to Passover and thus the LORD's atonement and **resurrection**, but it has no direct tie to the LORD's birthday, including the teachings of Joseph Smith. Most experts on the life of Christ point to His birth in the fall, on Rosh Hashanah or Tabernacles. Both are **holy days** on God's own calendar. God said:

> "And this day [Passover and other Holy Days] shall be unto you for a **memorial**; and ye shall keep it a feast to the LORD throughout your generations; ye shall keep it a feast by **an ordinance <u>for ever</u>**" (Ex. 12:14).

Because too many of the Saints rely on mortal leaders like Talmage more than God and His written word in scripture (including the Old Testament), too few are aware of the idolatry present among us in the calendar changes made by Constantine, the later Popes (see Daniel 7:25), and our own people. Most believe they are part of the Law of Moses, a law fulfilled by Christ's mission. Scripture says that the Holy Days on God's calendar are to be observed **<u>forever</u>**, that we might **remember** our LORD, much like the Sacrament. Both are an **ordinance**. They, like the Ten Commandments, and other portions of God's word and law, were not to be done away with. Instead, the primary portion of the Law of Moses that was "fulfilled" was blood sacrifice, completed in Christ's blood offering in Gethsemane, the scourging, and the cross. He came to establish His law, keeping **the Ten Commandments** and **the Holy Days** in place. Though there was much adulation for Pres. Nelson at the spring 2018 General Conference, wise virgins look to the LORD and to His return as the Bridegroom. The unfaithful bride will be shut out.

Assumption 9: *What is <u>God's</u> Definition of <u>His</u> Church? Is the LDS church True to this Defintion Today?*

This 9th assumption has two parts. Part I addresses church organization today, whereas Part II addresses God's definition of **His church**. Together, both point to what portions of it are "**true**" to this defintion.

Part I Today, fifteen men called "apostles" (the Twelve and the First Presidency) oversee the entire church. We have become entirely accustomed to this management method, when God's word in D&C 107 (and other scripture) teaches that we should have four equal priesthood quorums leading us, **not one** (which today is the Quorum of the Twelve, with one man within it leading us as a senior member of this quroum). This method came to us from changes made by Brigham Young. This system is **not** found in the God's word nor in those of Joseph Smith. The judge in the Temple Lot Case addressed the management system implemented by Young in his final verdict (see pages 128-30). In chapter 4 we saw how Brigham Young took control of the church quickly and in *crafty* ways following the murder of the three Smith brothers. He became the sole, one-man leader over the church. He then made changes to lift up the Twelve as administrative leaders over the church, rather than God's role for them as **traveling missionaries** – *serving out in the mission field* (see chap. 4). God put in place the four equal quorums structure to avoid man's natural tendency to exert **power** over other men (see D&C 121). God's plan provided instruction on how to remove those in power, if sin or abuse of it became evident. God warned the Prophet Joseph Smith and the Saints about this in D&C 3:6-11; 5:21-22; 35:17-18; 64:5; 93:47.

The Twelve today **maintain** Brigham's new model, one clearly going **against** God's directives in D&C 107. It may be the primary reason why the current church narrative is maintained…one that claims Joseph was a polygamist and that Brigham Young was the rightful heir to lead the church. The current system is threatened by an illegitimate transition of power from Joseph, to Brigham, and then to the Twelve (chap. 4). Too few understand the succession of power struggle that occurred with Joseph's murder (chap. 4). Ignorance is a useful tool for those holding power.

Paul the Apostle is a good example of what one of the Twelve is to do. He preached repentance and coming unto Christ out in the mission field. He sacrificed greatly to do so (see 2 Cor. 11). He did not sit in the comfortable **9**like King Noah and his replacement priests, all with many wives (a type for Brigham and those following him). Speaking of laborers for Christ, Paul asked, "Are they ministers **of Christ**? . . . in *labours* more abundant, in *stripes* above measure, in *prisons* more frequent, in *deaths* oft. Of the Jews five times received I *forty stripes* save one. Thrice was I *beaten* with rods, once was I *stoned*, thrice I suffered *shipwreck*, a night and a day I have been *in the deep*; In journeyings often, in *perils* of waters, in *perils* of robbers, in *perils* by mine own countrymen, in *perils* by the heathen, in *perils* in the city, in *perils* in the wilderness, in *perils* in the sea, in *perils* among **false brethren**; In *weariness* and *painfulness*, in *watchings* often, in *hunger* and *thirst*, in *fastings* often, in *cold* and *nakedness*. Beside those things that are without, that which cometh upon me daily, the *care* of all the churches" (2 Cor. 11:23-28). Paul gloried in his sufferings for the LORD's sake. He loved him. The Twelve today are pampered and lifted up as lights.

God defines the duty of the Twelve as traveling missionaries, not managers over the corporate assets of the church. Today the "apostles" enjoy celebrity status. They author books and oversee many for-profit businesses within "**The Coporation** of the President of the Church of Jesus Christ of Latter-day Saints." They sit in the high seats at General Conference, administrating over the affairs of the church (see 3 Ne. 9:20; 12:1; JST Mat. 3:38; JST John 1:28; D&C 33:15). Higher seating for them began with Brigham Young (see below). The Twelve and other General Authorities now receive salaries and perks (see Assumption #4, Chap. 6). Young put his secret chamber in place after making war on the Smith bloodline to obtain it - that he and those with him might maintain polygamy and enjoy the luxuries of the chief seats. The first eight verses of Mosiah 11 provide a very good point of comparison between Brigham Young *and* King Noah. Both built many buildings, bringing honor to themselves. Seven new temples were announced at Spring Gen. Conf. in 2018. Abraham paid tithes to Melchizedek for one reason, **to help the poor** (JST Gen. 14:38).

Chief Seats at the Kirtland House of the LORD

Historian Scott Faulring revealed how Joseph Smith's journal was *later changed* regarding seating for the Twelve at the Kirtland house of the LORD for the dedication of this structure on March 27 of 1836. Joseph desired that various leaders of the church be seated in the west pulpit-altars, on the first floor of the House of the Lord at Kirtland. To their left was the High Council, and to the right, the Twelve. Brigham Young didn't like this arrangement. Years after Joseph's murder, Brigham had editors cross out Joseph's words, creating **a new seating arrangement for the Twelve**, where they were given **the top row of seating**, with placement of **others below them**. The added words included "**highest seats**" and "**below**," suggesting that the Twelve be lifted up above other quorums. The authority and celebrity status of the Twelve today is the modern legacy of Brigham Young's rise to prominence (see chap. 4 and endnotes 15 & 17). **Real power**, however, is apparent in **the gifts** and **fruits of the Spirit**, and especially *charity*. Speaking of *false prophets*, Christ revealed how we can know them: by their "**fruits**" (see Matt. 7:15-20).

Part II: Is the LDS Church True? *More Importantly - what is the LORD's definition of His church?*

God said that most churches are "built up to get gain" and "not unto **me**" (2 Ne. 28:3; Morm. 8:33; 1 Ne. 22:23; 2 Ne. 26:20-23; D&C 10:46-70). In 1828 the LORD provided a clear definition of **His church** in D&C 10. It is not a financially successful, large corporation, but a community of believers who heed His invitation to "**repent** and **come unto me**" (D&C 10:67-68, 93:1; 1 Ne. 10:18-19; 2 Ne. 9:23-24; 28:31-32; Jacob 1:7; Alma 5:33-34; Ether 4:7-19; Mor. 7:34; 3 Ne. 9:14, 22, 51; 11:14; 12:19-20, 23-24; 27:5-21; 30:1-2). His church is thus made up of humble **followers** ("disciples") who love the LORD and seek to honor **His will** (Mosiah 5:5; D&C 10:56). He said those who *don't* **repent** and **come unto me** are "**under the bondage of sin**" (D&C 84:50-51). The Old Testament separates God's **will** into *Commandments* (a charge to be observed), *Judgments* (the way to handle a situation), and *Statutes* (an enactment, decree, or ordinance). All are God's *Law* – his wise directions or instructions, given in love.

When Christ came among those gathered at Bountiful in the Book of Mormon, we see that He first taught them (1) "the *doctrine* of Christ." He then presented (2) "the fullness of His *gospel*" to them. After these, He then addressed what (3) His *church* was and is. Our word "church" comes from the Greek word "**Eccelsia**," which means, "**an assembly**

called together." It is an assembly of receptive sheep who **recognize** and **follow His will** as the Good Shepherd (John 10). They are **the bride** of the Lamb or Bridegroom. Three scriptures provide more clarity

(1) *Christ's Church* Mortal men baptize other men and women into *their* churches today, but in the church of Christ or the Lamb, it is **He** who brings together His people. They are cleansed and purified **by Him** and thus become apart of the church of the Firstborn or the Lamb. He said, "after that ye are baptized with water, behold, **I will baptize you** *with fire and the Holy Ghost*" (3 Ne. 12:1 & 3 Ne. 9:20). No man can imitate this spiritual baptism. God does it Himself, **baptizing us into His church**. All other churches are preparatory lesser churches created by men. Nephi said, "Behold, there are save **two churches only**; the one is **the church of the Lamb of God**, and the other is the church of the devil; wherefore, whoso belongeth **not** to the church of the Lamb of God belongeth to that great church, which is the mother of abominations; and she is the whore of all the earth."

(2) *Adding Members* God regularly adds repentant believers into **His church** Himself, doing so in and outside of men's churches today. Acts 2:47 tells us, "**The LORD added** to the church daily such as should be **saved**." In other words, those **redeemed by Him** and His blood receive **His fiery baptism** and are brought into **His church**. The churches of men are often "built up unto **themselves to get gain**" (see D&C 10:56; 1 Ne. 22:23; 2 Ne. 26:20-23, 28:3; Morm. 8:33; Moses 5:29-31). The Brighamite church, like others, is a *preparatory* church of men. Mormon said **all** churches in our day are **polluted** (Morm. 8:36). Nephi confirms this saying, "**all** have gone out of the way" (2 Ne. 28:11). Jacob said "**all**" trees in the LORD's vineyard are corrupt (Jacob 5:42, 47). Any believing Christian who "repents" and "comes unto the LORD" can be part of **the church of the Lamb** (D&C 76:54, 67, 71, 94). They offer up the sacrifice **He** has chosen, a "**broken heart** and a **contrite spirit**" (3 Ne. 9:20; Psalm 51:17).

(3) *In God's name* A third definition for God's church is given us in 3 Ne. 27:1-12, where Christ said that **His church** is called in **His name** and will *only be* **His church if** "it is **built upon His gospel**" (the fullness of which is the two baptisms and **His** gifting of the Holy Ghost, D&C 5:16; 33:11-15; 39:6 & chap. 7). They are those who *see* and *enter* heaven (John 3:3-6). We are to be immersed in the character and attributes of Godliness. These are evident in "**the works of the Father**" or the gifts *and* fruits of the Spirit. They are manifestations of God's approval and are listed in D&C 46 (the LORD's list), 1 Cor. 12 (Paul's list), and Moroni 10 (Moroni's list). The **fruits** of the Spirit are "love, joy, peace, longsuffering, gentleness, goodness, faith, meekness, temperance: against such there is no law" (Gal. 5:22-23). These things, along with visions, prophecy, healings, angels, etc., follow **real believers** in Christ's church. God has said that the churches of men built up to get gain have joy in their work "*for a season* and then cometh the end when they are **hewn down and cast into the fire**" (3 Ne. 27:11).

The April 6 1830 Gathering at the Peter Whitmer Farm: *Six "Elders" are Rebaptized*

By 1829, there were three branches of the early church in operation with seventy converts. The "**church of Christ**" **was** in successful operation. According to Joseph Smith, Oliver Cowdery, and David Whitmer, the gifts and fruits of the Spirit were very evident between 1828 and 1830, **prior to April 6 of 1830**. Joseph, Oliver, and David received (1) the **lesser priesthood** and were baptized in water, (2) **receiving the baptism of fire and the Holy Ghost** immediately thereafter in 1829 (see Joseph Smith History 1:72-74). And (3) they had **the Holy Ghost** with them. Note that all three of these things existed **before** April 6 of 1830 – **before** *the ways of an institutionalized church* – run according to the rules, laws, and ways of men, began creeping in. The "**church of Christ**" **was** in successful operation between 1828-30, the evidence being, (1) priesthood, (2) the Holy Ghost (coming by way of God's second fiery baptism), and (3) the gifts and fruits of the Spirit! David Whitmer later left the church because of Danite coercion tactics in Missouri, increasing polygamy, and a lessoning of spiritual gifts (see Gal. 5:16-25). His name has now been removed from this early record. Since the Church was already in existence and didn't need to be "organized," let's examine what occurred on April 6 of 1830 at the Peter Whitmer farm.

On April 6 of **1830** six "elders" were all re-baptized in full view of the rest of "the church." From a spiritual perspective, the church was already functioning well according to the LORD's definition (supplied previously). The gathering at the Peter Whitmer farm in Fayette New York featured some seventy people and had five purposes. Prior to this date, Joseph Smith **was admonished** by a couple of the brothers to organize the church *according to* local New York State law - **to give the church legitimacy** amongst the locals. This was prayed about and voted upon, and then the proper paperwork for this was met. Joseph received a revelation for the re-baptisms to occur on this day. They were of two types; (1) "**baptism unto renewal**" (or a covenant of "re-committment" for the six elders), and (2) "**baptism unto repentance**" for those not previously baptized (including Joseph Smith's parents).

The six "elders" were the "spiritual teachers" of those in the church and were re-baptized as part of their **re**-commitment (or **re**newal) **to the LORD**. They included Joseph, Hyrum, and Samuel Smith, along with David, John, and Peter Whitmer Jr. The gathering accomplished five primary purposes, one of which was *recognition according to men* in the laws of New York State, as Joseph said it was done "agreeable to **the laws** of our country." These six men had been teaching the doctrine and gospel of Christ. The gifts and fruits of the Spirit were evident with them, including revelation, prophecy, and speaking in tongues, etc. Some of the six men **had the Gift of the Holy Ghost**, specifically Joseph Smith, Oliver Cowdery, and David Whitmer. Some had been baptized but had **not** yet received this important gift. This one another purpose for the gathering. Paul did the same basic thing in Acts 19:1-6.

The gathering date of April 6 was not Christ's birthday (which has now become an LDS tradition), but on or near the date of His **re**surrection in Jerusalem (three days after Passover). It signaled **re**newal for those with faith in Christ, those **re**penting of their sins. Church records *today* say that it was "the precise day upon which, according to his will and comandment, we would proceed to organize his Church *once more* here upon the earth" (HC 1:64-70). It was thus a **re**surrection or "**re**-organization." It is **not** clear if this was a modified statement later added to our historical record.

Each of the six "elders" had previously been baptized into **the church of Christ** *before* 1830, according to the LORD's own words in D&C 10:67. They followed God's admonition to "repent and come unto me," D&C 10, 1828. Some of those previously baptized, did **not** yet have the baptism of fire event in their lives, and thus the gift and power of **the Holy Ghost** to guide them, as did Joseph, Oliver, and David (see Assumption #5, Chap. 6). It represents "the fullness" portion of His gospel. Paul recognized the same problem with those previously baptized in Acts 19:1-6. Others needed a watery baptism first, like Joseph's parents. At some point in the April 6 meeting, Joseph ordained Oliver an elder in the church before the people ("a spiritual teacher," not today's "elder in the Melchizedek Priesthood). Oliver then ordained Joseph. He also ordained him as a "prophet, seer, and revelator" *to the church*, something which concerned David Whitmer (addressed farther below). A **vote** was then taken to approve the men as "spiritual teachers" or "elders" among the people (D&C 28:13). The **Sacrament** was then administered to all those baptized, perhaps the first time this was done among the Saints collectively.

Joseph said, "Several persons…became convinced of the truth and came forward shortly after, and were received into the Church; among the rest, **my own father and mother were baptized**, to my great joy and consolation. …" (HC 1:79). Joseph, Oliver, and David already had the Holy Ghost and the Aaronic priesthood (an **1829** event). Both men baptized each other earlier, receiving the priesthood under the hands of an angel – John the Baptist (who may have come later as Elijah, with greater priesthood power in 1836, see D&C 110). They also experienced the important baptism of fire and the Holy Ghost event (see JSH 1:73-74), receiving the gift and power of the Holy Ghost from God. Both men had already been brought into God's church in this **sanctifying** event, as it is God who baptizes us with His fiery Spirit, prior to receiving the unspeakable gift of the Holy Ghost. Following sanctification, Joseph, Oliver, and David were empowered by **the Holy Ghost**. What were the five reasons for the April 6, 1830 meeting?

(1) **Authoritatively Invite Others to Receive the Holy Ghost** The gathering at the Peter Whimer home provided a place for the *authoritative* "laying on of hands" ordinance for some who did **not yet** have the Holy Ghost (like Joseph's parents). It must be done by someone with *authority* to do so. Joseph, Oliver, and David were **apostles** ("sent ones") of the LORD Jesus Christ. They used their **apostolic authority** to *invite* those there who did not yet have the gift and power of the Holy Ghost - to actually receive it from God. Technically, they may have been "disciples of Christ, like the twelve "disciples" called in the Book of Mormon by our LORD (see 1 Ne. 12:9-10; 3 Ne. 19:4, 28:4-10; John 8:32), as the twelve "apostles" in Jerusalem maintain this position over the whole earth). Inviting others with *authority* - to *actually receive* the Holy Ghost from God is an *official duty* for those called as "apostles" (New Testament) or the (12) "disciples" of Christ in the Book of Mormon (see D&C 20:38-43; 3 Ne. 18:36-38: Moroni 2:2).

Receiving the Holy Ghost is the Father's "endowment of **power** from on high" (see Luke 24:49 & Acts 1 & 2; D&C 95:8-9, 97:12-18, 105:10-12). It completes "the Everlasting Covenant" made at baptism in water, that they might then receive the second, fiery spiritual baptism conducted by the LORD Himself, as He and the Father provide the Holy Ghost to us, not any man (see 3 Ne. 9:20, 12:1; 2 Ne. 31:12; 3 Ne. 11:35; JST Mat. 3:38; JST Luke 3:16; JST John 1:28; 15:26; D&C 33:15). This second baptism by God is part of the "fullness" portion of the gospel that is rejected by so many today (3 Ne. 16:10). Those sanctified in the *blood* of Christ (His atonement) are cleansed by His fiery *Spirit*, after they are first baptized in *water* (a demonstration of real faith, following real repentance with "a broken heart and contrite spirit" [3 Ne. 9:20]). Such are then gifted with *access to* "the unified mind of the Father and Son" (this is the definition of "the Holy Ghost" in the 5th Lecture on Faith. This meeting (and all others in God's church) was to be conducted by "**the Spirit**" (Mor. 6:9; D&C 46:2). Most of the Saints today believe they are already saved or redeemed of God. Most believe they already have the Holy Ghost. Have you been baptized by fire, a recognizeable event? Do you have clear access to "the unified mind of the Father and Son" – and to their pure revelation?

(2) **Public Vote for their Spiritual Teachers** The re-baptisms of the six "elders" signified their new beginning as teachers before the people. Why? In order to meet the law of the LORD"s own doctrine, gospel, and church, a public **vote** must be obtained from those served (D&C 26:2). The six "elders" were then **approved** to be the "spiritual teachers" or "elders" of the people (the LORD called Oliver an "**apostle**," an "elder," and "the first preacher" unto "this church of Christ," D&C 21:10:12). Modern corporations and governments have a single dictator or president making decisions for the people **without a vote** or input from them. This is what is occurring today.

(3) **Authoritative Ordinations & Confirmations** The rites of the priesthood needed to be carried out in the prescribed manner. This included ordination to the Aaronic priesthood and confirmation – an authoritative priesthood *invitation* to receive the gift and power of the Holy Ghost. Joseph, Oliver, and David were "apostles" and newly voted on "elders" or "spiritual teachers" for the people. They were inviting others to receive this gift *from* God.

(4) **Partake of the Sacrament as a Group** This gathering may have been the first time the sacrament was administered to a group of followers. It was to occur regularly thereafter so that Christ's disciples would have His Spirit to be with them, a part of their regular "remembering" of him and His commandments to them (D&C 20:75).

(5) **Be Recognized as an Independent Religious Society** The *newly ordained* "elders" **desired** to become *licensed ministers*, "elders" or "spiritual teachers" according to New York State law. There was no legal requirement for this, however. They believed this would allow them to conduct marriages and other rites lawfully. In reality, any license is only a piece of paper, whereas the Holy Ghost is what actually qualifies the actions of the LORD's servants in **His church** (God's mind & will). Those part of His doctrine, gospel, and church must "**repent** and **come unto him**" (Christ is the head of the church), and be **sanctified** and **empowered** **by Him**. It is to receive the gift and power of the Holy Ghost to guide them ("the unfied mind and will of the Father and Son via pure revelation).

It has long been thought that Joseph Smith applied to the State of New York for the church to be licensed or incorporated under state law, due to the words "it being regularly organized and established agreeable to the laws of our country…" etc. Note the wording "agreeable to" not "pursuant to" or "subject to." There were no statutes requiring churches to be licensed by any state. How could there be? For a church to petition a state for permission to exist would put the church of Jesus Christ under government control, which would violate the First Amendment. Instead, what Joseph and Oliver did was "organize" the church as a "religious society," after which **the Church** (not the government) issued licenses to the traveling elders for the purpose of identifying them as emissaries of a specific denomination sent out to preach the gospel of Christ. It would have been more accurate had Oliver Cowdery, when he wrote D&C 20, to use the wording "agreeable to the customs of our country," since the organization of this newly formed church followed the customs of the Methodists, Episcopalians, Presbyterians, and Baptists whenever they entered an area of the country to form a new religious society. Like those other denominations, the church of Christ was "organized" at its founding, not "incorporated." See David K. Stott, Legal Insights into the Organization of the Church in 1830, BYU Studies Vol. 49, No. 2.

Addressing the special April 6th gathering and its purposes, Joseph spoke specifically about the need for a vote, taking the sacrament, ordaining each other, and obtaining the Holy Ghost. "We were, however, commanded to defer our ordination [before the people] until such time as it should be practicable to have our brethren, who had been and who should be baptized, assembled together, [1] when we must **have their sanction** to…ordain each other, and have them decide **by vote** **whether they were willing to accept us as spiritual teachers or not**; when also [2] we were commanded to bless **bread** and break it and to take **wine**, bless it, and drink it with them; afterward [3] proceed to *ordain each other* according to commandment; then call out such men **as the Spirit should dictate**, and [4] ordain them; and then attend **to the laying on of hands for the gift of the Holy Ghost**, *upon all those whom we had previously baptized*, doing all things *in the name of the Lord*" (HC 1:60–61). Note how *everything was to be done* **by the Spirit**, not a handbook of instructions (especially the more secretive second handbook, for select higher leaders only). To do so, you must first have "**the Spirit**," in the gift and power of the Holy Ghost, which may attend those who "**repent** and **come unto him**" (D&C 18:11). They must be sanctified in the second baptism to receive it. All meetings are to be conducted by "**the Spirit**" (Mor. 6:9; D&C 46:2).

Early Idolatry in the Church – *the Great Sin of our Day*

The 1887 final testimony of David Whitmer is useful in trying to make sense of early church history, including the April 6th, 1830 gathering at the Peter Whitmer home, which the church today says is the date when "the church" was "organized." David's final testimony before his death was about his belief in Christ and the Book of Mormon, not the church that evolved from Joseph Smith's early work, a church later modified by Brigham Young. The judges in both the Kirtland Temple Suit and The Temple Lot case stated that Brigham Young had **changed the church** brought forth by Joseph Smith, and that the Utah church was **not** the legal successor church to the one Joseph had founded (see their final verdicts, pages 124-26). Whitmer's thoughts are credible and insightful. **God chose** him to be one of three witnesses for the gold plates of the Book of Mormon. He was also second in command (Assistant President of the Church in Zion) for a time in Missouri, President of the High Council in Zion, and an early Stake President there. In addition, he and Oliver had responsibility to find and call *the first set of twelve* "disciples" in **the church of Christ** as part of the Restoration (D&C 18:17-28). They were true "disciples" (followers) of Christ with Joseph Smith. They called the first "twelve disciples."

Hyrum Andrus (former Dean of the BYU Religion Dept., and Assistant church Historian, stated, "Joseph Smith ordained David Whitmer to be the President of the church in Missouri and his own **successor** should Smith 'not live to God.' This was on July 7 of 1834 (see Hyrum L. Andrus, Doctrines of the Kingdom, Bookcraft, 1973, p. 195). Later statements by the LORD in the D&C point to Joseph's successor being of the Smith bloodline (D&C 43:3-5; 124:58-59). As seen in chapter 4, succession did go to Joseph Smith III. Corruption later entered into this group as well, a major spilt occurring in 1984. Some 30 "restoration branches" were latter formed.

David Whitmer had discernment in the gift and power of **the Holy Ghost**. He has credibility because of God's calling and his experiences in the church with Joseph in the early Restoration. Though he left the church later (primarily over the Danite secret combination that entered into the church in Missouri), he never denied the reality nor importance of the Book of Mormon, nor his strong **faith in Christ** (it is the first principle and ordinance of the gospel of Christ). He was committed to both, but not to a man or to the later, changing church, the one evolving from the early days. Christian churches are to bring us to **Christ**. They are not be *the focus* of our faith, **replacing Christ**. This is what has occurred in the LDS Church. David identified the cause of this idolatry in Mormonism. It is one reason other believers often suggest we are not "Christians." The first statement in the Handbook of Instructions states that the purpose of the church is to bring its members **to Christ** (I had a copy of Book 1 when I was a Stake High Councilor). David's words hereafter provide insights into early church history available nowhere else. Joseph, Oliver, and David were all baptized in the same month that they were shown the gold plates (June, 1829), receiving their fiery baptism and **the Holy Ghost** at that point in time. This is very significant, for it defines the fullness of the gospel of Christ! The three men had repented and come unto Christ. This is the definition the LORD Himself has given us for **His church** in D&C 10:67 (1828). The April 6 1830 event at the Peter Whitmer home occurred two years later. David Whitmer was the third person baptized prior to this gathering. He was baptized into **the church of Christ**! The three men were very young, yet they led the church. Joseph and David were only 23 years old. Pride and inexperience were part of their learning. Pray as you read the words that follow, to know both the truth and any errors in David's words.

"Now, when April 6, 1830, had come, we had then established three branches of the 'Church of Christ,' in which three branches were about seventy members: One branch was at Fayette, N.Y.; one at Manchester, N.Y., and one at Colesville, Pa. It is all a mistake about the church being **organized** on April 6, 1830, as I will show. We were as *fully organized* — **spiritually** — before April 6th as we were on that day. The reason why we met on that day was this; **the world** had been telling us that we were not a *regularly organized church*, and *we had no right to officiate* in the *ordinance of marriage*, *hold church property*, etc., *and that we should organize according to the laws of the land*. **On this account** we met at my father's house in Fayette, N.Y., on April 6, 1830, to attend to this matter of organizing according to the laws of the land; you can see this from Sec. 17 Doctrine and Covenants: the church was organized on April 6th 'agreeable to *the laws of our country*.' It says **after** this, 'by the will and commandments of God;' [were these words added later?] but this revelation came through Bro. Joseph as 'mouthpiece.' Now brethren, how can it be that the church *was any more organized* — **spiritually** — on April 6th, than it was before that time? There were *six elders* and about *seventy members* before April 6th, and the same number of elders and members after that day. We attended to our business of organizing, **according to the laws of the land**, the church *acknowledging us* six elders as their ministers; besides, a few who had recently been baptized and *not confirmed* were **confirmed** on that day . . ."

"I do not consider that the church was *any more organized* or established **in the eyes of God** on that day than it was previous to that day. I consider that on that day *the first error* was introduced into the Church of Christ, and that error was Brother Joseph being ordained as 'Prophet Seer and Revelator' to the church [sole leader]. *The Holy Ghost was with us in more power during the eight months previous to April 6, 1830, than ever at any time thereafter. Almost everyone who was baptized received* **the Holy Ghost in power**, *some prophesying, some speaking in tongues, the heavens were opened to some, and all the signs which Christ promised should follow the believers were with us abundantly. We were an humble happy people, and loved each other as brethren should love.*"

"Just before April 6, 1830, **some** of the brethren began to *think* that the church should have **a leader**, just like the children of Israel [and modern churches in their day] *wanting a king*. Brother Joseph finally inquired of the Lord about it. *He must have had a desire himself to be their leader* **[an idol in his heart]**, *which desire in any form is not of God*, for Christ said, 'If any man desire to be *first*, the same shall be **last** of all, and **servant** of all. He that would be great, let him be your servant. For he that is least among you all, the same shall be great.'"

"A true and humble follower of Christ *will never have any desire* **to lead or be first**, *or to seek the praise of men or brethren. Desiring any prominence whatever is not humility*, but it is **pride**; *it is seeking praise of mortals instead of the praise of God.* Joseph received a *revelation that he should be the leader; that he should be ordained by Oliver Cowdery as 'Prophet Seer and Revelator' to the church, and that* **the church should receive his words as if from God's own mouth**. *Satan surely rejoiced on that day, for he then saw that in time he could overthrow them* [via idolatry in raising men up as our light]. Remember, '**Some revelations are of God; some revelations are of man, and some revelations are of the devil**' [the three ways we may receive revelation]. *God allowed them to be answered according to their erring desires [of their hearts]*. They were like the children of Israel *wanting a king, and God gave them a king*, but it was to their final destruction."

"He gave the church a leader, but it proved their destruction and final landing of the majority of them in the Salt Lake valley in **polygamy**, **believing that their leader** [Brigham] **had received a revelation from God to practice this abomination**. *This* [making Joseph our sole leader] *was the first error that crept into the church.* None of us detected it then. We had all confidence [trust] in Brother Joseph, thinking that as God had given him so great a gift as to translate the Book of Mormon, that *everything he would do must be right* [Bill Hickman believed the same thing about Brigham Young]. That is what I thought about it. You see how **we trusted too much in man** instead of **going to God in humility** [for *pure* revelation], and to **his written word** [D&C 18:3-5], to see if we were proceeding rightly. It grieves me much to think that I was not more careful, and **did not rely upon the teachings of Christ in the written word**. But we were then **young** in years, and all of us were mere **babes in Christ**. Brother Joseph and myself were only twenty-five years of age . . . After Sydney Rigdon came into the church — or in the spring of 1831 — we began to make proselytes faster; but great numbers coming into the church does not always signify great *spiritual* prosperity."

"I want the brethren [and all today] to understand me concerning this error of ordaining Brother Joseph to that office on April 6, 1830. Not at all do I mean to say that I believe the church was then rejected of God [see D&C 124:32]. What occured on that day was this: One of the elders of the church (Joseph) was led into a grievous error; and **the** [other] **members acquiesced in it**. In time it proved to be a most grievous error, being the cause of the trouble which afterwards befell the people of God [**idolatry**, replacing God and His direction, with that of one man]. They put their **trust** in Brother Joseph [a man] and received his revelations **as if from God's own mouth**. (Jer. 17:5) 'Thus saith the Lord: **cursed** be the man that trusteth in man, and maketh flesh his arm; and whose heart **departeth from the Lord**' [see also 2 Ne. 28:31-32; Jer. 2:13, 17:5-13]. **This has been the great curse of the work of God in these last days.** Nearly all of the church have continued to heed the words of **men as if from God's own mouth** — following man into one error in doctrine after another — from year to year — even on down into the doctrine of **polygamy**" (see David Whitmer, *An Address to All Believer's in Christ, http://www.utlm.org/onlinebooks/address1.htm*).

According to God's 1833 revelation to Joseph in the Book of Commandments (chap. 5:4), Joseph's primary job was to bring forth **more of God's word**, *not* become the sole **head** of the church. **Christ is that head** (see Mosiah 5:5-8; Eph. 1:22, 2:20:15, 5:23). David Whitmer knew that "**idols in one's heart**" can dramatically affect one's ability to receive pure, undefiled revelation. He noted that Joseph made changes to some revelations that were given to all three men (Joseph, Oliver & David), as a group. He believed Joseph's ordination as "prophet, seer, and revelator" to the Church in 1830 resulted in an increase in *pride* (Joseph was only 23 years old). David knew that it was Satan's desire to corrupt the church and that idolatry would be a useful tool for this. He also knew that Joseph's *primary role* was to bring forth **God's precious word in scripture** (see 2 Ne. 3:8 – "**none other work**"). Note one scripture change.

> "And he (Joseph) has a gift to translate the Book and I have commanded him that **he shall pretend to no other gift, for I will grant him no other gift**" (early 1833 Book of Commandments, 5:4; 2 Ne. 3:8).

In the 1835 D&C, Joseph amended this scripture (without input from Oliver or David) changing the words in italics.

> "And *you have* a gift to translate *the plates, and this is the first gift that I bestowed upon you*, and I have commanded *you* that *you should* pretend to **no other gift**, *until my purpose is fulfilled in this*; for I will grant *unto you* **no other gift** *until it is finished*" (1835 and later editions of the D&C , verse 4; a total of 31 changed words).

Scripture doesn't hide the weaknesses of men and women, including Adam and Eve, Abraham and Sarah, David, and others. It gives us hope today, that our Savior can make us clearn too. It is ironic that after Joseph's murder, Joseph's words in journals were later changed by Brigham Young and others to reflect a pro-polygamy stance. Between July of 1833 and August of 1835 revisionist history began occurring (see http://greatandmarvelouswork.com/the-book-of-commandments-vs-the-doctrine-and-covenants-part-1/). The LORD warned Joseph to not follow "the dictates of his **own will** and *carnal desires*" (D&C 3:1-9). Joseph was **not** to "walk in crooked paths" nor boast "in his own strength."

Whitmer's words point to the start of **idolatry** in Mormonism, an inherited *iniquity* passed down to us, further magnified today in the single man – President Nelson – who manages "**the corporation sole**." He has sole power to do as he pleases, just like the Pope, and **without** the vote of the people. The management instructions for this "Corporation of the President" is the Handbook of Instructions (one for top leaders and another for lower leaders). They have replaced God's holy word as the source of guidance.

Is the LDS Church "True" *and to What or Who?*

A better question to ask is, what are those in this organization **true** to – to Christ and the fullness of the doctrine He taught, or to the ways of men, including Brigham Young? There is truth in the Brighamite church today (available in scripture) and many errors too. There are wise virgins, sleeping virgins, wheat growing with **tares**, *and* **wolves** among the sheep. In the next chapter we will see that different "churches" existed among the Saints simultaneously. The church and its leaders are not our light, nor "**the gate**," **Christ is**! King Benjamin said Christ **must be our** "**head**" (see Mosiah 5:8-15). Many today have a testimony of the church or its President. Neither grants us salvation. We are to abide in **Christ** and bear fruit in **Him**, "fruit meet for the Father's [celestial] kingdom" (D&C 84:58).

Many in the institutional (corporate) church seek "gain," including control and the honors of men (1 Ne. 22:23; D&C 121). A few practice real love and are good people. According to the LORD Himself, His church is made up of those that "**repent** and **come unto Him**" (1 Ne. 10:18; D&C 18:11). Thus, those in the Brighamite church and any Christian church for that matter, may be part of **His** church if they choose by *turning* to **Him**. It is the choice **wise** virgins make in any church. Ours has survived under rejection (D&C 124:32), and condemnation (D&C 84:54-58), doing so with and without "*the fullness*" of the gospel of Christ (3 Ne. 16:10; 30:2). For a time it did a good job of sending the Book of Mormon forth to the world. Today the baptism rate is at its lowest point in recorded history (1.4 baptisms per missionary, down from 8 in 1989, see endnote 4). Many are leaving the Brighamite church. Some are turning to home-based worship (see https://churchwithoutwallsinternational.org/what-is-house-church/).

A significant reason for the decline (besides lies and deception) is that missionaries convert people to "**the church**," rather than to the message of the Book of Mormon, which is entirely centered upon **Christ**. We read repeatedly there and in other scripture of God's invitation to "**<u>repent</u>**" [of our idolatry] and "**come unto <u>me</u>**" (D&C 10:67-68, 93:1; 1 Ne. 10:18-19; 2 Ne. 9:23-24; 28:31-32; Jacob 1:7; Alma 5:33-34; Ether 4:7-19; Mor. 7:34; 3 Ne. 9:14, 22, 51; 11:14; 12:19-20, 23-24; 27:5-21; 30:2). Brigham Young diminished this message (Morm. 8:36). His version of the church has been rejected and condemned. Even those in Joseph's early restoration movement rejected "the fullness" of what God wanted to restore (see 3 Ne. 16:10; 30:2). The Brighamite church retains some truths, but most of it is found in **scripture**. If we feast upon God's words there *and* in prayer, we can find **Christ** and receive **His** salvation.

President Grant made the church a corporation in 1923. Like Pres. Woodruff before him, he needed money and turned to worldly bankers for it (Assumption #5). And now, because of "the carrot" of our tax exempt 501(c)3 status, the corrupt U.S. Government and the IRS wield a huge "stick" over the LDS church. There is too much focus on getting "gain" at the top. The corruption filters down to the people. Zion can only be created by focusing on purifying our hearts, loving God and one another. Our tax exempt status explains why there is **silence** from leaders on important moral issues forced down our throats by the Federal Government (like the 2015 Supreme Court decision forcing all 50 states to marry gay couples). The **great and abominable church** controls our government and many others, and because of the carrot of tax-exempt status (money), they control most churches too. The evil one (D&C

93:39) targeted Joseph and what he was trying to restore (the fullness of the gospel of Christ, see D&C 38). It has resulted in **compromise**, **change**, and **pollution**, especially through Brigham Young, polygamy, and Masonry.

God's definition of **His church** is what matters, **not** men's definition of it. Collectively, too many are in the cursed "awful situation" described in the Book of Mormon (both Mosiah 2:36-41 and Ether 8:24), primarily because too many look to **men** to lead them rather than **God** (1 Ne 8:5-8). He said He will be our King in the Millennium. Mortal leaders are often weak and imperfect and are rarely grounded in God's holy **word** (scripture and direct, *pure* revelation from Him). Some are evil and turn to the lord of this world, including some in the LDS church. Prayer is often the only way we can know about such things. Turning to God, in humility and repentance is our only hope. We must seek His sanctification, that we might obtain the gift and power of the Holy Ghost. Wise virgins have this **oil** in their lamps. It is essential to discern light from darkness (the focus of the latter part of D&C 38). Only God provides this important discerning gift. In 1828, before significant pollution began entering in, God told the Prophet Joseph: "For, behold, **I will gather them** [My humble followers] as a hen gathereth her chickens under her wings, **if they will not harden their hearts**; Yea, **if they will come**, **they may**, and **partake of the waters of life freely**. Behold, this is **my doctrine**—whosoever **repenteth** and **cometh unto me**, the same is **my church**. Whosoever declareth more or less than this, the same is **not of me**, but **is against me**; therefore he **is not of my church.** And now, behold, whosoever is of **my church**, and endureth of **my church** to the end, **him will I establish upon my rock**, and the gates of hell shall **not** prevail against them" (D&C 10:65-69).

Assumption 10: *Will the Saints be Spared in the coming judgment?*

The ancient Israelites believed they were the LORD's special covenant people and that they would be spared from the judgments spoken of in scripture. Instead, because of the their own actions, they were slaughtered, captured, and scattered to the four winds. They had **forsaken God** (Jer. 2:13). Many of the Saints today are collectively heading in the same direction, as history repeates itself. The LORD Jesus came in the meridian of time to save **the repentant** as the Lamb of God. He will return as a powerful Lion in perfect justice and judgment, cleansing the earth of all filth. Will *you* be able to stand in His fiery presence at the great and dreadful day of the LORD?

Shepherds are to feed and care for the sheep. According to many scriptures, especially those in Isaiah and Jeremiah, many watchmen on the tower have fallen asleep and are feeding themselves at the sheep's expense. Many have quit building up **the high tower** at the center of the vineyard. That high tower is **Christ** in seven different scriptures (see Psalm 18:2, 61:3 & 144:2; 2 Sam. 22:3 & 51; Prov. 18:10, and D&C 97:20). "The Master [Father] of the vineyard" commanded that the tower be built up at the CENTER of the vineyard (see D&C 101:43-66). Instead, the shepherds lift themselves up as lights before the people (see 3 Ne. 18:24). It is priestcraft, especially when there is money and other gain involved (2 Ne. 26:29-31). They then become as **salt that has lost its savor**, good for nothing but to be cast out and trodden under the feet of men (Mat. 5:13; 3 Ne. 12:13; JST Matthew 21:35-56). Like the Jews of old, pride keeps many Latter-day Saints believing that we are the only ones who will be saved, as we have temples among us and we continually hear the mantra that we are part of "the only true church." In Jeremiah 7, we read that the Jews of old believed they would be saved, as they too had the temple of the LORD. This scripture is worth reading again:

> "**Thus saith the LORD of hosts, the God of Israel**, **Amend your ways** and your doings, and I will cause you to dwell in this place. **Trust ye not in lying words**, saying, *The temple of the LORD, The temple of the LORD, The temple of the LORD*, are these. For if ye thoroughly amend your ways and your doings; if ye thoroughly execute judgment between a man and his neighbor; If ye oppress not the stranger, the fatherless, and the widow, and shed not innocent blood in this place, neither walk after other gods to your hurt [men lifted up to lead you]: Then will I cause you to dwell in this place, in the land that I gave to your fathers, for ever and ever" (Jer. 7:2-7).

The Prophet Hosea revealed much about the two of the houses of Israel, east and west, ancient and modern.

> "For **Israel** [mostly of Ephraim] **hath forgotten his Maker**, *and* **buildeth temples**; and Judah hath multiplied fenced cities: but I will send a fire upon his cities, and it shall devour the palaces thereof" (Hosea 8:14).

Lands Cursed through Sexual Sin

The words of 2 Ne. 19:9-17 address coming judgment upon the Gentile Ephraimites (the Saints and others) on this land, those who have **forsaken Christ**. It is often because of sexual perversion, secret combinations, and for making and breaking covenants. All three are tied to remaining on the LORD's two Promised Lands, places of inheritance for the covenant people of Abraham, Isaac, Jacob, and Joseph. Some will be cursed and removed from them. It happened frequently with ancient Israel in the Bible, and is addressed three times in connection with this land; (1) the Jaredites (Ether 2:7-12, 8:16-26), (2) the Nephites (Hel. 2:12-13), and **the future destruction** of the Gentiles here (JST Mat. 21:35-56; Ether 2:7-12, 8:15-26). Blessing or cursing is the decree of God for the eastern lands promised Abraham (Deut. 19:8-9), and for the promises made to Joseph of Egypt on this land in the west, as repeated by Moroni (Ether 2:9-12), by Alma (Alma 37:31, 4515-16), by Nephi (2 Ne. 1:7), and by Mormon (Morm. 1:17).

Today, like Sodom and Gomorrah of old, many on our land are rapidly descending into gross sexual sin (see endnote 1). They are second only in seriousness to murder and blasphemy against the Holy Ghost. Many tolerate and embrace this growing evil among us. We are at the point where the immorality of the wicked is openly flaunted before us. Speaking of this in our day, Isaiah stated, "they declare their sin as Sodom" (Isaiah 3:9). He added that many make evil look good, and good evil. Those who do not embrace the new ways – "the new order of things" - are characterized as <u>intolerant, out of touch, even evil</u>. Things are turning upside – down (2 Ne. 27:27). Isaiah pronounced a "woe" upon such, stating, "Woe unto them that call evil good, and good evil; that put darkness for light, and light for darkness…they have cast away **the law of the LORD** of hosts, and despised **the word of the Holy One of Israel**. Therefore is the anger of the LORD kindled against **his people**, and he hath stretched forth his hand against them…" (Isa. 5:20, 24-25). The use of the **raised hand** or **stretched out arm** (by the LORD here) with the use of the word "**woe**" (three times) by the great Prophet Isaiah (the watchman for our day) is noteworthy, perhaps a representation of **the sealing power** in an official **cursing** by Him. Those who repent are blessed.

Our choices are closely linked to blessings of liberty, prosperity, and protection - upon choice, Promised Lands, or curses that take them away. Many in both the general U.S. population and in churches are being deceived into tolerating the gay lifestyle (and the wickedness associated with it), out of a sense of false love and tolerance for the people. Some of it is also tied to avoiding persecution, or not fitting in, and of increasing pressure to be politically correct. In a 2017 PEW Research Center survey, 62% of Americans stated that they support gay marriage. The group with the highest percentage of change *from anti to pro-gay marriage* was **Latter-day Saints** (see endnote 4). In speaking of the collective voice of the people, Helaman stated, "and **they who chose evil** were more numerous than they who chose good, therefore **they were ripening for destruction**, for **the laws had become corrupted**" (Hel. 5:2). In 2015 the U.S. Supreme Court made gay marriage a **requirement** for all fifty states - the **stick**, tied to *tax exempt status.*

In the Bible, homosexuality is a great abomination presented early on in Genesis 19, and Leviticus 18 and 20. It is tied to desolation, as there is no creation or increase in it. It is the exact opposite of Godly power, He who has power to create worlds! Two men or two women cannot create life. In the old world those who could not have children were sometimes called "desolate" or "barren." Sarai (wife of Abram) was aged and unable to have children. Later, she was miraculously blessed by God with the son Isaac when she was 90 and Abraham 100 years old. Many do extraordinary, even desperate things to obtain posterity, like the daughters of Lot. Gay couples today seek children from others. Scripture reveals that when people are ripe in sin, they are removed from the choice lands they reside on. The first example is that in the first book of the Bible with **Adam and Eve**. They were expelled from Eden after their transgression, the land *cursed* for their sakes (Gen. 2:23; Moses 4:23). It then produced briars and thorns, etc. The last book of the Bible, Revelation, informs us that many in the last days will be harvested (judged) in the great winepress that is the wrath of God, a huge last-days cleansing. We read in D&C 112, verses 24 through 26:

> "Behold, vengeance cometh speedily upon the inhabitants of the earth, a day of wrath, a day of burning, a day of desolation, of weeping, or mourning, and of lamentation; and as a whirlwind it shall come upon all the face of the earth, saith the LORD. And upon **my house** *shall it begin*, and **from my house** *shall it go forth*, saith the LORD; *First among those among you*, saith the LORD, **<u>who have professed to know my name</u> and have <u>not</u> known me**, and have blasphemed against me in the midst of **my house**, saith the LORD" (see1 Peter 4:17-18).

If there is no repentance, the land is cleansed from such wickedness. Note the three following examples. Leviticus tells us that the land "**vomits**" or "**spues out**" those who "**defile**" it with *sexual sins* (Lev. 18:19-30). In Moses 7, the earth, Enoch, and the LORD were all crying together. Mother Earth was desperately awaiting the day of her *purification* through her Creator - Christ, known there as "**the Righteous**" (see Moses 7:45, 47). Mother Earth said:

> "Wo, wo is me, the mother of men; I am pained, I am weary, because of the **wickedness** of my children. When

shall I rest, and **be cleansed** from the *filthiness* which is gone forth out of me? When will my Creator **sanctify me**, that I may rest, and righteousness for a season abide upon my face?" (see Moses 7:28-52).

The Saints were driven from Nauvoo for polluting what the LORD called "mine holy grounds" (see D&C 124:45-48). **The church was rejected** with its dead **for their sins** (3 Ne. 30:2; 16:10) and for not doing as the LORD directed, nor in His timeframe (v. 36). The **leaders** of the people implemented polygamy among the people, and half the population were the unwise virgins, marrying multiple women to them in the temple, many on the same day. This whoredom increased in Utah. Sexual sin is often one reason people are swept off their lands in scripture (Morm. 1:17; Ether 2:8-12; 8:21-26; 9:28). When many of the Saints were removed from Nauvoo it was a fulfillment of the LORD's **promise** in D&C 124:28-32, 43-48. Note what He said earlier in D&C 42 in 1831, in connection with His higher law, which included (1) the law of consecration and (2) the law of monogamy. Both were rejected by many people.

> "Thou shalt love thy wife with all thy heart, and shalt cleave **unto her and none else**. And he that looketh upon a woman to lust after her shall *deny the faith*, and shall **not have the Spirit**; and if he repents not he shall be cast out" (D&C 42:22-23).

> "I, the Lord, am not pleased . . . I gave commandments and many have *turned away from my commandments* and have not kept them. There were among you **adulterers** and **adulteresses**; some of whom have turned away from you, and others remain with you.... And verily I say unto you, as I have said before, He that looketh on a woman to lust after her, or if any shall *commit adultery in their hearts*, they shall **not have the Spirit**..." (DC 63:12–16)

Chapter 6 Summary

Wise virgins everywhere are invited to awake, arise, and repent in preparation for the tough times that *are* coming. Turning to the President of the corporation sole rather than the living God will have dire results. Our only hope is Christ the LORD. Note the words of three Prophets; Joseph Smith, Mormon, and Isaiah.

> "**The Church must be cleansed**, and I proclaim against **all iniquity**. A man is saved no faster than he gets knowledge [D&C 131:6], for if he does not get knowledge, he will be brought into captivity by some evil power in the other world, as evil spirits will have more knowledge, and consequently more power than many men who are on the earth. Hence it needs revelation to assist us, and give us knowledge of **the things of God**." (HC 4:588).

> "Jesus Christ hath shown **you** unto me, and I know **your** doing. And I know that ye do walk in the **pride** of your hearts; and there are none save a few only who do not lift themselves up in the pride of their hearts . . . and your **churches**, yea, even **every one**, have become polluted because of the pride of your hearts. For behold, ye do love money, and your substance, and your fine apparel, and **the adorning of your churches**, more than ye love **the poor** and **the needy**, the sick and the afflicted. O ye pollutions, ye hypocrites, ye teachers, who sell yourselves for that which will canker, why have ye **polluted the holy church of God**? Why are ye ashamed to take upon you the name of Christ?. . .Yea, why do **ye build up your secret abominations to get gain** . . . Behold, the sword of vengeance hangeth over you" (Mormon 8:35-41).

> "Woe be unto **the pastors** that destroy and scatter the sheep of my pasture! saith the LORD . . . For the land is full of adulterers . . . Ye have scattered my flock, and driven them away, and have not visited them: behold, I will visit upon you the evil of your doings, saith the LORD. For both **prophet** and **priest** are profane; yea, in my house have I found their wickedness, saith the LORD. ...Mine heart within me is broken because of the **prophets**...they commit **adultery**, and walk in lies: they strengthen also the hands of evildoers . . . they are all of them unto me as **Sodom**, and the inhabitants thereof as **Gomorrah**...they speak **a vision of their own heart**, and not out of the mouth of the LORD... I have not sent these prophets...I have not spoken to them, yet they prophesied...I have heard what the prophets said, that prophesy **lies** in my name, saying, I have dreamed...they are prophets of **the deceit of their own heart**. Which think to cause my people to forget my name by their dreams...*as their fathers have forgotten my name* **for Baal** [see endnote 1]...Therefore, behold, I am against the prophets, saith the LORD ...Behold, I am against them that prophesy false dreams, saith the LORD, and do tell them, and cause my people to err by **their lies**...yet **I sent them not**, nor commanded them: therefore they shall not profit this people at all, saith the LORD...And I will bring an everlasting **reproach** upon you, and a perpetual shame, which shall not be forgotten (Jer. 23, select verses 1-40).

"Woe to the crown of **pride**, to the drunkards of **Ephraim**, whose glorious beauty is a **fading flower** . . .Ephraim, shall be trodden under feet . . . But they . . . are out of the way; the priest and the prophet have erred . . . they err in vision, they stumble in judgment...Wherefore hear the word of the Lord, ye scornful men, that rule this people . . . Because ye have said, We have made a covenant with death, and with hell are we at agreement; when **the overflowing scourge shall pass through**, it shall **not** come unto us: for [with these things] **we have made <u>lies</u> our refuge**, and under falsehood have we hid ourselves" (Isa. 28:1, 3, 7, 14-15).

Idolatry was the first sin of half the Saints at Nauvoo, leading them into the second sin – **polygamy** later in Utah. They trusted in **men** rather than God and followed Brigham and the Twelve into what the LORD called a whoredom an iniquity, a grosser crime, and an abomination. Rather than relying on God's word (scripture *and* pure revelation), too many sheep then and today are **deceived** by the *craftiness* of wolves dressed in sheep's clothing (see 1 Ne. 22:23).

1. Brigham and the Twelve **took all power** at Nauvoo, going against God's model of four equal priesthood quorums leading the church (see D&C 107). Two quorums lead at home: (1) the First Presidency, and (2) the Stake High Councils, and two more in the mission field (3) the Twelve, and (4) the Seventy. One quorum was **never** to lead (see chap. 4 and endnote 17). Brigham also ignored Joseph's words. Joseph said, "The Twelve shall have **no right** to go into Zion or any of its stakes and there undertake to **regulate the affairs** thereof **where there is a standing high council**. But it is their duty to *go abroad* and regulate all matters relative to the different branches of the church." The Prophet cautioned the high council to stay off the apostles turf, stating, "No standing high council has authority to go into the *churches abroad* and *regulate the matters thereof*, for this belongs to the Twelve" (Joseph Smith, Kirtland Council Minute Book, p. 112). See also the summary on the bottom of p. 114.

2. The Twelve took upon themselves the **title "apostle"** when the LORD did not give it to them. He called them "disciples" (or "*followers*") in the early portion of the Restoration, along with Twelve he chose at Bountiful in the Book of Mormon. He reserved the term "apostle" ("*sent one*") for the Twelve He chose, empowered, and sent out into the world at Jerusalem (see 1 Ne. 12:9-10, 3 Ne. 19:4, 28:4-10, and John 8:32). The Twelve in early church history replaced the word "disciple" in the 1833 Book of Commandments, with the word "apostle" in the 1835 Doctrine and Covenants. With their new title, they lifted themselves up as *sent* lights before the people, rather than *followers of* the Master. Brigham had the Twelve *repositioned physically above other quorums* in their seating (see p. 217), as well as in their callings. The LORD said, "the *servant* is **not** greater than his LORD" or his "Master" (John 13:16 & 16:20). God chose the twelve apostles in the Holy Land. Oliver Cowdery and David Whitmer chose the first set of twelve disciples in 1829 (D&C 18), by seeking God's inspiration. In the Reed Smoot hearings Pres. Joseph F. Smith said men chose other men to be part of the twelve in his day, unlike the days of the Prophet Joseph when they were chosen by God through **revelation** (see Assumption #3).

3. The Twelve **took on new roles**. They changed the responsibility the LORD gave them to be **traveling missionaries**, like Paul, bearing a powerful witness of Him and His gospel. In Matthew 10, we read, "And when he had called unto him his **twelve disciples**, **he gave them power** against unclean spirits, to *cast them out*, and to *heal all manner of sickness and all manner of disease*." In verse 8, He charged them to, "*heal the sick, cleanse the lepers, raise the dead, cast out devils*." Where is the evidence of this **power** today? The twelve are to preach pure doctrine in the fullness of our LORD's gospel – *which is faith on the LORD Jesus Christ* and *repentance*. They are to teach the two necessary baptisms (one physical and one spiritual), the result being the reception of the Holy Ghost ("the endowment of **power** from on high"). Modern men calling themselves "Apostles" have **lifted themselves up in the chief seats** to receive the honors of men and the things of the world (D&C 121:34-46; 1 Ne. 22:23). They are now administrators, overseeing the business affairs of a "**corporation**" (the LDS church was incorporated in 1923). Do they share prophecies, visions, and revelations with us? God said, "By their fruits ye shall know them" (Mat. 7:16-20). Do they exhibit charity for the sheep, sacrificing for them, as did Paul (see 2 Cor. 11). Do they seek "gain" or "the welfare of Zion" (see 2 Ne. 26:29)? Are they seeking the LORD's face in the "apostolic charge"? God told leaders in his day that they were not "entering in" (to His ways). They were also discouraging those who were trying to do so - from it (Mat. 23:13; JST Luke 11:53). The same is occurring today. It is our responsibility to discern true servants from false ones. God told us how to identify **His** servants, saying, "**by their fruits ye shall know them**" (Mat. 7:16-20; 3 Ne. 14:15-16).

4. The Twelve **redefined what qualifies them** to be a true "disciple," citing their "**calling**" by other men to the apostleship as sufficient. God calls all to "repent" and **receive Him** ("come unto me"), that they might be empowered and sent by Him, but few do. Hence, "many are called but few "**chosen**," "**empowered**," or "**sent**" by

God. Why? "Because their hearts are set on the things of the world" and because "they aspire to the honors of men" (see D&C 121:34-46). Such are powerless and do not bear "fruit meet for the Father's kingdom" (D&C 84:58). Joseph Smith and Oliver Cowdery gave the Twelve "**the apostolic charge**" to become actual witnesses of Christ and His reality, as did Paul the Apostle and other "special witnesses" of Christ. They were to **see Him**, **know Him**, and brings souls **to Him** (JST Matt. 7:33; 25:9-10). They are to see and feel the marks of the atonement in His side, hands, wrists, or feet – the infallible proofs of His love for us all. Today they no longer bear this type of "**special witness**" of the LORD to the world, and are thus no different than other church members in their testimony of Christ.

5. The Twelve have become **paid ministers**, living off the sheep. Scripture warns us about those practicing *priestcraft* for *gain* (2 Ne. 26:29). Christ told the Twelve of His day, "Provide neither gold, nor silver, nor brass in your purses, Nor scrip for your journey, neither two coats, neither shoes, nor yet staves: for the workman is worthy of his meat" (Mat. 10:9-10). God's spirit is given to those who **sacrifice** *for Him in loving service to others*. They can then teach, heal, cast out devils, and raise the dead - with **power** and **authority** (Mosiah 18:26). God's salvation is free (2 Ne. 2:4), available without money or price. Satan says we can have anything in this world for our money. Today, "tithing settlement" determines if one gets a temple recommend. Bishops and Stake Presidents work without pay, while the Twelve receive salaries, perks, and praise. Scripture provides a different model.

6. Joseph's "**last charge**" to the Council of Fifty, when he vigorously shook his clothing before them, was a warning and a condemnation upon many of the Twelve present at this private meeting. It was also a transfer of **responsibility** - of the blood and sins of his generation - off of Joseph's shoulders and onto **theirs**. Paul, King Benjamin, Alma, and Moroni also shook their garments free of the blood and sins of **those they taught**, **transferring responsibility to them** (see Acts 18:6; 2 Ne. 9:44-45; Jacob 1:19, 2:2 & p. 113 #4). Moroni **transfered responsibility** to **us** in the latter-days in Ether 12:37-41. He taught **the doctrine of Christ**. We must now act.

Watchman On the Tower

The men who lead us at the top are not who they say they are. The Saints have responsibility to exercise righteous judgment and discernment via the Spirit, or they will be *deceived*, inheriting lesser kingdoms in their decisions (see D&C 76:75). God said, "the inhabitants of Zion shall judge all things pertaining to Zion. And liars and hypocrites shall be proved **by them**, and they who are **not** apostles and prophets shall be known" (D&C 64:38-39). Ask God about these things and about those who the lead in its highest counsels. The LORD said:

> "**My sheep hear my voice**, and I know them, and **they follow me**: And **I** give unto them eternal life; and they shall never perish, neither shall any man pluck them out of my hand" (John 10:27-28).

God wants us to have **the truth**. This is why He **commanded** us to **diligently search Isaiah** in the Book of Mormon. He stated, "Ye ought to search these things. Yea, a commandment I give unto you that ye search these things diligently; for great are the words of Isaiah. For surely he spake as touching all things concerning **my people** which are of the house of Israel…And all things that he spake **have been** and **shall be** . . . Therefore give heed to **my words**... " (3 Ne. 23:1-3, see also 20:11-12; D&C 5:5; 56:3). The great Prophet Isaiah is an important watchman for our day, along with Jeremiah, Daniel, Ezekiel, John the Revelator, and Joseph Smith. During the Middle Ages the words of "watchmen" were scarce. Many leaders purposely kept the people in the "dark" for the purpose of control and gain. They fed themselves on the backs of the people, like the "shepherds" of Ezekiel 34 or Jeremiah 23. Scripture tells us that without knowledge of God, there is ignorance, captivity, and destruction (Hosea 4:6; Isa. 5:13). Unwise stewards are chastised by the LORD throughout scripture. Because too many watchmen are asleep, distracted by the things of the world, or in the employ of the enemy, darkness advances. We are there. God said:

> "**O my people, they who lead thee cause thee to err** and destroy the way of thy paths." (Isa. 3:12; 2 Ne. 13:12).

Too many leaders - at all levels - have **not sought *nor* experienced the transformational spiritual change** of being **born again** in Christ (chapter 7). Because of the false narrative of the church today (that Joseph is a polygamist, Assumption 7), many of them do not believe that he was an inspired prophet, and thus they don't internalize the important Book of Mormon message he brought forth. This book, Joseph, and even Christ, are then thrown out by many. **Leaders** must be **spiritually born of God**, teaching others the same, or **the blind lead the blind** (Mat. 15:14).

In chapter 34 of Ezekiel we read; "Son of man, prophesy against the shepherds of Israel…neither did my shepherds search for my flock, but **the shepherds fed themselves**, and fed not the flock…Therefore will **I** save my flock, and they shall no more be a prey; and I will Judge between cattle and cattle. And I will set up one shepherd over them, and he shall feed them . . . and he shall be their shepherd. And **I the Lord will be their God**." Scriptures addressing leaders negatively are a sign for those who have eyes to see. It is part of waking up to our "awful situation." They include Isaiah **1:5**, **3:12**, **9:16**, **19:14**, **28:1, 3, 7, 15**; 29:10, 56:10; Jeremiah 2:8, 13; 5:3-13, 26-31; 10:21; 14:14-15; 23:1-32; **Ezek. 34:1-3**, 8, 22-24, 27; 37:22-28; Hosea 2:16-17, 3:4-5; JST Luke 12:54; **2 Ne. 19:16**, 26:29; 28:3-4, 2, 11-15, 21, 24-25, 31, and D&C 64:38-43; 85:7-9; 89-95; 101:44-61, 90; 124:24-26 101:44-61, 90.

In these verses we are invited to open our eyes. They say the "**head** is sick," that the leaders "cause the people to **err**," that they are "**out** of the way," making "**lies** their refuge." They are "**blind**" and "**asleep**." In Mosiah 23:14 we are taught to trust **no man** to lead us, unless he is a "just man," a "man of God," one who keeps the commandments of God, all of them. King Benjamin was such a leader. He didn't say "follow me," but taught that Christ is to be our "**head**," (Mosiah 5:8), our source of light. Among us today are *three types of leaders* in the LDS church. They include:

(1) Many local *and* lower level General Authorities do their best, based on their current understanding of the gospel, and how it is put forth through **the Handbook of Instructions**. God's word teaches that meetings and dealings with each other *are better* led by "**the Spirit**" (D&C 20:45; Mor. 6:9) and by **His holy word** in scripture.

(2) Many upper level General Authorities do **not** believe the Restoration story of Joseph Smith and yet they continue to promote the current church narrative because they believe the Saints *need* the church as it is. They rise up in leadership positions *only* if they are "church broke" (with the same *unbelief*). Some do not even believe in Jesus Christ. Many are sincere and well-meaning people, even though they don't believe in Joseph's Restoration story or have *faith in Christ.* Some believe the anti-Mormon messages, which are strengthened by the false narrative put forth by the church itself through Brigham Young, that Joseph was a polygamist (and all the other **lies** going with it), rather than the saving message of the Book of Mormon. It encourages us to be **born again** in Christ. The false narrative is put forth to maintain their comfortable lifestyle, salary, and the acclaim of their position. Upper level leaders also receive a large financial gift at he start of their ministry. The perks keep everything in place.

(3) There are also wolves in sheep's clothing leading the Saints today. The promotion of the insideous "be one" movement (endnote 1) reveals a false veneer of love in acceptance for all. Those in Sodom and Gomorrah were destroyed because they embraced sexual sin, while ignoring the plight of the poor. One General Authority I have met has revealed that the Church makes monthly payments to the Roman Catholic Church, clearly tying us to the Great Whore of 1 Nephi 14:10. How long this has been occurring is unknown. We do know that in March of 2019 a new LDS Temple will be dedicated in Rome Italy, the capital of Roman Catholicism. It is a symbol of solidarity and more.

Speaking to General Authorities candidly about these things and their personal beliefs is very enlightening. It confirms our "**awful situation**" today – that addressed in the Book of Mormon. Though I don't agree with Palmer's assessments of Joseph and the Restoration in his book, *Restoring Christ: Leaving Mormon Jesus for Jesus of the Gospels*, his chapter 13, entitled, *Meetings with an LDS General Authority, 2012-14*, has insights consistent with the General Authority I have met. In, Palmer's book he addresses a meeting he had with an unnamed Seventy, Mission President, and upper level General Authority. Each of them did not believe the Restoration story of Joseph Smith. Palmer stated:

> "The GA said the church is like a weakened dam. At first you don't see the cracks on the face; nevertheless, things are happening behind the scenes. Eventually, small cracks appear, and then the dam will explode. When it does, he said, the members are going to be shocked and will need scholars and historians like myself [Palmer] to educate them regarding **the Mormon past**. The Mission President and the Seventy both said they attend church every Sunday, but feel like *hypocrites who are trapped.* The GA said his ward treats him like a king and when he gives Firesides and speaks to LDS congregations, they have high expectations of him. **He would like to do more in getting the truth out** *besides raising a few questions when speaking and gifting my book* [Palmer's anti-Mormon book] to others when feeling uncomfortable. Perhaps this is why he [the GA] has reached out to me [Palmer]. As stated previously, I think he is honestly telling me what **he believes** to be the truth" (Palmer, *Restoring Christ*, chap. 13).

For Palmer, "**the Mormon past**" believed by many LDS leaders, is the false narrative put forth by Brigham and those following him into polygamy, the one put forth today that weakens trust in Joseph's work and thus the very important

Book of Mormon message – **that each of us must be born again in Christ to be redeemed of Him**. Brigham's lies about Joseph and our early history have taken our focus off **faith in the LORD Jesus** and **His salvation**, and instead made Joseph out to be a polygamist, a cheat, and a liar, so that Brigham and others could practice polygamy freely for some 60 years. It is consistent with Satan's plan to **lie** and **deceive** us. The "handbook" of instructions has replaced the Lectures on Faith, God's holy word - in **scripture**, and individual **pure revelation**. There is a better way.

In Mormon 8:36 we read of the pollution of last-days churches, including ours. Just before Joseph Smith was murdered, he removed his garment and encouraged the Twelve to do the same. They would not. He went to William Marks (Stake Pres.) expressing remorse over his own errors and those of the Saints. Freemasonry, polygamy, idolatry and other sins among the Saints were creating havoc in the Church. In 1830 Joseph was lifted up as the sole church leader. He latter became Nauvoo's Mayor, General of the Nauvoo Legion, etc. It may have been the beginning of our idolatry, now greatly etrenched. Young and Kimball introduced secrecy and the oath of Cain into the temple rites (borrowed from Masonry). These oaths and their penalties were useful in implementing spiritual wifery and getting gain. Today ties are being established to Catholicism, its False Prophet, and the beast of Revelation 13 and 17. Idolatry is rampant in both cultures, as both the Pope and the President of the Corporation Sole are lifted up as lights before the people. Leaders in high places in both groups are accused of pedophilia, SRA, and more. Much is swept under the rug as *lawyers, judges*, and *high priests* (3 Ne. 6:27) are in collusion with one another, having made secret blood oaths to protect themselves, their gain, and their corporations ("the Great and Abominable" one of 1 Ne. 14:10). This unholy alliance has allowed the LDS Church to build a temple in Rome, but at great cost.

In the March 2019 meeting between Pres. Nelson and the Pope, Pres. Nelson called him "**His Holiness**." The Pope's primary mission today is to create a "**one world church**" (a goal of the United Nations, see p. 186), an unholy alliance of Catholicism, Islam, and all world relgions, which now may include Mormonism. The teachings of this first Jesuit Pope counteract God's word in scripture. He supports Darwin's evolution theory, not the Genesis creation account. He states all believers can go to heaven, including those embracing the LGBTQ movement and atheists, saying good works take us there not faith in Christ. He has spoken about forgiving abortion (something only God can do in Prov. 28:13; 2 Chron. 7:14; Isa. 55:7). He and his priests provide "indulgences" to earn God's mercy (see Deut. 10:17). He made a mass murderer (Junipero Serra) a "Saint" (see Psalm 85:8). He says criticizing Islam is a form of terrorism, whereas scripture teaches that we all are to exercise righteousness judgment (see Eph. 5:11; Isa. 58:1; Rev. 3:19). He says proselytizing is poison, whereas Christ taught His disciples to go out into the world and give all people a choice (Matt. 28:19-20; Mark 16:16). And he teaches a 1st day Sunday Sabbath, not a 7th day of rest (see Ex. 20:8-40).

In Revelation 13:3 John said the last days "beast" would receive a "deadly wound." It was the Reformation movement aided by the invention of moveable type printing presses. It allowed God's holy word in the Bible to go forth into the world. God's word is a powerful dividing sword, separating light from darkness. Too many today are not consulting it. In the same verse, John said that the "deadly wound" was eventually **healed**. It is occurring before our eyes today in the alliances Pope Francis is creating! The beast has risen up again, stronger than ever, but behind a curtain of deceit, like the wizard of Oz. The illuminated elite use **secrecy**, **lies**, and **deception** to *murder, get gain, and maintain control.* The Jesuits lead out in this effort, along with leaders of governments, media, schools, *and* churches, with enforcement by the CIA, the FBI, and many "*judges, lawyers,* and *high priests*" among us. Note what 3 Nephi 6 has to say about this.

> "Now it came to pass that those **judges** had many *friends* and *kindreds;* and the remainder, yea, even **almost all the lawyers** and the **high priests**, did gather themselves together, and unite with the kindreds of those **judges** who were to be tried according to the law. And they did **enter into a covenant one with another**, yea, even into that **covenant** . . . *administered* **by the devil**, *to combine against all righteousness*" (3 Nephi 6:27-28).

Nephi said there are "**two churches** only" (1 Ne. 14:10), one focused on Christ, one focused on gain. The "corporation sole" of both the Catholic and LDS church originates in ancient Roman law. It and covenants the Saints make are effective tools to get "gain" (see Moses 5:40, Alma 34:35 & Rev. 9:3-4 *versus* Ezek. 9:4, Mosiah 5:15, Rev. 7:2-3, 14:1, 22:4 & D&C 133:17-18). Isaiah spoke of "the drunkards of Ephraim" making "**lies** *our refuge*." He said *we* "have made a **covenant with death**" (Isa. 28:15). Is this the "covenant" the Saints make in temples wearing the green apron, a symbol of Satan's power and priesthoods? Or is it the one made to support leaders who appear to have made a recent alliance and covenant with the Jesuit Pope Francis? Are the Saints now under this covenant too *and* with their subtle consent (**see p. 174**)? Are they part of the binding chains and cords of hell spoken of in 2 Nephi 1:13 and 9:45?

Chapter Seven

The Doctrine of Christ

The Fullness & Its Rejection

After darkness each night there is the light of a new day. This chapter provides relief from the darkness of previous chapters by addressing the great light available in the saving "**doctrine of Christ**" in its fullness. God loves us and wants us to receive salvation and a fullness of His blessings. He sent His precious **Son** to show us "**the way**." It begins with understanding and embracing "**the way**" of salvation. Too few know *what* it is, or *how* to obtain it, as many churches (religions) keep their people in ignorance to **get gain** (1 Ne. 22:23). It is both accidental by some and puposeful by others, depending upon those who lead. Embracing the full portion of the doctrine and gospel of Christ is what was sacrificed in Brigham's push to implement his "new order of things" focused on spiritual wifery. Embracing Christ fully leads us into His church. It is made up of those whom He says "**repent** and **come unto me**" (D&C 10:67). They embrace "**the New and everlasting covenant**" which is Him and His will.

In its simplest, pure from this "**covenant**" can be defined as seeking and embracing **God's <u>will</u>** rather than our own (see JST Gen. 9:21; Mosiah 5:5, 8, 18:10; 2 Ne. 32:3, 6; D&C 22 & 84:35-48). This covennt extends throughout eternity. In this life we are to make a willing covenant with God out of love for Him, as did the people of King Benjamin (see Mosiah 5:5). We do so in a baptism where we are *fully aware of what we are promising to do*, one where we *truly* **repent** in *humility* and *sincerety* – one where we offer up a **broken heart** and a **contrite spirit** to God. In it *we willingly* **submit our will to God's will**, and thus take the LORD's **name** *upon us* as our "**head**" (see Mosiah 5). Few eight-year olds *or* adults understand these things and do them. Too often baptism is about joining a church and doing things others expect us to do - the *dead works* of men spoken of by Nephi (2 Ne. 25) and Paul the Apostle (Heb. 6:1, 9:14). We are invited instead to become "alive in Christ."

Hereafter, this chapter is divided into three parts to help us better understand "**how**" to come unto Christ, be alive in **Him**, and be **saved**. In Part I: *Rejecting God & His Will* we see how the fullness of the gospel of Christ (3 Ne. 16:10) was rejected early on, leading to our "awful situation" today. In Part II: *The Rejection at Sinai*, we read nine important scriptures that reveal similarities between the children of Israel and modern Saints. And in Part III: *Understanding the Doctrine of Christ,* we learn how to reverse our course and return to light in a fruitful relationship with Jesus Christ.

Part I: Rejecting God & His Will

In chapter 6 David Whitmer cited five things he saw corrupting the early church. The first was a secret combination that rose up in power in 1838 among the Danites. The second was spiritual wifery that took root in Kirtland and which latter exploded at Nauvoo. The third was changes he saw being made to scripture, the foundation of pure doctrine. The fourth was the rise of idolatry in the church, where the Saints became dependant upon Joseph, and later the Twelve led by Young, rather than upon God as "**the rock**," and His written *and* revealed **word**. Whitmer knew that Joseph's primary responsibility was to bring forth more of **God's word** to the people via scripture, and that he was not to be their **source** of light or doctrine - **God was**. With Joseph's murder, increasing trust was placed in men (the Twelve) with Brigham as leader eventually making polygamy official church doctrine, one required for exaltation. The changing of **doctrine** *to support sexual sin* was a great "abomination," patterned after "the Nicolaitan band" (D&C 117:11; Rev. 2:14-15). Whitmer had a final fifth concern. It was *deception* also tied to idolatry but on a more personal level. He noted how "**idols in one's heart**" affected the ability of he, Joseph, and Oliver to receive *pure*, undefiled revelation **from God**, as opposed to two other *false* revelation sources leading to deception. Pride and self will lead to believing our own thoughts and impressions, or those from Satan and false spirits, are "revelation" to us.

King Benjamin was a wise, holy man. He brought his people to Christ as their "head" by putting them under an important ovenant to obey **God's will** not *his will* (Mosiah 5:5-8). Doing one's own will and mixing it with the supposed things of God was the way of Cain and Brigham Young. King Benjamin wisely taught that Christ alone is our "**head**" (see Mosiah 5:8; Eph. 1:22, 2:20:15, 5:23). He said:

> "And now, because of the covenant which ye have made [in the two baptisms] ye shall be called the children of Christ, his sons, and his daughters; for behold, this day he hath **spiritually begotten you** [in the 2nd fiery baptism]; for ye say that **your hearts are changed** through *faith* on **his name** [not that of King Benjamin or Joseph Smith] therefore, ye are **born of him** and have become **his** sons and his daughters. And under **<u>this head</u>**

ye are made free, and there is **<u>no other head</u>** whereby ye can be made free. There is **<u>no other name</u>** given whereby **salvation** cometh; therefore, I would that **ye should take upon you <u>the name of Christ</u>**, all you that have **entered into the covenant <u>with God</u>** that *ye should be obedient* unto the end of your lives" (Mosiah 5:7-8).

Though Joseph brought forth much scripture and many revelations, he also made mistakes, freely admitting them (see D&C 3:6-11; 5:21-22; 35:17-18; 64:5; 93:47). Others cover them up. Mantras common today, like, "follow the Prophet" and "we cannot and will not lead you astray" are dangerous, as they introduce false doctrine and point to people to men, not God for light. Searching the phrase "*follow the prophet*" reveals three scriptures refuting how it is used falsely today to prop up men (see Deut. 18:20-22; Ezek. 13:3; 3 Ne. 20:24). Jesus is THE Prophet we are to follow as addressed 7 times in 1 Nephi 22. Too often men want honor, power, and money, resulting in "priestcraft" (see D&C 121:34-46). "He [God] commandeth that there shall be no priestcrafts; for, behold, priestcrafts are that men preach and set themselves up for a light unto the world, that they may get gain and praise of the world; but they seek not the welfare of Zion" (2 Ne. 26:29). The LORD added, "Behold I am the light which ye shall hold up—that which ye have seen me do" (see 3 Ne. 18:24). His ways were and are wise, full of love. He is worthy of our focus.

A. Rejecting the Fullness of His Word

When Christ came to those gathered at Bountiful in the Book of Mormon (following the great destruction), He taught them correct **doctrine** first, then he addressed the fullness of His **gospel**. Later he concluded His instruction detailing what His **church** was and is (see Assumption #9, pps. 215-223, chap. 6). An important contributor to our downfall has been ignoring, changing, or removing God's correct **doctrine** in scripture. Note the summary below:

1. There are 450 English "translations" of the whole Bible alone (the Saints use the King James Version), and 670 different language translations, all with their own variations. The New Testament has been translated into 1,521 languages. Much of this work is pure, but portions of it have been modified, polluted, or removed.
2. Royal Skousen has documented many changes to the Book of Mormon in its various printings. Five of many are presented below. It remains mostly pure today, however.
3. There were a total of 2,643 changes made to the D&C between the 1833 and 1835 editions (see endnote 22). Note one made by Joseph Smith in 1834 (top, p. 224). Brigham added pro-polygamy Section 132, while removing anti-polygamy Section 101, both in 1878 and with no Church vote. There are many other examples.
4. Joseph Smith's re-translation of the Bible was completed but not published prior to his murder. It was his firstborn son who published it in 1867 as President of the RLDS Church. It and the Book of Mormon did not go forth together into the world as the LORD directed, *except* through the RLDS Church.
5. LDS Church historian and polygamist Orson Pratt made changes to thr wording of portions of the Book of Moses when he made a copy of portions of the copyrighted and printed RLDS JST Bible. See p. 234.
6. The Lectures on Faith were removed from the D&C in 1923 by a committee of men, and with no church vote.
7. Today many of the Saints value the words of men over God's words in scripture. He has told us repeatedly to "**rely**" **on** that which is "**written**" in them and to "not trust in the arm of flesh." He commanded those reading the Book of Mormon to diligently search Isaiah (3 Ne. 23:1-3), which reveals the corruption among us today.

Book of Mormon Changes In chapter 1, the author referenced a 1981 change to Jacob 3:5, providing subtle support for polygamy. It reads, "Behold, the Lamanites . . . are more righteous than you; for they have **not** forgotten the commandment of the Lord, which was given unto our **fathers**" (*plural*, 1830 version). In the 1981 printing of the Book of Mormon, the word "**fathers**" (plural) was changed to "*father*" (singular, Lehi only). Note the additional Book of Mormon changes below, those introduced between the first 1830 New York edition and the second 1837 Kirtland edition. I believe they contribute to *diminishing* **Christ as God** and the **Father of the our salvation**. Though He **is** a Son (below right, 1837), He is also our **Savior** and **Jehovah**, **God** of the Old Testament. Our LORD is also the great **Creator**, **Judge**, and **King**. He will cleanse the Earth at His return. Are you prepared for this great and dreadful day?

	Original 1830 Book of Mormon	*Modified* 1837 Book of Mormon
1 Ne. 11:18	"the mother of **God**"	"mother of **the son of** God"
1 Ne. 11:21	"**the Lamb** of God, yea even the Eternal Father"	"the lamb of God, yea even **the son of** the Eternal Father"
1 Ne. 11:32	"**the Everlasting God** was judged of the world"	"**the son of** the Everlasting God was judged of the world"
1 Ne. 13:40	"**the Lamb of God is the Eternal Father**"	"the Lamb of God is **the son of** the Eternal Father"

Various verses in the Book of Mormon reveal why Christ is "**the Eternal Father**" – **of our salvation**. Besides the 1 Nephi verses above, **other** verses feature the clarifying words "son of" later added to them (see Mosiah 13:28, 34-35, 15:1-4 & 16:15; Alma 11:38-39; Hel. 14:12; Ether 4:7, 12). Note one other changed phrase - "**sword of justice**." It was later replaced in 1837 with, the "**word of justice**" (compare 1 Ne. 12:18 to Alma 26:19; 60:29; Hel. 13:5; 3 Ne. 29:4). The **word of God** is **a dividing sword** separating truth from error (1 Ne. 21:2). Most prefer the earlier, original translation in each of these five examples. Many more changes are documented in Royal Skousens' work, *The Book of Mormon: The Earliest Text*, Yale Univ. Press. The Bible has many more modifications, and because of this, the LORD had Joseph Smith re-translate it just after he completed the Book of Mormon. It has many significant improvements.

The Inspired Joseph Smith Re-Translation of the Bible Relatively few know that the Book of Mormon (completed in 1830), together with Joseph Smith's *entire* re-translation of the Bible (mostly completed by 1834) were intended to be printed and sent out into the world **together** (1 Ne. 13:41) in Joseph's Smith's day, along with the oracles (revelations to Joseph) in the Doctrine and Covenants. The Lord referred to them collectively as "*the fullness* of **my scriptures**" (D&C 42:12, 15, 56-59; 93:53), as well as "*the fullness of* **the scriptures**" (JST Luke 11:53), or "**my holy word**" (D&C 124:89). Together, they provide us "**the key of knowledge**" necessary to receive our LORD and His greatest gift, eternal life. Their truths are priceless. They help restore many *plain* (simple) and *precious* (sacred) things back to us, those things *changed* or *removed* from the Bible by evil and designing men. The *changed things* address both **how** to be *saved* by our LORD" and **how** Satan tries to stop this work with *secret combinations* and their *blood oaths*. The whole Book of Enoch was removed from the Bible to keep such things hidden. Addressing the importance of His **word**, God said:

> "Behold I give unto you a commandment, that you **rely upon** the things **which are written**; for in them [this fullness] are *all things* written, concerning **my church, my gospel**, and **my rock**. Wherefore if you shall build up **my church** and **my gospel**, and **my rock** [me and my teachings], the gates of hell shall not prevail against you" (early, *unchanged* 1833 Book of Commandments, chapter 15).

> "**my scriptures** . . . shall be preserved in safety [Emma's safekeeping] . . . And I give unto you a **commandment** that then **ye shall teach them unto all men**; for *they shall be taught* unto all nations, kindreds, tongues and people. Thou shalt take the things which thou hast received, which have been given unto thee in **my scriptures for a law, to be my law to govern my church**" (D&C 42:56-59). Not men's laws.

> "And after they had been received unto baptism, and were *wrought upon* and *cleansed by the power of the Holy Ghost,* they were numbered among the people of **the church of Christ**; and their *names* were taken, that they might be might be remembered and **nourished by the good word of God**, to keep them in *the right way*, to keep them *continually watchful unto prayer*, **relying alone** upon the merits of **Christ**, who was **the author and the finisher of their faith**" (Moroni 6:4).

> "And now, my beloved brethren, *after ye have gotten into this strait and narrow path*, I would ask if all is done? Behold, I say unto you, Nay; for ye have not come thus far save it were by **the word of Christ** with *unshaken faith in* **him, relying wholly upon the merits of him who is mighty to save**" (2 Ne. 31:19, see also 1 Ne. 10:6; Alma 25:16, 26:27-29).

Note that the LORD **did not say** that we were to **rely** on modern leaders, *the arm of flesh* – something which those practicing *priestcraft* do say now in statements like "*we cannot and will not lead you astray*" (see 2 Ne. 26:29; 3 Ne. 18:24). Turning to men always results in curses and *idolatry* and thus "the gates of hell" **prevail** against those who do **not** feast upon **the fullness of God's written word**.

In God's holy word He teaches that we are to **rely** instead on the "fullness" of **God's word** already given us - in both sets of scripture (the full JST Bible *and* the Book of Mormon), in combination with the *modern unchanged revelations* **given to Joseph Smith** in the early oracles of the Book of Commandments and many of the non-doctrored verses of the Doctrine and Covenants. Today, the Saints falsely rely on men and themselves (*the arm of flesh*, 2 Ne. 4:34, 28:31-32; Jer. 17:5) for their doctrine. It has continually changed since the days of Joseph. Relying on men to lead us results in ignorance of **truth** – and specifically "**the way**" of salvation of our God. It is His will and way.

In Christ's day it was the Rabbis as *academics*, the Sadducees as *philosophers*, and the Pharisees as *lawyers* who polluted the church. Satan, with the help of evil and designing men takes away light via disobedience (D&C 93:39), along with the passed down **iniquities** of "*fathers, priests,* and *kings.*" These iniquities include false teachings and traditions. Looking to men often "**corrupts**" and "**pollutes**" the church, the two words used by Nephi (2 Ne. 28:11) and Mormon when addressing **us** and **our** day (Morm. 8:36). Nibley said corruption always comes from within (p. 211). God said **His word is the law to govern His church** (D&C 42:59).

In The Far West Report, "Brother Joseph Smith, Jr. said . . . that God had often **sealed up the heavens** because of covetousness in the Church...and except the Church receive **the fullness of the Scriptures that <u>they would yet fail</u>**" (Far West Report, p. 16, TPJS, p 9). Joseph added that "**the salvation of the elect**" was dependent upon the **fullness of truths** being delivered to the world in a future **one-volume publication** of both the Book of Mormon **and** the JST Bible (D&C 35:20; 1 Ne. 13:41). The RLDS church had this fullness in the full JST Bible *and* the Book of Mormon for some time, but problems later entered into their leadership too, after their Twelve (like the Twelve under Brigham) took power away from the Smith family bloodline. The Utah Saints have never been encouraged to use the full version of Joseph's re-translation of the Bible, as the LDS Church did not hold copyright to it. The purity and fullness of God's whole word did not go out into the world via the LDS Church, thus fulfilling the LORD's prophecy.

Being grounded upon the **rock** of truth in pure doctrine from the LORD - is a must, otherewise the gates of hell prevail against us (see JST Mat. 16:16-19). The majority of the Brighamite Saints today know little about the complete JST version of the Bible, and thus they don't use it. Our salvation as a people is aided by it. It was Pres. Joseph Smith III of the RLDS church that published the full JST in **1867**, as the original manuscript for it remained in the hands of his mother Emma Smith for good reason. In her safe-keeping Brigham Young was unable to change its words to support polygamy. Copyright to this work remains in the hands of the Community of Christ (formerly the RLDS church). Their leadership had the full JST Bible and the Book of Mormon for **151 years** but departed from God's ways too. The Utah Saints still don't have it. We have a meager 16 pages (select verses chosen for us by leaders) of this precious re-translation. These 16 pages only became part of our scriptures in **1979**. It wasn't a church leader that brought this important work to our attention, but Robert J. Matthews, a professor at BYU. He has revealed that Polygamist Orson Pratt, as LDS Church Historian, simply copied a *copyrighted* and *printed* RLDS JST Bible so that the Brighamite Saints might have a more complete Book of Moses (for more on this subject see pps. 85-86).

In 2016 I remember being shocked to hear David Bednar quote two JST scriptures in General Conference that year. Both are **not** in our scriptures (though present in the RLDS JST Bible). Both address **the necessity** of coming to "**know**" the LORD (see JST Mat. 7:33 & 25:9-11). Alma knew the great value of **God's word** saying, "the preaching of **the word** had a great tendency to lead the people to do that which was **just**—yea, it had had more powerful effect upon the minds of the people **than the sword, or anything else**..." (Alma 31:5). To be "**justified**" in scripture is to be saved or redeemed. It is of critical importance to all who love God – the wise virgins.

Changes to the Doctrine and Covenants The D&C has seen the most *troubling* changes, over 2,500 of them,[27] like Brigham Young's addition of pro-polygamy Section 132 and the simultaneous removal of the original anti-polygamy Section 101 addressed in chapter 1. The Saints were not allowed to vote on these actions. The removal of *The Lectures on Faith* in 1923 (also without a vote of the church) took away important doctrine too, that tied to (1) The character and attributes of God that *give us good* **reason to have faith in the Father and the Son**; (2) The critical nature of developing *strong* **faith**, wherein there is **power** to do "all things" - as in healing the sick, raising the dead, casting out demons, etc.; And (3) The importance of **faith in Christ** *sufficient* to part the veil of our unbelief and receive Him in this life as our Second Comforter. **Faith** is the power behind all things in the doctrine, gospel, and church of Christ.

The word "disciple" was changed to "apostle" along with other changes made from the 1833 Book of Commandments *to* the 1835 D&C. Jesus called the Twelve in the Book of Mormon "disciples" *not* "Apostles" (see 1 Ne. 12:9-10, 3 Ne. 19:4, 28:4-10, and John 8:32 & p. 191). Desiring to have the honors of men appears to be the reason for the change (see D&C 121:34-46). God's written and revealed word to us is our "iron rod," our lifeline to **Him** in troubled times – those that are surely coming. John taught us that we are to abide in **Christ** as the True Vine. As long as we don't ask amiss (because of idols in our heart – from self will & pride), it can be a clear source of truth.

Remvoing the Lectures on Faith Having **strong faith** in **God** (the Son and the Father) is correct doctrine, as faith is where all **power** originates (Heb. 11:3). Verse 1 of *Lecture on Faith 1*, states that *The Lectures on Faith* are "**the doctrine of Christ.**" They were the curriculum for the School of the Prophets in February of 1833. Both this school and the seven lectures part of it were put in place by *the command of God* (see D&C 88:127, 136-41; 90:7). They were also put into our canon of scriptures by a vote of the whole church. They were later removed from the D&C in 1921 by a committee of men, without a vote of the church; an action going against the LORD's instruction in D&C 26:2 (the law of "common consent"). Subsequently the important doctrines of the Godhead, the Holy Ghost, *and* the necessity to develop strong faith in God necessary to receive salvation, have all been diminished, ignored, or put away.

Three major points are addressed in these lectures; (1) *What faith is* - "Now **faith** is the substance [assurance] of things hoped for, the evidence of things not seen . . . **the principle of action in all intelligent beings**" (LF 1:8-9); We also learn (2) *What we are to put our faith in* - **God, because of His superior, character, perfections, and attributes** (LF 2-4). We also learn that the "Godhead" is the Father and the Son (the *two* members of the Godhead as addressed in LF 5). And we learn that having the Holy Ghost is having access to their unified mind – that of the Father and the Son; And (3) We learn *What the effects of faith are* – or the outcome of real faith, and the sacrifice to obtain it (LF 6), and that is our **assimilation of the attributes of Godliness into our lives**, where we become **one with them**, inheriting **salvation** (in its highest form, LF 7). Christ is the prototype of a "**saved**" being. We believe Him, follow Him, and put our faith and trust in Him. With faith we can do all things. Faith is **power** (see http://lecturesonfaith.com).

Strong **faith** is necessary to part the veil of our *unbelief* and come to **know** God personally, experiencing Him and the gifts and fruits of the Spirit in our lives now. It is to be followed by real, heartfelt repentance, and then – after a covenant is made with God - to serve Him and obey His will - we are to be baptized in both water *and* then by fire – or in God's Holy Spirit (addressed later in this chapter). This puts us through **the gate** and onto the path to partake of the fruit of the Tree of Life. Too many of the Saints are failing in the very first step "in **the way** of salvation of our God" – and that is by **not** having strong "**faith in Christ,**" **the power** inherent in **His** doctrine, gospel, and church.

God the Father invites us to develop a trusting **relationship** with **Him** through **the Son**, our Mediator, Intercessor, and Advocate *with* the Father. This is the reason for the marriage symbolism sprinkled throughout scripture. Jesus is the Bridegroom and believers are His bride. False doctrine and traditions, resulting from our idolatry, have led us away from **the Rock** of our salvation, and **His** saving truths. We then wander into forbidden paths. Nephi said:

> "I know **in whom** I have trusted. **My God** hath been my support…He hath filled me with **his love**, even unto the consuming of my flesh…he hath heard my cry by day, and he hath given knowledge by visions in the nighttime… And upon the wings of his spirit hath my body been carried away upon exceedingly high mountains. And my eyes have beheld great things…Oh LORD, I will praise thee forever; yea my soul will rejoice in thee my God, and **the rock** of my salvation. Oh LORD, wilt thou redeem my soul?...May the gates of hell be shut continually before me, because that my heart is broken and my spirit is contrite! . . . Oh LORD, wilt thou encircle me around in the robe of thy righteousness!...Oh LORD, I have trusted **in thee** and I will trust **in thee** forever. I will **not** put my trust in the arm of flesh; for I know that **cursed** is he that putteth his trust in the arm of flesh. Yea, **cursed** is he that putteth his trust in man or maketh flesh his arm. Yea, I know that God will give liberally to him that asketh. Yea, my God will give me, if I ask *not amiss*; therefore I will lift up my voice unto thee, my God, **the rock** of my righteousness. Behold, my voice shall forever ascend up unto thee, **my rock** and mine everlasting God. Amen" (2 Ne. 4:19-35).

Too many Saints ignore God's written word in favor of the words of leaders. Thus the gates of hell prvevail. It is far easier to listen to leaders twice a year, believing they give all that is needed than to work out our salvation with God.

B. Rejecting the Fullness of His Law

God's **word** is His **law** (D&C 42:59). The fullness of God's higher **law** of **love** is necessary to establish Zion. It is summarized in the two great commandments (1) to **love** God with all our hearts, and (2) to **love** one another (see Mat. 22:36-40). D&C 42 (1831) features two primary portions of His law. They are (1) **the law of marriage** (vs. 22-23), and (2) **the law of consecration** (vs. 30-35). The law of marriage was focused on real love and moral purity between **one** man and **one** woman (monogamy), as found in the book of Jacob and D&C 63:13. Satan successfully polluted much of real love among the Saints via the introduction of "**spiritual wifery**" at Kirtland and Nauvoo.

The higher **law of consecration** insured that there were **no poor** among the Saints. In JST Genesis 14:38 we read of *one reason* for Abraham to pay tithing to Melchizedek, and that was *to help the poor.* With contention and a focus on carnal things, including materialism, living God's higher law of marriage and consecration were both *collectively* rejected among the Saints. The *mighty change of heart*, where we become capable of greater love, occurs as we are *born again* in Christ (addressed later in this chapter). Had more of the early Saints experienced this life changing event, they may have been able to live God's higher laws of **love**. Zion cannot be established without a fullness of God's word, law, and prieisthood. With them, a fullness of the LORD's **rest** or presence is possible, in a peaceful and just Zion society.

C. Removal of the Fullness of the Priesthood

Joseph Smith taught that there are three orders of priesthood, roughly associated with the telestial, terrestrial, and celestial levels of progression in our **relationship** with God. They are; (1) The Aaronic and Levitical orders (man – telestial); (2) The Melchizedek order (terrestrial – the Son); and (3) The Patriarchal order (celestial – the Father, see JST Gen. 14; Alma 13; D&C 84 & 107). In 1829, John the Baptist confirmed the Aaronic or lineal Priesthood upon Joseph and Oliver (after it was first given by the *voice* of God Himself, according to His will). He stated that, "this [lesser priesthood] **shall never be taken again from the earth**, until the sons of Levi do offer again an offering unto the Lord in righteousness" (JSH 1:35). After Joseph and Oliver were given the Aaronic Priesthood, the two men baptized each other and immediately received **the baptism of fire and the Holy Ghost**, a rare thing today. A similar outpouring occurred with the LORD's disciples in 3 Ne. 19:9-22. The change for all was **profound**. Joseph said:

> "Immediately on our coming up out of the water after we had been baptized, we experienced great and glorious blessings from our Heavenly Father. No sooner had I baptized Oliver Cowdery, than the Holy Ghost fell upon him, and he stood up and *prophesied* many things which should shortly come to pass. And again, so soon as I had been baptized by him, I also had *the spirit of prophecy*, when, standing up, I *prophesied* concerning the rise of this Church…we were **filled with the Holy Ghost**, and rejoiced in the God of our salvation. Our minds being now enlightened, we began to have **the scriptures laid open to our understandings**, and **the true meaning and intention of their more mysterious passages revealed unto us** in a manner **which we never could attain to previously, nor ever before had thought of**" (JS History 1:73-74).

Joseph and Oliver received two gifts of **power** at this time (1829), the lesser **priesthood** from John the Baptist, to baptize each other, and **the gift and power of the Holy Ghost** (from God) *to enlighten them.* Both were part of an "**endowment of power from on high**" (see chap. 6). Receiving these two gifts followed their sincere repentance, and God's purging of their sins through His fiery Spirit. With greater purity, they were allowed to have **access** to what we call today the Holy Ghost. Too many have not paid the price to receive this necessary gift, believing that a simple inviting ordinance at eight years old granted them this unspeakable gift. As we saw in chapter 6, our current definition of this gift is incorrect. In early church history, and as taught by Joseph Smith and others in the School of the Prophets, the early definition of the Holy Ghost was having **access** to the unified mind of the Father and the Son (*Lectures on Faith* 5), not a male personage of Spirit with unknown identity (see Assumption #5, chap. 6).

Later God desired that **the greater Melchizedek priesthood** be given to Joseph, Oliver and others, as was and is needed to bring again Zion and perform various priesthood ordinances (see JST Gen. 14; Alma 13; D&C 20, 84, 88 & 107). One of the most important of these is the authoritative **power** to invite others to receive the baptism of fire, and thereafter, the gift and power of the Holy Ghost, as part of the confirmation (laying on of hands) ordinance (see 3 Ne. 18:36-39; Mor. 2:2). A calling, ordination, or anointing (by man or an angel) precedes **real empowerment by God**, when a portion of God's power is sealed upon us by Him. It is the LORD Jesus who seals the lesser symbolic acts done by men on the earth, Himself. He does this acting in the capacity of the Holy Spirit of Promise (endnote 32). Our **relationship** with God and our faith in Him determines whether any of His power may be present in us, not just a preparatory ordination by men. The greater the **relationship** with God, the greater the potential priesthood. God revealed to Joseph that a secret combination would come among the Saints in the future (see D&C 38:11-13 and 28). Satan's power would be in it. God provided a way for the Saints to combat this darkness in verses 31-42. He called it a *gift* or "*endowment* of **power** *from on high.*" In Kirtland, we see that the phrase an "*endowment* of **power** *from on high*" involved **three things** given the Saints over time, and in the order listed hereafter (note the dates). They include the greater priesthood, special cleansing rites (like the washing of feet), and the gift and power of the Holy Ghost.

(1) *The Greater Priesthood* (1831) God provided the opportunity to receive the greater priesthood and its power to select men in 1831, offering both to 23 men called to the Morley Farm Conference (outside of Kirtland) in June of 1831. This is the first time that men were **called** *and* ordained to the office of High Priest in the church. Actual **power** in this office is given only by God and by via His direct **voice**. It is a separate matter. Many are **called** to various

offices, but few are **chosen** by God to receive power in the office because their hearts are "set on the things of the world" and "they aspire to the honors of men" more than God (see D&C 121:34-46). Thus, only 3 of the 23 men called at the Morley Farm conference of 1831 were actually **chosen** to receive **power** from God in their symbolic *ordinations* (a physical invitation to do so). They were Joseph Smith, Lyman Wight, and Harvey Whitlock. Note that this event – where an ordination for the greater priesthood was offered – came after God provided a fullness of His **written word** first (in the Book of Mormon and the JST Bible), and where a fullness of His higher **law** was also present (the law of monogamy and the Law of Consecration, D&C 42). Thus real **power** or "**strength**" (a term for the higher priesthood in scripture) comes only to those God trusts, as He alone knows their hearts. Such power, strength, or a "fullness of priesthood is used to defeat all enemies. It becomes a hedge of protection for the Saints against Satan and secret combinations (see D&C 38).

The authority of the greater Melchizedek priesthood is used to *invite* others to receive the gift and power of the Holy Ghost - **from God** - in a symbolic ordinance we call "confirmation" done by the laying on of hands. Jesus authorized only select servants to do this in 3 Nephi 18:36-38, by touching them (see also Moroni 2:2). Priesthood **power** (in a trusting **relationship** with God), along with **faith in Christ** are the two things used to bless, heal, and cast out, and toinvite others to received the Holy Ghost and all *according to God's will* (JST Gen. 14; Alma 13; D&C 20, 84, 88 & 107). Satan was seen at the Morley Farm Conference, and was cast out. The Father and the Son were seen by some there. D&C 124:28, given in 1838, informs us that the opportunity for the fullness of priesthood was lost or removed. In **that same year** the Danites (secrecy, oaths, revenge) emerged within the Church to avenge the persecution of the Mormons by Missourians. It represents one of the first *secret combinations* in the Church. "Love, relationship," "godliness," and "holiness of character" are useful substitite words for "priesthood." No gender is attached to it. In our "fallen state," ego has taken over. D&C 121:29 states, "Almost all men, as soon as they get a little authority, as they suppose, they will immediately begin to exercise unrighteous dominion."

(2) *Special Cleansing Rites* (1833) Along with opportunity for the greater priesthood, God inspired Joseph Smith to implement various symbolic cleansing rites, including "washing and anointings" that served as preparation for many of the Saints to receive the real thing, or God Himself and His best gifts (1833-36). It began with the "washing of feet" ordinance for those in the School of the Prophets (upper floor, Whitney Store, 1833), then moved to the Kirtland House of the LORD in 1836. These rites were performed before and after the Kirtland House of the LORD was built. Today we tie washing rites to what we now call the temple endowment. See D&C 84 and 88.

(3) *The Gift and Power of the Holy Ghost* (1836) God later provided a group gifting of the endowment of power or a group gifting of some of the gifts of the Spirit, including the Holy Ghost. They came from God or "from on high," and were given at a specific place *and* time (for those prepared to receive them). It was the dedication of the House of the LORD at Kirtland on March 27 of 1836. There were angels present, a great pillar of fire seen over the House of the LORD, cloven tongues of fire seen over the heads of some individuals, and speaking and interpretation of tongues (see Karl Ricks Anderson, Joseph Smith's Kirtland, Deseret Book). Signs of God's power followed both the believers at Kirtland and in those of the New Testament on the "Day of Pentecost" (see chap. 5, and endnote 22).

The Relationship of Priesthood Orders & Church Names

Early on the Lord called the church **His** in 1830, allowing it to be called after His holy **name** (the church of Christ). It was His church *collectively* at this time. He said that **His** power was in it "…power to lay the foundation of this church, and to bring it forth out of obscurity, and out of darkness, the only true and living church upon the face of the whole earth, with which I the Lord am well pleased, speaking unto the church *collectively* and not *individually*" (D&C 1:5). God changed the name of the church four times in early church history to reflect the growing troubles among the Saints (endnote 2). Names and titles in scripture typically reflect character, behavior, and the standing of the Saints before God from 1831 – 41. The four different names include; 1. *The church of Christ* (Mar. 1829 – June 1831); 2. *The church of God* (the Father, June 1831- Dec. 1834); 3. *The church of the Latter-day Saints* (God's name or title is removed, Dec. 1834 – Sept. 1836); And 4. *The Church of Jesus Christ of Latter-day Saints* (when God's name may have been re-inserted without His permission, Sept. 1836 – Jan. 1841).

From 1831 to 1834, the Saints were given the greater things and thus they were part of "the church of Christ." It contained a fullness of His doctrine and gospel. By 1834, rejection of this fullness began as God prophesied in 3 Ne. 16:10. The Lord appears to have taken His name away from the church. It then became "the church of the Latter-day Saints" (endnote 2). *Collectively* the lesser things remained for most, but *individually* some maintained or were given the greater priesthood. Thus there were different "orders of priesthood" present simultaneously among a limited number of the Saints. Though many were **called** to receive God's greater power, few were **chosen** to do so. There were those who (1) were members of "the church of the firstborn," with its call to the greater priesthood and actual empowerment in it; (2) those in "the church of Christ" who had received the two baptisms, and then the gift of the Holy Ghost; And (3) those in "the church of the Latter-day Saints." All existing at the same time. The exterior plaque for the house of the LORD at Kirtland expressed the state of most Saints in 1836, those in "the church of the Latter-day Saints." Christ's name had been removed. There were those among them who had the baptism of fire and the Holy Ghost. They rose to a higher level of spirituality in "the church of Christ." Latter it appears that the general body of the Saints reinserted the name "of Jesus Christ" into their lesser church and without God's permission.

How was the Fullness of the Priesthood Rejected?

D&C Section 124 (1841) features the promise that the church (at Nauvoo) and its dead would be rejected if the Saints didn't repent and turn to God fully, demonstrated by completing the Nauvoo House and a "house **to his name**," and in his time frame. This was a second chance to receive the fullness of God's various blessings and Him personally, both of which required the greater priesthood. Verse 28 below reveals that the offer for it was taken away (for most). This is because the Kirtland Saints collectively rejected the higher law of *unconditional, unfeigned* **love** – in "**the law of consecration**." Some were also breaking the law of monogamy (see Section 42). Given this second chance at Nauvoo, the Brighamite Saints were "moved out of their place" to Utah Territory. In D&C 124, God said:

> "...build a house to my name [at Nauvoo], for the Most High to dwell therein. For there is not a place found on earth that he may come to and **restore again that which was lost** unto you, or **which he hath taken away**, even **the Fullness of the priesthood** (v. 28)...I command you, all ye my saints, to build a house **unto me**; and I grant unto you a **sufficient time** to build a house unto me; and during this time your baptisms shall be acceptable unto me. But behold, **at the end of this appointment** your baptisms for your dead shall not be acceptable unto me; and if you **do not these things at the end of the appointment ye shall be rejected as a church, with your dead**, saith the Lord your God...If ye labor with **all your might**, I will consecrate that spot that it shall be made holy. And if my people will **hearken unto my voice**, and unto the voice of **my servants whom I have appointed** to lead my people [Joseph & Hyrum], behold, verily I say unto you, they shall **not** be moved out of their place...But if they will **not hearken to my voice**, nor unto the voice of **these men whom I have appointed**, they shall not be blest, because they pollute mine holy grounds, and mine holy ordinances, and charters, and **my holy words** which I give unto them. And it shall come to pass that if you build a house **unto my name**, and, I will not perform the oath which I make unto you, neither fulfil the promises which ye expect at my hands, saith the Lord. For instead of blessings, ye, by your own works, **bring cursings, wrath, indignation, and judgments** upon your own heads, by your follies, and by all your **abominations**, which you practice before me, saith the Lord (D&C 124:27-28, 31-32, 44-48).

The LORD's answers to questions in D&C 113 address the return of the greater priesthood. "What is *the root* of Jesse spoken of in the 10th verse of the 11th chapter? Behold, thus saith the Lord, it is a *descendant of Jesse, as well as of Joseph*, unto whom **rightly** belongs the priesthood, and *the keys of the kingdom* [in the greater priesthood] for an ensign, and for **the gathering of my people in the last days**. Questions by Elias Higbee: What is meant by the command in Isaiah, 52nd chapter, 1st verse, which saith: Put on thy **strength**, O Zion? And what people had Isaiah reference to? He had reference to those whom **God should call** *in the last days*, who should hold the **power** of [the greater Melchizedek] priesthood [after the Holy Order of the Son of God] **to bring again Zion**, and the redemption of Israel; and to put on her [their] **strength** is to put on the authority of the priesthood, which she (Zion) has a right to by **lineage** [Aaronic priesthood]; also to return to that [greater Melchizedek priesthood] **power which she had lost**. What are we to understand by Zion loosing herself from the bands of her neck: 2nd verse? We are to understand that the scattered remnants are exhorted to **return to the Lord** *from whence they have fallen*, which if they do, the promise of the Lord is that he will speak to them, or give them revelation" (and blessings and power, etc., see D&C 113:5-10). We have lost the greater things. We are a fallen people *collectively*, yet there is hope for the wise, humble, and repentant virgins among us, those who choose to "return to the LORD" by honoring **His will**.

Part II: The Rejection Taking Place at Sinai (9 scriptures as a type for modern Israel, the Latter-day Saints)

Sadly, like the Israelites of old who were camped at the base of Sinai, the LORD offered the modern Saints his fullest blessings early on at Missouri and Ohio. This included His presence in the establishment of Zion. It was God's desire that Zion be brought forth, that His people might dwell with Him. Zion is a place of unity, peace, and real unconditional love, beginning with real love of God. Sadly, God saw that we, the Gentile Saints, would reject the fullness He offered. It all begins with rejecting **Him**, very much like the Israelites of old. God gave us the following nine scriptures to illustrate the similar path we have taken. Again the Joseph Smith translation comes into play.

1. JST Exodus 34:1-2 The Israelites rejected God's *rest* (a *fullness* of *His glory*) at Sinai. The first higher law or commandments were then taken, a lesser law then given. Moses was later taken from the people too, like Joseph.

> "And the Lord said unto Moses, Hew thee two other tables of stone, like unto the first, and I will write upon them also, the words of the law, according as they were written at the first on the tables which thou brakest; but it shall **not** be according to the first, for **I will take away the** [higher] **priesthood out of their midst**; therefore my **holy order**, and the ordinances thereof, shall not go before them; for **my presence shall not go up in their midst**, lest I destroy them [in His great light]. But I will give unto them the law as at the first, but it shall be after the law of a carnal [lesser] commandment; for I have sworn in my wrath, that they shall **not enter into my presence**, into **my rest**, in the days of their pilgrimage . . ." (JST Ex. 34:1-2).

2. D&C 84:23-27, 47-57 The Saints also provoked God in similar ways by rejecting His invitation to receive Him literally, early on (and today). It too includes the fullness of His rest and glory. Verses 47-57 address our condemnation for **not** valuing the Book of Mormon and its primary message, which is to "repent," be "born again" and "come to me." Our rejection of repenting and then literally receiving **Him** places us under "**the bondage of sin**." (D&C 84:50-51). Note the definition of the wicked, versus the righteous below.

> "Now this Moses **plainly taught** to the children of Israel in the wilderness, and sought diligently to **sanctify** his people that they might **behold the face of God**; But they *hardened their hearts* and could not endure his presence; therefore, the Lord in his wrath, for his anger was kindled against them, swore that they should not enter into his rest while in the wilderness, which rest is **the Fullness of his glory**. Therefore, he took Moses out of their midst, and the Holy Priesthood also; And the lesser priesthood continued, which priesthood holdeth the key of the ministering of angels and **the preparatory gospel** [*not His Fullness*]; Which gospel is the gospel of repentance and of baptism, and the remission of sins, and the law of carnal commandments, which the Lord in his wrath caused to continue with the house of Aaron among the children of Israel *until John*, whom God raised up, being filled with the Holy Ghost from his mother's womb...And **every one that hearkeneth to the voice of the Spirit cometh unto God, even the Father**. And the Father teacheth him of the covenant which he has renewed and confirmed upon you, which is confirmed upon you for your sakes, and not for your sakes only, but for the sake of the whole world. And the whole world lieth in sin, and groaneth under darkness and under the bondage of sin. And **by this you may know they are under the bondage of sin, because they come not unto me. For whoso cometh not unto me is under the bondage of sin**. And whoso **receiveth not my voice** is not acquainted with my voice, and is not of me. And by this **you may know the righteous from the wicked**, and that the whole world groaneth under sin and darkness even now. And your minds in times past have been darkened because of **unbelief**, and because **you have treated lightly the things you have received**—Which vanity and unbelief have brought the whole church under condemnation. And this condemnation resteth upon the children of Zion, even all. And they shall remain under this condemnation until they repent and remember **the new** [fuller] **covenant**, even **the Book of Mormon** and the **former commandments** which I have given them, not only *to say*, but to **do** according to that which **I have written**—That they may **bring forth fruit** meet for their Father's kingdom; otherwise there remaineth a scourge and judgment to be poured out upon the children of Zion" (D&C 84:23-27, 47-58).

Moses called Seventy "elders" to assist him early on. Many continued to believe they held the higher priesthood, including the 70 members of the San Hedrin later in Jerusalem. It is no different today in the LDS church, and the "restoration branches" that separated from the RLDS church in 1984. With changes among both groups east and west, there was a loss of the higher priesthood.

3. Hebrews 3 & 4 In these two chapters Paul reveals that God was provoked when the Israelites rejected Him and His greater light. They provide additional witnesses to JST Exodus 34 and D&C 84, centered on **not** practicing the sin of **unbelief**, which is to have a *hard heart* - rather than a broken receptive heart and contrite, humble spirit. This is what led the Israelites to not enter into the Lord's rest. Paul's last testimony there reads, "Let us therefore come **boldly** unto the throne of grace [or divine nature], that we may obtain *mercy*, and find *grace* to help in time of need" (Heb. 4:16).

4. Jacob 1:6-8 God's provocation is addressed once again by Jacob in the Book of Mormon. He also connects this rejection with God's **higher law of monogamy** in Jacob chapters 2 and 3 (see also D&C 42:22-23). Jacob stated, "we labored diligently among our people, that we might persuade them to come unto Christ, and partake of the goodness of God, that they might enter into his rest…" (Jacob 1:7).

5. Mosiah 13:13-14, 25-35 Abinadi addressed **idolatry** (or formalism) and false gods (men and things) with King Noah and his priests. They too were rejecting the living God for lesser things. Abinadi stated:

> "Thou shalt not bow down thyself unto them, nor serve them; for I the LORD thy God am a jealous God, visiting the **iniquities** of the fathers upon the children, unto **the third and fourth generations** of them that hate me; And showing mercy unto thousands of them that love me and keep my commandments" (Mos. 13:13-14). Abinadi then added, "salvation doth **not** come by the law alone; and were it not for the atonement, which God himself shall make for the sins and **iniquities** of his people, that they must unavoidably perish, notwithstanding the law of Moses…they did not all understand the law; and this because of the hardness of their hearts; for they understood not that there could **not any man be saved except it were through the redemption of God**…[that] God himself [Jesus is God, and the Son of God the Father] should come down among the children of men, and take upon him the form of man, and go forth in mighty power upon the face of the earth…that he should bring to pass the resurrection of the dead, and he, himself, should be oppressed and afflicted" (Mos. 13:28-35).

Rejecting **God** [Jesus] led to "deadness" in looking to the lesser laws of men. The Jews of the LORD's day were experts in the Law – a replacement for Him. We are similar. We look to leaders, programs, and doctrines rather than to **Christ the LORD**, our personal God. Paul teaches against this in the New Testament. Men, church programs, the temple, and laws have become the god of many Latter-day Saints. Idolaters do not become "**alive in Christ**" (see 2 Nephi 25), as they do not **abide** in the True Vine (a **relationship** with God). The gifts and fruits of His Spirit are thus not active within them. *Lesser* things in the law then dominate the people, as *the fullness* of Christ's gospel is forgotten and downplayed. This is our plight today and the reason for this book. The fullness was taught by Joseph early on (see D&C 5:16, 33:11-15, 39:6).

> **6. 2 Nephi 2:3-11, 15-16, 27-28** Speaking to his son Jacob, Nephi stated, "I know that that thou art **redeemed**…thou hast beheld in thy youth **his glory**; wherefore thou art **blessed**…**redemption** cometh in and through the Holy Messiah; for his is full of grace and truth. Behold, he offereth himself a sacrifice for sin, to answer the ends of the law, unto all those who have **a broken heart and a contrite spirit**; and unto **none else** can the ends of the law be answered…there is no flesh that can dwell in the presence of God, save it be through the *merits*, and *mercy*, and *grace* **of the Holy Messiah**, who layeth down his life according to the flesh…" (2 Ne. 2:3-11, 15-16, 27-28).

After these words, Nephi addressed the two opposing trees of Genesis, a representation of *the doctrine of two ways*; lesser or greater, life or death, blessings or cursings. We are enticed by one type of fruit or another. We have agency to choose. Nephi said the choice is between "liberty and eternal life through **the great Mediator** of men, or…captivity and death." Too many today have inherited curses – lesser things – because they choose the lesser ways of men.

7. Moroni 6:4 We are easily deceived today as few are "*born again*" **in Christ**, receiving the cleansing necessary to be given new hearts *and* the Holy Ghost. Most Saints assume they already have this second gift and thus don't seek to be made *new* **in Christ**. Only He can make us new. Ask God to see if you have been "born again." Ask to see if you have the Holy Ghost. It is the iron rod (revelation from God) that takes us to the Tree – **to Him** and Father and Mother. Few Saints know what being "born again" is, including leaders. It is to be **redeemed** by God, cleansed by His fiery Spirit, receiving "the mighty change of heart" - a recognizable event, a great spiritual outpouring compared to no other. **Joy** is the only word to describe it. Though many are baptism, receiving a confirmation ordinance, few realize that this physical rite is only a symbolic invitation to receive the *fiery spiritual baptism* and the gift of the Holy Ghost thereafter. God gives it, not men, and only if we fully **submit**, **repent**, and **come unto Him**.

> "And after they had been received unto baptism, and were *wrought upon* and *cleansed* by **the power of the Holy Ghost** [a powerful, recognizable, spiritual event] they were numbered among the people of **the church of Christ**;

and their names were taken, that they might be remembered and nourished by **the good word of God** [pure revelation thereafter] to keep them in **the right way**, to keep them continually watchful unto **prayer**, relying alone upon **the merits of Christ**, who was **the author and the finisher of their faith**."

Note that there is **no** statement about leaders or a church. It is entirely **Christ**-centered for good reason. Without pure revelation from God – heeding His words (JST Gen. 9:21, Mosiah 5:5, 8, 18:10; 1 Ne. 22:20; 2 Ne. 1:13, 9:21, 10:24, 32:3, 6 & endnote 31), we will not have access to His Spirit as guidance. This **gift** or "**endowment** *of power from on high*" is "the iron rod." It is what guides us to the Tree of Life (see 2 Ne. 31:13-21, 32:1-6). Turning to God is full submission to His will is the only way to receive both gifts (the Holy Ghost as Christ as "the Heavenly Gift"). We thus remain in **the bondage of sin** and in darkness or ignorance (see D&C 84:50-51). A large percentage of the Saints are in this category. They are virgins, but not **wise** virgins who **oil** (the Spirit of God) in their lamps. It is no wonder so many remain *deceived* and unware of the *awful situation* they are in (being "unsaved").

8. JST Matthew 16:16-20 The LORD has taught us that *pure* revelation from the Father and Him are essential, to guide us back home. Jesus is **the rock** or foundation we must build our houses upon. He will guide us to the Tree after the born again event. Turning to men instead causes the gates of hell to prevail against us, the heavens remaining closed. Talking to His disciples, Jesus asked:

"…whom say ye that I am? And Simon Peter answered and said, Thou art the Christ, the son of the living God. And Jesus answered and said unto him, Blessed art thou Simon Barjona, for flesh and blood hath not revealed this unto thee, but my Father who is in heaven. And I also say unto thee, That thou are Peter, and upon **this rock** [the Father and I, and **revelation** from us] I will build **my church**, and the gates of hell shall not prevail against it" (JST Mat. 16:16-20).

9. 2nd Nephi 27:5 In this last, 9th scripture we have a prophecy of the LORD. It says that the heads of the seers would be covered. Does it apply to Joseph and Hyrum at Nauvoo before their death? The covering has continued today to the fourth generation. This Book of Mormon verse is based on Isaiah 29:10 (part of 21 chapters of Isaiah in the book). Note the additional words added to Isaiah's words, as found in both the Book of Mormon and the JST version of Isaiah 29. It reveals **why** the heads of the seers were and are covered - the **iniquity** of the people.

"For behold, all ye that doeth **iniquity**, stay yourselves and wonder, for ye shall cry out, and cry; yea, ye shall be drunken but not with wine, ye shall stagger but not with strong drink. For behold, the Lord hath poured out upon you *the spirit of deep sleep*. For behold, ye have closed your eyes, and ye have rejected the prophets and **your rulers**, and **the seers** hath he **covered** because of *your* **iniquity**" (2 Ne. 27:4-5; Isaiah 29).

A primary passed down iniquity among the Saints is *idolatry*. Too many are not worshipping the living God **Jesus Christ**, seeking salvation at His hands. We know revelation to Joseph began to lessen in his later years. Many believe his head was covered because of wickedness at Nauvoo (3 Ne. 16:10; 30:2). A quick glance at the revelations given early on (the first 3.5 years of the Restoration), versus those later on, reveal much less revelation in Joseph's later life. His teachings and speech changed too. Some accussed him of being a fallen prophet. Brigham Young used this to his advantage. Note that the word "**iniquity**" is used twice by Isaiah in the verse above, potentially tied to spiritual wifery in early Mormonism, and idolatry among the Saints.

The word "**iniquity**" is found 1,129 times in scripture. It is tied to three concepts, potentially associated with the whoredom and abomination of polygamy. It cuts us off from God.

(1) *Moral Sin* Iniquities are first defined as serious "**moral sins**" meriting punishment. They are premeditated, escalating sins tied to immorality, as opposed to virtue and goodness.

(2) *Generational Curses* A second definition for iniquities is inherited or **generational curses** tied to the sins of our fathers, **those passed down to us** through their and our idolatry, and related false teachings and traditions. Joshua stated that, "your fathers" (because of their traditions) were led to serve other Gods. He added, "Choose you this day whom ye will serve...As for me and my house, we will serve the LORD" (Josh. 24:2, 14-15). Scripture tells us that in addition to "fathers," civil and religious leaders also set traditions, for better or worse. Speaking of people being led astray, Zeniff said, "Yea, and they [the people] also became **idolatrous**, because they were deceived by the vain and

flattering words of the king and priests" (Mos. 11:7). Thus – those that lead us - "**fathers, priests**, and **kings**" give us our false teachings and traditions. They are the iniquities we often inherit.

(3) *Inequality* A third definition for iniquities is "**inequality**." It is placing oneself above others in **pride, causing oppression**. Christ's primary mission was to relieve us of oppression of all kinds, and deliver us from sin, death, and hell (separation from God). He said, "If ye are not one, ye are not mine" (D&C 38:27).

Spiritual wifery at Nauvoo involved all three of these things. We are given "a pattern in all things that we might not be **deceived**" (D&C 52:14). And we are to "seek the best gifts" from Him that "we might not be deceived" (D&C 46:8). Paul said that we are "to take heed that **no man deceive** you" (JS Mat. 1:5). Many are being deceived, falling away just before the Lord returns. It is *not* falling away from the church and its leaders, it is falling away from **Christ the LORD** our Redeemer, Father's representative. They are the whole focus of Christianity not churches and their leaders. Many have received "**strong delusion**," **believing a lie** rather than the truth, as they take pleasure in unrighteousness (2 Thess. 2:3, 11-12). Too many are "**blinded** by those who lie in wait to **deceive**" (Ephesians 4: 14; D&C 123:12). They are *crafty* and **lie** for the sake of gain (1 Ne. 22:23; Moses 5:29-31; Ether 8:15-16, 18). Honorable men and women, even the elect are **deceived** in this way. They then inherit lesser glory as they are "**blinded by the craftiness of men**," having not received "**the testimony of Jesus**" in this life. This is the meaning of D&C 76:74-75. Paul said there are "**false apostles, deceitful workers**" among us (2 Cor. 11:13). He warned us, "Let no man **deceive** you with vain words" (Eph. 5:6). We as lay members in the body of Christ, the "inhabitants of Zion shall judge all things pertaining to Zion. And **liars** and **hypocrites** shall be proved by them, and they who are **not apostles** and **prophets** shall be known" (D&C 64:38-39). For God has, "commandeth that there shall be no *priestcrafts*; for, behold, *priestcrafts* are that men preach and **set themselves up for a light** unto the world, that they may **get gain** and **praise** of the world; but they **seek not the welfare of Zion**" (2 Ne. 26:29).

Part III: Understanding the Doctrine of Christ: *Being Born Again in Christ*

Eternal life is God's gift at the end of "**the way**" to the Tree of Life. He said, "I am **the way**, and the truth, and the life." He added that no one comes to the Father except through Him (John 14:6). Before we can get onto the path to this Tree, holding onto the "**rod of iron**" to get there, we must first find and get through **the gate** that places us on this path. The "**iron rod**" is next to the path to the Tree. Christ is that gate or door onto the path, and He requiress a sacrifice from us to get through this gate. It is that of a "**broken heart** and **a contrite spirit**" (2 Ne. 2:7; 3 Ne. 9:19-22; 12:19; Ether 4:15; D&C 59:8, 97:8). It is in God's fiery cleansing baptism that we are born again in Him and become part of **His** church. If we continue to progress thereafter, we are invited to receive Him as the Heavenly Gift, and latter, Father and Mother in heaven. It is in being "**born again**" that we are cleansed from all sins. They are remitted, that we might be **sanctified** and made whole, able to receive **the gift and power of the Holy Ghost** as our guide in this life – our ability to access the unified mind of the Father and the Son. We can then abide with the Son and the Father. To have the Holy Ghost is to have "the endowment of **power** from on high." It is the oil in the lamps of "**wise**" virgins. The light and influence of the unified mind of the Father and the Son is that pure revelation called "the iron rod" in the Book of Mormon. It takes us further on the path to our LORD Jesus and to Father and Mother. They are "God." Their magnificent love is the sweet, white fruit of the Tree of Life. Nothing tastes better. Nothing is more joyful to experience! Six notable ones are quoted hereafter to explain being "**born again**" in Christ.

1. Jesus Christ Speaking to Nicodemus, a learned Rabbi who came to Christ at night, our LORD said, "except a man be **<u>born again</u>** he cannot **<u>see</u>** the kingdom of God…Except a man be born of **water**, *and* of **the Spirit** [fire], he cannot **<u>enter</u>** into the kingdom of God" (John 3:3-6). Nicodemus came in *the dark of night*, and *left that way*. He did not understand nor accept this doctrine. Besides John 3:3-6 and 8, the best Bible scriptures on being "born again" include *JST Matt. 5:3-5*; John 5:24; 2 Cor. 5:17; Gal. 4:29; Rom. 12:2; 1 John 2:29, 3:9, 4:7, 5:1, 4, 18; Rev. 21:5.

One of our LORD's most important teachings includes the **12** Beattitudes of JST Matthew 5 *and* 3 Nephi 12 (Matthew listed 9 "blessed" traits and Luke 4). They represent God's higher *spiritual* law, adding to the *lesser physical law* given Moses in Deuteronomy chapters 27-30, where there are **12 blessings** and *12 cursings* tied to keeping or ignoring God's **will** in His directives. The "born again" event is found in **the first 3 Beattitudes**. These "plain and precious" things were removed (1 Ne. 13:29)! The LORD taught these higher truths at the start of His mission in Capernaum (Matt. 5) *and* again at Bountiful (3 Nephi 12). The Prophet Joseph Smith restored them in JST Matt. 5:3-4. They read:

#1 v. 3 **<u>Blessed</u>** are they who shall **<u>believe on</u>** me [the way of salvation *begins* with **faith** and **trust** in Christ];
#2 and again, *more* **<u>blessed</u>** are they who shall **<u>believe on your words</u>** [the 12 apostles or the disciples He

chose], when ye [these 12 witnesses] shall **testify that ye have seen me and that I am.**
#3 v. 4 Yea, **blessed** are they who shall **believe on your words**, and **come down into the depth of humility**, and be **baptized in my name**; for **they shall be visited with fire and the Holy Ghost**, and **shall receive a remission of their sins** [3 Ne. 12:1 states, "**I will baptize you** *with fire and the Holy Ghost,*" endnote 33].

Note that it is Christ who does this baptizing and bestowal of the Holy Ghost (3 Ne. 9:20, 12:1; D&C 33:15).

Turning to Deut. 28:3-14 we see that 4 of the **12** "*blessing*" verses there begin with the word "**Blessed**" also. The number **12** in scripture is tied to "**governance**" in God's kingdom via the measure of "*space*" (12 inches to a foot) "*time*" (12 hours of light and darkness at the 2 equinoxes in a 24-hour "day") and in God's higher *law*. He governs by "*light*" including the 144,000 last-days servants addressed in Revelation and D&C 77 (12 x 12 x 1000=144,000 a number representing "the speed of light harmonic" or "144,000 minutes of arc per grid second" (Bruce Cathie, *Bridge to Infinity*, p. 8). These **12** "**blessed**" traits of those of *light* represent the higher law given to wise virgins (endnote 33).

2. Moses In Joseph's inspired translation of Genesis we read of Moses's account of Adam's fiery baptism. In it we read **two times** that it is a **commandment** that we **teach these things to our children** (vs. 57-58). Not only is it the doctrine of Christ, but it is the covenant of the Father, later called "the new and everlasting covenant."

Moses stated, "Wherefore teach it unto your children, that **all men**, **everywhere**, **must repent**, or they can in nowise inherit the kingdom of God, for no unclean thing can dwell there, or dwell in his presence; for, in the language of Adam, Man of Holiness is his name, and the name of his Only Begotten is the Son of Man, even Jesus Christ, a righteous Judge, who shall come in the meridian of time. Therefore I give unto you a commandment, to teach these things freely unto your children, saying: That by reason of transgression cometh the fall, which fall bringeth death, and inasmuch as ye were born into the world by **water**, and **blood**, and **the spirit**, which I have made, and so became of dust a living soul, even so ye must be **born again** into the kingdom of heaven, of **water**, and of the **Spirit**, and be cleansed by **blood**, even the blood of mine Only Begotten; that ye might be **sanctified** *from all sin*, and enjoy *the words of eternal life in this world*, and eternal life in the world to come, even immortal glory;

For by the **water** ye keep the commandment; by the **Spirit** ye are justified, and by the **blood** ye are **sanctified**; Therefore it is given to abide in you; *the record of heaven*; *the Comforter* [or *the Holy Ghost*]; *the peaceable things* of immortal glory; *the truth of all things*; that which *quickeneth* all things, which *maketh alive* all things; that which *knoweth* all things, and hath *all power* according to wisdom, mercy, truth, justice, and judgment.

And now, behold, I say unto you: This is **the plan of salvation** unto all men, through the blood of mine Only Begotten, who shall come in the meridian of time. And behold, all things have their likeness, and all things are created and made to bear record of me, both things which are temporal, and things which are spiritual; things which are in the heavens above, and things which are on the earth, and things which are in the earth, and things which are under the earth, both above and beneath: all things bear record of me.

And it came to pass, when the LORD had spoken with Adam, our father, that Adam cried unto the LORD, and he was caught away by the Spirit of the LORD, and was carried down into the **water**, and was laid under the water, and was brought forth out of the water. And thus he was baptized, and **the Spirit** of God descended upon him, and thus he was **born of the Spirit**, and became **quickened in the inner man**. And he heard a voice out of heaven, saying: Thou art baptized with **fire**, and with the Holy Ghost. This is the record of the Father, and the Son, from henceforth and forever; And thou art after the order of him who was without beginning of days or end of years, from all eternity to all eternity . . . thou art one in me, a son of God . . . all become my sons. Amen" (Moses 6:57-68).

3. John the Baptist "I indeed baptize you with water, *upon your repentance*; and when he of whom I record cometh, who is *mightier* than I, whose shoes I am not worthy to bear, (or whose place I am not able to fill,) as I said, I indeed baptize you before he cometh, that when he cometh **he may baptize you with the Holy Ghost and fire**. And it is he of whom I shall bear record, whose fan shall be in his hand, and he will thoroughly **purge** his floor, and gather his wheat into the garner; but in the **fullness** of his own time will burn up the chaff with unquenchable fire. Thus came John, preaching and baptizing in the river of Jordan; bearing record, that he [Christ] who was coming after him **had power to baptize with the Holy Ghost and fire**" (JST Mat. 3:38-40).

4. Joseph Smith "The baptism of water, without the baptism of fire and the Holy Ghost attending it, is of no use . . . They are necessarily and inseparably connected. An individual **must be born of water and the spirit** in order to get into the kingdom of God...You might as well baptize a bag of sand as a man, if not done in view of the **remission of sins** and **getting of the Holy Ghost**. *Baptism by water is but half a baptism, and is good for nothing without the* *other half*—that is, the baptism of [fire and] the Holy Ghost" (HC, 6:316). Men's dead works mean little in comparison to being "alive in Christ" (see 2 Ne. 25).

In one of the last public sermons of the Prophet Joseph Smith, known as the King Follett discourse (General Conference, April 7, 1844, two months before his murder), Joseph quoted Moses 6:59-60, and then said, "A man must be born of water *and* the Spirit in order to get into the kingdom of God. In the German Bible is found a text that bears me out the same as the revelations which *I have given and taught for fourteen years* about baptism. My testimony has been true all that time. You will find it in the declaration of John the Baptist…Here, I can render an even plainer translation: '**I Baptize you with water, upon your repentance**, but when Jesus Christ – of whom I bear record – comes, who has the power and keys, **He will administer the baptism of fire and the Holy Ghost**.'" This later amalgamated account of the King Follet Discourse was pieced together from four sources; William Clayton, Willard Richards, Wilford Woodruff, and Thomas Bullock. The Prophet Joseph's official re-translation of Matthew 3:38-40 (quoted earlier) was completed in the early 1830's, and is worded differently.

Continuing with his April 7 (1844), General Conference (King Follett) address, Joseph added, "Now where is all the sectarian world? If this testimony is true, they are all damned as clearly as any anathema ever was. I know the text is true. I call upon all you Germans who know that it is true to say, Aye. (Shouts of "Aye.") Alexander Campbell, **how are you going to save people with water alone? For John said his baptism was good for nothing without the baptism of Jesus Christ, that is, the baptism of fire and the Holy Ghost.**

Many talk of any baptism not being essential to salvation, but this would lay the foundation of their damnation. The Apostle [Paul] tells us, 'Therefore not leaving the principles of the doctrine of Christ, let us go on unto perfection; not laying again the foundation of repentance from dead works, and of faith toward God, Of the doctrine of baptisms, and of laying on of hands, and of resurrection of the dead, and of eternal judgment. And we will go on unto perfection, if God permit' [Heb. 6:1-3]. There is one God, one Father, one Jesus, one hope of our calling, one baptism; that is, all three baptisms make one" [water, fire, and blood, see Moses 6:57-68 & JS History 1:73-74].

Born Again Scriptures - *New Heart / Justified / Made Perfect in Chris*

1 Sam. 10:9 / New heart
Jer. 24:7 / A heart to know me
Ezek. 11:19, 18:31, 36:26-27 / New heart & Spirit
John 3:3 / All men must be born again
John 5:24 / Those made new have everlasting life
Rom. 12:2 / Renewed mind
2 Cor. 5:17 / A new creature
Eph. 2:15 / A new man
1 Peter 1:3 / God hath begotten us
1 John 2:29 / The righteous are born of Him
1 John 3:9, 5:18 / Born of God not commit sin
1 John 4:7 / Those who loveth are born of God
Rev.2 1:5 / I make all things new
Enos 1:8 / Thy faith had made thee whole
Mosiah 3:19 / Put off natural man, become a Saint
Mosiah 4:13 / Have no mind to injure one another
Mosiah 5:2 / No more desire to do evil
Christ / "Born of water and the Spirit" (John 3:3-5)
Joseph Smith HC 6:316 / "the remission of sins" and "getting the Holy Ghost"
Mos. 5:7 / Born of Him, become His sons & daughters
Mos. 27:25 / Must be born again, born of God, "being redeemed of God," on "the path to eternal life" (2 Ne. 31:17-18)
Alma 5:12-13 / The mighty change of heart
Alma 5:14 / Have ye spiritually been born of God 5:1- 16, 26-28, 49; 7:14
Alma 19:33, 36:23, 38:6, 50:28 / Hearts changed
Moses 6:59 / Born again into Kingdom of Heaven
Moses 6:65 / Born of Spirit, the inner man quickened
D&C 76:69 / Such are just men made perfect in Him
Gal. 3:24 / Such are justified in Christ the LORD
2 Ne. 31:17-18 / Baptism of fire and the Holy Ghost, "entered in by the gate or the way"

5. Nephi "…know the gate by which ye should enter. For the gate by which ye should enter is [1] repentance and [2] baptism by water; and [3] then cometh **a remission of your sins by fire and by the Holy Ghost**. And then are ye in this strait and narrow path which leads to eternal life; yea, ye have entered in by **the gate**; ye have done according to the commandments of the Father and the Son; and ye have received the Holy Ghost, which witnesses of the Father and the Son (and their divine character), unto the fulfilling of the promise which he hath made, that if ye entered in by **the way** ye should receive…Wherefore, ye must press forward with a steadfastness in Christ, having a perfect brightness of hope, and a love of God and of all men. Wherefore, if ye shall press forward, feasting upon the word of Christ, and endure to the end, behold, thus saith the Father: Ye shall have eternal life. And now, behold, my beloved brethren, this is **the way**; and there is *none other way nor name given under heaven whereby man can be saved in the kingdom of God.* And now, behold, this is **the doctrine of Christ**, and **the only** and **true doctrine** of the Father, and of the Son, and of the Holy Ghost, which is one God, without end. Amen" (2 Ne. 31:17-18, 20-21).

"Wherefore…feast upon the words of Christ; for behold, **the words of Christ will tell you all things what ye should do**. Wherefore, now after I have spoken these words, if ye cannot understand them it will be because ye ask not, neither do ye knock; wherefore, ye are not brought into the light, but must perish in the dark. For behold, again I say unto you that if ye will *enter in by* **the way**, and receive the Holy Ghost, **it will show unto you all things what ye should do**. Behold, **this is the doctrine of Christ**..." (2 Ne. 32:5-6).

6. Alma the Younger ". . . I have repented of my sins, and have been **redeemed** of the LORD; behold I am **born of the Spirit**. And the LORD said unto me: Marvel not that all mankind, yea, men and women, all nations, kindreds, tongues and people, must be born again; yea, **born of God**, changed from their carnal and fallen state, to a state of righteousness, being **redeemed** of God, becoming his sons and daughters; And thus they become **new creatures**; and unless they do this, they can in nowise inherit the kingdom of God…Nevertheless, after wading through much tribulation, *repenting nigh unto death*…**I am born of God** (Mos. 27:24-28). The chart below features *signs* typically accompaning those "born again." The signs below left are reported in the Book of Mormon. Our own unique experiences with this event (and its related gifts) may be different.

Signs tied to being Born Again in Christ / *They follow the Believers*

Signs Follow Believers	**Hel. 5**	**2 Ne. 31-32**	**Alma 5**	**Alma 18 /19**	**Alma 36**	**3 Ne. 17 / 19**	**Mosiah 5**
Faith in Christ	41, 47	13	4-7, 15	41	17, 18	8	8, 10 (4:5, 20)
Repent, Cry for Mercy	29, 32	11	32-34, 49-52	41	18	2	
Heavens Open	48	15		/34, 48	22	24 / 14	
See God				/13	22	25 / 15	
Spirit Sent Down	45	12, 15, 18		/6	24	/13, 20	3
Quickening / HG given						/9,13, 20-21	
Fire Present	44, 45	13, 14		/43-45	24 /14	/13-14	
Angels Minister	39, 48			/34, 48	24 /15	/14	
Joyful Praise	44, 45	13	26	/14, 30, 33	20, 21, 22, 28	17, 18	3
(see also Alma 5:26-34)							
Gift of Tongues	45	13, 14		/30, 45	13, 14	/ 24	3
Fall Down - Submission				42 /15, 16	7, 11		(4:1) 1
Reborn, Sins Remitted	50, 51	17	12-14, 19	/51	5, 23	/ 33	2, 7, 15
Heart purified, gifted with charity (see Mor. 7:48)							

These things represent many of the "plain and precious things" taken out of the Bible. (1 Ne. 13). Early D&C scriptures on being "**born again**" include 5:16, 19:31, 20:41 33:11-15 and 39:6. See also JSH 1:73-74. Note three.

> "And behold, whosoever believeth on **my words**, them will **I visit with the manifestation of my Spirit**; and they shall be **born of me**, even of *water* and of **the Spirit**" (D&C 5:16, 1829).

> "Yea, repent and be baptized, every one of you, for a remission of your sins; yea, be baptized even by water, and then cometh the baptism of fire and of the Holy Ghost. Behold, verily, verily, I say unto you, this is **my gospel**; and remember that they shall have faith in me or they can in nowise be saved; And upon **this rock** I will build **my church**; yea, upon **this rock** ye are built, and if ye continue, the gates of hell shall not prevail against you. And ye shall remember the church articles and covenants to keep them. And whoso having faith you shall confirm in **my church**, by the laying on of the hands, and **I will bestow the gift of the Holy Ghost** upon them. And the Book of Mormon and the [JST] holy scriptures are given of me for your instruction; and **the power of my Spirit quickeneth all things.** Wherefore, be faithful, praying always, having your lamps trimmed and burning, and oil with you, that you may be ready at the coming of the Bridegroom" (D&C 33:11-17; see also 3 Ne. 9:20, 12:1).

> "And this is **my gospel** – repentance and baptism by *water*, and then **cometh the baptism of fire and the Holy Ghost**, even the Comforter, Which *showeth all things*, and *teacheth the peaceable things* of the kingdom" (D&C 39:6, see also verse 11).

The Doctrine of Christ Rejected

The way of **salvation** of our God, or **redemption** – is clearly presented in God's word, but it is not backed up by traditional church instruction and teaching manuals any longer. Some replacement doctrines presented us now are false. One is that being "born again" is a process, when in reality it is an **event**. A pregnancy involves the growth of the baby over time, a process, but the birth of the child itself is an **event**. This is why the spiritual rebirth in Christ is called being "**born again**" or "the mighty change of heart."

The fullness of "the **doctrine** of Christ" is presented in **His gospel**. Those embracing both are brought into **His church** – the church of Christ. Those who continue to progress become part of the church of the Lamb or the Firstborn (D&C 76:54, 67, 71, 93:22). Christ doctrine is intimately tied to receiving Him and His best gifts. This path is summarized well in the beattitudes, especially those in 3 Nephi 12. To be "**blessed**" is to receive God literally in this life, as did many in scripture like *Lehi* (1 Ne. 2:1; Alma 50:20), *Nephi* (1 Ne. 3:8), *Jacob* (Jacob 5:75), *Enos* (Enos 1:5, 27), *Alma* (Mosiah 16:15-19, Alma 8:15), and *the twelve disciples* of Christ (3 Ne. 17:20). They turned to Christ and repented (Hel. 13:11), keeping His commandments (1 Ne. 13:37; Mosiah 3:41, 18:30; Alma 5:16; Ether 4:19; D&C 30:8). They entered into a "**blessed state**" (the *higher law* of the Beattitudes). It involves being on a strait and narrow pathway, wherein we receive two baptisms; one physical in water by men, followed by a fiery spiritual one of God. In them we are made new in Christ, giving us opportunity to receive the unspeakable gift of the Holy Ghost (see D&C 5:16; 20:41; 33:11-15; 39:6; 2 Ne. 31:13-21; 32:1-6; Mor. 6:4). Such aree part of the church of Christ or the Firstborn.

> "And after they had been received unto baptism, and were **wrought upon and cleansed by the power of the Holy Ghost**, they were numbered among the people of **the church of Christ**..." (Mor. 6:4).

Men on earth symbolically baptize other men and women, utilizing the symbolism of burial (or immersion) in water. It is a preparatory earthly baptismal ordinance. The second greater, spiritual baptism, is done by God Himself with His fiery Spirit. Most have only received the lesser, Aaronic portion of the covenant today. Too many times the first baptism is not done or perceived correctly. It needs to be preceded by real **faith** in Christ and a turning of the heart fully and completely to the LORD Jesus. Eight-year olds today rarely exhibit (1) strong faith in Christ, (2) in connection with heartfelt real repentance, (3) leading to full submission to God, (4) as seen in a broken heart and a contrite spirit, and (5) the covenant with Him to remember Him always, and keep His commandments. All five steps are necessary to experience the second, greater spiritual baptism by God. Too many have not been "**baptized unto repentance**." This type of baptism is especially clear in the Book of Mormon (Mosiah 26:22; Alma 5:62; 6:2; 7:14; 9:27; 48:19; 49:30; Hel. 3:24; 5:17 & 19; 3 Ne. 7:26; Mat.. 3:11). Instead, many are baptized into a church to fulfill pressures from parents and leaders, rather than because they have a moving faith in Christ. Real "repentance" involves giving up our fallen and carnal nature (changing)...and replacing it with a "divine nature" (Lecture 7:16-17).

Many out of the box Mormons who know and love scripture have become familiar with "the doctrine of Christ." Many are re-baptized as adults, in a private act to show the LORD they really love Him and want to be part the church of believers addressed by Alma in the Book of Mormon, where the gifts and fruits of the Spirit are clearly evident. Their symbolic baptism in water by men in the physical world, **after heartfelt repentance**, is done in a conscious effort to show God they love Him. They desire God's fiery baptism with all their hearts, crying out to Him for His mercy, just like Alma (see 3 Ne. 9:20; 12:1; JST Mat. 3:38; JST John 1:28; D&C 33:15). Re-baptism must be done secretly today, as President Grant stopped re-baptism during his administration. It was a common in the Book of Mormon (Alma 5:62) *and* in early church history. Alma said he was "**baptized unto repentance**" (Alma 7:14).

Church meetings, ministering, and temple attendance don't save us. God does. We must change and take advantage of the LORD's atonement. The LORD repeatedly invites us to receive **Him**, stating, "**repent** and **come unto me**" (D&C 10:67-68, 93:1; 1 Ne. 10:18-19; 2 Ne. 9:23-24; 28:31-32; Jacob 1:7; Alma 5:33-34; Ether 4:7-19; Mor. 7:34; 3 Ne. 9:14, 22, 51; 11:14; 12:19-20, 23-24; 27:5-21; 30:2). Doing so in sincere repentance helps us be born again (Alma 5; Mos. 27:24-27; 5:49; 7:14; 36:23-26; John 3:3-6). There is no other way to real salvation. The LORD said it is the only way we will **see** and **enter** heaven (John 3:3-6). Nephi told us that we are not even through the gate and onto the path ("**the way**") to eternal life **until** we are born again in Christ Jesus (2 Ne. 31:17-18). Our LORD is this gate! He employs **no** servant there. He or the Father are the ones baptizing us with their fiery Spirit (3 Ne. 9:20; 12:1; JST Mat. 3:38; JST John 1:28; D&C 33:15). They also provide the Holy Ghost (2 Ne. 31:12; 3 Ne. 11:35; John 15:26). In D&C 33:15, the LORD Jesus said that He bestows the gift (or endowment) of the Holy Ghost to us (see also 3 Ne. 12:1).

For review, five simple steps are summarized below. Satan and evil, designing men have removed these *plain* and *precious* truths from us, all for the sake of gain (D&C 93:39; 1 Ne. 22:23; Moses 5:29-31). The JST Bible and Book of Mormon re-introduce these *simple* and *sacred* things back to us, all based on God's superior will, wisdom, and love!

A. Faith in the LORD Jesus Christ, the FIRST principle and ordinance of the gospel, not faith in men and churches. See the important Lectures on Faith (removed 1921).

B. Repentance (confess one's sin to God and forsake them) – real heartfelt sorrow for sin, and letting go of our fallen and carnal nature, and then immersing ourselves in God's divine nature.

C. Baptism in water (3 types) An outward earthly sign of one's inward commitment, a **covenant** with God to remember Him and do **His will** (given in scripture & personal revelation). It is a preparatory, symbolic, physical ordinance. It should be *Baptism unto repentance* with ties to remission of sins (the wording Christ gave us for the baptism prayer in the Book of Mormon is no longer used, see 3 Ne. 11:25). "Baptism unto renewal" and "baptism unto healing" are two other kinds of baptism in scripture and early church history (endnote 27).

D. Baptism by fire and the Holy Ghost In this purging event our sins are remitted, our hearts made new. Our LORD baptizes us in the Spirit (3 Ne. 9:20, 12:1; D&C 33:15, endnote 33). With this sanctification we may then be given the gift and power of the Holy Ghost (greater access to the Holy Ghost). This gift is "the endowment of power from on high" spoken of in scripture. The "**born again**" event is the gate to the pathway to eternal life.

E. Receive Christ Those made new in Christ have "entered in at the gate" (via Christ). We are then placed on the pathway ("the way") to the Tree. It is well defined in the beattitudes of 3 Nephi 12. Such hold tight to "the iron rod" on "the way" that leads to the Tree of Life in Lehi's vision (1 Ne. 8 and 11). This iron rod is direct revelation from God via the Holy Ghost (our connection to the unified mind of the Father and the Son). It leads us into the holy presence of the LORD, our Second Comforter. He becomes our guide or mentor thereafter. In His presence we see, feel, and come to know of His reality, like those of 3 Nephi 11 and Acts 1 and 2. Both groups of believers became sure witnesses of God's reality. He became the father of their salvation. Such have "the testimony of Jesus" (Rev. 12:17, also Rev. 19:10; D&C 46:13-14; 76:51, 101; 88:4, 74-75; Mor. 10:8).

A The Fullness of God's Presence

God desires a loving, marriage-like relationship with each of us. It is to enter into His holiness. This is why we are called the bride (often an unfaithful bride) throughout scripture. He desires that we receive a *fullness* of His love, light, and spiritual gifts. He wants us to **know** Him from the inside-out. The first gift **He** lists for us in the thirteen gifts of the Spirit found in D&C 46, is He Himself – **the Heavenly Gift**. He can be our Second Comforter - our mentor and friend. According to the Prophet Joseph, if you have not "**the testimony of Jesus**" then you have little assurance of **salvation** or **eternal life** in this world. The testimony of Jesus is not a Sacrament meeting testimony of Christ, but His sure testimony to you (a decree from God) that **you** have **eternal life**! It is one of four types of "testimony" tied to our LORD Jesus. The first two are testimonies *of* Him. The third and fourth are **of Him** and **by Him**.

(1) Many good Christians believe that Jesus is our loving Savior. They read about Him, but haven't come to know Him. Religion teaches us about the LORD, but a real relationship with God requires more (see the Lectures on Faith).

(2) A second is a surer witness of Him as provided by the Holy Ghost. Its primary role as "the first comforter" is to bear witness of truth in all things, including the Father and the Son. When we bear witness of Christ or the Father under the influence of their Spirit (the unified mind of the Father and the Son [Lecture on Faith 5], we do so speaking with greater power of the Holy Ghost or "the tongue of angels" (received after the fiery baptism).

(3) The third testimony of our LORD is the most desirable. It is to receive Him as our "Second Comforter," typically done in an ascent into our Lord's presence in heaven (though He can do as He pleases here or anywhere). There we develop real knowledge, beyond belief - that He is real. Before this we must be completely cleansed from "the blood and sins of this generation" to receive Him (see Rev. 12:17, 19:10; D&C 46:13-14; 76:51, 101 & 88:4, 74-75). He does this in the baptism of fire and Holy Ghost event, a significant part of the **sanctifying** process. Christ's blood in the atonement completes this process (the third step, of *water*, *fire*, and then His *blood*). Brought to heaven, as King Benjamin says, we "are **sealed his**," becoming His son or daughter. There **we** have opportunity to see and feel the marks of the atonement in our LORD's body and become a witness for Him, like so many did in 3rd Nephi 11. It is to enter His "**rest**" (D&C 84:24) or to receive Him as "**the heavenly gift**" in this life (4 Ne. 1:3; Ether 12:8; Heb 6:44). It has ties to receiving salvation at His hands, or receiving "the more sure word of prophecy," from Him that we have eternal life normally heard from His own lips. It is the prophetic statement from Jesus as THE PROPHET

and the Great HIGH PRIEST that we have eternal life. It can only come from Him, He who went into the Holy of Holies of Gethsemane by His own free will, alone, to tread the winepress there for **you** and **I**. It is to have the day of judgment advanced in this life, by The Judge – Jesus Christ (the Father committed all judgment into His hands [John 5:22]). God pronounces us clean here in mortality via His *mercy* and His *blood* (not our good works). Our calling to know Him and receive His greatest gift, has resulted in our election to receive both – because of His great love for us.

(4) There is a fourth testimony. Such are the blessed souls whose names are written in the Book of Life. Such are sealed up to eternal life and have obtained the "**testimony of Jesus**" before the Father (as our Advocate and Mediator). This knowledge becomes an "anchor to the soul" when we are experiencing difficult times and trials. This is the **sealing** we should seek, a sealing to the Father of our salvation directly (see Mosiah 5:15), as most all scriptures using the word "seal" are tied to this concept via His promise of eternal life (see John 6:27; 2 Cor. 1:21-22; Eph. 1:13, 4:30; Rev. 7:3-4; Mos. 5:15; Hel. 10:7; Alma 34:35; D&C 1:8, 68:12, 76:51-54). Our LORD said:

> "Wherefore, **I now send upon you another Comforter**, even upon you **my friends**, that it may *abide* in your **hearts**, even *the Holy Spirit of promise*; which other Comforter is the same that I promised unto my **disciples**, as is recorded in the testimony of John. This Comforter is **the promise** which I give unto **you** of **eternal life**, even the *glory* of **the celestial kingdom**; Which glory is that of **the church of the Firstborn**, even of God, the holiest of all, **through Jesus Christ his Son**" (D&C 88:3-5).

Such then transition from the church of Christ to the church of the Firstborn. John provides us a second witness. Quoting the LORD, he stated:

> "And I will pray the Father, and he shall give you **another Comforter**, that he may *abide* with you for ever; Even the Spirit of **truth**; whom the world cannot receive, because it **seeth** him not, neither **knoweth** him: but ye **know** him; for **he dwelleth with you**, and **shall be in you**. **I will not leave you comfortless**: **I will come to you.** Yet a little while, and the world seeth me no more; **but ye see me**: because I live, ye shall live also. At that day ye shall know that **I am in my Father, and ye in me, and I in you**" (John 14:16-20). This can occur as we immerse our thoughts, words, and deeds, into the holiness of God's character and attributes (see D&C 93:23-24).

Jesus is the light, life, and truth of the world.

> "The Spirit of truth is of God. **I am the Spirit of truth**, and John bore record of me, saying: He received a **fullness of truth**, yea, even of **all truth**" (D&C 93:26).

Christ is "**the Spirit of truth**" and thus the "other" or **Second Comforter**, according to D&C 88:3 and **the Holy Spirit of Promise**. The Prophet Joseph Smith clarified these concepts further. After quoting John 14:16-23, he stated:

> "Now what is this *other comforter*? It is no more nor less than **the Lord Jesus Christ Himself**; and this is the sum and substance of the whole matter; that when any man obtains this last Comforter, he will have the personage of **Jesus Christ to attend him**, or appear unto him from time to time, and even He will manifest **the Father** unto him, and *they will take up their* **abode with him**, and the visions of the heavens will be opened unto him, and the **LORD** *will teach him* **face to face**, and *he may have a perfect knowledge of the mysteries of the Kingdom of God*" (HC, p. 381).

This is when a new glorious journey begins, one where we are mentored by the LORD personally, for our mission.

Ascent-Vision

We normally receive Christ by being brought to heaven spiritually. This kind of ascent-vision experience is, "seen and understood by the power of the Holy Spirit, which God bestows on **those who love him**, and **purify themselves before him** [through heartfelt sincere repentance]. To whom *he grants this privilege* of **seeing** and **knowing** for themselves; That *through the power and manifestation of the Spirit, while in the flesh*, **they may be able to bear his presence** *in the world of glory*" (D&C 76:116-18).

In the sixth verse of the very first chapter of the Book of Mormon, we read of Lehi **ascending to heaven** in an "ascent vision" experience. There are three basic types of visionary experience.[28] During Lehi's ascent-vision he saw God sitting upon His throne in heaven, surrounded by numberless concourses of angels, singing, praising, and worshipping Him. Later in chapter 8 we read of another vision of Lehi, that of the related, but more symbolic Tree of Life. In it, Lehi **first followed a man** *dressed in white*, who asked that he follow him (idolatry). Lehi is **led by this man into darkness** (1 Ne. 8:5-12; 2 Ne. 7:10-11; Isa. 50:7-11). After many hours, Lehi finally *calls out to God for* **His mercy**. Only then is He delivered by God. He then sees the Tree of Life which is at the end of "the way" – a straight and narrow path leading to the Tree. Many prideful ones that think they know, mock him, pointing their fingers at him from the great and spacious building (these are those who will not awake out of their sleep and deception). Lehi in his wisdom (a wise virgin) holds tightly to the rod of iron near the path (scripture and *pure* revelation from God, via the Holy Ghost – the unified mind of the Father and the Son). This iron rod safely takes Lehi through **the mists of darkness** (man's lies and deception [3 Ne. 16:10 & 30:2]) until he finally arrives at the Tree, partaking of its sweet, white fruit. The taste is incredible, pure **love** and **joy**. Nothing else is comparable. Alma describes God's love using the word "joy" five times in Alma 36:20-25). Lehi then desires that his family also taste this fruit. You can too!

The fruit is God Himself and his **great love** for you and I. It is a life-changing experience. Three chapters later in 1 Nephi 11, we read of his Son Nephi's desire to see, understand, and experience the fruit of this Tree himself too. He does so, because He **believed** his father's words. We read that he too was caught up to heaven, ascending on eagles wings, while he sat pondering on the things of God. Nephi also had an "ascent vision" of God upon His throne in heaven, like many others in scripture (see the experiences of Enoch, Abraham, Isaiah, Ezekiel, Daniel, Moses, John the Revelator, Joseph Smith, etc.). It is a spiritual, inner, "ascent vision" or **revelation** directed by God's Spirit, often initiated by our own faith and belief in God – and our love for Him and desire to be with Him. **Child-like faith, belief**, and **love** for Christ the LORD and the Father are essential for this to occur. Equally helpful is learning to praise and worship God. But most important, is **repentance**! It is the first part of God's five word statement defining His doctrine, gospel, and church, which is to "**repent** and **come unto me**," in combination with denying all ungodliness within us (Mor. 10:32). God then takes over our initial faithful effort in **meditation, pondering, or imagination** (as he did with Nephi), doing so within our minds-eye. We may then be brought to heaven spiritually and "**sealed" His** (Mosiah 5:15).

God controls **this gate** to heaven. **He**, in fact, **is the gate** and **employs no servant there** (2 Ne. 9:41). **He** baptizes us in fire and the Holy Ghost (see 3 Ne. 9:20, 12:1). The five steps on "**the way**" of salvation lead us to full **redemption** from the fall. This fall resulted in our *separation* from God. Returning to Him (His presence, rest, and glory) – or the Tree - completes this **fuller redemption**, like that of the Brother of Jared in Ether 3:13. It is the focus of the Book of Mormon message, the one not grasped, leading to condemnation (D&C 84:49-59). The effects of **Faith in** *and* **love for Christ our Redeemer -** is what parts the veil of our unbelief and brings us home to Him (Lec. on Faith 7). The idolatry of leader and church worship blocks this path. Mormon and Moroni saw our day, stating that *unbelief* was a great sin among us (Morm. 1:14; Ether 4:13; D&C 3:18, 20:15. 63:17). For many, "unbelief" means they do not believe they can experience these things. For others, it is belief in *the wrong things*, like polygamy, or that we should follow our leaders to heaven. Salvation is an individual thing, tied to our relationship with Jesus first, then Father and Mother. Note three simple and short statements where our LORD continually invites us to receive **Him**:

(1) "**Awake and arise**" (Moroni 10:31; D&C 117:2; D&C 133:10; Judges 5:12; Isaiah 51:9, 52:1; Ephesians 5:14; Proverbs 6:9 and Habakkuk 2:19).

(2) "**Come follow me**" (2 Ne. 31:12; Luke 9:23, 59; John 10:27, 12:26; D&C 38:22, 100:2). As we love Him and desire to follow Him, we are led to receive Him while in mortality, as encapsulated in His five-word summary of the fullness of His "doctrine," "gospel," and "church" - where He invites us to receive Him literally, saying:

(3) "**Repent** and **come unto me**" (D&C 10:67-68, 93:1; 1 Ne. 10:18-19; 2 Ne. 9:23-24; 28:31-32; Jacob 1:7; Alma 5:33-34; Ether 4:7-19; Mor. 7:34; 3 Ne. 9:14, 22, 51; 11:14; 12:19-20, 23-24; 27:5-21; 30:1-2). It is time we awaken out of our deep sleep, our unbelief and deception and embrace Christ the LORD! The LORD said:

> "For they that are **wise** and have received **the truth**, and have taken **the Holy Spirit for their guide** [the iron rod, Holy Ghost] and have **not been deceived**—verily I say unto you, **they** shall not be hewn down and cast into the fire, but shall abide the day" – the great and dreadful day of His coming in judgment first (D&C 45:57).

God described **who the righteous are** among us, those **who will abide this day**, versus those who are *wicked* and are under "*the bondage of sin*" (D&C 84:50-51). They will be burned with all unproductive fruit trees. These are the trees in the LORD's vineyard that do not heed His invitation to come to Him. They do not "**bear fruit meet for the father's** [celestial] **kingdom**" (D&C 84:58; Alma 12:15, 13:12-13, 32:40-43). Their fruit is bitter or they have no fruit. Such are destined for lesser kingdoms, often because they are **deceived by the craftiness of man** (D&C 76:75). God said:

> "And by this you may know *they are under* **the bondage of sin**, because **they come not unto me**. For *whoso cometh not unto me* is under **the bondage of sin**. And whoso receiveth not my voice is not acquainted with my voice, and is not of me. *And by this you may know the righteous from the wicked*" (D&C 84:50-53).

> "**I have commanded**...that ye should **come unto me**, that ye might **feel** and **see**; even so shall ye do unto the world; and **whosoever breaketh this commandment** *suffereth himself to be led into temptation*" (3 Ne. 18:25).
> "For it shall come to pass, saith the Father, that at that day **whosoever will not repent and come unto my Beloved Son**, *them will I cut off from among my people*, O house of Israel" (3 Ne. 21:20).

> "**No man can come unto me**, *except he doeth* **the will** *of my Father who hath sent me.* And this is **the will** of him who hath sent me, that **ye receive the Son** [and His divine attrributes, John 17]; for the Father beareth record of him; and **he who receiveth the testimony**, and *doeth* **the will** *of him who sent me*, **I will raise up in the resurrection of the just**. And he said, Therefore said I unto you, that **no man can come unto me**, *except he doeth* **the will** *of my Father who hath sent* **me**" (JST John 6:44 - 45).

For the humble and repentant, there is hope and deliverance in the LORD Jesus Christ. He said:

> "**He that cometh to me shall never hunger; and he that believeth on me shall never thirst**" (John 6:35).

False leaders teach false things, "But in vain **they teach for doctrine the commandments of men**" (Mat. 15:9). Such deny the real power of God, and the Holy Ghost He provides us. He made a similar statement to Joseph Smith in his First Vision. Many good people (including leaders) are often ignorant of these **fuller** things, while corrupt men **keep them from the sheep for the sake of gain** (1 Ne. 22:23) and the honors of men (D&C 121:34-35). God said:

> "And when the times of the Gentiles is come in, a light shall break forth among them that sit in darkness, and it shall be **the fullness of my gospel**; But *they receive it not; for they perceive not the light, and* **they turn their hearts from me because of the precepts of men.** *And in that generation shall the times of the Gentiles be fulfilled*" (D&C 45:28-30).

Satan and secret combinations lead us away from a fullness of light (D&C 93:39). This fullness is offered to you. God said the Gentiles would reject it, a process beginning in our early history. It expanded at Nauvoo and continues today.

> "And thus commandeth the Father that I should say unto you: At that day when **the Gentiles** shall sin against my gospel, and shall **reject the Fullness of my gospel**, and shall be lifted up in *the pride of their hearts* above all nations, and above all the people of the whole earth, and shall be filled with all manner of **lyings**, and of **deceits**, and of mischiefs, and all manner of hypocrisy, and murders, and priestcrafts, and whoredoms, and of secret abominations; and if they shall do all those things, and shall **reject the Fullness of my gospel**, behold, saith the Father, **I will bring the Fullness of my gospel from among them.** And then will I remember my covenant which I have made unto **my people, O house of Israel**, and I will bring **my gospel** unto **them**"(3 Ne. 16:10).

The Lord is taking His **fullness** to the house of Israel, those sheep who will seek out the Master Shepherd and listen to Him. It is happening to Jews, Muslims, Christians, and others all over the world. Are you one of them?

Chapter 7 Summary: *Becoming One with God*

In the Old Testament, things or places were holy that were set apart for sacred purposes. The opposite of holy is something common or profane (1 Sam. 21:5; Ezek. 22:26; 42:20; 44:23; 48:13–15). Under the guidance of inspired teachers Israel was taught that what distinguished Jehovah from the gods of the heathen was His **personal character**. The word "holy" therefore came to refer to **moral character** (Lev. 11:44; 19:2; 21:8; Isa. 6:3–8). Israel must be holy in character because the God of Israel was holy (Jer. 7:4–7; Matt. 5:48). The Law of **Holiness** (Lev. 17–26) shows how the attempt was made via ceremonial observances to secure this holiness of character. This attempt **failed** because the later Jews [and many Saints today] observed the letter of the law and neglected its spirit. They attached more importance to the ceremonial (symbols) than to the moral; and the result was a lapse into formalism [a type of idolatry]. But in the writings of the Prophets it is clearly laid down that the value of worship in the eyes of God depends upon **the personal character of the worshipper** (see Holiness, LDS Bible Dictionary).

In February of 2015, I chose to try and be more clean before God. I found other like-minded men Latter-day Saint men and began meeting with them to learn more of God's ways and adhere to them. All of us were starving for more. Each of us knew scripture enough to recognize that what was being taught us at church fell far short of what could be. In faith, we met early each Sunday morning for a couple of hours at one brother's house. This continued for two years. We did so to search out God's word in scripture, to worship Him, and to receive pure revelation from Him, collectively and individually. We then went home, shared what we learned with our wives, and took our families to church. Our goal was to personally obtain the blessings addressed in scripture, namely the mighty change of heart, and Christ the LORD as our teacher and mentor, and encourage our wives and children to do the same. We moved forward in faith and experienced the gifts and fruits of the Spirit, as a group and personally. It was a time of great growth for us all. What united us was our of the LORD Jesus and our desire for more. We advanced quickly because of our unity of belief, faith, and trust in the LORD. He is our Savior and Mediator with the Father. We purified ourselves and relied on action and revelation to guide us every step of the way. We were all active Latter-day Saint men in the church. Most were returned missionaries. We approached the LORD in real faith and repentance, and as a result we received the mighty change of heart (at different points in time), and have received, or are on track to receive, the LORD personally, as did those who bore testimony of Him powerfully in the Book of Mormon.

The difference for us, was real **faith that we could have these things**, **not fear** of what others might think. We sought and received what is offered in the holy word of God. Moving forward with **faith**, not fear was one of the best decisions in my life and has led to much of the understanding of the doctrine of Christ presented here. We searched out these things in scripture, together. We supported one another in real love and unity. It was a little piece of Zion. I saw my brothers experience these things, and I have experienced some of them too. Together with scripture, they represent three witnesses of truth. Apply God's invitation. Put your faith in Him. Fear (love, trust, honor) **God**, not man, and wonderful things can happen to you, but also keep in mind that there is always a price to pay for the things of God in this telestial, dark world. Much opposition will be presented you, but it is all worth it.

The Kingdom of God is Within YOU

In D&C 93, God speaks of "true worship," involving not only "**who**" but "**how**" to worship. In the Lectures on Faith, we learn of the "*effects*" of faith that come *from* **within us**. Thus, the attributes of godliness, the holiness of character, and the perfecting of them - comes only from a desire existing **within us** to know and love God. Luke said, "**the kingdom of God is within you**" (Luke 17:21). All through the Old Testament ancient Israel was continually reminded of "**how**" to worship. God said, "**Sanctify yourselves** therefore, and **be ye holy**: for I *am* the LORD your God." (Lev. 20:7; Ex. 19:2; Lev. 11:44; Num. 11:18; Josh. 3:5, 7:3; 1 Sam. 16:5; 1 Chron. 15:12,14; 2 Chron. 29:15,34; 30:3, 15, 24; 31:18; 35:6; Ezek. 38:23; John 17:17-23; D&C 43:11, 16; 88:68, 74; 133:4-5, 62). "And unto him that **repenteth** and **sanctifieth himself** before the Lord shall be given eternal life" (D&C 133:62).

Jeremiah lamented that his people became focused on the law, dead works, and the temple as idols, saying the people trusted in the **lying** words of men. "The temple of the LORD, The temple of the LORD, The temple of the LORD, are these." He recommended that we "thoroughly amend" our "ways" by caring for one another and looking to God for salvation (Jer. 7:3-8). Both ancient and modern Israel became the unfaithful bride. The Prophet Hosea married a prostitute as a type to show how God is merciful to wayward Israel. He stated, "**My people are destroyed for lack of knowledge** [of God]: because thou hast rejected knowledge [of me], I will also reject thee (Hosea 4:6). Modern idolatry severely limits our necessary **faith** and **trust in the LORD Jesus Christ.** Thus there is little or no *power* among us as a people (the gifts and fruits of the Spirit). Jesus is "**the way**" of life and salvation. Paul reveals this in the first chapter of Ephesians. Every verse there but one is entirely focused on **the Master**. We are to "work out" our own salvation "with fear and trembling" **before the LORD Jesus** (Philippians 2:12). When Christ said "come follow me" He was inviting us to forsake the world and develop a willingness to give up **all things** in it. This includes **all material possessions, family** (spouse, children, and parents, Mat. 10:35-40, 19:29; JST Luke 14:26), *and* **all the idols in our heart** (leaders, churches, things). We are to place our trust only **in the LORD**, or *cursings result* (2 Ne. 4:34; 28:31-32; Jer. 17:5). We are to stand on our own, **not relying** on *man, laws, institutions,* or our own *dead works* to save us (JST Mark 9:41-45), as there is **no other name, way, or means to be saved**, *only* in and through **the name of Christ** the LORD (2 Ne. 9:41; Mosiah 3:17; Alma 38:9; Hel. 5:9; D&C 22:2). His arms remain stretched out still.

Chapter Eight

A Coming Reformation

Inviting Zion

As we look back into our history, we might ask, did the LORD work the **reformation** He spoke of in 1833? Did it occur later at Nauvoo? Has it occurred since then? I believe this reformation is right around the corner, as the **fourth generation** since Joseph Smith's murder is ending. In 1833, God told Joseph Smith:

> "And thus, if the people of *this generation* harden not their hearts, I will work a **reformation** among them, and I will put down all **lyings**, and **deceivings**, and priestcrafts, and envyings, and strifes, and idolatries, and sorceries, and all manner of **iniquities**, and I will establish **my church**, like unto the church which was taught by my disciples in the days of old. And now if this generation do harden their hearts against **my word**, behold I will deliver them up unto Satan, for he reigneth and hath power at this time, for he hath got great hold upon *the hearts* of the people of this generation: and **not far from the iniquities of Sodom and Gomorrah**, do they come at this time: and behold the sword of justice hangeth over their heads, and if they persist in the hardness of their hearts, the time cometh that it must fall upon them" (Book of Commandments, 4:5-6, 1833, changed now in D&C 5:19).

As we saw earlier, "**Lies**" and "**deception**" (or "**lyings**" and "**deceivings**") are listed **first** *and* **second** by God in a number of scritpures (see chap. 6, pps. 188-89). In 1834, God told Joseph and the Saints to "**rely** on the things which were written" (in the JST Bible, the Book of Mormon & the *unmodified* oracles given Joseph). The two verses given to Joseph in revelation in 1833 above were omitted in the 1835 Doctrine and Covenants, replaced with what is now D&C 5:19 (see endnote 27).

The Forgotten Remnant

The Brighamite Saints as a whole appear to have been delivered up to Satan following the dark Nauvoo years, the natural result of the influences of Freemasonry, polygamy, and idolatry. A forgotten example of this rejection is "the Walker Lake event" in 1890, where Christ is said to have visited some 200 Native American representatives at a special gathering in western Nevada. This visit was not to leaders in Salt Lake City. The U.S. government tied this event to "The Messiah Craze," the year many battles rose up between Native Americans and the U.S. Army. Those at Walker Lake claimed that Christ invited them there and then came to them, teaching many things in the Spring of 1890. One was that He had been **rejected** 2,000 years earlier by religious leaders at Jerusalem, a statement that hinted at His rejection by leaders of the Saints and others here too. The LORD spoke to the posterity of Lehi (through Joseph of Egypt and Lehi) on this land about peace and real brotherhood among all peoples, including the white man. Though unbelievers generally, they did not embrace *polygamy* nor *secret combinations* and were thus preserved on this land (Jacob 3:5-6). The LORD taught those gathered a special dance designed to bring them healing and hope. Other Native Americans not at the gathering created a counterfeit dance, *corrupting* the one at Walker Lake. It was a dance of war designed to exact revenge on the oppresive whites who had pushed the Native Americans off their lands.

The LORD's "Dance of Peace" was transformed by many into what is now called "the Ghost Dance." It became the focus of a crackdown by the federal government and its army on "the Ghost Dance religion" which was believed to be the cause of many new battles out west in 1890. Today most have forgotten that the increasing battles with the whites (from those not at the Walker Lake Gathering) *and* a simultaneous period of great peace and hope among other Native Americans (who were part of the gathering), both resulted from Christ's visit and teaching. His visit to the "remnant of Jacob" on this land was the cause of "the Messiah Craze." He, the visit, and the Native peoples have been forgotten. Looking back, however, we see that the Walker Lake event was reported in newspapers and magazines all across the country in 1890. The Smithsonian Institution sent an ethnologist west to investigate it, resulting in an 1136 page report, complete with details on the dance Christ taught to Wovoka (a Piaute Indian from the area) and others. The purpose behind the LORD's dance was healing, peace, and hope for the oppressed Book of Mormon "remnant." They remain the forgotten focus of the Book of Mormon itself and their future role among the Gentiles of this land (for more on "the Walker Lake event," see the author's book, *The Remnant Awakens*, Amazon).

According to the Title Page of the Book of Mormon, it was written to **the Native American Remnant of Jacob** (along with Jews and Gentiles), that the promises God made to *their* "fathers" might be revealed to them and then fulfilled in time. They were to be fulfilled around 100 years after the gathering. The LORD did not come to church leadership in Salt Lake City. He had been rejected among them, as His statement to those gathered at Walker Lake implies. Pres. Wilford Woodruff was aware of Walker Lake gathering. He sent three men from Utah to listen to one Cheyenne Native American by the name of Porcupine following the event. Porcupine said he was one of twelve men Christ called there to be special witnesses of Him, one who was to spread peace and brotherhood among the native people. Christ's visit to them appears to have been partial fulfillment of 3 Nephi 16:10-12, where that fullness which had been rejected by the Saints (via sins described in 3 Ne. 16:10 and 30:2), resulted in taking a portion of the "fullness" to the Lamanite "remnant" instead. The great latter-day conversion of Native American people - to the LORD - did not happen in 1890, however. It is yet future, along with a great scourging of the Gentiles when they go through them as "lions" among the sheep (3 Ne. 16:15, 21:12). Their great future conversion to Christ (1 Ne. 15:14), their building of the New Jerusalem Temple (3 Ne. 21:23-24), and the return of stolen, covenant land are all part of the forgotten prommises in the Book of Mormon message. So too is our collective rejecting, denying, and forsaking the LORD, a natural result of embracing worldly ways in Freemasonry, sexual sin, and idolatry, a pattern presented us throughout scripture and among us again.

Secret Combinations Support Lawlessness (*to murder & get gain*)
Freemasonry Becomes Widespread, a Brotherhood of Secrecy (*lawyers, judges, high priests & others, 3 Ne. 6:21 & 27)*
Embracing Secret Blood Oaths (to maintain control via fear and coercion, with retribution)
Two-Tier Deception; An innocent Public Face at bottom, with Lucifer Worship at the top (false lord of the earth)

Sexual Perversion is Put in Place (*loss of the Spirit and God's choice blessings*)
Old Testament Baal worship involving fornication, adultery, same-sex practices, and child sacrifice
New Testament mix of false religious practices *with* sex among the Nicolaitans (reproach brought on the church)
Modern Sexual Perversion Reintroduced with the Cochranites, the Mormons, and now the LGBTQ movement

Idolatry Becomes Institutional (*"men in white" are lifted up in place of God and lead the people into darkness, 1 Ne. 8:5-8*)
Rabbis lifting themselves up as leaders of the Jewish people
The Pope leading the world's Catholics and soon the "one world church"
The Pres. of "the Corp. Sole" leading Mormons instead of **THE PROPHET** Jesus (*see this 7 x in 1 Nephi 22*)

False shepherds are a frequent problem throughout scripture (see Jer. 23; Ezek. 34; Isa. 1 & 28). In time leaders in the Josephite tradition also rejected the pure teachings of God's word in scripture. Usurpers again took control, rejecting the Joseph Smith *bloodline* for their leadership just like the Brighamites, installing themselves as Twelve administrators who sit in the chief seats (like King Noah), rather than sacrificing all for Christ as missionaries (like the Apostle Paul). Today these leaders embrace women in priesthood and those of the LGBTQ movement. All "restoration" Saints (pro or anti-polygamy) and good Christians everywhere must become one in their unity *and* love for God *via following* **His ways**. He said, "If ye love me, *keep my commandments*" (John 14:15). Awakened wise virgins transcend the curses, finding salvation in Christ. Many hearts are yet hardened against "**the word**" - **the LORD Jesus** and *both* His written word in scripture *and* His *pure* **revelation** available to us. Searching **the Word** provides answers (Acts 17:11; John 5:39; Jacob 7:23; Alma 14:1, 17:2, 33:2) and direction (2 Ne. 32:6). It is a powerful, dividing sword, separating truth from lies and deception. God has let tares and wolves in sheep's clothing (and those following **them** into idolatry) **have their own way** according to the "**idols of their hearts**." Curses thus continue to follow.

Too many have treated "lightly" the things presented in the Book of Mormon **covenant** made at baptism (to do the LORD's **will** rather than their own, Mosiah 5:5). This has led to the two "*awful situations*" spoken of in this book; (1) To be surrounded by **secret combinations** that control us for gain (Ether 8:24); And (2) Remaining in an *awful* **undredeemed state** (generally) because of ignorance of what "the fullness" of the gospel is (Mosiah 2:36-41). We *cannot* be saved in this ignorance (D&C 131:6). Over the last four generations we have inherited the **iniquities** of our fathers, priests, and kings, passed down to us as false teachings and traditions. Note the three uses of the word "**iniquity**" in the Isaiah verses used by Mormon and Moroni in the Book of Mormon.

> "But, behold, in the last days, or **in the days of the Gentiles**—yea, behold all the nations of the Gentiles and also the Jews, both those *who shall come upon this land* and those who shall be upon other lands, yea, even upon all the lands of the earth, behold, they will be **drunken with iniquity** and all manner of **abominations**...For behold, all ye that doeth **iniquity**, stay yourselves and wonder, for ye shall cry out, and cry; yea, ye shall be drunken but not with wine, ye shall stagger but not with strong drink. For behold, the LORD hath **poured out upon you the**

> **spirit of deep sleep**. For behold, ye have closed your eyes, and ye have rejected the prophets [the ones in scripture that have taught us to have one wife]; and your rulers, and **the** [real] **seers** hath he covered because of *your* **iniquity**" (2 Ne. 27:1, 4-5; Isa. 29).

We have been left without a gifted prophetic leader like Joseph for four generations. We have had the written word with us, however. In it God told us to "**rely upon the things that are written**" (D&C 18:3). All of scripture is a multi-layered Urim and Thummim for each of us, no matter what our age is. To understand His word without private interpretation (2 Pet. 1:20), requires the Spirit to receive the intended message. Sprinkled throughout His word is chastisement of wicked leaders, a verse here, a verse there. All together they speak of those who **use** the sheep for gain (see Watchman on the Tower, page 222). Brigham Young in his day, and many leaders today diminish both Christ and the truths which scripture provides, exposing error and priestcraft. Those claiming to be living prophets, seers, and revelators, claim we should listen to them **rather than** the written word. The two **are** to go hand-in-hand, not cancel each other out. Joseph and Hyrum Smith taught things that were consistent with God's written word, not new things that went against scripture. They were rejected and murdered at Nauvoo for preaching against polygamy. And like so many others in scripture, their lives were taken because their message didn't mesh with those who wanted power and other forms of gain. As we look at scripture, nearly every major figure in it was a courageous rebel, speaking against the status quo, calling the people to repentance. Most suffered for this. Those who value safety and the status quo remain in the great and spacious building. The valiant ones speak up. They fear God more than man.

Today, things are "upside down." Evil is put forward as good - and vice versa. So says additional verses in this same Isaiah chapter that was put in the Book of Mormon by men of God (2 Ne. 27:27). Judgment and cleansing are both coming (vs. 1-3). Note verses 6-26, where a sealed portion of the Book of Mormon will be coming forth (verses 6-14). With it and a special "servant," the LORD will do a "**marvelous work and wonder**" – **His** "**strange act**" (D&C 95:4, 101:95; Isa. 28:21). The sealed portion of the Book of Mormon has been "sealed" as a result of wickedness and abominations among **us** (v. 8). It includes a revelation from God, from the beginning of the world to its end (v. 7). It will provide much needed light for us in our day of darkness, deception, and ignorance. We are in that period spoken of by the Apostle Paul, when a great **falling away** occurs in the latter days. It is a falling away from **the LORD Jesus** and His fuller gospel of truth, not from men's modified churches. Many receive not,

> "the love of **the truth**, that they might be **saved**. And for this cause God shall send them **strong delusion**, that they should **believe a lie**: That they all might be *damned* who believed **not the truth**, but had pleasure in unrighteousness" (2 Thess. 2:11-12).

Paul was very concerned with the apostasy he saw creeping in the church in his day, and by those **leading** the church. It was a departure from **pure doctrine** and from **Jesus the Christ**. He talked about "grievous wolves entering in . . . speaking perverse things" (Acts 20:29-30). They would be part of "**another gospel**," that would "pervert the gospel of Christ" from within (Gal. 1:6-7). Peter called them "false teachers" with "damnable heresies" (2 Pet. 2:1). Paul addressed this apostasy **away from Christ** ("the first love," Rev. 1:4-5), and **His truth** (to the ways of men) in a number of scriptures. It came by **leaders** who embraced the ways of the world, the academics, and philosphers, etc. (see 2 Thess. 2:3, 7; 1 Tim. 4:1; 2 Tim. 1:15, 3:13, 4:3-4, see also John's words in Revelation 2:2, 14-15, 20, 3:16, and those of Jude in Jude 1:3-4). Hugh Nibley was also a "watchman" on the tower in his day, stating that he was concerned over changes he saw in the LDS temple, for example, changes to "accommodate to greater convenience, comfort, efficiency and complacency." He stated that, "apostasy never came by renouncing the gospel but always by **corrupting** it" from within (see p. 211).

For too long we have been "**upside down**" in our beliefs, believing a "**lie**," a "**strong delusion**" (see 2 Ne. 27:27; Acts 17:1; 2 Kings 21:13; Isa. 24:1, 29:16). It wasn't just polygamy either, but the false belief that leaders cannot lead us astray, and that their church, and their temple work can save us. Such **idols** replace the living God. Too many embraced **idolatry** and then **polgamy**. The idolatry remains. In many ways, we have followed the path of the ancient Israelites. That is why Mormon and Moroni put 22 chapters of Isaiah in the Book of Mormon. It is a type for us and our day. The LORD prophesied that latter day Israel would delight in their "**abominations**" [a word tied to polygamy in Jacob 2 and 3], therefore, God would give them the "**strong** delusion" they desired. It has led to a *great falling away* from **Christ the LORD** and His higher ways, as the Saints have been taught by their leaders to place their **trust** in them rather than the Savior of the world. Those in the church office building call the falling away they see "the Google Apostasy," as readily available "on-line" information counteracts the desired narrative they have put before us

– one that states "follow the Prophet," and "we cannot and will not lead you astray." These statements express the wrong message and are in fact false doctrine, a form of idolatry and priestcraft. Some 2,500 Latter-day Saints resigned from the church in August 2018 alone, for a variety of reasons. Others have been pushed out of the church, and many of them for their loyalty to the LORD rather than to church leaders. Something is very wrong here. **Jesus** is our only hope! He is **the Rock** and **the High Tower**, **the Light and Life of the world**, the **only name** under heaven wereby **men can be saved**! When tough times come, we will need Him, not the corporation and its president. Isaiah saw all of this coming. Brigham Young and many of the Saints cast away the law of the LORD, preferring instead the idols in their hearts and the teachings of men. Isaiah added these somber statements:

> "Yea, **they have chosen <u>their own ways</u>**, and their soul delighteth in their **abominations**. I also will choose their **delusions**, and will bring their fears upon them; because when **I called, none did answer**; **when I spake, they did not hear**: but they did evil before mine eyes, and chose that in which I delighted not" (Isa. 66:3-4).

> "At the noise of the tumult the people fled; at the lifting up of thyself the nations were scattered. The LORD is exalted; for he dwelleth on high: **he hath filled Zion with judgment and righteousness**. Behold, their valiant ones shall cry without: the ambassadors of peace shall weep bitterly. The highways lie waste, the wayfaring man ceaseth: he hath broken the covenant, he hath despised the cities, he regardeth no man. The earth mourneth and languisheth: Lebanon is ashamed and hewn down: Sharon is like a wilderness; and Bashan and Carmel shake off their fruits. Now will I rise, saith the LORD; now will I be exalted; now will I lift up myself. Ye shall conceive chaff, ye shall bring forth stubble: your breath, as fire, shall devour you. And the people shall be as the burnings of lime: as thorns cut up shall they be burned in the fire. Hear, ye that are far off, what I have done; and, ye that are near, acknowledge my might. **The sinners in Zion** are afraid; fearfulness hath surprised the hypocrites. Who among us shall dwell with the devouring fire? who among us shall dwell with everlasting burnings? He that walketh righteously, and speaketh uprightly; **he that despiseth the gain of oppressions**, that shaketh his hands from holding of bribes, that stoppeth his ears from hearing of blood, and shutteth his eyes from seeing evil . . . **For the LORD is our judge, the LORD is our lawgiver, the LORD is our king; he will save us**" [the righteous who seek Righteousness – even Jesus Christ] (Isa. 33:3, 5, 7-15).

> "I will tell you what I will do to **my vineyard**; **I will take away the hedge thereof**, and it shall be eaten up; and break down the wall thereof, and it shall be trodden down; And I will lay it waste: it shall not be pruned, nor digged; but there shall come up briers and thorns: I will also command the clouds that they rain not rain upon it…Therefore **my people** are gone into captivity, *because they have* **no knowledge** [of Me and my ways]…Therefore as the fire devoureth the stubble…so their root shall be as rottenness, and their *blossom* shall go up as dust: because **they have cast away <u>the law</u> of the LORD of hosts**, and **<u>despised the word</u>** of the Holy One of Israel" (Isa 5:5, 13, 24).

The righteous shall inherit the deserted cities of the Gentiles (3 Ne. 22:3). They are made desolate by the LORD. He comes with a dividing sword (Matt. 10:34). We must choose wisely. Any power present in a church today is centered in the LORD Jesus Christ, not men. He came first as a merciful lamb in the meridian of time, but when He returns against it will be as a just and powerful Judge, the Creator of heaven and earth, a King over His cleansed kingdom. There will be blood upon His robes, and it won't be His this time (D&C 133:51). The bride willingly cleanses herself in preparation for the coming of the Bridegroom.

Wheat and Tares – *the Coming Harvest of Souls*

Note the following seven sets of scripture tied to the LORD's vineyard. They are related and address the "wheat and tares" growing together among us in the last days. The great harvest of souls is coming. Too many are not saved (see D&C 45:2, 56:16, and Jer. 17:11). Too many trees are not bearing "*fruit* meet for the Father's kingdom" (D&C 84:58).

1. The first set of scriptures is Matthew chapter 13, where the LORD instructed His disciples about the coming harvest, doing so via the parable of the sower. As soon as God and His servant sowed the good seed of **His** gospel light – "the fullness," Satan came to corrupt it and take *the fullness* away (Mat. 13:19; D&C 93:39), introducing **tares** among the **wheat**, choking it. Men's false doctrines cause the choking. It diminishes the fuller doctrine and gospel of Christ. Many are **deceived by the craftiness** of men and their teachings (D&C 76:75; 123:12; Psalm 83:1-4), causing the hearts of the Saints to wax gross. Our ears become dull of hearing, our eyes closed to God's truth. God wants to root out these things and heal us (v. 15). Too many are not grounded in Christ, but in **<u>things</u>** that will not save them

(v. 21). Those who embrace **the Word** bear fruit in Him (v. 23). Speaking of our day, the time when the wheat and tares grow together, Jesus said:

> "**Let both grow together** until the harvest: and in the time of harvest I will say to the reapers, Gather ye together **first the tares**, and bind them in bundles to burn them: but **gather the wheat into my barn**" (Mat. 13:30).

In the final weeks of his life, Joseph Smith had three highly symbolic dreams. The first of these prophetic dreams was four months prior to his death and involved a *sinking steamboat.* Then two days before his death he had another *sinking steamboat* dream. Finally, the night before his death, while in Carthage jail, the Prophet Joseph Smith had his last dream, one about a **barn** he built in Kirtland. It had become dilapidated, various people fighting over what was left of it. Joseph **got out of this barn** in his dream and *out of the two sinking boats* (the later one was on fire), thus preserving his life in all three dreams. On the night of June 26, 1844, imprisoned in jail, Joseph dreamed the following dream.

> "I was back in Kirtland, Ohio, and thought I would take a walk out by myself, and view my old farm, which I found grown up with weeds and brambles, and altogether bearing **evidence of neglect** and want of culture. I went into the barn, which I found without floor or doors, with the weather - boarding off, and was altogether in keeping with the farm. While I viewed the **desolation** around me, and was contemplating **how it might be recovered** from the **curse upon it**, there came rushing into the barn a company of furious men, who commenced to pick a quarrel with me. The leader of the party ordered me to leave the barn and farm, stating **it was none of mine**, and that I must give up all hope of ever possessing it. I told him the farm was given me by the Church, and although I had not had any use of it for some time back, *still I had not sold it*, and according to righteous principles it belonged to me or the Church [meaning the members]. **He then grew furious and began to rail upon me, and threaten me, and said it never did belong to me nor to the Church**. I then told him that *I did not think it worth contending about*, that I had no desire to live upon it **in its present state**, and if he thought he had a better right I would not quarrel with him about it but leave; but my assurance that I would not trouble him at present did not seem to satisfy him, as he seemed determined to quarrel with me, and **threatened me with destruction** of my body. While he was thus engaged, pouring out his bitter words upon me, *a rabble rushed in and nearly filled the barn, drew out their knives, and began to quarrel among themselves for the premises*, and for a moment forgot me, at which time I took the opportunity to walk out of the barn about **up to my ankles in mud**. When I was a little distance from the barn, I heard them screeching and screaming in a very distressed manner, as it appeared they had engaged in a general fight with their knives. While they were thus engaged, the dream or vision ended" (HC, 6:609–10).

In D&C 88, the LORD said the "**tares**" are "that great church, the mother of abominations, that made all nations drink of the wine of the wrath of her fornication, that persecuteth the saints of God, that shed their blood…**she is the tares of the earth**" (D&C 88:94). The great whore of the earth (symbol of immorality) has invaded and polluted the things of God.

2. The **tares** are part of a second set of scriptures revealing more in Alma 37. Their darkness will be **exposed** and removed. According to Alma 37:23, the special mission of "Gazelem" will be to "discover," reveal, or bring out into light, the *increasing darkness* tied to **secret combinations** among the Saints and others today. There are wolves in sheep's clothing among us, some of whom are our "**brethren**," according to Alma 37. Gazelem's mission is about to unfold. The meaning of the name-title Gazel**e**m had roots in *Gaz* – a **stone** – and *Aleim*, a name of God as a **revelator.** Thus it may signify "**one who gazes**" (into a stone or a urim and thummim) receiving God-given knowledge. Alma 37:23 states:

> "And the Lord said: I will prepare unto my servant Gazel**e**m a *stone* which shall shine forth in darkness [ignorance] unto light, that I may discover unto **my people** *which serve me* – that I may discover *unto* **them** the works of *their* **brethren**, yea, their **secret works**, their works of darkness, and their wickedness and abominations" (Alma 37:23).

Joseph (Gazel**am**, note the spelling) was removed by a secret combination in 1844 (see D&C 38:13 & 28). This appears to be a different servant in our day. He will do a mighty work among his people, and among those of Ephraim that will listen to him. Samuel the Lamanite may be a type for him. He brought many to Christ our Redeemer. He will expose those among us who are part of the secret combinations that Moroni, Alma, and Mormon warned us of in the Book of Mormon. It may involve additional records that will be brought forth in our day for this purpose. They may include the Brass plates of Laban, the full account of John's Revelation, and the full account from the book of Ether, all that many more might be brought to Know our LORD. And there is another "**wise purpose**," **to reveal the secret works of darkness among our brethren**. It will be given him by way of the stone (revelation) which he comes to possess. The wicked ones among us (the tares) will be **exposed** as part of the fullness of the record of Ether's 24 plates (Alma 37:21).

> "And now I Moroni proceed to give an account of those ancient inhabitants which were *destroyed* by the hand of the Lord upon the face of this north country [the Jaredites]. And I take mine account from the twenty and four plates...which is called *the book of Ether*...**I do not write those things** which transpired from the day of Adam until that time. But they are had upon the plates; and whoso findeth them, the same will have power that he may get the **full account**" (Ether 1:1-4).

Gazelem appears to use the ancient Liahona or "director" to find these plates. He then uses the power the LORD has given him as a "prophet" and "seer" to "get the **full account**" of **the wickedness** of those destroyed anciently - as a way to reveal similar wickedness among our "**brethren**" today using this record. This "**full account**" will include the "**secret plans of their oaths and their covenants**," those that have been kept away from "*this people*" in the Book of Mormon up to this time (the Gentiles in the Book of Mormon or "*this people*," versus "*my people,*" the remnant of Jacob in the book, or believing Israel). The interpreters, the sealed portion of the Book of Mormon, and the knowledge addressed in Alma 37:23 will **not** go forth until "the the day that they [the Gentiles] shall repent of their **iniquity** [is this polygamy], and become clean before the LORD" (Ether 4:6). We are also to "rend that veil of unbelief which doth cause you to remain in your awful state" (Ether 4:15-19). Note three examples of chiastic structure in Alma 37.

Alma 37:9-19

(A) The brass plates convinced many thousands of Lamanites and brought them to a knowledge of the truth
- (B) Records will be the means of bringing many thousands to the knowledge of the truth
  - (C) Records are preserved for a wise purpose
    - (D) God counsels in wisdom – His paths are straight
      - (E) Keep the commandments and ye shall prosper
        - (F) Keep not the commandments and ye shall be cut off
          - (G) **Things which are sacred are preserved for a wise purpose**
        - (F) Transgress the commandments and ye shall be delivered up unto Satan
      - (E) Keep the commandments and no power on earth or in hell can take the plates from you
    - (D) God fulfills all the promises he makes unto you
  - (C) God preserves these records for a wise purpose
- (B) That He might show forth His power to future generations

(A) Even to the restoration of many thousands of the Lamanites to the truth

Alma 37:21-25

(A) Preserve these directors (changed to interpreters in later editions)
- (B) The Lord saw that His people began to work in darkness, yea work secret murders and abominations
  - (C) The Lord said, if they do not repent, they should be destroyed from off the face of the earth
    - (D) **And the Lord said: I will prepare unto my servant Gazelem, a stone which shall shine forth in darkness unto light**
  - (C) That I may discover unto them the works of their brethren
- (B) Yea, their secret works, their works of darkness and their wickedness and abominations

(A) These *directors* were prepared (changed to *interpreters* in later editions)

3. The third set of scriptures is D&C 86 (Dec. 1832), a revelation given as Joseph was re-translating the Bible. Here the LORD explained that,

> "the tares choke the wheat and drive **the church into the wilderness**" (D&C 86:3).

Many in our spiritual "wilderness" today have had to worship the LORD in more private ways, as too many in the church delight in **idolatry** (homage to men rather than Him). In the last-days "the blade [of believing wheat] is springing up and is yet tender." They exist side by side with "the tares [wicked ones] until the harvest is fully ripe" (v. 7). A number of committed believers in the Master are "**hid from the world** with [or in] Christ in God" (v. 9). They have "priesthood" and are "lawful heirs" because of their devotion to Him (not to men and their churches). They are awaiting "**the restoration of all things**" (v. 10) as part of God's "**strange act**" or "**marvelous work**." They have been a "light unto the Gentiles [asleep Latter-day Saints] through this priesthood [their relationship with God], a savior unto **my people** Israel" [the asleep Saints in the church and elsewhere who have not fully turned to Christ]. They have been trying to wake up others who will listen. Their numbers are "few," as too many fear what men can do.

4. The fourth set of scriptures is D&C 101 (1833). Here Joseph Smith was given a revelation in connection with the Saints who were "afflicted, persecuted, and cast out" from their lands in Missouri, as a result of "**their transgressions**," some of them had "lustful and covetous desires" (v. 2). What good are a people who claim to know God but don't? They are as salt that has lost is savor. In D&C 101 we read:

> "...they must needs be chastened and tried...[as] there were jarrings, and contentions, and envyings, and strifes, and **lustful and covetous desires** among them; therefore by *these things they polluted their inheritances*. They were slow to hearken unto the voice of the Lord their God; therefore, the Lord their God is slow to hearken unto their prayers, to answer them in the day of their trouble...Mine indignation is soon to be poured out without measure upon all nations; and this will I do when the cup of their *iniquity* is full. And in that day all who are found upon the watch-tower, or in other words, all mine Israel, shall be saved...When men are called unto mine everlasting gospel, and covenant with an everlasting covenant, they are accounted as the salt of the earth and the savor of men; They are called to be the savor of men; therefore, **if that salt of the earth lose its savor**, behold, it is thenceforth **good for nothing only to be cast out and trodden under the feet of men**..." (D&C 101, select verses from 2-41, 1833).

The LORD then addressed His vineyard today and the servants in it. It is a "very choice piece of land." Twelve olive trees were planted in it. The husbandmen tending it were told to "**build a tower** that mine olive trees may not be broken down when the enemy shall come" (vs. 44-45). In time, "they became very slothful, and they hearkened not unto the commandments of their LORD" (v. 50). The High Tower – is **Jesus**. He was not built up at the center of the vineyard. Men were lifted up in place of Him [including Brigham and the Twelve], or inbetween them and God. In **seven** different scriptures we read that Christ is "the high tower" all of us must build up **at the center of our lives** (see Psalm 18:2, 61:3 & 144:2; 2 Sam. 22:3 & 51; Prov. 18:10 & D&C 97:20). Some say the Nauvoo Temple was that high tower. It was never finished. Its architecture was an illustration of the bride, the Lamb's wife. She became *unfaithful* at Nauvoo, rejecting her husband. This building was destroyed.

5. The fifth set of vineyard scriptures is JST Matthew 21. It also addresses last-day servants in the LORD's vineyard. They too became very slothful. This chapter begins with a discussion of the daughter of Zion and the triumphal entry of the LORD Jesus into Jerusalem just prior to Passover and His Atonement. Later in this chapter we read that God let out His vineyard unto the husbandmen. They too were to build a high tower. Instead, the husbandmen took the LORD's servants and "beat one, and killed another, and stoned another" (they are servants like John the Baptist, Abinadi, Samuel the Lamanite, and others who call the wicked to repentance). Last of all, the LORD of the vineyard sent His **Son** to those in the vineyard. They seized Him as the Heir and killed Him (the LORD's atonement). He is Christ. He is "the stone which the builders [of the temple] rejected" (vs. 44). In the remaining verses we read of coming judgment in our day - upon this last-days vineyard - us.

> "Verily, I say unto you, **I am the stone**, and those wicked ones **reject me**. *I am the head of the corner*. These Jews [in the meridian of time] shall fall upon me, and shall be broken. And the kingdom of God shall be taken from them, and shall be given to a nation bringing forth the fruits thereof; (meaning **the Gentiles**.) Wherefore, on whomsoever this stone shall fall, it shall grind him to powder. And when the LORD therefore of the vineyard cometh, he will destroy those miserable, wicked men, and will **let again his vineyard** unto *other husbandmen*, even in **the last days**, who shall render him the fruits in their seasons. And then understood they the parable which he spake unto them, that **the Gentiles should be destroyed also**, when the Lord should descend out of heaven to reign in his vineyard [prior to the Millennium], which is the earth and the inhabitants thereof" (JST Mat. 21:5156).

6. Our sixth set of scriptures is Jacob 5 and 6 of the Book of Mormon. There we read about who corrupted the LORD's vineyard in the last days.

"Is it not **the loftiness** of thy vineyard [**pride** of leaders and others]—have not the branches thereof overcome the roots which are good? And because the branches have overcome the roots thereof, behold they grew faster than the strength of the roots, taking strength unto themselves. Behold, I say, is not this the cause that the trees of thy vineyard have become corrupted?" (Jacob 5:48). "And the day that he shall set his hand again the second time to recover his people, is the day . . . the last time, that the servants of the Lord shall go forth in his power [their priesthood or relationship with God], to nourish and prune his vineyard; and after that the end soon cometh" (Jacob 6:2).

Changes are coming soon in cleansing judgment, followed by a full "restoration of all things." Isaiah points out that a special servant will arise to call many to repentance. Correct doctrine will be taught. The everlasting covenant with its two baptisms will once again be put forth, insuring a mighty change of heart and giving of the gift of the Holy Ghost. Christ the LORD will be our Head, Judge, and King. He has decreed it (see 2 Ne. 10:14). Consistent with this, a *spiritual* "call out" has been occurring for some time and will continue to strengthen among those who love the LORD, as they – "the LORD's sheep" - respond to His voice (John 10:27-28). Truth will soon triumph. It will be shouted upon the housetops. And that truth is **Jesus Christ**. He is the way, the truth, and the life! The entire remnant of Jacob all around the world will be gathered to Him – their Redeemer. It is God's "**strange act**" (Isa. 28:21; D&C 95:4, 101:95) and His "**marvelous work and wonder**" (1 Ne. 22:8, 2 Ne. 25:17; 29:1, 3 Ne. 29:9).

7. This leads us to our last, seventh scripture. Many years later, Like King Benjamin before him, who cleansed the church of "false Christs," "false prophets, and false preachers and teachers" (Words of Mormon 1:15-16), Alma the younger also cleansed the church. He became the High Priest over the church of Christ. He saw problems rising up among his people, in the church his father Alma had also cleansed during the time of wicked King Noah. As a result, Alma the younger saw the need to conduct a great **reformation** in the land among those who were **members of the church**. Alma **commanded** that they – the **members** of the church - be **re-baptized**, revealing their re-commitment **to the LORD** in this symbolic, renewing act.

> "I speak by way of **command** unto you that **belong to the church**; and unto those who *do not belong to the church I speak by way of invitation*, saying: Come and be **baptized unto repentance**, that ye also may be partakers of the fruit of the tree of life" (Alma 5:62).

A great **reformation** must occur, like the seven examples of a group reformation given us in the Book of Mormon. The **renewal of covenants** was the original purpose of **re-baptism** throughout the early history of the church until President Grant (endnote 29). It was taken away without a revelation from God. Records show that nearly 8,000 **re-baptisms** were done inside four early LDS temples during the five-year period from 1877 to 1893 alone, with many more done outside temples - in streams, rivers, lakes and other pure water settings. In chapter six we learned that Joseph, Oliver, David and three others did this on April 6 of 1830, and so too Brigham Young and the entire church leadership in 1856. Both groups did so to recommit themselves, but for different reasons. Alma invited non-members to make a new covenant with the LORD, whereas members **renewed their** existing **covenants** with the living God. Both were part of the "**everlasting covenant**." It is not well understood today (see endnote 31).

Reformation and renewal begins individually within our hearts, where we turn completely to the LORD Jesus, the Father of our salvation. It requires being "**baptized unto repentance**" before we can be sanctified in a fiery baptism (Alma 5:54). Sincere repentance from our sins, iniquities, idolatry, and unbelief must be freely offered up to the LORD – as part of full submission to Him. Alma did this. He and his people were successful in separating themselves from the evil around them (v. 57), first from King Noah and his priests, and second from the ways of the world that crept in the church of his day. It is time for wise virgins everywhere to leave behind their dead works and the ways of babylon and become **alive in Christ**. Moroni and other prophets in the Book of Mormon have taught us correct doctrine. They are free of our blood (see Ether 12:37-40). Like King Benjamin, Mormon, and Moroni, Alma also desired that his people embrace "the way of salvation" and become redeemed of the LORD, that they might receive a new heart. He wanted them "to sing the song of redeeming love." He asked his people, "**have ye spiritually been born of God**. Have ye received **his image** in your countenances? Have ye experienced this "**mighty change in your hearts**?" Have you received a new heart? Do you have access to the unified mind of the Father and the Son?

Crying out to God is the great example of Joseph Smith, of Alma, and others in the Book of Mormon. It is the primary reason we have this important book today, as it is filled with "the plain and precious things," the saving truths that were removed from the Bible, by men who sought to control others for the sake of **gain**. Those who will listen to the voice of the Good Shepherd leave behind the ways of King Noah and his priests. It means embracing Christ the LORD - instead of men - in whatever situation you are in. It is good to listen to and respect mortal leaders, comparing what they say to what God says, but we are to fear (respect, honor, and love) God **more** than man. Those who do may receive the great endowment known as the Holy Ghost to guide them to the Tree of Life. Those who do are clothed with God's light as a covering (immersed in His divine attributes), the real wedding garment of the bride. So clothed, the bride may enter into the wedding chamber, while the unwise virgins are shut out (they never came to **know** Him, mirroring His divine image, JST Mat. 7:33; 25-9-10).

When Moses learned of God's intention to destroy the Israelites for their sins, he interceded for them (Ex. 32:11-13), offering himself as an atonement for his sinful people (v. 30). He stated that he was willing to have his name "blotted out of God's book," if He would only spare the people. Although God refused Moses' offer, He did spare the people, allowing some to continue on into the Promised Land after forty years of wandering in the wilderness. An angel led them now, rather than God Himself. Some believe Joseph Smith offered himself as a sacrifice for his people too, just like Moses in Exodos 32. Twenty-three years after Joseph's death, his firstborn son Joseph Smith III finally brought forth his father's inspired re-translation of the Bible among those who stayed behind. Then, with twenty-three more years, the Manifesto of 1890 was put in place by Pres. Wilford Woodruff. It signaled the success Joseph Smith III had in stopping much of the polygamy in Utah with the help of the Federal Government. The curses of it have remained in place for some four generations following his father's murder.

The Unfaithful Bride is invited to Awake & Arise

The great prophet Isaiah used the phrase "awake, awake" two times in his 66 chapters (Isa. 51:9, 52:1). It is an invitation for all to awaken out of their slumber, and prepare for the arrival of the Bridegroom. Although the condemnation and cursing the Saints received in D&C 84 and 124 remains upon the Utah Saints, God's merciful hand is stretched out still. After cleansing judgment (addressed in earlier chapters of Isaiah), the Bridegroom in His kindness will return His bride to Him. This is the hopeful message of Isaiah 54. It first addresses the **reproach** of his *unfaithful bride.* As the merciful husband, the LORD takes her back. **His kindness has never departed from her.** The Brighamite Saints and other Christians *are the unfaithful bride* of Christ, forsaken by Him for a time - three to four generations - since Joseph's death. The idolatry of some led to their polygamy. The curses end, after a cleansing.

> "For thou shalt break forth on the right hand and on the left; and **thy seed shall inherit the** [wicked] **Gentiles**, *and make the desolate cities to be inhabited.* Fear not; for thou shalt not be ashamed: neither be thou confounded; for thou shalt not be put to shame: **for thou shalt forget the shame of thy youth**, and shalt not remember the **reproach** of thy widowhood any more. For thy Maker is thine husband; the LORD of hosts is his name; and **thy Redeemer** the Holy One of Israel; The God of the whole earth shall he be called. For the LORD hath called thee as *a woman forsaken and grieved in spirit, and a wife of youth, when thou wast refused* [for a time – when the gates of hell prevailed against us, because of our choices], saith thy God. **For a small moment have I forsaken thee; but with great mercies will I gather thee. In a little wrath I hid my Face from thee for a moment; but with everlasting kindness will I have mercy on thee**, saith the LORD thy Redeemer (Isa. 54:3-8).

Consider taking a moment to listen to Rob Gardner's stirring piece of music entitled, "My Kindness Shall Not Depart from Thee" https://www.youtube.com/watch?v=Zq-KhxsUxNo&list=PLEVK55xNpj5SwS1CImoCdy0UpiBCPOqRs

Book Summary

A reformation **is** coming. It is part of the pattern God said He would given us in all things, that we might avoid **deception** (D&C 52:14). Martin Luther was part of a major reformation in 1517 with his 95 Theses. He addressed his 95 concerns to leaders of the powerful Catholic church. It had become a huge, corrupt business without spiritual gifts and prophetic leadership. The word of God in scripture was kept from the masses to protect the power and wealth of those leading the church, as God's word would expose them. Luther stood firm in scripture, knowing it was the key to change. He translated the Hebrew and Greek versions of the Bible into German for his people (the New Testament in 1522, the Old Testament in 1534). Those in pride, arrogance, and wealth demanded homage, obedience, and submission from the people. Luther wanted them educated in God's word, that they might have real salvation in Christ and His atoning blood. Joseph Smith said, "It is impossible for a man to be saved in ignorance" (D&C 131:6).

Threats to the power of the church in Luther's day often resulted in excommunication, imprisonment, torture, and death, but Luther feared God more than men and refused to be compelled to honor those who desired to control him. His 95 Theses addressed corruption of the church from within and departure from Christ the LORD, the Savior of men. Luther was also aware that, "He that entereth not by the door [Christ] into the sheepfold, but climbeth up some other way, the same is a thief and a robber" (John 10:1), as "the scripture cannot be broken" (John 10:35). Like the Bible, the Book of Mormon message reveals this same pattern of apostasy and then reformation (or restoration). Lehi escaped Jerusalem and possible death from those leading the people there, after he preached repentance among them. Later, in the New World, Nephi approached the LORD for understanding of his father's actions, and gained his own testimony of the living God. He then preached repentance to his brothers, explaining that his father had done so wisely in Jerusalem. Laman and Lemuel complained that those at Jerusalem were righteous, and that "all was well." They believed there was no need to leave Jerusalem. They **would not enquire** of the LORD about these things.

In time the division worsened between the two groups in Lehi's family. Nephi and those following him had to leave for safety's sake. In JST Matthew 10:30-31, Jesus said, "Think not that I am come to send peace on earth; I came not to send peace, but a sword. For I am come to set a man at variance against his father, and the daughter against her mother, and the daughter-in law against her mother in-law; and a man's foes shall be they of his own househould." Truth has always been a dividing sword. Some want it. Others want the status quo.

King Benjamin gathered his people that he might bring into the everlasting covenant. First he had to do away with **false Christs**, **false preachers**, and **false teachers** among his own people. He and "the holy men . . . did speak **the word of God** with power and with authority . . . using much sharpness because of the stiffneckedness of the people" (v. 17). Eventually, by "laboring . . . with the faculty of his whole soul, and also the prophets he [King Benjamin] did once more establish peace in the land" (v. 18). See Words of Mormon 1:15-18. Removing darkness comes prior to bringing greater light. In JST Matthew 21 God tells us that He will perform His "strange act," His "marvelous work." King Benjamin's greatest work was bringing his people our of darkness and into the greater light of Christ and **His** salvation. He taught the people that the LORD was their **head**, not him or any man (Mosiah 5:8). Three chapters later in Mosiah 8, we learn about the 24 plates of the Jaredite people who were destroyed on this land for their wicked ways (Ether 1:1-2). One among them was King Riplakish. He had many wives and put heavy tax burdens upon his people to support his lavish lifestyle, and the construction of many spacious buildings. He killed and imprisoned those that would **not** support him in his whoredoms, abominations, and high taxes. He was cut off from the LORD (see Ether 10:5-11), as was King Noah (Mosiah 11), and later Brigham Young. All practiced priestcraft and whoredoms.

Alma was a priest in King Noah's court, among a people that had fallen into corruption once again. He was moved by Abinadi's powerful testimony of salvation available in Christ and then escaped the wickedness of those leading the people in sin. They tried to kill him. We later read about his heartfelt repentance, how he cried out to God for His mercy, and that he later was "born again" in Christ. He was "**baptized unto repentance**." Alma then established "the church" among his people, those who responded to the Savior's invitation to "repent and come unto me." Two other examples of those preaching repentance are John the Baptist and the LORD Himself at Jerusalem. Both men were killed by those in charge of the corrupt church at this time. Christ was arrested and tried **secretly** before the Sandedrin (the people weren't involved and had no "vote"). The Sanhedrin had charge of a beautiful temple. It was a source of pride. Christ cleansed it two times; at the beginning and end of his ministry. He performed many miracles among the people there, and taught them with power and authority. False witnesses were brought against Jesus by those wishing to protect their power, prestige, and income (like Joseph Smith in his day). They accused Jesus of "**sorcery**" (for his miracles of healing, raising the dead, etc.), and for "enticing Israel into **apostasy**," as He preached powerful doctrine, unfamiliar among the fallen people at this time (see Sanhedrin 43a, Babylonian Talmud). He was then turned over to civil authorities (the Romans) for torture and execution. The LORD knew it would all occur and allowed it to be so to fulfill all righteousness. His murder was part of a mission of love and redemption for all those who have faith **in Him** and truly **repent**. Lies, deception, whoredoms, secret abominations, and murder, are all listed by the LORD in His description of similar sins among us in our day (see 3 Nephi 16:10 and 30:2). This pattern of corruption among leaders is all throughout scripture, for those with eyes to see.

Those who don't read the word of God today rely on leaders for their version of "salvation." They support the ones who are deceiving them, the ones who claim authority, but who do not teach the people the true "way of salvation." This same irony is presented us in the movie the Matrix, addressed at the start of this book. The "Judas" character in this story is "Cipher" in the movie. He is one of the bad guys. He turned on those who have escaped the deception of the Matrix. Cipher desires to return to "wonderland" for the **comfort** it gave him, even though it was deception. He didn't have to think or make difficult decisions. The reality of the deception was too difficult for him to accept. He thus chose to remain in it and re-insert himself back into the matrix after he had "woke up." Wise virgins are those who choose truth instead, with all its challenging ramifications. It requires courage, but in the end, it provides freedom from various chains that hold us captive, along with true salvation at the hands of God.

Because of the false Brighamite narrative put forth by the LDS church today, many are rejecting Joseph Smith and the Book of Mormon message he brought forth. Some are choosing to become atheists, or to embrace the same old Sodom and Gomorrah morality of the Old Testament. The lies about Joseph Smith are a huge stumbling block of deception for far too many. Paul spoke of our day as "*perilous times*" (2 Tim. 3:1-6). He addressed "**another gospel**" that replaces the pure one (Gal. 1:6; 2 Cor. 11:4). People are leaving the LDS church today in droves because of these lies and other reasons. It is a crisis of faith - in Christ (see endnote 4). He has been replaced with churches built up to get gain. The sad irony is that many earnestly seeking the LORD are being pushed out of the church by local leaders who follow the Brighamite enforcement cry for obedience and homage **to leaders**, those who are raised up as our light (see 3 Ne. 18:24). The LORD taught His followers a better way.

> "Master, which is **the great commandment** in the law? Jesus said unto him, Thou shalt **love the Lord thy God** with all thy heart, and with all thy soul, and with all thy mind. This is the first and great commandment. And the second is like unto it, Thou shalt **love thy neighbour** as thyself. On these two commandments hang all the law and the prophets" (Mat. 22:36-40).

Joseph Smith was innocent of polygamy. The great lie of his polygamy has been an effective tool of Satan to lead many Saints away from the LORD Jesus and the way of Salvation of our God. It is clear in scripture that God's form of marriage is one man with one woman. Throughout this work we have seen that all men and women are imperfect and fallible, whereas God is worthy of our faith, trust, and love. Go to Him in prayer. Seek His superior wisdom regarding all that has been presented in this work. Ask Him about Joseph, Brigham, polygamy, and those leading the LDS church today. Learn to receive pure revelation with a broken heart, a contrite spirit, and a desire to conform to God's will. Pure revelation from Him will be an essential in the near future. "If any of you lack wisdom, **let him ask of God**, that giveth to all men liberally, and upbraideth not; and it shall be given him" (James 1:5).

Accepting the truth about our leaders in government *and* churches reveals our "*awful* situation." Jacob, in the powerful chapter of 2 Nephi 9, spoke of that "*awful* monster" death and hell, and our need to overcome them by coming unto the LORD, the Holy One. He *pronounced* **10 "wo's"** upon the Gentile Saints of our day – those who have been given the things of God, but ignore them. Like Paul the Apostle and Joseph Smith, Jacob taught us correct doctrine and then **shook his garments free** of our blood, sins, and iniquities, along with those of his own people in his day. The responsibility is now upon our shoulders to embrace truth and act. Later in 2 Nephi 28, Jacob's brother Nephi pronounced **12 "wo's"** upon the rebellious, saying we will "**deny**" the LORD *and* the gift and power of the Holy Ghost. Both brothers addressed the "whoredoms" among us as well. I encourage you to read 2 Nephi 9 and chapters 25-32. Nephi substituted the word "**curse**" for the 11th "**wo**" in 2 Nephi 18:31. Note verse 15:

> "O the wise, and the learned, and the rich, that are puffed up in **the pride of their hearts**, and all those who **preach false doctrines**, and all those who commit **whoredoms**, and pervert the right way of the Lord, **wo, wo, wo** be unto them, saith the Lord God Almighty, for they shall be thrust down to hell!" (2 Ne. 28:15).

Truth is available to us in **God's word**. Our LORD gave us a "**commandment**" to "**rely on what is written**" in the law (the first five books of the Bible), and the prophets (the remaining Old Testament books that prophesy of the coming of Christ), along with more light in what He calls "the fullness of **my** scriptures," the JST Bible and the Book of Mormon, and the unmodified oracles given Joseph Smith (D&C 42:12, 15, 56-59). Without this **rock** or sure foundation, the gates of hell prevail against us.

> "I give unto you a commandment, that you **rely upon the things which are written**; For in them are all things written concerning the foundation of **my** church, **my** gospel, and **my** rock. Wherefore, if you shall build up **my** church, upon the foundation of **my** gospel and **my** rock, the gates of hell shall not prevail against you" (D&C 18:3-5). In 1828, God defined His church in five words, those who "**repent** and **come unto me**" (D&C 10:67).

He added that we the Saints are under **condemnation** for not valuing and adhering to the message of "the new covenant" made with God, as contained in the Book of Mormon (see D&C 84:49-59). We lift up men instead. Answers from God come to us as we remove our pride and will - our fallen, carnal nature - and seek truth in **God's will**, His divine, holy nature. David said, "If I regard **iniquity** in my heart, the LORD will **not** hear me" (Psalm 66:18, see also Isaiah 59:2). Jeremiah was more blunt. He said, "The heart is deceitful above all things, And desperately wicked; Who can know it?"(Jer. 17:9). The word "heart" in Greek is "*kardia*," meaning "the thoughts or feelings" (see #2588, the New Strong's Expanded Dictionary of the Bible).

(1) 63 And this I do that I may establish **my gospel**, that there may not be so much contention; yea, Satan doth stir up the hearts of the people to contention concerning the points of **my doctrine**; and in these things they do err, for they do **wrest the scriptures** and do not understand them.
(2) 64 Therefore, I will unfold unto them this great *mystery*;
(3) 65 For, behold, I will gather them as a hen gathereth her chickens… if they will not harden their hearts;
(4) 66 Yea, **if** they will **come**, they may, and partake of the waters of life *freely*.
(5) 67 Behold, this is **my doctrine**—whosoever **repenteth** and **cometh unto me**, the same is **my church**.
(6) 68 Whosoever declareth *more* or *less* than this, the same is **not** of me, but is against me; therefore he is not of **my church**.
(7) 69 And now, behold, whosoever is of **my church**, and endureth of **my church** to the end, him will I establish upon **my rock**, and **the gates of hell shall not prevail against them**.
(8) 70 And now, remember the words of him who is the life and light of the world, your Redeemer, your Lord and your God. Amen (D&C 10:63-70).

Our LORD said those who reject His invitation to receive Him and His ways "**are under the bondage of sin**" (D&C 84:49-51). Like Alma 37, this portion of the Oath and Covenant of the Priesthood has similar chiastic structure.

(1) 49 And the whole world lieth in sin, and groaneth under darkness and under the bondage of sin.
(2) 50 And by this you may know they are under the bondage of sin, because they come **not** unto me.
(3) 51 **For whoso cometh not unto me is under the bondage of sin.**
(4) 52 And whoso receiveth not my voice is not acquainted with my voice, and is not of me.
(5) 53 And by this you may know **the righteous from the wicked**, and that the whole world groaneth under sin and darkness even now.

God wants to bless you and I with a fullness of His light and love. Through Isaiah He states, "Awake, awake; put on thy *strength*, O Zion" (Isa. 52:1). Jesus is our Strength, our Rock, High Tower, and Light. We are to "wear" this Light as a warm covering. He awaits our sincere, heartfelt prayers and our repentance – that He might open the windows of heaven to us. I have felt His pure love. There is nothing more joyful in this life! A faith-filled trusting **relationship** with **Him** is the key to unlock these and other incredible possibilities. We can be made **new** in our LORD. Our salvation depends upon **Him**. He said:

"And whoso treasureth up **my word**, shall not be deceived" *(JST Mat. 1:37).*

"If ye continue in **my word** [Christ, written scripture & pure revelation], then are ye **my disciples** indeed;
And ye shall know **the truth**, and **the truth** shall make **you free**" *(John 8:32).*

End Notes (pages 264-84)

---

1 *Baal Worship: Idolatry, Sexual Sin & Murder* Sexual sin has frequently been the downfall of society and individuals. It was so anciently in scripture and is becoming prominent again today. The acceptance by the church of those involved in LGBTQ movements is an ominous sign of the return of ancient Baal worship. Idolatry was a central part of it, leading to sexual sin, child abuse and sacrifice, and murder generally. Sacrifices of children were made anciently to Baal. There have been some 60 million abortions since Roe versus Wade was instituted in 1973 (see http://www.numberofabortions.com/), 3,200 in Utah in 2017. Innocent children are not just (1) killed in abortions and (2) in Satanic Ritual Abuse (SRA), but they are also used (3) for sex slavery, and (4) for money as their body parts bring lots of cash on the black market. Children are part of a huge black market business, and the wars that western countries are involved in. They feature tens of thousands of refugee children. Some 18,000 Syrian children were taken into Turkish camps where their organs were harvested and sold (see https://youtu.be/uy0bF-PFpFI).

The innocent blood of children has another purpose, (5) to provide light or energy to those in darkness, those without it. This may be another reason for SRA with children, sustaining evil and prolonging lives.

Tax Exempt Status Oversight of civil leaders, those installing the laws of our land over us, should be a priority for Christian

Gay & Lesbian Agenda In the listing below, note the consistent month of June (Gay Pride month) and the specific date of **June 26** (or near it) for most of the Supreme Court decisions below, all tied to supporting sexual sin in modern-day Baal worship. The watchmen in high places – both civil and ecclesiastical – will be exposed for who they are and eventually replaced. Over the last 50 years we have seen dark forces at work to bring in more immorality and make it acceptable in our culture, our churches, and our legislative bodies, consistent with the month of June a specific date, **June 26**.

June 26, 1945 / The Charter for creation of the *United Nations* was signed by the representatives of 50 countries
June 25, 1962 / The U.S. Supreme Court banned prayer from public schools
June 29, 1963 / The date of the formal enthronement of the fallen angel Lucifer in the Vatican, the Roman Catholic Citadel, according to former Jesuit priest, Catholic theologian, and Vatican-Masonic whistle-blower Malachi Martin (a suspicious death in 1999). A complimentary "Black Mass" installation ceremony was conducted at the same time in Charleston, S.C., the Masonic "Mother Lodge of the World." This lodge is the U.S. Supreme Council of Scottish Rite Freemasonry, headed by Satanist Albert Pike. Masonry has infiltrated nearly all major institutions. June 29 is "The Feast of Saints *Peter* and *Paul*." A total of 33 days (a Masonic sacred number) after the installation of Pope John Paul (the VI), Jesuit Pope Francis was installed, perhaps the last Pope - the "False Prophet" of Revelation. He has spoken of a One World Church repeatedly.
June 1, 2009 / Pres. Barak Hussein Obama declared June as "Lesbian, Gay, Bi-sexual and Transgender Pride month." It was put in place by executive order.
June 26, 2003 / The U.S. Supreme Court invalidated sodomy laws for all 50 states
June 26, 2013 / The U.S. Supreme Court overturned The Defense of Marriage Act (DOMA)
June 26, 2015 / The U.S. Supreme Court re-defined marriage for all 50 states

Walls of Morality Breached **June 26** is the 9th of Tammuz on the Hebrew Calendar (in their 4th month). Tammuz was a Babylonian God, said to be the reincarnation of Nimrod, enemy to God (the Jews were held captive in Babylon for a time and took portions of their calendar from them, including the name of the 4th month). Baal religion is a form of Satan worship which began with Nimrod. Nimrod means, "he rebelled" or literally, "he returned to Baal" or Satan. The people of Babylon built the Tower of Babel, which was a tower to their god Baal, and a ladder to reach heaven and destroy God, **taking His power** (Gen. 10:8-12, 11:2). On the **9th of Tammuz** (or **June 26**) in 423 BCE, king Nebuchadnezzar's army **breached the walls** of Jerusalem, entering the Holy City Jerusalem. Eight days later on the 17th day of Tammuz, the Temple services were disrupted and the daily sacrificial offerings were discontinued. Finally, one month later, **Solomon's Temple was destroyed on the 9th of Av** (Av is the 5th month). The Jews were then exiled to Babylon for 70 years. As a result, this day became a day of fasting and mourning. Upon return to their homeland, the second temple was later built (that of Zerubabbel). Some 500 years later Jerusalem fell again, this time on the 17th of Tammuz, just prior to destruction of Herod's Temple (again on **the 9th of Av**).

It is clear that Satan and the secret combinations of our day are aware of this ancient date, somehow coordinating advances on this day for **gay rights** and the legalization of other **sexual perversion**. The day of **June 26th** is thus associated with the **breaching of the protective walls of the ancient Holy City** and her temple! It begins with **idolatry**, forsaking God , and then turning to darkness in sexual perversion (polygamy for the Saints). It resulted in the loss of their *covenant lands, homes, and possessions, and the freedom of the Irsraelites*, *many losing their lives*. It was followed by 70 years of *captivity* in Babylon. This represented a **10-fold time punishment** for not honoring the Sabbatical Year of Release every 7th year - when the land was to rest, when slaves were to be set free, and when all debt is forgiven. Christ's mission of redemption was designed to relieve oppression. All who are humble and repentant are granted a **release** from *sin, death, and hell* ("hell" being separation from God).

Polygamy was a tool of the adversary to attack the fullness of the gospel of Christ early on. It was conceived in "**secret chambers of hidden darkness**" (see D&C 38:13 & 28). See http://www.lorendavis.com/news_articles_Baal_Satanism.html.

Baal Gates Set Up (Ba'al, means "father of lies," John 8:44) In 2016, a replica of the Gate of Baal (from Palmyra Syria) was set up in five cities; New York City, London, Florence, Dubai, and Arona (Italy). Many believe this "gateway," "portal," or "antennae" is an invitation for Baal, Nimrod, the man of sin, or the Anti-Christ to come to earth through these cites.

Dates tied to LGBTQ Support in the LDS Church According to a recent Pew research center report, Latter-day Saints have changed their stance more than any Christian group in America relative to gay rights over the last seven years (2008 to 2015). LDS support for gay marriage has doubled since then. There were 3 pro-LGBTQ events in June 2018 (Gay Pride month).

June 25, 2018 / Tim Seelig, director of the San Francisco Gay Men's Chorus was invited by LDS church leaders to be a guest conductor for the Mormon Tabernacle Choir and Orchestra on this date at the Shoreline Amphitheatre in Mountain View, California. Mixed in with the Tabernacle Choir were those of Gay Men's Chorus (see 3 Ne. 16:10 & 30:2).
June 13, 2018 / LDS Church announces that the Family Search database will now add same-sex families to their Family Tree structure, a recognition of same-sex couples and families. The church immediately acknowledged the legality of same sex marriage in the United States after the U.S. Supreme Court legalized it in **June** of 2015. President Dallin H. Oaks, now in the First Presidency, counseled church members and people of faith to submit to the law because it had been "sustained by the highest available authority." Not so, God has not sustained it to my knowledge.
June 1, 2018 / LDS First Presidency sponsors the "Be One" event, saying it is "Time to Renew Our Commitment to Be One."

This is the first day of Gay Pride Month, as set aside by Pres. Barak Hussein Obama.
See https://www.lds.org/media-library/video/2018-06-1000-be-one-a-celebration-of-the-revelation-on-the-priesthood?lang=eng

2017 / LDS church offers statement of support for the LoveLoud Festival. The goal of the festival is to put differences aside between the LGBTQ and faith communities to promote love and acceptance of LGBTQ youth.

2016 / The official Mormons and Gays website was revised and moved to mormonandgay.lds.org. The update supported members in identifying as gay and noted that therapy focusing on changing sexual orientation is unethical.

June 6, 2015 / LDS Payson Temple Youth Celebration at BYU with Church Approved Rainbow Colors. Took place in the middle of Gay Pride celebrations held in Provo and Salt Lake between June 4 and 7th.

July 2, 2015 / Church Donates to the Utah Pride Center, the first official financial donation by the LDS Chruch to an LGBT cause, given to the Utah Pride Center of Salt Lake City.

2015 / Kentucky County Clerk Kim Davis would not issue a marriage license to gay couples in 2015 because it violated her Christian beliefs. "The [LDS] church's tone shifted slightly but *significantly* on Tuesday, when a high-ranking church leader said in a speech that Davis was wrong to shirk her responsibilities by invoking her religion. Public officials, "*are not free to apply personal convictions* -- religious or other -- in place of the defined responsibilities of their public offices," said Dallin H. Oaks [now of the First Presidency]. He added, "Government officials must not apply these duties selectively according to their personal preferences -- whatever their source" (Yahoo News, Oct. 21, 2015). Mat Staver, a lawyer for Davis, told the Assoc. Press that the Mormon Church's tactic "may sound nice, but it ends up not pleasing anyone. You need to stand on principle."

2015 / LDS Apostle D. Todd Christopherson states that Mormons who support gay marriage are not in danger of losing their temple privileges or church membership. They would only be in trouble for "supporting organizations that promote opposition or positions in opposition to the church's." In a later news conference he said, "In our view, it doesn't really become a problem unless someone is out attacking the church and its leaders.....and trying to get others to follow them." He also acknowledged that LDS leaders have evolved in their thinking about homosexuality. Todd's brother Tom is a "gay" active Mormon who teaches Gospel Doctrine in his Ward. His book on being gay and a Mormon is sold at Desert Book. It is entitled, "*That We May Be One*."

2013 / Boy Scouts of America votes to allow openly gay youth to have BSA membership, but maintains ban on openly gay adult leaders. The LDS church supported this decision.

2013 / Church Approves Gay Support Club at BYU. It is estimated that 2-3000 BYU students have some connection to gay or lesbian tendencies or activism within a Church supported school largely funded by the tithing of its members.

2013 / Provo Herald front page article, "Provo's first Gay Pride event" (Aug. 23). It took place on Sept. 21 of 2013.

2013 / Steve Young BYU & NFL Hall of Fame BYU quarterback and wife Barb give keynote addresses at the Affirmation's International Conference promoting acceptance of gays and lesbians within the church and community (Sept. 13-15).

2011 / BYU Honor Code removes ban on advocacy and promotion of homosexual behavior as being morally acceptable

2009 / LDS Church supports new Utah law banning gay discrimination in public housing.

Child Abuse Today modern Baal worship is expressed in not only greater acceptance of the LGBTQ agenda, but in the sexual abuse of children in multiple ways. The Catholic Church has a long history of the abuse of children (mostly male) by priests. The protest efforts of former Bishop Sam Young have called attention to similar problems in Mormonism, via leading questions that are asked children by some bishops. It is a reflection of our declining morality generally.

Who is Leading the Church? Many Saints are choosing to be an atheist or to embrace the ways of Sodom and Gomorrah, largely because the fifteen men leading the Brighamite church do not experience nor teach **the doctrine of Christ** and other early doctrines found in the Book of Mormon, those shared by the Prophet Joseph. Some honor another god. They say we shouldn't talk about seeking an audience with the LORD Jesus in this life, yet Joseph publicly declared that God had visited him, even to non-believers. He said, "Oh! I beseech you to go forward, go forward and make your calling and your election sure; and if any man preach any other Gospel than that which I have preached, he shall be cursed; and some of you who now hear me shall see it, and know that I testify the truth concerning them" (TPJS p. 366). A different gospel is preached today, one corrupted early on by Brigham Young and those following him. It wasn't and isn't the gospel of love preached by the Master. Abinadi was killed because he preached Christ. Wicked leaders then said, "we have found an accusation against thee, and thou art worthy of death. For thou hast said that God himself should come down among the children of men; and now, for this cause thou shalt be put to death unless thou wilt recall all the words which thou hast spoken evil concerning me and my people" (Mosiah 17:7-8).

The Lectures on Faith teach us (1) what faith is, (2) who we should have faith in and why, and (3) what the effects of faith are in our lives. This important instruction was once a part of "**the doctrine**" contained in the Doctrine and Covenants. Lecture 1, verse 1 says it is "**the doctrine of Christ**." The Lectures on Faith were put in the D&C by a vote of the whole church, then later removed secretly without any vote. Lecture 2:56 states, "We have now clearly set forth how it is, and how it was, that **God became an object of faith** for rational beings; and also, upon what foundation the testimony was based, which excited the enquiry and diligent search of the ancient saints, to seek after and **obtain a knowledge of the glory of God**: and we have seen that it was human testimony, and human testimony only, that excited this enquiry, in the first instance in their minds—it was the credence they gave to the testimony of their fathers—this testimony having aroused their minds **to enquire after the knowledge of God**, the enquiry frequently terminated, indeed, always terminated, when rightly pursued, in the most glorious discoveries, and eternal certainty." And that certainty is that He is real and He loves you and I. His invitation is, "**repent** and **come unto me**" (3 Ne. 9:22), and "**deny yourselves of all ungodliness**" (Moroni 10:32). Such are made new and gain real knowledge of His reality.

Nephi got it right when he pointed out that, "**there are save two churches only**." In the revealing listing of scriptures found on pages 183-84 of this book, we see what has become of the church originally founded by God through Joseph, then modified by Young and others. It is the reason so many are leaving the church today. Grant Palmer, in his book, *Restoring Christ: Leaving Mormon Jesus for Jesus of the Gospels*, points out who it is that is lifted up before the Saints today. Though I do not agree with Palmer's assessments of Joseph Smith and the Restoration in this book, his chapter 13 entitled, *Meetings with a LDS General Authority*, 2012-14, reveals much. It is consistent with what I have come to know about some of our top leaders. Many of them are who or what the Saints think they are (see Mat. 23:13; JST Luke 11:53). Jesus said, **I am the light which ye shall hold up**—that which ye have seen me do" (3 Ne. 18:24). The LORD Jesus (Yeshua) came here to redeem us. He is worthy of our love and devotion. He is returning soon as King and Judge to cleanse the earth.

[2] *Changing Church Names & the Scattering 7 Ways* The succession crisis of who would lead the church after the murders of the three Smith brothers led to the scattering of the Saints in seven directions early on, perhaps in fulfillment of Deut. 28:25. More divisions resulted later. Like the scattered Israelites of old, the Prophet Joseph prophesied that before the kingdom would be established among the Saints, they would first be scattered, driven, gathered again, and then *re-established.* Joseph stated, "I prophecy that the day will come when you will say Oh that we had given heed... the people will not hearken nor hear and bondage, death and destruction are close at our heels. The kingdom will not be broken up but we shall be scattered and driven, gathered again and then dispersed, reestablished & driven abroad and so on until the Ancient of days shall sit and the kingdom and power thereof shall be given to the Saints and they shall possess it forever and ever..." (Words of Joseph Smith, p. 67).

Many other divisions have been identified (perhaps 20 up to 1984 and another 20 thereafter). Most who followed Brigham and his polygamy westward were new converts (unaware of his secretive polygamy, my relatives included). They were from the British Isles where a controlling king oversaw the land. Many of the older, more seasoned Saints at Nauvoo (free of the monarchy in England) rejected Young, polygamy, and the new temple doctrines. Note the seven *original* factions arising from Young's "new order of things," which included polygamy and his strong hand of leadership:

1. The Church of Jesus Christ - William Bickerton
2. The Rigdonites - Sidney Rigdon
3. The Church of Christ (Temple Lot) - Granville Hedrick
4. A. The Church of Jesus Christ of Latter-day Saints (Strangite) - James Strang. Many from this movement latter became part of the RLDS movement (now the Community of Christ).
   B. The Reorganized Church of the Jesus Christ of Latter-day Saints (RLDS), now the Community of Christ; the bloodline of the Prophet Joseph was passed on to some in it through Joseph Smith III, Alexander Hale Smith, and David Hyrum Smith. In 1984, changes were introduced allowing women into the priesthood, resulting in further sub-divisions, including as many as twenty "independent branches of the restoration" from the RLDS movement. They are seeking to restore original truths tied to the Book of Mormon and Joseph Smith, as do many who have or are departing from the LDS church headquartered in Utah.
5. The Church of Jesus Christ of Latter-day Saints - Lyman Wight (Texas)
6. The Church of Jesus Christ of Latter-day Saints - Brigham Young (Utah); the bloodline of Hyrum Smith was passed on to some in this church. Unorganized "movements" of dissatified Latter-day Saints have sprung up, some having discovered the writings of Denver Snuffer, who traces the corruptiion in the church after deaths of Joseph, Hyrum, and Samuel. In 2013 a document was created for LDS church leaders to address growing "resignations" from the LDS Utah church. The exodus has dramatically incresed since then. See "**LDS Personal Faith Crisis**" in endnote 4. This book has been written primarily to this group of people.
7. The Church of Jesus Christ of Latter-day Saints - fundamentalist polygamists (mostly west and south)

Names Reflecting the Status of the Church Names and titles in the Bible typically reflect character and acts performed. This is also true of four consecutive name changes for the LDS church presented hereafter. They coincide with events from 1831 – 41, reflecting the character of the Saints and their church at that point in time. It should be noted that in times when the church was cursed with the lesser priesthood and lesser law, there have been individuals who lived higher ways among them. Those today that receive the first and second comforters (via the baptism of fire and the Second Comforter experiences) may become part of the church of the Firstborn. This celestial church has not been put in place officially upon the earth as of yet, but will be in the LORD's way and timing. Much of what follows, and that above, was obtained from "The Watcher" and his blog posts (see https://onewhoiswatching.wordpress.com). Pray to determine the truth in what is presented hereafter.

1. The church of Christ The LORD's church is named by Him in a revelation in D&C 20, where the name "the Church of Christ" is mentioned by the LORD 6 times. It appears to have lasted two years (Mar. 1829 – June 1831), a time when **47** revelations were received. The LORD's church came out of the wilderness of darkness on the Earth. A foundation was laid for the future church of God and its Zion via the coming forth of the Book of Mormon (Zion is the pure in heart). Those in the church of Christ attempted to live the higher Law of the Celestial Kingdom (place of the Father) via living the Law of Consecration. It was at this time that missionary work was first implemented and sent to the Book of Mormon remnant – to

Native Americans on this land. Historically, the "*Church of Christ*" name shows up in modern revelation at the very beginning of the formal establishment of the church. "It shall be the duty of the several churches, composing the church of Christ..." (D&C 20:81). This revelation was given in April of 1830, and features the first formal name of the church in the D&C. It is also the first formal name given the church in the Book of Mormon.

2. The Church of God (also called the church of the Firstborn) This is the church of God the Father, representing a "*Fullness*" that is restored to administer the Gospel of Christ. It may have lasted 3.5 years (June 1831- Dec. 1834) during which time there were **58** revelations received (the most of the four name periods). It was at this time that "*the Fullness*" of the higher Melchizedek Priesthood was offered to those gathered at the Morley Farm Conference, where the first high priests in the church were ordained (ordinations are invitations by men to receive the real thing, coming only from God). They were part of a church called "the Church of God" (a church within a church). The Father and the Son were both seen by some at this time, so too the "man of sin." The Saints had five years to redeem Zion in "the stronghold" that was Kirtland (from Sept. 11, 1831 to Sept. 11, 1836, see D&C 64:21-22). Their strength was to come in this higher priesthood power, *sufficient to defeat all enemies*. This "*Fullness*" of priesthood was to become a hedge of protection (D&C 38), but only if righteousness was present. The right to have it was later removed (D&C 124:28). Other names tied to this particular "church" include "the church of the Firstborn" (D&C 76:54, 101; 88:5; 107:80) and the "church of Zion."

Historically, the "Church of God" name begins to show up in modern revelation shortly after the Melchizedek priesthood opportunity is restored at the Morley Farm in June of 1831, resulting in the High Priests retroactively becoming the leading administrative body of the church. They had administrative authority in the Church of Christ over the "presiding elders" who were not High Priests (few if any actually obtained this power from God, however, though it did come with some via their prior preparation, see Alma 13). Most assume that this name is another name for the church of Christ, but a careful reading of the historical timeline - in context - reveals that it refers to those called to live the higher Law of Consecration, as well as practice a higher priesthood. Thus they and the name are tied to a higher church. Those faithful in this higher "church of God" were and are part of what is also called "the church of the Firstborn. D&C 107:80 refers to these higher administrative privileges generally, stating, "And after this decision it shall be had in remembrance no more before the LORD; for this is the highest council of the church of God, and a final decision upon controversies in spiritual matters." This higher law, priesthood, and church is reflected in D&C 84:17, where we read, "Which priesthood continueth in the church of God in all generations, and is without beginning of days or end of years."

Note also D&C 70:5, "Wherefore, I have appointed unto them, and this is their business in the church of God, to manage the concerns thereof, yea, the benefits thereof..." Note also verse 10, "And behold, none are exempt from this law who belong to the church of the living God..." They "are they who are the church of the Firstborn" (D&C 76:54). In Section 88, verse 5, we read, "Which glory is that of the church of the Firstborn, even of God, the holiest of all, through Jesus Christ his Son." Verse 22 of D&C 93 states, "And all those who are begotten through me are partakers of the glory of the same, and are the church of the Firstborn. Power in the priesthood is directly related to the level of our relationship with God.

3. The church of the Latter-day Saints Note that **the LORD's name was removed from the church at this time**. This new name appears to have lasted two years (Dec. 1834 – Sept. 1836), wherein **6** revelations were received (the lowest). God's hedge of protection in "*the Fullness*" was apparently rejected and removed from among the Saints for not living the higher law (see 3 Ne. 16:10; D&C 14:10; 124:28). Christ's name was removed and condemnation pronounced on the Saints, remaining on us today. All name changes for the church are well documented in the seven-volume history of the church, wherein a church conference was called in 1834. There, by unanimous vote, the name of the church was changed. "During a conference held on May 3, 1834, with Joseph Smith acting as moderator, "a motion was made by Sidney Rigdon, and seconded by Newel K. Whitney, that this Church be known hereafter by the name of 'The Church of the Latter-day Saints.' Remarks were made by the members, after which the motion passed by unanimous vote" (HC, vol. 2, pps. 62-63, 73). Shortly thereafter, the LORD informed the Saints that they were under condemnation and must have a reformation in all things. This new name for the church, without "Christ" in it, is documented on **the face of the Kirtland house of the LORD** in Ohio, *and* in the first edition of the Doctrine and Covenants. Some accused Joseph of apostasy for making this change.

4. The Church of Jesus Christ of Latter-day Saints The Saints appear to have renamed the church in 1836, **re-inserting Christ's name back into its title, and without God's permission** (Sept. 1836 – Jan. 1841). There were 11 revelations received by Joseph at this time (second lowest). The name reflects a continued rejection of "*the Fullness*" by the Saints, as seen via **the** whoredom of unlawful polygamy practices and in the Nauvoo house of the LORD never being completed. These and other sins led to the rejection described by God in D&C 124:32 and 3 Nephi 16:10.

In the dedicatory prayer of the Kirtland house of the LORD (D&C 109, April 1836), the Prophet Joseph Smith - on behalf of the Saints, appears to be petitioning the LORD to once again put his name back upon the condemned church (1832, D&C 84:58). In verse 79 we read, "And also this church, **to put upon it thy name**. And help us by the power of thy Spirit, that we may mingle our voices with those bright, shining seraphs around thy throne, with acclamations of praise, singing Hosanna to God and the Lamb!" The very first time "The Church of Jesus Christ of Latter-day Saints" shows up in modern revelation is section 115 in 1838. Historians use section 115 as the scriptural justification for using the current church name.

The Saints may have already re-inserted the name of Christ back into the name of the Church years before this particular revelation was given, however, perhaps demonstrating that Section 115 is not so much a directive from the LORD to re-insert

Christ's name into the church again, but rather a prophesy by the LORD that the Saints *would do so of their own accord.* After the Gentile church rejected the higher Law of Consecration, and the Fullness of the priesthood, sometime around 1834, Joseph was instrumental in renaming and establishing the Church of the Latter-day Saints (without Christ's name in it). This name was later changed, perhaps by a misinterpretation of section 115, to our current name - the Church of Jesus Christ of Latter day Saints, the later name referring to the saints who are then in a scattered and unconsecrated condition, presided over by an elder or elders. How much priesthood remained, if any (because of the abomination of polygamy) is unclear.

Note that the LORD said that the Saints "shall [future tense] be called" by this name. Verses 3-5 of D&C 115 state, "And also unto my faithful servants who are of the high council of my church in Zion, for thus it shall be called, and unto all the elders and people of my Church of Jesus Christ of Latter-day Saints, scattered abroad in all the world; For thus shall my church be called in the last days, even The Church of Jesus Christ of Latter-day Saints. Verily I say unto you all: Arise and shine forth, that thy light may be a standard for the nations." Today the official name of the incorporated LDS church is, "The Corporation of the President of the Church of Jesus Christ of Latter-day Saints. See also Assumption #9, chap. 6.

[3] *Smith Statements – Emma (wife), Lucy Mack Smith (mother), Katharine (sister), Hyrum, Samuel, William (brothers)* The Smiths are too often ignored as witnesses when it comes to Joseph Smith's innocence as a polygamist. There are always two sides to any story. If we listened to only Hillary Clinton, we would believe she is innocent of all wrongdoing tied to her and her husband over the last 25 years. They tell lies to cover the truth and smear the opposition with lies. The Smith family (the Josephites) is made out to be the enemy by the Brighamites. I choose to believe all of the Smiths rather than Brigham Young and those repeating his original lies. They have formed the narrative of the LDS church and its people today.

Emma Smith Statements (wife of the Prophet Joseph) Brigham Young made Emma Smith out to be an evil woman, a favorite tactic of liars. He did so in a General Conference address. Emma's version of history is consistent in the multiple interviews of her, and in direct opposition to Brigham Young's words. Young, Wilford Woodruff, and Willard Richards (all church leaders, all in "the secret chamber," all polygamists, all Masons, and many in England together during 1839-40) stated that Emma Smith burned the revelation later known as D&C 132, after Joseph Smith showed it to her. She consistently refuted these claims (below). She said she did not see any words tied to Young's Section 132 creation until 1856. Brigham Young had Orson Pratt write the pro-polygamy tract called "The Seer"in 1852, wherein the supposed "revelation" is contained. Emma first saw "The Seer" 9 years after her husband was murdered [1853]. Wilford Woodruff's story states, "After Joseph had been to Bishop Whitney's he went home, and Emma began teasing for the revelation. Said she – 'Joseph you promised me that revelation, and if you are a man of your word you will give it to me.' Joseph took it from his pocket and said – 'Take it.' She went to the fire-place and put it in, and put the candle under it and burnt it, and she thought that was the end of it, and she will be damned as sure as she is a living woman. Joseph used to say that he would have her hereafter, if he had to go to hell for her, and he will have to go to hell for her as sure as he ever gets her" (JD 23:131, p. 132 Wilford Woodruff, May 14, 1882).

A few questions from four different interviews of Emma Smith are presented hereafter. They are quoted from the book, *The Exoneration of Emma, Joseph and Hyrum,* by Ronald Meldon Karren (Amazon).

Emma Interview 1 by Jason Briggs J.W.B. Question - Mrs. Bidamon (Emma's new married name), have you seen the revelation on polygamy, published by Orson Pratt, in the Seer, in 1852 [Section 132 in the Utah Doctrine and Covenants]? A - I have. J.W.B. - Have you read it? A - I have read it, and heard it read. J.W.B. - Did Joseph Smith ever teach you the principles of polygamy as being revealed to him, or as a correct and righteous principle? A - He never did. Q - J.W.B. - What about the statement of Brigham Young, that you burnt the original manuscript of that revelation? A - **It is false in all its parts**, made out of whole cloth without any foundation in truth. Q: Sister Emma, is it not a fact that Joseph Smith received a revelation favoring polygamy and spiritual wifery? A: No, sir; **there was no revelation given through him on either spiritual wifery or polygamy. Nor was that abominable doctrine taught either privately or publicly** [by Joseph] **before Mr. Smith's death**. Q: How about Brigham Young's statement to the contrary—that Joseph Smith did receive the polygamy and Adam-god revelation, and that he presented it to you by the hand of a Mr. Clayton, and that after reading it you got mad, tore it up, and burned it? A: That is a base falsehood made out of whole cloth.

Emma Interview 2 by J. C. Chrestensen J.C.C. Question - Have you ever seen and read that feigned and assumed revelation on polygamy? A: Yes, sir. Q: When and where did you first see and read that polygamy revelation? A: **Right here in Nauvoo in the year 1853**, published in Washington, District of Columbia, **in a paper called The Seer**, by Orson Pratt of the Utah Church [Saints' Herald 65:1044–1045].

Emma Interview 3 by Dixon's Report An English author and traveler named William Hepworth Dixon visited Emma and wrote in 1869: Emma, Joseph's wife and secretary, the partner of all his toils, of all his glories, coolly, firmly, permanently denies that her husband ever had any other wife than herself. She declares the story to be false, the revelation a fraud. She denounces polygamy as the invention of Young and Pratt—a work of the devil—brought in by them for the destruction of God's new church. On account of this doctrine, she has separated herself from the Saints of Utah, and has taken up her dwelling with what she calls a remnant of the true church at Nauvoo [New America, Chapter 30, 1869; Saints' Herald 48:165–166].

Emma Interview 4 by Joseph Smith the III This account in February, 1879, was only two months before Emma's death. Question: What about the revelation on polygamy? Did Joseph Smith have anything like it? What of spiritual wifery? A: **There was no revelation on either polygamy, or spiritual wives**. There were some rumors of something of the sort, of which I asked my husband. He assured me that all there was of it was, that in a chat about plural wives, he had said, "Well, such a system might possibly be, if everybody was agreed to it, and would behave as they should; but they would not; and, besides, **it was contrary to the will of heaven**. No such thing as polygamy, or spiritual wifery, was taught, publicly or privately [by him], before my husband's death, that I have now, or ever had any knowledge of. Q: Did he not have other wives than yourself? A: **He had no other wife but me**; nor did he to my knowledge ever have. Q: Did he not hold marital relation with women other than yourself? A: He did not have improper relations with any woman that ever came to my knowledge. Q: Was there nothing about spiritual wives that you recollect? A: At one time my husband came to me and asked me if I had heard certain rumors about spiritual marriages, or anything of the kind; and assured me that if I had, that **they were without foundation; that there was no such doctrine, and never should be with his knowledge, or consent. I know that he had no other wife or wives than myself, in any sense, either spiritual or otherwise** [Saints' Herald 26:289–290].

Emma Interview #5 by Mark Forscutt Forscutt was a secretary to Brigham Young in Utah, until Brigham insisted that he take a plural wife. Forscutt **refused and was forced to escape from Utah to save his life**. Later he became an apostle in the Reorganization—and still later he interviewed Emma to get her testimony concerning the polygamy question. He recorded in his diary: Thur. Sep. 13/[18]77 Spent day visiting at Nauvoo, Sister Emma (widow of the Martyr) told me that she remembered Joseph having said in answer to a question from Sister [Brackenbury], Mother of the Brothers Brackenbury, as to whether Brigham would not lead the church in case of his (Joseph's) death,—"**I would pity the people that should follow Brigham as a leader**," and in answer to another question as to why he would pity them, Joseph answered, "**Because he would lead them to hell**." She also related that after Brigham came into power in Nauvoo, she sought several times to see him; but did not succeed, and finally sent for him. He came, bringing witnesses with him, and enquired what she wished. She asked him why he was teaching or allowing to be taught the doctrines and practises [sic] he was [spiritual wifery and polygamy], to which he replied he knew of nothing of the kind she referred to, and if she knew of any one indulging in such practises, and would **inform** on them, they should be taken up and dealt with. She replied, 'Why, Brigham you need not talk like that; you know these things are done. It is so plain, that even a stranger can not come and walk through our streets without witnessing it. You know too that Joseph in my presence told you [Brigham] that you had been teaching such things while he was alive, and that **he commanded you in the name of the LORD, to teach them no more**, or judgments would overtake you.' He left and she had no conversation with him afterward" (*Mark Forscutt's Diary*, pages 81–82).

Virtue Will Triumph There were four overflowing meetings of members of the Female Relief Society at Nauvoo to adddress accusations against the women of Nauvoo (each meeting being composed of different members that all might have the opportunity of expressing their feelings). They were held on March 9 and 16 of 1844. The following remarks were read and unanimously adopted at each meeting by President of the Relief Society, Emma Smith.

The Voice of Innocence from Nauvoo (Mar. 20, 1844) President Emma Smith stated, "it becomes us, in defence of our rights, for the glory of our fathers; for the honor of our mothers; for the happiness of our husbands; and for the welfare of our dear children, in rebuke such an outrage upon the chastity of society: to thwart such **a death blow at the hal'owed marriage covenant**...Resolved unanimously, That while we render credence to the doctrines of Paul that neither the man is without the woman neither is the woman without the man in the LORD, yet **we raise our voices and hands against John C. Bennett's "spiritual wife system" as a scheme of profligates to seduce women**...wherefore, **while the marriage bed, undefiled is honorable, let polygamy, bigamy, fornication, adultery, and prostitution, be frowned out of the hearts of honest men to drop in the gulf of fallen nature**, where the worm dieth not and the fire is not quenched!" and let all the saints say. Amen!" Emma Smith, Pres., women's Relief Society, Nauvoo, in Ronald Karren, *The Exoneration of Emma, Joseph & Hyrum: Part One.*

President Emma Smith (of the Nauvoo female Relief Society) used some 25 different names in her speech for those practicing *spiritual wifery* at Nauvoo, calling them, "debauchers, vagabonds, ungodly wretches, miserable dupes, poisoned daggers, tormentors, blood thirsty pimps, fag ends of creation, canker worms, serpents, sharks, putrid bodies, vultures, eagles, wolves, rotten flesh, rotten hearted ravens, rubbish, carrion, seducers, slanderers, defamers, cowardly assassins, and profligates" (shamelously immoral). Compare her 25 negative terms to the 13 name-titles used by those embracing polygamy later in Utah, those trying to hide it via a form of *institutional deception*, as reported in an 1887 *Deseret News* article (see p. 190).

For Emma Smith's words on the succession of power from her husband to Brigham Young, see endnote 17.

Hyrum Smith's China Creek Statement Hyrum stated, "To the brethren of the Church of Jesus Christ of Latter Day Saints, living on China Creek, in Hancock County, greeting: Whereas brother Richard Hewitt has called on me to-day, to know my views concerning some doctrines that are preached in your place, and states to me that some of your elders say, that a man having a **certain** [additional or secret] **priesthood**, may have as many wives as he pleases, and that doctrine is taught here: I say unto you that that man teaches false doctrine, for there is no such doctrine taught here. **And any man that is found teaching privately or publicly any such doctrine, is culpable, and will stand Council, and lose his license and membership** also: therefore he had better beware what he is about. And again I say unto you, an elder has no business to undertake to preach mysteries in any part of the world, for God has commanded us all to preach nothing but the first principles unto the world. Neither has any elder any authority to preach any mysterious thing to any branch of the church unless he has a direct commandment from God to do so..." (Co-President Hyrum Smith, *Truth will prevail*, Vol. V. No. 6, Nauvoo, Mar. 15, 1844, in Whole No. 90, History of Joseph Smith, Nauvoo, March 15, 1844).

Samuel Smith Statement Note the journal entries of Samuel Smith, brother to Joseph, Hyrum, and William Smith, all leaders in the church. "June 1829, 1832, Baptized three: Augusta Cobb, Elizabeth Harendeen and __________ Porter." Augusta Cobb would later become Brigham Young's third wife. Prior to their marriage, Augusta named her last child "Brigham." He was born May 17, 1843, and died on the way to Nauvoo to join Brigham and the Saints there (Augusta abandoned her husband and five of her children). The conception date is 9 months earlier, around August of 1842 (a full year before Joseph's purported "revelation" on plural marriage).

William Smith's Words Having quoted William Smith in much of this book, I do not repeat them here. See pages 131-37.

Emma Smith's Words See pages 72-73, also endnote 17 *Lucy Mack Smith's Words* See pages 73-75

Katharine Smith's Words See pages 107-8 & 133

4 *Record Decline* Numbers don't lie. The chart *on the next page* shows the least growth in LDS church recorded history (1.6% in 2016, 1.4% in 2017). Membership statistics were not given over the pulpit for 2016 and 2017 (in 2017 and 2018) perhaps because of this continuing decline and the growing exodus of so many Saints from the church for a variety of reasons (some say 2,500 left in August of 2018 alone). Note that though the LDS church had more missionaries than ever in 2014 (85,000), convert baptisms per missionary were down from a high point in 1989 of 8 converts per missionary, to just 3.5 in 2013 and 14. The highpoint year was 1989, the time of Pres. Benson's leadership, when he focused the Saints upon **the Book of Mormon**, in connection with His call to **eliminate pride** in our lives and our need to **repent**. These three pillars should be our focus today, plus one more – **Christ the LORD**. Decreasing faith and trust in Christ, and thus the loss of the gifts and fruits of the Spirit, are the result of dwelling too much on leaders and "the church" itself (see Psalm 118:8; 2 Ne. 4:34). There is also little teaching about Him and His gifts of the Spirit. Moral decline and an increase in the control of secret combinations is thus rampant.

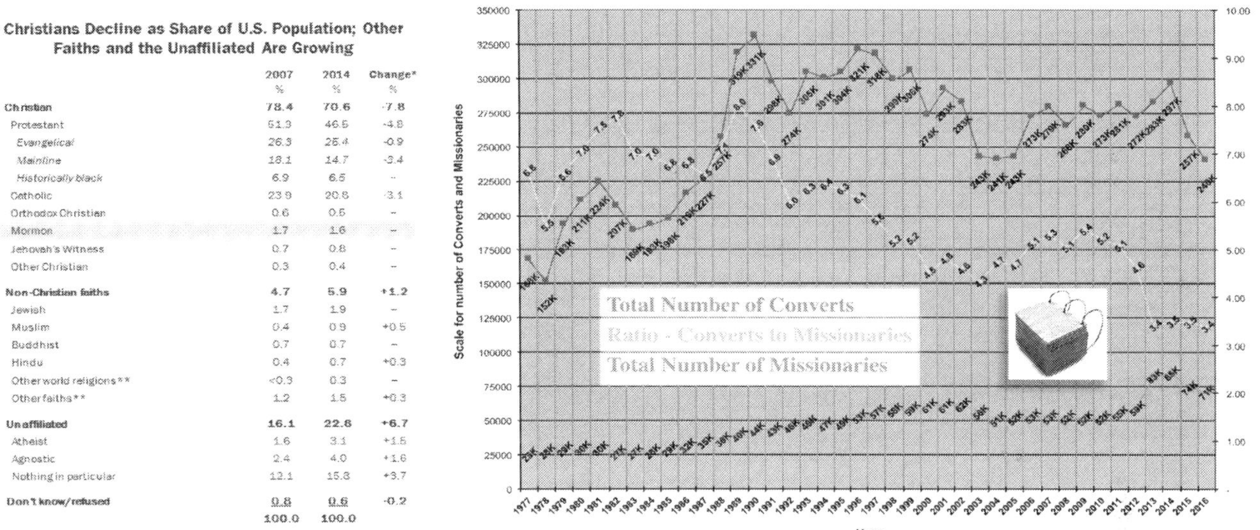

Christians Decline as Share of U.S. Population; Other Faiths and the Unaffiliated Are Growing

	2007 %	2014 %	Change* %
Christian	**78.4**	**70.6**	-7.8
Protestant	51.3	46.5	-4.8
Evangelical	26.3	25.4	-0.9
Mainline	18.1	14.7	-3.4
Historically black	6.9	6.5	-
Catholic	23.9	20.8	-3.1
Orthodox Christian	0.6	0.5	-
Mormon	1.7	1.6	-
Jehovah's Witness	0.7	0.8	-
Other Christian	0.3	0.4	-
Non-Christian faiths	**4.7**	**5.9**	**+1.2**
Jewish	1.7	1.9	-
Muslim	0.4	0.9	+0.5
Buddhist	0.7	0.7	-
Hindu	0.4	0.7	+0.3
Other world religions**	<0.3	0.3	-
Other faiths**	1.2	1.5	+0.3
Unaffiliated	**16.1**	**22.8**	**+6.7**
Atheist	1.6	3.1	+1.5
Agnostic	2.4	4.0	+1.6
Nothing in particular	12.1	15.8	+3.7
Don't know/refused	0.8	0.6	-0.2
	100.0	100.0	

The decline of belief, and lower church growth, is offset by the Pentecostals who have the strongest growth among Christians generally. There are more than 600 million charismatic Pentecostal believers worldwide, the second-largest group of Christians after Catholics. Like David of old, many of them really know how to worship Christ. Those who enjoy various gifts of the Spirit among them, seek Him and His charismatic gifts, including the gift of tongues (in August of 2018 the LDS Articles of Faith were changed. "Summary Article of Faith #5" was changed to **not** support **faith** in visions, prophecy, the gift of tongues, etc., see https://www.mormon.org/beliefs/articles-of-faith). According to the Pew Research Center, "Pentecostals and charismatic churches are by no means a small, fringe movement; on the contrary, they form the fastest-growing religious movement in the world. The gift of tongues is not reserved for a select few. Paul made it clear in 1 Cor. 14:5 that he wanted every believer to pray in tongues (for personal edification) and prophesy (to edify the church)." Paul stated, "I would like every one of you to speak in tongues, but I would rather have you prophesy." See http://www.charismamag.com/spirit/supernatural/21237-5-things-you-need-to-know-about-speaking-in-tongues Note also that while the percentage of traditional Christians in America is declining over the last 7 years, Christianity in Russia has doubled in the last 17 years, going from 31% of the total population to 72% today. In 2013 the Russian parliament voted 436 to 0 in favor of an anti-gay bill. In addition, Patriarch Kirill (of the Russian Orthodox Church) stated that recent Western "legislation of single-sex marriages is bringing the apocalypse closer." Will Russia, with their moral superiority be like the Lamanites in the book of Jacob, who loved their families and conquered the declining Nephites (they had more than one wife at this time). The Pew research report also showed that Latter-day Saints have changed their stance more than any Christian group in America relative to gay rights over the last seven years (2008 to 2015). LDS support for gay marriage has doubled since then.

2013 LDS Crisis of Faith Report A 2013 report created for LDS Church leaders entitled ***LDS Personal Faith Crisis***, detailed reasons for the exodus of many Latter-day Saints from the church. It stated that the number one cause for the "crisis of faith" in

2013 was "**dissemination of non-correlated materials on the Internet.**" The real root cause for the continuing, worsening exodus today (2018) is a lack of moving faith by leaders *and* many members **in the LORD Jesus Christ**. He is to be the head of His church, not men (see 3 Ne. 18:24). Faith in Christ is the first principle and ordinance of the gospel of Christ, as identified in Article of Faith 1. This author believes idolatry is the root cause of our current "crisis of faith." It is the lifting of of men, programs, and the ways of the world in place of the LORD Jesus. The 2013 report repeatedly addresses "the church," a wealthy corporation today (incorporated in 1923 during the administration of Heber J. Grant). It is revealing that the authors of the report mention the name Jesus Christ one time (those leaving the church mention Him more). Note one statement in the report, "When factoring median income for these Faith Crisis respondents, the Church incurs an estimated **tithing-revenue loss** of $281 Million over ten years (at $2.5 million per chapel, that represents a theoretical loss of 112 chapels)." This report was screated for the board of directors of the corporation "**doing business as**" a church. Money lost in the "faith crisis" was a key concern. See here:https://faenrandir.github.io/a_careful_examination/documents/faith_crisis_study/Faith_Crisis_Report_R24B.pdf?fbclid=IwAR2vGUnJrkFV6XilKNuKixFbpVtqwa5fpwb0rs22XO12Eq8_wfB7v8sL4IU

[5] See *Ronald Meldon Karren*, The Exonerataion of Emma, Joseph, and Hyrum: Part One, introduction. In his words, Karren's book was created using "solely pro-Mormon sourcing and publicly-available artifacts. It is pro-Mormon sourced, using pro-Mormon documents, and pro-Mormon history. It is an excellent source on how early LDS church history was changed, and by whom and how. Information on the secret chamber is also very insightful. Like all authors, Mr. Kerran writes from his perspective. He experienced abuse from some leaders in the LDS church, and thus often carries this tone. It is an excellent LDS history resource.

[6] *The Fanny Alger Story* In their *2014 Essays*, the LDS church used a quote from **one anti-Mormon to another to serve as evidence of Joseph Smith's first involvement in polygamy.** It states, "After receiving the commandment, he [Joseph] taught a few associates about it, but he did not spread this teaching widely in the 1830s" (LDS.org, Plural Marriage in Kirtland and Nauvoo, 2014). The citation for this claim is by *another anti-Mormon*, Ezra Booth (excommunicated Mormon) as found in one of 9 letters between Booth and Ira Eddy, *another anti-Mormon* (both were former preachers in other faiths). The citation is from Dec. 6, 1831, as found in Ohio Star Dec. 8, 1831. The "one thing" is Joseph's supposed relationship with Fanny Alger, which according to one alleged letter from Oliver Cowdery to his brother Warren was a "dirty, nasty, fillthy affair of his and Fanny Alger's" (Oliver Cowdery to Warren Cowdery, Jan. 21, 1838). The LDS church *later claimed this was not adultery but a marriage* performed by Oliver Cowdery. There are too many discripancies and contradictions in the accounts of all those involved for this to be true, and is typical of the claims against Joseph Smith with regard to polygamy. WHO we believe determines WHAT we believe.

[7] *Nephi & Moroni* A variety of church history sources cite Nephi rather than Moroni as *the first angel* to visit Joseph Smith on Rosh Hashanah of 1823. But he was apparently not the angel who delivered the plates to him four years later. That angel is thought to be Moroni. Joseph had a number of angels visiting him, preparing him for his mission. The first story teller in the Book of Mormon was Nephi - a Prophet and King as well. Moroni later wrapped up the Book of Mormon message, burying the plates and then later delivering them to the Prophet Joseph Smith in 1827. To avoid confusion today, it is probably best to leave the identity of the first angel visiting Joseph in 1823 as Moroni, rather than Nephi.

[8] *Hot Iron Story* Emma Josepha Smith McCallum's hot iron story was told to Richard Price in June of 1986. See http://restorationbookstore.org/articles/nopoligamy/jsfp-visionarticles/harrisonsagers.htm .

[9] *Brigham's Early Wives* By June 27 of 1844, Brigham Young had four wives. See Kate B. Carter, *Brigham Young—His Wives and Family*, 12–15; Stewart, *Brigham Young and His Wives*, 84–86; Utah Genealogical Magazine 11 [April 1920]: 52–54). For confirmation of Lucy Ann Decker's marriage to William Seely, see the records of Isaac Perry Decker and Harriet Page Wheeler Decker in the Genealogical Society Library in Salt Lake City, Utah.

[10] *Mary Fielding Smith* Mary Fielding Smith, the second wife of Hyrum Smith, Co-President of the church (after his first wife Jerusha died), followed Brigham Young west and is thus lifted up in the Utah church as a heroic historic figure. She married Heber C. Kimball in Nauvoo, becoming his fourth polygamous wife. She went from the #2 woman in the non-polygamy church to wife #4 of Heber in the pro-polygamy church. Why? Unlike Emma Smith who was a strong, valiant leader, true to principle and her husband Joseph, Mary appears to have been shy and easily influenced. She was friends with John Taylor in England, coming to Toronto Canada, where she and Taylor were in the same Methodist congregation. They converted to Mormonism there and came to Kirtland and then Nauvoo. She met Heber there. Heber became the 1st counselor to Brigham Young in the First Presidency later in Utah. His claim to fame in Mormonism was his establishment of five Masonic Lodges in the Utah area as part of his "church work." Mary was fully aware of her former husband Hyrum's anti-polygamy work in Nauvoo, yet she joined with his enemies ten weeks after his death, perhaps because of her long-established friendship with Taylor, who became the fourth president of the Utah church. He was also the fourth most important leader in the secret chamber in Nauvoo (after Brigham, Heber, and Willard Richards). Taylor may have taken part in the actual murder of the Prophet Joseph with Willard Richards in the Carthage jail. Some believe Mary was a reluctant spy for the secret chamber. She died in Utah seven years after marrying Heber. Compared to Emma, she did little to provide any lasting legacy, though the last of the Smith bloodline in

leadership in Utah did come through Mary, via the last church Patriarch, Eldred G. Smith. He and his position as "Patriarch over the church" (the highest office in the church, according to the Prophet Joseph) was first diminished, and then finally eliminated by the Twelve in Utah. The Brighamites had succeeded in overcoming the Josephite bloodline challenge to their power.

11 *Augusta Adams Cobb* https://www.findagrave.com/memorial/60955658/augusta-cobb

12 *Spiritual Wifery for Some of the Twelve in England* Thomas Stafford (an LDS Seventy serving with the Twelve in England and later Nauvoo) observed Brigham Young in both locations. On August 24, 1891, he wrote a letter to another Seventy, Gomer R. Wells, stating, "The seeds of polygamy was sown, and Brigham the sower...I was present at a meeting in a grove [at Nauvoo], about three weeks before Joseph and Hyrum were murdered, when Joseph made a public statement in the presence of three thousand people, that polygamy was being practiced secretly by some; that it had crept into the church secretly and **must be put down speedily or the church would be driven from Nauvoo**." This sermon is suppressed among the Brighamites.

In this letter, Stafford accused Young of indiscretions with women in England and Nauvoo. "But I am fully convinced, as I was then, that Brigham (Young), was in adultery in Manchester, England, in the fall, winter and spring of 1840 and 1841. Elizabeth Mayer is the person with whom Brigham was then committing adultery. My reasons are these: We lived next door to her, under the same roof....This Elizabeth Mayer had a father and a brother who were gard[e]ners; they took their dinners, as they worked a long piece from home. After they had left for work, Brigham would step into the house, she would then lock the door and pull down the blinds and curtains, which to me was strange. He never came to see our folks, although not five steps apart; and when he left he was always in a hurry, and she never came to the door with him when he was leaving. This same thing occurred in Nauvoo with a woman and Brigham. Her name was Greenough; her son was about my age, was always driven out when Brigham came, the door was shut and the curtains lowered. I was puzzled to know why he acted so, if he had a good heart, and was engaged in the business of teaching the truth, why drive the boy out? Why not come also and see my mother, only a few steps apart? I am satisfied that Joseph was not in favor of it (polygamy) at all. Would swear to all I have stated" (R. C. Evans, *Autobiography of Elder R. C. Evans*, pps. 334–335).

See Richard and Pamela Price, "Joseph Smith Fought Polygamy," Vol. 1, chapters 1-5, in http://restorationbookstore.org/articles/nopoligamy/jsfp-vol1/chp1.htm See also Uncle Dale's Readings in Early Mormon History (n.d.). (Newspapers of New England): Retrieved from http://sidneyrigdon.com/dbroadhu/NE/miscne00.htm). For evidence of the indescretions of Heber C. Kimball and William Clayton during their English missions, see Ronald Meldon Kerran, *The Exoneration of Emma, Joseph, and Hyrum: Part I*, https://www.amazon.com/product-reviews/B07728CX7N

13 *John Taylor Editing of William Smith* Apostle William Smith eventually became Patriarch to the Church (he claimed he was Presiding Patriarch *over* the church). He wanted to be church President too. William was a "wild card" in more ways than one. After the murder of his three brothers, William went head to head with Brigham Young to claim leadership. He also disclosed the actions of Brigham Young and some of the Twelve who were secretly practicing polygamy and polyandry at Nauvoo. He shared this knowledge with Joseph. Had William not been part of the secret chamber (later leaving Nauvoo), he too may have been murdered by this secret combination. Both William and Brigham discredited each other at times. We know the "official" LDS church records were in the hands of the Brighamites later in Utah, where they could be modified to discredit William Smith, making his testimony against secret chamber members less believeable. By his own admission, William was an adulterer, as he practiced polygamy on two occasions. He later repented, becoming part of the RLDS church with others in the Smith Family.

John Taylor Editing It is clear that secret chamber member **John Taylor kept imporatant truths about the Twelve practicing spiritual wifery – out of the two newspapers he edited and printed** (he owned one of them). **The Law group bought their own press to publish** to the Saints their belief that Joseph *and* the Twelve were secretly practicing spiritual wifery at Nauvoo. Both the Law group and the secret chamber (Brigham and some members of the Twelve) were using Joseph's name to push their own agendas. Taylor used his two newspapers to present partial truths and to discredit William Smith, who was challenging Brigham Young for leadership of the church (William was also a rogue member of the secret chamber). Taylor discredited William publicly at least four occasions in his publications. It was necessary, as on June 28, 1845, William announced, in the company of Patriarch John Smith and Apostle George A. Smith (both relatives), that he was President of the church. His mother, Lucy Mack Smith said she had three visions where she saw William Smith was President of the church by virtue of his office of Presiding Patriarch. Earlier, on may 29th, William said, Brigham Young was President of the church only by courtesty.

(1) Taylor's first articles to discredit William was on June 23, 1845. In it, Taylor countered William's claim to lead the church by subordinating the role of the office of Patriarch to the church. William was ordained a Patriarch by the Twelve, not by his father, as he should have been (D&C 86:10, see also Quinn, *Mormon Heirarchy*, Signature Books, p. 219). Neither William (because of sin and his lack of ordination by his father), nor the Twelve, had a lawful right to this office according to D&C 86:10.

(2) Taylor's second attempt to publicly discredit William was in July of 1845 (July 1st & 15), when the Times and Seasons published two articles, two weeks apart, revealing William's patriarchal blessing, where his father (Presiding Church Patriarch at the time) stated that he [William] had a "rebellious spirit" because of the "pride of his heart" (Quinn, p. 221). The second article eliminated the "rebellious spirit" phrase after William complained.

(3) The third discrediting article was Taylor's Dec. 1, 1845 piece in the Times and Seasons where he stated, that while William was serving in his eastern states mission, he "carried on the work of seduction" there (polygamy, Quinn, p. 223). There were complaints made about William's polygamous behavior in various branches of the Church at that time. Taylor's article did not disclose the fact, however, that the Twelve already knew of this **when they ordained William as Patriarch to the church**. They apparently allowed this action to keep him quiet about their own secret behavior with spiritual wives.

(4) Fourth and last, because William had been a loose canon about his freelance spiritual wifery (without Brigham's approval), along with that of the Twelve, he was given one of the typical warnings directed to dissenters of the secret chamber. It was a marking or "anointing" of William's newly built wooden benches created for a public speech he was to give near his mother's home. Each of the benches was marked or "anointed" with "refuse [human excrement] from "*Aunt Peggy's privy cabinet*" (or from an outhouse). His mother Lucy Mack Smith and sister in law Emma Smith were soon telling others that the Twelve authorized this "anointing." John Taylor ran an article in the Nauvoo Neighbor on May 7 of 1845 in the Deacon's Reports section of the paper, where he said that **another dissenter**, "has been introduced to '*Queen Peggy's privy cabinet*" (Quinn, p. 222). It was a clear **fear-based warning** to William and others of who was in charge at Nauvoo. The "Deacons" involved in this intimidation effort, were like those of "*the whistling and whittling brigade.*" They were not young boys, but older adults from 17-years old up. These later enforcers used bowie knifes to whittle their wood blocks and sticks with blades as long as 14 inches, while they also whistlling, letting those know nearby that they were being watched. Many were beaten and run out of Nauvoo. The next level of intimidation was the Nauvoo police and men like Hosea and Allen Stout, former Danites in Missouri. Murder or "blood atonement" was the final verdict, as it was with Hosea Stout and Bill Hickman later in Salt Lake City. Brigham's new doctrine was later repudiated.

John Taylor's Lying & Polygamy John Taylor was ordained an Apostle by Brigham Young. Besides editing and printing the two primary newspapers in Nauvoo from 1842-46, Taylor was also a Master Mason, a member of the Council of 50, and a member of the Nauvoo City Council. He became the third President of the church after Brigham Young. He was also a known, accomplished liar, and is suspected of being part of the murders of Joseph and Hyrum in Liberty Jail. Taylor repeatedly lied about his polygamy, the most notable being his mission in France in 1850, where he openly lied about it in a public debate with three noted ministers over the course of three nights. He denied that both he and Joseph were polygamists. Marriage records reveal that **he had three wives before Joseph was murdered**, going on to have sixteen total. Eight of them were taken in 1846 alone.

See https://restorationbookstore.org/articles/nopoligamy/jsfp-visionarticles/twoconspiracies.htm

See also https://restorationbookstore.org/articles/nopoligamy/jsfp-visionarticles/JSFP-Vision69.htm

William Smith's Polygamy William's first monogamous marriage to a 16 year-old girl was performed by Brigham Young. Young stated in his August 8, 1844 diary entry, that he (Brigham) married William to a 14 year-old girl in a polygamous relationship. William's own Patriarchal Blessing Book states that he gave two of his polygamous wives blessings earlier (Quinn, Mormon Heirarchy, Signature Books, p. 221). He apparently had at least three total wives at one point in time. William's cousin, Apostle George A. Smith complained at Nauvoo that he [William] was "committing intiquity, but "we have to sustain him against our feelings." In anger earlier in 1835, William resigned from the Apostleship, later physically attacking his brother Joseph.

William never accused his brother Joseph of polygamy, even though angry with him at one point. Accussed of insubordination, William was dropped from the Quorum of the Twelve for a time, then later reinstated. Two women accused William Smith and John Bennett of adultery in 1841. They said William claimed his brother Joseph approved of their spiritual wifery. Though troubled early on, William repented, providing key information on the secret chamber in his insightful writings. They are invaluable in speaking behind the curtain in Nauvoo. See http://olivercowdery.com/smithhome/WmSmith1.htm

14 *What Was Said in the Expositor?* The Expositor was the first and last issue of a four-page publication designed to call attention to Joseph Smith's errors and the direction the church was going under him. It was printed on **June 7, 1844**, in Nauvoo Illinois. Three of its principle contributors included; William Law (former first counselor in the First Presidency of the Church of Jesus Christ of Latter-day Saints to Joseph Smith, with Sidney Rigdon), his brother Wilson Law (Brigadier General of the Nauvoo Legion), and Robert D. Foster. They and others were excommunicated by the Prophet Joseph two months earlier in a church court that may have not proceed in the prescribed manner as given in the D&C. According to them, they were not present at the court held for them, nor were they informed of it by Joseph Smith.

In response to this publication, Joseph Smith, by his signature (representing the Nauvoo City Council) declared the paper "a public nuisance," and ordered the press destroyed. William Smith said that Joseph was coerced into signing this order by John Taylor and Willard Richards, in a visit with Joseph, in which William was present (from a letter sent to his Nephew Joseph Smith III, President of the RLDS Church). They knew it would get Joseph jailed, and appears to be part of a greater plan that these two men later carried out at the Carthage jail, to silence Joseph (and his brother Hyrum). The town marshal carried out the order during the evening of June 10. The destruction of the press led to charges of riot against Smith and other members of the Council. After Joseph Smith surrendered on the charges, he was also charged with **treason against Illinois.** Seventeen days later on June 27th of 1844, Joseph and his brother Hyrum were murdered at Carthage Jail.

The editors were writing to the Latter-day Saints at Nauvoo to seek a reformation by expressing their concerns over Joseph Smith's behavior and what they believed were false doctrines, traditions, and actions being put forth by him and others. Five principle concerns of fifteen total included, (1) the **illegal excommunication** of William Law and others (Resolution #1); (2) the "blasphemous" doctrine of "**plurality of Gods**" and "**exaltation**" (Resolutions #2 & 14); (3) the "disease," "abomination," and "whoredom" of "**plurality of wives**" (spiritual wifery, Resolution #14); (4) the non-religious aspect of "**secret societies**, and combinations under **penal oaths and obligations**" (Resolution #11); (5) **and** the opinion that as church president, Nauvoo mayor, General over the Nauvoo Legion, etc., **Joseph Smith held too much power** and desired to create a theocracy (the Council of Fifty, etc., Resolution #3).

Desipte the schism with Joseph, the authors of the Expositor maintained their belief in "the religion of the Latter Day Saints," as originally taught by Joseph Smith. This single-issue publication (4 pages total) consisted of four parts; (1) an Introduction by its editors, (2) a Preamble, (3) **Fifteen Resolutions** or criticisms, and (4) Affidavits attesting to the truthFullness of their testimony. The publishers of The Expositor were Charles Ivins, Colonel Francis M. Higbee (of the Nauvoo Legion), Chauncey L. Higbee, Robert Foster, and Charles Foster. The Senior editor was Sylvester Emmons, a non-Mormon part of the Nauvoo City Council.

To limit length, I have included a few paragraphs from the Preamble addressing polygamy only. For the full account, see https://www.fairmormon.org/answers/Primary_sources/Nauvoo_Expositor_Full_Text

The remaining paragraphs below are from the Preamble. It is a commentary on **the plight of innocent female converts** that were exposed to polygamy for the first time by leaders of the church at Nauvoo.

The Shock of the Spiritual Wives Doctrine "It is absurd for men to assert that all is well, while wicked and corrupt men are seeking our destruction, by a perversion of sacred things; for all is not well, while whoredoms and **all manner of abominations are practiced under the cloak of religion** . . . It is a notorious fact, that many females in foreign climes . . . have been induced, by the sound of the gospel, to forsake friends, and embark upon a voyage across waters that lie stretched over the greater portion of the globe, as they supposed, to glorify God . . . But what is taught them on their arrival at this place? They are visited by some of the Strikers [a Masonic term] . . . and are requested to hold on and be faithful, for there are great blessings awaiting the righteous . . . They are visited again, and what is the result? They are requested to meet brother Joseph, or some of the Twelve, at some insulated point, or at some particularly described place on the bank of the Mississippi, or at some room, which wears upon its front - Positively NO Admittance. The harmless, inoffensive, and unsuspecting creatures, are so devoted to the Prophet, and the cause of Jesus Christ, that they do not dream of the deep laid and fatal scheme which prostrates happiness, and renders death itself desirable; but they meet him, expecting to receive through him a blessing, and learn the will of the LORD concerning them, and what awaits the faithful follower of Joseph, the Apostle and Prophet of God, When in the stead thereof, they are told, after having been sworn in one of the most solemn manners, to never divulge what is revealed to them, with a penalty of death attached that God Almighty has revealed it to him, that she should be his (Joseph's) Spiritual wife; for it was right anciently, and God will tolerate it again: but we must keep those pleasures and blessings from the world, for until there is a change in the government, we will endanger ourselves by practicing it - but we can enjoy the blessings of Jacob, David, and others, as well as to be deprived of them, if we do not expose ourselves to the law of the land . . ."

15 *The Doctrinal Legacy of Brigham Young* Note the doctrines of Joseph Smith (listed first) versus those of Brigham Young (second) below. This nine-part list is supplied by The Watcher, https://onewhoiswatching.wordpress.com/

1. Joseph taught that a prophet is only speaking as a prophet when the spirit of prophecy descends on him and that the person was otherwise giving their personal opinion. Brigham taught that everything in his sermons was worthy of being called scripture.

2. Joseph accepted the literal interpretation of the creation story, with Adam being created from the dust of the earth. He even provided other books of scripture to verify it. Brigham taught that the creation story in Genesis was a fairytale and that Adam was transported to this earth as a resurrected being.

3. Joseph taught that the Joseph Smith Translation of the Bible would be an integral part of Gospel Law and needed to be published to the world before Zion could be redeemed but Brigham scoffed at the importance of the inspired version and taught that the King James version of the Bible was sufficient for the Saints.

4. Joseph taught the literal New Testament account that Mary conceived the baby Jesus as a virgin as a result of the Holy Spirit overshadowing her. Brigham and Orson taught that the Father descended in a physical body and had sexual relations with her.

5. Joseph taught that the Father was a personage of Spirit in Lectures on Faith 5. Brigham, using the alleged words of Joseph, taught that the Father is a personage of tabernacle with flesh and bones (see D&C 1).

6. Joseph taught that the Holy Spirit is the mind of the God and not a personage of spirit. Brigham taught that the Holy Ghost is a personage of spirit.

7. Joseph taught that Christ created Adam. Brigham taught that Adam was the father of Christ (the Adam-God theory).

8. Joseph taught that it was contrary to gospel law to take a person's life. He openly worried that some of his enemies might die in their sins before they had the opportunity to repent. Brigham, on the other hand, taught that if someone was evil, it was a merciful act under his version of the law of blood atonement to send them on their way. Young ordered the murder of many "dissenters, apostates," and "enemies." Men like Hosea Stout and Bill Hickman carried them out.

9. Joseph taught that God knows all things and that there is not anything that he does not know. In fact he taught that it is impossible to have enough faith to be saved if you did not believe that God knows all things… and could not make a mistake. Brigham taught that God does not know all things and that God is always learning new things. He taught that God was once a man. This was also part of Joseph's teaching in the King Follett Discourse.

Oppression of Women Damage occurs in marriage when one or more parties holds back any portion of their heart. The thought of polygamy can cause this to occur in the man or woman. Though the U.S. government stopped polygamy, it still occurs in LDS temple sealings, and thus retains its subtle damaging influence. Pro-polygamist men may hold back a portion of their heart form an imperfect wife, holding out for more wives, or a better wife in their future. Married LDS women may avoid a too-intimate relationship with their husband, believing he is never destined to be exclusively hers. Others put away any thought of polygamy from their minds to avoid contention, fear, or other issues. Polygamy may also subvert a close relationship with God for both parties. Men practicing this abomination cut themselves off from God. And those LDS men who want it in their future retain it as an idol in the heart. They were "without natural affection" (Romans 1:17-32), which is one man with one wife only. Polygamy severs a stronger relationship with the first wife, and with God. Sin cuts us off from Him. Some women find it difficult to develop an intimate relationship with God as they believe He designed a system that punishes them for being female. They feel subordinate. All of this is brought on by the thought that polygamy could be part of their future, or the next life. Only in Utah Territory (under Brigham Young) did two great evils coexist side by side in the late nineteenth century; oppression for women in polygamy and for blacks in slavery. Few know that:

1. On March 9, 1845, Brigham Young said that women, "have not right to meddle in the affairs of the Kingdom of God...they never can hold the keys of the Priesthood apart from their husbands" (Quinn, *Mormon Hierarchy*, Signature Books, p. 650).

2. Later in 1845, Brigham Young eliminated the Female Relief Society after Joseph's murder. He then re-established it his way, 22 years later as an "auxiliary."

3. Following the murder of the three Smith brothers, Lucy Mack Smith (Joseph Smith's mother) spoke in General Conference (October 8, 1845). She was **the last woman to do so in General Conference for 143 years**.

4. Oppression continued in 1906 when the Presiding Bishopric took possession of Relief Society Building assets. In 1918 their grain storage supply was sold by Church leadership. In 1946, Pres. Joseph Fielding Smith stopped women from giving blessings to each other via the laying on of hands. In 1971, the Relief Society Magazine was eliminated. In 1978, all financial assets for the Relief Society were transferred to the First Presidency. In 1997, the manual designed for Relief Society instruction was replaced with Teachings of the Presidents of the Church, making idolatry (male leader worship) complete. Thus, as D&C 121:36-40 tells us, "Amen to the priesthood or the authroity of that man" (D&C121:36-40).

16 *Removing, Shaking & Rending Garments* Joseph's directive to the Twelve to **remove** their endowment garment was given on June 20th of 1844, one week before his murder on the 27th (see HC 6:519). It may have had ties to the corruption of the temple endowment that was either beginning to take place or would take place later under Young and Kimball. Joseph's directive was recorded by Heber C. Kimball in his diary (Dec. 21, 1845, written by William Clayton). See *An Intimate Chronicle: The Journals of William Clayton,* p. 224. See also D. Michael Quinn, *The Mormon Hierarchy: Origins of Power*, Signature Books, p. 145.

Shaking Garments Free of Blood & Sin When the Prophet Joseph Smith **shook his garments clean** of the blood and sins of his people at a private meeting of **the Council of Fifty** prior to his murder in 1844, now known as "**the last charge**," he was **not** empowering the Twelve with priesthood keys of leadership (like the sealing power to seal multiple wives to one man). Instead, **he was placing the burden of the sin** for spiritual wifery squarely upon the shoulders of those of the Twelve who were practicing it, some of whom were present at this meeting. It had become an **abomination**, as they were justifying it via new church doctrine. The shaking of garments (free of blood and sin) is for *covenant people*, whereas the shaking off of dust from one's feet (with the washing of feet following) is for *unbelievers* (see D&C 24:15, 60:15, 75:19-22, 84:88-93, 99:2-4; Mat. 10:14; Luke 9:5; Acts 13:51). Joseph knew that some among the Twelve would betray him and take power after his murder, as indicated by his sister Katherine's statements on pages 104 & 129 (this statement was made 3 days prior to his murder).

According to John Taylor (D&C 135), Hyrum Smith quoted Ether 12:37-40 the day he and Joseph were on their way to Carthage Jail (June 25, 1844). This is one of two sets of scripture by Moroni where he freed himself of our blood and sin (the other is Mormon 9:35), as Moroni had taught us correct doctrine in the Book of Mormon, saying, "**my garments are not spotted with your blood**." Paul the Apostle also "**shook** his raiment" free of blood against those Jews (the *covenant* people) who were rejecting his testimony of Christ as Messiah. They tried **to kill Paul** (see Acts 18:6). In addition, Paul also "shook off" the **dust** from his feet against *unbelieving* Jews at Antioch (Acts 13:50-51).

Like Joseph Smith and Paul the Apostle, King Benjamin, Alma, and Moroni of the Book of Mormon didn't want the blood and sins of their people to be upon their garments either. In chapters 6-10 of 2 Nephi, the Prophet Jacob in chapters 1-3 tells us that he was able to discern the "**abominable thoughts**" of his people. He observed that they had **hard hearts of pride**. The Nephites were embracing the wicked practices of David and Solomon in "**desiring many wives, and concubines**." They sought to **excuse themselves in this sin** via the examples of both kings. Jacob also taught his people **correct doctrine**, shaking **his garments free** of their blood and sins. He stated, "O, my beloved brethren, remember my words. Behold, **I take off my garments, and I shake them before you; I pray the God of my salvation that he view me with his all-searching** eye; wherefore, ye shall know at the last day, when all men shall be **judged of their works**, that the God of Israel did witness that **I shook your iniquities from my soul**, and that I stand with brightness before him, and **am rid of your blood**. O, my beloved brethren, turn away from your sins; **shake off the chains** of him that would bind you fast; come unto that God who is the rock of your salvation" (2 Nephi 9:44-45). See also **Jacob 1:19** and **2:2.** Jacob's statements appear to be in connection with his teaching against the whoredom of many wives and concubines among his people. He added that all are to "**shake off**" the "**awful chains**" of **sin** that cut all off from God, in 2 Nephi 1:13-23 and 2 Nephi 4:31. God said he would "**shake**" up false churches that **seek to get gain in our day** in D&C 10:56. Of special note are the adulterers and false prophets and false priests whose hearts are not broken, those who use the people for filthy lucre and gain (see Jeremiah 23:9-11; see also Isaiah 52:2-3).

Like many other historical documents, Joseph's words in the "**last charge**" were later modified to fit Brigham Young's narrative, implying that both Brigham and the Twelve held all power and keys of priesthood, power supposedly given them by Joseph at this meeting, including the power to seal many women to one man. Some versions of Benjamin F. Johnson's letter to George Gibbs have been modified too. The changes represent more lies created to protect early polygamy and the power the Twelve had taken (see the list of 15 lies in Assumption #7, chap. 7). The stories of Parley P. Pratt and Wilford Woodruff (polygamists) of "**the last charge**" don't match reality. They claim that (A) the Twelve were given **all power** by Joseph, and (B) that Brigham Young was given sole management of "**the sealing power**" over the whole earth (to seal polygamous marriages). Pratt stated, "He [Joseph] proceeded to confer on Elder Young, the President of the Twelve, **the keys of the sealing power**, as conferred in the last days by the spirit and power of Elijah, in order **to seal the hearts of the fathers to the children, and the hearts of the children to the fathers**, lest the whole earth should be smitten with a curse" (Parley P. Pratt, *Millennial Star*, 5:151, March 1845). Woodruff added, "I have had sealed upon my head every key, every power, every principle of life and salvation that God has ever given to any man who ever lived upon the face of the earth . . . Now," said he [Joseph] **addressing the Twelve**, "I tell you, **the burden** of this kingdom **now rests upon your shoulders**; you have got to bear it off in all the world." In reality, the Prophet Joseph, like Jacob in the Book of Mormon, was placing **the burden of the sin of polygamy** upon their shoulders (see *Teachings of Presidents of the Church: Wilford Woodruff* [2004], p. 32).

The current church narrative of "the last charge" reveals a lack of understanding of; (1) how God alone provides sealing power to His servants; (2) how the church is governed (see D&C 107); and (3) the fact that Joseph was transferring responsibility of **sin** to those present, **not** priesthood sealing power, something which God alone does. Scripture patterns reveal these truths.

Rending Garments Rending or tearing a garment had ties to great mourning, sorrow, and hopelessness, in connection with repentance. The rent garment no longer covers (as in Christ's blood). In relation to Israel's kings, it often symbolized that the kingdom of a particular wicked king would be **rent from them**. Such was the case with King Saul (2 Sam. 3:31) and King Solomon's posterity (1 Kings 11:11-13, 29:31; 2 Chron. 34:27; see also D&C 84:118, 133:40; Gen. 37:29-30; Eccl. 3:7; Ezra 9:3-5; Joel 2:12-13; Amos 9:11; Colossians 1:21-23; 1 Peter 1:3).

Captain Moroni rent his garment and made it an ensign of freedom or liberty, tied to the covenant **not to forsake the LORD**. Those who took this covenant stated that if the time came that they became **ashamed** of the LORD's name (Morm. 8:38), that the LORD would **rend them** for their actions. Moroni equated his **torn garment** to **the torn coat of Joseph of Egypt**, his distant relative. He was a **remnant** of Joseph. We know the LORD will gather **the remnant of Jacob** throughout the world in the last days. See Alma 46:21-27. Those who love the LORD today are encouraged to **rend the veil of unbelief** and experience what the brother of Jared did in the book of Ether. Too many today remain in this awful state of wickedness (Ether 4:15).

The instruction of Moses to priests to **not** rend their garments as part of **mourning** in **repentance**, was because they were representatives of God (the Great High Priest). They were to provide **hope** for the people - via their repentance in connection with the Atonement of Christ (see Lev. 10:6, 21:10). The High Priest Caiaphas broke this law of Moses when he rent his outer robe ***and*** his inner tunic, after Christ said he was the Messiah in his presence (Mat. 26:64-66). There was no repentance on his part, no despair in his standing before God, only pride and disdain for the Master.

While on the cross, the LORD's clothing was parted four ways, while his one piece tunic (an undergarment) was left intact, taken by a soldier in a lottery (John 19:23-24). Upon His death, a veil-like curtain hanging in front of the temple was rent in two (Mat. 27:51). When Christ returns, He will set foot first upon the Mount of Olives, the setting of His atonement. It will be **rent** or cleave in **twain** (D&C 45:48). His garments were stained with His own blood there in Gethsemane. At His second coming they will be stained with the blood of the wicked instead (Isa. 63:1-3; D&C 133:46-52).

[17] *Twelve Individuals Back up Joseph's Statement* Twelve individuals claimed they had first hand knowledge that Joseph Smith made this statement. They include Joseph Thorn, David Dickson, James Whitehead, Catherine Huntington, Hannah Lytle, John and Priscilla Conyers, Mary Ralph, S.L. Crain, E. H. Morse and W. W Smith.
See https://restorationbookstore.org/articles/nopolygamy/jsfp-vol2/2chp14.htm

More on Succession of Power Stake President William Marks had no interest in becoming Church President, as the church was falling apart after Joseph's murder. One half of the Nauvoo Saints saw what Pres. Marks saw. They recognized Young's blind ambition to grab all power and wouldn't follow him west. One was former senior Seventy President, Hazen Aldrich. He said, "You will see by the Book of Covenants that the 12 are a traveling high council and are entirely out of their place in attempting to assume the First Presidency & dictate the affairs of the whole church" (Quinn, *Origins of Power*, p. 388).

There was no revelation making Young or any church president after Joseph the leader of the church? This false tradition originated with Young. God chooses His servants, whereas usurpers choose themselves and other men. The LORD said, "The president of the church, who is also the president of the council, **is appointed by revelation**" (D&C 102:9). Joseph was God's chosen servant. Pres. Joseph Fielding Smith said, "The senior apostle **automatically** becomes the presiding officer of the church, and he is so sustained by the Council of the Twelve which becomes the presiding body of the Church when there is no First Presidency" (Doctrines of Salvation, 3:156). BYU professor Casey Griffiths clarifies this tradition, stating, "**This is simply a historical precedent first set by President Brigham Young**, and despite there being nothing in the Doctrine and Covenants about prophetic succession, this pattern [**tradition**] of sustaining the most senior apostle as church president has been followed so consistently that **it might as well be doctrine**."

The Prophet Joseph knew that the Twelve were not to lead. He stated, "The Twelve shall have **no right** to go into Zion or any of its stakes and there undertake to **regulate the affairs** thereof **where there is a standing high council**. But it is their duty to *go abroad* and regulate all matters relative to the different branches of the church." Conversely, the prophet cautioned the high council that they were to stay off the apostles turf, "No standing high council has authority to go into the *churches abroad* and *regulate the matters thereof*, for this belongs to the Twelve" (Joseph Smith, Kirtland Council Minute Book, p. 112).

It was Christ as head of His Church who gave Joseph the authority to appoint anyone he wanted to succeed him as President. Joseph chose Hyrum from **the Stake High Council**, not one of the Twelve, stating, "If I should now be taken away, I had accomplished the great work the Lord had laid before me, and that which I had desired of the Lord; and that I had done my duty in organizing the High Council, through which council the will of the Lord might be known on all important occasions, in the building up of Zion, and establishing truth in the earth" (HC 2:124). Joseph reorganized the First Presidency **several times** but never **once** did he call one from among the Twelve.

Like her husband, Emma Smith knew God's word and will regarding succession. Her son Joseph Smith III was too young to lead at that time, so she looked to Pres. Marks to lead, "Whereas it is the business of the First Presidency, more particularly to govern the church at Zion, and the members abroad have a right to that quorum from the decisions of the Twelve. Now as the Twelve have **no power** with regard to the government of the Church in the Stakes of Zion, but **the High Council have all the power**, so it follows that on removal of the first President, the office would devolve upon the President of the High Council in Zion [William Marks at the time], as the first President always resides there, and that is the proper place for the quorum of which he is head; thus there would be no schism or jarring. But the Twelve would attend to their duties *in the world* and not meddle with the government of the church *at home*, and the High Council in Zion and the First Presidency would attend to their business *in the same place*...Mr. Rigdon is not the proper successor of President Smith, being only his counselor, but Elder Marks should be the individual as he was not only his councilor at the time of his death, but also President of the High Council" (Emma Smith to James M. Monroe, quoted in Newell and Avery, *Mormon Enigma: Emma Hale Smith*, pps. 206-207). Emma's knowledge of God's word and will was a threat to Brigham's power grab, a primary reason why he opposed her so strongly.

Today, volume two of the Encyclopedia of Mormonism (by authors Lynn England and Keith Warner) modifies God's word in D&C 107:22 to support the Twelve in their usurpation of power, deliberately deceiving readers. According to Brewster, "There have always been false prophets and self proclaimed would-be leaders who have sought to establish their own claim to presiding authority...One's eternal salvation depends upon the ability to recognize and know the true servants of God - those who are authorized to preach His gospel and administer the sacred and saving ordinances thereof" (Hoyt W. Brewster, *Prophets, Priesthood Keys, & Succession*, Deseret Book, 1991, p. 38, see also D&C 124:45-46). Joseph Smith said, "The moment we revolt at anything that comes from God, the devil takes power" (TPJS p. 181, see also D&C 93:39).

[18] *Joseph Smith III* James Whitehead was the private secretary of the Prophet Joseph the last two years of his life and was present in the Red Brick Store in Nauvoo in 1844, when young Joseph was ordained by his father to lead. In the Temple Lot Case of 1894, He stated, "I became a member [of the RLDS Church]...because I knew that Joseph Smith [III] was the right man to lead that church; I knew that he had been **ordained and set apart by his father as his successor in office**, and he came out and made that proclamation to the conference of the Saints, and they received it. The ceremony of the ordination of young Joseph Smith [III] by his father was performed at Nauvoo. Young Joseph [III] was called into the meeting, anointed with oil by his Uncle Hyrum Smith, Patriarch of the church. Newell K. Whitney, the Bishop of the church, held the oil [in another statement Whitehead said, Whitney poured the oil on the boy's head], and Joseph Smith, his father, laid his hands upon him, and blessed him and ordained him **to be his successor** in office...The church did take action as a body on the question of the ordination of young Joseph [III] as his father's successor; **the church consented to it**. That was **done first by the endorsement of the High Council, and then it was brought up before the whole body of the congregation, the whole people** . . . That was done at the meeting held in the grove at the east end of the temple. I should think there were three thousand (3,000) there. There **was a record** kept of it, but the record was taken to Salt Lake. I was present on that occasion . . . A negative vote was taken, but nobody voted in the negative; Joseph Smith had been preaching that day, and at the close of the sermon made the announcement to the congregation, that his young son Joseph [III] had been appointed as his successor. The question was submitted to the congregation for approval or rejection . . . The time that elapsed between the selection of Joseph Smith as his father's successor and the time of the public announcement, was four or five days. The selection and confirmation was on **Wednesday** evening, and on the **Sunday** following, after the sermon was delivered . . . **It was the regular preaching service** every Sunday afternoon, there was no calling about it. They gathered to hear the preaching and at that meeting it was declared by Joseph Smith himself that the selection and ordination of his son Joseph as his successor in office had been made, and the people agreed to it, **by a vote in the usual way**, voting by the uplifted hand" (James Whitehead testimony, the Temple Lot Case, pps. 31-44).

President of the RLDS Church Three events in the life of Joseph Smith III led him to finally accept the leadership position of the RLDS Church. The first was in the fall of 1853 when an English convert to Mormonism in Nauvoo told Joseph Smith III that God had given him a duty to unify and purify the Church, adding that he was, "possibly doing a great wrong in allowing the years to go by unimproved." He suggested that Smith prepare himself through study and prayer for the work of the LORD. This caused him to turn to the LORD, study the work of his father, determine if he was a polygamist, etc.

The second event was a vision he had, where a choice was presented him between two opposite lifestyles; one of honor and renown among a busy people in cities and towns, or one in a quieter place, among a "country of happy people." A number of factions from Joseph's Restoration wanted Joseph III to lead them, including some from the Brighamite movement. They knew of the blessing from his father, and wanted young Joseph to lead them. Brigham welcomed Joseph to join the Saints in Utah, but only if he would submit to the authority of he and the Twelve (and potentially live polygamy).

The third event was an answer to his solemn prayer of what direction to go in. He stated, "I heard a slight noise like the rush of the breeze…I turned my gaze slightly upward and saw descending towards me a sort of cloud; funnel-shaped with widest part upwards. It was luminous and of such color and brightness that it was clearly seen, though the sun shone in its summer strength. It descended rapidly and settling upon and over me enveloped me completely so that I stood within its radiance." In this light, Smith said he was told to have nothing to do with the Utah Mormonism, because "the light in which you stand is greater than theirs." Though Emma would not let Joseph III have anything to do with Mormonism early on, in time both of them felt the time to lead the RLDS Church had arrived. This was after two representatives from this faction invited Joseph to consider leading them. He did not become part of the RLDS church until he was brought low in the dust with the death of his new daughter Eva. In prayer he was told, "the Saints reorganizing at Zerahemla and other places, is the only organized portion of the Church accepted by me. **I have given them my Spirit and will continue to do so while they remain humble and faithful.**" Joseph then accepted the invitation to lead the RLDS people. For more on Joseph Smith III, see Roger D. Launius, Joseph Smith III: Pragmatic Prophet, Univ. of Illinios Press, pps, 66, 99-100, 109, 111, 117). So began the 54 years of leadership of Joseph Smith III. William Marks became a counselor to Joseph Smith III in the RLDS First Presidency.

19 *Witnesses in the Temple Lot Case* The credibility of witnesses was the single most important factor in the outcome of the case. There was 597 pages of evidence in this court case. Some of it is testimony of those physically present at the trial. Some of the evidence was also in the form of Affidavits (witness testimony in writing, not physically present). The RLDS church utilized Pres. Joseph Smith III, Presiding Bishop E. L. Kelley, W. W. Blair (Editor of Saints Herald), and James Whitehead (Joseph Smith's private secretary). The Utah LDS church utilized Pres. Wilford Woodruff, Lorenzo Snow (Pres. of the Twelve), Lyman O. Littlefield, James Noble, Joseph C. Kingsbury (scribe of the copy of the supposed "revelation" now known as D&C 132), and three supposed wives of Joseph Smith, one being Mary Rachael Thompson.

Useful Sources for the Temple Lot Case Include:

Verdict, Judge Phillips, Temple Lot Case: https://archive.org/details/decisionofjohnfp00philrich

Credibility of Witnesses – a Mormon History Association Paper, *The Temple Lot Case: Fraud in God's Vineyard* http://mormonpolygamydocuments.org/wp-content/uploads/2015/01/JS1018.pdf

Testimonies of Joseph Smith III, James Whitehead & William Smith http://www.olivercowdery.com/smithhome/1880s-1890s/1893_TLot.htm

Two simple summaries of the case: http://www.centerplace.org/library/study/court.htm http://restorationbookstore.org/articles/heritage/articles/churchincourt.htm#start

Full Text: https://archive.org/details/TempleLotCase

20 RLDS Conference Talks, http://olivercowdery.com/smithhome/BroBill/KStestimony.htm, see also Salisbury, I.G. Davidson interview of Katharine Smith, Fountain Green, Ill., May 1894, http://olivercowdery.com/smithhome/BroBill/KStestimony.htm

David Hyrum Smith Emma Smith was six-months pregnant with a third Smith son, David Hyrum Smith, when his father and his two uncles were murdered in 1844. According to Blair, the Prophet Joseph said that David, "will yet be a prince" (William W. Blair Diary, 17 June 1874, RLDS Research Library and Archives). Was he another potential heir to his father? The Prophet Joseph was apparently made a king by the theocratic Council of Fifty in Nauvoo in the Spring of 1844 (this was a heavenly role for him as Dispensation Head, not an earthly role). Some say that because David was born under "the covenant" tied to the Second Anointing ordinance of Joseph and Emma (conducted outside of the non-completed Nauvoo Temple), that he too should be considered a legitimate heir with Joseph Smith III. Unlike his older brother, however, David was not the firstborn son, nor was he anointed and blessed by his empowered uncles as was Joseph Smith III. David later developed mental issues, necessitating commitment to an asylum. Brigham Young conducted the first temple rites tied to the Second Anointing in the never-completed Nauvoo Temple. He and John Taylor were apparently also anointed kings, yet neither were of the Smith bloodline (though Brigham was a distant cousin).

21 *Patriarch Duties Early On* In the early days of the church founded by the Prophet Joseph, ordained church patriarchs, among other duties, were authorized to give blessings **only** to the "fatherless" of the church, in respect to family patriarchs. The Brighamite branch of the church took away the lineal right of all fathers in the church to bless their children as Patriarchs, making it a controlled practice of the church itself. Today Stake Presidents give "Patriarchs" counsel on the content of the blessings. The Handbook of Instructions states, "The stake president presides over the stake patriarch and supervises his work as outlined in Information and **Suggestions for Patriarchs** . . . The stake president interviews the patriarch at least twice a year. He also

reviews the blessings the patriarch has given at least twice a year. As needed, the Stake President may make **general suggestions about the content** of the patriarch's blessings." Revelation from God – through the Patriarch - to the one receiving the blessing was the older, purer standard. Recipients of blessings are today cautioned to not share them widely. Some who have compared their blessings complain that they are very similar, especially among those of the same Stake. Guidance from leaders appears to be part of the problem.

22 *The Dedication of the Kirtland House of the LORD* For additional historical sources on the spiritual events at Kirtland Ohio, see Joseph Smith, Kirtland Revelation Book, June 1, 1833; pps. 59-60; pages 97-98, of this same book, 22 June 1834; Kirtland Council Minute Book, 14 Feb. 1835; Oliver Cowdery's Kirtland, Ohio Sketch Book, 17 Jan. 1836; Joseph Smith Diary, Mar. 30, 1836; Autobiography of Milo Andrus, 1814-1875. In the following historic accounts, we read of Pentecostal outpourings of the Spirit, and even visitations by Christ and the Father outside of a "house of the LORD" (see Joseph Smith, HC, 1:176-77; John Whitmer, HC 1:176; John Corrill, *History of the Mormons* [1839], p. 18; Zebedee Coltrin diary, 24 Jan. 1833, and Minutes, Salt Lake City School of the Prophets, Oct. 3, 1883).

23 *The Testament of the Twelve Patriarchs, the Sons of Jacob* One British LDS elder, a Mr. Samuel Downes, reprinted an ancient Greek manuscript, entitled, *The Testament of the Twelve Patriarchs, the Sons of Jacob* in 1843. Some 100 copies of this book were sold in the church's Millennial Star office in Liverpool England. A short review of it was published in The Millennial Star 4 (Oct. 1843, 96). It may have had a strong influence upon some Apostles serving in England. Downes revealed that he showed the book to some of the apostles. Apparently, some urged him to publish it. The book's preface states, ".... **Having shewn it to many of my brethren, and it having met with their approbation, they are wishful to possess themselves of it also. I now at their solicitation for the church**, and for mankind in general, **send it forth** unto the world; and my heart's desire to God is, that the sublime truths contained in it may cause the hearts of the saints to rejoice and the wicked to see . . . Art thou a Bishop, a Minister? Look upon Jacob, O ye parents, peruse the twelve **godly fathers** in time and order. Learn of him and his to pray aright" (Preface to *The Testament of the Twelve Patriarchs, the Sons of Jacob*).

24 *House, Chapel, Temple* Joseph Smith referred to the "Kirtland **chapel**" some 50 times in his personal journal entries, never as a "temple." These were later changed to the "Kirtland **temple**" by Brighamite editors. Was there a desire to tie Joseph Smith's name to the new temple theology of the secret chamber and to the Freemasonry "temple," to help ensure that polygamy and funding for the temple be maintained? Note how the LORD uses the word "house" below, versus men's use of the word temple. Houses built by men may transition to a "temple built to the **LORD's name**," if our hearts are centered on Him.

251 Total uses of "**house**" in the D&C LORD's words – Section Revelation **231**X Men's Words - Introduction **20**X
49 Total uses of "**temple**" in the D&C LORD's words – Section Revelation **19**X Men's Words - Introduction **30**X

Tabernacle 1 / Temple 3	D&C 93 – "whatsoever temple is *defiled*, God shall *destroy* that temple"
House 100%	D&C 95 – "endow those whom I have chosen with power from on high"
House 3 / *unholy* Temple 1	D&C 97 – Pattern for house for my people / my glory, my presence, see God
House 100%	D&C 105 - Elders must be "endowed with power from on high"
House 100% / Temple - *Intro* 2	D&C 109 - Dedication prayer (Joseph Smith) at Kirtland "house of the LORD"
House 100% / Temple - *Intro* 2	D&C 110 - Visitation of Christ, Moses, Elias & Elijah at Kirtland "house of the LORD"
House 100%	D&C 115 – Commandment to build a house at Far West
House 100% / Temple - *Intro* 3	D&C 124 – Command to build the "Nauvoo house" and a "house of the LORD"

25 *Lucifer in the Bible* According to Robinson, the original Hebrew text of Isaiah 14:12 became corrupted with the Latin term Lucifer. How did this happen? "In Roman astronomy, Lucifer was the name given to the morning star (the star we now know by another Roman name, Venus). The morning star appears in the heavens just before dawn, heralding the rising sun. The name derives from the Latin term *lucem ferre*, 'bringer, or bearer, of light.' In the Hebrew text the expression used to describe the Babylonian king before his death is *Helal*, son of *Shahar*, which can best be translated as 'Day star, son of the Dawn.'... The scholars authorized by the militantly Catholic King James I to translate the Bible into current English did not use the original Hebrew texts, but used versions translated from the Catholic Vulgate Bible produced largely by St. Jerome in the fourth century. Jerome had mistranslated the Hebraic metaphor, 'Day star, son of the Dawn,' as 'Lucifer,' and over the centuries a metamorphosis took place. Lucifer the morning star became a disobedient angel, cast out of heaven to rule eternally in hell. Theologians, writers, and poets interwove the myth with the doctrine of the Fall, and in Christian tradition Lucifer is now the same as Satan, the Devil, and—ironically—the Prince of Darkness'...So 'Lucifer' is nothing more than an ancient Latin name for the morning star, the bringer of light. That can be confusing for Christians who identify Christ himself as the morning star, a term used as a central theme in many Christian sermons. Jesus refers to himself as the morning star in Revelation 22:16: 'I Jesus have sent mine angel to testify unto you these things in the churches. I am the root and the offspring of David, and the bright and morning star'...And so there are those who do not read beyond the King James version of the Bible, who say 'Lucifer is Satan: so says the Word of God,' while others with knowledge of the Latin and Hebrew texts say, 'No, Lucifer is the classical Roman name

for the morning star, and now Jesus is the morning star'" (See John J. Robinson, A Pilgrim's Path: Freemasonry and the Religious Right, M. Evans and Company, NY).

[26] *Wilford Woodruff's Wives* Pres. Wilford Woodruff died unexpectedly, days after making a presentation to members of the Boehmian Grove in 1898. He was seeking funding for the struggling LDS church, following very difficult times that resulted from the abomination of polygamy and the Manifesto of 1890 that followed.

Fifty-two years earlier at Nauvoo, as a 39-year old Apostle, Wilford Woodruff, took two teenage wives (besides the two he already had) on the same day, August 2nd of 1846. They were wives 3 and 4 (Mary C. Barton, age 17 & Sarah E. Brown, age 18). Both were divorced from Woodruff four weeks later on approval of Brigham Young (Young didn't become Church President **until 1847**). According to Woodruff, the two new brides were spending too much time with boys their own age. Woodruff suspected infidelity. Enforcer Hosea Stout was sent to "whip" the boys. Woodruff thought the girls, "deserved similar punishment" as well, but settled on "expulsion" (divorce) as approved by Young. Woodruff would end up with ten wives total (not all concurrent) and 34 children. There were four divorces. He became the fourth President of the church in 1889, dying in 1898, just after his Bohemian Grove visit. He is best known for issuing the Manifesto in 1890, ending polygamy on paper. Despite it, Woodruff continued to secretly encourage, or at least allow, new plural marriages to be performed in Mexico, Canada, and upon the high seas (neutral ground). The church did not fully renounce the practice of plural marriage until Joseph F. Smith's Second Manifesto of 1904 (he also conducted a polygamous marriage on the neutral ground of the ocean after his Manifesto). Besides the 1890 Manifesto, Woodruff is also known for changing the sealing of individuals to church leaders - by adoption (called "the law of adoption"), to only those who were their direct blood ancestors. This genealogy-based temple work is now the tradition among the Saints. No revelation is cited for the change. His Founding Fathers story has proven to be a fabrication. Their work had already been done by others, and though an avid record keeper, he did not record this miraculous visit in his journals. See http://puremormonism.blogspot.com/2013/04/wilford-woodruffs-pants-are-on-fire.html

[27] *Book of Commandments vs the D&C* The 1833 "Book of Commandments" focused on the saving ordinances and the "Law of the Gospel," including the law of monogamy and the law of consecration, all in connection with the establishment of Zion. It was addressing God's people who had the fullness of Gospel and the greater priesthood. It included the necessary laws to live to establish Zion. In the later 1835 "Doctrine and Covenants" this book was modified and expanded. Besides documenting historical events, it revealed the condemnation of the saints, and the fact that Christ's name was taken from it. One major concern for some is that revelations Joseph claimed were given by God to him, Oliver Cowdery, and David Whitmer were revised by both him and others later, including Sidney Rigdon and Orson Hyde, and without the consent of Oliver Cowdery and David Whitmer. Both men were present with Joseph when some of the first revelations were received (like Sections 17 & 18). They became concerned with the changes. One of many changes to the 1833 Book of Commandments was chapter 4, verse 4 which originally read, "And he (Joseph) has a gift to translate the Book and I have commanded him that he shall pretend to no other gift, for I will grant him no other gift" (note the changes made later to this verse in D&C 5:4). Another change is the word "disciple" later changed to "apostle." The LORD had Oliver and David locate the first set of twelve "disciples" in 1829. The LORD reserved the title "apostle" for those He chose in Jerusalem (the Twelve in the Book of Mormon were also called "disciples" by Christ there, not "Apostles"). See Assumption #2 in chap. 6 for more on this topic. According to Mervin J. Petersen, in the 1835 D&C some 703 words were changed, 1,656 new words were added, and 453 words deleted. In total, there were 2,643 changes made between the 1833 and 1835 editions. And by the 1921 edition of the D&C, 159 more changes were made, in 8 different additions thereafter (see p. 121 chart in his 1955 Master's Thesis). More changes are apparent since then (see *A Study of the Nature of and the Significance of the Changes in the Revelations as Found in a Comparison of the Book of Commandments and Subsequent Editions of the Doctrine and Covenants*, Master's thesis, BYU, 1955, p. 140, 147). A document citing the changes from the 1833 Book of Commandments to the 1835 Doctrine & Covenants is available at: https://drive.google.com/file/d/0B6ItuDdVWOO8X2JqTlVCb3E5dTg/view
See also David Whitmer's understanding of the changes in *An Address to All Believers in Christ* http://www.utlm.org/onlinebooks/address1.htm

[28] *Three Types of Vision* Experiencing a "vision" can be classified into three types of experiences. The first two normally occur within our own body and do not require one to be "*born again*" or "*sanctified*" (via the baptism of fire and the Holy Ghost), whereas the third requires *sanctification* and *transfiguration*. It typically occurs as one's Spirit typically leaves their body.

The first level *Type 1 Vision* provides less clarity and detail but there is a clear "knowing" that one has seen or experienced something of significance "in the Spirit," and often in heaven or in another setting. It is difficult to identify most specifics in this first level visionary experience, but it is nevertheless very real to the one experiencing it. In a *Type 2 Vision*, there is more vivid detail, brightness, and clarity. One may experience the vision spiritually or even physically with another being. Joseph's Smith's experience in the First Vision in 1820, and with the angel on Sept. 22-23 of 1823, appear to be *Type 2 Visions*. The experience of the 2,500 believers at Bountiful may have been a *Type 2 Vision* as well (a collective one). Individuals experiencing this higher level vision are often *transfigured* by God so that they might endure His powerful, fiery glory or that of another glorified being. In a Type 3 Vision, there may be ascension into a higher realm of glory. This requires both *sanctification* and *transfiguration* and tpically involves the spirit leaving the body. Moses in Moses chapter 1 appears to have experienced this third level of vision. It is in this state that one may have the full Second Comforter experience, entering the rest of the LORD in a fullness of His glory.

[29] *Water Baptisms for the Living* Scripture and Church history reveals that baptism was **not** intended to be a one-time event, but instead a rite that could also be used for recommitment purposes after an initial baptism, as well as healing. Hebrews 6:2 speaks of "the doctrine of baptisms," addressing a *plurality* of baptisms in both water and by fire or the Spirit. We sin and are in need of continual repentance and renewal, as well as the continual cleansing and renewal of the Spirit of God.

(1) "**Baptism unto repentance**" is done for remission of sins in pure streams, rivers, and lakes (Mosiah 26:22; Alma 5:62, 7:14; Hel. 5:17, 19; 3 Ne. 1:23; 7:25-26; Acts 19:1-6). It is always to be preceeded by real *faith in Christ* (see the Lectures on Faith), sincere heartfelt *repentance,* and *covenant-making* with the Lord. Those baptized were and are to be fully *accountable* (or of age), doing so as a *free-will* offering to the LORD, not by coercion of parents, leaders, or others. It is also to be performed by one *having authority.* We should ask God "who" should perform it via prayer and revelation. With this rite, one becomes part of **the church of Christ** (Mos. 26:22; Mor. 6:1-4). The specific words to use for this rite, to stop all disputations, were given us by the LORD Himself in the Book of Mormon. They utilize the words, "*having authority given me* of Jesus Christ" (3 Ne. 11:25), **not those** used today, which are, "*having been commissioned* of Jesus Christ" (D&C 20:73). Oliver Cowdery made this change in the 1835 D&C. In D&C 18:1-4, God tells us to "rely on the words which were written" (in the Book of Mormon, the "most correct book on earth," according to Joseph Smith, HC 4:461). We remain under condemnation for not relying on God's word in it (see D&C 84:43-58).

(2) "**Baptism unto renewal**" is tied to personal *renewal of covenants.* Six early church "elders" were **re-baptized** at the Peter Whitmer gathering on April 6, 1830 in New York (see chap. 6, assumption #9). It was done to allow them to *renew their covenants* with God in baptism publically, and allow the people to vote for them as their "spiritual teachers" in the law of common consent (D&C 28:13). Re-baptism is apparent in Revelation 2:2 (returning to Christ [their **first love**] and to "the first works" - faith, repentance, and re-baptism), and in Acts 19:1-6. It was also a part of seven group *reformation* efforts in the Book of Mormon.

Alma (the elder) / 120 BC / Mosiah 25:19; 26:15-33
Alma (the younger) / 83 BC / Mosiah 27:13; Alma chapters 5-16
Helaman / 73 BC / Alma 45:22
Helaman / 57 BC / Alma 62:46
Samuel the Lamanite / 6 BC / Helaman chapters 13-16
Jesus – Nephi / 34 AD / 3 Nephi 11:23-27; 19:9-15
Moroni / 410 AD / Moroni 6:1-7; 8 25

For years, many were re-baptized prior to a mission or becoming a Bishop, Stake President, or Apostle. It also preceeded ordinances like the endowment and marriage sealings (see Quinn, *The Mormon Hierarchy: Origins of Power*). Other reasons for re-baptism included lost records, and entering the United Order. In 1893, Church leaders encouraged members to be re-baptized prior to attending the dedication of the Salt Lake Temple on April 6, 1897. Brigham Young had the whole church re-baptized in 1856-57 (a useful tool to enforcing his new "order of things" including polygamy).

(3) "**Baptism unto healing**" was done in temple baptismal fonts in early church history. Joseph re-baptized Emma in both the Mississippi River, Oct. 5, 1842 (before the temple font was completed) and in the Nauvoo Temple font on Nov. 1, 1842 because of sickness. Temple records from four early Utah temples (1877 to 1893, 5 years) reveals 22,403 baptisms performed for "*health*" reasons, and 7,788 re-baptisms for "***renewal.***" "*Baptisms unto repentance*" were done outside of temples, whereas those for "*renewal*" and "*healing*" were done inside them (see D. Michael Quinn, *The Mormon Heirarchy*, Signature Books, pps. 632-33).

A new false tradition has arisen among modern Saints. It claims that the Sacrament renews baptismal covenants. This was and is the primary purpose for **re-baptism**, now discontinued. Pres Woodruff stopped re-baptisms outside of temples in 1897. Pres. Grant stopped those inside of temples in 1922. No revelation from God was cited for either decision.

[30] *The Necessary Sacrifice of All Things* The last-days reformation, in which all Christian believers must become **one** in Christ and the Father - in the unity required for Zion, requires each of us to remove **all the idols** held in our hearts, including the **pro**-polygamy idols among the Brighamites, and the **anti**-polygamy idols among the Josephites. Following God's **will** in "pure" revelation from Him was the example Christ set for us in seeking always to do **the will of the Father**. It may require us to do that very thing that is **most abominable** to us - to prove ourselves worthy of God's greatest gifts. Such was the case with Abraham and the distasteful *idolatry* of his father, *idolatry* where his father nearly sacrificed him, and where Abraham was required to sacrifice his own precious son on an altar. Abraham passed this test, even though it was most distasteful to him, more than any other thing. All of us must learn to **love** one another, whether we are polygamists or monogamists, and allow God in His greater love, wisdom, and righteousness to bring us together in His way *and* timing, for who knows but that He required certain things of some to test them. He is the Judge. I have presented the Book of Mormon approach to polygamy throughout this book purposely - that it is a "grosser crime," a "whoredom," and an "abomination," because it is written to mostly the Utah Saints and is already complex enough without this caveat. I recognize that God may allow it or even require it of some for reasons that I don't understand. He is God and can do as He pleases. Certainly if some desire it (especially women in some unique situation), and it is not oppressive to them, because the man tied to it does so in great love and wisdom, *and* via **the will of God**, then so be it. Who am I to judge and go against God? The reason this is not addressed earlier in this work is because it opens a "can of worms," a dangerous "**justification**" that can be used by those seeking to practice this relationship without the love, growth, wisdom, and permission of God. Such must "enter in at the gate." He is Christ Jesus. I do not believe Brigham Young entered in at **this** gate.

[31] *The New and Everlasting Covenant* Brigham's New and Everlasting Covenant of *plural marriage* is a perversion of truth. God defines this covenant as "the fullness" of His gospel (see D&C 22; 39:18; 45:9, 66:2; JST Gen. 9:21-25). We make a "New and Everlasting Covenant" with God at baptism. It is a covenant to serve God, keep His commandments, and *obey* **His will**, whether

given in the *written word* or in His *revealed word* to us personally. The tie of this covenant to **God's will** is clearest in the following scriptures; JST Gen. 9:21; Mosiah 5:5, 8, 18:10; 2 Ne. 32:3, 6; D&C 22 & 84:35-48. The doctrine of the two ways (Deut. 30:16-19) reveals either obedience to God and His superior will and wisdom - because of our love for him (Abel & "*the children of obedience*" – Eph. 2:2-3, 5:6; Col. 3:6; D&C 93:39, 121:17), versus disobedience in connection with self will (Cain & "*the children of disobedience*"). God gave the priesthood to Israel to serve others, not to be above others (see Matt. 20:25-28; Num. 25:13; Jer. 31:31-34; Ezek. 37:26; D&C 84:35-48). The best service to one another is clearly that where we follow and obey *the superior will and wisdom of God.* Honoring and obeying God's superior will is the simplest, best definition of the New and Everlasting Covenant.

32 *Christ as the Holy Spirit of Promise* Our LORD has many name-titles all describing different parts of His overall mission of **love.** In His role as the Holy Spirit of Promise, He seals upon worthy sons and daughters all the promised blessings tied to **eternal life**. It is granted by **Him alone** as **He** is the author and finisher of our faith, and **the Father of our Salvation**. Those who sincerely repent can come into the Church of Christ, receive their Baptism of Fire and the Holy Ghost, and then *receive their Calling and Election*, bringing them into the terrestrial level church. Such have their Gentile blood burned out of them, so that they become the pure blood of Israel and the Elect of God. Christ seals this ordinance upon us Himself as the Holy Spirit of Promise. To progress further and come into the Celestial level church, we are invited to come into the presence of Jesus Christ in His Glory and then receive *our Calling and Election,* that it might be *made sure.* God's invitation to receive Him and His fuller blessings is like a funnel that becomes narrower as fewer and fewer seek to follow and obey God. Receiving Christ as the Second Comforter is part of receiving the promise of eternal life, or to have one's *Calling and Election made sure.* It is part of coming into the Church of the First Born, the Church of God the Father (see Eph. 1:12-13; D&C 88:3-5). Enos approached God in mighty prayer about his state of righteousness. Because of his mighty prayer, a wrestle with God, he received answers, forgiveness, and a remission of his sins, pointing to a baptism of fire and the Holy Ghost. We too should ask regarding our state before God. Ask, seek, knock.

33 *Plain & Precious Truths Restored* The Prophet Joseph Smith's primary mission in "the Restoration" was to bring forth more of God's precious, saving truths in the Book of Mormon and his re-translation of the Bible, specifically "*the plain and precious things*" taken out of the Bible (1 Ne. 13:28-29). They were removed by evil and designing men who desired to keep the people in ignorance for the sake of gain (power, money, the honors of men, sex, etc., 1 Ne. 22:23). The simple and sacred truths removed included three things; (1) How to be saved (spiritually "born again" or made new, Rev. 21:5); (2) Specific ways in which Satan and evil men fight against God's salvation (including the blood oaths of secret combinations, presented in three witnesses; the Book of Enoch, the Book of Moses [JST Gen.], and the Book of Mormon); And (3) The covenants or promises God made to "the fathers," men like Adam, Enoch, Noah, Abraham, Isaac, Jacob, and Joseph sold into Egypt. We can inherit these promises too. The most important of them is the promise of eternal life. We as "the children" are to "*turn, seal,* or *remember*" these covenants and seek to receive the same promises from God ourselves, those tied to real salvation (see Joseph Smith History 1:39 and chap. 5).

At the very start of our LORD's mission in Capernaum near the Sea of Galilee in the New Testament (Matthew 5), and in the Book of Mormon at the city of Bountiful (3 Nephi 12), Christ the LORD taught *the higher law* of **the Beattitudes** to His most *trusted followers* or "*disciples.*" Both the JST Matthew 5 account and the 3 Nephi account list **12 Beattitudes**, whereas the Matthew account today has only 9 "*blessed*" traits (Luke has only 4 of them). They are tied to those who love **God's** and follow **His will** and commandments (see the 12 "*blessings*" and 12 cursings in Deut. 27 & 28; 4 of the "blessing" verses there begin with the word "*Blessed*"). John addresses these wise ones in Revelation. Many of them are the 144,000 last days servants who gather the elect to God (see also D&C 77). Researcher Bruce Cathie points out that the number 144,000 is one of three ways to record the speed of *light* (see *Bridge to Infinity,* p. 8). It is **12** x 12 x 1000 = 144,000. Whether it is space, time, law, or light, the number 12 is tied to "*governance*" in God's word and kingdom. God through the Prophet Joseph restored **the first three Beattitudes** to JST Matthew 5. Jesus taught them again in 3 Nephi 12. In these two "restorations" *the first three blessed traits* there lead to being "*born again*" or made new in our Savior (Rev. 21:5). It is to receive *salvation, a remission of sins,* and *the Holy Ghost* – and from **Him** (see 3 Ne. 9:20, 12:1; D&C 33:15). They provide our entrance into **His** church, *the church of the Lamb* (or the Firstborn). He does the baptizing in the Spirit to become part of **His** church. In 3rd Nephi 12, the LORD Jesus taught his "disciples" (followers) the following:

1. "**Blessed** are ye if ye shall give heed unto the words of these twelve whom *I have chosen* from among you to minister unto you, and *to be your servants*; and unto them *I have given power* that *they may baptize you with water*, and *after* that ye are *baptized with water*, behold, **I will baptize you with fire and with the Holy Ghost**; therefore **blessed** are ye **if ye shall believe in me** and be baptized, *after that ye have seen me and know that I am.* 2. And again, more **blessed** are they who shall *believe in your words* because that *ye shall testify that ye have seen me*, and that ye *know that I am.* Yea, **blessed** are they who shall *believe in your words*, and come down into *the depths of humility* and *be baptized*, for *they shall be visited with* **fire and with the Holy Ghost**, and shall receive a *remission of their sins.* 3. Yea, **blessed** are the poor in spirit **who come unto me**, for theirs is the kingdom of heaven. 4. And again, **blessed** are all they that mourn, for they shall be comforted. 5. And **blessed** are the meek, for they shall inherit the earth. 6. And **blessed** are all they who do hunger and thirst after righteousness, for **they shall be filled with the Holy Ghost**. 7. And **blessed** are the merciful, for they shall obtain mercy. 8. And blessed are all the pure in heart, for they shall see God. 9. And **blessed** are all the peacemakers, for they shall be called the children of God. 10. And **blessed** are all they who are persecuted *for my name's sake*, for theirs is the kingdom of heaven. 11. And **blessed** are ye when men shall revile you and persecute, and shall say all manner of evil against you falsely, *for my sake*; 12. For ye shall have *great* **joy** and be exceedingly glad, for great shall be your reward in heaven; for

so persecuted they the prophets who were before you. 13. Verily, verily, I say unto you, I give unto *you to be the salt of the earth*; but if the salt shall lose its savor [lose of *the fullness* of the gospel] wherewith shall the earth be salted? The salt shall be thenceforth good for nothing, but to be cast out and to be trodden under foot of men. 14. Verily, verily, I say unto you, I give unto you to be the **light** of this people [the 144,000 & others]. A city that is set on a hill cannot be hid."

Sources for this Book

Trustworthy Sources on Polygamy in the LDS Church / *Joseph was Innocent*

1. What the LORD calls "*the fullness of my scriptures*" - the JST Bible & the Book of Mormon (see D&C 42:12, 15, 56-59), along with the unchanged oracles of the early 1833 Book of Commandments (see 3 Nephi 16:10, 21:19, 30:2 & Book of Commandments 4:5-6)
2. Prayer and pure revelation that originates in a heart free of idols, as one seeks **God's will** in all things
3. Website: *Joseph Smith Fought Polygamy*, https://restorationbookstore.org/jsfp-index.htm / Joseph Smith was innocent, excellent sources *Cochranite spiritual wifery:* https://restorationbookstore.org/articles/nopolygamy/jsfp-vol1/chp1.htm
4. Book: *The Exoneration of Emma, Joseph, and Hyrum*, by Ronald Meldon Kerran, Part One / Focus on faulty sources, and the secret chamber
5. Book: *Joseph Smith Fought Polygamy*, volumes 1-3 , https://restorationbookstore.org/
6. Paper: *Joseph Smith's Monogamy* http://anonymousbishop.com/wp-content/uploads/2015/11/JosephSmithsMonogamy1.pdf
7. Paper: *A Bibliography on Joseph Smith III: The Mormon Prophet-Leader*, Enid Stubbart DeBarthe, Master's Thesis, N. Illinois Univ., 1969
8. Website: *An Evaluation of D&C 132* https://onewhoiswatching.wordpress.com/2009/09/01/analysis-of-section-132/
9. Website: *Marriage and Polygamy* www.MarriageAndPolygamy.com
10. Websites: defendingjosephsmith.org
11. Website: defendingjoseph.com
12. Website: latterdaytruth.org

Good Sources on Brigham Young's Rise to Power

1. Podcast: *Apostolic Coup d'état: How The Twelve Apostles, In a Breathtaking Power Grab, Assumed Absolute and Complete Control of the Church of Jesus Christ of Latter-day Saints,* Part I - http://puremormonism.blogspot.com/search?updated-max=2017-10-22T14:52:00-07:00&max-results=1 , Part II http://puremormonism.blogspot.com/2017/10/brigham-youngs-hostile-takeover.html
2. Paper: *The Temple Lot Case* http://restorationbookstore.org/blog/TLCtestimonies.pdf
3. Video: *The Carthage Conspiracy* https://www.youtube.com/watch?v=pTuu6Y6C0o4&t=4320s
4. Article: *The Making of a Mormon Myth: The 1844 Transfiguration of Brigham Young* https://www.dialoguejournal.com/wp-content/uploads/sbi/articles/Dialogue_V34N0102_171.pdf
5. Book: *The Mormon Hierarchy: Origins of Power*, D. Michael Quinn, Signature Books / believes Joseph was a polygamist
6. Book: *Bill Hickman: Brigham Young's Destroying Angel*, John H. Beadle ed., https://books.google.com/books?id=9-wQAAAAIAAJ
7. Article: Will Bagley, *One Long Funeral March: A Revisionist's View of the Mormon Handcart Disasters*
8. Article: Polly Aird, *You Nasty Apostates. Clear out: Reasons for Disaffection in the Late 1850's,* in Journal of Mormon History, vol. 30, issue 2, article 1). Available at http://files.lib.byu.edu/mormonmigration/articles/YouNastyApostatesJMHVOL30_NO2.pdf

Other Supporting Information

1. *An Address to All Believers in Christ* David Whitmer's Last Testimony http://www.utlm.org/onlinebooks/address1.htm
2. *William & Katherine Smith writings* http://olivercowdery.com/smithhome/WmSmith1.htm
3. *Revisionist History in the D&C* http://greatandmarvelouswork.com/the-book-of-commandments-vs-the-doctrine-and-covenants-part-1/
4. *Reed Smoot Hearings* https://wheatandtares.org/2018/02/04/the-reed-smoot-hearings/
5. *The False Story of the Founding Fathers visit at the St. George Temple* http://puremormonism.blogspot.com/2013/04/wilford-woodruffs-pants-are-on-fire.html
6. *The Plan to Destroy Christianity from Within* http://www.goodnewsaboutgod.com/studies/spiritual/home_study/church_destroy.htm
7. *Freemasonry ritual signs* http://www.ephesians5-11.org/handshakes.htm
8. *Secret Oaths & the Watchers* http://mormonyeshiva.blogspot.com/ Parts I Dec. 30, 2018, II Jan. 6, Part III Jan. 9, 2019 (Rob Kay)
9. *Changes - 1833 Book of Commandments to the 1835 D&C* https://drive.google.com/file/d/0B6ItuDdVWOO8X2JqTlVCb3E5dTg/view
10. *The True Location of the Atonement & the Temple,* chap. 6 (how truth was changed and manipulated among the Israelites anciently)
11. *House Church* https://churchwithoutwallsinternational.org/what-is-house-church/
12. *LDS Personal Faith Crisis* - 2013 report to LDS Church leaders - download this report at the web address found in endnote 4

Relationship with Christ Books

1. What the LORD calls "the fullness of my scriptures" - the JST Bible & the Book of Mormon (see D&C 42:12, 15, 56-59), along with the unchanged oracles of the early 1833 Book of Commandments
2. The Lectures on Faith http://lecturesonfaith.com
3. *How to Have Your Second Comforter* (www.digitalegend.com)
4. *Faith in the LORD Jesus Christ,* John and Jennifer Orten
5. *Wait as Eagles*, Sadhu Sundar Selvaraj, jesusministries.org
6. *Heaven Can't Wait*, by Lewis Clementson, amazon.com
7. *Seek Ye This Jesus*, by Robert Smith, upwardthought.blogspot.com
8. *The Rabbi, The Secret Message, and the Identity of Messiah*, Carl Gallups
9. *Beautiful Outlaw* (chapter 1 of all 18 youtube videos) - https://www.youtube.com/watch?v=hmUK0-mwMsk
10. *Jews converted to Christ* https://www.oneforisrael.org/met-messiah-jewish-testimonies/

General Awakening Websites & Blogs

1. http://upwardthought.blogspot.com
   free book download, *Teaching for Doctrines the Commandments of Men*
   https://drive.google.com/file/d/0B6t-rQr3iLAsekRiMW05QUVvR1U/view
2. https://www.7witnesses
3. http://ldsperfectday.blogspot.com
4. https://purerevelations.wordpress.com
5. http://puremormonism.blogspot.com
6. http://www.besacredspace.com
7. http://www.mormonyeshiva.blogspot.com

Printed in Great Britain
by Amazon